A DICTIONARY
OF ADVANCED
JAPANESE GRAMMAR

A DICTIONARY OF ADVANCED JAPANESE GRAMMAR

日本語文法辞典【上級編】

Seiichi Makino
and
Michio Tsutsui

the japan times PUBLISHING

A Dictionary of Advanced Japanese Grammar
日本語文法辞典【上級編】

2008 年 5 月 20 日　初版発行
2022 年 10 月 5 日　第 15 刷発行
著　者　牧野成一・筒井通雄
発行者　伊藤秀樹
発行所　株式会社 ジャパンタイムズ出版
　　　　〒 102-0082 東京都千代田区一番町 2-2
　　　　一番町第二 TG ビル 2F

ISBN978-4-7890-1295-9

First edition: May 2008
15th printing: October 2022

Typesetting: guild
English copyreading: Sara Harris
English copyreading and editorial assistance: Sharon Tsutsui
Cover art: Akihiro Kurata
Printing: Nikkei Printing Inc.

Published by The Japan Times Publishing, Ltd.
2F Ichibancho Daini TG Bldg., 2-2 Ichibancho, Chiyoda-ku, Tokyo 102-0082, Japan
https://jtpublishing.co.jp/

ISBN978-4-7890-1295-9

Printed in Japan

Preface

This is a dictionary of advanced Japanese grammar, a companion volume to *A Dictionary of Basic Japanese Grammar* (1986) and *A Dictionary of Intermediate Japanese Grammar* (1995). More than two decades have passed since we began this grammar dictionary project. During that time we have received numerous comments from our readers, many of whom kindly encouraged us to write a third volume. And here it is as the final volume in the set.

This book is designed for students and teachers of advanced-level Japanese. After examining upper-level textbooks, reference books, and our own teaching materials, we have collected some 230 main entries which we believe to be highly important grammatical items for advanced Japanese learners. As in the previous dictionaries, we have provided detailed explanations for each item and have included comparisons with synonymous items (approximately 430 items in all). The writing tasks were shared between us with each of us preparing first drafts of half of the items which we then exchanged for comments. Our second drafts were reviewed by The Japan Times editors and, following that, the final draft was completed.

There is one important difference between this volume and the preceding ones, however. For both *DBJG* and *DIJG* we wrote the example sentences ourselves, but for this volume we have also used the Internet as a resource in collecting and creating sentences which reflect natural usage. In situations where it is common practice, we use kanji. For the reader's convenience, pronunciations are provided in *hiragana* for characters defined as levels 1 and 2 in the Japanese Language Proficiency Test (*Nihongo-nōryoku-shiken*) except for those kanji which are regularly introduced in beginning- and intermediate-level textbooks.

We are clearly indebted to the many scholars and teachers whose works are referenced here. In addition to them, there are a number of individuals we wish to acknowledge. Foremost, we thank Chiaki Sekido, The Japan Times editor. We are deeply grateful for her thorough and critical reading of our drafts, for her numerous constructive comments on them, and for her tireless effort in preparing this volume for publication. We thank Sarah Harris, the English editor, for patiently transforming our English in the first draft to make it more natural. In addition, we owe a great deal to Sharon Tsutsui, who read the galley proofs carefully and critically and helped us to improve the readability of the final version. Our thanks go to our colleagues at Princeton University and the University of Washington, who kindly answered our questions about the naturalness of the example sentences, and also to our students, who used the early versions of some of the entries in class and gave us valuable feedback. Finally, we express our sincere gratitude to our wives, Yasuko and Sharon, who have been so helpful in every possible way during the seven years of this project.

Completing *A Dictionary of Advanced Japanese Grammar* was not an easy task to say the least. We are very pleased that we are now able to dedicate this volume to those students and teachers around the globe who are studying and teaching Japanese language with unceasing enthusiasm. Our sincere hope is that this dictionary will be a useful tool in their endeavors.

Spring 2008

Seiichi Makino
Michio Tsutsui

Table of Contents

To the Reader

This dictionary consists of the following parts:

A. *Grammatical Terms* contains brief explanations or informal definitions of the grammatical terms used in this book. If readers find that they are not familiar with these terms, it is suggested that they read this section first.

B. *Special Topics in Advanced Japanese Grammar* discusses selected topics: Adjectives in Japanese; Interpretation of "N₁ *no* N₂"; Politeness and Formality in Spoken and Written Language; Rhetorical Questions; Metaphors in Japanese; and Number Marking. The section introduces readers to a number of important concepts with which they should be familiar in order to improve their reading, writing and speaking skills.

C. *Main Entries* constitutes the core of this volume. Each entry is organized as follows:

---

① [entry name]   ② [part of speech]   ③ [usage restriction]

④ [meaning / function]   ⑤ [English counterpart(s)]

⑥ [related expression(s)]

⑦ ◆ **Key Sentence(s)**

⑧ **Formation**

⑨ **Examples**

⑩ **Note(s)**

⑪ **[Related Expression(s)]**

---

① [entry name]: Each entry is given in romanized spelling followed by its *hiragana* version. Entries are alphabetically ordered based on their romanized spellings.

② [part of speech]: Each entry is followed by its part of speech.

③ [usage restriction]: <s> or <w> is provided when the entry item is used only in spoken Japanese or only in formal written Japanese and formal speeches, respectively.

④ [meaning / function]: The basic meaning or function of the entry item is given in the box below the entry name.

⑤ [English counterpart(s)]: English expressions equivalent to the entry item are given to the right of the box.

⑥ [related expression(s)]: Items which are semantically related to the entry item are listed as **[REL.** *aaa*; *bbb*; ***ccc*]**. Expressions in plain type like *aaa* are explained in the entry under **[Related Expression(s)]** (⑪). Expressions in bold type like ***ccc*** contain comparisons to the entry item under **[Related Expression(s)]** for ***ccc***.

⑦ ◆ **Key Sentence(s):** Key sentences present typical sentence patterns in frames according to sentence structure. The elements that form the sentence patterns are printed in red and the elements which commonly occur with them are printed in bold-faced type.

⑧ **Formation:** The word formation rules / connection forms for each item are provided with examples. The entry elements are printed in red.

⑨ **Examples:** Example sentences are provided for each entry.

⑩ **Note(s):** Notes contain important points concerning the use of the item.

⑪ **[Related Expression(s)]**: Expressions which are semantically close to the entry item are compared and their differences are explained.

(⇨ *aaa* (DBJG / DIJG: 000-000)) in Note(s) and Related Expression(s) indicates that the item which was referred to (i.e., *aaa*) is explained on pp. 000-000 of the companion volumes: *A Dictionary of Basic Japanese Grammar* (DBJG) or *A Dictionary of Intermediate Japanese Grammar* (DIJG).

D. *Indexes* provides both a Japanese index and an English index. The Japanese index includes the main entries, the items explained in Related Expression(s), and the items covered in *A Dictionary of Basic Japanese Grammar* and in *A Dictionary of Intermediate Japanese Grammar*. The English index includes the English counterparts of the main entry items.

List of Abbreviations

Adj(*i*) = *i*-type adjective (e.g., *takai, yasui*)
Adj(*i*)cond = conditional form of *i*-type adjective (i.e., *takakere* of *takakere-ba, yasukere* of *yasukereba*)
Adj(*i*)stem = stem of *i*-type adjective (i.e., *taka* of *takai, yasu* of *yasui*)
Adj(*na*) = *na*-type adjective (e.g., *genkida, shizukada*)
Adj(*na*)stem = stem of *na*-type adjective (i.e., *genki* of *genkida, shizuka* of *shizukada*)
Adv. = adverb
Aff. = affirmative
Aux. = auxiliary
Comp. prt. = compound particle
Conj. = conjunction
Cop. = copula (e.g., *da, desu*)
DBJG = *A Dictionary of Basic Japanese Grammar*
Dem. adj. = demonstrative adjective (e.g., *kono, sonna*)
Dem. pro. = demonstrative pronoun (e.g., *kore, sore, are*)
DIJG = *A Dictionary of Intermediate Japanese Grammar*
Gr. = Group
Int. = interjection
Irr. = irregular
KS = Key Sentence
N = noun
Neg. = negative
Nom. = nominalizer (e.g., *no, koto*)
NP = noun phrase
Phr. = phrase
Prt. = particle
REL. = Related Expression
S = sentence
<s> = usually used in conversation
Sinf = sentence that ends with an informal predicate
S.o. = someone
S.t. = something
Str. = structure
Suf. = suffix (e.g., *-sa, -ya*)
V = verb
Vcond = conditional stem of verb (e.g., *hanase* of *hanaseba, tabere* of *tabereba*)
Vinf = informal form of verb (e.g., *hanasu, hanashita*)

V*masu* = *masu*-stem of verb (e.g., *hanashi* of *hanashimasu*, *tabe* of *tabe-masu*)

VN = stem of *suru*-verb, i.e., noun which forms a verb by affixing *suru* (e.g., *benkyō*, *yakusoku*, *nokku*)

Vneg = informal negative stem of verb (e.g., *hanasa* of *hanasanai*, *tabe* of *tabenai*)

VP = verb phrase

Vpot = verb potential form (e.g., *hanaseru*, *taberareru*)

V*te* = *te*-form of verb (e.g., *hanashite*, *tabete*)

Vvol = volitional form of verb (e.g., *hanasō*, *tabeyō*)

<w> = usually used in formal writing and formal speech

Wh-sentence = a sentence that contains a Wh-word

Wh-word = an interrogative word (e.g., *nani*, *doko*)

List of Symbols

⇨ = Refer to.

? = The degree of unacceptability is indicated by the number of question marks, two being the highest.

* = ungrammatical or unacceptable (In other words, no native speaker would accept the asterisked sentence.)

{ A / B } C = AC or BC (e.g., { V / Adj(*i*) } inf = Vinf or Adj(*i*)inf)

ø = zero (In other words, nothing should be used at a place where ø occurs. Thus, Adj(*na*) { ø / *datta* } *kamoshirenai* is either Adj(*na*) *kamoshirenai* or Adj(*na*) *datta kamoshirenai*.)

Grammatical Terms

The following are brief explanations of some of the grammatical terms used in this dictionary.

Auxiliary Adjective   A dependent adjective that is preceded by and attached to a verb or another adjective. The auxiliary adjectives in the following sentences are printed in bold-faced type.

(a) 私はジョンに行って**ほしい**。
     (I want John to go there.)

(b) この辞書は使い**やすい**。
     (This dictionary is easy to use.)

(c) 私はすしが食べ**たい**。
     (I want to eat *sushi*.)

(d) ベスは大学を出た**らしい**。
     (Beth seems to have graduated from college.)

(e) 花子は寂しい**ようだ**。
     (Hanako looks lonely.)

(f) このお菓子はおいし**そうだ**。
     (This cake looks delicious.)

Auxiliary Verb   A verb which is used in conjunction with a preceding verb or adjective. The bold-faced words of the following sentences are typical auxiliary verbs.

(a) ビルは今手紙を書いて**いる**。
     (Bill is writing a letter now.)

(b) 窓が開けて**ある**。
     (lit., The window has been opened. (= The window is open.))

(c) 僕は宿題をして**しまった**。
     (I have done my homework.)

(d) 私は友達にお金を貸して**あげた**。
     (I loaned money to my friend.)

(e) このコンピューターは高すぎる。

(This computer is too expensive.)

(f) ジョージはスポーツカーを欲^ほしがっている。

(lit., George is showing signs of wanting a sports car. (= George wants a sports car.))

(g) あっ！雨が降^ふってきた！

(Gee! It's started to rain!)

Compound Particle   A particle which consists of more than one word but functions like a single particle. For example, the compound particle *to shite wa* consists of the particle *to*, the *te*-form of *suru* and the particle *wa*, but it is used like a single particle to mean "for."

Conditional   A word, phrase, or clause which expresses a condition, as in (a)-(c).

(a) 翻訳^{ほんやく}の仕事ならやります。

(I will take it on if it's a translation job.)

(b) 安ければ買うかもしれない。

(I might buy it if it is cheap.)

(c) 山田^{やまだ}さんから電話があったら知らせて下さい。

(If Mr. Yamada calls me, please let me know.)

Continuative Form   Forms of verbs, adjectives and *da* which signal that the sentence is continuing. They do not indicate tense or politeness level. These forms include the following:

(a) *Affirmative forms:*

V*te*	話して (s.o. talks/talked/etc. and)
V*masu*	話し (s.o. talks/talked/etc. and)
Adj(*i*)stem く (て)	おいしく (て) (s.t. is/was delicious and)
Adj(*na*)stem {で / であり}	便利^{べんり}{で / であり} (s.t. is/was convenient and)
N {で / であり}	学者{で / であり} (s.o. is/was a scholar and)

Adj(*i*)stem く is also the adverbial form, as in 早く寝る (to go to bed early) or うまく話す (to talk skillfully).

(b) *Negative forms:*

Vneg ず   話さず (s.o. does/did/etc., not talk and)

Adj(*i*)stem くなく   おいしくなく (s.t. is/was not delicious and)

Adj(*na*)stem {じゃ / では} なく   便利 {じゃ / では} なく (s.t. is/was not convenient and)

N {じゃ / では} なく   学者 {じゃ / では} なく (s.o. is/was not a scholar and)

These forms are also used with certain words/phrases to convey more specific meanings, as shown in (c).

(c) *Other uses:*

V*te* いる   話している (s.o. is talking)

V*masu* やすい   食べやすい (easy to eat)

Adj(*i*)*te* 仕方がない   暑くて仕方がない (unbearably hot)

Adj(*na*)stem ではいけない   日本語が下手ではいけない (it's not good if s.o. is bad at Japanese)

N でもよい   英語でもよい (English would be all right)

Vneg ずに   寝ずに (without sleeping)

Coordinate Conjunction   A conjunction that combines two sentences without subordinating one to the other. A typical coordinate conjunction is *ga* "but."

(a) 走っていますが、ちっともやせません。
     (I'm running, but I haven't lost any weight at all.)

Demonstrative   A pronoun or adjective which specifies someone or something by pointing it out, as in (a) and (b).

(a) {これ / それ / あれ} は何ですか。
     (What is {this / that / that over there}?)

(b) {この本 / その本 / あの本} は私のです。
     ({This book / That book / That book over there} is mine.)

The interrogative words which correspond to demonstrative pronouns and demonstrative adjectives are *dore* and *dono*, respectively.

Dependent Noun　　A noun which must be preceded by a modifier, as in (a) and (b).

(a)　A: 明日田中先生に会うつもりですか。

(Are you going to meet Prof. Tanaka tomorrow?)

　　　B: はい、そのつもりです。

(Yes, I am.)

(b)　サンドラはトムを知っているはずだ。

(I expect that Sandra knows Tom.)

Direct Object　　The direct object of a verb is the direct recipient of an action represented by the verb. It can be animate or inanimate. An animate direct object is the direct experiencer of some action (as in (a) and (b) below). An inanimate direct object is typically something which is created, exchanged or worked on, in short, the recipient of the action of the verb (as in (c)-(e) below).　　　　　　　　　　　　　　　　(cf. Indirect Object)

(a)　山口先生は学生をよくほめる。

(Prof. Yamaguchi often praises his students.)

(b)　かおりは一郎をだました。

(Kaori deceived Ichiro.)

(c)　僕は本を書いた。

(I wrote a book.)

(d)　一郎はみどりにスカーフをやった。

(Ichiro gave a scarf to Midori.)

(e)　私はドアを開けておいた。

(I kept the door open.)

Although direct objects are marked by the particle *o*, nouns or noun phrases marked by *o* are not always direct objects, as shown in (f) and (g).

(f)　花子は一郎の大学入学を喜んだ。

(Hanako was glad that Ichiro entered college.)

(g)　トムはその時公園を歩いていた。

(At that time Tom was walking in the park.)

($\Rightarrow$ *o*[2] (DBJG: 349-51); *o*[4] (DBJG: 352-54))

Embedded Question   A question within a sentence. (a)-(c) provide examples (printed in bold-faced type):

(a)   郵便局がどこにあるか教えてください。

(Please tell me where the post office is.)

(b)   彼女がいつ結婚するか知っていますか。

(Do you know when she is getting married?)

(c)   来年日本へ行くかまだ決めていません。

(I haven't decided yet whether to go to Japan next year.)

Formal / Informal Forms   Formal forms are the forms which are used in such situations as polite conversation and business/personal letters. Informal forms are the forms used in such situations as casual conversation, newspapers, and academic papers. Examples of these forms can be seen in the following chart:

Formal Forms	Informal Forms
行きます	行く
大きいです	大きい
元気です	元気だ
学生です	学生だ

Informal forms are required in some grammatical structures.

(⇨ Appendix 4 (DBJG: 589-99))

Gr. 1 / Gr. 2 Verbs   Gr. 1 and Gr. 2 Verbs are Japanese verb groups: If a verb's informal, negative, nonpast form has the [*a*] sound before *nai* as in (a), the verb belongs to Group 1, and if not, as in (b), it belongs to Group 2. There are only two irregular verbs (i.e., *kuru* "come" and *suru* "do") that belong to neither Gr. 1 nor to Gr. 2.

(a)   Gr. 1 Verbs: 切らない [kir*a* - *nai*]
    読まない，書かない，待たない，死なない，会わない，話さない

(b)   Gr. 2 Verbs: 着ない [k*i* - *nai*], 食べない [tab*e* - *nai*]
    いない，起きない，できない，寝ない

Hearer　The person who receives a spoken or written message. In this dictionary the term "hearer" is used in a broader sense to mean the person to whom the speaker or the writer communicates.

Imperative Form　A conjugated verb form that indicates a command, as in *Hanase!* "Talk!," *Tabero!* "Eat it!," *Shiro!* "Do it!," or *Koi!* "Come!"

Indefinite Pronoun　A pronoun which does not refer to something specifically. *No* in B's sentence in (a) is an indefinite pronoun. Here, *no* is used for *jisho* "dictionary," but does not refer to a specific dictionary.

(a)　A: どんな辞書が欲しいんですか。

　　　　(What kind of dictionary do you want?)

　　　B: 小さいのが欲しいんです。

　　　　(I want a small one.)

Indirect Object　The indirect object of a verb is the recipient of the direct object of the main verb, and is marked by the particle *ni*. In (a), for example, the indirect object is Midori, the recipient of a *scarf,* which is the direct object of the verb *yatta*. It can be inanimate, as in (b). The main verbs which involve the indirect object are typically donative verbs (as in (a) and (b)).　　　　　　　　　　　　　　　　　(cf. Direct Object)

(a)　一朗はみどりにスカーフをやった。

　　　(Ichiro gave a scarf to Midori.)

(b)　台風は九州地方に多大な被害を与えた。

　　　(The typhoon brought great damage to the Kyushu area.)

Informal Form　(⇨ Formal / Informal Forms)

Intransitive Verb　A verb which does not require a direct object. The action or state identified by the intransitive verb is related only to the subject of the sentence. For example, the verb *hashitta* "ran" in (a) is an intransitive verb because the action of running is related only to the subject.　　　　　　　　　　　　　　　　　(cf. Transitive Verb)

(a)　鈴木さんは走った。

　　　(Mr. Suzuki ran.)

Intransitive verbs typically indicate *movement* (such as *iku* "go," *kuru* "come," *aruku* "walk," *tobu* "fly," *noru* "get onto"), *spontaneous change* (such as *naru* "become," *kawaru* "change," *tokeru* "melt," *fukuramu* "swell," *hajimaru* "begin"), *human emotion* (such as *yorokobu* "rejoice," *kanashimu* "feel sad," *omou* "feel"), and *birth/death* (such as *umareru* "be born," *shinu* "die").   (⇨ Appendix 3 (DBJG: 585-88))

I-type Adjective   An adjective whose nonpast prenominal form ends with *i*. Examples of *i*-type adjectives are *takai* "high; expensive" and *tsuyoi* "strong," as seen in (a) and (b).   (cf. *Na*-type Adjective; *No*-type Adjective)

  (a)   高い本 (an expensive book)

  (b)   強い人 (a strong person)

I-type adjectives are further subdivided into two types: *i*-type adjectives which end with *shi-i* and those with non-*shi-i* endings. Most adjectives with *shi-i* endings express human emotion (such as *ureshii* "happy," *kanashii* "sad," *sabishii* "lonely," *kurushii* "painful"); the non-*shi-i* adjectives are used for objective descriptions (such as *kuroi* "black," *shiroi* "white," *hiroi* "spacious," *takai* "high; expensive").

Main Clause   When a sentence consists of two clauses, one marked by a subordinate conjunction (such as *kara*, *keredo*, *node* and *noni*) and the other not marked by a subordinate conjunction, the latter is called a main clause. The main clauses in sentences (a) and (b) are printed in bold-faced type.   (cf. Subordinate Clause)

  (a)   山田は頭が痛いのに**学校に行った**。
        (*Yamada went to school*, although he had a headache.)

  (b)   和子は夫が優しいから**幸福**だ。
        (*Kazuko is happy*, because her husband is kind.)

When a sentence has a relative clause, the non-relative clause part is also referred to as a main clause, as in (c).

  (c)   **私はきのう**、友達から借りた**ビデオを見た**。
        (*Yesterday I watched a video* which I borrowed from my friend.)

Na-type Adjective   An adjective whose nonpast prenominal form ends with *na*. For example, *shizukada* "quiet" and *genkida* "healthy" are *na*-type adjectives, as in (a) and (b).   (cf. *I*-type Adjective; *No*-type Adjective)

  (a)   静かな家 (a quiet house)

  (b)   元気な人 (a healthy person)

Na-type adjectives are very similar to nouns. Some *na*-type adjectives can be used as nouns, as shown in (c) and (d). All *na*-type adjectives behave as nouns when they are used before the copula *da*, as shown in (e).

(c) 健康は大事ですよ。

(Health is important, you know.)

cf. 健康な人

(a healthy person)

(d) ご親切は忘れません。

(I'll never forget your kindness.)

cf. 親切な人

(a kind person)

(e) この人は元気／学生｛だ／です／だった／でした／じゃない／じゃありません／じゃなかった／じゃありませんでした｝。

(This person｛is/was/isn't/wasn't｝healthy／a student.)

Nominalizer   A nominalizer is a particle that makes a sentence into a noun phrase or clause. There are two nominalizers, *no* and *koto*: the former represents the speaker's/writer's empathetic feeling towards an event/state expressed in the nominalized noun phrase/clause; the latter indicates no empathy on the part of the speaker/writer towards an event/state.

(⇨ *no*³ (DBJG: 318-22); *koto*² (DBJG: 193-96))

Noun Phrase / Clause		Particle	Predicate
Sentence	Nominalizer		
日本語を読む	の／こと	は	難しい。
(Reading Japanese is difficult.)			

The nominalized sentence can be used in any position where an ordinary noun or a noun phrase/clause can be used.

***No*-type Adjective**   An adjective whose nonpast prenominal form ends with *no*.

(a) 一流の大学 (prestigious university)

(b) 特定の国 (specific country)

 (c) 一般の人 (people in general)

 (d) 普遍の法則 (universal rule)

 (e) がら空きの野球場 (mostly empty baseball stadium)

No-adjectives can occur in the predicate as well.

 (f) この大学は**一流だ**。
   (This university is prestigious (lit., first-class).)

 (g) この野球場はいつも**がら空きだ**。
   (This baseball stadium is always mostly empty.)

No-adjectives look like nouns, but they do not have the critical properties of nouns (e.g., they cannot be marked by the subject marker *ga* or the direct object marker *o*).

Many *no*-type adjectives can be classified by meaning, as shown below.

Excellent:
出色 (excellent), 抜群 (preeminent), 屈指 (outstanding), 一流 (first-class), だんとつ (by far the best), 指折り (distinguished), ぴかいち (superb), 上等 (high-class), 上々 (excellent)

Unique/Selected:
独自 (of one's own), 独特 (unique), 特有 (peculiar), 固有 (proper), 特定 (specific), 特別 (special) (cf. 特殊**な** (special))

Common:
普通 (common), 一般 (general), 並 (ordinary), ありきたり (ordinary), 常套 (common), 当たり前 (natural)

Unchanging:
一定 (constant), 普遍 (universal), 不変 (unchanging), 永遠 (eternal)

A common semantic property of *no*-adjectives is that they do not describe relative attributes such as height and quietness. Thus, unlike *i-* and *na-* adjectives, the suffix *sa* "the degree of" (e.g., *taka-sa* "height," *shizuka-sa* "quietness") cannot be affixed to *no*-adjectives.

          (cf. *Na*-type Adjective; *I*-type Adjective)

Certain prefixes and suffixes also form *no*-adjectives, as shown below.

Prefixes:

無-:　　　無人 (unattended), 無敗 (undefeated)

　　　　　*The following are *na*-adjectives: 無理 (impossible), 無知
　　　　　(ignorant), 無能 (incapable), 無遠慮 (impertinent), 無頓着
　　　　　(indifferent; careless), 無意味 (nonsensical)

未-:　　　未知 (unknown), 未完 (unfinished), 未踏 (unexplored)

最-:　　　最高 (the best), 最悪 (the worst), 最新 (the newest),
　　　　　最大 (maximum)

Suffixes:

-向き:　　子供向き (suitable for children)

-向け:　　携帯機器向け (for portable devices)

-用:　　　練習用 (for practice)

-入り:　　蜂蜜入り (with honey (as an ingredient))

-付き:　　ガレージ付き (with a garage)

-風:　　　スペイン風 (Spanish-style)

-だらけ:　間違いだらけ (full of errors)

-まみれ:　泥まみれ (covered with mud)

-気味:　　太り気味 (rather overweight)

-め:　　　大きめ (larger than expected, than usual, etc.)

Note: In the Formation section in each grammar entry, the formation rules for nouns apply to *no*-adjectives.

Potential Form   A verb form that expresses competence in the sense of "can do s.t." The formation is as follows:

Gr. 1 Verbs:	Vcond + る	e.g. 話せる (can talk)
Gr. 2 Verbs:	Vstem + られる	e.g. 食べられる (can eat)
	Vstem + れる	e.g. 食べれる (can eat)
Irr. Verbs:	来る	来られる, 来れる (can come)
	する	できる (can do)

Predicate   The part of a sentence which makes a statement about the subject. The core of the predicate consists either of a verb, an adjective, or a noun followed by a form of *da.* Optionally, objects and other adjectival and/or adverbial modifiers may be present. In (a)-(c), the predicates are printed in bold-faced type.

(cf. Subject)

(a) 松本さんはよく映画を見る。
(Mr. Matsumoto sees movies often.)

(b) 私の家はスミスさんのより新しい。
(My house is newer than Mr. Smith's.)

(c) ジョンは日本語の学生です。
(John is a Japanese language student.)

Prefix / Suffix   A dependent, non-conjugational word attached to nouns or the stems of verbs and adjectives in order to form new independent words. Prefixes are attached to the beginnings of nouns, etc., as in (a), and suffixes are attached to their endings, as in (b).

(a) 超特急 (superexpress), 副大統領 (vice-president), 無関心 (indifference)

(b) 映画化 (cinematization), 読み方 (how to read), 高さ (height)

Prenominal Form   The verb/adjective form which precedes a noun and modifies it. The bold-faced verbs and adjectives in (a)-(d) are prenominal forms.

(a) 私が**読む** / **読んだ**新聞
(the newspaper I read)

(b) **大きい** / **大きかった**家
(a big house / a house which used to be big)

(c) **立派な** / **立派だった**建物
(a magnificent building / a building which used to be magnificent)

(d) **おいしそうな** / **おいしそうだった**ケーキ
(a delicious-looking cake / a cake which looked delicious)

Stative Verb   A verb which represents the state of something or someone at some point in time, as in (a).   (⇨ Appendix 2 (DBJG: 582-84))

(a) ある (exist (of inanimate things)); いる (exist (of animate things)), いる (need), できる (can do)

Subject   An element of a sentence which indicates an agent of an action in active sentences (as in (a)) or an experiencer of an action (as in (b)) or someone or something that is in a state or a situation (as in (c)-(f)). The subject is normally marked by the particle *ga* in Japanese unless it is the sentence topic.

(a) ジョンがりんごを食べた。 (John ate an apple.)

(b) メアリーが先生にほめられた。 (Mary was praised by her teacher.)

(c) ナンシーはきれいだ。 (Nancy is pretty.)

(d) ドアが開いた。 (The door opened.)

(e) 机が一つある。 (lit., One table exists. (= There is a table.))

(f) 空が青い。 (The sky is blue.)

Subordinate Clause　　A clause which is embedded into a main clause with a subordinate conjunction. Typical subordinate conjunctions are *ba* "if," *kara* "because," *node* "because," *keredo* "although" and *noni* "although." Thus, in (a) below, the bold-faced clause with the subordinate conjunction *node* is embedded into the main clause *Nakayama-san wa gakkō o yasunda* "Mr. Nakayama was absent from school."　　(cf. Main Clause)

(a) 中山さんは**頭が痛かったので**学校を休んだ。

(Mr. Nakayama was absent from school *because he had a headache*.)

The informal form of a verb/adjective is usually used in a subordinate clause.

Suffix　　(⇨ Prefix / Suffix)

***Suru*-verb**　　A verb which is composed of a noun and *suru*, as in (a) and (b), or a single word and *suru*, as in (c). Nouns preceding *suru* are mostly Chinese-origin words. *Suru*-verbs conjugate in the same way as *suru*.

(a) 勉強する (to study), 掃除する (to clean), 夜更かしする (to stay up late)

(b) ノックする (to knock), サインする (to sign)

(c) 熱する (to heat), 察する (to guess)

Transitive Verb　　A verb that requires a direct object. It usually expresses an action that acts upon someone or something indicated by the direct object. Actions indicated by transitive verbs include *giving/receiving* (such as *ageru* "give," *morau* "receive," *kureru* "give"), *creating* (such as *tsukuru* "make," *kaku* "write," *kangaeru* "think"), *communicating* (such as *hanasu* "speak," *oshieru* "teach," *tsutaeru* "convey a message") and others. Note that some English transitive verbs are intransitive in Japanese.

(cf. Intransitive Verb)

(a) 私は車が**ある**。
    (lit., With me a car exists. (= I have a car.))

(b) 僕はお金が**いる**。
    (lit., To me money is necessary. (= I need money.))

(c) スミスさんは中国語が**分かる**。
    (lit., To Mr. Smith Chinese is understandable. (= Mr. Smith understands Chinese.))

(d) 私はフランス語が少し**できる**。
    (lit., To me French is a bit possible. (= I can speak French a little.))

(e) 木下さんは東京でお父さんに**会った**。
    (Mr. Kinoshita met his father in Tokyo.)

(f) 私にはベルが**聞こえなかった**。
    (lit., To me the bell wasn't audible. (= I wasn't able to hear the bell.))

(g) ここからは富士山が**見えますよ**。
    (lit., From here Mt. Fuji is visible. (= We can see Mt. Fuji from here.))

(h) 私たちは新幹線に**乗りました**。
    (We rode a bullet train.)

(i) 私は母に**似ている**らしい。
    (It seems that I resemble my mother.)

Volitional Sentence   A sentence in which a person expresses his/her will. The main verb in such sentences is in the volitional form, as in (a).

(a) 僕が**行こう / 行きましょう**。
    (I will go.)

Wh-question   A question that asks for information about *who*, *what*, *where*, *which*, *when*, *why* and *how*, as exemplified by (a)-(g) below.

(a) 誰が来ましたか。
   (Who came here?)

(b) 何を食べますか。
   (What will you eat?)

(c) どこに行きますか。
   (Where are you going?)

(d) どの建物が図書館ですか。
   (Which building is the library?)

(e) いつ大阪へ帰りますか。
   (When are you going back to Osaka?)

(f) どうして買わないんですか。
   (How come you don't buy it?)

(g) 東京駅へはどう行きますか。
   (How can I get to Tokyo Station?)

Wh-word　An interrogative word which corresponds to the English words *who*, *what*, *where*, *which*, *when*, *why* and *how*. The following are examples.

(a) 誰 (who), 何 (what), どこ (where), どの (which), いつ (when), どうして / なぜ (how come / why), どう (how)

Note that Japanese Wh-words are not always found in sentence-initial position; they are frequently found after a topic noun phrase, as shown in (b) and (c) below.

(b) 昨日のパーティーには誰が来ましたか。
   (lit., To yesterday's party, who came there? (= Who came to yesterday's party?))

   cf. 誰が昨日のパーティーに来ましたか。
       (Who came to yesterday's party?)

(c) 日本では何をしましたか。
   (lit., In Japan what did you do? (= What did you do in Japan?))

   cf. 何を日本でしましたか。
       (What did you do in Japan?)

Special Topics in Advanced Japanese Grammar

1. Adjectives in Japanese

Japanese adjectives are commonly classified into two groups: *i*-adjectives and *na*-adjectives. However, there is yet another group of adjectives, which can be called *no*-adjectives. (See *No*-type Adjective in Grammatical Terms.) (1) presents some examples of this type of adjective.

(1) a. 一般の人 (people in general)

b. 特定の国 (specific countries)

c. 永遠の真理 (eternal truth)

d. 並の選手 (average player)

e. 一流の大学 (prestigious university)

f. がら空きの野球場 (mostly empty baseball stadium)

No-adjectives are just like nouns in terms of their syntactic rules (e.g., they require *no* when they modify nouns), but they cannot be marked by case particles such as *ga* and *o*. In other words, they are not nouns. The only syntactic difference between *na*-adjectives and *no*-adjectives is that *na*-adjectives take *na* before nouns whereas *no*-adjectives take *no*.

However, some words can take either *na* or *no*, as shown in (2).

(2) a. 特別｛な / の｝治療 (special treatment)

b. 様々｛な / の｝衣装 (various costumes)

Some nouns can also be used as *no*-adjectives, as demonstrated in (3) and (4).

(3) a. 病気の母に手紙を書いた。 [*no*-adjective]
(I wrote a letter to my sick mother.)

b. 父の病気が悪化した。 [noun]
(My father's illness worsened.)

c. 蚊が人にこの病気をうつす。 [noun]
(Mosquitoes transmit this disease to people.)

(4) a. 私は水色のブラウスを買った。 [*no*-adjective]

(I bought a light blue blouse.)

b. 居間は水色を基調にした。 [noun]

(We chose light blue as the base color for the living room.)

Thus, *na*-adjectives, *no*-adjectives and nouns form a spectrum, as shown in Chart 1.

Chart 1: Spectrum of *na*-adjectives, *no*-adjectives and nouns

	Parts of speech	Examples	Prenominal form	Predicate form	Case particles
(a)	*Na*-adj.	静か (quiet) 便利 (convenient)	X-*na* N	X-*da/desu/ datta/*etc.	NA
(b)	*Na/No*-adj.	特別 (special) 様々 (various)	X-*na/no* N		
(c)	*No*-adj.	一般 (general) 並 (ordinary)	X-*no* N		
(d)	*No*-adj./ Noun	病気 (ill, illness) 水色 (blue)			X-*ga/o/* etc.
(e)	Noun	地球 (earth) ジョン (John)			

While the predicate form of *na*-adjectives and nouns is the same, both the predicate and the prenominal forms of *i*-adjectives are significantly different from those of *na*-adjectives. From this, it can be said that *i*-adjectives are "pure" adjectives. However, a handful of adjectives can take either *i* or *na*, as shown in (5). (The difference between the *i*-version and the *na*-version is subtle, but the *i*-version tends to be used when the speaker describes something objectively whereas the *na*-version is used when the speaker describes something with strong emotion.)

(5) a. 大き{い / な}うち (large house)

b. 柔らか{い / な}体 (limber body)

c. おかし{い / な}話 (strange/funny story)

d. まん丸{い / な}月 (round moon)

The overlapping categories of adjectives and nouns can be depicted as follows:

(6)

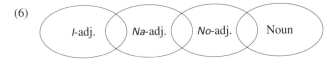

2. Interpretation of "N₁ *no* N₂"

Noun phrases with the structure "N₁ *no* N₂" often have multiple meanings. For example, (1) can mean "book(s) Hemingway wrote," "book(s) Hemingway owned" or "book(s) about Hemingway."

(1) ヘミングウェーの本

(book(s) Hemingway wrote / book(s) Hemingway owned / book(s) about Hemingway)

In the first two interpretations, N₁ (= Hemingway) is interpreted as the subject and N₂ (= book(s)) as the direct object, but in the third interpretation neither N₁ nor N₂ receives case interpretation. (Here, the term "case" refers to the grammatical property of a given noun which determines its role in the sentence in connection with the predicate, for example, as a subject, direct object, place, time, means, etc. When a noun is interpreted to have one of those properties, we say that it receives case interpretation.)

As another example, (2) means "the president's arrival," where N₁ (= the president) is the subject of the action represented by N₂ (= arrival). In this example, only N₁ receives case interpretation.

(2) 大統領の到着

(the president's arrival)

In general, "N₁ *no* N₂" can be categorized into four groups according to whether or not N₁ and N₂ receive case interpretation.

(3) "N₁ *no* N₂"

Group 1: Both N₁ and N₂ receive case interpretation

Group 2: Only N₁ receives case interpretation

Group 3: Only N₂ receives case interpretation

Group 4: Neither N₁ nor N₂ receives case interpretation

Group 1: Both N₁ and N₂ Receive Case Interpretation

(4) presents examples in which both N₁ and N₂ receive case interpretation.

(4) a. 奈津子のドレス

= {奈津子が着ているドレス (the dress Natsuko is wearing) /
奈津子が持っているドレス (the/a dress(es) Natsuko owns) /
奈津子が作ったドレス (the/a dress(es) Natsuko made)/etc. }

b. 京都の叔父

= 京都に住んでいる叔父 (the uncle (who lives) in Kyoto)

c. ９時の会議

= ９時に始まる会議 (the meeting that begins at 9 o'clock)

d. 名古屋の万国博

= 名古屋で開かれた万国博 (the world expo held in Nagoya)

Sometimes case markers appear between N_1 and *no* to clarify the meaning of the phrase, as demonstrated in (5). (The interpretations given in (5) are not necessarily exhaustive. (5b), for example, can also mean "the game that was held in Osaka.")

(5) a. ボーイフレンドからのメール

= ボーイフレンドから来たメール

(the e-mail that came from my boyfriend)

b. 大阪での試合

= 大阪で行われる試合

(the game that will be held in Osaka)

c. ニューヨーク・フィルとの競演

= ニューヨーク・フィルとした競演

(the performance (I) gave with the New York Philharmonic)

d. 今週末までの学会

= 今週末まで続く学会

(the academic conference that lasts through the end of this week.)

The case markers *ga*, *o* and *ni* never occur between N_1 and *no*. However, sometimes *ni* is replaced by a case particle with a similar meaning, as shown in (6).

(6) a. ガールフレンドへの手紙

= ガールフレンドに書いた手紙

(the letter I wrote to my girlfriend)

b. 学生たちからの贈り物

= 学生たちにもらった贈り物

(the gift I received from my students)

Group 2: Only N₁ Receives Case Interpretation

Example (2) belongs to this group, and (7) presents additional examples. In these examples, N_1 is the subject or direct object of an action represented by N_2.

(7)   a. 山村さんの参加

    ＝山村さんが参加｛する／した｝こと

       (Mr. Yamamura's participation)

   b. 遺伝子の研究

    ＝遺伝子を研究｛する／した｝こと

       (a study of genes)

   c. 列車の遅れ

    ＝列車が｛遅れる／遅れた｝こと

       (the train's delay)

   d. 給料の振り込み

    ＝給料を｛振り込む／振り込んだ｝こと

       (the (bank) deposit of someone's salary)

Group 3: Only N₂ Receives Case Interpretation

(8) presents examples of this category. As shown in the translations, in these examples, N_1 and N_2 are interpreted as predicate noun and subject, respectively.

(8)   a. パイロットの福井さん

    ＝パイロットである福井さん

       (Mr. Fukui, who is a pilot; (among two or more Fukuis,) the Fukui who is a pilot)

   b. 病気の妻

    ＝病気である妻

       (my wife, who is ill)

(9) presents another set of examples in this category. Here, the *suru*-verb stem N_1 represents an action, and N_2 represents the subject of the verb, as in (9a), or the procedure for creating a document, as in (9b).

(9) a. 流行のヘアスタイル

   = 流行しているヘアスタイル

   (the hairstyle that is popular)

   b. (文書)作成の手順

   = (文書を)作成する手順

   (the procedure by which someone creates a document)

It should be noted, however, that this type of noun phrase is not acceptable for any N_1. For example, the phrases in (10) are not acceptable.

(10) a. *到着の旅行者 (a/the traveler(s) who {will arrive / arrived})

   b. *削減の予算 (the budget that {will be / was} reduced)

   c. *研究の遺伝子 (the genes someone {will study / is studying / etc.})

Interestingly, a qualified N_1 can be grammatically acceptable in cases where the more general term isn't, as demonstrated in (11).

(11) a. <u>5時到着</u>の旅行者

   = 5時に到着{する / した}旅行者

   (a/the traveler(s) who {will arrive / arrived} at five)

   b. <u>本年度削減</u>の予算

   = 本年度削減{される / された}予算

   (the budget that {will be / was} reduced this year)

Group 4: Neither N_1 nor N_2 Receives Case Interpretation

Examples in this group can be further sub-grouped according to the relationship between N_1 and N_2.

A. Qualifier and Dependent Noun

The meanings of nouns such as *ue* "upper part; the area on top (of something)," *ichibu* "a part," *chosha* "author," *kekka* "result" and *tsumori* "intention" are not complete in themselves. In this respect, these nouns are dependent nouns. In the "N_1 *no* N_2" examples in this group, N_1 qualifies N_2 and gives it context and meaning, thus completing the meaning of N_2, as demonstrated in (12).

(12) a. テーブルの上 (the surface of the table; the space above the table)

    b. 計画の一部 (a part of the plan)

    c. 『老人と海』の著者 (the author of "The Old Man and the Sea")

    d. 試験の結果 (the result of the test)

    e. 出席のつもり ((someone's) intention to attend)

B. Appositive Relationship

In this group, N_1 indicates (a) specific member(s) of the group indicated by N_2, as shown in (13).

(13) a. サクラの木 (cherry tree(s))

    b. 51番の背番号 (lit., the back number 51 (= the number 51 on the back of an athlete's uniform))

    c. これらの書類 (these documents) (これら is a demonstrative pronoun.)

C. Inclusion Relationship

In this group, N_2 is part of (or an attribute of) N_1, as shown in (14).

(14) a. ロボットの脚 (the legs of a/the robot(s))

    b. ニューヨークのダウンタウン (New York's downtown area)

    c. 日本人の心 (the Japanese people's mind)

    d. 京都の気候 (the climate of Kyoto)

D. Relevance Relationship

In this group, N_2 represents something related to N_1 and the phrase means "N_2 {on / about / related to / etc.} N_1," as demonstrated in (15).

(15) a. イラク戦争の記事 (an article on the Iraq War)

    b. エネルギーの問題 (an energy problem / the energy issue)

    c. 健康保険の制度 (the health insurance system)

E. Time-Specified Noun

In this group, N$_1$ specifies a time frame for N$_2$, as demonstrated in (16).

(16) a. 明治の日本 (Japan in the Meiji Period)

b. 大学時代の理恵 (Rie in her college days)

c. 新婚当時の妻 (my wife when she was a newlywed)

As seen in (1) and other examples above, in many cases "N$_1$ *no* N$_2$" by itself means more than one thing; however, the hearer/reader usually determines the intended meaning from the context and/or situation.

3. Politeness and Formality in Spoken and Written Language

In Japanese, politeness and formality are different concepts. The use of *da* after nouns and *na*-adjective stems illustrates this difference, as shown in Chart 1.

Chart 1: Politeness and formality of *da*

		Plain	Polite
Non-formal	affirmative form	だ だった	です でした
	negative form	じゃない じゃなかった	じゃありません じゃありませんでした
	te-form	で	でして
Formal	affirmative form	である であった	であります でありました
	negative form	ではない ではなかった	ではありません ではありませんでした
	te-form	であって	でありまして

As seen above, *da* has four distinct sets of forms to show different levels of politeness and formality. The examples in Chart 2 and Chart 3 show the situations where these forms are used in spoken and in written language.

(Here, we do not discuss situations in which plain forms are required for grammatical reasons, e.g., *Kono atari <u>da</u> to tsūkin ni benri desu.* (この辺り<u>だ</u>と通勤に便利です。) "If (you live) around here, it's convenient to commute to work.")

Chart 2: Spoken language

Non-formal	Plain	Casual conversation: ・この辞書、便利だよ。 (This dictionary is convenient.) ・亜紀は来ないんだね。 (Aki is not coming, right? / Aki's not coming, is she? / You're not coming, right, Aki?)
	Polite	Ordinary polite conversation; speeches, lectures and presentations: ・この辞書は大変便利です。 (This dictionary is very convenient.) ・亜紀さんは来ないんですね。 (Aki is not coming, is she? / You're not coming, are you, Aki?)
Formal	Plain	(Not used in spoken language.)
	Polite	Formal speeches, lectures and presentations: ・木村君は我が校の誇りであります。 (Mr. Kimura is the pride of our school.) ・このような行為は絶対に許せないのであります。 (We cannot tolerate such conduct by any means.)

Chart 3: Written language

| Non-formal | Plain | News articles; academic papers; reports; essays:
・この価格設定は極めて不合理だ。
(This (practice of) price setting is extremely unreasonable.)
・結果はやり方次第だ。
(The result depends on the way you do it.)

Most books for adults use this form, which sets a neutral tone. This form may also be used in letters and e-mails to intimate friends.
・今のアパートは便利だよ。
(My current apartment is convenient.) |

Non-formal	Polite	Ordinary business or personal letters and e-mails; business documents for customers; books for young children: ・添付は必要経費の見積もりです。 (Attached is an estimate of the necessary expenditures.) ・真理ちゃんのお父さんはお医者さんです。 (Mari's father is a doctor.) Some books for adults use this form, which sets an intimate tone. This form is also used for letters and e-mails to one's family members and friends. ・今のアパートは便利です。 (My current apartment is convenient.)
Formal	Plain	News articles; academic papers; essays; reports; government reports; legal documents: ・これは助詞省略の一例である。 (This is an example of particle omission.) ・昨年の経済成長率は2.5％であった。 (The economic growth rate last year was 2.5 percent.) *De aru* is more formal in tone than *da*. In many cases both *de aru* and *da* are used within one document.
	Polite	Formal business letters; formal business documents for customers: ・この度の事故につきましては、当社は全力をあげて原因を究明する所存であります。 (We (lit., Our company) will do our utmost to investigate the cause of the recent accident.)

While verbs and *i*-adjectives have distinctive forms to indicate different politeness levels (e.g., *hanasu* and *hanashimasu*; *takai* and *takaidesu*), they do not have distinctive forms to indicate the formality level that corresponds to *de aru*; therefore, the same forms are used for both non-formal and formal situations. In other words, *da* and its variants are critical indicators of formality level.

4. Rhetorical Questions

Of all the types of questions, including Yes-No Questions, Wh-Questions, Choice Questions, Tag-Questions and Hypothetical Questions, only Rhetorical Questions (RQ hereafter) do not seek or accept an answer. RQs elicit the hearer's/reader's mental recognition and acceptance of an underlying claim. In other words, RQs look like a question on the surface but in actuality, they are an assertion.

The examples in (1) and (2) are some typical RQs used in spoken Japanese. As the English translations show, the RQ is essentially the same in Japanese as in English. The direct non-RQ versions are provided by examples with a prime mark. The sentences in (1) take the form of Yes-No Questions, and in (2), Wh-Questions.

(1) a. 俺にそんな汚い仕事をさせようって言うのか。
     (Are you going to make me do that kind of dirty job?)

   a'. 俺はそんな汚い仕事はしたくない。
     (I don't want to do that kind of dirty job.)

   b. そんなこと僕が知っているわけがないじゃないか。
     (How should I know that sort of thing?)

   b'. そんなことは僕は知らない。
     (I don't know that sort of thing.)

   c. お前はそれでも大学生か。
     (Are you really a college student?)

   c'. お前は大学生とは思えない。
     (You're no college student.)

   d. お前、気が狂ったんじゃないか。
     (Are you crazy?)

   d'. お前は気が狂っている。
     (You're crazy.)

   e. それはよかったじゃないか。おめでとう！
     (Wasn't that great? Congratulations!)

   e'. それはよかった。おめでとう。
     (That was great! Congratulations!)

(2) a. いつまでテレビを見ているの。勉強しなさい。

(Hey, how long are you going to watch TV? Do your homework!)

a'. もうテレビを見てはいけないよ。勉強しなさい。

(Don't watch TV now. Do your homework!)

b. 誰がそんな安い給料で仕事をするもんか。

(Who would do the job for such a low salary?)

b'. 誰もそんな安い給料で仕事はしないよ。

(No one will do the job for a salary that low.)

c. どうして私の考えも聞いて下さらないのですか。

(Why won't you listen to what I have to say?)

c'. どうぞ私の考えも聞いて下さい。

(Please listen to what I have to say.)

d. 日本語がやさしいなんていつ僕が言った？

(When did I tell you that Japanese is easy?)

d'. 日本語がやさしいなんて言ったことはないよ。

(I've never said that Japanese is easy.)

e. どうしていつも私のせいにするの？

(Why are you always blaming me?)

e'. いつも私のせいにしないで下さい。

(Don't always blame me.)

Depending on the context, RQs can express anger or frustration, as in (1a-c) and (2a, b); surprise, as in (1d); joy, as in (1e); a plea, as in (2c); denial, as in (2d); or accusation, as in (2e).

RQs are also used in written language. However, usually they are not used to express the writer's emotion, but rather to express the writer's views in an indirect way. Take (3a), for example. The writer may well be convinced that the Japanese are excessively optimistic about robots, but he is hesitant about writing that as straightforwardly as it's stated in (3a').

(3) a. 日本人はロボットに過大な期待を持っているのではないだろうか。

(Don't Japanese people have excessive expectations regarding robots?)

　　　　a'. 日本人はロボットに過大な期待を持っている。

　　　　（I think that Japanese people have excessive expectations for
　　　　robots.）

In all the examples in (4), the writer is not emotive about the subject. The
writer simply refrains from stating his/her belief in a straightforward manner. Depending on the context, an RQ may express the writer's humble
cautiousness or lack of straightforwardness. In Japanese formal or public
writing, RQs are used quite frequently.

(4)　a. 人間と動物の関係からもっと学べることはあるのではないだろうか。

　　　　（Can we not learn more from the relationship between people
　　　　and animals?）

　　　　a'. 人間と動物の関係からもっと学べる。

　　　　（We can learn more from the relationship between people and
　　　　animals.）

　　　b. 技術の醍醐味というものは、できないことを可能にするところにあ
　　　　　るのではないだろうか。

　　　　（Is it not those technologies that make the impossible possible
　　　　that show what is truly attractive about technology?）

　　　b'. 技術の醍醐味というものは、できないことを可能にするところにあ
　　　　　る。

　　　　（Those technologies that make the impossible possible show
　　　　what is truly attractive about technology.）

　　　c. 一体誰がこのような過激な思想に賛同するだろうか。

　　　　（Who in the world would agree with such a radical ideology?）

　　　c'. 誰もこのような過激な思想に賛同しない。

　　　　（Nobody would agree with such a radical ideology.）

Note that the endings of RQ sentences usually take one of five forms, as
shown below. (ii) can be interpreted either as a RQ or a self-directed question meaning "I wonder if ~."

(i)　　～（ない）｛（の）では／（ん）じゃ｝｛ない／ありません｝か

　　　Ex.　知っている（の）では｛ない／ありません｝か。
　　　　　　知っている（ん）じゃ｛ない／ありません｝か。
　　　　　　（Isn't it the case that he knows it?）

知らない (の) では ｛ない / ありません｝か。
知らない (ん) じゃ ｛ない / ありません｝か。
(Isn't it the case that he doesn't know it?)

(ii)　〜(ない) ｛の / ん｝ ｛だろう / でしょう｝か

Ex.　知っている ｛の / ん｝ ｛だろう / でしょう｝か。
(I doubt that he knows it. (lit., Could it be the case that he knows it?))

知らない ｛の / ん｝ ｛だろう / でしょう｝か。
(I believe that he knows it. (lit., Could it be the case that he doesn't know it?))

(iii)　〜(ない) ｛のでは / んじゃ｝ ない ｛だろう / でしょう｝か

Ex.　知っているのではない ｛だろう / でしょう｝か。
知っているんじゃない ｛だろう / でしょう｝か。
(I believe he knows it. (lit., Isn't it the case that he knows it?))

知らないのではない ｛だろう / でしょう｝か。
知らないんじゃない ｛だろう / でしょう｝か。
(I believe that he doesn't know it. (lit., Isn't it the case that he doesn't know it?))

(iv)　〜｛と / って｝ ｛言う / 言わない｝ ｛の (です) / んです｝か
　　　〜｛と / って｝ ｛思う / 思わない｝ ｛の (です) / んです｝か

Ex.　知っていると言うのですか。
知っているって言うのか。
(I bet he doesn't know it. (lit., Are you (really) saying / Would you say that he knows it?))

恥ずかしいと思わないのか。
(Shame on you! (lit., Don't you feel ashamed?))

(v)　(Wh-word)〜｛の (です) / んです｝か

Ex.　知っているの (です) か。
(I bet he doesn't know it. (lit., Does he (really) know it?))

どうして知らないのか。
(You should know it. (lit., Why don't you know it?))

5. Metaphors in Japanese

Seto (1995) used a triangle to classify five major types of metaphor, as shown below.

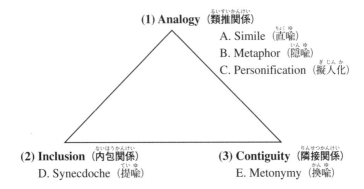

(1) Analogy （類推関係）
A. Simile （直喩）
B. Metaphor （隠喩）
C. Personification （擬人化）

(2) Inclusion （内包関係）
D. Synecdoche （提喩）

(3) Contiguity （隣接関係）
E. Metonymy （換喩）

The triangle shows that these five figures of speech are defined by three types of relationships between two objects, X and Y: (1) Analogy, (2) Inclusion and (3) Contiguity. A list of the three types, their metaphorical categories and the respective examples are provided below.

(1) Analogy （類推関係）

X is perceived to be similar to Y, although X and Y don't show any outward similarity.

A. Simile （直喩）

X is likened to Y using the pattern "X *wa* Y *no yōda*" or "X *wa* Y *mitaida*" (X is like Y).

(1)   a. 彼女はお人形のようだ。
      (She is like a doll.)

      b. 人生は旅のようだ。
      (Life is like a journey.)

      c. あの男はへびみたいだ。
      (That man is like a snake.)

  d. 彼の顔はお月さん**のようだ**。
   (His face is like the moon.)

  e. 私たちはモルモット**みたいだ**。
   (We are like guinea pigs.)

B. Metaphor （隠喩）

X is likened to Y using the pattern "X *wa* Y *da*" (X is Y).

(2) a. 彼女は人形だ。
   (She is a doll.)

  b. 人生は旅だ。
   (Life is a journey.)

  c. あの男はへびだ。
   (That man is a snake.)

  d. 彼の顔はお月さんだ。
   (His face is the moon.)

  e. 私たちはモルモットだ。
   (We are guinea pigs.)

C. Personification （擬人化）

X isn't human, but is likened to a person or a part of the human body.

(3) a. <u>ハワイ</u>があなたを**招いている**。
   (Hawaii is beckoning (lit., inviting) you.)

  b. <u>ひまわり</u>が風の中で**お辞儀をしている**。
   (Sunflowers are bowing in the wind.)

  c. <u>嵐</u>が**走り去った**。
   (The storm passed. (lit., The stormy wind ran away.))

  d. <u>この木</u>は**元気**だね。
   (This tree is healthy.)

  e. <u>小雪</u>が**舞っている**。
   (The small flakes of snow are dancing.)

f. この<u>机</u>の<u>脚</u>は弱い。

(The legs of this table are weak.)

g. この家は人に<u>優</u>しそうだ。

(This house looks kind to people.)

h. この<u>やかん</u>の<u>口</u>は小さすぎるな。

(The mouth of this kettle is a bit too small.)

(2) Inclusion（内包関係）

D. *Synecdoche*（提喩）

A specific example describes an entire category of nouns, as in (4), or a general category term is used to mean a specific example within that category, as in (5).

(4)　a. 週末は上野公園に<u>花見</u>に行ってきた。

(I went to Ueno Park for flower viewing (= cherry blossom viewing).)

b. 毎日お弁当にゆで<u>卵</u>を持っていきます。

(Every day I bring a boiled egg (= chicken egg) for lunch.)

c. <u>トリ</u>はあまり好きじゃないんだよ。

(I don't like chicken (lit., bird) so much, y'know.)

(5)　a. 人は<u>パン</u>だけで生きるのではない。

(Man doesn't live by bread (= food in general) alone.)

b. 晩ご<u>飯</u>は何時からですか。

(What time is dinner (lit., cooked rice)?)

Note that *hana* in (4a), *tamago* in (4b) and *tori* in (4c) describe the general categories of flowers, eggs and birds, but they are used to mean specific examples, i.e., cherry-blossoms, a chicken egg and chicken, respectively. Note, however, that *pan* (bread) in (5a) and *gohan* (cooked rice) in (5b) are examples of food and a meal, respectively, and are used to indicate the general category of food.

(3) Contiguity （隣接関係）

E. Metonymy （換喩）

Y of "X *no* Y" is omitted because X is closely related to or is part of Y.

(6) a. 自転車（のタイヤ）がパンクした。
         (The bicycle had a flat tire. (lit., The bicycle was punctured.))

   b. やかん（のお湯）が沸騰している。
         (The (hot water in the) kettle is boiling.)

   c. ピアノ（の音）が聞こえてくる。
         (I can hear the (sound of the) piano.)

   d. 風でローソク（の火）が消えた。
         (The wind extinguished the (flame of the) candle.)

   e. モーツアルト（の音楽）を聞くのが好きだ。
         (I like to listen to (the music of) Mozart.)

   f. きのう村上春樹（の小説）を2冊買った。
         (Yesterday I bought two (novels by) Murakami Haruki(s).)

The above examples of metonymy appear to be the result of the deletion of Y in "X *no* Y" (i.e., the nouns in parentheses). Metonymy is used only when the speaker gives more semantic saliency to X than Y.

All humans, it seems, have metaphorizing competence. In other words, they are all capable of perceiving analogy, inclusion and contiguity. The surface forms, that is, the phonetic shapes, are different from language to language, but as one notices in the examples above, Japanese metaphors frequently translate directly into English.

(7) is a list of some of the metaphorical idioms that are common to Japanese and English. There is always a possibility that Japanese borrowed the expressions from English or vice versa, but as far as we know, there is no evidence that they were the result of borrowing. Even if there is borrowing, it simply shows that any language has linguistic soil that is fertile for such metaphors from outside.

(7) 火に油を注ぐ (add fuel to the fire)
     絹のように滑らか (as smooth as silk)
     ～と波長が合う (be on the same wavelength)
     血が凍る (blood freezes)

～に幕を下ろす　(bring the curtain down on ~)

自分の耳を疑う　(can't believe one's ears)

～に目をつぶる　(close one's eyes to ~)

明るみに出る　(come to light)

～の言葉に踊らされる　(dance to someone's tune)

指一本動かさない　(don't lift a finger)

一線を引く　(draw a/the line)

目が飛び出るほど　(eyes pop out (of one's head))

穴をうめる　(fill some (of the) holes)

壁にぶつかる　(hit (up against) the/a wall)

財布の紐を握る　(hold the purse strings)

手綱を締める　(keep a tight rein on ~)

～に手を貸す　(lend a hand to ~)

～に耳を貸す　(lend one's ears to ~)

水と油のようだ　(like oil and water)

波風を立てる　(make waves)

～の道を開く　(open the way for ~)

ざるに水を注ぐ　(like water through a sieve)

(From Makino/Oka (Forthcoming))

Oka (2004) has shown that the frequency of metaphor use becomes higher as the learner's oral proficiency level goes up. For learners of Japanese, this suggests they should use metaphorical expressions as much as possible when they speak or write Japanese and pay special attention to metaphors when they read Japanese writings. As with Japanese onomatopoeia, the use of idiomatic metaphors makes communication more effective and often more creative.

6. Number Marking

Unlike Indo-European languages, Japanese does not have grammar rules requiring countable nouns to indicate number, such as "~s" or "a" in English. Thus, we cannot tell, for example, how many frogs jumped into the old pond in the *haiku* composed by the famous *haiku* poet, Matsuo Basho, which reads *Furuike ya kawazu tobikomu mizu no oto* (古池や 蛙飛び込む 水の音). Probably 99% of Japanese people would say one, but English translations are split between a frog and frogs: "The ancient pond / A frog leaps in / The sound of water" (Donald Keene), or "Old pond—frogs jumped in —sound of water" (Lafcadio Hearn). The choice isn't grammatical, but aesthetic. In daily conversation, the situation is the same. Marking a noun with regard to number is always optional in Japanese. But, as listed, by Martin (1975: 143-54), there are at least six ways to indicate plurality, as in (1a-f).

(1) a. *Repetition of Nouns*
人々(ひとびと) (people), 山々(やまやま) (mountains), 島々(しまじま) (islands), 家々(いえいえ) (houses), 木々(きぎ) (trees), 枝々(えだえだ) (branches), 店々(みせみせ) (stores), 神々(かみがみ) (deities), 花々(はなばな) (flowers), 日々(ひび) (days), 世々(代々)(よよ)(だいだい) (generations), 町々(まちまち) (towns)

b. *Suffixing*
-たち: 男の子たち (boys), 子供(こども)たち (children), 学生たち (students), 教師(きょうし)たち (teachers), 私たち (we), 加藤(か とう)(さん)たち (Kato and his group)

-ら[等]: 子供ら (children), 私ら (we), 彼(かれ)ら (they), こいつら (these guys), これら (these)

-ども[共]: 者ども(guys), 鬼(おに)ども (demons), 犬ども (dogs), 私ども (we)

-方(がた): 先生方 (teachers), 先輩(せんぱい)方(がた) (seniors), お客様(きゃくさま)方(がた) (customers)

c. *Chinese Prefixes*
多(た)- : 多文化(ぶんか) (many cultures), 多民族(みんぞく) (many races), 多方面(た ほうめん) (many directions), 多言語(た げんご) (multiple languages)

諸(しょ)-: 諸物価(しょぶっか) (various prices), 諸学問(しょがくもん) (various branches of learning), 諸制度(しょせい ど) (various systems), 諸事情(しょ じじょう) (various circumstances), 諸活動(しょかつどう) (various activities), 諸理論(しょ りろん) (various theories), 諸大学(しょだいがく) (various universities), 諸政党(しょせい とう) (various political parties)

d. *Noun-Modifying Phrases*

いろいろな人 (various people), 様々な考え (all sorts of ideas), たくさんの魚 (a lot of fish), 大勢の観光客 (many tourists), 数々の功績 (innumerable contributions), 複数の犯人 (more than one criminal)

e. *Verbal/Adjectival Predicates*

集まる／集める (gather), たむろする ((people) gather, get together), 散る／散らす (scatter), 片づく／片づける (be put in order／put s.t. in order), （数）多い (many), おびただしい (a large number of), 数え切れない (countless)

f. Quantifier Expressions

日本語の学生が約100人いる。 (There are about 100 students of Japanese.)

ねずみが五匹いる。 (There are five mice.)

本を五冊買った。 (I bought five books.)

三匹の子豚 (three little pigs)

The examples of noun repetition are restricted almost entirely to those listed in (1a). There are also restrictions regarding the use of the Sino-Japanese prefix plural markers in (1c). For the prefix *ta-* (多) there are more examples such as *tajō* (多情) "lit., many sentiments," *tasai* (多才) "lit., many talents" and *tagei* (多芸) "lit., many arts," but all these are usually used as the stem of *na*-adjectives meaning "passionate," "multi-talented" and "versatile," respectively.

The verbal and adjectival predicates in (1e) imply that the subject or direct object is plural, as shown in (2).

(2)   a. 僕は切手を**集めている**。
      (I am collecting stamps.)

b. 桜の花が**散って**しまった。
      (The cherry blossoms have already scattered.)

c. 情報サイトの数は**数え切れない**。
      (The number of information sites is countless.)

d. 勉強をしない大学生が**多い**。
      (Many college students don't study.)

The noun-modifying phrases in (1d) also imply that the subject is plural, as shown in (3).

(3)　a. 公園にはいろいろな花が咲いていた。

　　　　(In the park, all sorts of flowers were in bloom.)

　　b. その池にはたくさんの鯉が泳いでいた。

　　　　(In the pond, a lot of carp were swimming.)

　　c. この一年、様々な出来事が起きた。

　　　　(In the past year, all kinds of incidents occurred.)

Number can also be indicated with suffixes, as shown in (1b). The examples in (4) are cases where the plural marker -*tachi* must be used if the speaker wants to express plurality. Note that in such cases, the element that takes -*tachi* is either a proper name, as in (4a), or a pronoun, as in (4b-e). In (4), the suffix always means a "person and his/her group."

(4)　a. 山田さんたちが会いに来た。

　　　　(Yamada and his friends came to see me.)

　　b. 私たちは車でニューヨークに行った。

　　　　(We went to New York City by car.)

　　c. 彼女たちは同じレストランで働いている。

　　　　(Those women work in the same restaurant.)

　　d. 彼たちはいつも一緒に酒を飲む。

　　　　(They always drink together.)

　　e. あなたたちは夏はどうするの。

　　　　(What will you all be doing this summer?)

Kurafuji (2004) noted that there are cases where -*tachi* cannot be attached to a noun, as shown in (5).

(5)　a. 川本と柴田は大学の教師 (*たち) だ。

　　　　(Kawamoto and Shibata are college professors.)

　　b. 彼には子供 (*たち) がある。

　　　　(He has a child / children.)

Except in the above cases, the attachment of the suffix -*tachi* is optional. Its use is less appropriate when talking about animals; however, the plural marker can be attached to practically any noun if the speaker/writer feels close to whatever is expressed by the noun. (For details, see Makino (2007: 109-130).)

Another suffix, the plural marker *-ra* can be used interchangeably with *-tachi*, and, like *-tachi*, it cannot be used in the examples in (5). But in colloquial speech, *-tachi* tends to be used more frequently. Either *-ra* or *-tachi* may be preferred with certain personal pronouns, as shown in (6)-(8), or demonstrative pronouns, as in (9).

(Note: "A>B" indicates that A is used more frequently than B, and "A>>B" indicates that A is used far more frequently than B.)

(6)   a.   わたし｛**たち** >> **ら**｝は何も知らなかった。
         (We didn't know anything about it.)

      b.   わし｛**ら** >> **たち**｝は酒が大好きだ。
         (We love *sake*.)

      c.   わたくし｛**たち** >> **??ら**｝はこの大学の卒業生です。
         (We are alumni of this college. / We graduated from this
         college.)

      d.   われ｛**ら** / ***たち**｝は平和主義者だ。
         (We are pacifists.)

(7)   a.   あなた｛**たち** > **ら**｝はどこから来たの。
         (Where did you come from?)

      b.   あんた｛**ら** >> **たち**｝はここで何してんの。
         (What are you up to here?)

(8)   a.   彼｛**ら** >> **たち**｝は銀行員だ。
         (They are bankers.)

      b.   彼女｛**たち** > **ら**｝はよく仕事をする。
         (They work very hard.)

(9)   a.   これ｛**ら** / ***たち**｝はすべて優れた研究だ。
         (These are all (examples of) excellent research studies.)

      b.   それ｛**ら** / ***たち**｝は現実的な問題だ。
         (Those are realistic problems.)

      c.   あれ｛**ら** / ***たち**｝は全部フィクションです。
         (Those are all fiction.)

Finally, the plural suffix *-domo* has its unique usages. For one, it indicates the speaker's humbleness when used with the first person pronoun, as shown in (10).

(10) a. 私どもは先生のご講演を楽しみにしております。

(We (lit., I and my in-group members) are looking forward to your lecture.)

b. 私どもの大学には世界の各地から留学生が来ております。

(Students are coming from all over the world to study at our university.)

c. 私どもの店ではお客様に気に入っていただける商品を廉価で販売しております。

(Our store sells (selected) merchandise at low prices to please our customers.)

The second and the third person pronouns and the demonstrative pronouns cannot be used with -*domo*, as shown in (11)-(13), respectively.

(11) a. <u>あなた</u>｛たち / ら /*ども｝はどこから来たの。(= (7a))

b. <u>あんた</u>｛ら / たち /*ども｝はここで何してんの。 (= (7b))

(12) a. <u>彼</u>｛ら / たち /*ども｝は銀行員だ。(= (8a))

b. <u>彼女</u>｛たち / ら /*ども｝はよく仕事をする。(= (8b))

(13) a. <u>これ</u>｛ら /*たち /*ども｝はすべて優れた研究だ。(= (9a))

b. <u>それ</u>｛ら /*たち /*ども｝は現実的な問題だ。(= (9b))

c. <u>あれ</u>｛ら /*たち /*ども｝は全部フィクションです。(= (9c))

It is interesting that -*domo* can also be used to indicate that the speaker is looking down on people or, more frequently, on animals, as shown in the following examples.

(14) a. 一体この国の政治家どもは何をしようとしているのか。

(What in the world are the politicians of this country up to?)

b. 今どきの若者どもは敬語を知らない。

(Young people these days don't know how to use polite expressions.)

c. 近所の犬どもがうるさくて仕方がない。

(The dogs in our neighborhood are unbearably noisy.)

Among the three plural suffixes, -*tachi* is the most widely and frequently used and -*ra* is next. The use of -*domo* is limited.

A DICTIONARY
OF
ADVANCED
JAPANESE
GRAMMAR

(Main Entries)

日本語文法辞典〈上級編〉

aete あえて   *adv.*

an adverb that expresses the speaker's/ writer's desire or will to dare to do s.t. in spite of difficulty, danger or opposition	daringly; boldly; dare to ~; venture to ~; force oneself to ~ 【REL. *omoikitte*; *shiite*】

◆ **Key Sentences**

(A)

部長は	あえて	社長に反対意見を述べた。

(The department head boldly expressed his opposing view directly to the company president.)

(B)

			V*masu*		
私は	あえて	大がかりな研究計画を	**立て**	たい	と思う。

(I would like to take on a large-scale research proposal.)

(C)

		V*vol*	
あえて	先生の理論に異議を唱えて	**みよう**	と思う。

(I think I will try to oppose my professor's theory.)

(D)

	V*cond*		
あえて	**言え**	ば	あなたの考えは机上の空論だ。

(If I dare to say so, your idea is an unrealistic, ivory tower theory.)

(E)

			V*neg*		
君の言うことに	あえて	反対は	し	ない	よ。

(I don't dare oppose what you're saying.)

Formation

あえてV

あえて反対する　(s.o. dares to disagree)

Examples

(a) アメリカでは黙っていると損をするので、私は日本人としてあえて自己主張
をすることにしている。

(In the U.S., if I keep silent I lose out, so as a Japanese, I'm making a
point of asserting myself.)

(b) 委員会の賛同を得るのは難しいとは知りつつも、あえて新機軸の計画を提案
した。

(Although I knew that it was hard to get approval from the committee, I
dared to propose a brand new plan.)

(c) 彼の両親があえて住居を変えたのは彼の教育を考えた上であった。

(It was after his parents thought about his education that they made the
bold move to change their residence.)

(d) 悪いとは思いつつも、あえて先輩の非をとがめたら、やっぱりそれ以後、そ
の先輩は私と口をきかなくなった。

(While I knew I shouldn't have done so, I ventured to criticize my
senior partner's wrongdoings. And, sure enough, he's stopped talking to
me since.)

(e) 私はあえて人とは違った道を進みたいと思っている。

(I'm thinking of daring to follow a path different from others.)

(f) 時代の流れにあえて抗おうとしたが、徒労に終わった。

(I dared to resist the flow of the times, but it was all in vain.)

(g) あの男は能力がないけれど、あえて長所を拾えば、人のよさだろう。

(That man has no talent, but if I force myself to single out his strong
point, it would be his fine personality.)

(h) あえて日本の政治を一言で批判すると、派閥の行動ということになるだろう。

(If I ventured to find fault with current Japanese politics, it would be to
criticize the behavior of factions.)

(i) でもいいことばかりでもなかったです。あえて今言いませんが、いやなこと
　　もたくさんありました。

　　(Not everything went well. I won't venture to say now what, but there
　　were many unpleasant things.)

Notes

1. *Aete* is an adverb with which the speaker/writer expresses his/her desire
   or will to do something daringly, in spite of the fact that he or she is
   aware of the difficulty, danger or opposition in executing it.

2. The person who dares to do something has to be a person one is very
   familiar with, including the speaker/writer himself/herself. For example,
   in (1) *watashi* and *chichi* are acceptable, but *ano tsūkōnin* is not, because
   the speaker/writer is not on familiar terms with a passerby.

   (1) ｛私／父／??あの通行人｝は赤信号だったのにあえて道を渡った。

   　　(｛I／My father／??The passerby｝ boldly crossed the street, even
   　　though the signal was red.)

[Related Expressions]

I. *Omoikitte*, which means "to do s.t. hard to do with strong determination," is similar in meaning to *aete*. The crucial difference, however, is
   that *aete* is used when one dares to do something that runs contrary to
   common sense in spite of difficulty, danger or opposition, but *omoikitte*
   is used when one resolutely does something which is difficult to do.
   So in KS(A)-(D) and Exs.(a)-(h) *aete* can be replaced by *omoikitte*,
   but with a slight change in nuance; that is, the *aete* versions don't
   imply strong determination, but the *omoikitte* versions do. As shown
   in [1] below, *aete* in KS(E) and Ex.(i) cannot be replaced by *omoikitte*,
   because the latter can be used only with an affirmative predicate.

   [1] a. 君の言うことに｛あえて／*思い切って｝反対はしないよ。(= KS(E))

   　　　b. でもいいことばかりでもなかったです。｛あえて／*思い切って｝今言
   　　　　いませんが、いやなこともたくさんありました。(= Ex.(i))

   There are also cases in which only *omoikitte* can be used, as in [2],
   because *aete* is used when one does something that runs counter to
   common sense, whereas *omoikitte* is used when one does something
   difficult to do, regardless of whether it is common sense or not. It is
   quite natural for a person to speak in English with an American as in [2a]
   or to talk to a girl as in [2b].

[2] a. ｛思い切って /＊あえて｝アメリカ人と英語で話してみたら、通じたのでとても嬉しかった。

(I ventured to talk with an American in English and, because he understood, I was very happy.)

b. ｛思い切って /＊あえて｝彼女に声をかけたら、にっこりと笑ってくれたんだ。

(When I ventured to talk to her, she gave me a big smile!)

II. Another adverb with similar meaning is *shiite*, the V*te* of the verb *shiiru* "force s.o. to do s.t." *Shiite* is used to mean "to force oneself to do s.t." The crucial difference between the two is *aete* implies that an action may be met with opposition, danger, etc., but *shiite* doesn't have such an implication.

[3] a. どちらの絵の方がいいかは言いにくいけれど、｛強いて /??あえて｝言えば、このセザンヌの方だ。

(It is hard for me to say which painting is better, but, if I have to choose one, I would say this Cezanne.)

b. これと言って趣味はないんですが、｛強いて /??あえて｝言えば、音楽鑑賞ですかね。

(I don't have any particular hobby, but, if you pressed me, I could say music appreciation.)

Conversely, in a context where choice doesn't exist, the use of *shiite* becomes marginal.

[4] a. 彼は｛あえて /?強いて｝危険を冒してイラクの戦場に出かけて行った。

(He went to the war zone in Iraq at great risk.)

b. 彼女は｛あえて /??強いて｝両親の反対を押し切って彼と結婚した。

(She dared to oppose her parents and married him.)

ageku (ni) あげく（に）   *adv. / conj.*

| an adverb/conjunction indicating that one spends an extended period of time before reaching a result | in the end; finally; eventually; after 【REL. *ue de*; *sue (ni)*; *kekka*】 |

◆ **Key Sentences**

(A)

	Vinf.past			
さんざん	**考えた**	あげく	（に）	大学院へ進学することにした。
(After thinking for a long time, I decided to go on to graduate school.)				

(B)

	Vinf.past			Noun	
彼女の離婚は数年	**悩んだ**	あげく	の	**決断**	だった。
(Her divorce was a decision she made after agonizing for several years.)					

Formation

(i)   Vinf.past あげく（に）

     話したあげく（に）   (after s.o. talked)

(ii)   Vinf.past あげくの N

     考えたあげくの決断   (a decision made after deliberation)

Examples

(a) 私はさんざん悩んだあげくに最初に勤めていた会社を辞めた。

     (I quit the company where I first worked after thinking very hard (about what to do).)

(b) 彼はアジア、ヨーロッパ、北米などいろいろな国の女性とつき合ったあげくに、結局は生涯独身で過ごした。

     (He dated women from various countries in Asia, Europe and North America, but in the end he spent his entire life single.)

(c) 妻はあの靴がいい、この靴がいいと、いろいろと履いてみたあげくに、どれ
も買わずに店を出た。

(Saying "I like this one" or "I like that one," my wife tried on all sorts of shoes, but after all that, she left the store without buying any of them.)

(d) 山田は私の車を一か月も使ったあげく、返す時お礼の一言も言わなかった。

(After using my car for a whole month, Yamada didn't say even a word of thanks when he returned it.)

(e) さんざん迷ったあげく、一年休職してアメリカに留学することにした。

(After weighing my options for a long time, I finally decided to take a one-year leave from my company to study abroad in the U.S.)

(f) 彼女は既婚の男性との恋に溺れたあげくに、自分の人生を台無しにしてしまった。

(After falling in love with a married man, her own life was in ruins.)

(g) どのテレビを買おうかと迷ったあげく、何も買わずに帰ってしまった。

(I couldn't decide which television I should buy, so (in the end) I went home without buying any.)

(h) 彼が自殺したのはよくよく悩みぬいたあげくのことだったのであろう。

(It must have been after really agonizing that he committed suicide.)

(i) 無料のネットサービスには、登録時に住所、氏名、電話番号、生年月日、あ
げくの果てには学歴、年収、家族構成など、様々な個人情報を要求してくる
ものがある。

(There are some free Internet services that require at the time of registration your address, name, telephone number, date of birth, and at the end, all sorts of personal information such as educational background, annual income and family size, etc.)

Notes

1. *Ageku (ni)* indicates that one spends an extended period of time before reaching some result. The verb preceding *ageku (ni)* has to be a Vinf.past. Notice that the entire verb phrase Vinf.past *ageku (ni)* usually represents something troubling, as shown in the KS and Exs. The following unacceptable sentences prove this point.

(1) *彼は３時間ぐらい友達とテニスを楽しんだ**あげく（に）**、家に帰った。

(After enjoying tennis with his friend, he went home.)

cf. 彼は３時間ぐらい友達とテニスを楽しん｜で／でから／だ後で｜、家に帰った。

(2) *１週間よく考えた**あげく（に）**、その仕事を引き受けることにした。

(After thinking hard for one week, I decided to take that job.)

cf. １週間よく考え｜て／てから／た後で｜、その仕事を引き受けることにした。

2. Since the *ageku (ni)* construction indicates two past events in sequence, it cannot be used for events in the future.

(3) *いろいろ口論をした**あげくに**二人は別れることにするだろう。

(After having argued a lot, the two will decide to separate.)

3. As shown in KS(B) and Ex.(h), the pre-nominal form is "Vinf.past *ageku no.*"

4. All the uses of *ageku (ni)* in the KS and Exs. can be rephrased using *ageku no hate ni (wa)* when the eventual outcome is a rather extreme one. Note that *ageku no hate ni (wa)* may be used without a preceding Vinf.past. Examples follow.

(4) a. 父は長年自分の車を自分で直し続けたが、**あげくの果てには**、とうとう自分で車を作ってしまった。

(My father had been repairing his own cars for many years, and in the end he made a whole new car himself.)

cf. 父は長年自分の車を自分で直し続けた**あげくに**、とうとう自分で車を作ってしまった。

b. キャシーは京都の舞子の生活に強い興味を持ち、**あげくの果てには**一年間祇園で舞子と寝食をともにして、その生活を観察した。

(Cathy was deeply interested in how the *maiko* live in Kyoto, and eventually she observed their lives while living under the same roof with them for a year in Gion.)

cf. キャシーは京都の舞子の生活に強い興味を持った**あげくに**、一年間祇園で舞子と寝食をともにして、その生活を観察した。

【Related Expressions】

There are three related expressions: *ue de*, which expresses a preparatory action for a relatively important action, *sue (ni)*, which indicates the end of a period, and *kekka*, the neutral expression "as a result of s.t." The following examples show similarities and differences among these synonyms.

[1] a. 私はさんざん悩んだ{あげくに/末に/結果/*上で}最初に勤めていた会社を辞めた。(= Ex.(a))

b. 彼はアジア、ヨーロッパ、北米などいろいろな国の女性とつき合った{あげくに/末に/*上で/*結果}、結局は生涯独身で過ごした。

(= Ex.(b))

c. よく考えた{上で/*末に/*結果/*あげくに}行動に移しなさい。
(Put it into action after you have given it careful thought.)

d. 一郎は両親とよく相談をした{上で/結果/*末に/*あげくに}アメリカの大学に入学することにした。
(After he had discussed it thoroughly with his parents, Ichiro decided to enroll in an American college.)

e. 電車は車を引きずって約200メートル走った{末に/*上で/*結果/*あげくに}ようやく止まった。
(The train finally stopped after dragging a car about 200 meters.)

Ue de is ungrammatical in [1a, b, e] because in these examples no preparatory action for an important action is expressed. *Ageku (ni)* and *sue (ni)* are ungrammatical in [1c, d], because S_2 refers to an event not yet realized. In [1d] *ue de* is grammatical because the first event, i.e., discussion with his parents, is a preparatory action for an important action, i.e., choosing a college. *Kekka* is ungrammatical in [1b, c, e] because in these sentences the second event is not a direct result of the first event. In [1e], *ageku ni* is unacceptable because the agent of the action is not explicitly human.

(⇨ **(no) ue de** (DIJG: 547-50); **sue (ni)** (in this volume); **kekka** (DIJG: 121-23))

akumade mo   あくまでも   *adv.*

an adverb that represents the idea of "to the utmost degree"

to the end; persistently; insist; strictly; just; under any circumstance; absolutely; never; completely; ultimately
【REL. *doko made mo*; *saigo made*】

◆ **Key Sentences**

(A)

江本氏は	あくまでも	自説を変えなかった。

(Mr. Emoto persistently maintained (lit., didn't change) his opinion.)

(B)

これは	あくまでも	小説であって	実話ではない。

(lit., This is strictly fiction and not a true story.)

(C)

彼女は	あくまでも	自分に正直だった。

(She was true to herself to the end.)

Examples

(a) 私はあくまでも彼の無実を信じる。
    (I will believe in his innocence to the end.)

(b) 彼はあくまでも日本の参戦に反対を唱え続けた。
    (He kept opposing Japan's entry into the war up to the end.)

(c) あくまで一人でやると言うのならあえて手助けはしない。
    (If you insist on doing it by yourself, I won't venture to assist you.)

(d) 反乱軍はあくまでも抵抗を続けた。

(The insurgent troops continued their resistance to the end.)

(e) 君がそういう風にあくまで話し合いを拒否するのならこちらにも考えがある。

(If you persistently refuse to have a discussion (with me) like that, I'll make another plan.)

(f) ケイトはあくまでも自分の外見にこだわった。

(Kate was always particular about the way she looked.)

(g) 理論はあくまで理論であって、現実がその通りになるという保証はどこにもない。

(Theories are strictly theories; there is no guarantee that reality turns out the way they predict.)

(h) ここに書かれた費用はあくまでも目安であり、サービスによっては異なる場合があります。

(The cost written here is strictly an estimate. It may differ depending on the service (you choose).)

(i) これはあくまでも私の直感なんですが、山田さんは近々この会社を辞めるんじゃないかと思います。

(This is just what my sixth sense tells me, but I think Mr. Yamada will quit this company soon.)

(j) 少しお金を貸していただきたいのですが、家族にはあくまで内緒にしていただきたいのです。

(I'd like to borrow some money from you, but I'd appreciate it if you would keep it absolutely secret from my family.)

(k) 空はあくまでも青く澄みきっていた。

(The sky was completely blue and clear.)

Notes

1. *Akumade mo* can modify verbs, as in KS(A), Exs.(a)-(f), (j) and (k), adjectives, as in KS(C) or nouns followed by a copula, as in KS(B) and Exs.(g)-(i).

2. *Akumade mo* literally means "as much as one gets tired of," but the common meaning in today's use is "to the utmost extent." The specific meanings vary depending on the context, as seen in the examples above.

3. The meanings of *akumade mo* can be roughly grouped into four categories. (Some sentences can have more than one interpretation.)

    (i)　"to the end; persistently; always" (KS(A), (C), Exs.(a)-(f))

    (ii) "strictly; just" (KS(B), Exs.(g)-(i))

    (iii) "under any circumstance; absolutely" (KS(A), Ex.(j))

    (iv) "completely; ultimately" (Ex.(k))

4. When *akumade mo* means "to the end," it is used only in contexts where someone does something despite the fact that the situation is against him/her. In Ex.(a), for example, the speaker maintains a position contrary to the opinion of others. Thus, *akumade mo* cannot be used in (1). (See Related Expression II.)

(1) a. 僕は明日のマラソンで絶対｛*あくまでも／最後まで｝走り抜くつもりだ。

    (I'll keep going (lit., run to the end) by any means in tomorrow's marathon.)

   b. 地球上に｛*あくまでも／最後まで｝生き残る生物は何だろう。

    (I wonder what kinds of creatures will be able to survive on the earth until the end.)

5. The final *mo* sometimes drops, but the meaning or nuance does not change.

【Related Expressions】

I.　*Doko made mo* "to a limitless degree" is synonymous with *akumade mo* and can be used for *akumade mo* when it means "to the end; persistently; strictly; ultimately," as in [1].

  [1]　a. 江本氏は｛あくまでも／どこまでも｝自説を変えなかった。(= KS(A))

    b. 私は｛あくまでも／どこまでも｝彼の無実を信じる。(= Ex.(a))

    c. 理論は｛あくまで／どこまでも｝理論であって、現実がその通りになるという保証はどこにもない。(= Ex.(g))

    d. 空は｛あくまでも／どこまでも｝青く澄みきっていた。(= Ex.(k))

II.　*Saigo made* "until the end" can also be used for *akumade mo* when *akumade mo* means "to the end."

[2] a. 私は｛あくまでも／最後まで｝彼の無実を信じる。(= Ex.(a))

b. 彼は｛あくまでも／最後まで｝日本の参戦に反対を唱え続けた。

(= Ex.(b))

anagachi ~ nai あながち～ない   *str.*   <w>

~~~~~~~~~~~~~~~~~~~~~~~~~~~~~~~~~~~~~~
a structure that indicates that s.t. is not necessarily the way the speaker/writer thought
~~~~~~~~~~~~~~~~~~~~~~~~~~~~~~~~~~~~~~

(not) necessarily; (not) always 【REL. *kanarazushimo ~ nai*】

◆ **Key Sentence**

彼の推理も	あながち	間違ってい	ない	のかもしれない。
(His guess may not necessarily be wrong.)				

Formation

あながち～ない

あながち間違いではない   (~ isn't necessarily wrong)

Examples

(a) バーチャル指揮者ソフトが売れているところを見ると、一度は指揮者になってみたいというのは、あながち僕だけの願望ではないらしい。

(Judging by how well virtual conducting software has been selling, apparently I'm not necessarily the only one who'd like to try orchestra conducting at least once in my life.)

(b) 最後の一章はやや蛇足とも思えるが、そのエピソードは読んでいて気分がいい。ということは、あながち蛇足とは言えないということか。

(I felt like the last chapter wasn't quite necessary, but it feels good to read it. So, I guess it's not so superfluous after all.)

(c) 皮膚のpHが体調によっても変わるとすれば、「気分次第で色が変わる口紅」というのもあながち嘘ではない。

(If it's true that the pH of your skin changes depending on your health, then "the lipstick that changes its color depending on your mood" isn't necessarily a lie.)

(d) 完全に男女平等な社会が来るのは困るというのも、あながち偽った気持ちではない。

(It wouldn't be a total lie for me to say I would have difficulty with a society in which men and women are completely equal.)

(e) この俳優の演技はうまいが、時々違和感を覚えるのは、あながち演出のせいとばかりは言えない。

(This actor is talented, but sometimes his performances come off a little strange, and I don't think it's necessarily always the fault of the producer.)

(f) 生死の境をさまよっていた人が手術中の会話を鮮明に覚えていたりすることから、幽体離脱現象もあながち否定できない。

(Since some people who've come close to dying say that they can clearly recall what was being said around them while they were on the operating table, we can't simply deny the occurrence of out-of-body experiences.)

Note

The adverb *anagachi* is used with a negative predicate, indicating that the proposition implied in the context is not necessarily false. The writer of Ex.(a), for example, initially thought that there were not many people who would want to conduct an orchestra. But because software for virtual conducting is selling well, he modified his initial judgment.

【Related Expression】

The adverb *kanarazushimo ~ nai* can also mean "not always" and can replace all the uses of *anagachi ~ nai* in the KS and Exs. But there are cases where *kanarazushimo ~ nai* cannot be replaced by *anagachi ~ nai*, as shown in [1], where the speaker/writer doesn't give some objective reason. In [2], where the speaker/writer gives an objective reason in the preceding context, both adverbs can be used.

[1] a. 光るもの、{必ずしも /*あながち}金ではない。
(All that glitters is not gold.)

b. 金持ちは{必ずしも /*あながち}傲慢ではない。
(Rich people are not always arrogant.)

c. 日本人は{必ずしも /*あながち}丁寧ではない。
(Japanese are not always polite.)

d. 彼の話は{必ずしも /*あながち}真実ではない。
(He doesn't always tell the truth.)

[2] a. あの男は、傲慢だと言われているけど、僕の観察では時々非常に優しい面を見せる。{あながち /必ずしも}傲慢ではないのだ。(cf. [1b])
(They say that guy is arrogant, but sometimes I've seen him being very kind. He isn't always arrogant.)

b. UFOは全く根拠のないことだというのが常識だが、UFOの証拠写真を見ると、{あながち /必ずしも}真実ではないとは言い切れないようだ。(cf. [1d])
(It is widely believed that UFOs are sheer nonsense. But when you look at evidence of UFOs in photos, it seems that the claim isn't altogether groundless.)

(⇨ ***kanarazushimo*** (DIJG: 92-96))

aruiwa　あるいは　　　*conj.*

{ a conjunction that marks alternatives }　or; either ~ or; perhaps
【REL. *mata wa*; *moshikuwa*; *soretomo*; ***mata***; ***naishi (wa)***】

◆ **Key Sentences**

(A)

Noun₁			Noun₂		
ボールペン	(か)	あるいは	万年筆 まんねんひつ	で	お書き下さい。

(Please write either with a ballpoint pen or a fountain pen.)

(B)

		Sentence₁		
日本のような少子化社会では、 しょうしか		大学の数を少なくする かず	か、	あるいは

Sentence₂		
外国人の学生を増やす ふ	か	しなければなるまい。

(In a society like Japan where the number of children is decreasing, we may have to either reduce the number of colleges or increase the number of foreign students.)

(C)

	Adj(*i*)₁			Adj(*i*)₂		
性格が せいかく	明るい	か、	あるいは	暗い	か	によって、人生は非 じんせい ひ 常に変わってくる。 じょう か

(Depending on whether someone's personality is cheerful or gloomy, his or her life will change dramatically.)

(D)

すべての宗教は、 しゅうきょう	あるいは	アニミズムから 来ている	(の)	かもしれない。

(Perhaps all religions originate from animism.)

Formation

(i) N₁ (か)、あるいは N₂

父 (か)、あるいは母 (either my father or my mother)

(ii) V₁inf か、あるいは V₂inf か

   本を読むか、あるいはテニスをするか   (either reading books or playing tennis)

(iii) ｛Adj(*i*)inf / Adj(*na*)stem｝か、あるいは｛Adj(*i*)inf / Adj(*na*)stem｝か

   面白いか、あるいはつまらないか   (interesting or boring)

   民主的か、あるいは独裁的か   (democratic or dictatorial)

(iv) あるいは｛V / Adj(*i*)｝inf (の)かもしれない

   あるいは｛行く / 行った｝(の)かもしれない   (s.o. perhaps will go / went there)

   あるいは｛面白い / 面白かった｝(の)かもしれない   (s.t. is/was perhaps interesting)

(v) あるいは｛Adj(*na*)stem / N｝｛ø / だった (の)｝かもしれない

   あるいは｛元気 / 元気だった (の)｝かもしれない   (s.o. is/was perhaps healthy)

   あるいは｛先生 / 先生だった (の)｝かもしれない   (s.o. is/was perhaps a teacher)

Examples

(a) 社長は朝ご飯にはトーストかあるいはオートミールを召し上がる。

   (For breakfast, the company president has either toast or oatmeal.)

(b) 政治学あるいは経済学を専攻した学生を採用します。

   (We will hire a student who has majored in either political science or economics.)

(c) ご注文は電話か、あるいはインターネットでお願いします。

   (Please place your order either by phone or by Internet.)

(d) この会社は大規模なリストラをするか、あるいは、倒産するかしかない。

   (The only choice left for this company is to execute a large-scale re-structuring or else go bankrupt.)

(e) 定年になったら毎日川で釣りをするか、あるいはゴルフをしようと思っています。

   (Once I retire, I'm thinking of fishing at the river or playing golf every day.)

(f) 人々の大統領の評価は好きか、あるいは、嫌いかのどちらかだ。

(People's assessment of the president is split: They either love him or hate him.)

(g) 現在日本の政党は乱立しているが、将来あるいはアメリカのように二大政党になるかもしれない。

(Right now there are too many political parties in Japan, but in the future, perhaps there will be two big parties like in the States.)

Notes

1. *Aruiwa* is a conjunction that marks alternatives or possibility, depending on the structure. When *aruiwa* occurs with *kamoshirenai*, as in KS(D) and Ex.(g), it means possibility, but otherwise it connects alternatives, as shown in KS(A)-(C) and Exs.(a)-(f).

2. In Formation (i), the use of *ka* is optional.

3. In the "alternative" interpretation, *ka aruiwa* can be merely *ka*, but the use of *aruiwa* makes the utterance more formal.

(1) a. 社長は朝ご飯にはトースト**か(あるいは)**オートミールを召し上がる。

(= Ex.(a))

b. 政治学**か(あるいは)**経済学を専攻した学生を採用します。(= Ex.(b))

In the case of the "possibility" interpretation, *aruiwa* retains its basic meaning of alternatives. For example, in Ex.(g), the speaker is expressing the possibility of a two-party system as an alternative to a multi-party system.

[Related Expressions]

There are three conjunctions in addition to *aruiwa* with the meaning of "or": *mata wa*, *moshikuwa* and *soretomo*. All of them can replace *aruiwa* in the KS and Exs., in which the speaker is wondering which alternative is to be chosen, as shown in [1]. If not, *soretomo* cannot replace *aruiwa*, as shown in [2].

[1] a. 日本のような少子化社会では、大学の数を少なくするか、{**あるいは**/**または**/**もしくは**/**それとも**}外国人の学生を増やすかしなければなるまい。(= KS(B))

b. この会社は大規模なリストラをするか、{**あるいは**/**または**/**もしくは**/**それとも**}、倒産するかしかない。(= Ex.(d))

A

　　c. この本が間違っているか、{あるいは / それとも / または / もしくは}
　　　私が間違っているか、そのどちらかだ。
　　　(It's either that this book is wrong, or that I am wrong.)

[2]　a. ボールペン (か) {あるいは / または / もしくは / *それとも} 万年筆で
　　　お書き下さい。(= KS(A))

　　b. 政治学 (か) {あるいは / または / もしくは / *それとも} 経済学を専攻
　　　した学生を採用します。(= Ex.(b))

　　c. ご注文は電話 (か)、{あるいは / または / もしくは / *それとも} イン
　　　ターネットでお願いします。(= Ex.(c))

　　d. この会社は大規模なリストラをするか、{あるいは / または / もしく
　　　は / *それとも}、倒産するかしかない。(= Ex.(d))

The hierarchy of formality among the four conjunctions is roughly *moshi-kuwa* > *mata wa* > *aruiwa* > *soretomo*, with *moshikuwa* as the most formal conjunction and *soretomo* as the least formal conjunction. The first two in the hierarchy are seldom used in spoken language, as shown in [3].

[3]　冬休みはここにいますか。{あるいは / それとも / *または / *もしく
　　は}、旅行かなんかしますか。
　　(During winter break are you going to stay here? Or are you going
　　on a trip or something?)

Note also that neither *mata wa* nor *moshikuwa* nor *soretomo* can be used with *kamoshirenai*, as shown below. In other words, they cannot indicate possibility.

[4]　a. すべての宗教は、{あるいは / *または / *もしくは / *それとも} アニ
　　　ミズムから来ている (の) かもしれない。(= KS(D))

　　b. 現在日本の政党は乱立しているが、将来 {あるいは / *または / *もし
　　　くは / *それとも} アメリカのように二大政党になるかもしれない。

　　　　　　　　　　　　　　　　　　　　　　　　　　　　　　(= Ex.(g))

　　　　　(⇨ ***mata wa*** (DIJG: 171-74); ***moshikuwa*** (in this volume);
　　　　　　soretomo (DBJG: 421-22))

atakamo あたかも　　*adv.*　<w>

an adverb used to present a counter-factual statement emphatically	(just) as if ~ were; (just) as if ~ did ~; just like; just; exactly 【REL. *marude*; **ka no yōni**】

◆ **Key Sentences**

(A)

		Noun		
彼は	あたかも	責任者	のように	振る舞っている。

(He behaves as if he were the person in charge.)

(B)

			Vinf		
リニアモーターカーは	あたかも	氷の上を	すべる	(かの)ように	走る。

(The linear motor car runs as if it were gliding on ice.)

(C)

			Vinf		Noun
この装置を使って、	あたかも	現場に	いる	(かの)ような	感覚

で	現場にいるロボットを操縦できる。

(Using this device you can operate a robot at the site as if you were actually there.)

Formation

(i)　あたかも N の{ように / ような N}

　　　あたかも上司の{ように / ような言い方}　(as if s.o. were a supervisor; a way of talking as if s.o. were a supervisor)

(ii)　あたかも {V / Adj(*i*)}inf(かの){ように / ような N}

　　　あたかもよく知って{いる / いた}(かの){ように / ような言い方}　(as if s.o. knew / had known s.t. well; a way of talking as if s.o. knew / had known s.t. well)

あたかも ｛安い／安かった｝(かの)｛ように／ような言い方｝　(as if s.t. were / had been cheap; a way of talking as if s.o. were / had been cheap)

(iii) あたかも ｛N／Adj(*na*)stem｝｛である／であった｝(かの)｛ように／ような N｝

あたかも専門家｛である／であった｝(かの)｛ように／ような言い方｝ (as if s.o. were / had been a specialist; a way of talking as if s.o. were / had been a specialist)

あたかも上手｛である／であった｝(かの)｛ように／ような言い方｝　(as if s.o. were / had been good at s.t.; a way of talking as if s.o. were / had been good at s.t.)

Examples

(a) この磁石はあたかも永久磁石のように動作する。

(This magnet acts as if it were a permanent magnet.)

(b) リモートコントロールソフトは遠くのPCのデスクトップ画面をそのまま手元のPCに映し出し、あたかも自分のデスクトップのように操作することができる。

(A remote control software program displays the desktop of a remote personal computer on the computer in front of you and enables you to operate it as if it were your own computer's desktop.)

(c) 彼女はあたかも自分のうちにいるように振る舞っている。

(She behaves as if she were in her own house.)

(d) 上手な説明文は、あたかも目の前にその光景が広がっているように鮮明にイメージできるものです。

(With well-written explanatory sentences, the reader can get vivid images, as if the scenes were spread out in front of his eyes.)

(e) 彼はあたかも自分が上司であるかのように私に仕事を言いつける。

(He gives me assignments as if he were my boss.)

(f) 連結納税制度とは、企業グループがあたかも一つの法人であるかのように捉えて、納税させる仕組みです。

(The linked tax payment system is a mechanism by which a group of companies is viewed and made to pay taxes as if they were a single corporation.)

(g) この映画はコンピュータ・グラフィックスによって、あたかも人間が実際に
人の体の中に入って活動しているような効果を生み出している。

(Using computer graphics, this movie creates the effect of people
actually working and playing inside someone's body.)

(h) 私はあたかも空を飛んでいるかのような錯覚を覚えた。

(I felt as if I were flying (lit., I had the illusion of flying) through the
air.)

(i) この文章はあたかも我々が不正を行っているかのごとき印象を与える。

(These sentences give people the impression that we are doing something dishonest.)

Notes

1. *Atakamo* is used to introduce a counterfactual statement emphatically.
This means that what is described in the *atakamo* phrase/clause is
not real or true. *Atakamo* is usually paired with auxiliaries meaning
"appear," such as *yōda* and *gotoshi*. The use of *gotoshi*, however, is
limited to formal written language. The noun-modifying and verb-
modifying forms of *gotoshi* are *gotoki* (Ex.(i)) and *gotoku*, respectively.
(⇨ *gotoshi* (in this volume))

2. *Ka no* before *yōda*, *gotoshi* and their variations is optional. *Ka no*
emphasizes counterfactuality.

3. *Yōna* in "*yōna* N" and *gotoki* in "*gotoki* N" can be omitted when N
represents things like sensations and impressions. For example, (1a) and
(1b) are acceptable without *yōna* or *gotoki*, whereas in (1c) *yōna* cannot
be omitted.

(1) a. この装置を使って、あたかも現場にいる{ような / ø}感覚で、現場に
いるロボットを操縦できる。(= KS(C))

   b. この文章はあたかも我々が不正を行っているかの{ごとき / ø}印象を
与える。(= Ex.(i))

   c. この映画はコンピュータ・グラフィックスによって、あたかも人間が
実際に人の体の中に入って活動している{ような / *ø}効果を生み出
している。(= Ex.(g))

4. Besides the auxiliaries mentioned in Note 1, *atakamo* also occurs with
verbs of thinking and perception, such as *omou* "think," *kangaeru*
"think," *ninshiki-suru* "recognize," etc.

(2) a. この夜空の色は**あたかも**火事を<u>思わせる</u>。

    (The colors of the night sky make you think there is a fire.)

  b. 製品の特定部分の品質、性能等が著しく強調され、**あたかも**全体が優良であると<u>誤解させる</u>ような表示をしてはならない。

    (Product labels must not be designed to mislead us into believing that the product as a whole is excellent by overemphasizing the quality and performance of particular parts.)

5. *Atakamo* is also used to mean "just" when nouns refer to specific times, as in (3).

(3) a. 時は**あたかも**<u>就職</u>シーズンだ。

    (It lit., The time) is exactly job hunting season now.)

  b. 私が日本に来たのは、時**あたかも**桜が<u>満開の時</u>だった。

    (When I came to Japan, it was just the time the cherry blossoms were peaking.)

[Related Expression]

Sentences with *atakamo ~ yōda/gotoshi* can be rephrased with *marude ~ yōda/gotoshi* without changing the meaning, as shown in [1]. The only difference is that *atakamo* sounds more bookish.

[1] a. 彼は{**あたかも**／**まるで**}責任者のように振る舞っている。(= KS(A))

  b. リニアモーターカーは{**あたかも**／**まるで**}氷の上をすべる（かの）ように走る。(= KS(B))

  c. この文章は{**あたかも**／**まるで**}我々が不正を行っているかのごとき印象を与える。(= Ex.(i)))

bakari ni ばかりに *conj.*

> a conjunction indicating that a single factor causes a negative situation

simply because; just because; simply on account of ~

◆ **Key Sentences**

(A)

Subordinate Clause			Main Clause
	Vinf.past		
僕が一言変なことを	**言った**	ばかりに	彼女との関係は悪くなってしまった。

(Just because I said one nasty thing to her, my relationship with her deteriorated.)

(B)

Subordinate Clause			Main Clause
	Adj(*i*).inf		
あの子は、体が	**弱い**	ばかりに	クラスメートにいじめられている。

(That child is being bullied by his classmates simply because he is (physically) weak.)

Formation

(i) Vinf.past ばかりに

食べたばかりに (simply because s.o. ate it)

(ii) Adj(*i*)inf ばかりに

難し{い / かった}ばかりに (simply because s.t. is/was difficult)

(iii) Adj(*na*)stem{な / である / だった / であった}ばかりに

不便{な / である / だった / であった}ばかりに (simply because s.t. is/was inconvenient)

(iv) N{である / だった / であった}ばかりに

学生{である / だった / であった}ばかりに (simply because s.o. is/was a student)

B

Examples

(a) あの日たまたま休んでいたばかりに、大事な連絡を聞きそびれた。

(I missed a really important announcement just because I happened to be absent that day.)

(b) 彼女が会いたいと言ってきた時に会いに行かなかったばかりに、それが最後のチャンスになってしまった。

(Simply because I didn't go see her when she wanted to see me, it turned out to be my last chance to see her.)

(c) 遺言がないばかりに相続人の間で遺産争いに発展するということがよくある。

(Disputes among heirs over an inheritance often develop simply because there is no will.)

(d) お金がなかったばかりに、映画もろくに見られなかった。

(I couldn't even go to the movies just because I didn't have any money.)

(e) 医者の処置が不適切であったばかりに、助かる患者を死なせてしまった。

(Simply because the doctor's treatment wasn't appropriate, the patient, who could have been helped, lost his life.)

(f) 彼女は黒人女性であったばかりに人種差別と性差別を受けた。

(She suffered from racial and sexual discrimination simply because she was a black woman.)

(g) 姑との関係が悪いばかりに嫁はストレスが溜まり、よく病気になった。

(Just because her relationship with her mother-in-law was so bad, she often fell ill from the stress.)

(h) 両親が甘かったばかりに子供たちは自立心がない。

(Those children don't have a sense of independence just because they are spoiled so much by their parents.)

(i) 高校時代の教育がよくなかったばかりに、大学に入ってから苦労している。

(I'm having a difficult time in college all because my high school education wasn't good.)

Notes

1. The conjunction *bakari ni* is used to indicate that a single factor causes a negative situation.

2. The main clause indicates the resulting negative situation, but when the *bakari ni* clause takes the auxiliary adjective ~ *tai*, the main clause can indicate effort, as shown in (1).

(1) a. あいつは目立ちたいばかりに似合わない派手な背広を着ている。

(He is wearing a gaudy suit jacket that doesn't suit him just because he is so eager to stand out.)

b. ヤンキースの松井秀喜を見たいばかりに、わざわざ日本からニューヨークにやってきました。

(I came to New York all the way from Japan just to see the Yankees' Hideki Matsui.)

3. If *bakari ni* is preceded by the particle *to*, it has a totally different meaning "as if s.o. were saying ~."

(2) 彼は今がチャンスとばかりに彼女に言い寄った。

(Thinking that it was his best chance (lit., As if he were saying "now is my chance"), he made advances toward her.)

4. The negative of *aru* can be used either in the present tense, as in Ex.(c), or in the past tense, as in Ex.(d).

ba koso ばこそ *conj.* \<w\>

| a conjunction that emphasizes a reason | it is precisely because ~ that ~; only because ~; to the extent that ~ 【REL. *kara koso*】 |

◆ **Key Sentence**

	Vcond			
環境保護を支持して	いれ	ば	こそ	植林に力を入れているのだ。

(It is only because I support environmental protection so much that I put my efforts into planting trees.)

B

Formation

(i) {V / Adj(*i*)} cond ばこそ

　　読めばこそ　(it is only because s.o. reads s.t.)

　　面白ければこそ　(it is only because s.t. is interesting)

(ii) {Adj(*na*)stem / N} であればこそ

　　元気であればこそ　(it is only because s.o. is healthy)

　　先生であればこそ　(it is only because s.o. is a teacher)

Examples

(a) 「愛」があればこそ生きる喜びがある。

　　(Only because there is love is there joy for living.)

(b) 膨大な電力の需要があればこそ原子力発電を開発せざるを得ないのだ。

　　(It is precisely because of the enormous demand for electricity that we
　　cannot help but develop atomic power plants.)

(c) 中近東の和平を熱望すればこそ、国連の役割を強化しなければならないと思
　　う。

　　(It is only because I hope for peace in the Middle East as much as I do
　　that I think we have to strengthen the role of the UN.)

(d) 親友であればこそ君にこんなにずけずけとものが言えるんだよ。

　　(It is precisely because I'm your close friend that I can talk straight to
　　you like this.)

(e) ビジョンを持った社長であればこそ社員は張り切って仕事をしているのだ。

　　(It is precisely because he is a president with vision that his employees
　　are working with high spirits.)

(f) 人は一人でいるのが寂しければこそペットを飼うのだ。

　　(To the extent a person feels lonely when he/she is alone, he/she will
　　keep a pet.)

(g) 言論が自由であればこそ民主主義は育っていくのである。

　　(To the extent that there is freedom of speech, democracy will keep
　　growing.)

(h) 僕がこんなことを言うのも君を心配すればこそだ。

　　(It is because I am really anxious about you that I am telling you such a
　　thing.)

Notes

1. *Ba koso* is a subordinate conjunction that is used to give a precise reason.

2. In the *ba koso* structure, the main clause tends to end with *noda*, as shown in most of the examples, because the emphatic reason which *ba koso* represents and the function of *noda*, i.e., the function of involving the hearer/reader in his or her statement, are mutually complementary.

[Related Expression]

Ba koso can be replaced by *kara koso* which can be used in both spoken and written language. However, *kara koso* cannot always be replaced by *ba koso*, because the *kara koso* clause can be negative, but the *ba koso* clause cannot, as shown in [1].

[1] a. 英語が上手に {話せないからこそ / *話せなければこそ} 人より余計に練習しなければならない。

(It is precisely because you can't speak English well that you need to practice more than other people.)

b. 他の授業がそれほど {面白くないからこそ / *面白くなければこそ} この授業は面白く感じられる。

(Precisely because other classes are not so interesting I find this class interesting.)

---

bekarazu / bekarazaru   べからず / べからざる   *aux.*   \<w\>

an auxiliary verb that indicates a strong prohibition

shouldn't; must not; ought not to ~; cannot; Don't ~
【REL. Vinf.nonpast *na*; *o kinzu(ru)*; *-kinshi*; *te wa ikemasen*; *nai de kudasai*; *nai yōni shite kudasai*】

B

◆ **Key Sentences**

(A)

	Vinf.nonpast	
芝生に	入る	べからず。
(Keep off the lawn. (lit., Don't enter the lawn.))		

(B)

	Vinf.nonpast		Noun	
原子力はエネルギー源として	欠く	べからざる	もの	となっている。
(Atomic energy has become indispensable as a source of energy.)				

Formation

(i) Vinf.nonpast べからず。 (Exception: する→{す/する}べからず)

　　読むべからず。 (You shouldn't read it.)

　　食べるべからず。 (Don't eat (it).)

　　盗作をす(る)べからず。 (You shouldn't plagiarize.)

(ii) Vinf.nonpast べからざる N (Exception: する→すべからざる)

　　あるべからざる状態 (a situation that shouldn't exist)

　　必要欠くべからざるもの (an indispensable thing (lit., a thing that is necessary and that one cannot lack))

　　否定すべからざる事実 (an undeniable fact)

Examples

(a) 電車の中で携帯電話を使うべからず。

(You ought not to use your cell phone in the train.)

(b) ここで犬に糞をさせるべからず。

(Don't let your dog go (to the bathroom) here.)

(c) 授業中に隣の者と私語をするべからず。

(You shouldn't talk in class with your neighbors.)

(d) 無用の者、入るべからず。

(No trespassing. (lit., Don't enter if you aren't on business.))

(e) 虚言を吐くべからず。

(Don't tell a lie.)

(f) インターネットを使う時の「べからず集」からいくつか引用してみよう。プライバシーを公開するべからず。怪しげなファイルに触れるべからず。インターネットの向こうに人間がいることを忘れるべからず。

(Let me quote some of the Internet don'ts from this collection: Don't make private matters public. Don't touch suspicious-looking files. Don't forget that there are people on the other end of the Internet.)

(g) 彼は学生として許すべからざる行為を行ったとして大学を退学させられた。

(He was expelled from college because he committed an unpardonable act for a student.)

(h) この世の中には批判すべからざる学説はほとんどないと言ってよいだろう。

(One could say that there are very few theories we cannot criticize.)

(i) 奇跡とは一言にしていえば、起こり得べからざる事実が起こる場合のことである。

(In a nutshell, a miracle is when an utterly unexpected and unlikely event happens.)

Notes

1. *Bekarazu* is a negative form of *beshi* that means "should; ought to." It expresses a strong prohibition and is used only in written language.

2. The prenominal form of *bekarazu* is *bekarazaru*, which is the written version of *bekide nai*. Examples follow:

   (1) それは総理大臣としてす｛べからざる / べきでない｝発言だった。

   (It was a statement that the Prime Minister shouldn't have made. (lit., he shouldn't have made as Prime Minister.))

   (2) 児童虐待などは許す｛べからざる / べきではない｝行為だ。

   (Child abuse is an act that nobody should condone.)

   (⇨ *bekida* (DIJG: 11-15))

[Related Expressions]

There are expressions synonymous to *bekarazu* such as ~ *na*, ~ *o kinzu(ru)*, *-kinshi*, ~*te wa ikemasen*, ~*nai de kudasai*, and ~*nai yōni shite kudasai*.

B

[1] a. 芝生に{入るべからず/入るな/入ることを禁ず(る)/入ってはいけ
     ません/入らないで下さい/入らないようにして下さい}/芝生内立
     ち入り禁止。(= KS(A))

   b. 電車の中で携帯電話を{使うべからず/使うな/使うことを禁ず(る)/
     使ってはいけません/使わないで下さい/使わないようにして下さ
     い}/電車の中での携帯電話使用禁止。(= Ex.(a))

The six synonymous expressions can be ordered by the degree of prohibitive expression they express as follows: *na > bekarazu > kinzu(ru) >
-kinshi > te wa ikemasen > nai de kudasai > nai yōni shite kudasai.*

> (⇨ *na* (DBJG: 266-67); *~kudasai* (DBJG: 209-10);
> *~yōni suru* (DBJG: 562-64))

---

beku べく   *aux.*   <w>

the verb modification form of the auxiliary *bekida*, which is used to indicate a purpose or aim	in order to; to; for the purpose of; for; so that ~ (can) 【REL. *tame (ni)*】

◆ **Key Sentence**

	Vinf.nonpast		
この大学では、2学期制に	**変える**	べく	今準備が進められている。

(At this university, preparation is under way for changing (the current
system) to a semester system.)

Formation

Vinf.nonpast べく (Exception: する → {す/する}べく)

話すべく   (in order to talk (to s.o.))

勉強す(る)べく   (in order to study)

Examples

(a) K社は人件費を削減すべく大規模なリストラを行う予定だ。

(K Company plans to execute large-scale restructuring in order to reduce personnel expenses.)

(b) 当社はいち早くお客さまの多様なニーズに対応すべく、最新の設備を導入してまいりました。

(We (lit., our company) have installed the newest facilities so that we can quickly respond to our customers' various needs.)

(c) 二児の母親ですが、現在フットセラピストとして独立すべく勉強中です。

(I am a mother of two children and am currently studying to start my own practice as a foot therapist (lit., to become independent as a foot therapist).)

(d) 本学は、経済的な理由で大学教育を受けられない海外の優秀な学生にその機会を与えるべく、奨学金を供与している。

(We (lit., our university) provide scholarships to give educational opportunities to excellent students from overseas who cannot go on to higher education for financial reasons.)

(e) 重大な事故が発生した場合、お客様の安全確保を最優先として迅速な対応を行うべく、社内システムの見直しを行いました。

(We have reexamined our internal systems so that we can rapidly respond to major accidents in a manner that gives highest priority to customer safety.)

(f) より進んだ経営革新を行うためには、マネジメントシステム運用時の無駄を省くべく、システム間の重複をなくすことが重要である。

(In order to engage in management innovation that is more advanced, it is important to remove redundancy in management systems so that we can eliminate unnecessary operations.)

Notes

1. *Beku* is the verb modification form of *bekida* "should." However, when *beku* is used to modify the verbs of main clauses, it means "in order to" rather than "should."

2. *Beku* is a highly formal expression and is usually used in written language. (⇨ ***bekida*** (DIJG: 11-15))

[Related Expression]

B

Beku can be replaced with *tame (ni)* without changing the meaning of the sentence. *Tame (ni)* can be used in informal situations, too.

[1] a. この大学では、2学期制に変える{べく / ために}今準備が進められている。(= KS)

b. K社は人件費を削減{すべく / するために}大規模なリストラを行う予定だ。(= Ex.(a))

Note that *suru*, not *su*, precedes *tame (ni)* in this structure.

(⇨ ***tame (ni)*** (DBJG: 447-51))

beku mo nai   べくもない   *phr.*   <w>

a phrase meaning "it is impossible to do s.t."

impossible; there is no way for s.o. to ~; cannot be expected to

【REL. Vpot *wake ga nai*; Vpot *hazu ga nai*】

◆ **Key Sentence**

	Vinf.nonpast	
私が一億円の家を買うなど、	望む	べくもない。

(It is impossible for me to hope to buy a hundred million yen house.)

Formation

Vinf.nonpast べくもない   (Exception: する → {す / する}べくもない)

勝つべくもない   (it is impossible to win)

否定す(る)べくもない   (it is impossible to deny)

B

Examples

(a) 10年前に別れた女性の居どころなど知るべくもない。

(There is no way for me to know the whereabouts of the woman I split up with 10 years ago.)

(b) 終戦後は海外旅行など望むべくもなかった。

(In the post-war era, one could not even hope to make a trip abroad.)

(c) 初日は雨で山頂は望むべくもなかったが、翌日はすっかり晴れ、白銀に輝く山は神々しい美しさだった。

(On the first day, it was impossible to view the summit because of rain, but on the following day, the weather was perfect, and the mountain was shining silvery white. It was sublimely beautiful.)

(d) 我々のような弱いチームが優勝候補のTチームに勝つべくもない。

(A weak team like ours simply cannot be expected to beat Team T, one of the competitors for the championship.)

(e) その事件が起きた時私は海外旅行中で知るべくもなかった。

(The incident occurred when I was traveling abroad, so there was no way for me to know about it.)

(f) 最近は多忙で本を読む時間など期待すべくもない。

(Lately I've been so busy that it is impossible to find (lit., to expect to have) time to read books.)

Note

Beku mo nai means that there is "no way for s.o. to do s.t." The phrase is used exclusively in written Japanese. The verbs preceding the phrase appear to be limited to *nozomu* "desire," *shiru* "get to know," and *katsu* "win." In terms of frequency, *nozomu beku mo nai* appears to be the most frequently used.

【Related Expressions】

Vpot.inf.nonpast *wake ga nai* and Vpot.inf.nonpast *hazu ga nai* mean "there is no reason to believe that s.t. is possible" and "s.t. isn't expected to be possible," respectively. Verbs can be practically any verb for the two constructions. However, the verb of Vinf.nonpast *beku mo nai* is usually limited to *nozomu*, *shiru* or *katsu*, as stated in Note. So, *beku mo nai* can be replaced by *wake ga nai* and *hazu ga nai*, but not the other way around, as shown in [1] and [2], respectively.

B

[1]　a. 終戦後は海外旅行など {望むべくもなかった / 望めるわけがなかった / 望めるはずがなかった}。(= Ex.(b))

　　b. 我々のような弱いチームが優勝候補のTチームに {勝つべくもない / 勝てるわけがない / 勝てるはずがない}。(= Ex.(d))

[2]　a. こんな難しい日本語が {読めるわけがない / 読めるはずがない / *読むべくもない}。

　　　({There is no reason why I can / I cannot be expected to be able to} read such difficult Japanese.)

　　b. 僕に詩が {書けるわけがない / 書けるはずがない / *書くべくもない}。

　　　({There is no reason why I can / I cannot be expected to be able to} write poems.)

beku shite　べくして　*phr.*

{a phrase used when s.t. occurs/occurred exactly as expected}

exactly as expected
【REL. *yahari/yappari*】

◆ **Key Sentence**

	V₁inf.nonpast		V₂ (= V₁)
第二次世界大戦は	起こる	べくして	起こった。

(World War II occurred, exactly as expected.)

Formation

V₁inf.nonpast べくして V₂　(where V₁ = V₂)　(Exception: する → {す / する} べくして)

起こるべくして起こる　(s.t. occurs exactly as expected)

成功す(る)べくして成功する　(s.t./s.o. succeeds exactly as expected)

B

Examples

(a) 彼は大統領になるべくしてなった。

(He became president, exactly as expected.)

(b) 真知子は高校の時から成績が抜群によく、東大に入るべくして入ったという感じである。

(Machiko distinguished herself as an excellent academic achiever in her high school days. As expected, she got into the University of Tokyo.)

(c) 二人は性格、趣味、学歴がすべて一致している。二人は結婚するべくして結婚したのだ。

(Their personalities, hobbies and academic backgrounds match. Just as (we) expected, those two got married.)

(d) ゆみの運転はいつも荒っぽいし、エンジンもブレーキも調子が悪かった。事故は起こるべくして起こった。

(Yumi's driving was always wild, and her car's engine and brakes weren't in good condition. An accident occurred, exactly as expected.)

(e) あの会社は経営がずさんだったから倒産するべくして倒産したのだ。

(The management of the company has been so careless that it went bankrupt, exactly as expected.)

(f) 私は自宅が海のすぐ近くのため、釣り好きになるべくしてなったと言っていいでしょう。

(You could say that I became fond of fishing, exactly as expected, because my home is so close to the ocean.)

Notes

1. The phrase *beku shite* is used in the construction "V₁inf.nonpast *beku shite* V₂," where V₁ and V₂ are identical. The construction means s.t. was expected to happen and it actually did. For example, in KS, World War II was expected to occur and, in fact, it did.

2. *Beku shite* cannot be used with Adj(*i/na*) nor with N + Copula nor with Vneg *nai*, as shown in (1).

    (1) a. *日本のおすしは<u>おいしい</u>べくして<u>おいしい</u>。

        (As I expected, Japanese *sushi* is good.)

        cf. 日本のおすしは**やはり**おいしい。

B

b. *外見は日本人に見えるロイ・ヤマダさんも<u>アメリカ人である</u>べくして
<u>アメリカ人</u>だ。

(Mr. Roy Yamada, who looks Japanese, is really American.)

cf. 外見は日本人に見えるロイ・ヤマダさんも**やっぱり**アメリカ人だ。

c. *ベイリーさんは<u>来ない</u>べくして<u>来なかった</u>。

(As expected, Mr. Bailey didn't show up.)

cf. ベイリーさんは**やはり**来なかった。

3. Verbs that precede *beku shite* are limited to intransitive verbs such as *naru* "become," *okoru* "happen," *kawaru* "change," *hairu* "enter," *katsu* "win," *tōsan-suru* "go bankrupt," and others. Note that these verbs all represent something that goes beyond human control, except for *kekkon-suru* "get married" in Ex.(c). But notice that *musubareru*, a synonym for *kekkon-suru*, is a non-controllable verb.

Note also that a passive verb, which is in essence an intransitive verb, can be used, as in (2).

(2) 彼は<u>嫌われる</u>べくして<u>嫌われている</u>。

(He is hated, exactly as expected.)

4. *Beku shite* is used primarily in formal written language.

5. The phrase is usually employed with Vinf.past, but it is also used with Vinf.nonpast in a generic statement, as in (3).

(3) a. 実社会は、基本的に自分以外はすべて敵だから、勝つやつは<u>勝つ</u>べく
して<u>勝つ</u>し、負けるやつは<u>負ける</u>べくして<u>負ける</u>。

(In the real world, everybody is basically your enemy, so, as one would expect, the winners will win and the losers will lose.)

b. 社会通念は<u>変わる</u>べくして<u>変わる</u>のだから、地域社会の通念を行政的に改革しようとしても無理だ。

(It is impossible to revise the accepted ideas of a regional community by administrative means, because those ideas change anyway, as they are meant to.)

[Related Expressions]

All the examples of *beku shite* in the KS and Exs. can be rephrased by *yahari/yappari*, as shown in [1]. But there is an important difference between the two expressions. For example in [1b], in the *beku shite* version the underlying expectation is based more on objective facts, whereas in the *yahari/yappari* version it is based more on subjective intuition.

[1]　a. 第二次世界大戦は｛**起こるべくして** / **やはり** / **やっぱり**｝起こった。

(= KS)

　　b. 彼は大統領に｛**なるべくして** / **やはり** / **やっぱり**｝なった。(= Ex.(a))

　　c. 真知子は高校の時から成績が抜群によく、東大に｛**入るべくして** / **やはり** / **やっぱり**｝入ったという感じである。(= Ex.(b))

(⇨ *yahari* (DBJG: 538-40))

chinami ni ちなみに　*conj.*

a conjunction to indicate that what follows is additional information related to the previously stated main theme	incidentally; in this connection

◆ **Key Sentence**

Sentence₁	Sentence₂
彼の小説はポストモダン的で大変気に入っている。	解釈が読み手にゆだねられているところがよい。

	Sentence₃
ちなみに、	去年の作品はベストセラー第1位だった。

(I love his post-modern novels. I like the way he leaves the interpretation to the reader. Incidentally, his work published last year topped the best-seller list.)

Formation

S₁。 (S₂。……。) ちなみに Sₙ。

(⇨ KS)

Examples

(a) 先週から上野の美術館で印象派の絵画展が開かれており、ルノアール、モネ、マネなどの代表作が出品されている。ちなみに、入場料は大人3,500円、子供1,000円である。

(An exhibit of Impressionists' paintings opened last week at an art museum in Ueno and representative works of Renoir, Monet and Manet, among others, are displayed there. Incidentally, the admission fee is 3,500 yen for adults and 1,000 yen for children.)

(b) 先月の26日と27日に東京で国際建築学会が開かれた。建築の人間化というのがテーマだった。ちなみに参加者数は約1,500人だった。

(On the 26th and 27th of last month, there was an international conference on architecture in Tokyo. The theme of the conference was

"The humanization of architecture." Incidentally, about 1,500 people attended.)

(c) アメリカの大学教授は７年に一度、研究休暇をとることができる。その期間中に研究を集中的にやるわけである。ちなみにその間の給料は、休暇が１年間なら半額、半年ならば全額が支給される。

(A professor in the U.S. can take a sabbatical every seventh year. During that period the professor concentrates on research. Incidentally, professors are paid half their salary for a year's sabbatical or their full salary for half a year.)

Note

Chinami ni is a coordinate conjunction that is used to introduce an incidental remark related obliquely to the main theme of the preceding parts of the discourse. This conjunction is quite different from *tokoro de*, because the latter is used to change the subject while the former is used to give additional information without changing the subject.

dake だけ   *prt.*

| a particle meaning "to the extent that s.o. (can / wants to) do s.t. or s.t. can happen" | as much as; as ~ as possible; as much as one wants |

◆ **Key Sentences**

(A)

	V₁pot.inf. nonpast		V₂ (= V₁)	
若いうちに本を	読める	だけ	読んで	おいた方がよい。

(You'd better read as many books as you can while you are young.)

(B)

V₁inf. nonpast		V₂ (= V₁)		
食べる	だけ	食べる	と、	礼も言わずに帰ってしまった。

(After he had eaten as much as he wanted, he went home without even thanking me.)

(C)

V₁*masu*			V₂		
食べ	たい	だけ	食べる	のが	僕の主義です。

(My principle is to eat as much as I want to.)

(D)

	V₁inf.nonpast (intransitive)		V₂ (= V₁)	
うちの子は背が	伸びる	だけ	伸びた	感じです。

(It looks like my child has grown as much as he is going to.)

(E)

			Adverb	
修士論文の内容について	できる	だけ	詳しく	話して下さい。

(Tell me about your MA thesis in as much detail as possible.)

D

Formation

(i)　V_1pot.inf.nonpast だけ V_2　(where $V_1 = V_2$)

　　食べられるだけ食べる　(s.o. eats as much/many s.t. as he or she can)

(ii)　V_1inf.nonpast だけ V_2　(where $V_1 = V_2$)

　　言うだけ言う　(s.o. says as much as he or she wants to say)

(iii)　V_1inf.nonpast だけ V_2　(where V = non-volitional intransitive verb; $V_1 = V_2$)

　　膨らむだけ膨らむ　(s.t. swells as much as it can)

(iv)　できるだけ Adj(*i/na*) / Adv.

　　できるだけ大きいケーキ　(as big a cake as possible)

　　できるだけ速く歩く　(walk as fast as s.o. can)

Examples

(a)　きのうはすし屋ですしを食べられるだけ食べた。

　　(Yesterday I ate as much *sushi* as I could at a *sushi* restaurant.)

(b)　学生のうちに海外に行けるだけ行ってみたいと思います。

　　(I think I want to go abroad as often as I can while I'm a student.)

(c)　運転手さん、飛行機に遅れてしまうので、飛ばせるだけ飛ばして下さい。

　　(Driver, I may miss my plane, so please go as fast as you can.)

(d)　前から抱いていた不服を言うだけ言ったらすうっとした。

　　(When I freely gave vent to my longstanding complaints (lit., as much as I wanted to) it felt so good.)

(e)　お金は使うだけ使っても故障の少ない車が買いたい。

　　(I'd like to buy a trouble-free car no matter how much it costs.)

(f)　きのうは寝たいだけ寝たので、心も体もすっきりした。

　　(Yesterday I slept as much as I wanted, so my mind and body are refreshed.)

(g) 痛風になった時、私の足の親指は腫れるだけ腫れてしまいました。

(When I got gout my big toe really swelled up (lit., as much as it could swell).)

(h) 今まで都会の真ん中でとてもうるさかったので、今度はできるだけ静かなところに住みたいです。

(Until now, we have lived in the midst of a big, noisy town, so now we would like to live in as quiet a place as possible.)

(i) この会社に入りたい理由、また入社したらやりたいことは何ですか。できるだけ具体的にお書き下さい。

(Why do you want to join this company and what do you want to do once you join the company? Please write down your answers in as much detail as possible.)

(j) その学会にはできるだけ出席するようにします。

(I will do my best to attend the academic conference.)

Notes

1. *Dake* in "V$_1$inf.nonpast *dake* V$_2$" (V$_1$ = V$_2$) indicates the extent to which someone (can / wants to) do something or something can happen.

2. The V$_1$ can take a potential form explicitly, as in KS(A) and Exs.(a)-(c), or can have a potential meaning, as in KS(D) and Ex.(g), when the verb is a non-volitional intransitive verb such as *nobiru* (grow), *hareru* (swell), *chijimu* (shrink), *mori-agaru* (get lively), among others. More examples follow:

    (1) a. 洗濯したら、シャツが縮むだけ縮んでしまった。

    (When I washed the shirt, it shrank to nothing (lit., as much as it could).)

    b. 飲み会は盛り上がるだけ盛り上がった。

    (The drinking party grew very lively (lit., as lively as it could).)

    If the V$_1$ is a volitional transitive verb it means "as much as one wants to ~," as in KS(B), (C) and Ex.(f), or "as much as one can," as in Ex.(e).

3. *Dekiru* is a potential form of *suru*, but *dekiru dake* is a set phrase followed by an adjective or an adverb, as shown in KS(E), Exs.(h) and (i).

dake atte だけあって   *phr.*

| a phrase that means "and as one would expect" or "for good reason" | and as one would expect; so (naturally); for good reason 【REL. *dake no koto wa atte*; ***dake ni***】 |

◆ **Key Sentences**

(A)

	Noun		
彼女は	人気女優	だけあって	すごいうちに住んでいる。

(She is a popular actress and, as one would expect, she lives in a splendid house.)

(B)

	Vinf		
聡子は小さい時からバレエを	している	だけあって	体が柔らかい。

(Satoko has practiced ballet since she was a child, so naturally she is limber.)

(C)

	Vinf		
彼が	自慢する	だけあって、	彼のオフィスからの眺めはちょっとほかでは見られないものだった。

(He is proud of his office for good reason: The view is something you could never see from other offices.)

Formation

(i)   Vinf だけあって

　　　{教えている／教えていた}だけあって　(s.o. is/was teaching s.t., and as one would expect)

(ii) Adj(*i*)inf だけあって

　　　{若い／若かった}だけあって　(s.o. is/was young, and as one would expect)

(iii) Adj(*na*)stem{な / だった}だけあって

上手{な / だった}だけあって   (s.o. is/was good at s.t., and as one would expect)

(iv) N{ø / だった}だけあって

先生{ø / だった}だけあって   (s.o. is/was a teacher, and as one would expect)

D

Examples

(a) 日本は火山国だけあって年中地震が絶えない。

(Japan is a volcanic country, and, as one would expect, earthquakes occur constantly throughout the year.)

(b) この壺はさすが名工の作品だけあって色や形に気品がある。

(This pot was made by a master craftsman, so naturally its colors and shape are graceful.)

(c) オーストラリア南端の地だけあって8月のメルボルンは実に寒い。

(Melbourne, as one would expect from its location in the southern corner of Australia, is really cold in August.)

(d) さすが日本一の花火大会と言われるだけあって、規模も芸術性もすばらしいものだった。

((i) As one would expect from what people call the best fireworks in Japan, the scale and artistry were both amazing.

(ii) People call it the best fireworks show in Japan for good reason: Its scale and artistic quality were both excellent.)

(e) あのレストランは笠原さんのお薦めだけあっておいしかったです。

((i) Ms. Kasahara recommended that restaurant, and, as one would expect, the food was delicious.

(ii) Ms. Kasahara recommended that restaurant for good reason: The food was delicious. [Ms. Kasahara is known as a gourmet.])

(f) この鞄は高いだけあって材料もいいし作りもしっかりしている。

((i) As one would expect from the (high) price of this bag, the material is good and it's also well made.

(ii) This bag is expensive for good reason: The material is good and it's well made.)

(g) あのうるさい社長が信頼するだけあって、彼の秘書は実に有能だ。

((i) As you can guess from the way that president, who is so critical, relies on his secretary, she is truly capable.

(ii) That president, who is so critical, relies on his secretary for good reason: She is truly capable.)

Notes

1. Two interpretations are possible from *dake atte*. One is "and as one would expect; so, naturally" and the other is "for good reason." In some cases both interpretations are possible, as in Exs.(d)-(g).

2. The adverb *sasuga* sometimes occurs with *dake atte*, as seen in Exs.(b) and (d). This adverb indicates that the speaker is impressed by what S_2 represents.

[Related Expression]

Dake no koto wa atte, the *te*-form of *dake no koto wa aru*, can be used in place of *dake atte* without changing the meaning, as shown in [1].

[1] a. 彼女は人気女優だけ（のことは）あってすごいうちに住んでいる。

$$(= KS(A))$$

b. 聡子は小さい時からバレエをしているだけ（のことは）あって体が柔らかい。(= KS(B))

c. あのうるさい社長が信頼するだけ（のことは）あって、彼の秘書は実に有能だ。(= Ex.(g))

($\Rightarrow$ ***dake no koto wa aru*** (in this volume))

---

dake ni だけに   *phr.*

a phrase that carries the idea "as one would expect"	and as one would expect; so (naturally); because 【REL. *dake atte*】

◆ **Key Sentences**

(A)

	Noun			
ビルは	元フットボール選手	だけに	足が速い。	

(Bill used be a football player and, as one would expect, he runs fast.)

(B)

	Vinf		
ホワイトさんは長い間日本に	住んでいた	だけに	日本のことをよく知っている。

(Mr. White lived in Japan for a long time, so naturally he is very familiar with things related to Japan.)

Formation

(i)   Vinf だけに

　　　{教えている / 教えていた} だけに   (s.o. is/was teaching and as one would expect)

(ii) Adj(*i*)inf だけに

　　　{若い / 若かった} だけに   (s.o. is/was young and as one would expect)

(iii) Adj(*na*)stem {な / だった} だけに

　　　上手 {な / だった} だけに   (s.o. is/was good at s.t. and as one would expect)

(iv) N {ø / だった} だけに

　　　先生 {ø / だった} だけに   (s.o. is/was a teacher and as one would expect)

Examples

(a) 彼は元アナウンサーだけに声がよく通る。

(He used to be an announcer, so naturally his voice carries well.)

(b) 山内先生は英語の先生だっただけに英語の文法をよく知っている。

(As one would expect from her having been an English teacher, Ms. Yamauchi is very knowledgeable about English grammar.)

(c) 雅人は一人っ子だけについ甘やかしてしまう。

(Masato is our only child and, as you might expect, we tend to spoil him (without meaning to).)

(d) 孝夫は学生時代に相撲をやっていただけに体が大きい。

(Takao was a *sumō* wrestler when he was a student, so naturally he is big.)

(e) チェンさんはアメリカの大学を卒業しただけに英語が上手だ。

(Ms. Chen graduated from an American university, so naturally her English is good.)

(f) ハリスさんは日本の大学で長い間教えていただけに日本の大学の問題をよく知っている。

(Mr. Harris taught at a university in Japan for a long time so, as one would expect, he knows a lot about the problems of Japanese universities.)

(g) 春樹はジャズが何よりも好きなだけにジャズ・ミュージシャンの名前をよく知っている。

(Haruki likes jazz more than anything, so naturally he knows the names of many jazz musicians.)

(h) 彼女がとても忙しいことをよく知っているだけに、彼女にはこの仕事を頼みにくい。

(Because we know she's very busy, it's hard to ask her to do this job.)

Notes

1. "S₁ *dake ni* S₂" is used when S₂ is something that can be expected from S₁, where S₁ represents a fact.

2. The adverb *sasuga* sometimes occurs with *dake ni*. This adverb indicates that the speaker is impressed by what S₂ represents. *Sasuga* can be placed either before or right after the topic.

   (1) a. 彼はさすが元アナウンサーだけに声がよく通る。

      b. さすが彼は元アナウンサーだけに声がよく通る。(cf. Ex.(a))

   (2) a. 孝夫はさすが学生時代に相撲をやっていただけに体が大きい。

      b. さすが孝夫は学生時代に相撲をやっていただけに体が大きい。

(cf. Ex.(d))

Because *sasuga* indicates that the speaker is impressed by what S₂ represents, this adverb cannot be used with sentences like Exs.(c) and (h), where there is nothing impressive to the speaker in S₂.

(3) a. *雅人はさすが一人っ子だけについ甘やかしてしまう。(cf. Ex.(c))

    b. *さすが彼女がとても忙しいことをよく知っているだけに、彼女にはこの仕事を頼みにくい。(cf. Ex.(h))

(⇨ ***sasuga*** (DIJG: 374-78))

D

[Related Expression]

Dake atte is synonymous with *dake ni* when they are used to mean "as one would expect," as in [1].

[1] a. 山内先生は英語の先生だった｛だけに / だけあって｝英語の文法をよく知っている。(= Ex.(b))

    b. ハリスさんは日本の大学で長い間教えていた｛だけに / だけあって｝日本の大学の問題をよく知っている。(= Ex.(f))

However, "S₁ *dake atte* S₂" cannot be used when S₂ represents something undesirable, as in [2], or when a whole sentence is about a negative expectation, as in [3a]. Note that when a whole sentence represents a positive expectation, both *dake ni* and *dake atte* can be used, as in [3b].

[2] a. 雅人は一人っ子｛だけに / *だけあって｝つい甘やかしてしまう。

(= Ex.(c))

    b. 彼女がとても忙しいことをよく知っている｛だけに / *だけあって｝、彼女にはこの仕事は頼みにくい。(= Ex.(h))

[3] a. ジョージは仕事の覚えが遅い｛だけに / *だけあって｝昇進も遅かった。

(George was slow to learn (new) jobs and, as one would expect, his advancement was also slow.)

    b. ハリーは仕事の覚えが早い｛だけに / だけあって｝昇進も早かった。

(Harry was quick to learn (new) jobs and, as one would expect, his rise (in the organization) was also quick.)

Conversely, when X *dake atte* means "there is a reason for X," *dake ni* cannot be used, as in shown [4].

[4] a. 吉岡さんが薦める｛だけあって/*だけに｝ここの料理はちょっとそこ
らでは食べられない。

(Mr. Yoshioka recommended the food here for good reason (lit., There is a reason Mr. Yoshioka recommended the food here); you can hardly taste food of the same quality anywhere else.)

b. 彼が自慢する｛だけあって/*だけに｝彼のオフィスからの眺めは
ちょっとほかでは見られないものだった。

(He is proud of his office for good reason: The view is something you could never have in other offices.)

(⇨ **dake atte** (in this volume))

D

---

dake no koto wa aru   だけのことはある   *phr.*

| a phrase expressing an evaluative comment regarding how s.t. is contributing to an expected, remarkable result | don't do s.t. for nothing; ~ explains it; no wonder; it's no surprise |
| | 【REL. *dake atte*】 |

◆ **Key Sentences**

(A)

Sentence₁		Sentence₂	
明子は韓国語がとても上手だ。	さすがに	2年間ソウル大学に留学していた	だけのことはある。

(Akiko is very good at Korean. She didn't study at Seoul National University for two years for nothing.)

(B)

Subordinate Clause		Main Clause
毎日１キロ以上水泳をしてきた	だけのことはあって、	彼は90歳の今もかくしゃくとしている。

（He has been swimming more than 1 kilometer every day. No wonder he is still in such good shape at 90 (years old).）

Formation

(i)　{V / Adj(*i*)} inf だけのことはある

　　{読む / 読んだ} だけのことはある　(s.o. doesn't/didn't read s.t. for nothing)

　　{高い / 高かった} だけのことはある　(s.t. isn't/wasn't expensive for nothing)

(ii)　Adj(*na*) {な / だった} だけのことはある

　　好き {な / だった} だけのことはある　(it's no surprise s.o. likes/liked it)

(iii)　N {ø / だった} だけのことはある

　　プロゴルファー {ø / だった} だけのことはある　(it's no surprise s.o. is/was a professional golfer)

Examples

(a) 山田先生は日本語の教え方が上手だ。アメリカの大学で20年近く日本語を教えていらしただけのことはある。

(Prof. Yamada is good at teaching Japanese. She didn't teach it at a U.S. university for nearly 20 years for nothing.)

(b) チャンさんは世界の経済状況をよくつかんでいる。経済コンサルタントとして世界を飛び回っているだけのことはある。

(Ms. Chang has a firm grip on the world economic situation. She doesn't fly around the world as a finance consultant for nothing.)

(c) 隣の家の子供たちは実に行儀がいい。親のしつけが厳しいだけのことはある。

(The kids next door have very good manners. Strict parental discipline explains it.)

(d) 田中はさして才能もないのに昇進が早い。上司への気配りが巧みなだけのことはある。

(Tanaka's rise has been quick, although he isn't that talented. His careful attention to his boss explains it.)

(e) アインシュタインの理論は 21 世紀の現在でも死んでいない。さすがに 20 世紀最大の物理学者と言われるだけのことはある。

(Einstein's theory is still alive, even in the 21st century. No wonder he is called the greatest physicist of the 20th century.)

D

(f) 幸い日本で日本語を勉強して、かなり話せるようになりました。日本に行っただけのことはありました。

(Fortunately, I studied Japanese in Japan and now I can speak it fairly well. I didn't go to Japan for nothing.)

(g) 彼は若いころから俳句を作ってきただけのことはあって、さすがに自然に対する観察眼が鋭い。

(He has been composing *haiku* since his younger days. No wonder he has such a sharp eye for nature.)

Notes

1. *Dake no koto wa aru* is used to express an evaluative comment about how someone's achievement, skills, habits or experience contributes to an positively-expected, remarkable state of affairs. In short, in S *dake no koto wa aru*, S gives a reason. If there are two sentences, S_1 and S_2, as in KS(A) and Exs.(a)-(f), S_1 represents a remarkable result and S_2, a good reason for it. But if there is a single, coordinated sentence that consists of S_1 and S_2, as in KS(B) and Ex.(g), the subordinate clause represents a good reason for the remarkable result expressed in the main clause.

2. As in KS(A), Exs.(e) and (g), the adverb *sasuga ni* "as expected" is often used with *dake no koto wa aru* and *dake no koto wa atte*. By using both, the meaning of "expectedness" is doubly emphasized. Note that the adverb is located in S_2 in all the examples in which *sasuga* is used.
(⇨ *sasuga* (DIJG: 374-78))

3. *Dake no koto wa atte* is a continuative form of *dake no koto wa aru*. The continuative version means that what precedes the phrase naturally results in what follows it, as shown in KS(B) and Ex.(g). In fact, all the rest of the example sentences can be rewritten using *dake no koto wa atte* by reversing the order of S_1 and S_2.

(1) a. 2 年間ソウル大学に留学していただけのことはあって、さすがに明子は韓国語がとても上手だ。(cf. KS(A))

b. 経済コンサルタントとして世界を飛び回っているだけのことはあって、チャンさんは世界の経済状況をよくつかんでいる。(cf. Ex.(b))

D

dani   だに   *prt.*   <w>

a particle indicating that s.t. expressed by the preceding verb alone produces a certain feeling or the meaning "(not) even doing s.t.; doesn't even occur"

just; (not) even
【REL. *dake demo*; *sae*; *sura*】

◆ **Key Sentences**

(A)

	Vinf.nonpast		
あの時の大きな失敗は	思い出す	だに	恥ずかしい。

(Just remembering the big mistake I made at that time makes me feel embarrassed.)

(B)

	VN		
イチローが、84年間続いたジョージ・シスラーの最多安打記録を破るとは	想像	だに	しなかった。

(I couldn't (lit., didn't) even imagine that Ichiro would break George Sisler's 84-year-old record for the most hits in one season.)

Formation

(i) Vinf.nonpast だに

  思うだに   (just to think)

(ii) VN だにしない

  考慮だにしない   (s.o. doesn't even consider)

  注意だにしない   (s.o. doesn't even warn)

Examples

(a) 私の体脂肪率は今どれくらいあるんだろうか。考えるだに、恐ろしい。

(I wonder what my percentage of body fat is right now? Just the thought of it scares me.)

(b) 私が父の真似をしていたら、どんなことになったか。想像するだに心細いものがあります。

(What would have happened if I had followed in my father's footsteps? Just imagining it makes me feel uneasy.)

(c) この猛暑の中、友人は避暑地で休日を楽しんでいるとは、思うだにうらやましい。

(It makes me envious just to think that my friend is enjoying her holiday at a summer resort while I'm stuck here in this scorching heat.)

(d) アメリカの指導者たちの大多数は9/11のようなテロが発生する可能性を考慮だにしなかったらしい。

(It appears that the majority of U.S. leaders didn't even consider the possibility that terrorism like 9/11 could occur.)

(e) 若者たちは毎晩スケートボードで駅前のロータリーを走り回っているのに、警官は注意だにしない。

(Every night the young men skateboard around the rotary in front of the station, but the police don't even warn them not to.)

(f) 発表当時、彼の文献学的方法論は否定的評価を受けたが、彼の信念は微動だにしなかった。

(His philological method received negative reviews at the time it was published, but his faith has not wavered even an inch.)

(g) 小林は何か心配事があるのか、青い顔をして、こちらを一瞥だにしなかった。

(Kobayashi looked pale and didn't even cast a glance in my direction, seeming as if something was bothering him.)

(h) 人間は他の種を絶滅させるような環境を作り出しても一顧だにしない。

(Even though humans have created an environment that drives other species into extinction, they don't give it a second thought.)

Notes

1. The particle *dani* has two meanings. First, it can mean that just engaging in a cognitive process, expressed by cognitive verbs, such as

kangaeru "think," *omou* "feel," *omoidasu* "remember/recall" and *sōzō-suru* "imagine," produces a certain feeling such as shamefulness, fearfulness, uneasiness or happiness.

Secondly, *dani* can mean "even" with regard to the action expressed by a Sino-Japanese verb (i.e., Sino-Japanese word + *suru*), as shown in KS(B) and Exs.(d)-(h). Note that the Sino-Japanese verbs used with *dani* are mostly limited to *sōzō-suru* "imagine" (KS(B)), *kōryo-suru* "take s.t. into consideration" (Ex.(d)), *chūi-suru* "warn" (Ex.(e)), *bidō-suru* "budge; waver" (Ex.(f)), *ichibetsu-suru* "cast a glance" (Ex.(g)) and *ikkō-suru* "give s.t. a thought" (Ex.(h)). As pointed out in Formation (ii), the structure is VN *dani shinai*. Non-Sino-Japanese verbs cannot be used like Sino-Japanese verbs.

(1) a. *動きだにしない。　(cf. 微動だにしない。)

　 b. *見だにしない。　(cf. 一瞥だにしない。)

2. The particle *dani* is used almost exclusively in written Japanese.

[Related Expressions]

I. In sentences where *dani* is used to mean "just doing s.t.," *dake demo* can also be used interchangeably, as shown in [1]. But, as shown in [2], *dani* cannot replace *dake demo*, because the verb used before *dani* must be a cognitive verb, whereas there is no restriction on verbs used before *dake demo*.

[1] a. あの時の大きな失敗は思い出す{だに / だけでも}恥ずかしい。

(= KS(A))

　 b. 私の体脂肪率は今どれくらいあるんだろうか。考える{だに / だけでも}、恐ろしい。(= Ex.(a))

[2] a. 最近は新幹線で東京から京都まで行く{だけでも / *だに}疲れてしまう。

(Lately just going from Tokyo to Kyoto by *Shinkansen* makes me tired.)

　 b. 僕は彼女のそばにいる{だけでも / *だに}気持ちが安らぐ。

(Just being close to her makes me feel relaxed.)

II. In sentences where *dani* means "someone doesn't even do something," it can be replaced by *sae* or *sura*, but, as in [4], not all uses of *sae* and *sura* can be replaced with *dani*, because *dani* is used with a very limited number of Sino-Japanese verbs, while *sae* and *sura* can be used freely with any verb, noun or particle (except *ga*).

[3] a. イチローが、84年間続いたジョージ・シスラーの最多安打記録を破るとは想像｛だに／さえ／すら｝しなかった。(= KS(B))

　　b. 若者たちは毎晩スケートボードで駅前のロータリーを走り回っているのに、警官は注意｛だに／さえ／すら｝しない。(= Ex.(e))

[4] a. 父は散歩｛さえ／すら／*だに｝しない。
　　　(My father doesn't even go on walks.)

　　b. 彼はひらがな｛さえ／すら／*だに｝読めない。
　　　(He can't even read *hiragana*.)

Note also that *bidō dani shinai* (Ex.(f)), *ichibetsu dani shinai* (Ex.(g)) and *ikko dani shinai* (Ex.(h)) are idiomatic phrases. In these cases, *sae* or *sura* cannot be used in place of *dani*.

(⇨ **sae** (DIJG: 363-69))

dano　だの　　*conj.*

| a conjunction that lists nouns/quotes inexhaustively | and (~ and); or (~ or); and things like that 【REL. *toka*; *ya*】 |

◆ **Key Sentences**

(A)

	Noun₁		Noun₂		Noun₃	
庭には	すみれ	だの	チューリップ	だの	つつじ	だの、

花がたくさん咲いていた。

(In the garden, many flowers such as pansies, tulips, azaleas and others, were in bloom.)

(B)

	Sentence₁ (Quote)		Sentence₂ (Quote)
学生たちは	食堂のご飯がまずい	だの、	授業がつまらない
だの	と、	いつも不平を言っている。	

(The students are always complaining that the food at the cafeteria isn't good, or their classes are boring and so on.)

Formation

(i)　N₁ だの N₂ だの（N₃ だの）

そばだの、うどんだの、すしだの　(*soba* and *udon* and *sushi*, and things like that)

(ii)　{V / Adj(*i*)}₁inf だの {V / Adj(*i*)}₂inf だの

疲れるだの、おなかが空くだのと　(saying that s.o. gets tired or hungry, and things like that)

疲れただの、おなかが空いただのと　(saying that s.o. got tired or hungry, and things like that)

暑いだの、雨が多いだのと　(saying that it is hot or it rains too much, and things like that)

暑かっただの、雨が多かっただのと　(saying that it was hot or it rained too much, and things like that)

(iii)　{Adj(*na*)stem / N}{ø / だった}だの、{Adj(*na*)stem / N}{ø / だった}だのと

不健康{ø / だった}だの、非衛生的{ø / だった}だのと　(saying that s.t. is/was unhealthy and unhygienic, and so on)

ばか者{ø / だった}だの、腑抜け{ø / だった}だのと　(saying that s.o. is/was a fool or an idiot, among other things)

Examples

(a) 僕はそばだの、うどんだの、ラーメンだのといった麺類が大好きだ。
(I like noodles such as *soba*, *udon* and *rāmen*.)

(b) 今の高校生は携帯電話だのコンピュータゲームだのにはまっている。

(High school students now are addicted to things like cell phones and computer games.)

(c) 彼は僕が飲みに行こうかと誘っても、いつも頭が痛いだの、約束があるだの と言い訳をする。

(Whenever I invite him to go out for a drink, he has an excuse: he's got a headache or another appointment or something.)

(d) 彼女は仕事が好きだから結婚しても仕事を続けるだの、家庭生活と職業を両立できるだのと主張していた。

(She used to claim that she would keep working after she got married because she liked her work and could manage both family life and her career.)

(e) 彼女は自分がテニスが上手だの、ピアノがうまいだのと自慢ばかりしている。

(She's always boasting that she's good at tennis and (also good at) piano, and things like that.)

(f) 受験生たちは塾だのテストだのと忙しい毎日を送っている。

(Students preparing for the examination are spending busy days stuffed with cram school and tests.)

Notes

1. *Dano* is a marker of inexhaustive listing. The listed items can be either nouns, as in KS(A), Exs.(a), (b) and (f), or quotes, as in KS(B) or Exs.(c)-(e).

2. When *dano* is used in "~ *dano* ~ *dano to* ~," the speaker/writer is usually critical of the situations stated, as shown in KS(B) and Exs.(c)-(f).

[Related Expressions]

The conjunctions *toka* and *ya* can replace all but the final *dano* in the KS and Exs., as in [1].

[1] a. 庭にはすみれ{だの / とか / や}チューリップ{だの / とか / や}つつじ{だの /?とか /??や}、花がたくさん咲いていた。(= KS(A))

b. 僕はそば{だの / とか / や}、うどん{だの / とか / や}、ラーメン{だの /?とか /??や}といった麺類が大好きだ。(= Ex.(a))

As shown in [2], *ya* cannot replace *dano* when *dano* is followed by a quote, as in KS(B) and Exs.(c)-(e). Note also that the use of *toka* for the last quote should be avoided, but without the quote marker *to*, *toka* is acceptable.

[2] a. 学生たちは食堂のご飯がまずい{**だの** / **とか** / ***や**}、授業がつまらない{**だの** / ??**とか** / ***や**}と、いつも不平を言っている。(= KS(B))

cf. 学生たちは食堂のご飯がまずい**とか**、授業がつまらない**とか**、いつも不平を言っている。

b. 彼は僕が飲みに行こうかと誘っても、いつも頭が痛い{**だの** / **とか** / ***や**}、約束がある{**だの** / ??**とか** / ***や**}と言い訳をする。(= Ex.(c))

cf. 彼は僕が飲みに行こうかと誘っても、いつも頭が痛い**とか**、約束がある**とか**、言い訳をする。

(⇨ ***toka*** (DBJG: 488-90); ***ya*** (DBJG: 536-38))

datte[1] だって[1] *conj.* <s>

a conjunction that indicates a reason — because

◆ Key Sentence

A:
どうして会ってくれないの？
(Why won't you see me?)
B:
だって、 僕、今日忙しい んだ。
('Cause I'm busy today.)

Formation

(i) だって{V / Adj(*i*)}inf んだ({もの / もん})

だって{V / Adj(*i*)}inf{もの / もん}

だって{食べる / 食べた}んだ({もの / もん}) (because s.o. eats/ate s.t.)

だって{食べる / 食べた}{もの / もん} (because s.o. eats/ate s.t.)

だって{面白い/面白かった}んだ({もの/もん}) (because s.t. is/was interesting)

だって{面白い/面白かった}{もの/もん} (because s.t. is/was interesting)

(ii) だって{N/Adj(*na*)stem}{な/だった}んだ({もの/もん})

だって{N/Adj(*na*)stem}{だ/だった}{もの/もん}

だって学生{な/だった}んだ({もの/もん}) (because s.o. is/was a student)

だって学生{だ/だった}{もの/もん} (because s.o. is/was a student)

だって変{な/だった}んだ({もの/もん}) (because s.t./s.o. is/was strange)

だって変{だ/だった}{もの/もん} (because s.t./s.o. is/was strange)

Examples

(a) 母：さや、どうしてもっとご飯食べないの。
   (Mother: Saya, how come you aren't eating more?)
   さや：だっておなか、空いていないもん。
   (Saya: 'Cause I'm not hungry.)

(b) 妻：健太さん、今日はどうしてゴルフに行かないの。
   (Wife: Kenta, how come you're not going golfing today?)
   夫：だって、今日は客と銀座で昼食をとらなきゃならないんだ。
   (Husband: 'Cause I have to have lunch with a client in Ginza.)

(c) A: 路子、笑い事じゃないよ。
   (Michiko, it's no laughing matter!)
   B: だって二人の話しているのを聞いていると面白いんだもん。
   (But it's so funny just listening to you guys talk.)

(d) もう35度じゃ驚かないね。だって連日気温は35度、36度、37度が当たり前の状態なんだもの。
   (35º(C) isn't anything surprising, because the temperature is normally 35º(C), 36º(C), 37º(C) every day.)

(e) A: なんで、僕だけ烏龍茶なんですか？
   (How come you put oolong tea only in my glass?)
   B: だって、お前はまだ未成年だろう？
   (Because you are not an adult yet, are you?)

(f) 彼(かれ)がいるはずの店にやってきたが、入るべきかどうか迷(まよ)っていた。だって、ここに来るとろくなことがない。

(I came to the restaurant where I knew he'd be, but I wondered whether I should go in or not, because something bad always occurs there.)

D

Notes

1. *Datte* is a conjunction that indicates a reason for something in casual speech.

2. *Datte* is used only in highly colloquial speech in informal situations. Typically it is used in conversation between two very close people, such as close friends, as in the KS, parent and child, as in Ex.(a), or a married couple, as in Ex.(b).

3. *Datte* often ends with *nda*, *nda mon(o)*, or *mon(o)*, as in Exs.(a), (c) and (d). Note also that it can be used with *kara (da)*, as in (1).

(1) 一般的(いっぱんてき)に偏頭痛(へんずつう)の方がつらいらしいけれど、僕(ぼく)にはこの緊張型(きんちょうがた)の方がつらい。だって「頭(あたま)が痛(いた)い」というのがすでにストレスの一部(いちぶ)に荷担(かたん)しているから。

(Generally speaking, a migraine is supposedly harder to put up with, but to me these stress headaches are worse. That's because the headache just adds to the stress.)

4. There are two other uses of *datte* that are distinct from its use as a reason-conjunction. One is a concession-conjunction, as shown in (2), and the other is a hearsay-conjunction, as shown in (3). Note that *datte* as a reason-conjunction always comes at the sentence-initial position, but *datte* as a concession-conjunction or a hearsay-conjunction occurs at the end of a subordinate clause or the end of a sentence, respectively.

(2) a. 遠くて不便だってマイホームならかまいません。

=遠くて不便でもマイホームならかまいません。

(If it's my own home, it doesn't matter if it is far away and inconvenient.)

b. どんなにいい先生だって時々間違(まちが)います。

=どんなにいい先生でも時々間違います。

(No matter how good a teacher may be, he sometimes makes mistakes.)

(⇨ *-tatte* (DBJG: 461-63))

(3) a. 幸恵、来ないんだって。

   =幸恵は来ないそうです。

   (I heard that Yukie isn't coming.)

  b. 明日は雪だってさ。

   =明日は雪だそうです。

   (They say it's going to snow tomorrow.)

D

datte²   だって²   *prt.*   <s>

> a particle meaning "too" or "even"

too; also; (not) ~ either; even; any; no matter what/who/how/ etc.
【REL. *mo*; *demo*】

◆ Key Sentences

(A)

	Noun	Prt.		
この翻訳なら	私	に	だって	できます。

((i) I could do this translation, too. (lit., If it's this translation, I can do it, too.) (ii) Even I could do this translation. (lit., If it's this translation, even I can do it.))

(B)

	Noun		
数多いお客さんの中には難しい	人	だって	いる。

(In a large group of customers, there will be difficult people(, too).)

(C)

Noun	Prt.		
今	から	だって	遅くないから、彼に電話してみたら？

(It's not too late now (lit., It is not late, even from now), so why don't you call him?)

(D)

	Wh-word		
そんないい仕事だったら	誰 *だれ*	だって	やりたい。
(Anyone would want a good job like that.)

Formation

(i)   N (Prt.) だって

　　　彼だって　　(he, too; even he)
　　　かれ

　　　これからだって　　(from now on, too; even from now on)

(ii)　Wh-word だって

　　　誰だって買う　　(anyone would buy)
　　　だれ

Examples

(a) 君だって子供のことは考えているだろう。
　　きみ　　*こども*

　　((i) You're thinking about your children, too, aren't you?

　　(ii) Even you are thinking about your children, aren't you?)

(b) それは部長だって知らないことだ。
　　　　ぶちょう

　　((i) This is something the division head doesn't know, either.

　　(ii) This is something even the division head doesn't know.)

(c) 最近は忙しいので日曜だって休めないことが多い。
　　さいきん　*いそが*

　　((i) Because I have been very busy recently, often I haven't been able to take a day off on Sunday, either.

　　(ii) Because I've been very busy recently, often I haven't even taken Sunday off.)

(d) もういい加減に許してやれよ。彼だって悪気があってやったわけじゃないんだから。
　　　　かげん　*ゆる*　　　　*かれ*　*わるぎ*

　　(Why don't you forgive him now? He didn't mean anything bad when he did it.)

(e) これからだって彼にはいろいろ頼まないといけないんだから、そんなに彼のことを悪く言うもんじゃないよ。
　　　　　　かれ　　　　*たの*

　　(We're going to have to ask a lot of favors from him from now on, too, so don't talk so ill of him.)

(f) この間だってそうだ。僕のノートを借りたまま言われるまで返さないんだ。

(It happened the other day, too. He borrowed my notebook and didn't return it until I asked him to.)

(g) 一度だって僕が君に嘘をついたことがあるかい。

(Have I ever lied to you, even once?)

(h) それだけ日本語を知っていたら一人だってできるからやってごらん。

(If you know that much Japanese, you can do it even on your own, so give it a try.)

(i) 私は子供が欲しがるものは何だって買い与えた。今から思えばそれは間違いだったかもしれない。

(I bought my child anything he wanted. When I think about it now, I feel that might have been the wrong thing to do.)

(j) どっちだって同じだろう。早く決めちゃえよ。

(It's the same either way, isn't it (lit., Any one of which is the same, isn't it)? Make up your mind, quick.)

(k) いつだってあなたのやりたいことを優先してきたじゃないの。

(Haven't I always given priority to what you want to do?)

Notes

1. *Datte* is a particle that is used primarily in spoken language.

2. *Datte* means either "too" or "even," depending on the context. In some cases, *datte* can be interpreted either way, as in KS(A) and Exs.(a)-(c). The context and/or situation determines the meaning of the sentence.

3. In some cases, *datte* can be interpreted only as "too," as in KS(B) and Exs.(d)-(f), or only as "even," as in KS(C), Exs.(g) and (h).

4. When a Wh-word precedes *datte*, it usually means "any." *Nan datte* "why; how come," as shown in (1), is a different use.

(1) 何だってそんな馬鹿なことをしたんだ。

(How come you did such a stupid thing?)

【Related Expressions】

I. *Mo* "too; also; even" can replace *datte* in many situations, as shown in [1]. Note that when the meaning of the sentence is ambiguous, as in KS(A) and Ex.(a), *mo*'s meaning is limited to "too."

[1] a. この翻訳なら私に{だって/も}できます。(= KS(A))

　　　b. 数多いお客さんの中には難しい人{だって/も}いる。(= KS(B))

　　　c. 君{だって/も}子供のことは考えているだろう。(= Ex.(a))

　　　d. もういい加減に許してやれよ。彼{だって/も}悪気があってやった
　　　　わけじゃないんだから。(= Ex.(d))

However, when *datte* means only "even," *mo* cannot be used in its
place, as shown in [2].

[2] a. 今から{だって/*も}遅くないから、彼に電話してみたら？

　　　　　　　　　　　　　　　　　　　　　　　　　　　　　(= KS(C))

　　　b. 一度{だって/*も}僕が君に嘘をついたことがあるかい。(= Ex.(g))

　　　c. それだけ日本語を知っていたら一人{だって/*も}できるからやって
　　　　ごらん。(= Ex.(h))

Conversely, *datte* cannot be used in place of *mo* in the following situations, where *mo* is used as an emphatic marker:

[3] a. その集まりには500人{も/*だって}集まった。
　　　　(As many as 500 people joined the gathering.)

　　　b. パーティーに先生が一人{も/*だって}来なかった。
　　　　(Not a single teacher came to the party.)

　　　c. そんな簡単なこと{も/*だって}できないのか。
　　　　(Can't you do such a simple thing?)

　　　d. 課長は私のレポートを見{も/*だって}しなかった。
　　　　(My section chief didn't even look at my report.)

　　　　　　　　　(⇨ ***mo¹*** (DBJG: 247-50); ***mo²*** (DBJG: 250-53))

II.　*Demo* can be used in place of *datte* when *datte* means "even," as shown
　　in [4].

　　[4] a. 今から{だって/でも}遅くないから、彼に電話してみたら？

　　　　　　　　　　　　　　　　　　　　　　　　　　　　　(= KS(C))

　　　　b. 一度{だって/でも}僕が君に嘘をついたことがあるかい。(= Ex.(g))

c. それだけ日本語を知っていたら一人 ｛だって / でも｝できるからやってごらん。(= Ex.(h))

Demo can also replace *datte* when *datte* follows a Wh-word, meaning "any," as in [5].

[5] a. そんないい仕事だったら誰 ｛だって / でも｝やりたい。(= KS(D))

b. 私は子供が欲しがるものは何 ｛だって / でも｝買い与えた。今から思えばそれは間違いだったかもしれない。(= Ex.(i))

c. どっち ｛だって / でも｝同じだろう。早く決めちゃえよ。(= Ex.(j))

(⇨ ***demo*** (DBJG: 111-13))

---

de are であれ   *phr.*   <w>

> a conjunctive phrase that expresses the idea of concession

even; even if; even though; no matter what/who/how/etc. ~ may be; whatever/whoever/etc. ~ may be
【REL. *de mo*; *de atte mo*; *de arō ga/to*】

◆ Key Sentences

(A)

	Noun		
たとえ	**社長**	であれ、	そのような行為は許されない。

(Even the (company) president shouldn't be allowed to do things like that. (lit., Even if it is the president, such conduct should not be allowed.))

(B)

	Noun		
どんな	**問題**	であれ、	必ず私に報告して下さい。
(Whatever kind of problem it may be, please report it to me without fail.)			

(C)

		Adj(*na*)stem		
通勤が	いかに	**不便**	であれ、	今の家を変わるつもりはない。
(No matter how inconvenient my commute is, I do not intend to move (lit., from our current house).)				

(D)

	Adj(*i*)inf.nonpast	Noun		
いかに	**難しい**	**問題**	であれ	彼ならきっと解決できるはずだ。
(No matter how difficult the problem may be, he certainly should be able to solve it.)				

Formation

(i) N であれ

たとえ病気であれ   (even if s.o. is ill)

誰であれ   (no matter who it may be)

いかに弱いチームであれ   (no matter how weak a team it may be)

いかに静かなアパートであれ   (no matter how quiet an apartment it may be)

(ii) Adj(*na*)stem であれ

たとえ可能であれ   (even if s.t. is possible)

いかに不便であれ   (no matter how inconvenient s.t. may be)

Examples

(a) この練習は、たとえ数分間であれ、毎日することが大切です。

(It is important to practice this every day, even if it is only for a few minutes.)

(b) 彼の提言は、たとえそれが実行不可能であれ、聞くに値する。

(His suggestions are worth listening to even if they cannot be carried out.)

(c) 暗号技術については、たとえ短期間の使用であれ、その輸出入を規制している国があります。

(Some countries regulate the export and import of cryptographic technology, even when it is intended for short-term use.)

(d) 何事であれ、その仕事で生活するとなれば楽なものはない。

(Whatever kind it may be, if you make a living from it, there is no such thing as easy work.)

(e) どのような理由であれ、著作物を複製する時は、著作権の侵害に注意しなければならない。

(Whatever the reason (for making copies) may be, when you duplicate copyrighted materials, you have to be careful not to infringe on the copyright.)

(f) 当時の軍隊では上官の命令がいかに理不尽であれ、下級兵はそれに従うしかなかったのだ。

(In the army in those days, no matter how unreasonable the senior officers' commands, the soldiers under them had no choice but to obey them.)

Notes

1. *De are* is the imperative form of *de aru*. When *de are* is used in a subordinate clause, it indicates concession, i.e., "even if; even though."

   (⇨ ***ni shiro/seyo*** (in this volume); ***to wa ie*** (in this volume); ***de aru*** (DIJG: 30-33))

2. Only nouns and *na*-adjective stems precede *de are*.

3. The emphatic adverb *tatoe* "admitting, granting, supposing" often occurs with *de are* when *de are* is not preceded by a Wh-word (e.g., KS(A) and Exs.(a)-(c)).

4. The emphatic adverb *ikani* "how" occurs with *i*-adjectives or *na*-adjectives. When *ikani* occurs with *i*-adjectives, they are always noun modifiers, as in KS(D) and (1).

   (1) いかにいい運動選手であれ、優れたコーチがいなければ大成するのは難しい。

(No matter how good an athlete may be, it is difficult for him/her to become a great athlete without a good coach.)

5. *De are* is also used in the phrase "X *de are* Y *de are*" to mean "whether X or Y."   (⇨ ~ ***de are*** ~ ***de are*** (in this volume))

[Related Expressions]

De mo, *de atte mo*, and *de arō ga/to* can be used in place of *de are* without changing the meaning of a sentence. *De atte mo* is less formal than *de are*, and *de mo* is even less formal.

[1] a. たとえ社長｛であれ / でも / であっても / であろう｛が / と｝｝、その ような行為は許されない。(= KS(A))

b. どんな問題｛であれ / でも / であっても / であろう｛が / と｝｝、必ず 私に報告して下さい。(= KS(B))

c. 通勤がいかに不便｛であれ / でも / であっても / であろう｛が / と｝｝、 今の家を変わるつもりはない。(= KS(C))

(⇨ ***yō to/ga*** (in this volume))

~ **de are** ~ **de are**   ～であれ～であれ   *str.*   <w>

a structure that means "no matter which one is the case"	whether X or Y ; be it X or Y; or [REL. ~ *de arō to* ~ *de arō to*; ~ *de mo* ~ *de mo*; ~ **to iwazu** ~ **to iwazu**]

◆ Key Sentences

(A)

Noun₁		Noun₂		
男性 だんせい	であれ、	女性 じょせい	であれ、	人間としての権利は同じはずだ。 にんげん　　　　　けんり

(Whether one is a man or a woman, one's rights as a human being should be the same.)

(B)

Adj(*na*)₁stem		Adj(*na*)₂stem		
有名	であれ、	**無名**	であれ、	**人生**は短い。
(No matter if one is famous or nameless, life is short.)				

D

Formation

(i)   N₁ であれ、N₂ であれ

　　　夏であれ、冬であれ   (whether it is summer or winter)

(ii)   Adj(*na*)₁stem であれ、Adj(*na*)₂stem であれ

　　　便利であれ、不便であれ   (whether s.t. is convenient or inconvenient)

Examples

(a) ここは春であれ秋であれ美しいから観光に向いている。

(Whether spring or fall, this place is beautiful, so it is a good sight-seeing spot.)

(b) イスラエル人であれ、パレスチナ人であれ、平和を望んでいることでは同じはずだ。

(Whether an Israeli or a Palestinian, their hope for peace should be the same.)

(c) 彼は和食であれ、洋食であれ、何でも食べてしまう。

(He eats anything, Japanese- or Western-style food.)

(d) あの学者は哲学であれ、言語学であれ、人類学であれ、同じように精通している。

(That scholar is well-versed in a number of subjects, whether it be philosophy, linguistics or anthropology.)

(e) 平日であれ、週末であれ、健太は仕事に追われている。

(Whether weekday or weekend, Kenta is always pressed by work.)

(f) 写真であれ、コンピュータグラフィックスであれ、求められたイメージを表現するのはたいへん難しい。

(Whether in photography or in computer graphics, it is hard to produce an image as requested.)

(g) 場所が便利であれ、不便であれ、マイホームが持ちたい。

(Whether the location is convenient or inconvenient, I'd like to have my own house.)

Notes

1. "N₁ *de are* N₂ *de are*" is used to mean "whether it be N₁ or N₂."

2. If an *i*-adjective is used, the formation changes to "Adj(*i*)₁stem *kare* Adj(*i*)₂stem *kare*," which is almost limited to such phrases as *osokare hayakare* in (1a), *yokare ashikare* in (1b) or *ōkare sukunakare* in (1c). Those three are virtually idioms. The ending *kare* is a contraction of *ku are*.

(1) a. 遅かれ早かれ、この国でもIT革命が起こるだろう。

　　 (Sooner or later, the information technology revolution will take place in this country, too.)

　　 b. インターネットの使用で国境の意識が薄れるから、良かれ悪しかれ、国の概念も薄らいでいくだろう。

　　 (Because our awareness of national boundaries will fade due to our use of the Internet, for better or worse, the concept of nation will also continue to weaken.)

　　 c. 言語学者は多かれ少なかれチョムスキーの影響を受けている。

　　 (Linguists have been influenced to a greater or lesser degree by Chomsky.)

There are similar idiomatic phrases that take the form of "Adj(*i*)₁stem *karō to* Adj(*i*)₂stem *karō to*," as in (2).

(2) a. 彼はプロジェクトが難しかろうとやさしかろうと、同じような情熱でそれに挑む。

　　 (Whether a project is hard or easy, he tackles it with the same passion.)

　　 b. 暑かろうと寒かろうと、彼女は一年中泳ぐ。

　　 (Whether it is hot or cold, she swims all year round.)

　　 c. 値段が高かろうと高くなかろうとおいしいものが食べたい。

　　 (I want to eat good food, whether or not it is expensive.)

Note the contrast in meaning in (3a, b) and (4a, b).

(3) a. 日本は戦後アメリカから良かれ悪しかれ、いろいろな影響を受けてきた。

(For better or for worse, post-war Japan received all sorts of influence from the U.S.)

b. 結果が良かろうと悪かろうと、別にかまわない。

(Whether the result is good or bad, I don't care.)

(4) a. 私たちは多かれ少なかれ弱点を持っている。

(Whether many or few, we all have our weak points.)

b. 給料が多かろうと少なかろうと、その人の価値に違いはない。

(Whether someone's salary is high or low, his value as a person remains the same.)

【Related Expressions】

I. ~ de arō to ~ de arō to can replace ~ de are ~ de are without changing the meaning, as shown in [1].

[1] a. 男性で{あれ / あろうと}、女性で{あれ / あろうと}、人間としての権利は同じはずだ。(= KS(A))

   b. 有名で{あれ / あろうと}、無名で{あれ / あろうと}、人生は短い。

(= KS(B))

The second de {are / arō to} may change to the negative form (~ de) nakarō to, but nakare, the negative form of are, cannot be used, as shown in [2].

[2] a. 男性で{あろうと / あれ}、(男性で){なかろう / *なかれ}と、人間としての権利は同じはずだ。(cf. KS(A))

(Whether or not one is a man, one's rights as a human being should be the same as the next person's.)

   b. 有名で{あろうと / あれ}、(有名で){なかろうと / *なかれ}人生は短い。(cf. KS(B))

(Whether one is famous or not, life is short.)

II. ~ de mo ~ de mo can replace ~ de are ~ de are quite freely. The only difference between the two is that the former is used in both spoken and written Japanese while the latter is used primarily in written Japanese.

[3]　a. 男性で{あれ／も}、女性で{あれ／も}、人間としての権利は同じは
　　　ずだ。(= KS(A))

　　　b. 有名で{あれ／も}、無名で{あれ／も}、人生は短い。(= KS(B))

D

de mo / ja aru mai shi　でも / じゃ あるまいし　　*phr.*　\<s\>

> a phrase expressing the speaker's be-
> lief that s.o.'s action is based on mis-
> taken identity of himself/herself and
> also expressing the speaker's critical
> comments about s.o.'s behavior

you are not ~, so; it isn't ~, so

◆ **Key Sentences**

(A)

Noun		
幼稚園児	{でも ／ じゃ} あるまいし	一人で学校に行きなさい。

(You are not a kindergarten pupil. Go to school by yourself.)

(B)

	Vinf		
フランスに	行ける	わけ	{でも ／ じゃ} あるまいし、

どうしてそんなにフランス語を勉強しているの。

(There's no way you can get to France. How come you're studying
French so hard?)

Formation

(i)　N{でも ／ じゃ}あるまいし

　　　子供{でも ／ じゃ}あるまいし　(you aren't a child, so ~ (lit., you
　　　couldn't possibly be a child, so ~))

(ii)   Vinf わけ{でも /じゃ}あるまいし

プロ野球の選手に{なる /なった}わけ{でも /じゃ}あるまいし   (it isn't the case that s.o. will/has become a professional baseball player, so ~)

(iii)   Adj(*i*)inf わけ{でも /じゃ}あるまいし

{面白い /面白かった}わけ{でも /じゃ}あるまいし   (it isn't the case that s.t. is/was interesting, so ~)

(iv)   Adj(*na*)stem{な /だった}わけ{でも /じゃ}あるまいし

有名{な /だった}わけ{でも /じゃ}あるまいし   (it isn't the case that s.o. is/was famous, so ~)

(v)   N{である /だった}わけ{でも /じゃ}あるまいし

社長{である /だった}わけ{でも /じゃ}あるまいし   (it isn't the case that s.o. is/was a company president, so ~)

Examples

(a) 学生じゃあるまいし、仕事でも探したらどうだ。

(You are not a student; why don't you look for a job or something?)

(b) 政治家でもあるまいし、嘘をつかないで下さい。

(You aren't a politician. Don't tell a lie.)

(c) 犬じゃあるまいし、そんなに人にじゃれるようなことはやめなさい。

(You aren't a dog, you know. Stop being so playful with me.)

(d) お葬式でもあるまいし、そんなにしゅんとしないで下さい。

(It's not a funeral service. Don't be depressingly quiet!)

(e) 現地の英語学校に入ったら、日本人の女の子が英語で「分からないことがあったら聞いて」と言ってきた。授業中じゃあるまいし、日本語で言えばいいのに。

(When I went inside an English language school there, a Japanese girl said to me in English, "If you have anything you don't understand, ask me." It wasn't even a class. She could have talked to me in Japanese!)

(f) このうどん屋では注文してから、うどんがくるまで長く待たされ、いらいらする。フランス料理でもあるまいし……。

(At this noodle shop it takes so long from the time you order noodles to the time they bring them to the table that I get annoyed. It's not French cuisine, you know.)

(g) 息子は音楽を専攻しているんじゃあるまいし、ギターばかり弾いていて卒業
　　できるんだろうか。

(My son isn't majoring in music, but he's always playing the guitar. I
wonder if he can finish school.)

D

Notes

1. *De mo / ja aru mai shi* is a phrase expressing the speaker's belief that
   someone's action is based on mistaken identity of himself/herself, as in
   KS(A) and Exs.(a)-(c), and expressing the speaker's critical comments
   about someone's behavior, as in KS(B) and Exs.(d)-(g).

2. *De mo / ja aru mai shi* is preceded either by nouns or by a *wake* clause
   or *n* clause, as shown in KS(B) and Ex.(g).

3. The *de mo* of the phrase can be replaced by *ja* without changing the
   meaning.

4. *Wake* can be replaced by *n*. For the difference in meaning refer to *wake
   da* (DIJG: 570-74) and *no da* (DBJG: 325-28).

~ demo [Wh-word] demo　　～でも [Wh-word] でも　　　*str.*

| a structure indicating that what is expressed in the main/subordinate clause is applicable to anyone, anything, any place or any time | ~ whatever; ~ whoever; ~ whenever; ~ whichever |

◆ Key Sentence

	Noun		Wh-word		
そんなことは	子供	でも	誰	でも	知っているよ。
(That sort of thing is known even to a child or to anybody.)					

Formation

N (Prt.) でも、 (N (Prt.) でも、) Wh-word (Prt.) でも

　小学生 (に) でも、誰 (に) でも　((to) an elementary pupil or (to) anybody)

アフリカ(から)でも、どこ(から)でも   ((from) Africa or (from) anywhere)

すしでも、何でも   (*sushi* or whatever)

明日でも、いつでも   (tomorrow or whenever)

Examples

(a) 私ってマンガでも何でも読み出すと止まらないタイプなの。

(I'm the type of person who cannot stop reading *manga* or whatever once I start.)

(b) Tシャツの大きさはMでもLでも、どちらでもかまいません。

(It doesn't matter to me whether (the size of) the T-shirt is M or L (lit., or whichever).)

(c) 欧米では、バスでも地下鉄でも、車椅子でどこへでも行ける。どうしても助けが必要な時は、誰かに頼めばたとえ日本人にでも誰にでも手を貸してくれる。

(In Europe and America you can go anywhere in a wheelchair by bus or by subway. When you find you need help, just ask anyone. People there will lend a hand to anyone who asks, Japanese or otherwise.)

(d) 最近のパーティーは留学生でも日本人学生でも誰でも参加自由で、来る人は飲み物、音楽、自分の作った料理を持ってくるというようにしています。

(At our recent parties we've made it so all students, whether Japanese or from abroad, can freely participate and ask everyone to bring drinks, music or food they've made.)

(e) A: すみませんが、来週、検査の結果が出たら、もう一度来ていただけますか。

(Can you come back next week when we get the result of the examination?)

B: 分かりました。来週でもいつでも伺います。

(Yes, I can come next week or whenever.)

Notes

1. "~ *demo* [Wh-word] *demo*" can be used when what is expressed in the main/subordinate clause is applicable to anyone, anything, any place or any time.

2. As shown in the Formation, *demo* can be preceded by a particle. (1) provides more examples.

(1) a. この野球選手は小学生にでも、誰にでも人気がある。

(This baseball player is popular with elementary school students and everyone else.)

b. 彼は若い人とでも、年取った人とでも、誰とでもうまく話せる。

(He can talk comfortably with anyone, young and old alike.)

c. このプロジェクトは今月からでも、来月からでも、いつからでも始められる。

(We can begin this project this month, next month or whenever.)

dochira ka to iu to　どちらかと言うと　*phr.*

| a phrase indicating that the speaker/ writer chooses one alternative over another in a tentative way | rather; more like ~ ; more of ~ ; rather on the ~ side; rather than otherwise; more ~ than ~ 〖REL. *dochira ka to ieba*; *mushiro*〗 |

◆ **Key Sentences**

(A)

		Noun₁		Noun₂	
彼は	どちらかと言うと	教育者	というより (は)	研究者	だ。

(He is more like a researcher than an educator.)

(B)

		Adj(*na*)₁stem	
私は	どちらかと言うと	外向的	というより (は)

Adj(*na*)₂stem	
内向的	だ。

(I'm more of an introvert than an extrovert.)

(C)

		Adj(*i*)inf		
母は	どちらかと言うと、	おとなしい	方	です。
(My mother is rather on the quiet side.)				

(D)

		Noun		
洋食も悪くはないが、	どちらかと言うと、	和食_{わしょく}	の方	が	いい。
(It's not that Western-style food is bad, but I prefer Japanese-style food.)				

D

Formation

(i)　どちらかと言うと(X というよりは)Y。　(where X = N{ø / だ / だった} /
　　Adj(*i*)inf / Adj(*na*)stem{ø / だ / だった};Y = N{だ / だった} /
　　Adj(*i*)inf / Adj(*na*){だ / だった})

　　どちらかと言うと(詩人_{しじん}(だ)というよりは)学者だ。　(S.o. is more of a
　　　scholar than a poet.)

　　どちらかと言うと(詩人だったというよりは)学者だった。　(S.o. was
　　　more of a scholar than a poet.)

　　どちらかと言うと(悲_{かな}しいというよりは)寂_{さび}しい。　(I'm lonely rather
　　　than sad.)

　　どちらかと言うと(悲しかったというよりは)寂しかった。　(I was lonely
　　　rather than sad.)

　　どちらかと言うと(不便(だ)というよりは)便利_{べんり}だ。　(S.t. is convenient
　　　rather than incovenient.)

　　どちらかと言うと(不便だったというよりは)便利だった。　(S.t. was
　　　convenient rather than inconvenient.)

(ii)　どちらかと言うと、X 方{だ / だった}。　(where X = Vinf.nonpast /
　　Adj(*i*)inf.nonpast / Adj(*na*)stem な)

　　どちらかと言うと、本をよく読む方{だ / だった}。　(S.o. is/was an
　　　avid reader.)

　　どちらかと言うと、大きい方{だ / だった}。　(S.t./s.o. is/was rather on
　　　the big side.)

　　どちらかと言うと、親切な方{だ / だった}。　(S.o. is/was more of the
　　　kind type.)

(iii) どちらかと言うと、(X よりは) Y 方が〜。   (where X, Y = Vinf.nonpast / Adj(*i*)inf.nonpast / Adj(*na*)stem な)

> どちらかと言うと、(するよりは)見る方が好きだ。   (I like watching s.t. rather than playing it.)

> どちらかと言うと、先生は(厳しいよりは)優しい方がいい。   (I like a teacher to be kind rather than strict.)

> どちらかと言うと、ゲームは(単純なよりは)複雑な方が面白い。   (I like complex games rather than simple ones.)

(iv) どちらかと言うと、(N₁ よりは) N₂ (の方が)〜。

> どちらかと言うと、(犬よりは)猫(の方)が好きだ。   (I like cats rather than dogs.)

Examples

(a) 山本は決して呑気な男ではない。どちらかと言うと神経質な男だ。
(Yamamoto is far from easygoing. He's more of a nervous type of guy.)

(b) あの政治家のやり方はどちらかと言うと賢いというよりはずる賢い。
(The way that politician behaves is more cunning than wise.)

(c) 君はどちらかと言うと楽観的というよりは悲観的だね。
(You're more pessimistic than optimistic, aren't you?)

(d) 彼女はどちらかと言うと、仕事に生きるタイプで、精神的にも強い人間だと思う。
(More than anything, I think she's the type who lives to work, and is quite mentally strong.)

(e) あの大学はどちらかと言うと入学がやさしい方だ。
(Entering that college is rather easy.)

(f) 私はパーティーなどの集まりでは、どちらかと言うと、話し役ではなく、聞き役の方だ。
(At parties or other gatherings I am more of a listener than a speaker.)

(g) どちらかと言うと、夏目漱石よりは芥川龍之介の方が私の趣味に合っている。
(If I had to choose I'd say Ryunosuke Akutagawa matches my tastes better than Soseki Natsume.)

(h) この大学の日本語の学生は、どちらかと言うと目的を持って勉強しているというよりは趣味として日本語を勉強している。

(At this university the students of Japanese are studying it more as a hobby than for a certain objective.)

(i) 彼はどちらかと言うと話すより書く方が得意だ。

(He is better at writing than speaking.)

Notes

1. *Dochira ka to iu to* is a phrase used when the speaker/writer chooses one alternative over another in a tentative way.

2. When X and Y are used in Formation (i) and (iii) they are usually the same part of speech. But when an adjective is used, the combination of X (= Adj(*i*)) and Y (= Adj(*na*)) or X (= Adj(*na*)) and Y (= Adj(*i*)) is allowed, as shown in (1a, b) below.

   (1) a. 彼はどちらかと言うと頭脳明晰だというよりは要領がいい。

      (He is more of a shrewd person than a bright one.)

      b. 彼女はどちらかと言うと人に優しいというよりはおせっかいだ。

      (She is nosey rather than kind.)

3. According to Formation (ii), the past tense is expressed at the end of the sentence, but there is another version in which the past tense is expressed within X, as in (2). Virtually there is no difference in meaning between the two versions.

   (2) a. どちらかと言うと、本をよく読んだ方だ。

      b. どちらかと言うと、大きかった方だ。

      c. どちらかと言うと、親切だった方だ。

4. In colloquial speech *dochira* is often replaced by *dotchi*.

[Related Expressions]

I. *Dochira ka to iu to* can be replaced by *dochira ka to ieba*. Examples follow.

   [1] 彼はどちらかと {言うと / 言えば} 教育者というよりは研究者だ。

                                    (= KS(A))

   [2] 私はどちらかと {言うと / 言えば} 外向的というよりは内向的だ。

                                    (= KS(B))

Dochira ka to ieba sounds more formal than *dochira ka to iu to*. *Dochira ka to ieba* is used typically for public surveys, as shown in [3].

[3] あなたは他の人と比べて、「国を愛する」という気持ちは強い方だと思いますか。 1．非常に強い 2．どちらかと{言えば／?言うと}強い 3．どちらかと{言えば／?言うと}弱い 4．非常に弱い

(Compared to others, do you think your patriotism is strong?
1. Very strong, 2. Strong, 3. Weak, 4. Very weak.)

(⇨ **ba** (DBJG: 81-83); **to⁴** (DBJG: 480-83))

II. *Mushiro* indicates the speaker's/writer's choice of one alternative over another. This adverb implies a more definitive choice than *dochira ka to iu to*. In [4a, b] the use of *dochira ka to iu to* is unnatural because the speaker/writer here expresses a very definitive choice.

[4] a. この大学の日本語の学生は増えるどころか、{むしろ／??どちらかと言うと}減ってきている。

(The enrollment of Japanese language students at this college is far from increasing; it is rather on the decrease.)

b. あの人と結婚するぐらいなら、{むしろ／*どちらかと言うと}死んだ方がいい。

(I'd rather die than marry him.)

(⇨ **mushiro** (in this volume))

dō ka どうか   *adv.*

| an adverb indicating a polite yet very strong request | please [REL. *dōzo*] |

◆ **Key Sentences**

(A)

		V *te*	
どうか	私の言い分を	聞いて	下さい。
(Please listen to what I have to say.)			

(B)

		Vneg		
どうか	私を	見捨て	ないで	下さい。

(Please don't abandon me.)

(C)

		V*masu*	
どうか	お	許し	下さい。

(Please forgive me.)

Formation

どうか～{V*te*／V*neg* ないで／お V*masu*}下さい。

  どうか返して下さい。 (Please return it to me.)

  どうか行かないで下さい。 (Please don't go.)

  どうかお持ち帰り下さい。 (Please take it home.)

Examples

(a) どうかこれに懲りずにまたいらして下さい。
   (We'd love to have you over again. (lit., I hope you'll see fit to overlook our meager hospitality and come again.))

(b) どうか本当のことを話して下さい。
   (Please tell me the truth.)

(c) どうかお体を大切に(して下さい)。
   (Please take good care of yourself.)

(d) どうかお気を使わないで下さい。
   (Please don't bother.)

(e) 向寒の折から、どうかお体にお気をつけ下さい。
   (It's getting cold, so please take good care of yourself.)

(f) どうか命をお助け下さい。
   (Please spare my life!)

(g) どうか今後ともよろしくお願いいたします。

(lit., Please let me ask for your kind help and considerateness from now on, too.)

Notes

1. *Dō ka* is an adverb that expresses the speaker's/writer's polite yet very strong request or plea.

2. The final predicate is typically in polite request form such as V *te kudasai*, as in KS(A) and Exs.(a)-(c), or its negative version, Vneg *nai de kudasai*, as in KS(B) and Ex.(d), or *o* V *masu kudasai*, as in KS(C), Exs.(e) and (f). Exs.(a), (e) and (g) need some explanation. Ex.(a) is used when a host humbly refers to his or her hospitality. In essence, it means "Please come back again." Ex.(e) is used in written Japanese, more specifically in the final paragraph of a letter. Ex.(g) is used when one wants to formally and politely express one's desire for future assistance or cooperation.

[Related Expression]

Dōzo can replace all uses of *dō ka* in the KS and Exs. because both *dōzo* and *dō ka* can express request, but note that the former doesn't indicate a very strong request or plea, rather it is used to indicate politeness in making a request, extending an invitation or giving permission. Thus, there are many cases where *dō ka* cannot replace *dōzo*. [1] provides some examples.

[1] a. はじめまして、{どうぞ / *どうか}よろしく。[Request]

(I am pleased to meet you.)

b. {どうぞ / *どうか}お先に（いらして下さい）。[Request]

(Please go ahead.)

c. {どうぞ / *どうか}週末に遊びにいらして下さい。[Invitation]

(Please come and see us on the weekend.)

d. A: もう食べてもよろしいですか。

(Can I eat now?)

B: ええ、{どうぞ / *どうか}。[Permission]

(Yes, please go ahead.)

On the other hand, when one is pleading, *dōzo* can't be used.

[2] a. 先生、{どうか / ??どうぞ}母の病気を治して下さい！

(Doctor, please cure my mother's illness!)

b. 裁判長、{どうか / ??どうぞ}息子を死刑にしないで下さい。お願い
です。

(Honorable Judge, please don't sentence my son to death! I beg
you.)

dokoro de wa nai　どころではない　*phr.*

a phrase indicating that an action/state is simply impossible due to an adverse situation	cannot; be simply impossible; simply don't/doesn't have time; be far from ~; anything but ~; no way; far from; be out of question 【REL. *dokoroka*; *dokoro no hanashi de wa nai*】

◆ **Key Sentences**

(A)

		Vinf.nonpast	
自分のことで精一杯で、	人のことなど	**考える**	どころ ではない。

(I'm so busy with my own things that I simply can't think of other people's matters (right now).)

(B)

	Noun		
年末なのに多忙で、	**海外旅行**	(をする)	どころ ではなかった。

(I was so busy toward the end of the year that there was no way I could travel abroad.)

(C)

	Adj(*i*)inf. nonpast		
津波で愛する娘を亡くしたので、	悲しい	どころではない。	死にたい気持ちだ。

(I lost my beloved daughter in the tsunami. I'm not just sad. I feel like killing myself.)

(D)

	Adj(*na*)stem		
定年になっても	暇	どころではない。	毎日野菜作りに精を出している。

(I have retired, but I can't say I have any free time. Every day I put all my energy into vegetable gardening.)

Formation

(i) {V / Adj(*i*)} inf.nonpast どころではない

映画を見るどころではない　(s.o. simply doesn't have time to see a movie)

面白いどころではない　(s.t. is far from being interesting)

(ii) N(をする)どころではない　(where N is typically an action noun)

ゴルフ(をする)どころではない　(I simply don't have time to play golf)

散歩(をする)どころではない　(I simply don't have time to take a walk)

(iii) Adj(*na*)stem どころではない

自由どころではない　(s.t./s.o. is hardly free)

Examples

(a) 毎日の生活に汲々としていて、株を買うどころではありません。

(My everyday life is so tight financially that I simply can't consider buying stocks.)

(b) 私はテニスが大好きだが、最近大怪我をしてテニスどころではない。

(I love tennis, but I sustained a severe injury recently, and playing tennis is now out of the question.)

(c) A: おい、今晩、飲みに行こうか。

(Hey, why don't we go drinking tonight?)

B: それどころじゃないんだ。妻が入院したんだ。

(No way. My wife has been hospitalized.)

(d) 目下寝たきりの母の介護で、外出どころではないんです。

(Right now I'm taking care of my bed-ridden mother, so I simply don't have time to leave the house.)

(e) このところ学生の修論指導で研究どころじゃないんだよ。

(I've been advising MA students on their theses lately and I simply don't have time to do research.)

(f) 妻：あなた、この週末に熱海の温泉にでも行かない？

(Wife: Honey, why don't we go to the hot springs in Atami this weekend?)

夫：それどころじゃないんだよ。原稿の締め切りが来週の月曜日なんだ。

(Husband: No way! The deadline for the manuscript is next Monday.)

(g) スイカマラソンは、レース中やレース後にスイカが食べられる。でも、走り終わったら、へとへとで、とてもスイカを食べるどころではないそうだ。

(In the watermelon marathon, runners can eat watermelon during or after the race, but I hear that when they're done running they're so tired that there's no way they can eat the watermelon.)

(h) 今日は非常に暑かった。もう暖かいどころではない。

(It was extremely hot today. You can't just call it warm anymore.)

(i) ものすごい排気ガスを吸っているから、健康どころではない。

(I am breathing in all these awful exhaust fumes, so I am far from being healthy.)

Notes

1. *Dokoro de wa nai* is a phrase expressing that an action or state is simply impossible due to an adverse situation.

2. *Dokoro de wa nai* can be used in its contracted form *dokoro ja nai* in colloquial speech, as in Exs.(c), (e) and (f).

3. As shown in Exs.(c) and (f), the pronoun *sore* can replace s.t. expressed previously.

[Related Expressions]

I. The use of *dokoroka* "far from" is very similar to that of *dokoro de wa nai*. The former is a clause-final conjunction, and the main clause follows it, but *dokoro de wa nai* is a phrase that is used at the end of a sentence. The following examples demonstrate this point.

[1] a. A: 彼女、日本語、話せるの？

(Can she speak Japanese?)

B: いや、話せるどころ{じゃない。／か、}一度も勉強したことがないんだ。

(No, hardly. She's never studied it.)

b. 津波で愛する娘を亡くしたので、悲しいどころ{ではない。／か、}死にたい気持ちだ。(= KS(C))

c. 定年になっても暇どころ{ではない。／か、}毎日野菜作りに精を出している。(= KS(D))

(⇨ *dokoroka* (DIJG: 34-36))

II. *Dokoro no hanashi de wa nai* can always replace *dokoro de wa nai*. However, the former is more emphatic.

[2] a. 自分のことで精一杯で、人のことなど考えるどころ(の話)ではない。

(= KS(A))

b. 年末なのに多忙で、海外旅行どころ(の話)ではなかった。(= KS(B))

domo ども　　*conj.*　　\<w\>

a conjunction that indicates concession based on an actual state or action	even though; although; though; no matter how much/often/hard/etc. 【REL. *tomo*; *te mo*】

◆ **Key Sentences**

(A)

	Vcond		
この二つの文章{ぶんしょう}は言い方は	違{ちが}え	ども、	言おうとしていることは同じだ。

(Although the way in which these two compositions are written is different, their claims are the same.)

(B)

V₁cond		V₂cond (V₁ = V₂)		
行け	ども	行け	ども	人家{じんか}が見えてこない。

(No matter how far we go, we still can't see houses.)

Formation

Vcond ども

　行けども　(even though s.o. goes)

　見れども　(even though s.o. sees s.t.)

　すれども　(even though s.o. does s.t.)

　来{く}れども　(even though s.o. comes)

Examples

(a) 私{わたし}は知識{ちしき}はあれども学才{がくさい}がなく、今後{こんご}学問{がくもん}の世界でやっていけるとは思えない。

(Although I have (a good amount of) knowledge, I have no scholastic talent, so I don't think I can survive in academia (in the future).)

(b) 汲{く}めども尽{つ}きぬ泉{いずみ}のように、彼{かれ}は次々{つぎつぎ}と美{うつく}しい曲{きょく}を書{か}き続{つづ}けた。

(Just like a spring which never dries up no matter how much water is taken out, he kept writing beautiful songs, one after another.)

(c) 見慣{みな}れているものというのは、視{み}れども見えずで、毎日見ていてもその問題に気がつかないものである。

(Regarding things you are used to seeing, even though you look at them, you don't really see them. So, you don't notice their problems even if you see them every day.)

(d) 親といえども子供に対してそんな横暴は許されない。

(Even parents shouldn't be allowed to exercise such tyranny over their children.)

(e) 老いたりといえども、伊藤先生はまだ動きも速く、この剣道場の人は誰も先生に勝つことができない。

(Although Master Ito is old, he still moves swiftly, and no one at this Japanese fencing school can beat him.)

(f) 走れども走れども雪原が続いているだけだった。

(No matter how far I drove, the snow (lit., snowfields) never ended.)

Notes

1. *Domo* is a classical conjunction that carries the meaning of concession but is still used in contemporary Japanese. Its use is mostly limited to written language.

2. In "S$_1$ *domo* S$_2$," S$_2$ represents an actual state or action, meaning "Even though S$_1$, S$_2$."

3. For some reason, Gr. 2 verbs cannot be paired with *domo* as easily as Gr. 1 verbs and irregular verbs.

4. *Domo* often occurs as part of the phrase *to iedomo* "even though (lit., even though they say)," as in Exs.(d) and (e).

(⇨ to ie domo (in this volume))

5. When Vcond *domo* is repeated, it means "no matter how much/far/etc.," as in KS(B) and Ex.(f).

6. *Domo* occurs in proverbs and common phrases:

   (1) a. 「心ここに在らざれば、視れども見えず、聴けども聞こえず、食らえども其の味わいを知らず。」――孔子

   ("When the mind is not present, we look and do not see; we hear and do not understand; we eat and do not know the taste of what we eat."――*Confucius*)

   b. 王は君臨すれども統治せず。

   (The (British) sovereign reigns, but does not rule.)

   c. 声はすれども姿は見えず。

   (I hear someone, but don't see him.)

7. *Do* is another classical concessive conjunction, but in contemporary Japanese it appears only as part of proverbs or set phrases, as in (2).

(2) a. 笛吹けど踊らず。

(We have provided the music (lit., played the flute), but you have not danced.)

b. 待てど暮らせど彼女から返事が来なかった。

(Though I waited for so long, no reply came from her.)

【Related Expressions】

I. While *domo* always represents concession based on an actual state/action, *tomo* "even if; even though" can represent concession based on either an unknown (i.e., future or unknown present) state/action or an actual one, as shown in [1].

[1] a. 何が起ころうとも驚かない。

(No matter what happens, I won't be surprised.)

b. お金がないので海外旅行をしたくともできない。

(Even though I want to travel abroad, I can't do it because I have no money.)

(⇨ ***tomo*** (DIJG: 507-10))

II. *Te mo* is also a concessive conjunction. It can represent both concession based on an actual state or action and concession based on an unknown state or action. Thus, *domo* can be rephrased using *te mo*, as shown in [2]. Note that *te mo* is used in both spoken and written language.

[2] a. この二つの文章は言い方は{違えども / 違っても}、言おうとしていることは同じだ。(= KS(A))

b. {行けども行けども / 行っても行っても}人家が見えてこない。

(= KS(B))

(⇨ ***te mo*** (DBJG: 468-70))

dō ni mo ~ nai   どうにも～ない   *str.*

a structure indicating that no matter how hard s.o. may try, s.t. is impossible	not ~ by any means; no matter how hard ~ try, ~ cannot ~; there is no way to ~; cannot do ~ at all 【REL. *dō ni mo kō ni mo ~ nai*】

◆ **Key Sentences**

(A)

		Vpot.neg	
私には小説などは	どうにも	**書け**	ない。

(I'd never be able to write something like a novel, no matter how hard I try.)

(B)

		V*masu*			
この作文は間違いがひどくて	どうにも	**直し**	よう	が	ない。

(This composition has such awful mistakes that there is no way to fix it.)

(C)

		Noun			
最近は携帯がないと	どうにも	**仕事**	に	なら	ない。

(Lately we can't work without a cell phone.)

Formation

(i) どうにも Vpot.neg ない

　　　どうにも話せない (can't speak no matter how hard s.o. tries)

(ii) どうにも V*masu* ようがない

　　　どうにも食べようがない (there is no way to eat it)

(iii) どうにも N にならない

　　　どうにも勉強にならない (can't study at all)

Examples

(a) この書類は印刷が悪くてどうにも読めない。

(This document is printed so poorly, there's no way we can read it.)

(b) あの人はあまりにも内気でどうにも好きになれない。

(He is so introverted, I don't think I'll ever grow to like him.)

(c) 人の悪口をかげで言うなどということはどうにも許せない。

(I can't possibly tolerate someone speaking ill of me behind my back.)

(d) 会社経営で破綻寸前まで来るとどうにも救いようがない。

(When a company's management is on the verge of bankruptcy, there is no way to salvage it.)

(e) これだけストレスが溜まると、どうにも解消しようがない。

(When stress piles up this much, there's no way to relieve it.)

(f) バブル経済崩壊後の日本の経済の低迷ぶりはひどいものだけれど、どうにもならない。

(The Japanese economic slump since the bubble economy burst is terrible, but there is no help for it.)

(g) いろいろお礼の言葉を書こうと思っていたのですが、どうにも言葉になりません。今まで本当にありがとうございました。

(I was going to send you a thank-you note but I just couldn't find the words to say what I meant. Thank you very much!)

Note

Dō ni mo ~ nai is used to express the idea that s.o. cannot do s.t. no matter how hard he or she tries. The verb after *dō ni mo* is a Vpot.neg, as shown in KS(A) and Exs.(a)-(c), V*masu yō ga nai*, as shown in KS(B), Exs.(d) and (e), or ~ *ni naranai*, as shown in KS(C) and Ex.(g). However, there is an idiomatic phrase, *dō ni mo naranai*, used in the sense of *shikata ga nai*, as in Ex.(f).

【Related Expression】

Dō ni mo kō ni mo ~ nai, a more emphatic version of *dō ni mo ~ nai*, can replace the latter if emphasis is warranted, as in KS(B), Exs.(d) and (e).

[1] a. この作文は間違いがひどくて｛どうにも／どうにもこうにも｝直しようがない。(= KS(B))

  b. 会社経営で破綻寸前まで来ると｛どうにも／どうにもこうにも｝救い
   ようがない。(= Ex.(d))

  c. これだけストレスが溜まると、｛どうにも／どうにもこうにも｝解消
   しようがない。(= Ex.(e))

D

-dōshi 同士(どうし) *suf.*

a suffix that adds the meaning of "the same things/people"	each other; between/among (things/people of the same kind, group, etc.); together; with 【REL. *to*; *isshoni*】

◆ **Key Sentences**

(A)

	Noun			
磁石(じしゃく)の	N極(きょく)（またはS極）	同士(どうし)	は	反発(はんぱつ)する。
(North poles (or south poles) of magnets repel each other.)				

(B)

	Noun			
高校時代の	友達(ともだち)	同士(どうし)	で	海外旅行に行くことになった。
(We've decided that we high school friends will travel abroad together.)				

(C)

	Noun		Noun		
決勝戦(けっしょうせん)は	アルゼンチン選手(せんしゅ)	同士(どうし)	の	対決(たいけつ)	になった。
(The final turned out to be a battle between (two) Argentine players.)					

(D)

	Noun			
このケーブルを 使うと、	パソコン	同士 <ruby>同<rt>どう</rt></ruby><ruby>士<rt>し</rt></ruby>	を	<ruby>直接<rt>ちょくせつ</rt></ruby>つないで<ruby>高速<rt>こうそく</rt></ruby>ファイル転送 をすることができる。

(With this cable, you can connect personal computers directly and transfer files (from one computer to another) at high speed.)

D

Formation

N 同士（どうし）

友達同士　(the friends do s.t. to/for each other / together)

Examples

(a) たばこを吸（す）う者同士（ものどうし）は、何（なん）となく相手（あいて）に親（した）しみを感（かん）じやすい。

(Smokers somehow find it easier to feel close to each other.)

(b) 面白（おもしろ）いことに、隣（とな）り合（あ）った国同士（くにどうし）は仲（なか）が悪（わる）いことが多（おお）い。

(Interestingly, adjacent countries often have poor relations with each other.)

(c) 茨城沖（いばらきおき）で貨物船同士（かもつせんどうし）が衝突（しょうとつ）、２人死亡（しぼう）４人行方不明（ゆくえふめい）。[Newspaper headline]

(Two cargo ships collide off (the coast of) Ibaraki; two killed, four missing)

(d) これは分子同士（ぶんしどうし）が衝突（しょうとつ）して起（お）こる現象（げんしょう）だ。

(This is a phenomenon caused by molecules colliding (lit., against each other).)

(e) 男同士（おとこどうし）で旅行（りょこう）に行（い）ってもつまらない。

(It's boring if we travel together as a group of all men.)

(f) 韓国（かんこく）では1997年（ねん）に法律（ほうりつ）が変（か）わり同姓同士（どうせいどうし）でも自由（じゆう）に結婚（けっこん）できるようになった。

(In South Korea the laws changed in 1997, and people with the same family name can freely marry each other now.)

(g) この国（くに）ではいとこ同士（どうし）の結婚（けっこん）は法的（ほうてき）に認（みと）められている。

(In this country, marriage between cousins is legally recognized.)

(h) 何も知らない者同士が話し合ってもいい答えは出てこない。

(Discussions among those who don't know anything will never lead to a good solution.)

(i) 日本ではバレンタインデーに女の子が男の子にチョコレートを渡して愛を告白するのが一般的になっていますが、アメリカでは夫婦や恋人同士はもちろんのこと、友達や家族同士でもこの日、愛を言葉にします。

(It is common in Japan for girls to confess their love to boys on St. Valentine's Day by giving them chocolates. However, in America, not only married couples and lovers but also friends and family members verbally express their love to each other.)

(j) このタンパク質は細胞同士を結びつけるセメントのような役割をする。

(This protein acts like cement in joining cells.)

(k) モンスター同士を戦わせるコンピュータゲームが間もなく発売される。

(A computer game in which monsters fight against each other (lit., which makes monsters fight against each other) will be on sale soon.)

Notes

1. *Dōshi* itself means "fellow(s)." However, X-*dōshi* is used for both animate and inanimate things.

2. X-*dōshi* is used when two or more Xs do something to/for/against each other, as in KS(A), (C), Exs.(c), (d) and (f)-(i); do something together, as in KS(B) and Ex.(e); or are in a reciprocal relationship, as in Exs.(a) and (b). X-*dōshi* is also used when someone/something joins Xs together in some way, as in KS(D) and Ex.(j), or causes Xs to do something together or to/for/against each other, as in Ex.(k).

3. The interpretation of X-*dōshi* depends on the situation. When the action of X is a reciprocal action, such as *butsukaru* "to collide" or *kenka-suru* "to fight," X-*dōshi* means "between/among," or "(to) each other." When it is not a reciprocal action, X-*dōshi* means "together." When two or more Xs are in a reciprocal relationship, X-*dōshi* means "(to) each other."

4. When X-*dōshi* means "together," the action of the Xs must be interactive between the Xs. Thus, the sentences in (1) are unacceptable.

   (1) a. 学生 { ø / *同士 } が立ち上がった。

   (The students stood up together.)

　　b. 機動隊{ø /＊同士}が学生に襲いかかった。

　　　(The riot police attacked the students together.)

　　c. ヘリコプター{ø /＊同士}が飛び立った。

　　　(The helicopters took off together.)

5. Numbers do not occur before X-*dōshi*, as demonstrated in (2).

　　(2) a. 3台の車{ø /＊同士}が衝突した。

　　　　(Three cars collided with one another.)

　　　b. 5人の友達{ø /＊同士}で映画に行った。

　　　　(We five friends went to a movie together.)

However, note that numbers can follow X-*dōshi* when it means "together," as in (3).

　　(3) 友達{ø /同士}5人で映画に行った。

　　　(We five friends went to a movie together.)

6. As seen in the translations of KS(B) and Ex.(e), when X-*dōshi* means "together" and the subject is omitted, the sentence is considered to be in the first person unless there is some context to indicate otherwise, as in (4).

　　(4) 絵里子はよく旅行する。先月も友達同士で九州に行った。

　　　(Eriko travels often. Just last month she went to Kyushu with her friends.)

【Related Expressions】

I.　When X-*dōshi* means "(to) each other," it can be restated using the particle *to*, as shown in [1].

　　[1] a. 磁石のN極とN極（またはS極とS極）は反発する。(cf. KS(A))

　　　b. 決勝戦はアルゼンチン選手とアルゼンチン選手の対決となった。

　　　　　　　　　　　　　　　　　　　　　　　　　　　(cf. KS(C))

　　　c. 茨城沖で貨物船と貨物船が衝突、2人死亡4人行方不明。(cf. Ex.(c))

　　　　　　　　　　　　　　　　　　　　　（⇨ *to*¹ (DBJG: 473-76))

II.　When X-*dōshi* means "together," it cannot necessarily be rephrased using the synonymous adverb *isshoni* "together." For example, in [2], if the speaker/writer is male, the sentence is equivalent to Ex.(e).

However, if the speaker/writer is female, it means something different.

[2]　男と一緒に旅行に行ってもつまらない。(cf. Ex.(e))
　　　(It's boring to travel with a man (or men).)

D

ga hayai ka が早いか　*conj.*　<w>

a conjunction indicating that as soon as s.t. happens, s.t. else happens

as soon as; the moment; no sooner ~ than
【REL. *ya ina ya*】

G

◆ **Key Sentence**

		Subordinate Clause			Main Clause	
		Vinf.nonpast				Vpast (action)
彼は	朝	**起きる**	が早いか、		シャワーを	**浴びた**。

(As soon as he woke up he took a shower.)

Formation

Vinf.nonpast が早いか

食べるが早いか　(as soon as s.o. ate)

Examples

(a) 彼女は日本に着くが早いか友人に電話をかけた。
(The moment she arrived in Japan she called her friend.)

(b) 彼は私がいるのを見るが早いか、部屋を出て行ってしまった。
(As soon as he saw me, he left the room.)

(c) 猫はねずみを捕まえるが早いか、食べ始めた。
(The moment the cat caught the mouse, it started to eat it.)

(d) 電車はジョンが乗るが早いか、動き始めた。
(As soon as John got on the train, it started to move.)

(e) ディーンはきれいな女の子を見かけるが早いか、近寄って行って話しかけた。
(No sooner did Dean see the pretty girl than he approached her and started talking to her.)

(f) 子供たちはパンが焼けるが早いか、全部食べてしまった。
(As soon as the bread was baked, the children ate it all.)

(g) ひったくりは金を奪うが早いか、自転車で逃げた。

(As soon as the thief (lit. snatcher) snatched my money, he fled by bike.)

Notes

1. *Ga hayai ka* is a conjunctive phrase meaning that as soon as what is expressed in the subordinate clause (i.e., the clause that ends with *ga hayai ka*) takes place, what is expressed in the main clause takes place. For example, in the KS, getting up in the morning is followed almost immediately by taking a shower.

2. The tense of the main clause can't be nonpast in contrast to ~ *tara sugu* or ~ *to sugu* which can take both nonpast and past verbs in the main clause. Observe the following examples.

   (1) a. 彼は朝起きるが早いか、シャワーを{浴びた / ?浴びる}。(= KS)

   cf. 彼は朝{起きたら / 起きると}すぐ、シャワーを{浴びた / 浴びる}。

   b. 彼女は日本に着くが早いか友人に電話を{かけた / ?かける}。

   cf. 彼女は日本に{着いたら / 着くと}すぐ、友人に電話を{かけた / かける}。　　　　　　　　　　　　　　　　　　　　　　　(= Ex.(a))

3. The subjects for the subordinate clause and the main clause can be different, as in Exs.(d) and (f).

4. The subject of the main clause can't be the first person singular pronoun.

   (2) a. {彼女 / ??私}は日本に着くが早いか友人に電話をかけた。(= Ex.(a))

   b. {彼 / ??僕}は家に帰るが早いかビールを飲んだ。

   (As soon as {he / ??I} came home {he / ??I} drank beer.)

gai　がい [甲斐]

(⇨ *kai/gai* in this volume)

~ **ga** ~ **nara**   ～が～なら   *str.*

a structure presenting a counterfactual situation which indicates that things would be better if s.t. were really good or appropriate	if s.o./s.t. were a really good/ appropriate one; if s.t. is right

◆ **Key Sentence**

Noun₁		Noun₂ (= Noun₁)				
会社	が	会社	なら	もう少しましな給料を出してくれるの	だろう	が。

(If my company were a really good one, it would probably pay a bit better salary, but . . .)

Formation

N₁ が N₂ なら～（だろう / かもしれない）   (where N₁ = N₂)

病院が病院なら治っていた{だろう / かもしれない}   (if that hospital were a really good one, s.o. might have been cured)

Examples

(a) 大学が大学ならもっといい教育が受けられて、いい就職もできたのだろう。

(If the university had been a really good one, it would have given me a much better education, and I could have gotten a good job.)

(b) 友人が友人なら、役に立つ助言をしてくれたかもしれません。

(If your friend were a true friend, he might have given you useful advice.)

(c) 季節が季節なら、ここはすばらしい観光地なんですが、今は寒すぎて観光には向いていないんですよ。

(If we were here in the right season, this place would be a wonderful sightseeing spot, but now it's not a good place to take tourists because it is too cold. [It's winter now.])

(d) 時代が時代なら、そんな服装も悪くはないのかもしれないが、今ではおよそ古臭い。

(At the appropriate time, that sort of clothing would not have looked so bad, but now it is too old-fashioned looking.)

(e) 世が世なら、こんな情けない生活はしなくても済んだのに。

(If I were living in a really good time, I wouldn't need to live such a miserable life.)

G

Notes

1. N *ga* N *nara* is used to express a counterfactual situation indicating that things would be better if s.t. identified by N were a really good or appropriate one. Usually conjectural expressions such as *darō* or *kamoshirenai* occur with this clause, as shown in the KS, Exs.(a), (b) and (d).

2. Usually N in the construction is hypothesized as good, as shown in the KS and Exs., but sometimes it can be negative, as in (1). Note that there is no counterfactual meaning here.

(1) a. 親が親なら、子供も子供だ。

(The parents are really bad, but the children are the same.)

b. 医者が医者なら、看護師も看護師だ。

(The doctors are terrible, but the nurses are the same.)

gotoshi ごとし *aux. adj.* <w>

> an auxiliary adjective that indicates a resemblance of s.t./s.o. to s.t./s.o. or indicates how s.t./s.o. appears to speaker/writer

like; look like
【REL. *yōda*; *mitaida*; *ka no yōni*】

◆ **Key Sentences**

(A)

	Noun		
人生は じんせい	旅	の	ごとし。
(Life is like a journey.)			

(B)

	Vinf.nonpast		
その無謀な行為は火中に む ぼう こう い か ちゅう	飛び込む と こ	｛が／かの｝	ごとし。
(Acting recklessly like that is like jumping into the fire.)			

(C)

	Noun			
彼女は かのじょ	モナリザ	の	ごとく	いつも微笑んでいる。 ほほ え
(She is like Mona Lisa, always smiling.)				

(D)

	Noun₁			Noun₂	
X氏は し	超人 ちょうじん	の	ごとき	人	だ。
(Mr. X is like a superman.)					

(E)

	Vinf.nonpast			Noun	
彼女は僕のことを全然 かのじょ ぼく ぜんぜん	覚えていない おぼ	かの	ごとき	様子 よう す	だった。
(She looked as if she didn't remember me at all.)					

Formation

(i) N のごとし。

　　魚のごとし。　(S.o./s.t. is like (a) fish.)

(ii) Vinf.nonpast {が / かの} ごとし。

　　夢見る {が / かの} ごとし。　(It is like dreaming / as if s.o. were
　　　　dreaming.)

(iii) N (か) のごとく

　　魚のごとく泳ぐ　(s.o. swims like a fish)

　　魚かのごとく泳ぐ　(s.o. swims as if he/she were a fish)

(iv) N (か) のごとき N

　　夢のごとき人生　(life like a dream)

　　夢かのごとき人生　(life like a dream)

(v) {Vinf.nonpast / Nである} {が / かの} ごとき N

　　山に登る {が / かの} ごとき人生　(life like climbing a mountain)

　　夢である {が / かの} ごとき人生　(life like a dream)

Examples

(a) 光陰矢のごとし。

　　(Time flies like an arrow. (lit., Time is like an arrow.))

(b) 人生は航海のごとし。

　　(Life is like a voyage.)

(c) 東京人は万人走っているかのごとし。

　　(Tokyoites all look as if they were always running.)

(d) 日本の経済は、上述のごとく、今後しばらくは回復しない見込みである。

　　(As stated above, the Japanese economy is not expected to recover for
　　some time.)

(e) 彼女は女王のごとく芸能界に君臨している。

　　(She dominates the showbusiness world as if she were a queen.)

(f) 課長は当然のごとく女性の職員にお茶くみをさせている。

　　(The section chief has female staff members serve tea as if it were in
　　their job description (lit., as if it were a matter of course).)

(g) 夢のごとき新婚生活の後に悲劇が訪れた。

(Their dream-like, newly-wedded bliss was followed by tragedy.)

(h) 彼は平社員なのに社長であるかのごとき言動をするのでみんなに嫌われている。

(He is just a regular employee, but he talks and acts as if he were the president, so nobody likes him.)

(i) 皮膚の色だけで差別するがごとき行為は絶対にあってはならぬ。

(Behavior such as discriminating against people merely on the basis of skin color simply shouldn't exist.)

(j) 子供が大人のような犯罪を犯すがごとき風潮は何が原因なのだろうか。

(I wonder what causes trends such as children committing adult crimes.)

G

Notes

1. *Gotoshi* indicates similarity. As shown in the Formations, it changes form depending on its grammatical function. That is, the sentence-final form is *gotoshi*, as shown in Formation (i) and (ii); the adverbial form is *gotoku*, as in Formation (iii); and the noun-modifying form is *gotoki*, as in Formation (iv) and (v).

2. One of the functions of *gotoshi* is to mark a simile, as seen in KS(A)-(D), Exs.(a) and (b). When *ka* is inserted, as in KS(B), (E), Exs.(c) and (h), it adds the nuance of doubt on the part of the speaker.

3. *Gotoshi* and its variations are used exclusively in written language. In colloquial speech, *yōda* or *mitaida* is used. (See Related Expressions.)

4. *Jōjutsu no gotoku* "as stated above" (Ex.(d)) and *tōzen no gotoku* "as if it were a matter of course" (Ex.(f)) are idiomatic phrases.

[Related Expressions]

Yōda and *mitaida* can replace *gotoshi* as shown in [1]. Note that *mitaida* is highly colloquial.

[1]　a. 人生は旅｛のごとし / のようだ / みたいだ｝。(= KS(A))

　　　b. 東京人は万人走っている｛かのごとし / かのようだ / みたいだ｝。

(= Ex.(c))

c. 彼女は女王｛のごとく／のように／みたいに｝芸能界に君臨している。

(= Ex.(e))

d. 夢｛のごとき／のような／みたいな｝新婚生活の後に悲劇が訪れた。

(= Ex.(g))

e. 彼は平社員なのに社長である｛かのごとき／かのような／みたいな｝
言動をするのでみんなに嫌われている。(= Ex.(h))

(⇨ *yōda* (DBJG: 547-52); ***ka no yōni*** (in this volume);
mitaida (DBJG: 250))

hanmen 反面 *conj.* <w>

はんめん

a conjunction used to contrast the positive and negative sides of s.t./s.o.

while; on the other hand
【REL. *ni taishite*; *ni hanshite*; ***ippō (de)***】

◆ **Key Sentences**

(A)

Topic	Adjective₁		Adjective₂	
携帯電話は	便利な	反面、	わずらわしい	こともある。

(While cell phones are convenient, they are also sometimes annoying.)

(B)

Topic	Clause₁		Clause₂
この国は	個人の意思が尊重される	反面、	グループとしてのまとまりが弱い。

(In this society, while the individual's will is respected, group unity is weak.)

(C)

Topic	Clause₁			
この仕事は	面白くて収入もいい	が、	（その）	反面、

Clause₂
忙しくて自分の時間がなかなか持てないという問題もある。

(This job is interesting and pays well; on the other hand, being so busy, I hardly ever (lit., cannot) have time for myself and that is a problem.)

(D)

Sentence₁				Sentence₂
ここは海産物が安く、また 種類も多くて本土では食べ られない魚もあります。	（しかし、）	（その）	反面、	野菜や果物は 高いです。
(Seafood is cheap and plentiful in variety here, and there are also fish that you cannot eat on the mainland. On the other hand, fruits and vegetables are expensive.)				

Formation

(i) {V / Adj(*i*)} inf.nonpast 反面

　　 ～ができる反面　 (while s.o. can do ~)

　　 厳しい反面　 (while s.o. is strict)

(ii) Adj(*na*)stem {な / である} 反面

　　 便利 {な / である} 反面　 (while s.t. is convenient)

(iii) N である反面

　　 有利な投資である反面　 (while s.t. is a good investment)

Examples

(a) この仕事は厳しい反面、勉強になることも多い。

　　 (While this job is tough, it teaches me a lot.)

(b) 外食は手軽な反面、栄養が偏る恐れがある。

　　 (While eating out is easy, it can lead to an unbalanced diet.)

(c) この地域は商業や医療、文化施設などの利用が便利な反面、自然環境はあまり望めない。

　　 (In this region, while the commercial, medical and cultural facilities are convenient to use, you cannot expect much in terms of the natural environment.)

(d) アメリカンタイプのホテルは建物も比較的新しく部屋が機能的な反面、雰囲気に欠けるところがあります。

　　 (While American-style hotels provide functional rooms in relatively new buildings, they are somehow lacking in (good) atmosphere.)

(e) ポリエステルのカーテンは縮みにくく、熱にも強いが、反面、静電気が発生して汚れがつきやすい。

(While polyester curtains do not shrink easily and are heat-resistant, they attract dirt easily because of static electricity.)

(f) この磁石は優れた磁気特性を持ち、機械強度が大きい。反面、錆びやすく、高温での使用には適さない。

(This magnet has superb magnetic properties and excellent mechanical strength. On the other hand, it rusts easily and should not be used at high temperatures.)

(g) 理想主義はある面ではすばらしいが、その反面、それが行きすぎていろいろな問題が起こることもある。

(Idealism is wonderful in some ways; on the other hand, when it goes too far, it can cause problems.)

(h) インターネットの恋人探しサービスを使う場合、出会いという観点から見ると、こちらから積極的にアプローチをする方法はかなり効果的です。その反面、個人情報の流出という危険性もあります。

(When you use online services to search for a boyfriend or girlfriend, taking the active approach is quite effective in terms of meeting people. On the other hand, there is the danger that your personal information will be leaked.)

Notes

1. The literal meaning of *hanmen* is "the other side." *Hanmen* is used to contrast positive and negative sides of something or someone. The negative side is usually stated in the main clause or in a second sentence.

2. *Hanmen* can appear either at the end of the first clause or at the beginning of the second sentence. In the latter case, *sono* before *hanmen* is optional.

3. As seen in KS(D), *hanmen* is sometimes preceded by a demonstrative adjective. In this case, only *sono* can precede *hanmen*, as shown in (1).

(1) ここは海産物が安く、また種類も多くて本土では食べられない魚もあります。(しかし)、{(その) / *この / *あの} 反面、野菜や果物は高いです。

(= KS (D))

【Related Expressions】

I. *Ni taishite* is also used for contrasting statements. However, *ni taishite* is commonly used to contrast two different things rather than two sides of one thing. Thus, *ni taishite* and *hanmen* are not interchangeable, as shown in [1].

[1] a. 一般に、日本の学生は大学に入る前によく勉強する{のに対して / *反面}、アメリカの学生は大学に入ってからよく勉強するようだ。

(It appears that, in general, Japanese students study hard before entering college whereas American students study hard after entering college.)

b. この国は個人の意思が尊重される{反面 / *のに対して}、グループとしてのまとまりが弱い。(= KS(B))

(⇨ ***ni taishite/taishi*** (DIJG: 275-78))

II. *Ni hanshite* can be used to present two propositions in opposition. When *ni hanshite* presents two opposing propositions about one thing, *ni hanshite* and *hanmen* are interchangeable, but when *ni hanshite* presents two opposing propositions about two different things, *ni hanshite* cannot be replaced by *hanmen*, as shown in [2].

[2] a. 我が社はテレビの売れ行きが伸びている{反面 / のに反して}、オーディオ製品の売れ行きが下がっている。

(In our company, in contrast to the increase in sales of TV sets, sales of audio products are decreasing.)

b. 日本ではいい大学に入るのは難しいが卒業するのはやさしいと言われている。{これに反して / *その反面}、アメリカではいい大学でも入学は比較的やさしいが卒業するには相当勉強しなければならない。

(It is said that to enter a good university in Japan is difficult but to graduate is easy. In contrast, in America even good universities are relatively easy to enter, but students must study quite hard to graduate.)

(⇨ ***ni hanshite/hansuru*** (DIJG: 241-45))

hatashite はたして   *adv.*   <w>

> an adverb indicating that s.t. occurred as the writer expected, or expressing in a concession clause the writer's strong doubt

just as ~ thought; as expected; really; in fact; sure enough; indeed; at all; lo and behold 【REL. *yahari/yappari*; *an no jō*】

◆ Key Sentences

(A)

		Noun	
今年の冬も暖冬だと言われていたが、	はたして	暖冬	だった。

(They said this would be a warm winter, and indeed it has been.)

(B)

		Vinf			
はたして	日本の教育は	改革される	(の)	だろう	か。

(I wonder if Japanese education will really be reformed at all.)

(C)

		Vinf		
はたして	女性の地位が	改善される	としても	時間がかかるだろう。

(Even if women's status improves, as expected, it may take time.)

Formation

(i)   はたして {V / Adj(*i*)} inf.past

はたして失敗した   (s.o. failed as expected)

はたして安かった   (s.t. was indeed inexpensive)

(ii)   はたして {Adj(*na*)stem / N} だった

はたして立派だった   (s.o./s.t. really was magnificent)

はたして雨だった   (it rained (lit., it was rain), as expected)

(iii) はたして {V / Adj(*i*)} inf (の) だろうか

　　　はたして彼は {来る / 来た} (の) だろうか　(I wonder if he really is coming / came)

　　　はたして彼は頭が {いい / よかった} (の) だろうか　(I wonder if he really is/was smart)

(iv) はたして {Adj(*na*)stem / N} {ø / なの / だった (の)} だろうか

　　　はたして彼は元気 {ø / なの / だった (の)} だろうか　(I wonder if he really is/was healthy)

　　　はたして彼は学生 {ø / なの / だった (の)} だろうか　(I wonder if he really is/was a student)

(v) はたして {V / Adj(*i/na*) / N + Cop.} inf としても

　　　はたして彼が大統領に {なる / なった} としても　(even if he really becomes / became president)

　　　はたして彼が {若い / 若かった} としても　(even if he were / had been really young)

　　　はたして彼が {元気だ / 元気だった} としても　(even if he were / had been really healthy)

　　　はたして彼が {独身だ / 独身だった} としても　(even if he really were / had been a single)

Examples

(a) 東西ドイツ統一はいずれは起こると思っていたが、はたして予想通り起きた。

(I thought that sooner or later East and West Germany would be united, and, just as I expected, it happened.)

(b) 二人の仲は周知の事実で、いつかはゴールインすると思っていたら、はたしてその通りになった。

(Everyone knew about their relationship, and, just as we expected, they got married.)

(c) そこのレストランは魚料理で有名だったが、はたして思った通りのおいしい料理が出てきた。

(That restaurant was famous for its fish dishes, and the food really was as good as we had expected.)

(d) イスラエルとパレスチナ両国の間にはたして真の平和が訪れるのだろうか。

(I wonder if real peace will indeed come to Israel and the Palestinian territories.)

(e) はたして日本経済は近い将来に復興するだろうか。

(I wonder if the Japanese economy really will revive in the near future.)

(f) 21世紀ははたしてどの国の世紀になるのだろうか。

(To which country will the 21st century really belong?)

(g) はたして政治家たちの言うことがうわべだけのことであるとしても、多少の真実はあると考えたい。

(Even if what politicians say really is just lip service, I would like to think that there is some truth in it.)

Notes

1. *Hatashite* is used in three ways, as shown in KS(A), (B) and (C), but the basic meaning of "as expected" stays the same. The examples for Formation (i) (ii), (iii) (iv) and (v) are KS(A) and Exs.(a)-(c), KS(B) and Exs.(d)-(f), and KS(C) and Ex.(g), respectively.

2. *Hatashite* is used only in written or formal spoken Japanese. It could not be used in the following colloquial sentences.

   (1) a. *彼は来ないと思ったけど、**はたして**現れなかったよ。

   (cf. [1a] in Related Expressions)

   (I didn't think he was coming, and, just as I expected, he didn't show up.)

   b. *車の調子が悪いなと思っていたら、**はたして**会社に行く途中でエンストを起こしちゃったんだ。 (cf. [1b] in Related Expressions)

   (I thought something was wrong with my car, and, lo and behold, the engine stopped on my way to the office.)

[Related Expressions]

The colloquial adverb *yahari/yappari* can replace *hatashite* in Formation (i)-(iv), as shown in [1]-[3], but not in (v), as shown in [4], simply because *yahari/yappari* cannot be used in a dependent clause. There is another adverb, *an no jō*, which means "s.t. undesirable has occurred as expected." *An no jō* can replace *hatashite* in Formation (i) and (ii), if what occurred is undesirable, as shown in [1]. It cannot replace *hatashite*, however, if what occurred is recognized as desirable, as shown in [2]. In [3] and [4], in which something may occur in the future, *an no jō* is unacceptable, because it implies that something has already occurred as expected.

[1] a. 彼は来ないと思ったけど、｛はたして / 案の定 / やはり / やっぱり｝現れなかった。

(I didn't think he was coming, and in fact he never did show up.)

b. 車の調子が悪いなと思っていたら、｛はたして / 案の定 / やはり / やっぱり｝、会社に行く途中でエンストを起こしてしまった。

(I thought something was wrong with my car, and, lo and behold, the engine stopped on my way to the office.)

[2] a. 今年の冬も暖冬だと言われていたが、｛はたして / やはり / やっぱり / *案の定｝暖冬だった。(= KS(A))

b. 東西ドイツ統一はいずれは起こると思っていたが、｛はたして / やはり / やっぱり / *案の定｝予想通り起きた。(= Ex.(a))

[3] a. ｛はたして / やはり / やっぱり / *案の定｝日本の教育は改革されるのだろうか。(= KS(B))

b. ｛はたして / やはり / やっぱり / *案の定｝日本経済は近い将来に復興するだろうか。(= Ex.(e))

[4] a. ｛はたして / ??やはり / ??やっぱり / *案の定｝女性の地位が改善されるとしても時間がかかるだろう。(= KS(C))

b. ｛はたして / ??やはり / ??やっぱり / *案の定｝政治家たちの言うことがうわべだけのことであるとしても、多少の真実はあると考えたい。

(= Ex.(g))

(⇨ **yahari** (DBJG: 538-40))

---

hiite wa　ひいては　*adv.*

an adverb indicating that s.t. is perceived to eventually lead to a significant result	eventually (lead to) ~ ; even 【REL. *sara ni (wa)*】

◆ **Key Sentences**

(A)

	V *masu*		
イラクへの攻撃は アメリカの孤立を	招き、	ひいては	イスラム社会全体との戦争に発展していく恐れがある。

(There is fear that an attack against Iraq will bring about American isolation, and eventually will lead to a war with Muslim society as a whole.)

(B)

	Noun₁		Noun₂	
彼は同僚に	ライバル意識、	ひいては	殺意	すら抱いていた。

(He regarded his colleague as a rival, even to the point of considering murder.)

Formation

(i)　〜V *masu*、ひいては S。

　　　(⇨ KS(A))

(ii)　N₁、ひいては N₂

　　　(⇨ KS(B))

Examples

(a) 東京の産業構造を適切に転換していくことが、東京の産業を活性化させ、ひいては日本の経済力の強化につながっていく。

(Addressing the appropriate restructuring of Tokyo's industrial structure will revitalize Tokyo's industry and eventually lead to the strengthening of the Japanese economy.)

(b) 「誰もが自分自身の能力を最大限に活かして、自ら積極的に新しいことにチャレンジして、よりよく生きていく」という考えを、日本国内、ひいては世界に波及させたいと思っています。

(Life will improve when everyone uses their abilities to the greatest extent and actively takes on new challenges. I would like this idea to spread within Japan, and, eventually, in the world.)

(c) 世間では、企業経営から、教育、ひいては犯罪まで、話題はインターネットが独占しているという感じです。

(Throughout society, in business management and education, and even crime, it seems like the Internet is the dominant topic of discussion.)

(d) 道を歩いていて、奇妙な姿の人が向こうから歩いてくると、不安な気持ちになる。これは人間、ひいては動物の防衛機能の一つだろう。

(If a person with a strange figure walks towards you on the street, you might start to feel uneasy. This is a human defense mechanism, and is used even by animals.)

(e) 栄養価が高い旬のものをおいしく食べることは、ひいては病気を予防する。

(Food eaten in season is richer in nutrition, and thus can help prevent disease.)

(f) マスメディアが個人の名誉やプライバシーを不当に侵害する状況が続けば、ひいては報道に対して権力が介入する口実を与えることになる。

(If the media continues to violate people's reputations and privacy unjustly, some day it could provide an excuse for the government to intervene.)

Notes

1. The adverb *hiite wa* is used when it is believed something will eventually lead to some significant result. For example, in KS(A), "an attack against Iraq" causes "American isolation," but the speaker fears that in turn it will lead to "a war with Muslim society as a whole."

2. As indicated in Formation (ii), *hiite wa* can combine two or more nouns, as in KS(B) and Exs.(b)-(d). But strictly speaking, Formation (ii) is the result of ellipsis. For example, KS(B) and Ex.(d) are shortened from the forms shown in (1) below.

   (1) a. 彼は同僚にライバル意識(を抱き)、ひいては殺意すら抱いていた。

   (= KS(B))

   　　 b. これは人間(の**防衛本能の一つであり**)、ひいては動物の防衛機能の一つだろう。(= second sentence of Ex.(d))

3. The adverb *hiite wa* can be preceded by S *koto wa*, as in Ex.(e), or by Vcond *ba*, as in Ex.(f).

[Related Expression]

The adverb *sara ni (wa)*, "in addition," can replace the adverb *hiite wa* in all the KS and Exs. above. Meanwhile, *sara ni (wa)* can be replaced by *hiite wa* only when *sara ni (wa)* means "in addition." [1a] and [1b] below refer to number and quantity, respectively, so *hiite wa* cannot be used.

[1] a. 会員は37名だったが、{さらに/*ひいては}12名加わって49名になった。

(There were 37 members, but another 12 people joined, for a total of 49.)

b. 二人はすでにビールを十本も飲んでいたが、{さらに/*ひいては}ウイスキーも二瓶空けた。

(The two had already drunk 10 bottles of beer, but, in addition, they drank two bottles of whiskey.)

(⇨ ***sara ni*** (in this volume))

---

hito / ichi [Counter] **to shite ~ nai**   一 [Counter] として～ない
str.   <w>

<table>
<tr><td>a structure that means "not a single one"</td><td>not a single ~; not even one; not any ~
【REL. [Wh-word] *hito/ichi* [Counter] ~ *nai*; *hito/ichi* [Counter] *tari to mo ~ nai*】</td></tr>
</table>

◆ **Key Sentence**

		Counter			
うちの課には	一	人	として	英語を話せる者がい	ない。
(Not a single person in my section can speak English.)					

Formation

一 [Counter] として〜ない

一つとして使えない   (not a single one can be used)

Examples

(a) この資料室には一冊として役に立つ本がない。

(There's not a single useful book in this library.)

(b) 私が困っていた時、一人として私を助けてくれる者がいなかった。

(Not a single person helped me when I was having trouble.)

(c) この宗教は、この世の中には一つとして自分のものはないと教えている。

(This religion teaches that nothing in this world belongs to you.)

(d) 剣道の審判は一秒として気を抜くことは許されない。

(A *kendō* (Japanese fencing) judge will not be forgiven for losing his concentration for even a second.)

(e) 単身赴任中、一日として家族のことを思わない日はなかった。

(While I was assigned to another city (lit., When I lived on my own away from my family for business), there was not a single day I didn't think of my family.)

(f) 彼女の演奏は一音としておろそかに弾かれることはなく、どの曲も聴く者に深い感銘を与えないではおかない。

(In her performances, she never plays a single note carelessly, and no matter what the piece, her audience can't help being deeply impressed.)

Note

Hito/ichi [Counter] *to shite ~ nai* is used to indicate total negation, i.e., "not a single" or "not any."

[Related Expressions]

I.   A Wh-word followed by *hito/ichi* "one" and a counter expresses the same idea as *hito/ichi* [Counter] *to shite ~ nai*, as shown in [1].

[1]   a. うちの課には{一人として / 誰一人}英語を話せる者がいない。

(= KS)

b. この資料室には{一冊として／どれ一冊}役に立つ本がない。

(= Ex.(a))

c. この宗教は、この世の中には{一つとして／<ruby>何<rt>なに</rt></ruby>一つ}自分のものはないと教えている。(= Ex.(c))

II. Expressions with *tari to mo* are similar to *to shite*, as shown in [2].

[2]   a. うちの課には**一人**{として／たりとも}英語を話せる者がいない。

(= KS)

b. この宗教は、この世の中には**一つ**{として／たりとも}自分のものはないと教えている。(= Ex.(c))

H

c. 剣道の審判は**一秒**{として／たりとも}気を抜くことは許されない。

(= Ex.(d))

Tari to mo is more bookish than *to shite* and indicates even stronger negation than *to shite*.

Tari to mo is also used with *nanibito* or *nanpito* "anyone," as shown in [3].

[3]   <ruby>一部<rt>いちぶ</rt></ruby>のイスラム世界では、<ruby>女性<rt>じょせい</rt></ruby>は**<ruby>何人<rt>なんぴと</rt></ruby>たりとも**<ruby>髪<rt>かみ</rt></ruby>の<ruby>毛<rt>け</rt></ruby>を<ruby>他人<rt>たにん</rt></ruby>に見せることは<ruby>許<rt>ゆる</rt></ruby>されない。

(In part of the Muslim world, no woman is allowed to show her hair to others.)

hitotsu   ひとつ   *adv.*   <s>

an adverb used when the speaker intends to do s.t., or asks s.o. a favor, or makes a suggestion or gives advice to s.o.

give s.t. a try

◆ **Key Sentences**

(A)

		V*te*	
ひとつ	日本の小説の英訳を	やって	みよう。

(I will try to translate a Japanese novel into English.)

(B)

	Noun		Vinf.past		
ひとつ	ゴルフ	でも	やった	ら	どうですか。

(How about giving golf a try?)

(C)

		V*te*	
ひとつ	相談に	のって	下さい。

(Please give me your advice.)

Formation

(i) ひとつ V*te* みよう。

　　ひとつジョギングをしてみよう。　(I will give jogging a try.)

(ii) ひとつ N でも {V*te* は / Vinf.past ら} どうですか。

　　ひとつ散歩でも {しては / したら} どうですか。　(How about taking a walk or something?)

(iii) ひとつ V*masu* ませんか。

　　ひとつ話し合いませんか。　(How about discussing it?)

(iv) ひとつ V*te* 下さい。

　　ひとつ会いに来て下さい。　(Please come see me.)

Examples

(a) ひとつインターネットでもやってみよう。

　　(I will try the Internet or something.)

(b) ひとつ東大を受けてみたいと思います。

　　(I'd like to give the entrance exam for the University of Tokyo a try.)

(c) 「Shall we ダンス?」という面白い映画を見たので、ひとつ社交ダンスでも
やってみようかという気になった。

(Now that I've seen the (interesting) movie *Shall We Dance?*, I want to
give social dancing a try.)

(d) ひとつ映画でも見に行きませんか。

(Why don't we go see a movie?)

(e) ひとつ株でもやってみませんか。

(Don't you want to try stocks?)

(f) A: 君の言うことなど聞きたくないよ。

(I don't want to listen to what you have to say.)

B: まあ、そう言わないで、ひとつ聞いて下さいよ。

(Don't say that. Just give me a chance (lit., please try to listen).)

(g) そこのところを、ひとつよろしくお願いいたします。

(I'm well aware of the difficulty, but I would appreciate anything you
can do to help me.)

(h) じゃあ、この仕事をひとつやってもらいましょうか。

(So, can I ask for your help with this work?)

Notes

1. The Number-Counter combination *hito-tsu* "one piece" is used as an
   adverb when the speaker intends to do something, as in KS(A) and
   Exs.(a)-(c), asks a favor of someone, as in KS(C) and Exs.(f)-(h), or
   makes a suggestion or gives advice to someone, as in KS(B), Exs.(d)
   and (e). This expression seems to convey the meaning "give it a try."

2. The use of *hitotsu* in (1)-(3) below is different from that in the KS and
   Exs. because the adverb here somehow retains the meaning of "one
   piece." The sentences in (1) are negative potential sentences, and those
   in (2) are plain negative sentences. In both, the negative meaning is
   reinforced by *hitotsu*. That is, in both (1) and (2) the meaning of *hitotsu*
   is "(not) even one." (3) are affirmative sentences in which something is
   accomplished solely by its own virtues.

   (1) a. 彼女は手紙ひとつ満足に書けない。

      (She cannot even write a letter properly.)

      b. 息子はもう大人なのに、挨拶ひとつできない。

      (My son is already an adult, but he cannot even greet people
      properly.)

(2) a. このごろの若い子のファッションなんか**ひとつ**もいいとは思わない。

   (I don't like young people's fashion these days at all.)

   b. このマンガ、**ひとつ**も面白くないね。

   (This comic isn't interesting at all.)

   c. 彼は何**ひとつ**取り柄がない。

   (He doesn't have a single strong suit.)

(3) a. 彼女は美貌**ひとつ**で昇進していった。

   (She has been rising in rank simply because of her beauty.)

   b. 母は女手**ひとつ**で子供五人を育てた。

   (My mother brought up five kids all by herself.)

hitotsu ni wa 一つには   *adv.*

| an adverb meaning "partly" in a context where s.o. gives one or two objectives, benefits, examples or reasons for s.t. | partly; for one thing |

◆ **Key Sentences**

(A)

Topic		
大学教育の目的は、	一つには	幅広い教養と専門的な知識・能力を授けること、
一つには	社会に貢献する指導者を育成することだ。	

(The objective of college education is partly to provide broad schooling and professional knowledge and ability, and partly to train and produce leaders who will contribute to society.)

(B)

	Vinf			
彼が外国語を好んで	**勉強している**	の	は、	一つには、
異文化学習が好きだ	からだ。			

(One reason he likes studying foreign languages is because he likes to learn about different cultures.)

Formation

(i) 一つには～（もう）一つには～

　　　一つには自分のため、もう一つには家族のため　(partly for oneself and partly for one's family)

(ii) {V / Adj(*i*)} inf {の / 理由} は一つには～ {から / ため} だ。

　　　食べない {の / 理由} は一つにはまずい {から / ため} だ。　(One reason why s.o. doesn't eat s.t. is because it doesn't taste good.)

　　　食べなかった {の / 理由} は一つにはまずかった {から / ため} だ。　(One reason why s.o. didn't eat s.t. was because it didn't taste good.)

　　　おいしい {の / 理由} は一つには素材がいい {から / ため} だ。　(One reason why s.t. is delicious is because the ingredients are good.)

　　　おいしかった {の / 理由} は一つには素材がよかった {から / ため} だ。 (One reason why s.t. was delicious was because the ingredients were good.)

(iii) Adj(*na*)stem {な / だった} {の / 理由} は一つには～ {から / ため} だ。
　　　数学が得意な {の / 理由} は一つには好き {だから / なため} だ。　(One reason why he excels in math is because he likes it.)

　　　数学が得意だった {の / 理由} は一つには好きだった {から / ため} だ。 (One reason why he excelled in math was because he liked it.)

(iv) N {なの / である理由} は一つには～ {から / ため} だ。
　　　失敗 {なの / である理由} は一つには計画不足 {だから / のため} だ。 (One reason for the failure is lack of planning.)

(v) N だった {の / 理由} は一つには～ {から / ため} だ。

　　　失敗だった {の / 理由} は一つには計画不足だった {から / ため} だ。 (One reason for the failure was lack of planning.)

Examples

(a) 彼がよく家族と旅行に出かけるのは、一つには自分のため、一つには家族のためだ。

(He travels so frequently with his family, partly for himself and partly for his family.)

(b) 日本人が大人まで漫画を読んでいるのは、一つには、大人が十分味わえるような漫画があるからだ。

(One reason even Japanese adults read comics is because there are comics that adults can fully enjoy.)

(c) 彼がその子を好きな理由はいろいろとあるが、一つには彼女の話し方がいつも生き生きとしているためだ。

(He likes that girl for many reasons, but partly because her talk is always lively.)

(d) 私がアメリカに来た理由は、一つには、そこに学問の自由があると思ったからだ。

(One reason I came to the U.S. was because I thought there was academic freedom here.)

(e) 政治家が嫌われる理由は、一つには、選挙の時には魅力的な公約を言うのに、当選するとそれを実行しないからだ。

(Part of the reason politicians are disliked is because they make attractive promises when campaigning but don't put them into practice once they are elected.)

(f) 日本に来た外国人が体験するカルチャーショックにはいろいろあると思うが、一つには、日本人が彼らをガイジン、つまりソトの人と呼ぶということがある。

(Foreigners experience a variety of culture shocks when they come to Japan, one of which is being called *gaijin*, or "outside people," by the Japanese.)

(g) 「10年日記」をやってみたいとよく思うが、まだ始めていない。それは一つには、前の年の方がいい年だったらいやだからだ。

(I've often thought of keeping a "10-year diary," but I've never gotten around to doing it. That's partly because I wouldn't like it if the previous year was better.)

Notes

1. The adverb *hitotsu ni wa* is used either to give one reason, implying that there are more reasons, as in KS(B), Exs.(b)-(e) and (g), or to give one example, implying that there are more examples, as in Ex.(f), or to give objectives or benefits, as in KS(A) and Ex.(a).

2. The sentence ending can be other than ~ *kara da* or ~ *tame da*. Some examples follow.

    (1) a. アパートに決めたのは一つには学生寮に比べて居心地がいいということもあります。

    (One of the reasons I have decided on an apartment is that it is more comfortable than the students' dorm.)

    b. この国で別の大学への転学が容易に認められる理由の一つには、厳しい大学入試がないという事情がある。

    (One of the reasons that transferring to another university is easy (lit., readily approved) in this country is the fact that there aren't tough entrance examinations here.)

    c. その日本語の学生は、いろいろ問題があるのだが、一つにはまだ語彙が不足しているということがある。

    (That student of Japanese has many problems; one is his poor vocabulary.)

ichiō 一応 _{いちおう} *adv.* <s>

> an adverb indicating that an action or state is only temporary or tentative or is superficially conceived

for the time being; for the present; for now; tentatively; for formality's sake; nominally; kind of; sort of; although not perfect; just in case
【REL. *toriaezu*】

◆ **Key Sentence**

会議の日取りを ^{かい ぎ} ^{ひ ど}	一応 ^{いちおう}	来週の水曜日と決めておきましょう。 ^き

(Let's tentatively set our meeting date for next Wednesday.)

Examples

(a) 私は一応トムにその仕事を担当させることにした。
   ^{いちおう} ^{たんとう}

   (I've put Tom in charge of the project for the time being.)

(b) この問題についてはまだ議論の余地はあるとは思うが、一応ここでけりをつ
   ^{ぎ ろん} ^{よ ち} ^{いちおう}
   けたいと思う。

   (I believe that on this issue there is still a lot to be discussed, but I'd like to bring it to a close for the time being.)

(c) 一応大学を出ておいた方が都合がいいと思い、大学に進学したんです。
   ^{いちおう} ^{つ ごう}

   (I thought it would be better for me to graduate from college, to keep up appearances. That's why I went on to college.)

(d) A: コンピュータを使っていらっしゃいますか。

   (Are you using a computer?)

   B: はあ、まあ、一応は使っていますが。
     ^{いちおう}

   (Well, I'm kind of using one, but . . .)

(e) A: あなたは情報技術の研究者ですか。
     ^{じょうほう ぎ じゅつ}

   (Are you an IT researcher?)

   B: まあ、一応そういうことです。
     ^{いちおう}

   (Yes, sort of.)

(f) A: このお金どうするの？

(What are you going to do with this money?)

B: 俺が一応銀行に入れておくよ。

(I will put it in the bank for now.)

(g) 二人は兄弟と言うだけに顔は、まあ、一応似ている。しかし気性はかなり違う。

(The two are brothers, so their faces do sort of resemble each other. But, their temperaments are quite different.)

(h) すみません。これでも一応大学教師なんです。

(Sorry, (I know I don't look like one,) but I am in fact a college professor.)

(i) 滅多に買わない店だけど、名前くらいは一応覚えてもらっているから安くしてくれるかもしれない。

(It's a store where I seldom buy things, but they sort of know my name, so they might discount the price for me.)

Notes

1. *Ichiō* is an adverb used frequently and primarily in spoken Japanese. It means that an action or a state is temporary, tentative or superficially conceived.

2. The marker *mā* and *ichiō* are used together when the speaker wants to convey a sense of indecisiveness, as shown in Exs.(d), (e) and (g).

[Related Expression]

Toriaezu is an adverb used in spoken Japanese with a meaning similar to *ichiō*. It basically indicates that an action is temporary, tentative or introductory. It can replace *ichiō* in all instances except when the latter expresses a vague state, as shown below.

[1] a. 会議の日取りを｛一応／取りあえず｝来週の水曜日と決めておきましょう。(= KS)

b. 私は｛一応／取りあえず｝トムにその仕事を担当させることにした。

(= Ex.(a))

c. この問題についてはまだ議論の余地はあるとは思うが、｛一応／取りあえず｝ここでけりをつけたいと思う。(= Ex.(b))

    d. A: あなたは情報技術の研究者ですか。

       B: まあ、{一応 / *取りあえず} そういうことです。(= Ex.(e))

When *toriaezu* expresses an introductory action, as in [2], it cannot be replaced by *ichiō*.

[2] a. A: 何を飲もうか。
        (What shall we drink?)
    B: {取りあえず / *一応} ビールで始めようよ。
       (Let's start with beer for now.)

I

ichi [Counter] **to shite ~ nai** 一 [Counter] として～ない

(⇨ *hito/ichi* [Counter] ***to shite ~ nai*** in this volume)

ikan (da) いかん（だ）［如何（だ）］   *adv.*   <w>

| a classic form of the adverb *dono yō ni* "in what way" | how; what; (depending on) how/what; (according to) how/what; depend on 【REL. *shidai*; *ni yoru/yotte*】 |

◆ Key Sentences

(A)

	Noun Phrase		
私がこの会社に採用されるかどうかは、	面接の結果	いかん	だ。

(Whether or not I'll be hired by this company depends on the results of my interview.)

(B)

Noun Phrase			
今年の新車の売れ行き	いかん	{ で / によって }	この会社の将来が決まりそうだ。

(It looks like this company's future will be determined by this year's new car sales (lit., how new car sales are this year).)

(C)

Noun Phrase				
このテストの結果	いかん	によって	は	今年卒業できないかもしれない。

(Depending on the results of this test, I may not be able to graduate this year (lit., depending on what the result of the test is.).)

(D)

	Noun Phrase				
納入した学費は、	理由	の	いかん	{ を問わず / に関わらず }	返却しません。

(The tuition and fees you have paid will not be returned, no matter what the reason.)

Formation

(i)　N いかんだ

結果いかんだ　(s.t. depends on the result of s.t.)

(ii)　N (の) いかん { で / によって (は) / etc.}

理由 (の) いかんで　(depending on (what) the reason (is))

方法 (の) いかんによって (は)　(depending on (what) the means (is))

Examples

(a)　燃料電池自動車が普及するかどうかは価格とパワーいかんである。

(Whether fuel-cell cars spread or not depends on their price and power.)

(b) 子供の失敗をやる気に結びつけ成長への糧にできるかどうかは、その時の親の態度いかんだ。

(Whether or not children's failures can be connected to their motivation and cast as food for growth depends on their parents' attitude at the time.)

(c) 国や組織の将来はリーダーの知的能力いかんで決まると言える。

(We can say that the future of a country or organization is determined by the intellectual ability of its leader (lit., how strong the intellectual ability of its leader is).)

(d) 実験の結果いかんによっては、大発見になる可能性もある。

(Depending on the result of the experiment, this could be a great discovery.)

(e) 生活排水などの汚水は、その処理方法いかんによっては、周辺環境の悪化を招くこととなります。

(Depending on the treatment method, residential sewage and other wastewater can lead to the worsening of the surrounding environment.)

(f) 賞味期限のある食品類は開封・未開封のいかんに関わらず返品対象外となります。

(Food products with an expiration date are not returnable (lit., outside those which may be returned), (regardless of) whether the package has been opened or not.)

(g) このコンテンツの複製は、方法、媒体のいかんを問わず禁止されている。

(Copying this content is prohibited, regardless of the method or the medium.)

(h) 事態がここまで悪化しては、いかんともしがたい。

(Now that the situation has worsened to this extent, we cannot do anything (lit., in whatever way we do it, it's difficult).)

Notes

1. *Ikan* is derived from *ikani* "how; in what way." Thus, X *ikan* is equivalent to X *ga dō dearu ka* or X *ga dono yō dearu ka* "how/what X is."

2. Although X *ikan da*, as in KS(A), does not contain a word that carries the meaning of "to depend," it is equivalent to X *ikan ni yoru* "depend on how X is." Similarly, X *ikan de*, as in KS(B), is equivalent to X *ikan ni yotte* "depending on how X is."

3. *Ikan* has the property of a noun and is sometimes preceded by N *no*, as in KS(D).

4. *Ikan tomo* in Ex.(h) is equivalent to *dono yō ni mo* "in whatever way."

[Related Expressions]

I. When *shidai* means "depend on," it can be used in place of *ikan* except that *shidai ni yotte* is not acceptable, as shown in [1].

[1] a. 私がこの会社に採用されるかどうかは、面接の結果{いかん/次第}
   だ。(= KS(A))

   b. 今年の新車の売れ行き{いかんで/いかんによって/次第で/*次第に
   よって}この会社の将来が決まりそうだ。(= KS(B))

   (⇨ ***shidai*** (DIJG: 385-90))

II. *Ikan da* and *ikan de* can be rephrased using *ni yoru* "depend on" and *ni yotte* "depending on," respectively.

[2] a. 私がこの会社に採用されるかどうかは、面接の結果{いかんだ/によ
   る}。(= KS(A))

   b. 今年の新車の売れ行き{いかんで/によって}この会社の将来が決ま
   りそうだ。(= KS(B))

   (⇨ ***ni yotte/yori*** (DIJG: 292-301))

ikanaru   いかなる   *noun modifier*   <w>

> a noun modifier that means either "what kind of" or "no matter what"

what kind of ~; no matter what ~ ; whatever; any kind of 【REL. *donna*; *dono yōna*】

◆ **Key Sentences**

(A)

		Noun	
生物社会学とは	いかなる	学問分野	(なの)か。
(What kind of academic field is bio-sociology?)			

(B)

		Noun	Prt.		
彼は	いかなる	忠告	(に)	も	耳を貸さなかった。
(He didn't lend an ear to any kind of advice.)					

(C)

	Noun		
いかなる	理論	{でも / であれ / であろうと(も)}	穴はあるものだ。
(No matter what the theory is, it will have holes in it.)			

(D)

		Noun	Prt.	V*te*		
父は	いかなる	事態	に	なって	も	常に沈着だった。
(My father was always calm no matter what situation he found himself in.)						

(E)

		Noun	Prt.	Vvol		
重要な ことは、	いかなる	結果	が	出よう	と(も)	自分で決めたい。
(I would like to make my own decisions about important matters, no matter what happens as a result.)						

Formation

(i) いかなる N (Prt.) 〜か

いかなる政策を選ぶべきか (what kind of policy should we choose?)

いかなる政策(なの)か (what kind of policy is that?)

(ii) いかなる N (Prt.) も

いかなる図書館にも (at any kind of library)

いかなる図書館も (any library)

(iii) いかなる N {でも / であれ / であろうと(も)}

いかなる人 {でも / であれ / であろうと(も)} (no matter what kind of person (s.o. may be))

(iv) いかなる N + Prt. {V*te* も / Vvol と(も)}

いかなる大学で {教えても / 教えようと(も)} (at whatever college s.o. may teach)

Examples

(a) 日本語運用能力はいかなる基準で測るべきか。

(By what kind of standards should we assess proficiency in Japanese?)

(b) 厳しい父はいかなる口実も許してくれなかった。

(My strict father never allowed me to make any kind of excuse.)

(c) いかなる文化にも宗教は存在する。

(There is religion in any culture.)

(d) あの男はいかなる失敗にも負けず、不死鳥のように蘇る。

(No matter what the failure, he is undefeated, rising like a phoenix.)

(e) いかなる外国語学習でもその国の文化が好きになってくるものだ。

(When learning any foreign language, one will begin to like the country's culture.)

(f) スポーツはいかなるスポーツであれ、肉体だけではなく精神をも鍛えてくれる。

(Sports, no matter what kind, train not only your body but also your spirit.)

(g) いかなるアイディアでも、みんなで討議する価値がある。

(No matter what the idea is, it is worth discussing together.)

(h) いかなる社会を見ても女性の地位は徐々に向上している。

(No matter what society one observes, the status of women is gradually improving.)

(i) 私の研究がいかなる賞を得ようとも、その賞は私個人のものではなく、プロジェクトチームのものだ。

(No matter what prize my research may win, it is not mine alone; it belongs to my project team.)

(j) オリンピック・エリアにおいては、いかなる種類のデモも、いかなる種類の政治的、宗教的もしくは人種的な宣伝活動も認められない。

(In Olympic areas, no kind of demonstration nor any political, religious or racially-biased propaganda activities are allowed.)

Notes

1. *Ikanaru* is a noun modifier that is always followed by a noun. It means either "what kind of ~" or "no matter what ~," and is used in formal spoken and written language.

2. *Ikanaru* is primarily used in the four constructions shown in KS(A)-(E). The examples in Formation (i), (ii), (iii) and (iv) are KS(A) and Ex.(a), KS(B), Exs.(b)-(d) and (j), KS(C), Exs.(e)-(g) and (i), and KS(D), (E) and Ex.(h), respectively.

3. Formation (iii) and (iv) include alternative forms, i.e., *demo* vs. *de are* and V*te mo* vs. Vvol *to (mo)*, respectively. Both alternative forms are more formal than the original; i.e., *de are* is more formal than *demo*, and Vvol *to (mo)* is more formal than V*te mo*.

[Related Expressions]

Donna and *dono yōna* take the place of *ikanaru* in spoken and less formal written Japanese.

[1] a. 生物社会学とは{いかなる / どんな / どのような}学問分野なのか。

(= KS(A))

b. 彼は{いかなる / どんな / どのような}忠告にも耳を貸さなかった。

(= KS(B))

c. {いかなる / どんな / どのような}理論{でも / であれ / であろうと}穴はあるものだ。(= KS(C))

d. 父は{いかなる / どんな / どのような}事態になっても常に沈着だった。(= KS(D))

---

ikani いかに *adv.* <w>

| an adverb meaning "how" | how; how much; how hard 【REL. *donnani*; *nanto*】 |

◆ **Key Sentences**

(A)

		Adj(*i*)inf		
いかに	日本語が	難しい	か	は学習者の母語による。

(How difficult Japanese is (for someone) depends on the learner's mother tongue.)

(B)

	V*te*		
いかに	運動して	も	長生きできるとは限らない。

(No matter how hard one exercises, it doesn't guarantee a long life.)

(C)

	Vvol		
いかに	一生懸命	働こう	とも	一戸建ての家は買えない。

(No matter how hard I work I cannot buy a single house.)

(D)

		Adj(*i*)inf	
人生は	いかに	短い	ことか。

(How short life is!)

Formation

(i)　いかに {V / Adj(*i*)} inf か

　　いかに {生きる / 生きた} か　(how s.o. lives/lived)

　　いかに {美しい / 美しかった} か　(how beautiful s.o./s.t. is/was)

(ii)　いかに {Adj(*na*)stem / N} {ø / だった} か

　　いかに有名 {ø / だった} か　(how famous s.o./s.t. is/was)

　　いかに天才 {ø / だった} か　(how much of a genius s.o. is/was)

(iii)　いかに {V*te* も / V*vol* と(も)}

　　いかに勉強 {しても / しようと(も)}　(no matter how hard s.o. studies s.t.)

(iv)　いかにAdj(*i*)stem く {ても / とも}

　　いかにおいしく {ても / とも}　(no matter how delicious s.t. is)

(v)　いかに {Adj(*na*)stem / N} でも

　　いかに元気でも　(no matter how healthy s.o. is)

　　いかに天才でも　(no matter how much of a genius s.o. is)

(vi)　いかに Adj(*i*)inf ことか。

　　いかに {面白い / 面白かった} ことか。　(How interesting s.t. is/was!)

(vii)いかに {Adj(*na*)stem / N} {である / であった / だった} ことか。

　　いかにきれい {である / であった / だった} ことか。　(How pretty s.o. is/was!)

　　いかに天才 {である / であった / だった} ことか。　(What a genius s.o. is/was!)

Examples

(a)　いかに死ぬかはいかに生きるかと同じように大事だ。

　　(How one dies is as important as how one lives.)

(b)　ヒトゲノムの解読が病気の根本的な治療にいかに必要かが分かってきた。

　　(We began to understand how important decoding the human genome is for the basic treatment of illness.)

(c) クローン人間がいかに創られるのかは私には理解できないが、その倫理性についての論争には強い興味を覚える。

(I cannot comprehend how human clones are created, but I have a strong interest in the debate over the ethics of cloning.)

(d) 食べた物がいかにおいしかったかを言葉で適確に説明することは至難のわざだ。

(It is extremely difficult for one to describe in words how delicious the food he/she ate was.)

(e) いかに努力しても自分の才能のない領域だったら限界があるだろう。

(No matter how much effort you make, you will face limits when you deal with areas beyond your own talent.)

(f) いかに環境問題の重要性を強調しようとも強調しすぎることはない。

(No matter how much you emphasize the importance of environmental issues you can never emphasize it too much.)

(g) いかに天才でも、運が悪ければいい仕事はできない。

(No matter how much of a genius you may be, if you have bad luck, you won't be able to accomplish much.)

(h) 日本の経済はいかに脆いことか！

(How fragile the Japanese economy is!)

Note

Ikani means "how" and is used in three different structures, as shown in the KS and Exs., i.e., first in an embedded question, as in KS(A) and Exs.(a)-(d); second, in a "no matter how" sentence (sentence of concession), as in KS(B), (C) and Exs.(e)-(g); third, in an exclamatory sentence, as in KS(D) and Ex.(h). Note that in the second structure *ikani* means not "how" but "how hard/much."

[Related Expressions]

I. *Ikani* in Formation (i)-(v) can be replaced by *donnani*. *Donnani* can be used in both written and spoken Japanese.

　[1]　a. ｛いかに／どんなに｝日本語が難しいかは学習者の母語による。

(= KS(A))

　　　 b. ｛いかに／どんなに｝運動をしても長生きできるとは限らない。

(= KS(B))

c. 日本語が {いかに / どんなに} 難しく {ても / とも} 勉強を続けたい。
(No matter how hard Japanese is I would like to continue to study it.)

II. *Ikani* in Formation (vi) can be replaced by *nanto*. *Nanto* can be used in both written and spoken Japanese.

[2] a. 人生は {いかに / なんと} 短いことか。(= KS(D))

b. 日本の経済は {いかに / なんと} 脆いことか！(= Ex.(h))

I

ikura   いくら   *Wh-word*

a Wh-word that asks about the amount of s.t.

how much; how
【REL. *donnani*】

◆ **Key Sentences**

(A)

東京の 3DK のマンションは	いくら	ぐらい	ですか。

(Approximately how much is a 3DK (3 rooms with a dining room / kitchen) apartment in Tokyo?)

(B)

	V*te*		
いくら	働いて	も	お金が貯まらない。

(No matter how much I work I can't save money.)

(C)

			Verb
夏休みだから時間は	いくら	でも	ある。

(It's summer vacation, so I have tons of time.)

(D)

			Vneg	
ミルクはもう	いくら	も	残ってい	ない。
(There is barely any milk left.)				

(E)

今日は	いくら	か	気分がいい。
(I feel somewhat better today.)			

Formation

(i) いくら {Vte / Adj(*i*)stem くて / Adj(*na*)stem で} も

   いくら飲んでも (no matter how much s.o. drinks)

   いくら難しくても (no matter how hard s.t. is)

   いくらきれいでも (no matter how beautiful s.t./s.o. is)

(ii) いくらでも {Adj(*i/na*) / V}

   いくらでもいい (any amount of s.t. is fine)

   いくらでも結構だ (any amount is fine)

   お金はいくらでもある (there is an enormous amount of money)

(iii) いくらも Vneg ない

   いくらも買わない (s.o. doesn't buy much)

   いくらも食べない (s.o. doesn't eat much)

Examples

(a) その車はいくらでしたか。
   (How much was the car?)

(b) A: 寄付はいくらぐらいすればいいでしょうか。
   (About how much money should I donate?)
   B: いくらでも結構です。
   (Any amount would be fine.)

(c) いくら時間とお金をかけてもそのプロジェクトは終わるまい。

(No matter how much time and money we spend on this project, it probably won't end.)

(d) 会議はいくら長くても一時間ぐらいだろう。

(The meeting should last for an hour at the most (lit., no matter how long it may last).)

(e) いくら頭脳明晰でもよき指導者になれるとは限らない。

(No matter how bright someone is they won't necessarily become a good leader.)

(f) お酒はいくらでもありますから、どうぞたくさん飲んで下さい。

(There is really plenty of *sake*, so please drink as much as you like.)

(g) 私はまだ経験が浅いので報酬はいくらでもいいです。

(I don't have much experience, so any amount of compensation is fine.)

(h) 寄付はいくらでも大丈夫です。

(As for donations, any amount will be fine.)

(i) 僕みたいに毎日泳いでいる人間はいくらもいない。

(Very few people swim every day like I do.)

(j) 我々のように、いくらも休みがない人間だと、どんなに山登りをしたくても時間がないのである。

(People like us who don't have many days off can't afford the time to climb mountains, no matter how much we'd like to.)

(k) いくらか日本語の面白さが分かってきた。

(I have (now) come to appreciate some of the fascinating aspects of the Japanese language.)

Notes

1. *Ikura*, a Wh-word meaning "how much," can be used in five patterns with somewhat distinct meanings, as shown in the KS. KS(A) presents the straightforward question "how much?," as in Exs.(a) and (b). KS(B) is an example in which *ikura* is followed by the *te*-form of verbs or adjectives + *mo*, yielding the concessive meaning "no matter how much ~," as exemplified by Exs.(c)-(e). KS(C) is an example of the pattern where *ikura demo* is followed by the verb, as shown in Ex.(f), or Adj(*i/na*), as shown in Exs.(g) and (h). In KS(D), *ikura* is immediately followed by *mo* with a negative verb, meaning "not much/many," as

in Exs.(i) and (j). Lastly, KS(E) is an example of *ikura* followed by *ka* meaning "some; somewhat," as shown in Ex.(k).

2. *Ikura de mo aru/iru* is often shortened to *ikura mo aru/iru*, as in (1).

(1) a. 危険なものはほかにいくら(で)もある。

(There are plenty of other dangerous things.)

b. こんな仕事をしたい人はいくら(で)もいる。

(People who want to do this kind of work are quite common.)

【Related Expression】

In all the examples of *ikura ~ te/de mo* (i.e., Formation (i)), the expression can be replaced by *donnani ~ te/de mo*, as shown below.

[1] a. ｛いくら / どんなに｝働いてもお金が貯まらない。(= KS(B))

b. 会議は｛いくら / どんなに｝長くても一時間ぐらいだろう。(= Ex.(d))

c. ｛いくら / どんなに｝頭脳明晰でもよき指導者になれるとは限らない。
(= Ex.(e))

---

imasara いまさら ［今更］   *adv.*

> an adverb indicating that s.o. feels that it is too late to do s.t.　　too late (for/to ~); now 【REL. *ima ni natte*】

◆ Key Sentences

(A)

	Wh-word		Sentence (Aff.)	
この話は二年も前に話し合ったじゃないか。	なんで、	いまさら	同じ話を持ち出す	んだ。

(Didn't we discuss this issue two years back? How come you are bringing it up after such a long time?)

(B)

		Vneg	
いまさら	契約を解消するわけには	いか	ない。

(It is too late to cancel the contract.)

(C)

		V *te*			
いまさら	後悔	して	も	仕方が	ない。

(It is useless now to regret what you have done.)

(D)

		Vinf.past		
この問題を	いまさら	議論した	ところで	無意味でしょう。

(It would be meaningless to discuss this issue now.)

(E)

卒業してから 20 年だが	いまさら	ながら	母校の教育の質のよさが分かってきた。

(It's been 20 years since I graduated, (lit., it is too late) but now I've finally come to appreciate the educational quality of my alma mater.)

Formation

(i)   {いまさら + Wh-word / Wh-word + いまさら} + Predicate (Aff.)(か)。

   {いまさら何が / 何がいまさら}言いたいのか。 (What do you want to say now (at this late date)?)

(ii) いまさら + Predicate (Neg.)。

   いまさら行けない。 (It's too late to go (there).)

(iii) いまさら{Vても / Vinf.past ところで}+ Predicate (Neg.)。

   いまさら{見ても / 見たところで}仕方がない。 (It is no use looking at it now.)

Examples

(a) あなたはあの男とはきっぱり別れたはずなのに、いまさらなんで会おうとしているの。

(I thought you had broken up with that guy. Why in the world are you still trying to see him?)

(b) いまさらですが、「明けましておめでとうございます」。

(I'm afraid it is too late, but let me wish you a Happy New Year.)

(c) 今日の講師は皆さんよくご存じの方ですから、いまさらご紹介する必要はないとは思いますが……。

(All of you know today's lecturer very well, so I believe it is not necessary to introduce him now, but . . .)

(d) 会議の日程はすでに全員に電子メールで通知を出したのだから、いまさら変更することはできない。

(Because we have already e-mailed information on the conference schedule to everybody, it is impossible to change it now.)

(e) 喜んでプロジェクトに加わりたいと言った手前、いまさら断れないよ。

(Because I told them that I would participate in the project with great pleasure, I can't decline now.)

(f) がんがここまで進むと、いまさら手術をしても治らないと思います。

(With the cancer this far advanced, even if I operate now I don't think it will help.)

(g) 子供時代に過ごした村を訪ねたいと思っていますが、いまさら行ったところで、古いものは何も残っていないでしょうね。

(I'd like to visit the village where I spent my childhood, but even if I go, I guess nothing of the old times will still be there.)

(h) 母親を失って 10 年、自分も親になってみて、いまさらながら、親不孝だったことを反省しています。

(It has been 10 years since I lost my mother, and I am now a parent myself. It is too late, but I regret that I was not a devoted son.)

Notes

1. The adverb *imasara* that consists of *ima* "now" and *sara* "again" is used to indicate that someone is feeling it is too late to do something. The adverb is used in four ways. In KS(A), it is used with an affirmative

predicate, as also shown in Exs.(a) and (b). In most cases, such patterns yield a rhetorical question with a negative implication. So, KS(A) and Ex.(a) carry the implication that one shouldn't do what is indicated by the predicate (i.e., "bringing up the issue already discussed" in KS(A), and "meeting the guy you broke up with" in Ex.(a)). In KS(B), the adverb is used with a negative predicate, i.e., "not do s.t.," as also shown in Exs.(c)-(e). In some contexts, *imasara* is used with V*te mo* or Vinf.past *tokoro de* followed by a negative predicate, as in KS(C), (D), Exs.(f) and (g). *Imasara nagara* used in KS(E) and Ex.(h) means that someone feels belatedly thankful or sorry about something.

2. With the exception of *imasara*'s use in rhetorical questions with negative implications, as explained above, *imasara* cannot be used with affirmative predicates, as shown in (1). (See Related Expression.)

   (1) a. *いまさら問題が<u>はっきりした</u>。

       (The problem is now clear to me.)

      b. *いまさらなぜ彼女が僕を嫌ったかが<u>分かった</u>。

       (Now I understand why she hated me.)

3. *Imasara* is used when s.t. cannot be done due to certain circumstances created by a preceding action. KS(B), Exs.(d) and (e) are examples of this. The adverb cannot be used when someone is simply not in time for something, as shown in (2) below.

   (2) ｛もう／*いまさら｝その電車には乗れない。

       (I'm too late for the train.)

4. *Imasara nagara* in KS(E) is actually an idiomatic phrase, also used in Ex.(h), in which someone has strong feelings about something belatedly.

[Related Expression]

Ima ni natte can always be used in place of *imasara*, as shown in [1] below, with no semantic difference.

   [1] a. この話は二年も前に話し合ったじゃないか。なんで、｛いまさら／今になって｝同じ話を持ち出すんだ。(= KS(A))

      b. ｛いまさら／今になって｝契約を解消するわけにはいかない。

                                                    (= KS(B))

c. ｛いまさら／今になって｝後悔｛しても／したところで｝仕方がない。

(= KS(C))

As explained in Note 2, *imasara* cannot be used with affirmative predicates except when it is used in rhetorical questions with negative implications. However, *ima ni natte* does not have this restriction, as shown in [2].

[2] a. ｛今になって／*いまさら｝問題が<u>はっきりした</u>。(= (1a))

b. ｛今になって／*いまさら｝なぜ彼女が僕を嫌ったかが<u>分かった</u>。

(= (1b))

Ima ni natte can be used if the verb it modifies is present, as shown in [3].

[3] a. ｛いまさら／今になって｝<u>考えてみても</u>、どうしようもない。
   (It's no use thinking about it now.)

b. ｛いまさら／今になって｝<u>やろうと思っても</u>、無駄だよ。
   (It's waste of time trying to do it now.)

c. 何を｛いまさら／今になって｝<u>しようと言う</u>のかね。
   (What do you think you are going to do at this point?)

However, *ima ni natte* cannot be used if the verb it modifies has been omitted, as shown in [4]. This is not the case with *imasara*.

[4] a. ｛いまさら／??今になって｝どうしようもない。(cf. [3a])
   (You can't do anything about it now.)

b. ｛いまさら／??今になって｝無駄だよ。(cf. [3b])
   (It's waste of time to do it now.)

c. 何を｛いまさら／?今になって｝。(cf. [3c])
   (What are you going to do at this point?)

ippō (da)   一方（だ）   *phr.*   <w>

| a phrase indicating that "s.t. happens continuously" or "s.o does s.t. repeatedly" | only; always; continue to; keep ~ing; be steadily ~ing; become ~er and ~er 【REL. *bakari da*; *masumasu*; *dake*】 |

◆ **Key Sentences**

(A)

	Vinf.nonpast		
物価は	上がる	一方	だ。

((Commodity) prices are rising steadily.)

(B)

	Vinf. nonpast			
久子は私にものを	頼む	一方	で、	何もしてくれたことがない。

(Hisako is always requesting favors but has never done anything for me.)

Formation

(i)   Vinf.nonpast 一方だ

　　悪くなる一方だ　(s.t. only worsens)

(ii) Vinf.nonpast 一方の N

　　増える一方の財政赤字　(the fiscal deficit, which continues to increase)

Examples

(a) 電話や電子メールを利用した詐欺は巧妙化する一方だ。

　　(Telephone and e-mail fraud is becoming cleverer and cleverer.)

(b) この市は急増した人口にインフラ整備が追いつかず、犯罪も増える一方だ。

　　(Improvements to the infrastructure in this city have not kept pace with the sudden population increase, and crime keeps increasing as well.)

(c) ビジネスのグローバル化が進む今日、英語によるコミュニケーション能力の重要性は増す一方だ。

(English communication skills are becoming more and more important today as businesses continue to globalize.)

(d) サッカー熱は高まる一方だが、少年サッカーでひざの故障を起こすケースも増えている。

(People's enthusiasm for soccer is growing steadily, but the number of (cases of) knee injuries in youth soccer is also growing.)

(e) 深刻化する一方の医師不足に早急に何らかの対策が必要だ。

(We need some immediate countermeasures for the shortage of doctors, which is just getting worse.)

(f) 昨日のホッケーでは我々のチームは攻められる一方だった。

(In yesterday's hockey match, our team was always on the defensive.)

(g) 私たちはいつも子供や犬のことでお隣に迷惑をかける一方なので、申し訳なく思う。

(We feel sorry for our next door neighbors because our children and our dog are always giving them trouble.)

Notes

1. *Ippō* literally means "one direction." The phrase *ippō da* is used in two situations: (i) when describing a state that keeps progressing in a single direction (KS(A) and Exs.(a)-(e)), and (ii) when describing a state in which one party always does something to/for another, but not vice versa (KS(B), Exs.(f) and (g)).

2. *Ippō* is a noun; therefore, the noun modification form is *ippō no*, as in Ex.(e).

[Related Expressions]

I. *Bakari da* represents the same idea as *ippō da* except that *bakari da* is less formal.

[1] a. 物価は上がる{一方 / ばかり}だ。(= KS(A))

b. 久子は私にものを頼む{一方 / ばかり}で、何もしてくれたことがない。(= KS(B))

    c. 久子は私にものを頼んでばかりで、何もしてくれたことがない。

                                                       (cf. KS(B))

    (Hisako is always requesting favors but has never done anything
    for me.)

However, *bakari da* has other uses, as shown in [2], in which *ippō da*
cannot be used.

[2] a. あとはレポートを書く{ばかり/*一方}だ。

     (The only thing left to do is to write the report.)

    b. 稔は笑う{ばかり/*一方}で何も説明してくれない。

     (Minoru just laughs and doesn't explain anything to me.)

                                        (⇨ ***bakari*** (DBJG: 84-87))

II. *Masumasu* "more and more" is synonymous with *ippō da* when it
means "continue to; keep ~ing," as shown in [3].

[3] a. 物価はますます上がっている。(cf. KS(A))

     ((Commodity) prices are rising higher and higher.)

    b. 電話や電子メールを利用した詐欺はますます巧妙化している。

                                         (cf. Ex.(a))

     (Telephone and e-mail fraud is becoming cleverer and cleverer.)

III. *Dake* "only" can replace *ippō* when *ippō* means "always," as seen in [4].

[4] a. 久子は私にものを頼む{一方/だけ}で、何もしてくれたことがない。

                                                (=KS(B))

    b. 片方が何かをしてもらう{一方/だけ}の関係は長続きしないと思う。

     (I don't think a relationship in which one person always receives
     the favors from his/her partner will last long.)

When *ippō* means "keep ~ing; continue to" or when it means "always"
but is part of the main clause's predicate, *dake* cannot replace it, as seen
in [5].

[5] a. 物価は上がる{一方/*だけ}で、みんな困っている。

     ((Commodity) prices keep rising and everybody has a hard time.)

    b. 昨日のホッケーでは我々のチームは攻められる{一方/??だけ}だっ
     た。(= Ex.(f))

                                         (⇨ ***dake*** (DBJG: 93-97))

ippō (de) 一方（で）〔いっぽう〕　*conj.*　<w>

┌─────────────────────────────────────┐
a conjunction used to present two
concurrent actions/events/states or
contrastive situations
└─────────────────────────────────────┘

while; when; (but) at the same time; on the other hand; even though; although
【REL. *katawara*; *hanmen*】

◆ **Key Sentences**

(A)

	Vinf		
我々（われわれ）は化石燃料（かせきねんりょう）による環境汚染（かんきょうおせん）の問題に	対応（たいおう）する	一方（いっぽう）（で）、	新しいエネルギーの開発（かいはつ）に力を入れなければならない。

(We have to make more effort in developing new energy (sources) while countering the problem of environmental pollution caused by fossil fuels.)

(B)

	Adj(*na*)stem			
企業（きぎょう）は IT 投資（とうし）には	熱心（ねっしん）	な	一方（いっぽう）（で）、	セキュリティ意識（いしき）はまだ低（ひく）いところが多い。

(Many companies are still not very conscious about (information) security, even though they are eager to invest in information technology.)

(C)

	VN		
軍事予算（ぐんじよさん）	拡大（かくだい）	の	一方（いっぽう）（で）、	教育（きょういく）や社会福祉関連（ふくしかんれん）は大きく切（き）り捨（す）てられた。

(While the military budget has increased, budgets related to education and social welfare have been cut drastically.)

(D)

Sentence₁
日本は工作機械の分野では依然優位に立っている。

			Sentence₂
しかし	その	一方（で）、	最終製品の生産でシェアを下げつつある。

(Japan maintains its superiority in the field of machine tools. However (lit., However, on the other hand), its (market) share in the production of finished goods is falling.)

(E)

Sentence₁		Sentence₂
テレビはソファに深々ともたれ「後傾姿勢で受動的」に見る。	一方、	インターネットは椅子に浅く腰を掛け「前傾姿勢で能動的」にやる。

(Sinking into your sofa, you watch TV passively, while leaning back. On the other hand, the Internet is something you do actively in a forward-leaning position, while sitting on the edge of your chair.)

Formation

(i) {V / Adj(*i*)} inf 一方（で）

　　開発{する / した}一方（で）　(while developing s.t.)

　　{難しい / 難しかった}一方（で）　(while s.t. is/was difficult)

(ii) Adj(*na*)stem {な / だった / である / であった}一方（で）

　　顕著{な / だった / である / であった}一方（で）　(while s.t. is/was noticeable)

(iii) N{である / だった / であった}一方（で）

　　研究者{である / だった / であった}一方（で）　(s.o. is/was a researcher, and at the same time)

(iv) VN の一方（で）

　　強化の一方（で）　(while strengthening s.t.)

(v) S₁。一方、S₂。

　　イタリアは人口のほとんどがカトリックだ。一方、ドイツのカトリック人口は全体の約３分の１だ。　(In Italy most of its population is

Catholic. On the other hand, in Germany the Catholic population
is about one-third of the entire population.)

Examples

(a) 我が社は新製品を開発する一方で、多岐にわたる現在のモデルを少数に統合する計画だ。

(At our company we plan to consolidate our present broad range of models into only a few, while at the same time developing new products.)

(b) 政府は各種の予算を削減している一方、無駄遣いも目につく。

(While on the one hand the government is reducing its various budgets, on the other, its wasteful spending becomes more noticeable.)

(c) 就職できない若者がたくさんいる一方で、国民の生活に欠かせない仕事の分野で人手が不足しているそうだ。

(While a lot of young people cannot find a job, it is said that there is a shortage of manpower in fields essential for maintaining people's lifestyles.)

(d) 花粉症は完治が難しい一方、予防はしやすい。

(Although (lit., While) pollen allergies are hard to cure completely, they are easy to prevent.)

(e) 外国の食品がどこでも手に入るということは、便利な一方で、世界で食材不足を起こす危険性もある。

(It is convenient to be able to buy foreign foods anywhere but, at the same time, there is the danger of causing a shortage of foodstuff worldwide.)

(f) 日本では高齢人口が増加する一方、年少人口の減少が進んでいる。

(In Japan, the elderly population is increasing, while the population of young people is decreasing.)

(g) 今日では、海外に出かける日本人の数は、日本に来る外国人観光客の数の3倍もあります。しかしその一方で、海外から日本への観光客も、1970年以降、確実に増加しています。

(Today, the number of Japanese who go abroad is three times the number of foreign tourists who come to Japan. At the same time, the number of tourists who come to Japan from abroad has been increasing steadily since 1970.)

(h) 情報というものは簡単に複製し共有することができる。一方、物理的なモノ
の場合は、完全に複製するのは容易ではない。

(Information is something that can be easily reproduced and shared. Physical objects, on the other hand, are not so easily reproduced.)

Notes

1. *Ippō* is a noun but it functions as a conjunction with the meaning of "while; at the same time; on the other hand." It is connected to a sentence (KS(A) and (B)), the stem of a *suru*-verb (KS(C)), or the demonstrative adjective *sono* (KS(D)), or it is used as a sentence-initial conjunction (KS(E)).

2. When *ippō* is connected to another element, it may be followed by *de*.

3. Sentences with VN *no ippō (de)* can be rephrased using VN-*suru ippō (de)*, as in (1).

   (1) ｛軍事予算拡大の／軍事予算が拡大する｝一方（で）、教育や社会福祉関連
   は大きく切り捨てられた。(= KS(C))

4. When *ippō* is used as a sentence-initial conjunction, as in KS(E) and Ex.(h), the preceding sentence and the following sentence present two contrastive situations rather than presenting two concurrent actions, events, etc.

[Related Expressions]

I. *Katawara* "while" is synonymous with *ippō (de)*; thus, most of the sentences above can be rephrased using *katawara*, as shown in [1].

   [1] a. 我々は化石燃料による環境汚染の問題に対応する｛一方（で）／かたわ
   ら｝、新しいエネルギーの開発に力を入れなければならない。

   (= KS(A))

   b. 企業はIT投資には熱心な｛一方（で）／かたわら｝、セキュリティ意識
   はまだ低いところが多い。(= KS(B))

   c. 軍事予算拡大の｛一方（で）／かたわら｝、教育や社会福祉関連は大き
   く切り捨てられた。(= KS(C))

   d. 日本は工作機械の分野では依然優位に立っている。しかし｛(その)一
   方（で）／かたわら｝最終製品の生産でシェアを下げつつある。

   (= KS(D))

However, *katawara* cannot replace *ippō (de)* when it is used as a sentence-initial conjunction, as shown in [2].

[2] テレビはソファに深々ともたれ「後傾姿勢で受動的」に見る。｛一方／*かたわら｝、インターネットは椅子に浅く腰を掛け「前傾姿勢で能動的」にやる。(= KS(E))

II. *Hanmen* also means "while; on the other hand" and can replace *ippō (de)* in some situations, as shown in [3].

[3] a. 企業はIT投資には熱心な｛一方（で）／反面｝、セキュリティ意識はまだ低いところが多い。(= KS(B))

b. 日本は工作機械の分野では依然優位に立っている。しかしその｛一方（で）／反面｝、最終製品の生産でシェアを下げつつある。(= KS(D))

The difference is that *hanmen* is always used to state positive and negative sides of one thing (or person). This is not necessarily the case with *ippō (de)*. For example, in [4], the two parts of the sentence do not present positive and negative aspects of one thing. Rather, they simply present two actions that should be taken concurrently. In this case, *hanmen* cannot be used.

[4] 我々は化石燃料による環境汚染の問題に対応する｛一方（で）／*反面｝、新しいエネルギーの開発に力を入れなければならない。(= KS(A))

For the same reason, *hanmen* cannot be used when *ippō (de)* is used as a sentence-initial conjunction, connecting two sentences that present contrasting situations (see Note 4).

[5] テレビはソファに深々ともたれ「後傾姿勢で受動的」に見る。｛一方／*反面｝、インターネットは椅子に浅く腰を掛け「前傾姿勢で能動的」にやる。(= KS(E))

(⇨ ***hanmen*** (in this volume))

irai 以来〔いらい〕　*prt./conj.*

{ a particle/conjunction meaning "since" }　since
　　　　　　　　　　　　　　　　　　　　　　【REL. *kara*; *ikō*; *igo*】

◆ **Key Sentences**

(A)

	Noun		
大統領〔だいとうりょう〕の支持率〔しじりつ〕が	就任〔しゅうにん〕	以来	最低〔さいてい〕となった。

(The president's approval ratings have hit their lowest level since his presidency began.)

(B)

	Noun			
G 社が	創業〔そうぎょう〕	以来	初〔はじ〕めて	ホームページのデザインを変更〔へんこう〕した。

(Company G changed the design of its homepage for the first time since it opened for business.)

(C)

	V *te*		
肝臓〔かんぞう〕を	患〔わずら〕って	以来、	酒〔さけ〕はやめている。

(I've stopped drinking since I had my liver problem (lit., suffered from liver (disease)).)

(D)

	Noun Phrase		
植村〔うえむら〕に会うのは	10年〔ねん〕前の高校のクラス会	以来	だ。

(This will be the first time since our high school class reunion 10 years ago that I've seen Uemura.)

(E)

		Dem. pro.		
2年ほど前に重いスーツケースを持ち上げようとして腰を痛めてしまった。		それ	以来、	重いものは持てなくなった。
(About two years ago I damaged my back when I tried to lift a heavy suitcase. Since then I haven't been able to lift heavy things.)				

Formation

(i) N 以来　(where N indicates an event or a specific time)

そつぎょう
卒業以来　(since s.o.'s graduation)

5月3日以来　(since May 3)

(ii) V*te* 以来

帰って以来　(since s.o. returned)

(iii) Dem. pro. 以来

あれ以来　(since that time)

Examples

(a) 国の教育ローンの利用者が制度発足以来初めて300万人を超えた。

(The number of users of the state's education loan (program) has exceeded 3 million for the first time since the inauguration of the system.)

(b) 当ホテルは、明治42年創業以来90年の歴史を持っています。

(Our hotel boasts a 90-year history, having been established in the 42nd year of Meiji.)

(c) 琵琶湖の水位が今月6日、プラス31センチとなり、昨年7月21日以来、8か月ぶりに基準値に戻った。

(On the 6th of this month, the water level in Lake Biwa reached 31 centimeters above zero, returning to the standard level for the first time in eight months, or since July 21 last year.)

(d) 半導体市場は95年以来の二桁成長が予測されている。

(Two-digit growth is predicted in the semiconductor market for the first time since 1995.)

(e) ジョンソン氏が社長に就任して以来、この会社は次々に大きな改革を行った。

(Since Mr. Johnson became president, this company has carried out one major reform after another.)

(f) 生の舞台を見て以来、すっかり歌舞伎のファンになってしまった。

(Ever since seeing my first live performance, I've become a big fan of *kabuki*.)

(g) この空港始まって以来の大事故となった。

(This is the worst accident since this airport opened.)

(h) 先週清美と大げんかをした。それ以来、彼女とは口をきいていない。

(I had a ferocious quarrel with Kiyomi last week. Since then, I haven't talked to her.)

Notes

1. With a preceding noun or verb in *te*-form, *irai* makes an adverbial phrase or clause meaning "since X," where X refers to a specific time or an action or event in the past.

2. N *irai no* and V*te irai no* can modify nouns, as in Exs.(d) and (g).

3. The demonstrative pronouns *sore* and *are* can precede *irai*. *Are* is used when the speaker assumes that the hearer has knowledge about the event it refers to; otherwise, *sore* is used. Demonstrative pronouns before *irai* are sometimes omitted, as in (1a), unless *sore/are* and *irai* form a part of the predicate, as in (1b), or modify a noun, as in (1c).

   (1) a. 先週清美と大げんかをした。{それ / ø} 以来、彼女とは口をきいていない。(= Ex.(h))

       b. 植村には 10 年前に高校のクラス会で会った。彼に会うのは {それ / *ø} 以来だ。

       (I saw Uemura at our high school class reunion 10 years ago. This will be the first time I've seen him since then.)

       c. 植村には 10 年前に高校のクラス会で会った。今回は {それ / *ø} 以来の再会だ。

       (I saw Uemura at our high school class reunion 10 years ago. This will be our first meeting since then.)

4. *Irai* cannot be used with a time in the very recent past.

(2) a. 今朝{*以来 / から}頭痛がする。

    (I've had a headache since this morning.)

  b. 1時{*以来 / から}ずっとここで仕事をしていた。

    (I've been here working since one o'clock.)

  c. 昨日{*以来 / から}何も食べていない。

    (I haven't eaten anything since yesterday.)

5. *Irai no* N conveys the idea of "(for) the first time" or the notion of superlative (e.g., "the most," "the worst," etc.), as in Exs.(d) and (g). *Irai da* also conveys the idea of "for the first time," as in KS(D).

[Related Expressions]

I. *Kara* can replace *irai* when it is preceded by a verb in *te*-form.

  [1] a. 肝臓を患って{以来 / から}酒はやめている。(= KS(C))

    b. ジョンソン氏が社長に就任して{以来 / から}、この会社は次々に大きな改革を行った。(= Ex.(e))

Note that V*te kara* can also mean "after doing s.t.," but V*te irai* can only be used to mean "since."

Kara can be used to mean "since" with words that indicate a very recent time, while *irai* cannot. (See Note 4.)

                            (⇨ ***kara²*** (DBJG: 177-78))

II. *Ikō* "after; or later" looks similar to *irai*, but they are significantly different. While *irai* is used to indicate an action or event at a certain time (or a specific point in time) in the past and also to refer to the period since then and up to the moment of speech, *ikō* is used to indicate an action, event or state after a certain time (not necessarily in the past). Thus, *ikō* is unacceptable in [2].

  [2] a. 大統領の支持率が就任{以来 / *以降}最低となった。(= KS(A))

    b. 植村に会うのは10年前の高校のクラス会{以来 / *以降}だ。

                                  (= KS(D))

    c. 国の教育ローンの利用者が制度発足{以来 / *以降}初めて300万人を超えた。(= Ex.(a))

　　d. 当ホテルは、明治42年創業{以来 / *以降}90年の歴史を持っています。(= Ex.(b))

On the other hand, *ikō* can be used to refer to a point in time or an entire period after a certain point in time, as in [3]. In these sentences, *irai* cannot be used.

[3]　a. 訪問は来月{以降 / *以来}にして下さい。

　　　(Please make your visit next month or later.)

　　b. 5月{以降 / *以来}三度雨が降った。

　　　(We have had rain three times since May.)

　　c. 6月{以降 / *以来}はほとんど毎週出張があった。

　　　(I had a business trip almost every week starting in June.)

In the following contexts, both *ikō* and *irai* can be used, although there is a slight difference in nuance.

[4]　a. 6月1日{以来 / 以降}の雨

　　　(the first rain since June 1 / (any) rain after June 1)

　　b. 6月1日{以来 / 以降}雨が降っていない。

　　　(It hasn't rained since June 1 / It didn't rain after June 1.)

　　c. 第二次大戦{以来 / 以降}日本人の戦争観は変わった。

　　　(Japanese people's views about war have changed since World War II. / Japanese people's views about war changed after World War II.)

III. *Igo* "after; or later" is equivalent to *ikō* except that *igo* can be used alone, as in [5].

[5]　a. {以後 / *以降}注意するように。

　　　(Please pay more attention from now on.)

　　b. 知らずに女性言葉を使って恥をかいた。{以後 / *以降}同じ間違いはしなくなった。

　　　(I used female expressions without knowing it and I was embarrassed. After that, I didn't make the same mistake again.)

issai ~ nai   一切～ない   *str.*   `<w>`

~~~~~~~~~~~~~~~~~~~~~~~~~~~~~~~~~~~~
a structure that means "not at all"
~~~~~~~~~~~~~~~~~~~~~~~~~~~~~~~~~~~~

not ~ at all; absolutely not; not
~ whatsoever
【REL. *zenzen ~ nai*; *mattaku ~ nai*】

◆ **Key Sentence**

		Vneg	
飛行機事故の原因は	一切	分から	ない。

(We have no idea what caused the airplane accident.)

I

Formation

一切 Vneg ない

　一切食べない　(s.o. doesn't eat a thing)

　一切読まない　(s.o. doesn't read at all)

Examples

(a) この製品には遺伝子組み換え大豆は一切使用していません。

(For this product we haven't used any genetically modified soybeans at all.)

(b) 盗難に関しては当社は一切責任を負いません。

(Our company will not take any responsibility whatsoever for thefts.)

(c) 私はその汚職事件とは一切関係ない。

(I have nothing whatsoever to do with the bribery scandal.)

(d) 謝金は一切いただくわけにはまいりません。

(I couldn't possibly accept any honorarium at all.)

(e) 私は有害物質を一切含んでいない洗剤を使うことにしている。

(I make it a rule to use detergents that contain no harmful ingredients.)

Note

Issai is an adverb that is used with a negative verb to indicate absolute negation, that is, "not at all." The adverb cannot be used to negate Adj(*i/na*), as shown in (1) below.

(1) a. その教授の講義は{全然／全く／*一切}面白くなかった。

(The professor's lecture wasn't interesting at all.)

　　b. 僕の大学のキャンパスは{全然／全く／*一切}きれいじゃない。

(My college campus is not beautiful at all.)

【Related Expressions】

Zenzen ~ nai and *mattaku ~ nai*, meaning "not at all," can replace *issai* in practically all of the instances in the KS and Exs., as shown below.

[1] a. 飛行機事故の原因は{一切／全然／全く}分からない。(= KS)

　　b. この製品には遺伝子組み換え大豆は{一切／全然／全く}使用していません。(= Ex.(a))

　　c. 私はその汚職事件とは{一切／全然／全く}関係ない。(= Ex.(c))

However, in some idiomatic expressions, only *issai* is used. See [2].

[2] a. 盗難に関しては当社は{一切／??全然／??全く}責任を負いません。

(= Ex.(b))

　　b. 謝金は{一切／*全然／*全く}いただくわけにはまいりません。

(= Ex.(d))

Although *zenzen ~ nai* and *mattaku ~ nai* mean "not at all," they are different in the following way: *mattaku* can be used with affirmative and negative forms of V or Adj(*i/na*) in both spoken and written Japanese, but, as a rule, *zenzen* basically cannot be used with an affirmative V or Adj(*i/na*), as in [3a, b]. It can be used with an affirmative V or Adj(*i/na*) only in very casual, slang-like speech, as in [3c].

[3] a. 僕はあなたの意見に{全く／*全然}賛成です。

(I totally agree with your view.)

　　b. 父は{全く／*全然}健康だ。

(My father is completely healthy.)

c. 初めてよしもとばななの小説を読んだよ。もっと難しいと思ってたけど、{全く / 全然}面白い。

(I read a novel of Banana Yoshimoto's for the first time. I thought it would be much harder (to understand), but it was awfully interesting!)

Additionally, *issai* and *mattaku* can modify nouns with *no*, but *zenzen* cannot, as shown in [4] and [5]. The difference between *issai no* N and *mattaku no* N is that the former means "any instance of s.t.," whereas the latter means "a complete case of s.t." The difference can account for the reason why *mattaku no* N and *issai no* N are unacceptable in [4] and [5], respectively.

[4] a. 盗難に関しては当社は{一切の / *全くの / *全然の}責任を負いません。(cf. Ex.(b))

b. 両国は{一切の / *全くの / *全然の}外交関係を断ち切った。

(The two countries cut off all diplomatic relations.)

[5] a. {全くの / *一切の / *全然の}初心者も大歓迎です。

(We welcome complete novices.)

b. それは{全くの / *一切の / *全然の}誤解だと思います。

(I think it is a total misunderstanding.)

ittan　いったん [一旦]　*adv.*

an adverb meaning "once" or "for a short time"

once; for a time; temporarily; for the moment; for the present; now

【REL. *ichido*】

◆ **Key Sentences**

(A)

		Vinf.past		
この小説は	いったん	**読み始めた**	ら	やめられない。
(Once you begin reading this novel, you won't be able to put it down (lit., stop reading it).)				

(B)

		Vinf.past	
邦彦は	いったん	**やめた**	たばこをまた吸い出した。
(Kunihiko resumed smoking, which he had quit for a time.)			

(C)

			V*te*		
開演までまだだいぶ時間があるので、	いったん	ホテルに	**帰って**	から	出直そう。
(There's still a lot of time before the performance begins, so let's go back to the hotel (now) and come again later.)					

Formation

いったん V

   いったんやめる　(stop s.t. temporarily)

Examples

(a) この大学は、いったん入学してしまえば、そんなに勉強しなくても必ず卒業できる。

(Once you've entered this university, you will definitely be able to graduate, even if you don't study very hard.)

(b) この電子掲示板はいったん書き込むと消せないので、自分のメッセージを書く時に注意しないといけない。

(Once you write a message on this electronic bulletin board, you cannot delete it, so you have to be careful (when you write a message).)

(c) 石田は、いったん約束した以上は必ず守る男だ。

(Ishida is someone who keeps his promise (once he has made one), no matter what.)

(d) いったんこじれた我々の関係は、容易には元に戻らなかった。

(Our relationship, once it had become complicated, did not recover easily.)

(e) 予算が厳しくなったので、無料健康相談サービスをいったん中止します。

(Because the budget has become tight, we are going to discontinue our free health consultation service temporarily.)

(f) 新型ウイルスの被害はいったん終息したように見えた。

(It appeared that damage from the new virus had subsided temporarily.)

(g) ひょっとすると違う原因かもしれないので、今飲んでいる薬をいったんやめてしばらく様子を見てみましょう。

(There might be a different cause, so stop taking the current drug for the moment and see what happens.)

(h) 今使っているプログラムをいったん終了して、再起動してみて下さい。

(Please quit the current program (lit., the program you are using now) temporarily and reboot.)

(i) いったん日本へ帰って、親と相談してからアメリカで就職するかどうかを決めたい。

(I'd like to go back to Japan for a time and, (when I'm there) after talking to my parents, decide whether or not I'll look for a job in the U.S.)

Notes

1. *Ittan* is used in two situations: (i) a situation in which something takes place and the situation does not go back to the original state, and (ii) a situation in which something takes place and the situation changes, but it may go back to the original state. In the first case, *ittan* is interpreted as "once" (KS(A) and Exs.(a)-(d)), and in the second case, it is interpreted as either "for a time," "temporarily," "for the moment" or "now" (KS(B), (C) and Exs.(e)-(i)), depending on the context.

2. When *ittan* is used in conditional clauses, it means "once," as in KS(A), Exs.(a) and (b).

3. *Ittan* modifies only verbs.

[Related Expression]

Ittan can be replaced with *ichido* without changing the meaning of the sentence.

[1] a. この小説は｛いったん／一度｝読み始めたらやめられない。(= KS(A))

  b. 邦彦は｛いったん／一度｝やめたたばこをまた吸い出した。(= KS(B))

  c. 開演までまだだいぶ時間があるので、｛いったん／一度｝ホテルに帰ってから出直そう。(= KS(C))

Note that *ichido* cannot always be replaced by *ittan*, as demonstrated in [2].

[2] a. 私は韓国へ｛一度／*いったん｝行ったことがある。
   (I've been to Korea once.)

  b. ｛一度／*いったん｝医者に見てもらったらどうですか。
   (Why don't you go see the doctor (lit. have the doctor examine you)?)

  c. ｛一度／*いったん｝私のうちにも遊びに来て下さい。
   (Please come to my place, too.)

itte mireba   言ってみれば   *phr.*

a phrase signaling a comparison (including the use of simile and metaphor), a definition, or an explanation	figuratively speaking; so to speak; metaphorically speaking; in a manner of saying 【REL. *iwaba*; *tatoete ieba*; *(tatoete) iu naraba*】

◆ **Key Sentences**

(A)

	Sentence		
	じんせい こうかい 人生は航海	(のようなもの)	だ。
言ってみれば、			

(Figuratively speaking, life is (like) a voyage.)

(B)

		Noun		
かのじょ 彼女の家は、	言ってみれば、	しろ お城	のように	作られている。

(You could say her house is built like a castle.)

I

Formation

(i) 言ってみれば S。 (where S is a simile or a metaphor)

  言ってみれば、彼は熊(のような男)だ。 (Figuratively speaking, he is (like) a bear.)

(ii) 言ってみれば N のように〜。

  言ってみれば、彼は小説の神様のように見られていた。 (One could say that he was regarded as a god of novels.)

Examples

(a) 日本の文化には厳しいしきたりがあって、言ってみれば、それは宗教のようなものだ。

  (Japanese culture has a set of strict conventions; you could almost call it a religion.)

(b) 結婚は言ってみれば人生の墓場だ。

  (Marriage is, in a manner of speaking, the graveyard of life.)

(c) 医者と弁護士は、言ってみれば、神様のように振る舞う。

  (One could say medical doctors and lawyers act like God.)

(d) 学生たちが学んだ多くの知識は、頭の中に放置されたままで、言ってみれば、死んだ状態になっているのである。

  (A lot of the knowledge that students have learned remains piled up in their brains, and figuratively speaking, it is dead to them.)

(e) シリコンバレーも、結局は日本の、言ってみれば商店街なり地域作りの話と本質的には同じなんだと思いました。

(I would say Silicon Valley is, after all, essentially the same story as commercial district or community development in Japan.)

(f) 著作権とは、言ってみれば、創造者の権利を守る法律だ。

(Copyright can be thought of as a law to protect the rights of creators.)

(g) このブログは言ってみれば僕の絵日記のようなものだ。

(I like thinking of this blog as my picture journal.)

Note

Itte mireba (lit., "if I were to say (so)") is a phrase that signals a comparison, as in KS(A), (B), Exs.(a) and (c)-(e) or an explanation/definition, as in Exs.(f) and (g). A simile, as in KS(A), usually takes the form of N *no yōda* "s.o./s.t. is like N," or its variations N *no yōna mono da* or N *no yōni* (the adverbial form of *yōda*). A metaphor, as in Exs.(b) and (d), doesn't take *yōda*. (⇨ *yōda* (DBJG: 547-52))

[Related Expressions]

Iwaba "so to speak," *tatoete ieba* and *(tatoete) iu naraba* "if one compares s.o./s.t. to s.o./s.t. else" can replace all the *itte mireba* example sentences except for Ex.(f). This replacement is not acceptable because there is no comparison expressed in Ex.(f). In other words, *chosakuken* "copyright" is not likened to anything else. The only difference among these expressions is that *iwaba* is used primarily in written Japanese.

[1] a. ｛言ってみれば / 言わば / たとえて言えば / (たとえて)言うならば｝、人生は航海のようなものだ。(= KS(A))

b. 彼女の家は、｛言ってみれば / 言わば / たとえて言えば / (たとえて)言うならば｝、お城のように作られている。(= KS(B))

c. 著作権とは、｛言ってみれば / 言わば / ??たとえて言えば / ??(たとえて)言うならば｝、創造者の権利を守る法律だ。(= Ex.(f))

(⇨ *iwaba* (in this volume))

iu made mo nai 言うまでもない *phr.*

a phrase indicating that what the speaker/writer expresses is generally known but that he/she presents it as a reminder	it is needless to say that ~; needless to say; it goes without saying

◆ **Key Sentences**

(A)

Sinf	Nom.		
すしが日本の代表的な料理である	こと	は	言うまでもない。

(It goes without saying that *sushi* is representative of Japanese cuisine.)

(B)

	Sentence
言うまでもなく、	日本の社会は世界一の高齢化社会になっている。

(That Japan has become the most rapidly aging society in the world goes without saying.)

Formation

(i) {V / Adj(*i*)}inf + Nom. は言うまでもない。

{買う / 買った}{の / こと}は言うまでもない。 (Needless to say, s.o. will buy/bought s.t.)

つまらない{の / こと}は言うまでもない。 (It goes without saying that s.t. is boring.)

つまらなかった{の / こと}は言うまでもない。 (It goes without saying that s.t. was boring.)

(ii) Adj(*na*)stem{な / である / だった / であった} + Nom. は言うまでもない。

立派{な / である / だった}{の / こと}は言うまでもない。 (It goes without saying that s.t. is/was magnificent.)

(iii) N{な / である / だった / であった}のは言うまでもない。

教授{な / である / だった}のは言うまでもない。 (It goes without saying that s.o. is/was a professor.)

(iv) N{である／だった}ことは言うまでもない。

天才{である／だった}ことは言うまでもない。 (Needless to say, he is/was a genius.)

(v) 言うまでも{なく／ない(ことだ)が}、S。

言うまでも{なく／ない(ことだ)が}、日本は島国だ。 (Needless to say, Japan is an island country.)

Examples

(a) 少子化が日本の社会を変えていくことは言うまでもない。

(It goes without saying that the shrinking population of children will change Japanese society.)

(b) 「アジアの人々は貧しい」「貧しいのは可哀想」「開発援助しなくては」という固定観念が有害なのは言うまでもありません。

(The set of fixed ideas that "Asians are poor," "Being poor is pitiable," and "We should provide development assistance," is, needless to say, harmful.)

(c) 二人はパーティーで会って、すぐ意気投合しました。そのあと毎日のようにデートをしたのは言うまでもありません。

(The two met at a party, and right away they hit it off. I hardly need to mention that after that they went out on a date almost every day.)

(d) オープンネットワークコンピューティング環境では、日々増大するネットワークデータをいかに敏速にかつ効率よくバックアップするかが重要であることは言うまでもありません。

(Needless to say, in an open network computing environment, it is important how quickly and effectively you back up the continually expanding network data.)

(e) 言うまでもありませんが、大学の成績の優秀な学生が社会で成功するとは限りません。

(Needless to say, students whose grades in college were superb do not always succeed in society.)

(f) いまさら言うまでもなく、地球の温暖化は生態系に悪影響をもたらしている。

(It's obvious now, but global warming is having an adverse effect on the ecosystem.)

(g) 菜穂子はとびきりの美人でもなかったが、誰とでもにこやかに話し、いつも溌溂としていた。言うまでもないことだが、彼女の周りには人が自然に集まり、職場のみんなにも好かれていた。

(Nahoko was not especially beautiful, but she had a smile for everybody and was always cheerful. Needless to say, people spontaneously gathered around her, and everybody at her office loved her.)

1. *Iu made mo nai*, which means "it is needless to say that ~" is used in two ways. First, as shown in Formation (i)-(iv), it is used in a nominalized construction as exemplified by KS(A) and Exs.(a)-(d). Secondly, as shown in Formation (v), *iu made mo naku*, the adverbial form of *iu made mo nai*, meaning "needless to say," is used, as shown in KS(B) and Ex.(f). The non-adverbial version, *iu made mo nai (koto da) ga*, is shown in Exs.(e) and (g). The adverbial form is often inserted after the topic phrase, as in (1) below.

   (1) a. 麻薬は、言うまでもなく、肉体と精神を滅ぼす。

      (Drugs, needless to say, will destroy mind and body.)

      b. 英語は、言うまでもなく、国際語だ。

      (English is, needless to say, an international language.)

2. The reason for using this phrase is to remind the listener/reader about known facts, as in KS(A), (B), Exs.(a), (b) and (d)-(f) or results expected from the context, as in Exs.(c) and (g).

(⇨ *koto*[2] (DBJG: 193-96); *no*[3] (DBJG: 318-22))

iwaba 言わば　　*adv.*

an adverb that means "if I were to say it some way (or a different way)"	so to speak; as it were; like; sort of [REL. *itte mireba*]

◆ **Key Sentences**

(A)

		Noun Phrase	
この本は、	言わば	私のバイブル	だ。
(This is, as it were, my Bible.)			

(B)

		Sentence
この試験は	言わば	アメリカの大学に留学する際のTOEFLに当たる。
(This test is, so to speak, the equivalent of the TOEFL, which people take when they (want to) study at a university in the U.S.)		

Formation

言わば S。

　　言わば国の誕生日だ。　(S.t. is, as it were, the nation's birthday.)

　　言わば彼は二度死んだようなものだ。　(He died twice, so to speak.)

Examples

(a) ここまでは、言わばウォーミングアップのようなもので、ここからが本番だ。
(This has been sort of a warm-up, and starting now, the real business begins.)

(b) その判決は言わばこの国の良心を代弁したものだった。
(The court's ruling represented (lit., was something that represented) this country's conscience, so to speak.)

(c) 言わば趣味で始めたことがいつの間にか大きなビジネスになってしまった。
(What I started as sort of a hobby became a large-scale business before I knew it.)

(d) 当地区には、言わば幽霊人口である非合法居住者が 7 ～ 10 万人いますが、この人たちは補助金対象外となります。

(In this district there are 70,000 to 100,000 illegal residents, who form, as it were, a ghost population. These people are not eligible to receive assistance subsidies.)

(e) こうして見てみると、かつてはサダム・フセインも、ソ連やイランと戦ってきた、言わばアメリカの盟友だったわけである。

(When we view it this way, (we realize that) Saddam Hussein, who fought against Soviet Russia and Iran, used to be America's bosom buddy, so to speak.)

(f) ファッション写真は、1930 年代までは、言わば「新参者」の分野と見られていたらしい。

(Up to the 1930s, fashion photography was apparently considered a "newcomer" field, so to speak.)

(g) この酵素は、正常状態では必要な時だけ活性化して細胞を増殖させるのだが、がん細胞の場合は常に活性化し、言わばアクセルを踏みっぱなしの状態で、無秩序に細胞を増殖させてしまうのだ。

(In normal cells this enzyme is activated only when needed to promote cell multiplication. However, in cancer cells it is always activated, like a state, so to speak, in which a driver keeps his foot on the accelerator, so cells increase with no control.)

Note

Iwaba, a conditional form of the classic form of *iu* "say," literally means, "if I were to say." It is used when the speaker/writer explains or gives an example of the nature of a thing, person, action, state, etc., by comparing it with another thing, person, etc., or by describing it figuratively.

iwayuru いわゆる　　*noun modifier*

| a noun modifier that means "known generally by this term" | so-called; what we call; known as |

◆ **Key Sentence**

		Noun Phrase	
伊藤さんは	いわゆる	「エリート」の大学	を卒業した。
(Ms. Ito graduated from one of the so-called "elite" universities.)			

Formation

いわゆる N

　いわゆる天才　(what people call a genius)

Examples

(a) いわゆるリストラのために失業した人は非常に多い。

(Many people lost their jobs because of what is called restructuring.)

(b) 1986年から90年代初めにかけてのいわゆる「バブル経済」の時代には土地や株が高騰した。

(During the so-called "bubble economy," from 1986 through the early 90's, land and stocks prices soared.)

(c) 21世紀には多くの国でいわゆる安楽死が合法化されていくだろう。

(In the 21st century what is called euthanasia will be legalized in many countries.)

(d) いわゆる「いじめ」の問題は、自分と異なる人間を認めるメンタリティーが日本に根づかないと容易にはなくならないであろう。

(The problem we know as bullying will not easily be solved unless the mentality of accepting someone different from oneself takes root in Japan.)

(e) いわゆるIT、すなわち情報技術の開発に、日本政府は本腰を入れ始めた。

(The Japanese government has started to put its weight behind developing "IT," or information technology.)

(f) 内分泌撹乱化学物質、いわゆる環境ホルモンは、人間と野生生物へ悪影響を与えると言われている。

(Endocrine disrupting chemicals, also known as environmental hormones, are said to adversely affect humans and wildlife.)

Note

The noun modifier *iwayuru* originally came from the prenominal passive form of the old Japanese verb *iu*. It is not a regular adjective but a prenominal modifier, meaning "so-called." The modified noun has to be a word or a phrase that has been popularly used to refer to something known generally by that term. Note also that unlike "so-called" in English, *iwayuru* cannot be used to mean "falsely or improperly so named."

(1) ジョンは{自称/*いわゆる}占い師に騙された。

(John was deceived by a self-proclaimed fortune-teller.)

-jitai 自体   *n.*

a dependent noun that is used to emphasize the referent of the preceding noun	oneself; in and of itself; the very 【REL. *-jishin*; **sono mono**】

◆ **Key Sentences**

(A)

Noun			
インターネット	自体	は	情報の通路であって、内容は持たない。

(The Internet is a path for information and does not contain any content itself.)

(B)

	Sinf			
私にとっては	この試合に出られる	こと	自体	が光栄なことです。

(For me, being able to participate in this match in and of itself is an honor.)

Formation

(i) NP 自体

技術自体   (technology itself)

日本に行くこと自体   (the act of going to Japan (in and of) itself)

(ii) NP それ自体

素材それ自体   (the materials themselves)

Examples

(a) ケータイ自体には問題はない。問題は使う人のマナーや気配りだ。

(There is no problem with cell phones in and of themselves. The problems exist in the manners and considerateness of the users.)

(b) いまの仕事自体には満足していますが、職場の人間関係がうまくいかず悩んでいます。

(I'm satisfied with the job itself, but what troubles me is that I cannot maintain good relationships with the people at my workplace.)

(c) 音声データ自体に異常があるので、どのプレーヤーで再生してもノイズが入ってしまう。

(The sound data itself contains some defects, so no matter what player you use to play it back, you'll get noise.)

(d) 世の中が大きく変わった今、この組織の存在自体が疑われている。

(The world has changed greatly, and the very existence of this organization is now in doubt.)

(e) この広告は、販売より広告それ自体が目的だ。

(The goal of this advertisement is the advertisement (of the product) itself rather than sales.)

(f) 裁判所はこれらのファイル交換ソフト自体の違法性は認められないという判決を下した。

(The court ruled that these file-exchange software programs in and of themselves are not illegal.)

(g) そういうところから金を借りること自体が間違っている。

(The very act of borrowing money from that kind of place is wrong.)

(h) 問題は個々の差別表現自体ではなく、そういう表現が出てくる背景なのだ。

(The problem is not the individual discriminatory expressions themselves, but the context from which they arise.)

(i) 音楽のデジタル化やインターネット配信が音楽業界の主流になってきたが、私はそのこと自体は悪いことではないと思う。問題は、それによって不正コピーや大量配布がしやすくなったことだ。

(Music digitization and distribution via the Internet has become mainstream in the music industry, but I don't think that (lit., that fact itself) is a bad thing. The problem is that it has become easier to make illegal copies and mass-distribute them.)

Notes

1. X-*jitai* is used to emphasize X in the sentence. It is often translated as "X-self."

2. *Jitai* always follows a noun or a noun equivalent and does not occur alone. In this respect, it is a kind of dependent noun. A noun (or its equivalent) with *jitai* behaves like a noun in terms of the ways it is connected to particles.

3. Sometimes the demonstrative noun *sore* occurs between the preceding noun and *jitai*, as in Formation (ii) and Ex.(e). The meaning does not change with the insertion of *sore*.

[Related Expression]

Jishin is synonymous with *jitai*, and the way they are connected to nouns is the same. However, *-jishin* is more commonly used with human nouns while *-jitai* tends to occur with non-human nouns. This difference is especially true when the preceding noun refers to the speaker, the hearer, or a person with whom the speaker is empathetic, as seen in [1].

[1] a. あなた{自身／*自体}はこの事件についてどう思いますか。

(What do *you* think of this incident?)

b. 私{自身／*自体}は海外生活の経験がないので、異文化の問題はよく分かりません。

(I myself have no experience living abroad, so I don't know much about the problems of different cultures.)

c. 自分{自身／*自体}に挑戦してみよう。

(Let's challenge ourselves. / Challenge yourself!)

d. うちの子{自身／*自体}はアメリカには行きたがっていません。

(My child's own preference is not to go to America.)

kagiri da 限りだ *phr.* <w>

a phrase that indicates the extreme degree of the speaker's/writer's emotion—happiness, sorrow, envy, shame or loneliness, among others

extremely
【REL. *kono ue nai*】

◆ **Key Sentence**

	Adj(*i*)inf.nonpast (emotive)	
いろいろなところに行っておられるんですね。	うらやましい	限りです。

(You are traveling to all sorts of places. I'm extremely envious of you.)

Formation

Adj(*i*)inf.nonpast 限りだ (where Adj(*i*) = emotive adjective)

嬉しい限りだ (I am extremely happy)

Examples

(a) 電子メールでご連絡いただければ、嬉しい限りです。

   (I would be extremely happy if you would kindly contact me by e-mail.)

(b) 私の講演が皆様の知性を刺激できれば喜ばしい限りです。

   (If my lecture stimulates you intellectually, I will be extremely happy.)

(c) あなたの明るい顔が見られなくなって、寂しい限りです。

   (I cannot see your cheerful face any longer, and I couldn't feel lonelier.)

(d) 私がかいた絵をお見せするのはお恥ずかしい限りです。

   [a humble expression]

   (It really makes me feel embarrassed to show you my painting.)

(e) その頃は大阪に単身赴任で行っていたが、家族から離れて夜一人でアパートで食事をするのはわびしい限りだった。

   (During that time I was working in Osaka, but leaving my family behind and eating dinner alone in my apartment made me feel so miserable.)

Notes

1. *Kagiri da* indicates that the degree of emotion is extreme; *kagiri* means "limit." The *i*-adjectives used with *kagiri da* are limited to emotive adjectives that end with *-shii*. The most typical *i*-adjectives are *ureshii* "happy," *urayamashii* "envious," and *hazukashii* "embarrassed; ashamed."

   (⇨ *-shi-* (DBJG: 397-98))

2. *Na*-adjectives with emotive meaning can also be used with *kagiri da*, as in (1), but not as extensively as *i*-adjectives. Typical emotive *na*-adjectives such as *kōfukuna* "happy," *fukōna* "unhappy; unfortunate," *fukaina* "unpleasant," *fuyukaina* "unpleasant," *yūutsuna* "gloomy," *mendōna* "cumbersome," *taigina* "tiring," *okkūna* "bothersome," *sōkaina* "refreshing," *anshinna* "safe," *fuanna* "anxious," and *sinpaina* "anxious" cannot be used with *kagiri da*.

   (1) a. 試合中止とは残念な限りです。

      (I feel extremely sorry that the game has been suspended.)

      b. 木下さんはお母さんが交通事故に遭ったとか。お気の毒な限りです。

      (I heard that Ms. Kinoshita's mother got involved in a car accident. I feel terribly sorry for her.)

      c. 私の講演はお粗末な限りで、申し訳ございませんでした。

      (I am so sorry that my lecture turned out so poorly.)

   Compare the following sentences in which *kagiri da* cannot be used because the *na*-adjectives don't have emotive meaning.

   (2) a. この大学の建物は{*きれいな限り/とてもきれい}です。

      (The buildings at this college are extremely beautiful.)

      b. あの人は{*健康な限りだ/とても健康だ}。

      (He is extremely healthy.)

3. The only nouns that can take *kagiri da* are *kansha* "appreciation" and *kyōshuku* "gratefulness," as shown in (3).

   (3) a. 本プロジェクトを皆様のご協力により完成させることができましたことは誠に感謝の限りです。

      (I am extremely thankful that we could finish the project with your cooperation.)

b. つたない料理をお褒めいただき**恐縮の限り**です。

(I am extremely grateful to you for your praise of my humble cooking.)

kai / gai かい / がい ［甲斐］ *n.*

a dependent noun that means s.t. is worth s.o.'s effort

worth; meaning; effect; result

◆ Key Sentences

(A)

	Vinf			
日本語をよく	勉強した	かい	があって、	日本関係の会社に就職することができた。

(It was worth studying Japanese hard because (lit., and) I was able to get a Japan-related job.)

(B)

Noun Phrase				
社員一同の努力	の	かい	があって	一時低調だった会社も上向きになった。

(The combined efforts of the company employees paid off, and the company, which had been in a slump for awhile, started improving.)

(C)

	V*masu*			
あなたにとって	生き	がい	とは	何ですか。

(What makes life worth living for you?)

(D)

Sentence₁
彼は東南アジア諸国の旅行中、毎日詳しく日記をつけておいた。

Sentence₂

その	かい	があって、	日本に戻って旅行記を書く時にとても書きやすかった。

(He kept a detailed diary during his trip to South East Asia. It paid off, as (lit., and) it made it easy for him to write his travelogue when he returned to Japan.)

Formation

(i)   Vinf かいが {ある / ない}

　　来たかいがある   (it is worth coming here; coming here pays off)

　　薬を飲んでいるかいがない   (it isn't worth taking medicine)

(ii)   N のかいが {ある / ない}

　　徹夜のかいがある   (s.t. is worth staying up all night for / staying up all night pays off)

　　勉強のかいがない   (s.t. isn't worth studying)

(iii)   V*masu* がい

　　やりがい   (meaning/worth in doing s.t.)

(iv)   S₁。そのかいがあって、S₂。   (only その can precede かい)

　　毎日運動をした。そのかいがあって、体重がだいぶ減った。   (I exercised every day. And it was worth it; I lost quite a bit of weight.)

Examples

(a)   一生懸命やったかいがあって、マラソン大会ごとに順位が上がってきました。
(My efforts paid off, and I finished higher in the ranking with each race.)

(b)   寒い中待っていたかいがあって、見事な日の出を見ることができた。
(Waiting in the cold paid off, as I was able to see a wonderful sunrise.)

(c) せっかく富士山に登ったのに頂上からは下が全然見えず、登ったかいがなかった。

(I climbed Mt. Fuji with great effort, but I couldn't see anything from the summit, so it wasn't worth the climb.)

(d) 弟は看病のかい（も）なく5歳の短い生涯を閉じた。

(In spite of all the medical care (he received), my little brother's life ended when he was only five.)

(e) 辛抱のかいがあって、運が開けた。

(My perseverance paid off, and my fortunes have changed for the better.)

(f) この大学の学生はよく勉強するから、本当に教えがいがある。

(The students of this college study so hard that they are really worth teaching.)

(g) 私の料理をおいしく食べてくれる人がいるから、作りがいがあるのです。

(Because there are people who enjoy eating my cooking, it is worth doing it.)

(h) 交通事故で脚に大怪我をして、毎日リハビリに通うことになった。そのかいがあって、今では元どおり歩けるようになった。

(My legs were injured in a traffic accident, and I went to the hospital for rehabilitation every day. It paid off, and now I can walk as before.)

Notes

1. *Kai* is a dependent noun that means "worth." Notice in Formation (iii) that *kai* changes phonetically to *gai*, because V*masu gai* is a compound in which the initial sound of the second element is often voiced.

2. The English verb phrase "pay off" can often be used as a translation for *kai*, as seen in KS(B), (D), Exs.(a), (b), (e) and (h).

3. Although the dependent noun *kai* means "worth," it doesn't indicate an objective worth but rather is subjective. Therefore, as shown in (1), *kachi* "worth; value" and *imi* "meaning" used as impersonal general terms are acceptable, but *ikigai* used as personal worth is marginal.

(1) 植物人間になった場合、もはや人間として機能していないのだから、その人間に{?生きるかい／??生きがい／生きる価値／生きる意味}はないという立場もあろう。

(People may take the stance that when someone is in a vegetative state, he is no longer functioning as a human, so there is no {value to / meaning in} his living.)

4. *~ kai ga aru* is often used in the V*te* form, that is, *~ kai ga atte*, which functions as a kind of subordinate conjunction, as exemplified by KS(A), (B), (D), Exs.(a), (b), (e) and (h).

ka ina ka   か否か   *phr.*   \<w\>

| a conjunctive phrase indicating that the speaker/writer is wondering whether s.t. is the case or not | whether X or not
[REL. *~ ka ~ nai ka*; *~ ka dō ka*] |

K

◆ Key Sentences

(A)

	Vinf			
このソフトが役に	立つ	か否か	は	保証の限りではありません。

(I cannot say (lit., guarantee) whether this software is useful or not.)

(B)

	Noun				
選挙の時に、有権者は 候補者が倫理観のある	政治家	（である）	か否か	を	見抜かなけれ ばならない。

(In an election, the voter has to judge (lit., see through) whether or not a candidate is a politician of integrity.)

(C)

	Vinf.nonpast				
子供に携帯電話を	持たせる	べき	か否か	は	議論が分かれる。

(Opinions differ as to whether we should allow a child to have a cell phone.)

Formation

(i) {V / Adj(*i*)} inf か否か

　　{来る / 来た} か否か　(whether or not s.o. will come / came)

　　{面白い / 面白かった} か否か　(whether or not s.t. is/was interesting)

(ii) {N / Adj(*na*)} stem {ø / である / だった / であった} か否か

　　学生 {ø / である / だった / であった} か否か　(whether or not s.o. is/
　　was a student)

　　元気 {ø / である / だった / であった} か否か　(whether or not s.o. is/
　　was healthy)

(iii) Vinf.nonpast べき (である) か否か

　　{N / Adj(*na*)stem} であるべきか否か

　　行くべき (である) か否か　(whether or not s.o. should go there)

　　学生であるべきか否か　(whether or not s.o. should be a student)

　　質素であるべきか否か　(whether or not s.o. should be frugal)

K

Examples

(a) アメリカの大学では教授が外国人であるか否かは問題にならないが、日本で
はそれがよく問題になるようだ。

(In the U.S., whether or not a professor is a foreigner is not a problem,
but in Japan, it appears that it is frequently an issue.)

(b) 家を探す場合、その地域が安全であるか否かが一番大事なポイントになる。

(When you search for a house, whether or not the area is safe is the
most important point.)

(c) クラシック音楽を聞く時、私は旋律が美しいか否かよりその音楽が生命を感
じさせるか否かに注意を払う。

(When I listen to classical music, I pay attention to whether or not
it causes me to feel life rather than whether or not the melody is
beautiful.)

(d) 大学の入試要項をよく読んでから受験するか否かを決めるべきだ。

(You should decide whether or not to take the entrance examination
after reading the university's guidelines carefully.)

(e) 愛されたら愛しかえすべきか否かという疑問は愚問です。

(The question of whether or not one should return love when one is loved is a silly one.)

(f) 容疑者に遺体を見せると、真犯人か否かが分かることがある。

(There are cases in which you can tell whether or not a suspect is the real culprit when you show him or her the dead body.)

Notes

1. ~ *ka ina ka* "whether ~ or not" is a conjunctive phrase used as an embedded question marker.

2. *De aru* after nouns and *na*-adjective stems is often omitted, as shown in KS(B), Exs.(e) and (f).

3. *I*-adjectives can be freely used with ~ *ka ina ka* except for *ii*. With *ii*, *ka warui ka* or *ka dōka* is used, as shown in (1).

(1) 大学を出てすぐ就職するのがいいか{*否か / 悪いか / どうか}は一概に言えない。

(One cannot always tell whether or not getting a job right after graduation is good.)

[Related Expressions]

~ *ka ~ nai ka* or ~ *ka dō ka* can replace ~ *ka ina ka* without changing the meaning of the sentence, as shown in [1].

[1] a. このソフトが役に立つか{否か / 立たないか / どうか}は保証の限りではありません。(= KS(A))

b. 選挙の時に、有権者は候補者が倫理観のある政治家であるか{否か / ないか / どうか}を見抜かなければならない。(= KS(B))

Note that ~ *ka dō ka* cannot replace ~ *ka ~ nai ka* in colloquial speech, as shown in [2].

[2] a. あいつがやってくるか{こないか / どうか / *否か}分からないじゃん。

(We don't know if he is coming or not.)

b. 彼、一見若いのか{若くないのか / どうか / *否か}はっきりしないね。

(With just a glance, you can't tell if he is young or not.)

(⇨ ***ka (dō ka)*** (DBJG: 168-70))

kana かな *int.* \<w\>

| ~~an interjection that expresses deep-felt emotion~~ | how ~ !; what a(n) ~ !; to my/our ~; it is ~ that 【REL. *koto ni*】 |

◆ Key Sentence

Adj(*i*)inf.nonpast (emotive)		
悲<ruby>かな</ruby>しい	かな、	年を取って往年の記憶力がなくなってしまった。

(How sad (it is) that I no longer have as strong a memory as I had in my younger days.)

Formation

(i) Adj(*i*)inf.nonpast かな (where Adj(*i*) = emotive adjective)

惜<ruby>お</ruby>しいかな (How regrettable!)

(ii) Adj(*na*)stem なるかな

壮大<ruby>そうだい</ruby>なるかな (How spectacular!)

Examples

(a) 悲<ruby>かな</ruby>しいかな、自分の能力<ruby>のうりょく</ruby>を過大評価<ruby>かだいひょうか</ruby>する人間<ruby>にんげん</ruby>がいる。

(It's so sad that there are people who overestimate their ability.)

(b) インターネットを使うといろいろ面白<ruby>おもしろ</ruby>いことが分かるそうですが、惜<ruby>お</ruby>しいかな、私はコンピュータを買うお金がないんです。

(They say that you can find out many interesting things if you use the Internet, but, to my great regret, I don't have the money to buy a computer.)

(c) 画面<ruby>がめん</ruby>では絵も動きます。チャットもできます。惜<ruby>お</ruby>しいかな、全部<ruby>ぜんぶ</ruby>英語<ruby>えいご</ruby>ですが。

(On the screen, pictures move, and you can chat, too. Regrettably, everything is in English.)

(d) 秋<ruby>あき</ruby>の訪<ruby>おとず</ruby>れを知ると共<ruby>とも</ruby>に、大空<ruby>おおぞら</ruby>は広大<ruby>こうだい</ruby>なるかなと驚<ruby>おどろ</ruby>く。

(With the coming of autumn, I am astonished by how broad the sky is.)

(e) みんな退職後<ruby>たいしょくご</ruby>の生活<ruby>せいかつ</ruby>の甘<ruby>あま</ruby>いイメージを抱<ruby>いだ</ruby>いている。しかし、残念<ruby>ざんねん</ruby>なるかな、

現実_{げんじつ}には、熟年離婚_{じゅくねんりこん}や体_{からだ}の不調_{ふちょう}にさいなまれている。

(Everybody has a rosy image of post-retirement life. But, to our great regret, the reality is not as it seems; people are vexed by "vintage year divorce" and poor physical condition.)

(f) 途中_{とちゅう}に教会があったので期待_{きたい}して入ってみると、果_はたせるかな、クリスマス礼拝_{れいはい}で荘厳_{そうごん}な雰囲気_{ふんいき}であった。

(There was a church on my way, so I entered it, hoping (for a feeling of Christmas). Just as I expected, there was a solemn atmosphere for the Christmas service.)

Notes

1. *Kana* is an interjection to express something emotively. It is used with a limited number of *i*-adjectives of emotion, as in KS and Exs.(a)-(c), and *na*-adjectives, as in Exs.(d) and (e). *Hataseru kana* in Ex.(f) is the only set phrase that has a verb before *kana*. The *i*-adjectives that can be used with *kana* are limited to the ones used in the examples above, i.e., *kanashii* "sad" and *oshii* "regrettable." But the *na*-adjectives are not very limited: *yukai* "pleasant," *kōfuku* "happy," *tsūkai* "exhilarating," *sōretsu* "heroic; brave," *yūutsu* "cheerless," etc.

2. *Kana* as introduced in this entry is different from the sentence-final particle *kana*, which indicates a self-addressed question or a question addressed to an in-group member. (⇨ **kana** (DIJG: 90-92))

[Related Expression]

As shown in [1], {Adj(*i*)inf.nonpast / Adj(*na*)stem *na*} *koto ni* can replace ~ *kana* in all the examples above except for the set phrase in Ex.(f). But *koto ni* can be used with a greater number of adjectives, so there are many cases where *kana* cannot replace *koto ni*, as shown in [2].

[1] a. 悲_{かな}しい{**かな** / **ことに**}、年を取って往年の記憶力がなくなってしまった。(= KS)

b. せっかく富士山_{ふじさん}に登_{のぼ}ったのに残念_{ざんねん}{**なるかな** / **なことに**}雲_{くも}で下が見えなかった。

(Although I made the effort to climb up Mt. Fuji, to my regret, the clouds prevented me from seeing below.)

[2] a. 面白_{おもしろ}い{**ことに** / *****かな**}、日本人はやたらと英語の単語_{たんご}を使いたがる。

(Interestingly, Japanese people like to use English words indiscriminately.)

b. 恥ずかしい{ことに / *かな}、私は日本人でありながら日本の歴史を
ほとんど何も知りません。

(I'm ashamed that I know practically nothing about Japanese history even though I am Japanese.)

c. わびしい{ことに / *かな}、私は今一人暮らしなんです。

(It's miserable living all by myself.)

(⇨ **koto ni** (in this volume))

---

ka no yōni かのように   *phr.*   <w>

K

a conjunctive phrase that forms an adverbial clause which describes the way s.o./s.t. appears to the writer, contrary to reality

as if
【REL. *ka no gotoku*; *atakamo*】

◆ **Key Sentences**

(A)

			Vinf		
彼女は	(まるで)	整形手術を	した	かのように	きれいになった。

(Her looks improved (lit., She became beautiful), as though she had undergone cosmetic surgery.)

(B)

	Vinf		
彼女の病気は年内に	治る	かのように	見えた。

(It looked as though her illness would be cured before the end of the year.)

(C)

		Adj(*i*)inf		
あたかも	日本の製造業全体 の競争力は <small>せいぞうぎょうぜんたい</small> <small>きょうそうりょく</small>	**強い**	かのように	思われてきた。

(The competitiveness of the Japanese manufacturing industry has been perceived as (though it were) strong.)

(D)

	Noun Phrase			
彼は <small>かれ</small>	有能な政治学者 <small>ゆうのう　せいじ</small>	である	かのように	言われているが、実は無 能極まりない。 <small>じっ　む</small> <small>のうきわ</small>

(People say he is a capable political scientist, but actually he is extremely incapable.)

(E)

		Adj(*na*) stem			
あの男は不確 かなことを <small>ふたし</small>	あたかも	正確 <small>せいかく</small>	である	かのように	断言する。 <small>だんげん</small>

(That man speaks definitively about something uncertain as if it were a sure thing.)

Formation

(i)   (まるで / あたかも) {V / Adj(*i*)} inf かのように

   (まるで / あたかも) {怒っている / 怒っていた} かのように   (as if s.o.
   <small>おこ</small>
   were / had been mad)

   (まるで / あたかも) {正しい / 正しかった} かのように   (as if s.o./s.t.
   were / had been correct)

(ii)   (まるで / あたかも) {N / Adj(*na*)stem} {である / であった} かのように

   (まるで / あたかも) 神様 {である / であった} かのように   (as if s.o.
   <small>かみさま</small>
   were / had been God)

   (まるで / あたかも) ぜいたく {である / であった} かのように   (as if s.t.
   were / had been luxurious)

Examples

(a) その教師は私がまるでカンニングをしたかのように私を問いただした。

(The teacher pressed me hard as if I had cheated on the exam.)

(b) 彼は心理学のことは何も知らないのにあたかもよく知っているかのように心理学のことを話したがる。

(He doesn't know anything about psychology, but he likes to talk about it as if he knows it very well.)

(c) あたかも僕の心を解かすかのように、白くて透明な雪が降っている。

(White, transparent snow is falling as though it would melt my heart.)

(d) まるで私の結婚を祝ってくれているかのように空は完璧に晴れていた。

(The sky was perfectly clear, as if it were celebrating my wedding.)

(e) あの教師は学生が何を考えているかまるで意に介していないかのように見える。

(The instructor looks as if he didn't care at all about what his students are thinking.)

(f) 平凡でつまらないかのようにみえる彼らの人生とて起伏がないわけではない。

(Their life, which looks as if it were ordinary and boring, is not without its ups and downs.)

(g) 空港での持ち物検査の時、うっかりはさみをポケットに入れていたので、犯罪者であるかのように扱われた。

(When I went through the security check at the airport, I was treated as if I were a criminal because I inadvertently had put a pair of scissors in my pocket.)

(h) イスラム系組織のテロがあるからと言って、イスラム系の人があたかもすべて危険であるかのように考えるのは単純すぎる。

(It is simplistic to think that all Muslims are dangerous just because some terrorist acts are perpetrated by Islamic groups.)

Notes

1. *Ka no yōni* is a conjunctive phrase that forms an adverbial clause which describes the way someone or something appears to the writer, contrary to the reality.

2. The counterfactuality of *ka no yōni* can be emphasized by the adverbs *marude* and *atakamo*.

3. When the main predicate is *mieru*, *ka no yōni* can be reduced to *ka ni*, but this version loses its counterfactual meaning.

   (1) a. 彼女の病気は年内に治る**か**(**のよう**)**に**見えた。(= KS(B))

      b. あの教師は学生が何を考えているかまるで意に介していない**か**(**のよう**)**に**見える。(= Ex.(e))

4. The non-adverbial version of *ka no yōni* is *ka no yōda* at the end of the sentence and *ka no yōna* before a noun, as exemplified by (2a) and (2b), respectively.

   (2) a. まるで別世界に来た**かのようだった**。

       (I felt as if I had come to a totally different world.)

      b. 私は金_{かね}ですべてが解決_{かいけつ}する**かのような**考え方にはついていけない。

       (I can't accept that way of thinking, as if everything can be solved by money.)

【Related Expression】

Ka no yōni can be replaced by *ka no gotoku* in formal written Japanese, as in [1]. Note that *atakamo* instead of *marude* is used.

   [1] a. 彼女は**あたかも**整形手術をした**かのごとく**きれいになった。

                              (cf. KS(A))

      b. あの男は不確かなことを**あたかも**正確である**かの**{**ように** / **ごとく**}断言する。(= KS(E))

                         (⇨ ***atakamo***; ***gotoshi*** (in this volume))

---

kara itte　から言_いって　*phr.*

| a phrase that means either "in terms of" or "judging from" | in terms of; from the viewpoint of; judging from
【REL. *no ten de*; ***kara shite***】 |

◆ Key Sentences

(A)

Noun		
燃費<ruby>ねん<rt></rt></ruby>	から言って	この車は非常に経済的だ。

(In terms of gas mileage, this car is extremely economical.)

(B)

Noun Phrase		
学生の評価	から言って	鈴木先生はいい先生に違いない。

(Judging from his student evaluations, Prof. Suzuki must be a fine teacher.)

Formation

N から言って

効率から言って　(in terms of efficiency)

K

Examples

(a) 性能から言って、このエンジンを凌ぐものは少ない。

(In terms of performance, few engines can surpass this one.)

(b) この小説は内容から言って子供向きではない。

(The content of this novel is not suitable for children.)

(c) 仕事の効率から言って週休二日の方がいい。

(In terms of efficiency a five-day work week (lit., two days off a week) is better.)

(d) DNA鑑定から言って、彼が犯人であることは確実だ。

(Judging from the DNA evidence, there is no doubt that he is the culprit.)

(e) 顔の色つやから言って、父は間違いなく健康だ。

(Judging from his facial complexion, my father is definitely healthy.)

(f) 日本語能力試験の結果から言って、ジョンの日本語はすばらしいに違いない。

(Judging from the results of his Japanese Proficiency Test, John's Japanese must be superb.)

Note

N *kara itte* is used to express a criterion or basis for judgment and means "in terms of," as in KS(A) and Exs.(a)-(c), or "judging from," as in KS(B) and Exs.(d)-(f). In the latter case, N is used as the basis for someone's judgment.

[Related Expression]

When *kara itte* means "in terms of" it can be replaced by *no ten de*, which also means "in terms of," but when it expresses a basis for judgment, it cannot be replaced by *no ten de*, as shown in [1] and [2]. Note that *ten de* covers a much wider range of meaning than *kara itte*.

(⇨ ***ten (de)*** (DIJG: 458-61))

[1] a. 燃費{から言って／の点で}この車は非常に経済的だ。(= KS(A))

b. この小説は内容{から言って／の点で}子供向きではない。(= Ex.(b))

c. 仕事の効率{から言って／の点で}週休二日の方がいい。(= Ex.(c))

[2] a. 学生の評価{から言って／*の点で}鈴木先生はいい先生に違いない。

(= KS(B))

b. DNA鑑定{から言って／*の点で}、彼が犯人であることは確実だ。

(= Ex.(d))

c. 顔の色つや{から言って／*の点で}、父は間違いなく健康だ。

(= Ex.(e))

kara naru   からなる   *phr.*

a phrase indicating that s.t. consists of more than one member/constituent	consist of; be composed of

◆ **Key Sentences**

(A)

		Noun₁	
英語の "relax" は	ラテン語の	**"re-"（再び）**	と

Noun₂			
"laxare"（緩む）	と	からなっている。	

(The English word "relax" consists of the Latin "re-" (again) and "laxare" (to loosen).)

(B)

	Noun	
タンパク質は	アミノ酸	からなっている。

(Proteins are composed of amino acids.)

(C)

Noun₁		Noun₂		Noun₃		
夫婦	と	子供	からなる	世帯	は	今後減るのだろうか。

(I wonder if households that consist of a married couple and their children will decrease in the future.)

Formation

(i) (Xは) N₁ と N₂ (と……) (と)から {なる / なっている}

   委員会は男性 5 人と女性 7 人 (と)から {なる / なっている}　(the committee consists of five men and seven women)

(ii) (Xは) N から {なる / なっている}

   委員会は 12 名の教授から {なる / なっている}　(the committee consists of 12 professors)

(iii) N₁ (と N₂(と……)) (と)からなる N₃

   役員と理事 (と)からなる委員会　(a committee that consists of officers and board members)

Examples

(a) 日本の神社は拝殿と本殿とからなっている。

(A Japanese Shinto shrine consists of a front shrine and an inner shrine.)

(b) この大学の東洋学科は言語、文学と歴史からなっている。

(This university's East Asian Studies Department consists of language, literature and history (programs).)

(c) 日本は島国で、本州と北海道と四国と九州と沖縄とからなっている。

(Japan is an island country consisting of Honshu, Hokkaido, Shikoku, Kyushu and Okinawa.)

(d) 地球の内部構造は、何重もの階層構造からなっている。

(The structure of the inner part of the earth consists of multi-layered strata.)

(e) ブラームスのレクイエムは演奏に約1時間半を要する大作で、全7楽章からなっている。

(Brahms's Requiem is a *magnum opus* that takes about an hour and a half to perform and consists of a total of seven movements.)

(f) フィリピンは多くの島々からなっている。

(The Philippines is made up of many islands.)

(g) このボランティア団体は約150名の会員からなる団体です。

(This volunteer organization is a group made up of about 150 members.)

Notes

1. Formation (i), (ii) and (iii) can be seen in KS(A) and Exs.(a)-(c), KS(B) and Exs.(d)-(f), and KS(C) and Ex.(g), respectively.

2. The conjunctive particle *to* can be dropped entirely in a sentence where more than two nouns are listed, as shown in (1) below.

   (1) 日本は島国で、**本州、北海道、四国、九州、沖縄**からなっている。

   (= Ex.(c))

3. The *naru* of *kara naru* can take the stative expression *natte iru* except in noun modification clauses, as in KS(C) and Ex.(g). The *kara naru* version is more suitable in more formal spoken and written language.

So, in (2), both *kara naru* and *kara natte iru* are acceptable but the former is preferred because the writing is formal.

(2) a. 本誌の掲載原稿は、投稿原稿と依頼原稿とから{なる/なっている}。

(The manuscripts published in this journal consist of contributed manuscripts and commissioned work.)

b. 1個のモーラは、普通、1個の子音と1個の母音とから{なる/なっている}。

(One mora usually consists of one consonant and one vowel.)

4. *Yori* is used for *kara* in formal writing. Note that the last *to* in "X *wa* N *to* N *to* ~" does not occur with *yori*.

(3) 米国議会は上院と下院{(と)から/より/*とより}なる。

(The U.S. Congress consists of the Senate and the House of Representatives.)

K

kara ni wa からには *conj.*

~~~
a subordinate conjunction meaning
"now that," "once s.o. does / has done
s.t." or "so long as"
~~~
once; now that ~; as long as ~;
so long as ~; if
【REL. *ijō (wa)*】

◆ **Key Sentences**

(A)

Subordinate Clause			Main Clause
	Vinf		
いったん	引き受けた	からには	最後まで責任をもってやります。

(Once I take on (the job), I will fulfill my responsibility and complete it.)

(B)

Subordinate Clause			Main Clause
Quote			
裁判 さいばん	と言う	からには	弁護人が不可欠だ。 べん ご にん　ふ か けつ

(Since it is a trial, a defense attorney will be indispensable.)

Formation

(i)　Vinf からには

　　　行くからには　(so long as s.o. goes there)

　　　行ったからには　(once s.o. has gone there)

(ii)　Quote と言うからには

　　　戦争と言うからには　(as long as one calls it a war)
　　　せんそう

　　　見たと言うからには　(as long as s.o. said he saw it)

Examples

(a)　生まれてきたからには長生きしたい。
　　　　　　　　　　　ながい

　　　(So long as I'm here (lit., Since I was born), I'd like to live a long time.)

(b)　行くって言ったからにはちゃんと行かなきゃ駄目だよ。
　　　　　　　　　　　　　　　　　　　　だ め

　　　(Now that you've said you're going there, you have to go, OK?)

(c)　ネット上で文章を書いたからには、必ずそれを読む人が存在するのです。
　　　　　　　ぶんしょう　　　　　　かなら　　　　　　　　　そんざい

　　　(Once you write a passage on the Internet, there are definitely people who will read it.)

(d)　写真をカラーで撮るからには、色にこだわりたい。
　　　　　　　　　　と

　　　(As long as I am taking pictures with color film, I want to be very particular about the color.)

(e)　マラソンに出るからには、絶対に勝ちたい。
　　　　　　　　　　　　ぜったい　か

　　　(Now that I am taking part in the marathon, I absolutely want to win.)

(f)　アメリカに住んでいるからには郷に入っては郷に従えで、批判ばっかりしていたって仕方がない。
　　　　　　　　　　　　　ごう　い　　　　　したが　　　ひ はん

　　　(As long as you are living in the U.S., do as the Americans do; it won't help if you just complain.)

(g)「ブレーンストーミング」と言うからには、発言に制限を設けてはならない。

(Since you are calling it brainstorming, you shouldn't restrict statements people make.)

(h) 世界一周と言うからには、経度の基準点であるグリニッジ天文台から出発しようと決め込んだ。

(Because I was going to travel around the world, I decided to start my trip from London's Greenwich Observatory, which is the base point of longitude.)

Notes

1. When the phrase *kara ni wa* is used with Vinf.past, it means "once s.o. has done s.t.," as in KS(A), or "now that," as in Exs.(a)-(c) and (e). When it is used with Vinf.nonpast, it means "as long as; since; because," as in KS(B), Exs.(d) and (f)-(h).

2. *Kara ni wa* is frequently used with *to iu/itta*, as in KS(B), Ex.(b), (g) and (h). More examples are given in (1).

(1) a. 個性、能力を重視すると言うからには、教育改革が必要だ。

(If we declare that individuality and ability are to be regarded as important, then we will need educational reform.)

b. 一度すると言ったからにはちゃんとやってくれなければ困る。

(If you've already said once that you will do it, you should definitely do it.)

c. ビールの本場と言うからにはさぞおいしいだろうね。

(If this is the home of beer as they say, it should be tasty, indeed!)

3. *Ni* can be omitted in spoken Japanese, as shown in (2).

(2) a. 函館に来たからは……まずはやっぱ、函館ラーメン！

(Now that we are in Hakodate, let's go for Hakodate *rāmen* first!)

b. やるからは一生懸命にやりたい。

(If I do it at all, I want to do it whole-heartedly.)

c. 始めたからは死ぬまで続けてね。

(Keep doing it (until you die) once you have started, OK?)

[Related Expression]

Ijō (wa) can replace *kara ni wa* (regardless of the preceding element) without changing the meaning, as in [1].

[1] a. いったん引き受けた{からには / 以上(は)}最後まで責任をもってやります。(= KS(A))

b. 裁判と言う{からには / 以上(は)}弁護人が不可欠だ。(= KS(B))

c. 写真をカラーで撮る{からには / 以上(は)}、色にこだわりたい。
(= Ex.(d))

But the reverse is impossible when *ijō (wa)* means "as long as s.o. does s.t. continuously, either a good or a bad result ensues."

[2] a. 体をよく動かしている{以上(は) / *からには}、人間の体は衰えないらしい。

(It is said that so long as you are very active, your body stays strong.)

b. 酒を飲み続けている{以上(は) / *からには}病気は治らないよ。

(So long as you keep drinking, your illness won't be cured, you know.)

c. 僕が生きている{以上(は) / ??からには}お前に不自由させないよ。

(As long as I am alive I won't let you go without anything.)

d. 日本語のラジオを聞いている{以上(は) / ??からには}日本語を聞く力は低下しないでしょうね。

(So long as I am listening to Japanese radio, I presume my listening skills won't deteriorate.)

Notice that stative expressions like *sunde iru* "live," *kekkon-shite iru* "be married," *harete iru* "weather is clear," etc., can take both *kara ni wa* and *ijō (wa)*.

[3] a. アメリカに住んでいる{からには / 以上(は)}郷に入っては郷に従えで、批判ばっかりしていたって仕方がない。(= Ex.(f))

b. 結婚している{からには / 以上(は)}家庭を守る義務がある。

(So long as you are married you have a responsibility to protect your family.)

(⇨ *ijō wa* (DIJG: 64-66))

kara shite   からして   *phr.*

a phrase that singles out s.t. for emphasis or presents s.t. as a basis for judgment	even; judging from 【REL. *(de) sura*; *(de) sae*; *kara itte*; *kara mite*; **ni shite kara ga**】

◆ Key Sentences

(A)

Noun		
社長	からして	会社再建の意欲がないんだから、社員の志気が上がらないのは当たり前だ。

(Even the president has no desire to reconstruct the company; so, of course, his employees' morale is low.)

(B)

Noun Phrase		
あの日本語の話し方	からして	彼は日本に行ったことがあるに違いない。

(Judging from the way he speaks Japanese, he must have been to Japan.)

Formation

N からして

　大統領からして　(even the president)

　外見からして　(judging from the outward appearance)

Examples

(a) あの男は歩き方からして他の人と違う。

(Even in the way he walks, he is different from other people.)

(b) プロの銀行員からして、初歩的な経済の分析に必要な数学に弱い。

(Even professional bankers are weak in the math necessary for elementary economic analysis.)

(c) 週末の彼女とのデートでは、待ち合わせの場所からして間違えてしまった。

(When I went out on a date with her last weekend, I even got the meeting place wrong.)

K

(d) 沈没した原子力潜水艦を引き揚げるのは、その大きさからして技術的な限界に近い。

(Judging from its size, pulling up the sunken atomic submarine will be next to impossible technologically.)

(e) 「車は走る凶器」「飲んだら乗るな」の掛け声も、事故の実態からして死語同然となっている。

(Judging from the reality of car accidents, slogans like "A car is a running weapon," and "Don't drink and drive" are just empty (lit., dead) words.)

Note

X *kara shite* is a phrase that singles out X for emphasis, meaning "even X," as in KS(A) and Exs.(a)-(c), or presents a basis for judgment, meaning "judging from X," as in KS(B), Exs.(d) and (e). If X refers to a human being, the phrase always means "even X," but otherwise, the meaning depends on context. For example, (1a) and (1b) include exactly the same phrase, *hanashikata kara shite*, but (1a) and (1b) are translated as "even the way she talks" and "judging from the way she talks," respectively, because (1b) expresses the speaker's judgment but (1a) doesn't.

(1) a. 僕は彼女の話し方からして気に食わないんだ。

(I hate even the way she talks.)

b. 彼女はその話し方からして明晰な頭脳を持っていると思う。

(Judging from the way she talks, I think she is clearheaded.)

[Related Expressions]

When the phrase *kara shite* means "even," it can be replaced by *(de) sura* or *(de) sae*, as shown in [1].

[1] a. 社長{からして／(で)すら／(で)さえ}会社再建の意欲がないんだから、社員の志気が上がらないのは当たり前だ。(= KS(A))

b. プロの銀行員{からして／(で)すら／(で)さえ}、初歩的な経済の分析に必要な数学に弱い。(= Ex.(b))

The three phrases differ in that *kara shite* is used in the subject position, as in [1], but it cannot be used in the direct object position, as shown in [2a], nor in the indirect object position, as in [2b].

[2] a. あの男は自分の子供｛(で)すら／(で)さえ／*からして｝殴りつける。
(He hits even his own child.)

b. 彼女は両親に｛すら／さえ／*からして｝本当のことを言わない。
(She doesn't even tell her parents the truth.)

(⇨ *sae* (DIJG: 363-69))

When *kara shite* means "judging from," it can be replaced with *kara itte* or *kara mite* without changing the meaning.

[3] a. あの日本語の話し方から｛して／言って／見て｝彼は日本に行ったことがあるに違いない。(= KS(B))

b. 沈没した原子力潜水艦を引き揚げるのは、その大きさから｛して／言って／見て｝技術的な限界に近い。(= Ex.(d))

(⇨ *kara itte* (in this volume))

K

kari ni 仮に　*adv.*

an adverb that indicates the speaker's/writer's tentative supposition

supposing that; suppose; providing that; (even) if
【REL. *moshi (mo)*】

◆ **Key Sentences**

(A)

仮に	Sinf		
	1億円｛もらう／もらった｝	と｛したら／すれば｝	何に使いますか。
(Supposing you received 100 million yen, what would you use it for?)			

(B)

		Vinf	
仮_{かり}に	月収_{げっしゅう}が 30 万円	{ある / あった}	として、

どのようなアパートを借りることができるだろうか。			

(Supposing that I had an income of 300,000 yen, I wonder what kind of an apartment I could rent.)

(C)

	Sinf		
仮_{かり}に	これが日本の教育_{きょういく}の現状_{げんじょう}だった	ら、	構造改革_{こうぞうかいかく}の余地_{よち}は大_{おお}いにある。

(If this were the current state of Japanese educational affairs, a lot would have to be restructured.)

(D)

Subordinate Clause (concession)			Main Clause
		Vinf	
仮_{かり}に	手術_{しゅじゅつ}が	成功_{せいこう}{する / した}	としても、	高齢_{こうれい}だから父の体_{からだ}が元_{もと}に戻_{もど}ることはないだろう。

(Even if the operation is successful, my father, who is quite old, will probably not regain his original health.)

Formation

(i) 仮_{かり}に Sinf と {したら / すれば}

仮に {話す / 話した} と {したら / すれば}   (supposing (that) / if s.o. talks/talked)

仮に {高い / 高かった} と {したら / すれば}   (supposing (that) / if s.t. is/were expensive)

仮にきれい {だ / だった} と {したら / すれば}   (supposing (that) / if s.t./s.o. is/were beautiful)

仮に先生 {だ / だった} と {したら / すれば}   (supposing (that) / if s.o. is/were a teacher)

(ii) 仮に Sinf 場合

仮に{話す／話した}場合　(supposing (that)／if s.o. talks/talked)

仮に{高い／高かった}場合　(supposing (that)／if s.t. is/were expensive)

仮にきれい{な／だった}場合　(supposing (that)／if s.t./s.o. is/were beautiful)

仮に先生{の／だった}場合　(supposing (that)／if s.o. is/were a teacher)

(iii) 仮に Sinf として

仮に{話す／話した}として　(supposing (that) s.o. talked)

仮に{高い／高かった}として　(supposing (that) s.t. were expensive)

仮にきれい{だ／だった}として　(supposing (that) s.t./s.o. were beautiful)

仮に先生{だ／だった}として　(supposing (that) s.o. were a teacher)

(iv) 仮に Sinf.past ら

仮に話したら　(supposing (that)／if s.o. talks/talked)

仮に高かったら　(supposing (that)／if s.t. is/were expensive)

仮にきれいだったら　(supposing (that)／if s.t./s.o. is/were beautiful)

仮に先生だったら　(supposing (that)／if s.o. is/were a teacher)

(v) 仮に～{V*te*／Adj(*i*)stem くて}も

仮に～{Adj(*na*)stem／N}でも

仮に話しても　(even if s.o. talks/talked)

仮に高くても　(even if s.t. is/were expensive)

仮にきれいでも　(even if s.o./s.t. is/were beautiful)

仮に先生でも　(even if s.o. is/were a teacher)

(vi) 仮に Sinf としても

仮に{話す／話した}としても　(even if s.o. talks/talked)

仮に{高い／高かった}としても　(even if s.t. were expensive)

仮にきれい{だ／だった}としても　(even if s.o./s.t. were beautiful)

仮に先生{だ／だった}としても　(even if s.o. were a teacher)

K

Examples

(a) 仮にあなたがベンチャー企業の経営権を持っていたら、どのようなアプローチを取りますか。

(Supposing that you managed a business venture, what sort of approach would you take?)

(b) よくある質問ですが、仮にあなたが今小さい島で一人で暮らすとして、一冊だけ本を持って行けるとしたら、どの本を持って行きますか。

(This is a common question, but supposing that you were going to live alone on a small island and were allowed to bring only one book, what would it be (lit., which book would you take there)?)

(c) 仮に今の調子で老齢化が進むとすれば、21世紀後半には日本の人口の5割以上が65歳以上になる可能性がある。

(If Japan ages at the current rate, in the latter half of the 21st century more than half of the Japanese population will be 65 or older.)

(d) 仮に日本に1年ぐらい行って日本語を勉強すれば、君たちの日本語はすごく上達するよ。

(If you go to Japan to study Japanese for about a year, your Japanese will make an impressive progress.)

(e) 信号を待っている時、仮に前の車が青になったのに進まなかったとしても、クラクションは鳴らさない方がよいでしょう。

(When you are waiting for the light, even if the car in front of you doesn't move ahead when it turns green, it's better not to honk.)

(f) 仮に話を経済学の「理論」に限定するとしても、今日までのあらゆる経済学理論が結局においてはすべてゲーム理論だと言っていいだろう。

(Even if we limit the discussion to economic theory, I can safely say that all economic theories are, in the end, game theory.)

(g) 仮に仲介者を通して売る場合、利益が少なくなるのは当然だ。

(If you sell it through a go-between, your profit, of course, will become smaller.)

Notes

1. The adverb *kari ni* indicates a tentative assumption. KS(A)-(C), Exs.(a) and (b) are examples of counterfactual assumption. Exs.(c), (d) and (g) are conditional statements, and KS(D), Exs.(e) and (f) are examples of

concession. Note that the tense of the verbs (in bold style in the KS) has nothing to do with counterfactual interpretation.

2. *Kari ni* can be preceded by *moshi (mo)* "if" to emphasize the hypothetical nature of a statement, as shown in (1).

(1) a. もし（も）仮に1億円もらうとしたら何に使いますか。(cf. KS(A))

b. もし（も）仮にこれが日本の教育の現状だったら、構造改革の余地は大いにある。(cf. KS(C))

c. もし（も）仮に手術が成功したとしても、高齢だから父の体が元に戻ることはないだろう。(cf. KS(D))

3. In (2a), the probability of receiving 100 million yen is lowest when the past tense version, i.e., *moratta to shitara*, is chosen and highest when *morattara*, is chosen. *Morau to shitara* comes between the other two in terms of the probability. In (2b), the probability of a successful operation is lowest when the past tense version, i.e., *shita to shite mo*, is used and highest when *shite mo*, is used, and *suru to shite mo* comes in between the two.

(2) a. 仮に1億円｛もらったとしたら／もらうとしたら／もらったら｝何に使いますか。(= KS(A))

b. 仮に手術が成功｛したとして／するとして／して｝も、高齢だから父の体が元に戻ることはないだろう。(= KS(D))

4. When Vinf *ba'ai* is used the meaning changes according to the tense of Vinf. If it is nonpast, the action of the verb is incomplete, and if it is past, the action is complete. In (3), for example, if the nonpast verb *hairu* is chosen the costs include an application fee and other fees one has to pay before entering graduate school, and if the past verb *haitta* is chosen the costs include tuition and other fees one has to pay after entering graduate school.

(3) 仮に日本の国立大学の大学院に｛入る／入った｝場合、どのぐらいお金がかかりますか。

(Supposing I enter / have entered graduate school of a Japanese national university, how much does it cost?)

[Related Expression]

There is another adverb, *moshi (mo)*, which emphasizes the hypothetical nature of a statement. It can be used together with *kari ni*, as shown in (1), or it can be used alone, as shown in [1]. *Kari ni* indicates a tentative assumption, while *moshi (mo)* indicates low probability.

[1] a. ｛仮に／もし（も）｝1億円もらったと｛したら／すれば｝何に使いますか。(= KS(A))

b. ｛仮に／もし（も）｝これが日本の教育の現状だったら、構造改革の余地は大いにある。(= KS(C))

c. ｛仮に／もし（も）｝手術が成功したとしても、高齢だから父の体が元に戻ることはないだろう。(= KS(D))

ka to omou to　かと思うと　*phr.*

> a phrase indicating that an action or state in the dependent clause occurs very closely with another action or state in the clause, or causes another action or state in the main clause

as soon as (one notices that) ~; soon after; when one thinks/feels that ~

【REL. *ka to omoeba*; *ka to omottara*】

◆ **Key Sentences**

(A)

	S₁inf.past		Sentence₂ (non-emotive)
最近は、	肌寒くなった	かと思うと、	翌日には暖かくなったりする。
(These days, just when you think it's gotten chilly, the next day it turns warm again.)				

(B)

	S₁inf		Sentence₂ (emotive)
私の書いた小説が出版される		かと思うと、	とても嬉しい。
(When I think that the novel I wrote will be published, I feel very happy.)				

Formation

(i) S₁inf.past かと思うと、S₂。 (where the predicate in S₂ is non-emotive; the subjects in S₁ and S₂ are the same)

食べたかと思うと、家を出た。 (As soon as s.o. has eaten, he left home.)

(ii) S₁inf かと思うと、S₂。 (where the predicate in S₂ is emotive)

日本へ行けるかと思うと嬉しい。 (When I think that I can go to Japan, I am happy.)

馬鹿にされたかと思うと悔しい。 (When I think that I was despised, I feel distressed.)

Examples

(a) ハワイでは、雨が降ってきたかと思うと、すぐやんでしまう。

(In Hawaii, as soon as it begins to rain, it stops right away.)

(b) 花火は、あがったかと思うとすぐ消えてしまうからいいのだ。

(I like fireworks because they disappear as soon as they go up.)

(c) うちの小学生の子供は、テレビを見終わったかと思うと、コンピュータゲームをやり始める。

(Our elementary school child starts to play computer games soon after he finishes watching TV.)

(d) 妻がおいしい夕食を作ってくれているかと思うと、家に帰る足も速まる。

(When I think about my wife preparing a delicious dinner for me, I naturally start walking home faster.)

(e) 会社のリストラで職を失うのではないかと思うと、気が重いです。

(When I think about how I might be laid off because of restructuring at my company, I feel depressed.)

(f) 子供たちも大学を出て一人立ちしたので、もう学費もかからないかと思うと、ほっとします。

(When I think about how we no longer need to pay educational expenses because our children have graduated from college and are now on their own, I feel so relieved.)

Notes

1. The *ka to omou to* construction can be used in two ways. First, it carries

the meaning of "as soon as" or "the moment ~," when the predicate of the main clause is a non-emotive predicate, as in KS(A) and Exs.(a)-(c). Secondly, the phrase means "when I think that ~" when the predicate of the main clause is emotive, as in KS(B) and Exs.(d)-(f). Note that *ashi mo hayamaru* in Ex.(d) is an instance of an emotive predicate.

2. If it is a non-emotive predicate, the whole sentence describes a habitual action or state, as shown in KS(A) and Exs.(a)-(c). In a recollective context, the tense is past.

(1) a. 先月は、肌寒くなった**かと思うと**、翌日には暖かくなったりした。

(cf. KS(A))

(Last month, just when I thought it had turned chilly, the following day it got warm.)

b. 私の書いた小説が出版される**かと思うと**、とても嬉しかった。

(cf. KS(B))

(When I thought that my novel would be published, I felt very happy.)

3. As shown in Formation (i), when the predicate in S_2 is non-emotive, S_1 is always past. S_1 can be either nonpast or past when the predicate in S_2 is emotive.

[Related Expressions]

There are two related expressions, *ka to omoeba* and *ka to omottara*. They are different from *ka to omou to* only in the choice of conditional form. Both of them can replace *ka to omou to* when the predicate in S_2 is non-emotive, but not when it is emotive, as shown in [1] and [2] below.

[1] a. 最近は、肌寒くなったかと｛思うと／思えば／思ったら｝、翌日には暖かくなったりする。(= KS(A))

b. ハワイでは、雨が降ってきたかと｛思うと／思えば／思ったら｝、すぐやんでしまう。(= Ex.(a))

[2] a. 私の書いた小説が出版されるかと｛思うと／?思ったら／??思えば｝、とても嬉しい。(= KS(B))

b. 会社のリストラで職を失うのではないかと｛思うと／?思ったら／??思えば｝、気が重いです。(= Ex.(e))

katsu かつ［且つ］　*conj.*　<w>

~~~
a conjunction meaning "and" that connects words, phrases and sentences
~~~

and; and also; yet; but; and ~
as well; as well as; moreover
【REL. *to*; *ya*; *mata*; *sono ue*;
sara ni; *kuwaete*; *soshite*】

◆ **Key Sentences**

(A)

	Phrase₁		Phrase₂
スミス氏_しは	流暢_{りゅうちょう}な日本語を話し、	かつ	日本の歴史_{れきし}や文化_{ぶんか}にも明るい。

(Mr. Smith is fluent in Japanese and is also knowledgeable about Japanese history and culture.)

(B)

	Adjective₁		Adjective₂	Noun	
この本は、	分かりやすく、	かつ	味わい深_{ぶか}い	言葉_{ことば}	で書かれている。

(This book is written in language that is easy to understand but also profound.)

(C)

	Noun Phrase₁			Noun Phrase₂	
彼女_{かのじょ}は	一流_{いちりゅう}のピアニスト	で、	かつ	優_{すぐ}れた随筆家_{ずいひつか}	だ。

(She is a first-class pianist, as well as a fine essayist.)

(D)

	Adverb₁		Adverb₂	
外国語は、	楽しく、	かつ	効果的_{こうかてき}に	勉強したい。

(We'd like to study foreign languages in an enjoyable yet effective way.)

K

(E)

Phrase₁			Phrase₂		
英語ができる	こと、	かつ	ウェブサイトの 作成経験がある _{さくせいけいけん}	こと	がこの仕事の要 件だ。 _{よう} _{けん}

(Being able to speak English and having experience in constructing web-sites are the conditions required for this job.)

Formation

(i) ｛V*masu* / V*te*｝、かつ

   飲み、かつ　(s.o. drinks and)
   _の

   飲んで、かつ　(s.o. drinks and)

(ii) Vneg ず、かつ

   行かず、かつ　(s.o. will not go and)

(iii) Adj(*i*)stem く（て）、かつ

   面白く（て）、かつ　(s.t. is interesting and)
   _{おもしろ}

(iv) Adj(*na*)stem（｛で / であり / であって｝）、かつ

   経済的（｛で / であり / であって｝）、かつ　(s.t. is economical and)
   _{けいざいてき}

(v) N で（｛あり / あって｝）、かつ

   天才で（｛あり / あって｝）、かつ　(s.o. is a genius and)
   _{てんさい}

(vi) ｛Adj(*i*)stem く / Adj(*na*)stem で(は) / N で(は)｝なく、かつ

   面白くなく、かつ　(s.t. is not interesting and)

   便利で(は)なく、かつ　(s.t. is not convenient and)
   _{べんり}

   英語で(は)なく、かつ　(s.t. is not English and)

(vii) ｛Adj(*i*)stem く / Adj(*na*)stem（に）｝、かつ｛Adj(*i*)stem く /
   Adj(*na*)stem に｝

   早く、かつ正確に　(quickly and accurately)
   _{せいかく}

   慎重（に）、かつ迅速に　(prudently and rapidly)
   _{しんちょう} _{じんそく}

(viii)｛Sentence / Phrase｝₁ こと、かつ｛Sentence / Phrase｝₂ こと

   日本人であること、かつ区内に居住すること　(being a Japanese and
   _{くない} _{きょじゅう}
   living in the ward)

Examples

(a) パソコンさえあれば自宅ででき、かつ高収入の仕事をご紹介します。

(We will introduce you to jobs that not only pay well, but can be done at home, as long as you have a computer.)

(b) この図は、自動車を個人で利用できず、かつ家族とも共有できない65歳以上の高齢者の外出頻度を示している。

(This figure shows how often senior citizens over 65 who cannot drive a car and do not share one with their family get out.)

(c) 和太鼓による若々しく、かつたくましい演奏をご堪能下さい。

(Please enjoy the youthful, powerful performance on the Japanese drums.)

(d) 当店では、スタイリッシュで、かつシンプルなトレーニングウエアを各種取り揃えております。

(Our store has various kinds of training gear that are stylish yet simple in design.)

(e) ご注文のキャンセルについては、注文から24時間以内で、かつ注文されたご本人によりメールあるいはファックスでご連絡いただいた場合のみ認められます。

(We accept cancellations only within 24 hours of an order being placed *and* only when we receive notification via e-mail or fax by the person who has placed the order.)

(f) この仕事では大量の文献を速く且つ正確に読むことが要求される。

(This job demands that you read a large volume of material both quickly and accurately.)

(g) 当社は、個人情報を取り扱うにあたり、個人情報保護法はじめ適用される諸法令、規範遵守を徹底し、適切且つ慎重に管理いたします。

(At our company, when we handle personal information, we thoroughly observe the applicable laws and regulations, including the Personal Information Protection Law, and we manage the information properly and prudently.)

(h) 売主は、製品には欠陥またはきずのある材料の使用がないこと、且つ当該製品が売主の発行した仕様に合致するものであることを保証する。

(The seller guarantees that the product does not use materials with defects or blemishes and that the product meets the specifications issued by the seller.)

『Notes』

1. *Katsu* connects words, phrases or sentences. It means "and," "yet" or "but" depending on the context and emphasizes the following word, phrase or sentence.

2. The forms which precede *katsu* include continuative forms (e.g., the *masu*-stems of verbs, *i*-adjective stems + *ku* and *na*-adjective stems + *de*), adverbs or adverbial phrases, and *koto* clauses or phrases. The use of the *te*-forms of verbs and *i*-adjectives before *katsu* is not common. The *de* and *ni* after *na*-adjective stems often drop before *katsu*.

3. *Katsu* is commonly used in formal documents such as contracts and agreements.

[Related Expressions]

I. Unlike *to* "and" and *ya* "and," *katsu* is not used to simply connect two nouns.

[1] a. 中国{と / *かつ}韓国がその会議に参加した。

(China and Korea participated in the conference.)

b. マリアはスペイン語{と / *かつ}ポルトガル語を話す。

(Maria speaks Spanish and Portuguese.)

[2] a. 大統領はインド{や / *かつ}パキスタンを訪問した。

(The president visited India, Pakistan and other counties.)

b. 石田氏はカナダ{や / *かつ}オーストラリアに不動産を持っている。

(Mr. Ishida has real estate in Canada, Australia and elsewhere.)

Note that *to* and *ya* cannot connect verbs, adjectives, adverbs, phrases (except for noun phrases) or sentences.

(⇨ *to*[1] (DBJG: 473-76); *ya* (DBJG: 536-38))

II. *Mata* "also" can be used in place of *katsu*. *Katsu* can also precede *mata*.

[3] a. スミス氏は流暢な日本語を話し、{かつ / (かつ)また}日本の歴史や文化にも明るい。(= KS(A))

b. この本は、分かりやすく、{かつ / (かつ)また}味わい深い言葉で書かれている。(= KS(B))

c. 彼女は一流のピアニストで、｛かつ／(かつ)また｝優れた随筆家だ。

(= KS(C))

d. 外国語は、楽しく、｛かつ／(かつ)また｝効果的に勉強したい。

(= KS(D))

(⇨ ***mata*** (in this volume))

III. *Katsu* "and" is emphatic. In this respect, it is synonymous with *sono ue* "on top of that," *sara ni* "furthermore," and *kuwaete* "in addition," although *katsu* does not convey as much of a sense of "in addition" or "furthermore" as the other conjunctions do.

[4] a. スミス氏は流暢な日本語を話し、｛かつ／その上／さらに／加えて｝日本の歴史や文化にも明るい。(= KS(A))

b. 彼女は一流のピアニストで、｛かつ／その上／さらに／加えて｝優れた随筆家だ。(= KS(C))

Sono ue, *sara ni* and *kuwaete* cannot be used with noun-modifying or adverbial phrases/clauses.

[5] a. この本は、分かりやすく、｛かつ／*その上／*さらに／*加えて｝味わい深い言葉で書かれている。(= KS(B))

b. 外国語は、楽しく、｛かつ／*その上／*さらに／*加えて｝効果的に勉強したい。(= KS(D))

(⇨ ***sono ue*** (DIJG: 413-17); ***sara ni*** (in this volume); ***kuwaete*** (in this volume))

IV. *Soshite* "and" can convey the same idea as *katsu* when describing two properties or actions of a person (or a thing), as shown in [6]. In this case, the second sentence contains *mo* "also."

[6] a. スミス氏は流暢な日本語を話す。｛そして／*かつ｝日本の歴史や文化にも明るい。(cf. KS(A))

b. 彼女は一流のピアニストだ。｛そして／*かつ｝優れた随筆家でもある。(cf. KS(C))

Note here that *soshite* appears in the sentence-initial position, but *katsu* cannot. Also note that *soshite* can indicate the sequence of two actions or events in some context, whereas *katsu* does not indicate a time sequence.

(⇨ ***soshite*** (DBJG: 422-23))

kirai ga aru きらいがある   *phr.*   <w>

```
a phrase indicating that s.o. or s.t. has
an undesirable tendency
```
have a tendency to; tend to;
have a touch of ~; have a dash
of ~; smack of ~; be slightly ~
【REL. *-gachi*; *keikō ga aru*】

◆ **Key Sentences**

(A)

	Vinf	
彼は物事を単純に	考える	きらいがある。

(He has a tendency to think (about things) in simplistic terms.)

(B)

	Noun		
彼は	独断	の	きらいがある。

(He is slightly dogmatic (lit., has a touch of dogmatism).)

Formation

(i) Vinf きらいがある

結論を{急ぐ／急いだ}きらいがある (s.o. has/had a tendency to reach
   a conclusion hastily (lit., to hurry to rseach a conclusion))

飲み{すぎる／すぎた}きらいがある (s.o. has/had a tendency to drink
   too much)

(ii) N のきらいがある

過食のきらいがある (s.o. has a tendency toward overeating)

誇張のきらいがある (s.t. smacks of exaggeration)

Examples

(a) 我々はとかく自分に都合がいい意見だけに耳を傾けるきらいがある。
   (We tend to listen only to views that are convenient for us.)

(b) 今の子供たちは、夜遅くまでコンピュータゲームなどをして寝ないきらいがある。

(Children these days have a tendency to stay up late at night playing computer games and doing other things.)

(c) 主婦は毎日の雑事に追われて、自分の体調管理がおろそかになるきらいがある。

(Housewives have a tendency to neglect taking care of their own health because they are busy doing everyday chores.)

(d) 彼女は親切な人ですが、知らずに人を傷つけることを言うきらいがあります。

(She is a kind person, but she has a tendency to say things unwittingly that hurt people.)

(e) 私たちは、あまりに自分のからだを医者任せにしてきたきらいがあるのではないでしょうか。

(Don't you think that we have tended to entrust (the care of) our bodies too much to doctors?)

(f) これまでの日本の高等教育は、アジアとの共生を重視しなかったきらいがある。

(Japanese higher education so far has tended to attach little importance to Japan's coexistence with Asia.)

(g) 現在の日本の教育は、子供を社会から保護しすぎるきらいがある。

(Education in Japan today tends to overprotect children from society.)

(h) 彼は家庭環境が複雑なせいか、人間不信のきらいがある。

(Because he was brought up in a complicated family setting, he tends not to trust people (lit., tends towards mistrust of humans).)

(i) 彼は頭もよくて、仕事もばりばりやるけど、八方美人のきらいがあるね。

(He is sharp and works furiously, but he has a tendency to try to be everything to everybody.)

(j) 健康診断で白内障のきらいがあると医者に言われました。

(When I had a physical checkup, the doctor told me that I have cataracts developing.)

(k) 糖尿病のきらいがあるので、甘いものは控えています。

(I have a borderline case of diabetes (lit., have a tendency towards diabetes), so I am refraining from eating sweets.)

Notes

1. The phrase *kirai ga aru* indicates that someone has an undesirable tendency in the way he or she thinks or behaves, as illustrated in the KS, Exs.(a)-(e), (h) and (i). Exs.(f) and (g) are cases where a thing shows an undesirable tendency, and Exs.(j) and (k) are cases where someone's body has an undesirable tendency towards a particular illness.

2. In KS(A) and Exs.(a)-(g), a Vinf precedes the phrase, and in KS(B) and Exs.(h)-(k), a noun comes before the phrase.

3. "Vinf.past *kirai ga aru*" can usually be rephrased as "Vinf.nonpast *kirai ga atta*," as shown in (1).

    (1) a. これまでの日本の高等教育は、アジアとの共生を重視{しなかったき らいがある／しないきらいがあった}。(= Ex.(f))

    b. これまでの学力試験は、記憶力を試す問題が{多すぎたきらいがある／ 多すぎるきらいがあった}。
    (Achievement tests so far have tended to ask too many questions that only test students' memory.)

    However, if a tendency still persists at the time of the statement, as in Ex.(e), the final verb cannot be in the past tense, as shown in (2).

    (2) a. 私たちは、あまりに自分のからだを医者任せにして{きたきらいがあ る／*くるきらいがあった}のではないでしょうか。(= Ex.(e))

    b. これまで我が社は社員研修を軽視して{きたきらいがある／*くるきら いがあった}。
    (Our company has tended to attach little importance to employee training.)

4. The noun *kirai* comes from the V*masu* of *kirau* "dislike; hate," but the Chinese character 嫌 is seldom used.

[Related Expressions]

I. The suffix *-gachi* can also express an undesirable tendency in someone or something, and it can replace *kirai ga aru* if an informal nonpast verb is used before the phrase, as shown in [1].

    [1] a. 彼は物事を単純に{考えるきらいがある／考えがちだ}。(= KS(A))

　b. 我々はとかく自分に都合がいい意見だけに耳を｛傾けるきらいがある／傾けがちだ｝。(= Ex.(a))

　c. 主婦は毎日の雑事に追われて、自分の体調管理がおろそかに｛なるきらいがある／なりがちだ｝。(= Ex.(c))

However, "Vinf.past *kirai ga aru*" cannot be rephrased using *-gachi*, as shown in [2].

[2]　a. これまでの学力試験は、記憶力を試す問題が｛多すぎたきらいがある／*多すぎがちだった｝。(= (1b))

　b. 私たちは、あまりに自分のからだを医者任せにして｛きたきらいがある／*きがちだった｝のではないでしょうか。(= Ex.(e))

-gachi da cannot replace *kirai ga aru* when "N *no*" precedes *kirai ga aru* and the noun indicates something that tends to exist in someone.

[3]　a. 彼は独断｛のきらいがある／*がちだ｝。(= KS(B))
　　cf. 彼は独断をしがちだ。

　b. 糖尿病｛のきらいがある／*がちな｝ので、甘いものは控えています。
　　　　　　　　　　　　　　　　　　　　　　　　　　　　(= Ex.(k))

K

Briefly, N-*gachi* expresses a negative tendency in terms of frequency, but N *no kirai ga aru* expresses a negative tendency in terms of the existence of something in someone's mind or body.

　　　　　　　　　　　　　　　　　　　　(⇨ *-gachi* (DIJG: 47-50))

Furthermore, as demonstrated in [4], *-gachi* phrases cannot be replaced by *kirai ga aru* when the noun that precedes *-gachi da* indicates something that tends to occur very frequently, like *byōki* "illness" in [4a], *rusu* "absence from home" in [4b] or *enryo* "hesitation; restraint" in [4c].

[4]　a. うちの娘は病気｛がちで／*のきらいがあって｝、学校をよく休みます。
　　　(Our daughter is prone to illness and has to miss classes very often.)

　b. 先月は出張が多くて、留守｛がちだった／*のきらいがあった｝。
　　　(Last month I made a lot of business trips and wasn't at home most days.)

　　c. 彼は小さい時から遠慮｛がちな /*のきらいのある｝性格だった。

　　　(Since he was little, he has been reserved (lit., has had a reserved personality).)

II. The phrase *keikō ga aru* "have a tendency to" can replace *kirai ga aru* when the tendency is undesirable, as shown in [5].

　[5]　a. 彼は物事を単純に考える｛きらい /傾向｝がある。(= KS(A))

　　　b. 我々はとかく自分に都合がいい意見だけに耳を傾ける｛きらい /傾向｝がある。(= Ex.(a))

　　　c. 主婦は毎日の雑事に追われて、自分の体調管理がおろそかになる｛きらい /傾向｝がある。(= Ex.(c))

　　　d. 彼は独断の｛きらい /傾向｝がある。(= KS(B))

　　　e. 糖尿病の｛きらい /傾向｝があるので、甘いものは控えています。
　　　　　　　　　　　　　　　　　　　　　　　　　　　　　(= Ex.(k))

However, only *keikō ga aru* can be used when the tendency under focus is not undesirable, that is, either positive, as in [6a], or neutral, as in [6b].

　[6]　a. 研究的使用のための十全なデータベースが構築されてきた｛傾向 /*きらい｝がある。

　　　(There has been a tendency to construct complete databases for research purposes.)

　　　b. 日本では箸は使い捨てや個人専用など、使用者が箸を共用しない｛傾向 /*きらい｝がある。

　　　(In Japan, people tend not to share chopsticks, either using disposable ones and throwing them away or having their own individual pair.)

(k)kiri 〔っ〕きり   *conj. / prt.*   <s>

> a conjunction indicating that since s.t. occurred, nothing has happened and the resultant situation remains unchanged; a particle indicating a strict limitation in terms of number/quantity

since; only
【REL. *dake*; *mama*】

◆ **Key Sentences**

(A)

	Vinf.past		
山下氏は 1964 年に 日本を	出た	〔っ〕きり	日本には一度も帰っていない。

(Mr. Yamashita hasn't returned to Japan even once since he left in 1964.)

(B)

	Noun (time)		
ソウルにいるのも	今夜	きり	です。

(This is my last night (lit., the only night left) in Seoul.)

Formation

(i) Vinf.past 〔っ〕きり

> 出た〔っ〕きり〔帰らない〕 ((s.o. has never returned) since he left home)

> 買った〔っ〕きり〔使わない〕 ((s.o. has never used s.t.) since he bought it)

(ii) N きり   (where N = noun of time)

> 今日きり   (only today)

> 今週きり   (only this week)

> 今年きり   (only this year)

(iii) Dem. Pro. 〔っ〕きり

> これ〔っ〕きり   (only this much / only this time)

> それ〔っ〕きり   (only that much / only that time); since then

あれ（っ）きり　(only that much / only that time); since then

(iv)　Number + Counter （っ）きり

二人（っ）きり　(only two (students, etc.))

三枚（っ）きり　(only three (CDs, etc.))

四本（っ）きり　(only four (pencils, etc.))

Examples

(a) 彼女とは10年以上も前にパリで会ったきりで、その後どうしているのか、全然知らない。

(I haven't seen her since we met in Paris more than 10 years ago and I have no idea how she's been doing since then.)

(b) 小学校6年の時に別れたっきりの同級生に気づかれるなんて、ひょっとして私って小学校の時から顔が変わってないんだろうか。

(My classmate, whom I hadn't seen since we left 6th grade, recognized me. I wonder if I look the same as I did in elementary school (lit., my face has not changed since my grade school days).)

(c) フロイトの本はずいぶん前に読んだっきりなので、内容のほとんどは忘れてしまいました。

(It's been a long time since I read Freud's books, so I've forgotten almost all of the content.)

(d) 父は雪の日に倒れて、腰の骨を折ってから、寝たきりになってしまった。

(My father fell on a snowy day and broke his hip, and since then he's been lying in bed.)

(e) これっきりなの？ もっとたくさんちょうだい。

(Is this all (lit., only this much)? Give me more, please.)

(f) もう会うのはこれっきりにしましょう。

(Let's make this the last (lit., only) time we see each other.)

(g) 10年前に別れて二人はそれきりだった。

(The two parted 10 years ago and have never seen each other since.)

(h) 彼からはあれっきり何も連絡がないの？

(You haven't heard anything from him since then?)

(i) 夏休みも今日一日きりで終わっちゃうね。

(Today is the last day (lit., the only day left) of summer vacation, isn't it?)

(j) 私は母と二人っきりで暮らしています。

(I live alone with my mother.)

Notes

1. Vinf.past *(k)kiri*, as demonstrated in KS(A) and Exs.(a)-(d), is used to indicate that ever since someone did something in the past nothing has happened.

2. *Kiri* means "only" when it is used with N, Demonstrative Pronoun or Number + Counter, as in KS(B) and Exs.(e)-(j).

3. The *masu*-stem of the two verbs *kakaru* and *tsuku* are used to express someone's single-minded devotion to an action, which makes it impossible for him or her to do anything else.

(1) a. 領収書の整理や計算など、一日中、確定申告書の作成にかかり（っ）きりだった。

(Putting the receipts in order and calculating (the figures), I've been busy the entire day preparing the tax return (form).)

b. 一昨日、敏男が倒れてから、心配でたまらず、ずっとつき（っ）きりで看病していたのだ。

(Toshio collapsed the day before yesterday, and I have been attending to him ever since because I am so worried about him.)

4. The demonstrative pronoun *kore/sore/are* + *(k)kiri* is used to mean "only this/that much," as in Ex.(e), or "ever since this/that time," as in Exs.(f)-(h).

5. *Kkiri* is more colloquial and/or more emphatic than *kiri*, as is always the case with contrasts such as Adj(*i*)stem *kute* vs. Adj(*i*)stem *kutte*, *yahari* vs. *yappari*, among others.

6. *(K)kiri* is used to indicate strict limitation when it is used with Number + Counter. This combination is often followed by *da* and its variations, as shown in (2a, b) and Ex.(j). It is also used with "*no* N," as in (2c). When it is used with a verb, it often takes the form of *(k)kiri shika ~ nai*, as shown in (2d).

(2) a. その短編集に載った彼の短編は**四つきり**だった。

(A total of four of his short stories were included in the anthology.)

b. 僕が読んだ村上春樹の小説は『ノルウェイの森』**一作きり**です。

(The only one of Haruki Murakami's novels I have read is *Norwegian Wood*.)

c. 老後は妻と二人**(っ)きり**の生活を楽しもうと思う。

(I plan to enjoy old age alone with my wife.)

d. 今日はいつもと違ってビールを**2本きり**しか飲まなかった。

(Unlike my usual routine, today I drank only two bottles of beer.)

[Related Expressions]

I. The particle *dake* can replace *(k)kiri* when the latter indicates a strict limitation in terms of number/quantity, as in [1a, b], or emphasizes the end of a time period, as in [1c]. Note that *(k)kiri* is more emotive and is used mainly to spoken Japanese.

[1] a. これ{**っきり** / **だけ**}なの？ もっとたくさんちょうだい。(= Ex.(e))

b. 私は母と二人{**っきり** / **だけ**}で暮らしています。(= Ex.(j))

c. 今週{**っきり** / **だけ**}で今学期の授業は終わります。

(This week is the last week of class this semester.)

(⇨ ***dake*** (DBJG: 93-97))

II. Vinf.past *(k)kiri* can be replaced by Vinf.past *mama* and vice versa when the two actions/states expressed by the two verbs (i.e., the verb in the *kiri* clause and the verb in the main predicate) are not occurring simultaneously, as in [2].

[2] a. 山下氏は1964年に日本を出た{**(っ)きり** / **まま**}日本には一度も帰っていない。(= KS(A))

b. 彼女とは10年以上も前にパリで会った{**っきり** / **まま**}で、その後どうしているのか、全然知らない。(= Ex.(a))

c. フロイトの本はずいぶん前に読んだ{**っきり** / **まま**}なので、内容のほとんどは忘れてしまいました。(= Ex.(c))

d. 彼女はお金を借りた{**(っ)きり** / **まま**}返しません。

(She borrowed money, but she has never returned it.)

If the two actions/states are occurring simultaneously, as in [3], *mama* cannot replace *(k)kiri*.

[3] a. 靴をはいた｛まま／*(っ)きり｝家に入ってはいけません。

(Don't go into the house with your shoes on.)

  b. 電気をつけた｛まま／*(っ)きり｝寝てしまった。

(I fell asleep leaving the light on.)

(⇨ ***mama*** (DBJG: 236-40))

-kke つけ   *prt.*   <s>

⎧ a colloquial sentence-final particle ⎫   【REL. *ka*】
⎩ marking a question   ⎭

K

◆ **Key Sentences**

(A)

	Vinf.nonpast		
鈴木さんは英語が	**話せる**	んだ	っけ。
(Can you speak English, Mr. Suzuki? / Can Mr. Suzuki speak English?)			

(B)

	Vinf.past		
鈴木さんは英語が	**話せた**	(んだ)	っけ。
(Can you speak English, Mr. Suzuki? / Can Mr. Suzuki speak English?)			

Formation

(i) ｛V／Adj(*i*)｝inf.nonpast んだっけ

   ｛話す／おいしい｝んだっけ (Does s.o. talk? / Is s.t. delicious?)

(ii) ｛V／Adj(*i*)｝inf.past (んだ)っけ

   ｛話した／おいしかった｝(んだ)っけ (Did s.o. talk? / Was s.t. delicious?)

(iii) ｛Adj(*na*)stem / N / Wh-word｝(なん)だっけ

　　　｛元気 / 学生｝(なん)だっけ　(Is s.o. healthy / a student?)

　　　｛なん / 誰 / どこ / いつ｝(なん)だっけ　(What/Who/Where/When is it?)

(iv) ｛Adj(*na*)stem / N / Wh-word｝だった(んだ)っけ

　　　｛元気 / 学生｝だった(んだ)っけ　(Was/Is s.o. healthy / a student?)

　　　｛なん / 誰 / どこ / いつ｝だった(んだ)っけ　(What/Who/Where/When was/is it?)

Examples

(a) 今日は木曜日だ(った)っけ。
(Is today Thursday?)

(b) ジェーンさんはピアノが弾けた(んだ)っけ。
(Can you play the piano, Jane? / Can Jane play the piano?)

(c) パーティーは何時に始まるんだっけ。
(When does the party start?)

(d) スミスさんはワシントン大学の学生だったっけ。
(Are (Were) you a University of Washington student, Ms. Smith? / Is (Was) Ms. Smith a University of Washington student?)

(e) 僕が子供の頃はこの辺は林だったっけ。
(When I was a kid this area used to be a forest.)

(f) この映画、面白いんだっけ。
(Is this movie interesting?)

(g) あの人って、正直なんだっけ。
(Is he an honest person?)

Notes

1. *-kke* is a colloquial question marker.

2. When an informal nonpast verb or *i*-adjective is used, *n da* has to be used with *-kke*, as shown in KS(A), Exs.(c) and (f). Thus the sentences in (1) are all ungrammatical.

(1) a. *鈴木さんは英語が話せるっけ。 (cf. KS(A))

b. *ジェーンさんはピアノが**弾ける**っけ。(cf. Ex.(b))

c. *この映画、**面白い**っけ。(cf. Ex.(f))

If the verb is past, the use of *n da* is optional, as shown in KS(B) and Ex.(b), which is repeated here as (2).

(2) a. 鈴木さんは英語が**話せた**(**んだ**)っけ。(= KS(B))

b. ジェーンさんはピアノが**弾けた**(**んだ**)っけ。(= Ex.(b))

3. The verb before *n da-kke* can be either nonpast, as in KS(A), or past, as in KS(B). The difference between (3a) and (3b) is that the latter implies that the speaker is trying to confirm that Mr. Suzuki was able to speak English in the past, but the former doesn't.

(3) a. 鈴木さんは英語が**話せるんだ**っけ。(= KS(A))

b. 鈴木さんは英語が**話せたんだ**っけ。(= KS(B))

4. *-kke* is highly colloquial and can't be used in written or formal spoken Japanese.

5. The polite past form of verbs and the polite past form of *da* (i.e., *deshita*) can be used in place of the informal past form of verbs and *datta*, respectively.

(4) a. 鈴木さんは英語が**話せました**っけ。(cf. KS(B))

b. 今日は木曜日**でした**っけ。(cf. Ex.(a))

Note, however, that neither the formal past of *i*-adjectives, as in (5a), nor the formal *n desu*, as in (5b), can be used.

(5) a. あのレストランは{**おいしかった** / ***おいしかったです**}っけ。

b. あのレストランは{**おいしいんだ** / ***おいしいんです**}っけ。

6. Vinf.past-*kke* or N *datta-kke* can express nostalgic recollection, as in Ex.(e). More examples are in (6). *Nā* is also used in this situation.

(6) a. 子供の時は父とよくこの川に釣りに来た{**っけ** / **なあ**}。
(When I was a child I used to come to this river often to fish with my father.)

b. ここは昔、小学校だった{**っけ** / **なあ**}。
(A long time ago an elementary school stood here.)

[Related Expression]

The question marker *ka* is similar to *-kke* although *-kke* is used only in highly colloquial speech. When *-kke* is used with a nonpast verb or Adj(*i*)inf.nonpast, *n da* must be used. With *ka*, however, *n da* is optional.

(⇨ ***ka***[2] (DBJG: 166-68); ***no da*** (DBJG: 325-28))

Additionally, *-kke* can be used to recollect something, as in KS(B), but *ka* cannot. The *-kke* form with *desu* is unacceptable, but *desu ka* is acceptable.

kono ue nai　この上ない　　*phr.*　<w>

~~~~~~
a phrase that indicates that something　　extremely; utterly; very; so; can-
or someone is in an extreme state　　　　not be more; extreme; utmost
~~~~~~
【REL. *kiwamete*; *hijōni*; *jitsu-ni*; *kiwamari nai*; *kagiri da*】

◆ **Key Sentences**

(A)

		Adj(*na*)stem	
生まれたばかりの赤ん坊を車に残して買い物に行く	とは	非常識	この上ない。

(It is utterly senseless to leave a newborn baby in the car and go shopping.)

(B)

	Adj(*i*)inf.nonpast		
この部屋はクーラーも扇風機もなく、風も全然通らないので、	暑い	こと	この上ない。

(There is neither an air-conditioner nor a fan in this room, and no breeze, either, so it's extremely hot in here.)

(C)

		Noun	
大任を無事に果たして	この上ない	充実感	に浸っている。

(I'm enjoying the feeling of utmost fulfillment, having completed an important mission successfully.)

Formation

(i)　Adj(*na*)stem この上ない

　　　不便この上ない　(extremely inconvenient)

(ii)　{Adj(*i*)inf.nonpast / Adj(*na*)stem な}ことこの上ない

　　　嬉しいことこの上ない　(s.o. cannot be happier)

　　　危険なことこの上ない　(extremely dangerous)

(iii)　この上ない N

　　　この上ない幸せ　(extreme happiness)

K

Examples

(a)　最近よく食事時にセールスの電話がかかってくるが、迷惑この上ない。

　　　(We often get sales calls at dinnertime these days, which is extremely annoying.)

(b)　一人住まいの高齢者を狙って金を騙し取るなど卑劣この上ない。

　　　(It is utterly contemptible to target old people living alone and cheat them of their money.)

(c)　こんな大事な仕事をアルバイトにさせるなんて無責任この上ない。

　　　(It is extremely irresponsible to have a part-timer do such an important job.)

(d)　また選挙シーズンが来た。いつものことだが、選挙の車が連日うちの前を通り、マイクで候補者の名前を連呼する。うるさいことこの上ない。

　　　(Here we are again in election season. As always, the campaign cars pass by my house every day, shouting out their candidate's name repeatedly on the microphone. It's extremely noisy and annoying.)

(e)　このコンピュータは日本語入力の時、いちいち入力方式を指定しないといけないので、面倒なことこの上ない。

(Because we have to specify the input method on this computer every time we want to type in Japanese, it's extremely cumbersome.)

(f) 新しく入ったアパートはキッチンの流しが高くて、私のように背の低いものは使づらいことこの上ない。

(The sink in my new apartment is tall, which makes it extremely hard to use for someone short like me.)

(g) 一人でハワイに来て、この上ない解放感に満たされている。

(Having come to Hawaii by myself, I'm filled with a feeling of utmost freedom.)

(h) ご出席いただいた皆様からこの上ないお褒めの言葉をいただきました。

(I received the utmost praise from those who attended.)

(i) 彼とやっと一緒の生活を始めることができ、この上ない幸福感に浸っている。

(Finally, I can start living with my boyfriend; I couldn't be happier.)

(j) この国は、他の国の批判に耳を貸すこともなく、この上ないごう慢さをもって自国のイデオロギーを主張し続けている。

(This country keeps insisting with utmost arrogance on its ideology without paying attention to other countries' criticisms.)

Notes

1. *Kono ue nai* literally means there is "nothing above this." This phrase is used when something or someone is in a state beyond what is considered normal.

2. When *i*-adjectives are used with *kono ue nai*, *koto* always occurs in front of *kono ue nai*, as in (1).

    (1) 日本の選挙カーはうるさい{*ø / こと}この上ない。

    (The election campaign cars in Japan are extremely noisy.)

3. *Kono ue nai* is commonly used to describe undesirable situations but it can be used for desirable situations as well, as in KS(C) and Exs.(g)-(i). (2) provides more examples.

    (2) a. 旧友と酒を飲みながら話すのは愉快この上ない。

    (It is so much fun to talk with your old friends over a drink.)

    b. 皇室に待望の男の子が生まれて喜ばしいことこの上ない。

    (We are extremely happy that the royal family had a baby boy, (an occasion) everyone had been waiting for.)

【Related Expressions】

I. Adverbs such as *kiwamete* "extremely," *hijōni* "very" and *jitsuni* "really" can convey ideas similar to *kono ue nai* and sentences with *kono ue nai* can be rephrased using them, as shown in [1].

[1] a. 生まれたばかりの赤ん坊を車に残して買い物に行くとは{非常識この上ない／{極めて／非常に／実に}非常識だ}。(= KS(A))

 b. この部屋はクーラーも扇風機もなく、風も全然通らないので、{暑いことこの上ない／{極めて／非常に／実に}暑い}。(= KS(B))

II. *Kiwamari nai* is synonymous with *kono ue nai* and can be used in similar situations, as shown in [2].

[2] a. 生まれたばかりの赤ん坊を車に残して買い物に行くとは非常識{この上ない／極まりない}。(= KS(A))

 b. ここはバスが1時間に1本しか来ないので不便{この上ない／極まりない}。
 (Because the bus comes here only once every hour, it is extremely inconvenient.)

 c. 銃を子供が勝手に持ち出せるようなところに置いておくのは危険{この上ない／極まりない}。
 (It is extremely dangerous to keep a gun where children can get to it easily.)

 d. この部屋はクーラーも扇風機もなく、風も全然通らないので、暑いこと{この上ない／極まりない}。(= KS(B))

However, *kiwamari nai* is used only when the state is undesirable. Thus, its use in the sentences in [3] is not acceptable.

[3] a. 旧友と酒を飲みながら話すのは愉快{この上ない／*極まりない}。
 (= (2a))

 b. 皇室に待望の男の子が生まれて喜ばしいこと{この上ない／*極まりない}。(= (2b))

Note also that *kiwamari nai* cannot precede a noun that it modifies.

[4]　この国は、他の国の批判に耳を貸すこともなく、{この上ない /＊極^{きわ}まり

　　ない}ごう慢さをもって自国のイデオロギーを主張し続けている。

(= Ex.(j))

III. *Kagiri da* also means "extremely"; however, it is used only to express
the speaker's/writer's emotion. Thus, the sentences in [5] are acceptable,
but those in [6] are not.

[5]　a. 最近よく食事時にセールスの電話がかかってくるが、迷惑{この上な

　　　い / な限^{かぎ}りだ}。(= Ex.(a))

　　b. 皇室に待望の男の子が生まれて喜ばしい{ことこの上ない / 限りだ}。

(= (2b))

[6]　a. 生まれたばかりの赤ん坊を車に残して買い物に行くとは非常識{この

　　　上ない /＊な限^{かぎ}りだ}。(= KS(A))

　　b. この部屋はクーラーも扇風機もなく、風も全然通らないので、暑い{こ

　　　とこの上ない /＊限りだ}。(= KS(B))

(⇨ ***kagiri da*** (in this volume))

K

koto ka　ことか　　*phr.*　<w>

a sentence-final, exclamatory phrase used in written language	how ~ !; what a(n) ~ ! 【REL. *nē*; *nā*; *nan te/to ~ no/n da(rō)*】

◆ Key Sentences

(A)

	Wh-word	Prt.		Adj(*i*)inf	
カルフォルニアは	何	と	太陽^{たいよう}が	明るい	ことか。
(How bright the sun is in California!)					

(B)

		Counter		Vinf	
私は今までに	何	度	オーストラリアを	訪ねた	ことか。
(How many times I have visited Australia before now!)

Formation

(i) Wh-word + Prt. 〜 Adj(*i*)inf ことか。

何と{面白い / 面白かった}ことか。 (How interesting it is/was!)

どんなに{嬉しい / 嬉しかった}ことか。 (How happy I am/was!)

(ii) 何{Counter / と}〜 Vinf ことか。

何回{聞く / 聞いた}ことか。 (How many times we {are listening / have listened} to it!)

何とおいしく{食べる / 食べた}ことか。 (How we do/did enjoy eating!)

(iii) Wh-word 〜 Adj(*na*)stem{な / である / だった / であった}ことか。

いかに困難{な / である / だった / であった}ことか。 (How difficult s.t. is/was!)

(iv) Wh-word + Prt. 〜 N{である / だった / であった}ことか。

{いかに / 何と / 何たる}天才{である / だった / であった}ことか。
(What a genius s.o. is/was!)

(v) どれ{ほど / だけ}〜ことか。

どれほど望んだことか。 (How much s.o. has hoped for it!)

Examples

(a) アメリカの大学に比べると日本の大学は何と貧弱に見えることか。

(When compared with American universities, how unimpressive Japanese universities look!)

(b) ペダルを踏み替える時に膝がハンドルにぶつかる車がどんなに多いことか。

(How many cars are there in which the driver's knee hits the steering wheel whenever he switches pedals!)

(c) 日本語がよく読めるようになるためにどれぐらい勉強したことか。

(How much I studied in order to read Japanese well!)

(d) 新鮮な魚を探して何軒の魚屋を見て歩いたことか。

(How many fish shops I have gone to in search of fresh fish!)

(e) この数学の問題を解くのに何時間使ったことか。

(How many hours I have spent to solve this mathematical problem!)

(f) 日本人はいかにしばしば内と外の行動を区別することか。

(How often Japanese differentiate their behavior in inside and outside spaces!)

(g) 二人はどれだけ強く愛し合っていたことか。

(How strongly the two loved each other!)

Notes

1. The sentence-final phrase *koto ka* is an exclamation marker that is used with an interrogative alone, as in KS(A) and Exs.(a)-(c), an interrogative + Counter, as in KS(B), Exs.(d) and (e) or an interrogative + adverb, as in Ex.(f).

2. *Koto ka* is used only in written language.

[Related Expressions]

There are other exclamatory expressions in Japanese. Any word or phrase can be made exclamatory by using an emphatic intonation pattern, as in [1]. The use of *nē* or *nā* in the sentence-final position, as in [2], or the use of the pattern *nan te/to ~ no/n da(rō)*, as in [3], also creates exclamatory expressions.

[1] a. すごい！　(Wow!)

b. すごい美人！　((What a) gorgeous woman!)

c. やるーう！　(Good job!)

[2] a. あの木、大きい**ねえ**！　(What a big tree!)

b. あの車、かっこいい**なあ**！　(That car looks sharp!)

c. 映画、面白かった**ねえ**！　(The movie was so interesting!)

[3] a. **なん**{て／と}親切なんだろう！　(How kind he/she is!)

b. **なん**{て／と}ひどい話なんだ！　(What a horrible story!)

(⇨ *nā* (DIJG: 193-97))

koto kara   ことから   *phr.*   \<w\>

~~~
a phrase that expresses a reason or a
cause
~~~
because; due to; from the fact
that ~; cause; trigger
【REL. *kara*; *node*; **tokoro
kara**】

◆ **Key Sentences**

(A)

	Sinf		
彼は	アリバイが成立しなかった	ことから	犯行の嫌疑がかかった。

(Because (lit., from the fact that) he couldn't establish an alibi, he was
suspected of a criminal act.)

(B)

Adj(*na*)stem			
妙	な	ことから	二人の関係は悪化した。

(The relationship between the two people deteriorated due to strange
circumstances.)

Formation

(i)   {V / Adj(*i*)}inf ことから

　　{話す / 話した}ことから　(because s.o. talks/talked about s.t.;
　　　because of (lit., from) s.t. which s.o. talks/talked about)

　　{つまらない / つまらなかった}ことから　(because of s.t. trivial;
　　　because s.t. is/was boring)

(ii) Adj(*na*)stem{な / である / だった}ことから

　　不便{な / である / だった}ことから　(because s.t. is/was
　　　inconvenient)

(iii) N{である / だった / であった}ことから

　　学生{である / だった / であった}ことから　(because s.o. is/was a
　　　student)

Examples

(a) その教授は学生に高圧的だったことから、学生にひどく嫌われていた。

(The professor was so overbearing towards his students that he was thoroughly hated by them.)

(b) 今年は大学創立から 250 年に当たることから、盛大な記念祝典が開かれた。

(Because it is the 250th year since the founding of the college, there was a magnificent anniversary ceremony this year.)

(c) 私が余計なことを言ったことから議論が紛糾した。

(The discussion became complicated because I said something uncalled for.)

(d) 魚を水槽内で飼って行う研究は、長期的な観察が可能であることから、汎用性のあるデータが取得しやすい。

(Keeping fish in a tank for research allows us to obtain data for general use because long-term observation is possible.)

(e) 首相は不用意な言動が多かったことから、不信任案が議会で可決された。

(Because the prime minister was often careless in his statements and behavior, a no-confidence motion was passed in Parliament.)

(f) 本当にささいなことから会談は中止になってしまった。

(Because of a really trivial matter the conference broke up.)

Notes

1. The phrase ~ *koto kara* is used to express a reason, as in KS(A), Exs.(b), (d) and (e), or a cause, as in KS(B) and Exs.(a), (c) and (f).

2. *Koto* in the phrase *koto kara* can be either a nominalizer, as in (1a), or a noun which refers to an intangible thing, as in (1b).

(1) a. 彼が一つのアイディアについて話したことからプロジェクトが始まった。

(The project started because he talked about an idea.)

b. 彼が話したことから、プロジェクトが始まった。

(What he talked about triggered the project.)

【Related Expressions】

Kara and *node*, conjunctions of reason/cause, can replace Sinf *koto kara*. The use of *koto* adds the meaning of "based on the fact that ~."

[1] a. 彼はアリバイが成立しなかった{ことから / から / ので}犯行の嫌疑 がかかった。(= KS(A))

b. その教授は学生に高圧的だった{ことから / から / ので}、学生にひ どく嫌われていた。(= Ex.(a))

(⇨ ***kara***[3] (DBJG: 179-81); ***node*** (DBJG: 328-31))

koto ni ことに *phr.*

| a phrase that expresses the speaker's/ writer's emotion or subjective judgment | it is ~ that; I am ~ that ; we are ~ that; to my/our ~ ; ~ly 【REL. *to wa*; *ni mo*; ***kana***】 |

◆ **Key Sentences**

(A)

Adj(*i*)inf		
嬉しい	ことに、	今学期は祭日が3日もある。
(I'm glad that there are (as many as) three holidays this term.)		

(B)

Adj(*na*)stem			
残念	な	ことに、	この本は絶版で、普通の本屋では手に入らない。
(To my regret, this book is out of print and cannot be purchased at ordinary bookstores.)			

(C)

Vinf		
驚いた	ことに、	村田さんはあんなに気に入っていた会社を半年で辞めてしまった。

(I was surprised that Mr. Murata quit his job after six months—he seemed so excited about his work.)

Formation

(i)　Adj(*i*)inf ことに

　　{悲しい / 悲しかった} ことに　(it is/was sad that; sadly)

(ii)　Adj(*na*)stem {な / だった} ことに

　　幸い {な / だった} ことに　(it is/was fortunate that; fortunately)

(iii)　Vinf ことに

　　腹の {立つ / 立った} ことに　(I am/was mad that)

Examples

(a)　恥ずかしいことに、私は英文学専攻でありながら英語が話せない。

　　(It's embarrassing, but I can't speak English despite the fact that I'm an English literature major.)

(b)　面白いことに、ハワイの日系人の方が日本人より日本の古い伝統をよく守っているという。

　　(Interestingly, they say that Japanese-Americans in Hawaii maintain old Japanese traditions better than (Japanese) people in Japan.)

(c)　悪いことに、オーディションの前の日に風邪を引いてしまった。

　　(Unfortunately, I caught a cold the day before my audition.)

(d)　悔しいことに、私はロジャーに負けた。

　　(I was frustrated by my loss to Roger.)

(e)　吉岡さんのところの悦子ちゃんは、感心なことに、お母さんが仕事で遅くなる時は自分で晩ご飯を作るんだそうです。

　　(I'm so impressed with Etsuko, Yoshioka's daughter; they say she fixes dinner herself when her mother is late because of work.)

(f) 浄水器は濾過の過程で塩素をすべて取り去ってしまうため、濾過した瞬間から水は腐敗の危険にさらされる。さらに心配なことに、濾過材に残った水から大量に細菌が繁殖するといった問題が報道された。

(Because water purifiers remove all the chlorine in the purification process, from the moment it's been purified, there's a risk the water will get contaminated (lit., rot). What's even more worrisome, bacteria can multiply in the water left in the (purification) fixtures, according to media reports.)

(g) 厄介なことに、この種の詐欺は被害者が世間体のために警察に届けを出さないことが多く、これが犯人検挙を難しくしている。

(The trouble is, this kind of fraud is seldom reported to the police because the victims want to save face, which makes it hard to arrest the culprits.)

(h) 困ったことに、日本のDVDはアメリカのプレーヤーでは見られないのです。

(The problem is that Japanese DVDs cannot be viewed on American (DVD) players.)

(i) 腹の立つことに、私のフライトは5時間も待たされたあげく、キャンセルされた。

(It was maddening: After I was kept waiting for my flight for five full hours, in the end it was cancelled.)

Notes

1. With certain adjectives and verbs, *koto ni* links a situation, event or action with the speaker's/writer's feeling (e.g., *ureshii* "happy" or *kanashii* "sad") or his/her subjective judgment (e.g., *warui* "bad" or *omoshiroi* "interesting") about it. The adjectives and verbs that commonly occur with *koto ni* are as follows:

I-adjectives:

嬉しい (happy); ありがたい (thankful); 悲しい (sad); 寂しい (lonely); つらい (hard; painful); 情けない (shameful; pitiful); 悔しい (frustrating); 憎らしい (hateful); 腹立たしい (annoying); ばかばかしい (ridiculous); うっとうしい (depressing; annoying); わずらわしい (bothersome); 恐ろしい (scary); 恥ずかしい (embarrassing; shameful); 悪い (bad); 面白い (interesting)

Na-adjectives:

幸せな (happy); 幸いな (fortunate); 幸運な (lucky); 愉快な (fun); 不幸

な (unfortunate); 哀れな (pitiful); 残念な (regrettable); 面倒な (trouble-some); 厄介な (troublesome); 心配な (worrisome); 気掛かりな (worri-some); 感心な (admirable); 馬鹿な (stupid); 愚かな (stupid)

Verbs:

｛驚く / 驚いた｝(be surprised); びっくり｛する / した｝(be surprised); 困った (be in trouble); うんざり｛する / した｝(be fed up); 感激した (be moved); 失望した (be disappointed); 腹｛が / の｝｛立つ / 立った｝(be angry)

2. When adjectives are used with *koto ni*, their nonpast forms are common-ly used, even when the main clause is in the past tense. However, past forms are also acceptable, as shown in (1).

(1) a. ｛悲しい / 悲しかった｝ことに、彼は私を全然覚えていなかった。

(It is/was sad that he didn't remember me at all.)

b. 幸い｛な / だった｝ことに、私はその時携帯電話を持っていた。

(It is/was fortunate that I had a cell phone with me at the time.)

3. *Koto ni* usually expresses the emotion or subjective judgment of the first-person subject (i.e., I or we). However, if *koto ni* expresses someone's emotion and the topic subject is in the third person, it can express the emotions of the subject, as shown in (2).

(2) 恥ずかしいことに、ジョンは泳げなかった。

(John was ashamed that he couldn't swim.)

Note that if *koto ni* presents someone's subjective judgment and the topic subject is in the third person, it expresses the judgment of the speaker rather than the subject, as shown in (3). That is, in (3) it is the speaker who thinks it is interesting that Ken didn't know until recently that he was Japanese.

(3) 面白いことに、ケンは自分が日本人であることを最近まで知らなかった。

(Interestingly, Ken didn't know until recently that he was Japanese.)

In this case, the speaker is empathetic with the subject.

4. In general, in order to express the emotions of a third-person subject, different sentence structures are used, as demonstrated in (4).

(4) a. 久保先生はその本が絶版で普通の本屋では手に入らないことを残念に思っている。(cf. KS(B))

(Prof. Kubo thinks it's unfortunate that that book is out of print and cannot be purchased at ordinary bookstores.)

b. 渡辺さんは、村田さんがあんなに気に入っていた会社を半年で辞めてしまったので驚いた。(cf. KS(C))

(Ms. Watanabe was surprised that only after six months Mr. Murata quit his job, which he seemed so excited about.)

c. アンディーはロジャーに負けて悔しがった。(cf. Ex.(d))

(Andy was frustrated by his loss to Roger.)

d. 彼は、5時間も待たされたあげくフライトがキャンセルされて、腹を立てている。(cf. Ex.(i))

(After he was kept waiting for five full hours, in the end, his flight was cancelled, so he was very mad.)

[Related Expressions]

I. *To wa* is also used to express the speaker's/writer's emotion. Sentences with *koto ni* can be rephrased using *to wa*, as shown in [1].

[1] a. 今学期は祭日が3日もあるとは嬉しい。(cf. KS(A))

b. この本は絶版で、普通の本屋では手に入らないとは残念だ。

(cf. KS(B))

c. 村田さんがあんなに気に入っていた会社を半年で辞めてしまったとは驚いた。(cf. KS(C))

However, *to wa* is used to express the speaker's/writer's reaction to something he/she has only just learned about.

(⇨ *to wa* (in this volume))

II. *Ni mo* is also used to express the speaker's/writer's emotion or subjective judgment, as shown in [2].

[2] a. 幸いにも、私はその時携帯電話を持っていた。(cf. (1b))

(Fortunately, I had a cell phone with me at the time.)

b. 感心にも、吉岡さんのところの悦子ちゃんは、お母さんが仕事で遅くなる時は自分で晩ご飯を作るんだそうです。(cf. Ex.(e))

(I'm impressed with Etsuko, Yoshioka's daughter; they say she fixes dinner herself when her mother is late because of work.)

However, *ni mo* can be used only with a limited set of *na*-adjectives, including those in [3], and cannot be used with *i*-adjectives or verbs.

[3] 幸いにも (fortunately); 幸運にも (fortunately); 不幸にも (unfortunately); 感心にも (I admire; it's impressive); 愚かにも (it is stupid); 哀れにも (I am sorry); 不覚にも (in spite of oneself)

kuwaete 加えて   *conj.*   <w>

a conjunction that means "in addition to what has just been mentioned"

in addition; and additionally; what's more
【REL. *dake de naku ~ (mo)*; *bakari de naku ~ (mo)*; *sono ue (ni)*; *katsu*】

K

◆ **Key Sentences**

(A)

	Noun₁	Noun₂		Noun₃	
この冬のアメリカ東部は	雪、	雨、	加えて	強風	の被害が大きかった。

(This winter the East Coast of the U.S. suffered terribly from snow, rain and, in addition, strong winds.)

(B)

Sentence₁			Sentence₂
この辺は物価が安い。	(それに)	加えて	自然環境もすばらしい。

(Things are inexpensive in this neighborhood. What's more, the natural environment is amazing.)

Formation

(i) N₁、N₂、(……、) 加えて N

酒、ビール、加えてウイスキー (*sake*, beer, and on top of that, whisky)

(ii) S₁。（それに）加えて S₂。

　　彼は頭が切れる。（それに）加えて人柄もいい。　　(He is sharp. In addition, he has a good personality.)

Examples

(a) この作家の小説は想像力の豊かさ、鮮明な文体、加えて、極めて音楽的なリズム感がある。

(The novels of this author are richly imaginative, have a clear-cut style, and, in addition, have a highly musical rhythm.)

(b) 金融業の倒産、失業率の上昇、加えて、不安定な政治状況によって、この国の経済は沈滞している。

(The bankruptcy of financial institutions, the rise in the unemployment rate, and, additionally, political instability are causing the stagnation of this country's economy.)

(c) 健康維持には正しい食事、適度な運動、加えて人との温かいコミュニケーションが必要であろう。

(In order to maintain your health, a proper diet, moderate exercise and, what's more, amiable communication with other people are necessary.)

(d) 彼女はおしゃべりが好きで、とても明るい。それに加えて、なかなかユニークなキャラクターだ。

(She likes to chat and is very cheerful. In addition, she has a unique character.)

(e) 北海道の秋は紅葉がきれいだ。加えて、空気がからっと乾燥していて気持ちがいい。

(The fall foliage in Hokkaido is beautiful. In addition, the crisp, dry air feels good.)

(f) 京都は神社仏閣がたくさんある。加えて、魅力的な日本庭園も多い。

(Kyoto has many shrines and temples. In addition, it has many charming traditional gardens.)

Note

The conjunction *kuwaete* is the *te*-form of the verb *kuwaeru* "add." It can be used to combine nouns, as shown in KS(A) and Exs.(a)-(c), or to combine sentences, as in KS(B) and Exs.(d)-(f). In the latter case, *sore ni* can precede *kuwaete*; the demonstrative pronoun *sore* refers back to the content of S$_1$.

〖Related Expressions〗

I.　The phrase ~ *dake/bakari de wa naku* ~ *(mo)* "not only ~ but also ~" can replace the use of *kuwaete* in both Formation (i) and (ii) without changing the basic meaning, as shown below.

[1]　a. この冬のアメリカ東部は雪、雨｛だけ / ばかり｝ではなく、強風の被害が大きかった。(cf. KS(A))

　　　b. この辺は物価が安い｛だけ / ばかり｝ではなく、自然環境もすばらしい。(cf. KS(B))

Dake/bakari de wa naku ~ *(mo)* can be used in both spoken and written Japanese, but *kuwaete* is used only in written Japanese.

(⇨ ***dake de (wa) naku*** ~ ***(mo)*** (DBJG: 97-100))

K

II.　The conjunction *sono ue (ni)* "on top of that" can replace *(sore ni) kuwaete* in Formation (i) and (ii), as shown in [2] and [3], respectively, without a change in meaning. The particle *ni* of *sono ue ni* can be used in sentences using Formation (i), as shown in [2], but cannot be used in sentences using Formation (ii), as shown in [3].

[2]　a. この冬のアメリカ東部は雪、雨、｛加えて / その上 (に)｝強風の被害が大きかった。(= KS(A))

　　　b. この作家の小説は想像力の豊かさ、鮮明な文体、｛加えて / その上 (に)｝、極めて音楽的なリズム感がある。(= Ex.(a))

[3]　a. 彼女はおしゃべりが好きで、とても明るい。｛それに加えて / その上 / *その上に｝、なかなかユニークなキャラクターだ。(= Ex.(d))

　　　b. 京都は神社仏閣がたくさんある。｛加えて / その上 / *その上に｝、魅力的な日本庭園も多い。(= Ex.(f))

Sono ue (ni) can be used in both spoken and written Japanese.

(⇨ ***sono ue*** (DIJG: 413-17))

made (no koto) da　まで (のこと) だ　*phr.*

| a phrase indicating s.o.'s decision to cope with a negative situation, or a simple, straight forward reason for his/ her action | just; merely; only 【REL. *dake (no koto) da*】 |

◆ **Key Sentences**

(A)

		Vinf	
もし TOEFL の点が悪かったら	もう一度	受ける	まで (のこと) だ。

(If my TOEFL score isn't good, then I'll just take the test again.)

(B)

	Vinf	
日本語は面白そうだったので、	取った	まで (のこと) だ。

(I took Japanese language only because it looked interesting (not for any other reason).)

Formation

Vinf まで (のこと) だ

帰るまで (のこと) だ　(s.o. will just go home, and that's all)

言ったまで (のこと) だ　(s.o. just said s.t., and that's all)

Examples

(a) 結婚できなかったら、一生独身で仕事をするまでのことだ。

(If I cannot marry I will just stay single for the rest of my life and do my work.)

(b) 就職できなかったら、フリーターになるまでのことだ。

(If I cannot get a regular job, I will just become a permanent part-time worker.)

(c) バスが来ないんなら歩いて帰るまでだ。

(If a bus doesn't come, I will just walk home.)

(d) 夕食にどうぞと言われたから彼女のアパートに行ったまでだ。とやかく言われる筋合いはない。

(I went to her apartment just because she invited me over to dinner. You have no right to say such a critical thing to me.)

(e) 小説みたいなものを書いたが、別に小説家になりたいと思ったのではない。小説を書くということがどんなことか知りたかったまでのことだ。

(I've written something like a novel, but I never particularly thought I wanted to be a novelist. I just wanted to know what it was like to write a novel. That's all.)

(f) あなたに私の個人的なことを話したのは、あなたの将来に多少役立つかと思ったまでのことです。

(The reason I told you about my personal matters is just because I thought it would be useful for you in the future. Nothing more and nothing less.)

Notes

1. The phrase *made (no koto) da* is used to express the idea that the speaker's decision to do something to cope with a negative situation, as in KS(A) and Exs.(a)-(c), or a simple, straightforward reason for someone's action, as in KS(B) and Exs.(d)-(f), doesn't go beyond the decision/reason expressed in the preceding phrase.

2. The decision maker cannot be the second or third person, as shown in (1) below.

(1) a. 結婚できなかったら、{私 / ??あなた / ??彼}は一生独身で仕事をするまでのことだ。(cf. Ex.(a))

b. 就職できなかったら、{私 / ??あなた / ??彼}はフリーターになるまでのことだ。(cf. Ex.(b))

A person who gives a reason can be the third person, as shown in (2).

(2) a. {私 / 彼 / *あなた}は日本語が面白そうだったので、取ったまで（のこと）だ。(cf. KS(B))

b. {私 / 彼 / *あなた}は夕食にどうぞと言われたから彼女のアパートに行ったまでだ。(cf. Ex.(d))

【Related Expression】

The phrase *dake (no koto) da* can replace *made (no koto) da* as long as the former is used to mean the speaker's decision or the actual reason, as shown in [1].

[1] a. もしTOEFLの点が悪かったらもう一度受ける｛まで／だけ｝(のこと)だ。(= KS(A))

b. 日本語は面白そうだったので、取った｛まで／だけ｝(のこと)だ。

(= KS(B))

Dake (no koto) da cannot be replaced by *made (no koto) da* when the sentence means "all s.o. has to do is ~," as in [2].

[2] a. これは簡単な書類です。ここに名前と住所を書く｛だけ／*まで｝のことです。

(This is a simple form. All you have to do is to write your name and address here.)

b. 健康になるには規則的な生活をする｛だけ／*まで｝のことなんです。

(To become healthy you just need to live a regular life.)

M

---

mashite(ya) まして（や） *adv.*

| an adverb expressing the idea that because one statement is true, the subsequent statement is naturally true | to say nothing of; not to speak of; let alone; still more; much less; all the more reason why 【REL. *dokoroka*; *iwan'ya*】 |

◆ **Key Sentences**

(A)

Subordinate Clause		Main Clause
アパートの家賃を払うのが精一杯なのに、	まして（や）	家を買うなんて夢物語だ。

(I am just managing to pay the rent for my apartment; how much more of a dream it is to imagine buying my own house!)

(B)

Sentence₁		Sentence₂
彼女は日本語で講演もできる。	まして（や）	日常会話など問題ではない。

(She can give a speech in Japanese, to say nothing of (her ability to handle) everyday conversation.)

Formation

(i)　Subordinate Clause、まして（や）Main Clause。

　　　(⇨ KS(A))

(ii)　S₁。まして（や）S₂。

　　　(⇨ KS(B))

Examples

(a)　この小説は大人にも読みにくいのに、まして小学生に読めるはずがない。

　　　(This novel is hard even for adults to read much less elementary school students.)

(b)　彼は簡単な日本語すら話せない。ましてや、書くことなど思いもよらない。

　　　(He cannot even speak Japanese, let alone write it.)

(c)　僕は自転車さえ買えない。まして、車を買うなんて不可能だ。

　　　(I can't even buy a bike, let alone a car.)

(d)　国内での単身赴任でもつらい。ましてや、外国での単身赴任となるともっとつらい。

　　　(To be sent alone to a new post within Japan is hard. It is still harder to go overseas to work without one's family.)

(e) この数学の問題は教授でも解けないのだから、まして、学生の僕に解けるはずがない。

(Even a professor cannot solve this math problem much less a student like me.)

(f) 65歳の人が毎日1キロ泳いでいるんです。まして、32歳のあなたが同じことができないわけがないですよ。

(There's a 65-year-old man who swims one kilometer every day. All the more reason why a 32-year-old like you should be able to do the same.)

(g) ニューヨークのような大都市でも犯罪率を下げることに成功している。ましてや、中小都市なら十分可能だろう。

(Even a big city like New York has been successful in lowering the crime rate, which is all the more reason why mid- and small-sized cities should be able to lower theirs.)

(h) このちっぽけな蟻だって協力し合っているんです。まして、頭脳の発達した人間にそれができないわけはないでしょう。

(These tiny ants are cooperating with each other—all the more reason why humans with our developed brains should be able to do the same.)

Notes

1. The adverb *mashite(ya)* expresses the idea that because the statement before *mashite* is true, the statement that comes after *mashite* is naturally true.

2. *Mashiteya* is usually used in written language, but *mashite* can be used in both spoken and written language.

【Related Expressions】

I. The conjunction *dokoroka*, which expresses the idea that someone or something is very far from what is expected, can replace *mashite(ya)*, as shown in [1] below.

[1] a. 家を買う**どころか**、アパートの家賃を払うのが精一杯だ。(cf. KS(A))
(Far from being able to buy a house, all I can do is pay the (apartment) rent.)

b. この小説は小学生に読める**どころか**、大人にも読みにくい。(cf. Ex.(a))
(It is not just that an elementary school students cannot read this novel. It is hard to read even for an adult.)

　　　c. 彼女は日常会話など問題ではないどころか、日本語で講演もできる。

(cf. KS(B))

(She isn't just able to conduct daily conversation without any problem. She can even give a lecture in Japanese.)

(⇨ **dokoroka** (DIJG: 34-36))

II. There is another adverb, *iwan'ya*, that can replace *mashite(ya)*. It expresses the idea that because the statement before *iwan'ya* is true, the statement made after *iwan'ya* is also true, as shown in [2].

　　[2]　a. アパートの家賃を払うのが精一杯なのに、｛まして(や) / いわんや｝家を買うなんて夢物語だ。(= KS(A))

　　　　b. 彼女は日本語で講演もできる。｛まして(や) / いわんや｝日常会話など問題ではない。(= KS(B))

　　　　c. この小説は大人にも読みにくいのに、｛まして(や) / いわんや｝小学生に読めるはずがない。(= Ex.(a))

M

mata また　　*adv. / conj.*

an adverb/conjunction that indicates repetition or addition	again; also; too; (not) ~ either; and; additionally; or [REL. *aruiwa*; **katsu**]

◆ **Key Sentences**

(A)

		Verb
来年の春、	また	お会いします。
(I will see you again next spring.)		

(B)

Noun		Noun			Noun			Noun	
山田	も	東京出身	だ	が、	林	も	また	東京出身	だ。

(Yamada is from Tokyo, and Hayashi, too, is from Tokyo.)

(C)

	Nom.		Adj(*i*)	
机に座ってものを考える	の	も	いい	が、

	Nom.			Adj(*i*)
歩きながら考える	の	も	また	いい。

(Thinking while sitting at a desk is fine, but thinking while walking is also good.)

(D)

	Adj(*i*)stem			
この日本語の教科書は内容も	面白	く、	また	文法の記述が正確だ。

(This Japanese textbook is interesting, and the grammar explanations are also accurate.)

(E)

Sentence₁		Sentence₂
発表は英語でしてもよい。	また、	日本語でしてもよい。

(You may present your paper in English. Or, you may do so in Japanese.)

(F)

Sentence₁			Sentence₂
発表は英語でしてもよい	し、	また、	日本語でしてもよい。

(You may present your paper in English or you may do so in Japanese.)

Formation

(i)　また V　[repetition]

　　　また来る　(s.o. will come again)

(ii) N もまた [addition]

猫もまた (哺乳動物だ) (a cat is also a mammal)

(iii) Nom. もまた [addition]

酒をオンザロックで飲むのもまた (いい) (drinking *sake* on the rocks is not bad either)

文化を学ぶこともまた大切だ (studying culture is also important)

(iv) ～{V*masu* / Adj(*i*)stem く}、また、S。 [additional information]

彼女はピアノを巧みに弾き、また、歌もうまい。 (She plays the piano well, and also sings well.)

ここは景色もすばらしく、また、空気もきれいだ。 (The scenery is marvelous here, and the air is clean, too.)

(v) ～{Adj(*na*)stem / N}で(あり)、また、S。 [additional information]

彼女は聡明で(あり)、また、性格もよい。 (She is bright, and her character is also fine.)

彼はピアニストで(あり)、また、指揮者でもある。 (He is a pianist and also a conductor.)

(vi) S₁。また、S₂。 [additional information]

登録はあらかじめして下さい。また、当日も受け付けいたします。 (Please register beforehand. You can register (lit., We will accept your registration) on the day of the conference, too.)

(vii) S₁ し、また、S₂。 [additional information]

登録は学会の1か月前から受け付けますし、また、当日も受け付けいたします。 (We will accept your registration starting one month before the conference, but you can register on the day of the conference, too.)

Examples

(a) 今日もまた雪が降った。

(It snowed again today.)

(b) また風邪をひいちゃった。

(I caught a cold again!)

(c) 大統領もまた人間だ。過ちを犯すこともあるだろう。

(The president is also human. He may sometimes make mistakes.)

(d) 大学で勉強をするのはもちろん大切だが、生涯の友達を作るのもまた大切だ。

(Needless to say, it is very important to study at college, but it is also important to make lifetime friends there.)

(e) 彼は優れた研究者であり、また、優れた教育者でもある。

(He is a fine researcher, and he is also a fine educator.)

(f) 日本は失業率が高くなってきている。また、株価も急落している。

(In Japan, the unemployment rate is on the rise. And additionally, stock prices are rapidly dropping.)

(g) この会議には出席してもよい。また、出席しなくてもよい。

(You may attend this meeting. But, you don't have to attend.)

(h) 日中間の相互理解を図る上で、文化交流は大変重要だし、また大変有益だ。

(In achieving mutual understanding between Japan and China cultural exchange is very important, and beneficial as well.)

Notes

1. The adverb *mata* means repetition in the sense of "again," as shown in Formation (i). The conjunction *mata* expresses either repetition or addition, as shown in the five constructions in Formation (ii)-(vii). It can be used to express repetition of action, as in Formation (i) (and demonstrated in KS(A), Exs.(a) and (b)), or to express addition in the sense of "also; too," as in Formation (ii) (KS(B) and Ex.(c)) and Formation (iii) (KS(C) and Ex.(d)). In "S_1 *mata* S_2" where *mata* indicates additional information, S_1 can be either a sentence that ends with the continuative form, as in Formation (iv) and (v) (KS(D) and Ex.(e)), a complete sentence, as in Formation (vi) (KS(E), Exs.(f) and (g)), or a sentence that ends with the conjunction *shi*, as in Formation (vii) (KS(F) and Ex.(h)).

2. *Mata wa* "or" appears as part of the structure "S_1. *Mata wa* ~," as in (1), or "N_1 *ka*, *mata wa* N_2," as in (2). In (2), *mata wa* is optional and can be dropped because in this situation it is redundant.

   (1) a. 発表は英語でしてもよい。**また（は）**、日本語でしてもよい。(= KS(E))

   b. この会議には出席してもよい。**また（は）**、出席しなくてもよい。

   (= Ex.(g))

   (2) a. 山田**か（、または）**田中が代表で会議に出る。

   (Either Yamada or Tanaka will represent us at the meeting.)

b. 電子メール**か**(、**または**)ファックスで送って下さい。

(Please send it to me either by e-mail or by fax.)

c. 試験を受ける**か**(、**または**)レポートを提出しなければならない。

(You have to take an exam or submit a research paper.)

【Related Expression】

When *mata* expresses another choice, as in KS(E), (F) and Ex.(g), it can be
replaced by *aruiwa*.   (⇨ **aruiwa** (in this volume))

metta ni ~ nai   滅多に～ない   *str.*

~~~~~~~~~~~~~~~~~~~~~~~~~~~~~~~~~~~~
a structure that indicates extremely
low frequency
~~~~~~~~~~~~~~~~~~~~~~~~~~~~~~~~~~~~

rarely; seldom; hardly; almost
never
【REL. *tama ni wa*; *amari ~ nai*;
hotondo ~ nai; *toki tama shika
~ nai*; *zenzen ~ nai*; *mattaku ~
nai*】

◆ Key Sentence

		Vneg	
この辺りでは地震は	滅多に	**起き**	ない。

(Earthquakes seldom occur in this area.)

Formation

滅多に～ Vneg ない

　滅多に外国に行かない   (s.o. seldom goes abroad)

　滅多に肉を食べない   (s.o. seldom eats meat)

Examples

(a) 日本の父親は忙しいので、週末でも滅多にうちにいない。

(Japanese fathers are so busy that even on weekends they are seldom at
home.)

(b) 大学時代の同級生とは滅多に会えない。

(I can hardly ever see my college classmates.)

(c) 日本の車は滅多に故障しないので、海外で人気がある。

(Because Japanese cars rarely break down, they are popular abroad.)

(d) 汚染のためにこの川では滅多に魚が泳いでいるのを見られなくなった。

(Due to pollution, we almost never see fish swimming in this river now.)

Note

Metta ni ~ nai indicates an extremely low frequency of something. *Metta ni* is always used with a negative verb.

【Related Expressions】

I. Both *metta ni* and *tama ni wa* indicate an extremely rare occurrence; while *metta ni* focuses on negative aspects, *tama ni wa* focuses on positive aspects. For example, in [1a] the speaker is focusing on the negative aspect of not studying Japanese frequently, but in [1b] the speaker is focusing on the positive aspect of studying Japanese, in spite of the low frequency.

[1] a. ジョンは**滅多に**日本語を<u>勉強しません</u>。

(John seldom studies Japanese.)

b. ジョンは**たまには**日本語を<u>勉強します</u>。

(John studies Japanese every once in a while.)

II. The scale of frequency (from high to low) of the related adverbial phrases is as follows:

[2] あまり～ない ＞ ほとんど～ない ＞ ｛滅多に／時たましか｝～ない
　　　＞ ｛全然／全く｝～ない

Note that the adverbial phrases *amari ~ nai*, *hotondo ~ nai* and *zenzen/ mattaku ~ nai* do not exclusively indicate frequency, but *metta ni ~ nai* and *toki tama shika ~ nai* indicate frequency only. The adverbs in [3a], [4a] and [5a] express frequency, but those in [3b], [4b] and [5b] express a meaning other than frequency.

[3] a. 最近彼は**あまり**ゴルフをやってい**ない**。

(Lately he doesn't play much golf.)

b. この辞書はあまり役に立た**ない**。

(This dictionary isn't very useful.)

[4] a. 忙しくてほとんど映画を見てい**ない**。

(I'm so busy that I've hardly seen any movies.)

b. 中国のことは**ほとんど**何も知ら**ない**。

(I barely know anything about China.)

[5] a. 僕は{**全然**/**全く**}運動をしてい**ない**。

(I don't exercise at all.)

b. 彼女は政治には{**全然**/**全く**}興味が**ない**。

(She isn't interested in politics at all.)

(⇨ **amari** (DBJG: 72-73))

M

miru kara ni   見るからに   *phr.*

---

a phrase indicating that s.t. can be (obviously) recognized through visual cues

visibly; obviously; really look; can be easily recognized as; can tell just by looking at ~
【REL. *akiraka ni*; *ikanimo*】

◆ **Key Sentences**

(A)

		Adj(*i*)stem	
太陽の光をたっぷり浴びたみかんは、	見るからに	**おいし**	そうだ。
(The sun-bathed mandarin oranges look really delicious.)			

(B)

彼女が身につけているものは	見るからに	高級品だった。
(What she wears is obviously of high quality.)		

Formation

(i) 見るからに Adj(*i/na*)stem そうだ

見るからに面白そうだ　(s.t. is obviously interesting)

見るからに元気そうだ　(s.o. is obviously healthy)

(ii) 見るからに〜

見るからに日本人だ　(s.o. is obviously Japanese)

見るからに失望している　(s.o. is obviously disappointed)

Examples

(a) このパンは見るからに手作りという感じですね。

(This bread is obviously homemade.)

(b) その青年は見るからに聡明そうだった。

(You could tell just by looking that the young man was intelligent.)

(c) 老人が見るからに重そうな買い物袋を抱えて歩いている。

(The old man is walking with a shopping bag that is obviously heavy.)

(d) その写真には見るからに寂しそうな孤児たちが写っていた。

(In that picture the orphans were obviously lonely.)

(e) 阪神・淡路大震災の時は見るからに新聞記者らしい人たちが大勢写真を撮っていた。

(At the time of the Great Hanshin-Awaji Earthquake, a lot of people who could easily be recognized as news reporters were taking pictures.)

(f) 彼の顔は青黒くむくみ、見るからに健康を害していた。

(His face was pale, dark and swollen. You could tell just by looking at him that he was in poor health.)

(g) 見るからにジューシーなお肉にかぶりつくと、うまみが口の中に広がっていった。

(I took a big bite into a visibly juicy piece of meat. Delicious flavor started to fill my mouth.)

(h) このスープは野菜たっぷりで、見るからに体によさそう！

(This soup has plenty of vegetables and looks really healthy!)

(i) この男の人、見るからに誠実で優しそうね。

(This man looks really honest and kind, doesn't he?)

Notes

1. The adverbial phrase *miru kara ni* is used in two ways. The first use, with auxiliaries like *sōda* and *rashii*, describes the way someone/something looks or feels. Here *miru kara ni* emphasizes that X really looks ~ or really feels ~, as in KS(A), Exs.(a)-(e), (h) and (i). The second use indicates that the nature of something/someone can be recognized just by looking at it/him/her. Here *miru kara ni* conveys the meaning "visibly; obviously," as in KS(B), Exs.(f) and (g). (⇨ **rashii** (DBJG: 373-75))

2. *Miru kara ni* cannot be used with *yōda/mitaida*, because both phrases are expressions of conjecture based not just on visual cues but also on reasoning and judgment.

   (1) a. *太陽の光をたっぷり浴びたみかんは、見るからにおいしい｛よう／みたい｝だ。(cf. KS(A))

   b. *その写真には見るからに寂しい｛よう／みたい｝な孤児たちが写っていた。(cf. Ex.(d))

   c. ?このスープは野菜たっぷりで、見るからに体にいい｛よう／みたい｝だ。(cf. Ex.(h))

   d. ?この男の人、見るからに誠実で優しい｛よう／みたい｝ね。(cf. Ex.(i))

   (⇨ **yōda** (DBJG: 547-52))

3. *Kara ni* can also be used with *kiku* "hear; listen." *Kiku kara ni* indicates that it is easy to recognize something through auditory cues. Examples follow.

   (2) a. ゆったりした音楽を聞きながらたっぷりマッサージを受けるなんて、聞くからにリラックスできそうです。

   (Having a nice, long massage while listening to soft music . . . just hearing those words makes a person feel relaxed.)

   b. 「地獄谷」というのは、聞くからに身の毛がよだつ名前ですね。

   ("Valley of Hell": Just hearing the name makes my hair stand on end.)

【Related Expressions】

I. The adverb *akiraka ni* "obviously" cannot replace *miru kara ni* when it is used with *sō da* or *kanji da*, as shown in [1], because *akiraka ni* is used when someone is convinced that something is factual.

[1] a. 太陽の光をたっぷり浴びたみかんは、{見るからに / *明らかに} おいしそうだ。(= KS(A))

b. このパンは {見るからに / ??明らかに} 手作りという感じですね。
(= Ex.(a))

c. その青年は {見るからに / *明らかに} 聡明そうだった。(= Ex.(b))

But replacing *miru kara ni* is possible in situations like those below:

[2] a. 彼女が身につけているものは {見るからに / 明らかに} 高級品だった。
(= KS(B))

b. 彼の顔は青黒くむくみ、{見るからに / 明らかに} 健康を害していた。
(= Ex.(f))

II. The adverb *ikanimo* meaning "s.t. is indeed the case" can replace *miru kara ni* in all the KS and Exs., as shown in [3].

[3] a. 太陽の光をたっぷり浴びたみかんは、{見るからに / いかにも} おいしそうだ。(= KS(A))

b. このパンは {見るからに / いかにも} 手作りという感じですね。
(= Ex.(a))

c. 彼女が身につけているものは {見るからに / いかにも} 高級品だった。
(= KS(B))

d. 彼の顔は青黒くむくみ、{見るからに / いかにも} 健康を害していた。
(= Ex.(f))

But *miru kara ni* cannot replace *ikanimo* when the latter means "what you have said is indeed right," as shown in [4].

[4] A: 失礼ですが、千鶴子さんのお父さまですか。
(Excuse me, but are you Chizuko's father?)

B: ｛いかにも／*見るからに｝私は千鶴子の父親ですが、それがどうか
しましたか。
(Yes, indeed, I am Chizuko's father, but why do you ask?)

(⇨ ***ikanimo*** (DIJG: 66-70))

~ mo [V] ba ~ mo [V]   ～も [V] ば～も [V]   *str.*   <w>

a structure used to present typical examples of actions, events, situations,
people, or things among a number of
possibilities

there are times when ~ and/
or ~; sometimes ~ and sometimes ~; sometimes do things
like ~ and ~; some (people/etc.)
~ and some (people/etc.) ~
[REL. ~ *mo* [V] *shi ~ mo* [V];
~*tari ~tari suru*]

◆ **Key Sentences**

(A)

	V₁*masu*			V₂*masu*		
父は感情的な人ではな いが、時に	怒り	も	すれば	泣き	も	する。

(My father is not an emotional person, but there are times when he gets
angry and times when he cries.)

(B)

	Noun₁		V₁cond		Noun₂		V₂
私だって	ロック	も	聞け	ば	ダンス	も	する。

(Even I sometimes (do things like) listen to rock music and dance.)

(C)

	Noun₁	Prt.		V₁cond	
日本全国が担当地域なので	北海道	(へ)	も	行け	ば

Noun₂	Prt.		V₂
沖縄	(へ)	も	行く。

(Because my area of responsibility covers all of Japan, I may go to Hokkaido or Okinawa (or wherever else in Japan).)

(D)

	Noun Phrase₁				
	S₁inf				
交通事情によって	30分で行ける	こと	も	あれ	ば

Noun Phrase₂		
S₂inf		
1時間以上かかる	こと	も	ある。

(Depending on the traffic situation, sometimes it takes only 30 minutes to get there and sometimes it takes more than an hour.)

M

Formation

(i) V₁*masu* もすれば V₂*masu* もする

　　笑いもすれば泣きもする   (sometimes laugh and sometimes cry)

(ii) NP₁(Prt.) も V₁cond ば NP₂(Prt.) も V₂

　　古いのもあれば最新のもある   (some are old ones and some are the most recent ones)

　　映画も見ればコンサートへも行く   (sometimes do things like watching movies and going to concerts)

(iii) {Adj(*i*)₁stem く / Adj(*na*)₁stem に} も V₁cond ば {Adj(*i*)₂stem く / Adj(*na*)₂stem に} も V₂

　　やさしくもなれば難しくもなる   (sometimes become easy and sometimes difficult)

　　有利にもなれば不利にもなる   (sometimes become advantageous and sometimes disadvantageous)

Examples

(a) 円満な夫婦は口論もすれば不満も言い合う。

(A happy husband and wife may sometimes argue and sometimes complain to each other.)

(b) 私は子供をよく可愛いがるが、悪いことをしたら怒りもすれば叱りもする。

(I adore my children, but when they do something bad, sometimes I get mad and sometimes I scold them.)

(c) この学会では英語で発表する人もいれば日本語で発表する人もいる。

(At this conference some people give presentations in English and some give them in Japanese.)

(d) 人生は晴れの日もあれば雨の日もある。

(In life, there are sunny days as well as rainy days.)

(e) うちの会社は服装の規則がないので、スーツを着て行く時もあればセーターで行く時もある。

(Because my company has no dress code, sometimes I go in a suit and sometimes in a sweater.)

(f) 担当の先生が来られない時は、代わりの先生を頼むこともあれば、やむを得ず休講にすることもある。

(When the teacher in charge of the class cannot come, we sometimes ask a substitute to teach, and sometimes have no choice but to cancel class.)

(g) アイディアが突然湧き上がってくる時もあれば、全く出てこない時もある。

(Sometimes ideas well up all of the sudden, and sometimes nothing comes to mind (lit., comes out).)

(h) 外国語は勉強の仕方次第で、面白くもなればつまらなくもなる。

(Depending on the way you study it, a foreign language can be interesting or boring.)

Notes

1. "X *mo* V₁cond *ba* Y *mo* V₂" means that sometimes someone does one thing (or one thing happens) and sometimes he/she does another thing (or another thing happens). Although this construction involves a conditional form, it carries no conditional meaning. It is commonly used to present typical examples of actions, events, situations, etc., from among a number of possibilities.

2. In "X *mo* V₁cond *ba* Y *mo* V₂," "X *mo* V₁cond *ba*" can be either "V*masu mo sureba*" (e.g., *naki mo sureba* "sometimes cry") or "N *mo* Vcond *ba*" (e.g., *manga mo yomeba* "sometimes read comics"), and "Y *mo* V₂" can be either "V*masu mo suru*" (e.g., *warai mo suru* "sometimes laugh") or "N *mo* V" (e.g., *eiga mo miru* "sometimes watch movies"). Mixing patterns (i) and (ii) in the Formations is also possible (e.g., *okori mo sureba, monku mo iu* "sometimes get angry and sometimes complain").

3. "S₁ *koto/toki mo areba* S₂ *koto/toki mo aru*" is a common pattern involving the structure "X *mo* V₁cond *ba* Y *mo* V₂." In this case, X and Y are *koto* or *toki* clauses, which are noun equivalents.

[Related Expressions]

I. "*~ mo* V *shi ~ mo* V" carries the same meaning as "*~ mo* Vcond *ba ~ mo* V." The difference is that the former is more colloquial.

   [1] a. 父は感情的な人ではないが、時に怒りも｛すれば／するし｝泣きもする。(= KS(A))

   b. 私だってロックも｛聞けば／聞くし｝ダンスもする。(= KS(B))

   c. 日本全国が担当地域なので北海道へも｛行けば／行くし｝沖縄へも行く。(= KS(C))

   d. 交通事情によって30分で行けることも｛あれば／あるし｝1時間以上かかることもある。(= KS(D))

II. When X *~tari* Y *~tari suru* "do things like X and Y" represents habitual actions or situations, it is synonymous with "*~ mo* Vcond *ba ~ mo* V," as shown in [2].

   [2] a. 父は感情的な人ではないが、時に怒ったり泣いたりする。(cf. KS(A))
   (My father is not an emotional person, but sometimes he gets mad and sometimes he cries.)

   b. 私だってロックを聞いたりダンスをしたりする。(cf. KS(B))
   (Even I (do things like) listen to rock music and dance.)

   c. 日本全国が担当地域なので北海道へ行ったり沖縄へ行ったりする。
   (cf. KS(C))
   (Because my area of responsibility covers all of Japan, sometimes I go to Hokkaido and sometimes to Okinawa.)

M

d. 交通事情によって 30 分で行け**たり** 1 時間以上かかっ**たりする**。

(cf. KS(D))

(Depending on the traffic situation, sometimes it takes only 30 minutes to get there and sometimes it takes more than an hour.)

The major difference between the two expressions is that "X *mo* Vcond *ba* Y *mo* V" implies that the subject takes a number of actions in addition to X and Y, or that a number of situations other than X and Y occur, whereas ~*tari* ~*tari suru* does not carry that implication and simply lists actions non-exhaustively. For example, [3a] implies that a happy man and wife sometimes argue and sometimes complain to each other while they do many other things, most of which are happy. On the other hand, [3b] indicates that a happy man and wife do things like arguing and complaining to each other but does not imply more than that; therefore, the sentence is odd. Note that [3b] would be natural if *toki ni wa* "sometimes" were added, as seen in [3c].

[3] a. 円満な夫婦は口論**もすれば**不満**も**言い合う。(= Ex.(a))

b. ??円満な夫婦は口論**したり**不満を言い合っ**たりする**。

(A happy man and wife do things like arguing and complaining to each other.)

c. 円満な夫婦は**時には**口論**したり**不満を言い合っ**たりする**。

(A happy man and wife sometimes do things like arguing and complaining to each other.)

On the other hand, [4a] means that the weather will alternate between rain and no rain and does not imply more than that. In this case, "X *mo* Vcond *ba* Y *mo* V" cannot be used, as in [4b], because it implies that a number of other rain conditions will occur.

[4] a. 明日は雨が降っ**たり**やん**だりする**でしょう。 [Weather forecast]

(It will probably rain off and on tomorrow.)

b. ??明日は雨が降り**もすれば**やみ**もする**でしょう。

(Probably it will sometimes rain and sometimes stop.)

(⇨ ~***tari*** ~***tari suru*** (DBJG: 458-61))

mono de wa nai　ものではない　*phr.*

<table>
<tr><td>a sentence-final phrase indicating that one shouldn't do s.t., one could not possibly do s.t., or one naturally cannot do s.t.</td><td>shouldn't; not possibly; naturally cannot; cannot bear 【REL. *beki de wa nai*; *te wa ikenai*; *tōzen da*; *atarimae da*】</td></tr>
</table>

◆ Key Sentences

(A)

	Vinf.nonpast	
夜遅く人に電話を	かける	ものではない。

(You shouldn't call people late at night.)

(B)

	Vpot.inf.past	
彼の演奏は	聴けた	ものではない。

(We cannot bear listening to his performance (lit., His performance isn't something we could possibly listen to).)

(C)

	Vpot.inf.nonpast	
そんな時間のかかる仕事は	引き受けられる	ものではない。

(That kind of time-consuming work isn't something I can accept.)

M

Formation

(i)　Vinf.nonpast ものではない

　　食べるものではない　(one shouldn't eat s.t.)

(ii)　Vpot.inf.past ものではない

　　食べられたものではない　(one could not possibly eat s.t.)

(iii) Vpot.inf.nonpast ものではない

　　食べられるものではない　(one naturally cannot eat s.t.)

Examples

(a) 日本では先生と話す時に帽子をかぶったまま話すものではない。
(In Japan, one shouldn't wear a hat while speaking to one's teacher.)

(b) 日本では人のうちに訪ねて行く時には手ぶらで行くものではありません。
(In Japan, you shouldn't visit someone's house without bringing something with you.)

(c) 未成年者は酒を飲むもんじゃない。
(Minors shouldn't drink.)

(d) 女性に年齢を聞くものではない。
(You shouldn't ask a woman her age.)

(e) こんなつまらない小説、読めたもんじゃない。
(I could not possibly read such a boring novel!)

(f) 私のかいた絵なんか、あなたに見せられたものではありません。
(There's no way I could possibly show you the paintings I've done.)

M

(g) 辞書などはそう簡単に書けるものではない。
(It is natural that dictionaries can't be written so easily.)

(h) 現在の補助金の額で十分な研究ができるものではない。
(We cannot possibly do thorough research with the current amount of research funds.)

Notes

1. The sentence-final phrase *mono de wa nai* can be used to express three meanings: (i) "one shouldn't do s.t." because it violates common ethics, as in KS(A) and Exs.(a)-(d); (ii) "one couldn't possibly do s.t." because one believes that the quality is very poor, as in KS(B), Exs.(e) and (f); and (iii) "one naturally cannot do s.t." due to some obvious reasons, as in KS(C), Exs.(g) and (h).

2. When *mono de wa nai* is used to mean "one could not possibly do s.t.," the preceding potential verb is in the past. The nonpast version can express frequency, but not quality. For example, in (1a), the quality of "his performance" is awful, but in (1b), quality isn't an issue.

   (1) a. 彼の演奏は{おそまつで／*滅多に}聴けたものではない。(cf. KS(B))
       (His performance is so awful, it isn't worth listening to (it).)

b. 彼の演奏は｛滅多に /?おそまつで｝聴けるものではない。

(We seldom get a chance to listen to his (fine) performances.)

3. *Mon ja nai* used in Exs.(c) and (e) is a colloquial version of *mono de wa nai*. *Mono ja nai* can also be used in colloquial language, and *mon de wa nai* can be used in both written and colloquial language.

【Related Expressions】

I. When *mono de wa nai* is used to mean "one shouldn't do s.t.," it can be replaced by such sentence-final phrases as *beki de wa nai* and *te wa ikenai*. In terms of the degree of prohibitive force, *mono de wa nai* is the weakest and *te wa ikenai* is the strongest.

[1] a. 夜遅く人に電話を｛かけるものでは /かけるべきでは /かけてはいけ｝ない。(= KS(A))

b. 日本では先生と話す時に帽子をかぶったまま｛話すものでは /話すべきでは /話してはいけ｝ない。(= Ex.(a))

c. 日本では人のうちに訪ねて行く時には手ぶらで｛行くものではあり /行くべきではあり /行ってはいけ｝ません。(= Ex.(b))

(⇨ ***bekida*** (DIJG: 11-15); *~ wa ikenai* (DBJG: 528))

II. When the sentence-final predicate means "one naturally cannot do s.t.," it can be rephrased using *tōzen da* and *atarimae da*, as shown in [2]. *Atarimae* means "s.t. is a matter of course" and *tōzen* is a slightly formal version of *atarimae*.

[2] そんな時間のかかる仕事は引き受けられるものではない。(= KS(C))

→そんな時間のかかる仕事を引き受けられないのは｛当然だ /当たり前だ｝。

そんな時間のかかる仕事は当然引き受けられない。

mono ka[1]   ものか[1]   *phr.*   <s>

a rhetorical question marker that expresses a strong negative intention or disagreement	definitely not; absolutely not; impossible

◆ **Key Sentences**

(A)

	Vinf.nonpast	
あんなやつとは二度と	**会う**	ものか。
(I will never see that sort of guy again.)		

(B)

A: 彼は5年後には自分でコンピュータの会社をつくるって言っているよ。

	Vinf.nonpast	
B: そんなこと彼に	**できる**	もんか。
(A: He says he will establish a computer company by himself in five years. / B: I bet he can't. (lit., Can he do it?))		

Formation

(i)   {V / Adj(*i*)} inf.nonpast ものか

　　　行くものか   (s.o. definitely won't go there.)

　　　めずらしいものか   (s.t. definitely isn't rare)

(ii)   {Adj(*na*)stem / N} なものか

　　　便利なものか   (s.t. is definitely not convenient)

　　　病気なものか   (s.o. is absolutely not ill)

Examples

(a) あんなケチな男とはもうつき合うものか。

　　(Who really wants to spend more time with such a stingy fellow?)

(b) A: 鈴木、TOEFLが650点だったってよ。

      (I heard that Suzuki got 650 points on the TOEFL.)

   B: まさか！ そんなことがあるもんか。

      (Unbelievable! That can't be true.)

(c) 世話をしてもお礼の一言も言わないの。あんな人、もう世話をするもんですか。

(She didn't even thank me when I helped her out. Who really wants to help someone like that again?)

(d) A: 池田先生、親切な先生？

      (Is Prof. Ikeda a kind teacher?)

   B: 親切なもんか。

      (Definitely not kind.)

(e) A: そのパズル、やさしいんだろう。

      (Isn't that puzzle easy?)

   B: やさしいもんか。

      (Absolutely not.)

(f) A: あいつは自分のことをいっぱしの政治家だと思っているようだな。

      (He seems to think that he is a full-fledged politician.)

   B: あいつは政治家なもんか。政治屋じゃないか。

      (He is absolutely not a politician. He's just being political.)

(g) A: 黙って帰ったら彼に悪いだろう。

      (It's not right if we go home without saying a word to him, right?)

   B: かまうもんか。

      (Who cares?)

(h) A: みんな、あの政治家は信頼できるって言っているよ。

      (Everybody is saying that politician is reliable.)

   B: 分かるもんか。

      (How do they know?)

Notes

1. *Mono ka* is not a real question marker but a rhetorical question marker that expresses a strong negative intention or negative view. For example, KS(A) and Ex.(d) can be rephrased as (1a) and (1b), respectively. Note that the intonation in this sentence structure goes down rather than up, since *mono ka* isn't a real question marker.

(1) a. あんなやつとは二度と会うものか。(= KS(A))

→あんなやつとは二度と会うつもりはない。
(I don't have any intention whatsoever of meeting that sort of guy again.)

b. 親切なもんか。(= Ex.(d)-B)
→絶対に親切じゃない。
(I absolutely don't believe that he is kind.)

2. *Mono ka* becomes *mon ka* in male colloquial speech, as in KS(B), Exs.(b) and (d)-(h). In female colloquial speech, *mono ka* changes to *mon desu ka*, as in Ex.(c).

mono ka²   ものか²   *phr.*

a phrase indicating that the speaker wants to do s.t. or is wondering what one he/she should choose	wish; wonder if; should; 【REL. *tara ii noni*; *tara ii no da ga*; *tara ii ka*; *beki ka*】

◆ **Key Sentences**

(A)

	Vpot.neg		
もう少し広い家に	住め	ない	もの（だろう）か。

((i) I wish to live in a house that is a bit more spacious. (ii) I wonder if I can live in a slightly more spacious house.)

(B)

	Wh-word	Vinf.past			V (of thinking)
修士論文の題目を	どのように	決めた	ものか	（と）	迷っています。

(I am at a loss as to how I should choose my MA thesis topic.)

(C)

	Vneg		
もう少し真面目にこの問題に取り組んで	**くれ**	ない	もの (だろう) か。
(I'm wondering if they can handle this problem a little more seriously.)			

Formation

(i) Vpot.neg ないもの(だろう)か

　　食べられないもの(だろう)か (s.o. wishes to eat s.t. / s.o. wonders if he could (lit., couldn't) eat s.t.)

(ii) Wh-word + Vinf.past ものかと V (where V = verb of thinking)

　　どこへ行ったものかと{思う / 考える} (s.o. thinks about where he should go)

　　どうしたものか(と){迷う / 思案する} (s.o. wonders what to do)

Examples

(a) 何とかしてこの原稿を月曜日までに書き終われないものか。

(I would like somehow to finish writing this manuscript by Monday.)

(b) もう少し自由に休暇が取れないものだろうか。

(I'm wondering if I can take time off a bit more freely.)

(c) 東京の夏はやたらと暑い。もう少し涼しくならないものだろうか。

(Tokyo's summer is terribly hot. I wish it were a bit cooler.)

(d) 日本語を勉強したいんですが、どの大学を選んだものかと考えているところです。

(I want to study Japanese, and I'm wondering which university I should choose.)

(e) 今年の夏は海外旅行をしようと思っていますが、どの国に行ったものかと思案中です。

(We're thinking of making a trip abroad this coming summer, and we are trying to figure out which country to visit.)

(f) 子供が反抗期に入っている。その期間を問題なく乗り越えるにはどうしたものかと思っている。

(Our child has entered the rebellious stage of life. I'm wondering what we should do to get through this period without problems.)

(g) このところ体の調子が悪いので、医者に診てもらったものかと考えていると
ころです。

(I'm now wondering if I should go see a doctor because I don't feel well these days.)

(h) 日本の狭い社会から飛び出して海外移住でもしたものかと思っています。

(I'm wondering if I should escape from Japan's confining society and live abroad.)

(i) 人の性格は変わらないものだろうか。

(I wonder if a person's character ever changes? (Does a person's character never change?))

(j) 私も食事に注意しているのだから、少しはやせないものだろうか。

(I'm paying attention to my diet, so I wonder if I will lose some weight.)

(k) もうちょっと雨が降らないものだろうか。

(I wonder if there will be more rain.)

Notes

1. The phrase *mono ka* is either a sentence-final question marker, as in KS(A) and Exs.(a)-(c), or an embedded question marker, as in KS(B) and Exs.(d)-(h). Note that in the former the verb is Vpot.neg *nai* and in the latter it is Vinf.past.

2. In the use of *mono ka*, as in KS(A), the phrase often takes the negative potential form of a verb, but as shown in KS(C), Exs.(c) and (i)-(k), other verbs may also occur, such as those that express something that is beyond human control: *naru* "become," *kawaru* "change," *yaseru* "lose weight," *fukureru* "swell," V*te kureru* "s.o. does s.t. for me" and *ame ga furu* "it rains," among others.

3. In Formation (i), the meaning of desire expressed by *mono ka* is weakened if *mono darō ka* is used. See the two translations in KS(A), i.e. "I wish to live in a house that is a bit more spacious" vs. "I wonder if I can live in a slightly more spacious house." Both *mono ka* and *mono darō ka* are used in written language and can be used in both male and female speech. The spoken versions are *mono deshō ka* or *mono kashira*. The former is used in both male and female speech but the latter is used only in female speech.

(1) 東京の夏はやたらと暑いです。もう少し涼しくならないもの｛でしょう
か / かしら｝。(cf. Ex.(c))

4. In Formation (ii) the conjunction *to* is obligatory when the main verb is *omou* "think" or *kangaeru* "think," but it is optional when the verb is *mayou* "wonder" or *shian-suru* "wonder."

(2) a. 子供が反抗期に入っている。その期間を問題なく乗り越えるにはどうしたものか{と /*ø}思っている。(= Ex.(f))

b. 修士論文の題目をどのように決めたものか{と / ø}迷っています。

(= KS(B))

【Related Expressions】

I. *Mono ka* in KS(A) can be replaced by such phrases as *tara ii noni* or *tara ii no da ga* without changing the meaning, as in [1] below.

[1] a. もう少し広い家に住めたらいい{のに / のだが}。(cf. KS(A))
(It would be nice if I could live in a house that is a bit more spacious.)

b. 何とかしてこの原稿を月曜日までに書き終われたらいい{のに / のだが}。(cf. Ex.(a))
(It would be nice if I could somehow finish writing this manuscript by Monday.)

c. もう少し休暇が自由に取れたらいい{のに / のだが}。(cf. Ex.(b))
(It would be nice if I could freely take time off.)

II. *Mono ka* in KS(B) can be replaced by *tara ii ka* or *beki ka* without changing the meaning.

[2] a. 修士論文の題目をどのように{決めたもの / 決めたらいい / 決めるべき}か (と) 迷っています。(= KS(B))

b. 日本語を勉強したいんですが、どの大学を{選んだもの / 選んだらいい / 選ぶべき}かと考えているところです。(= Ex.(d))

c. 今年の夏は海外旅行をしようと思っていますが、どの国に{行ったもの / 行ったらいい / 行くべき}かと思案中です。(= Ex.(e))

mono nara ものなら   *conj.*

a conjunction indicating that the pre-   if; if ~ at all
ceding clause presents a hypothetical
situation that is unlikely to become a
reality

◆ **Key Sentences**

(A)

Subordinate Clause			Main Clause
	Vpot.inf.nonpast		
（もし）	一戸建ての家が	**買える**	ものなら	買いたい。
(If I could buy a single family house, I would like to.)			

(B)

Subordinate Clause		Main Clause	
	V₁pot.inf.nonpast		V₂te (V₁ = V₂)	
一人で	**やれる**	ものなら	**やって**	みろ！
(If (you think) you can do it by yourself, go ahead and do it!)			

V_1pot.inf.nonpast, V_2te ($V_1 = V_2$)

Formation

Vpot.inf.nonpast ものなら

　　行けるものなら　　(if I can/could go there)

　　読めるものなら　　(if I can/could read it)

Examples

(a) 近い将来における日本語の存在意義など、書けるものなら書いてみたい。

(If I could, I would like to write about the raison d'etre of Japanese
language in the near future.)

(b) 喫煙所の中でたばこを吸っている人たちを外から見ればまるで動物園……。
もしやめられるものならやめてみようかなあと思い始めたこの頃です。

(When I look at people smoking in smoking areas, I feel like I am at the
zoo. Lately, I have begun to think that, if I could, I would try quitting.)

(c) この新刊、もし町の図書館で借りられるものなら買わずに済むのに、まだ入っていないようだ。

(I wouldn't need to buy this new book if I could borrow it at the public library in my town, but it looks like it isn't available there yet.)

(d) 南極旅行は、気持ち的には、借金してでも行けるものなら行きたいんだが。

(I feel like I'd like to travel to the South Pole, even if I had to borrow money to do it.)

(e) もしできるものなら、もう一度生まれ変わりたい。

(If I could, I would like to be born again.)

(f) 西行じゃないけれど、願いがかなうものなら、満開の桜の下で春に死にたい。

(I am no Saigyo, but if wishes came true, I would wish to die in spring, under cherry trees in full bloom.) [Saigyo (1118-1190) is a famous *waka* poet and Buddhist priest who expressed in his poetry his desire to die under blooming cherry trees.]

(g) この曲がやさしいって言うんですか？ 何も分かっていないからそんなことを言うんですよ。弾けるものなら弾いてみなさい。

(Are you saying this piece is easy? You're saying that because you don't know anything about it. Go ahead and play it if you think you can!)

(h) 訴えるなんて言ってもちっとも怖くなんかありませんよ。訴えられるものなら訴えてごらんなさい。

(Even if you tell me that you're going to sue me, I'm not afraid at all. Sue me if you can!)

(i) カリスマのある哲学者が大学に来て講演をしようものなら、1万人を超える聴衆が集まる。

(If a charismatic philosopher did come to the university to give a lecture, more than 10,000 people would gather to listen to him.)

Notes

1. The conjunction *mono nara* is used to express a hypothetical situation that is unlikely to become a reality. The verb used before *mono nara* is often an informal potential nonpast verb, as shown in KS(A) and Exs.(a)-(e), but implicit potential verbs like *kanau* "be fulfilled" can be used, too, as in Ex.(f). The predicate in the main clause is often ~ *tai* "want to ~," as shown in KS(A), Exs.(a), (d), (e) and (f).

2. *Moshi* may be used with *mono nara*, as in KS(A), Exs.(b), (c) and (e), to strengthen the hypothetical nature of the statement.

3. Examples of the present counterfactual, i.e., a fact that runs counter to the present situation, can be turned into the past counterfactual, i.e., a fact that runs counter to a past situation, if the final predicate is in the past tense, as shown in (1). In this case, the sentence sounds more natural without *moshi*.

(1) a. 一戸建ての家が買える**ものなら**<u>買いたかった</u>のだが。(cf. KS(A))

(If I had been able to buy a single family house I would have liked to buy it, but . . .)

b. この新刊、町の図書館で借りられる**ものなら**買わずに<u>済んだ</u>のに。

(cf. Ex.(c))

(If I had been able to borrow this new book at the public library in my town I wouldn't have needed to buy it, but . . .)

4. When *mono nara* is used with imperative sentences, as in KS(B), Exs.(g) and (h), it indicates the speaker's challenge to the hearer and means "I bet you can't do it." The ending is always an imperative form of ~ *te miru* "try to ~." This use of *mono nara* occurs only in spoken language. Thus, the written version ~ *te miyo* is not acceptable, as shown in (2).

(2) 一人でやれるものならやって{**みろ**/*みよ}！(= KS(B))

5. See *yō mono nara* in this volume for the use of Vvol *mono nara*.

(⇨ **yō mono nara** (in this volume))

mono no　ものの　　*conj.*　<w>

┌──────────────────────────────┐
│ a conjunction that means "although" │
└──────────────────────────────┘

although; though; even though; but

【REL. *ga*; *keredomo*】

◆ **Key Sentences**

(A)

Sinf		
通訳の仕事を引き受けた	ものの、	うまくやれる自信がない。

(Although I accepted the interpreting job, I'm not confident that I can do it well.)

(B)

Sinf			
一人でいる方が気楽だ	とは言う	ものの、	やはり話し相手が欲しいと思うこともある。

(Although I say being alone is easier, sometimes I want someone to talk with.)

Formation

(i) {V / Adj(*i*)}inf ものの

{行く / 行った}ものの　(although s.o. will go / went)

{安い / 安かった}ものの　(although s.t. is/was cheap)

(ii) Adj(*na*)stem{な / で(は)ある / だった / であった}ものの

便利{な / で(は)ある / だった / であった}ものの　(although s.t. is/was convenient)

(iii) N{で(は)ある / だった / であった}ものの

大学生{で(は)ある / だった / であった}ものの　(although s.o. is/was a college student)

Examples

(a) 大学を卒業はしたものの、不況でなかなかいい仕事が見つからない。

(Even though I graduated from college, because of the recession I cannot find a good job (despite my effort).)

(b) マネージャーになって給料は上がったものの、急にいろんな仕事が増えてとても忙しくなった。

(Although I became a manager and got a raise, my work (of various kinds) quickly increased and I became very busy.)

(c) 市内を抜け出すまでは時間がかかったものの、高速に入ってからは渋滞もなく、4時前にホテルにチェックインすることができた。

(Although it took time to get out of the city, there were no traffic tie-ups after we got on the highway, and we were able to check in at the hotel before four o'clock.)

(d) 韓国産のハマグリは形はふくらみが少なく身がややかたいものの、うま味が強く、寿司ネタにも使われている。

(Clams from Korea are a little lean and tough, but they taste very good and are sometimes used for *sushi*.)

(e) 現地の子供たちは最初こそよそよそしかったものの、時間がたつにつれて慣れてきてとても親切にしてくれました。

(Although the local children were cold and unfriendly at the start, as time passed they got used to me and were very kind to me.)

(f) 小林氏は身のこなしが軽快で、髪こそ真っ白なものの、「若い」という印象を与える。

(Mr. Kobayashi's carriage is light and jaunty, and even though his hair is totally white, he gives the impression of being young.)

(g) 我がチームは出だしは好調だったものの、夏場で失速し、シーズンが終わってみれば、勝率5割を切るという不本意な成績に終わった。

(Even though our team started off well, we lost momentum over the summer, and when the season was over, to our regret we had won less than 50 percent of our games.)

(h) 彼は敬虔なイスラム教徒だったものの、ドイツ国内のイスラム主義団体との交流はなかった。

(Although he was a devout Muslim, he had no connection with Islamic groups in Germany.)

(i) 暦の上では秋とは言うものの、まだ真夏のような暑さが続いている。

(Although the calendar says that it is autumn, it's still hot like midsummer.)

(j) 同居していた息子の家族が県外に引っ越したので、やっと静かな生活に戻った。とは言うものの、孫の顔がいつも見られないのはちょっと寂しい。

(Our son and his family, who had been living with us, moved out of the prefecture, and we have finally returned to a quiet life. However, we feel a little lonely, not being able to see our grandchild all the time.)

Notes

1. When "X *mono no*" does not modify a noun, *mono no* functions as a conjunction meaning "although." "S₁ *mono no* S₂" is used when the following conditions are met:

   (i) S₂ represents a fact. That fact is generally the speaker's/writer's focus.

   (ii) Given the information in S₁, the fact presented in S₂ is generally unexpected.

(i) indicates that, in this construction, S₂ cannot be a question, as shown in (1), or a sentence which mentions a future action such as a command, a request, a suggestion, or a volitional sentence, as shown in (2).

(1) a. *彼は通訳の仕事を引き受けたものの、うまくやれるんですか。

   (Although he accepted the interpreting job, can he do that well?)

   b. *君は通訳の仕事を引き受けたものの、うまくやれるんですか。

   (Although you accepted the interpreting job, can you do that well?)

(2) a. *君はまだ日本語がうまくないものの、この翻訳をやってみなさい。

   (Although your Japanese is not good yet, try this translation.)

   b. *あなたはとても忙しいものの、この翻訳をやってもらえないでしょうか。

   (Although you are very busy, could I ask you to do this translation?)

   c. *あなたはあまり自由時間がないものの、少し運動をした方がいいですよ。

   (Although you don't have much free time, you'd better do some exercise.)

   d. *私はこの歌手のことをよく知らないものの、コンサートに行こうと思う。

   (Although I don't know much about this singer, I think I'll go to her concert.)

(In the sentences in (1) and (2), *ga* or *keredomo* can be used instead of *mono no*. See Related Expressions.)

M

2. In "S$_1$ *mono no* S$_2$," the subject of S$_1$ and that of S$_2$ must be the same.

3. *Mono no* is usually used in written or formal spoken language.

4. *To wa iu mono no* "lit., although I say; although it is said" functions as a conjunction meaning "although; even though; however." Unlike *mono no*, *to wa iu mono no* can be attached to a noun or a *na*-adjective stem, as in (3).

   (3) a. 先生とは言うものの　(although s.o. is a teacher)

   b. 便利とは言うものの　(although s.t. is convenient)

Note that *to wa iu mono no* can be in the sentence-initial position, as in Ex.(j). (⇨ **to wa ie** (in this volume))

[Related Expressions]

The conjunctions *ga* and *keredomo* are synonymous with *mono no* and can be used in its place, as shown in [1].

   [1] a. 通訳の仕事を引き受けた{ものの / が / けれども}、うまくやれる自信がない。(= KS(A))

   b. 韓国産のハマグリは形はふくらみが少なく身がややかたい{ものの / が / けれども}、うま味が強く、寿司ネタにも使われている。
   (= Ex.(d))

   c. 彼は敬虔なイスラム教徒だった{ものの / が / けれども}、ドイツ国内のイスラム主義団体との交流はなかった。(= Ex.(h))

However, *mono no* cannot replace *ga* or *keredomo* when either is used simply to connect sentences contrastively, with no positive or negative implication (see [2]).

   [2] a. ハリーはパーティーに行く{が / けれども / *ものの}、メアリーは行かない。
   (Harry is going to the party, but Mary is not.)

   b. ジョンは民主党{だが / だけれども / *であるものの}、ジョージは共和党だ。
   (John is a Democrat, but George is a Republican.)

Note that in the sentences in [2], the subjects of the two sentences connected by *ga* or *keredomo* are different, which is not the case with sentences connected by *mono no*.

Ga and *keredomo* are not bound to the conditions (i) and (ii) in Note 1. Thus, they are acceptable in the sentences in [3] and [4].

[3] a. 彼は通訳の仕事を引き受けた{が / けれども /*ものの}、うまくやれるんですか。(= (1a))

　　b. 君は通訳の仕事を引き受けた{が / けれども /*ものの}、うまくやれるんですか。(= (1b))

[4] a. 君はまだ日本語がうまくない{が / けれども /*ものの}、この翻訳をやってみなさい。(= (2a))

　　b. あなたはとても忙しい{が / けれども /*ものの}、この翻訳をやってもらえないでしょうか。(= (2b))

　　c. あなたはあまり自由時間がない{が / けれども /*ものの}、少し運動をした方がいいですよ。(= (2c))

　　d. 私はこの歌手のことをよく知らない{が / けれども /*ものの}、コンサートに行こうと思う。(= (2d))

(⇨ *ga²* (DBJG: 120-23); *keredomo* (DBJG: 187-88))

M

mono o　ものを　　*conj.*

a disjunctive coordinate conjunction expressing the meaning of "although" with the speaker's strong feeling of discontent	although; but 【REL. *noni*】

◆ **Key Sentences**

(A)

		Subordinate Clause				Main Clause
		Vcond		Adj(*i*)inf		
彼は	日本語を続けて	勉強すれ	ば	いい	ものを、	1年間やっただけでやめてしまった。

(Although he should have continued studying Japanese, he quit after only one year.)

(B)

	Subordinate Clause				
	Vinf.past			Vinf	
すぐ医者に	診てもらった	ら	簡単に	治っていた	ものを、

Main Clause
手遅れになってしまった。

(Had I gone to the doctor right away, I would have gotten better easily, but I acted too late.)

Formation

(i) Vcond ば {Adj(*i*) / Vpot} inf ものを

　　Vcond ば Adj(*na*)stem {な / だった} ものを

　　　行けば {いい / よかった} ものを　(s.o. should go / should have gone there but)

　　　注意すれば {安全な / 安全だった} ものを　(s.o. would be / would have been safe if he were / had been attentive)

　　　勉強すれば {行ける / 行けた} ものを　(s.o. could go / could have gone there, if he/she studied / had studied)

(ii) Vinf.past ら〜 Vinf ものを

　　　あったら {食べる / 食べた} ものを　(s.o. would/could have eaten s.t. if it were / had been there)

(iii) Vinf.past ら～{いい / よかった}ものを

行ったら{いい / よかった}ものを　(it would be / would have been good if s.o. went / had gone there)

Examples

(a) ゴルフかなんかして少しリラックスすればいいものを、父は週末でも会社の仕事を家でやっている。

(My father should play golf or something and relax a little bit, but he brings work home from the office even on weekends.)

(b) あのくだらない小説はちょっと読んだだけでやめればよかったものを、なんと最後まで読んでしまった。全くの時間の浪費だった。

(I should have stopped reading that cheap novel after a few pages, but believe it or not, I read it to the very end. It was an utter waste of time.)

(c) 居留守を使えばいいものを、彼女は気が弱いのでそうもできず、いやいや人に会うことになってしまうのだ。

(She doesn't have to answer the door, but she doesn't have the nerve to resist and ends up talking to people even though she doesn't want to.)

(d) 私のことが嫌いなら嫌いだともっと早くはっきり言ってくれたらよかったものを。

(He should have told me much earlier that he didn't like me (lit., if in fact he didn't like me).)

(e) 時間があったらいろいろな外国旅行ができたものを、いつも忙しく働いてきたので、外国はどこにも行っていない。

(Had I the time, I could have made trips to various foreign countries, but because I've been so busy working I have never been overseas.)

(f) 父があと１年生きていてくれたら私の結婚式に出てもらえたものを、私がぐずぐずしていたばかりに、父に私の晴れ姿を見てもらえず、とても残念です。

(Had my father lived one year longer, he could have attended my wedding ceremony, but just because I was indecisive for so long, I couldn't give him the chance to see me in my wedding dress. I feel so sorry!)

Notes

1. *Mono o* is a disjunctive conjunction that means "but" or "although." It expresses discontent, in general; the conjunction can also represent criticism, as in KS(A), Exs.(a), (c) and (d), or regret, as in KS(B),

Exs.(b), (e) and (f). All these describe counterfactual situations. Ex.(f) can be rephrased as (1) below.

(1) 父があと1年生きていてくれたら私の結婚式に出てもらえただろう。

(cf. Ex.(f))

(If my father had lived one year longer he could have attended my wedding ceremony.)

2. Sometimes the main clause is omitted, if the meaning can be recovered from the context of the sentence, as in Ex.(d). An example of the main clause is included in parentheses in (2), below.

(2) 私のことが嫌いなら嫌いだともっと早くはっきり言ってくれたらよかったものを(なぜ言ってくれなかったのか)。(cf. Ex.(d))

(He should have told me much earlier that he didn't like me, if in fact he didn't like me. (Why didn't he tell me so?))

【Related Expression】

In all of the KS and Exs., *mono o* can be replaced by the disjunctive conjunction *noni*, as shown in [1], but the former expresses the emotions of discontent, regret, etc., more strongly.

[1] a. 彼は日本語を続けて勉強すればいい{ものを/のに}、1年間やっただけでやめてしまった。(= KS(A))

b. すぐ医者に診てもらったら簡単に治っていた{ものを/のに}、手遅れになってしまった。(= KS(B))

However, the conjunction *noni* cannot be replaced by *mono o*, if the subordinate clause expresses a fact, as shown in [2].

[2] a. 毎日漢字を勉強している{のに/*ものを}よく覚えられない。

(Although I study kanji every day, I still haven't learned them well.)

cf. 漢字が面白かったら毎日漢字を勉強している{のに/ものを}、ちっとも面白くないのでよく覚えられない。

(If kanji were interesting (to me) I would study them every day, but since they aren't interesting at all, I haven't been able to learn them.)

b. 中学と高校で6年間も英語を勉強した{のに/*ものを}まだ英語が話せません。

(I studied English in junior and senior high school for a total of six years, but I still can't speak it.)

cf. 英語に興味があったらもっと一生懸命勉強した{のに / ものを}、興味もなかったのであまり勉強せず、そのためまだ英語が話せません。

(I would have studied English much harder if I had had an interest in it, but I didn't, so I still cannot speak English (lit., because I didn't study much).)

(⇨ **noni**[1] (DBJG: 331-35))

mo saru koto nagara もさることながら *phr.* <w>

a phrase used to mention something important and then introduce something more significant	~ is one thing, but; it is true that ~, but; it is the case that ~, but; but more importantly

M

◆ **Key Sentence**

	Noun Phrase		
この図書館は	蔵書の多さ	もさることながら	サービスが実にすばらしい。

(This library's large collection of books is one thing (lit., is so, too), but the services they provide are really something else (lit., really wonderful).)

Formation

NP もさることながら

教育もさることながら (education is one thing, but)

Examples

(a) 指圧やマッサージといった「タッチセラピー」が注目されている。身体への直接的な効果もさることながら、安らぎ感や癒やしといった心理的な効果も大きいようだ。

("Touch therapies," such as *shiatsu* and massage, are drawing people's attention. While they have a direct effect on the body (lit., Their direct effect is so, too), apparently their psychological effect, including feelings of relaxation and healing, is also great.)

(b) 高齢化が進むにつれ、認知症老人の介護が問題になっているが、これからは、介護のこともさることながらぼけをいかに予防するかがさらに重要だ。

(As the population has aged, the care of senile seniors has become a problem. It is true that from now on care will be an important issue (lit., care is so, too), but the question of how to prevent people from becoming senile is more important.)

(c) 障害者向け製品の価格が高いのは、技術的な困難もさることながら市場の小ささが大きな原因になっている。

(It is true that the high price of products for the handicapped is (partially) due to technical issues (lit., technical difficulties are so, too), but the major cause is a lack of demand (lit., the small market).)

(d) 下から眺めるテレビ塔やイルミネーションの美しさもさることながら、展望台に登って眺める市の夜景もまた格別です。

(The TV antenna tower and the lights on it viewed from below are a beautiful sight, but seeing the city at night from the observatory tower is really something special.)

(e) この合作映画は、作品の完成度の高さもさることながら、文化の異なる二国が協力して一つの映画を完成させたという事実が非常に意義深い。

(This jointly-produced movie is highly polished, but more importantly, the fact that two countries with different cultures worked together and completed a film (in and of itself) is quite significant.)

Notes

1. "X *mo saru koto nagara*" is equivalent to "X *mo sō de aru ga*," which literally means "although X is so, too; although it is also true with X."

   (⇨ **nagara(mo)** (DIJG: 199-202))

2. "X *mo saru koto nagara*" is used when it is important to mention X but there is a more significant thing to mention.

3. *Mo saru koto nagara* is usually used in written or formal spoken language.

moshikuwa もしくは   *conj.*   <w>

a conjunction to disjunctively connect two items or ideas

or
【REL. *soretomo*; *aruiwa*; *mata wa*; *ka*; **naishi (wa)**】

◆ **Key Sentences**

(A)

	Noun₁			Noun₂		
この申込書は	本人	(か)、	もしくは	保証人	が	記入しなければならない。

(This application has to be filled in by the applicant or by his/her guarantor.)

(B)

		Verb Phrase₁		
			Vinf.nonpast	
ワークショップに出席なさりたい方は	オンラインで		登録する	か、

	Verb Phrase₂
もしくは、	メールでお申し込み下さい。

(If you want to participate in the workshop, please register online or apply by e-mail.)

Formation

(i)   N₁ (か)、もしくは N₂

電子メール (か)、もしくはファックス   (e-mail or fax)

研究 (か)、もしくは教育   (research or education)

(ii) V₁inf.nonpast か、もしくは V₂

権利を売るか、もしくは譲渡する   (sell one's right or transfer it to s.o.)

Examples

(a) 基調講演者は日本研究もしくは関連領域の研究について話すことになっている。

(The keynote speaker is expected to talk about Japan studies or related areas.)

(b) この予算は研究費、もしくは研究補助費にのみ使用できる。

(This budget is to be used exclusively for research or research-related expenses.)

(c) 大学のプールは学生か、もしくは使用料を支払った大学関係者のみ利用できる。

(The college pool is open only to students or those affiliated with the college who have paid the fee.)

(d) 夏季のドライブシーズンを迎える頃には、ガソリンの在庫が昨年とほぼ同水準まで下がるか、もしくはそれ以下に減少する見通しである。

(It is predicted that by the time of the summer driving season, the reserves of gasoline will fall approximately to the same level as last year or will go below it.)

(e) 日本の経済力が弱まってきている現在、日本が世界で生き残る道はテクノロジーで時代の先取りをするか、もしくは、モノとしての日本の文化をより積極的に海外に輸出することであろう。

(These days Japan's economic strength has decreased. For Japan to survive in the world, it must either take leadership in the field of technology in the future, or export Japanese culture as a product more aggressively.)

Notes

1. *Moshikuwa* "or" is used to connect two or more alternatives—that is, items, as in KS(A) and Exs.(a)-(c), or ideas, as in KS(B), Exs.(d) and (e).

2. *Ka* "or" precedes *moshikuwa*. It is optional in the construction "N$_1$ *(ka)*, *moshikuwa* N$_2$," but obligatory in "V$_1$inf.nonpast *ka, moshikuwa* V$_2$."

3. *I/Na*-adjectives can be connected if it is part of a noun modifier as shown in (1a). But "Adj(*i/na*) *ka, moshikuwa*, Adj(*i/na*)" is unacceptable as part of a predicate, as shown in (1b).

(1) a. ご近所の、大きいか、もしくは、有名な病院に行くことをお勧めします。

　　　 (I recommend that you go to a large hospital or one that is well-known in your neighborhood.)

　　 b. *近所の病院は大きいか、もしくは、有名です。

　　　 (*The hospital in the neighborhood is large or famous.)

In contrast, "N₁ *ka, moshikuwa,* N₂ *da*" is acceptable, as shown in (2).

(2) 大学のプールの使用者は学生か、もしくは、大学関係者だ。(cf. Ex.(c))

　　 (The users of the college pool are either students or university employees.)

4.　This conjunction is used only in formal written Japanese.

[Related Expressions]

I.　In addition to *moshikuwa* there are other conjunctions meaning "or," such as *soretomo, aruiwa* and *mata wa,* among others. Out of these *aruiwa* and *mata wa* can replace *moshikuwa,* as shown in [1] below.

　　[1] a. この申込書は本人（か）、{もしくは / あるいは / または / *それとも} 保証人が記入しなければならない。(= KS(A))

　　　 b. ワークショップに出席なさりたい方はオンラインで登録するか、{もしくは / あるいは / または / *それとも}、メールでお申し込み下さい。

　　　　　　　　　　　　　　　　　　　　　　　　　　　　　　　　(= KS(B))

But in the embedded question *soretomo* can also replace *moshikuwa,* as shown in [2].

　　[2] 彼女は仕事を探すか、{もしくは / それとも / あるいは / または} 大学院に進学するか、迷っている。

　　　 (She is undecided about whether she should look for a job or go to graduate school.)

In a simple question only *soretomo* can be used, as shown in [3].

　　[3] ステーキにしますか。{それとも / *あるいは / *もしくは / *または} 魚にしますか。

　　　 (Would you like steak? Or, would you like fish?)

II.　As shown in Formation (i) and (ii), the conjunction *ka* meaning "or" is optional after a noun, but obligatory after Vinf.nonpast. Actually the same *ka* can be used without *moshikuwa,* as shown in [4].

[4] a. この申込書は本人か保証人が記入しなければならない。(cf. KS(A))

   b. ワークショップに出席なさりたい方はオンラインで登録する**か**、メールでお申し込み下さい。(cf. KS(B))

   c. 彼女は仕事を探す**か**、大学院に進学する**か**、迷っている。(cf. [2])

        (⇨ ***soretomo*** (DBJG: 421-22); ***aruiwa*** (in this volume); ***mata wa*** (DIJG: 171-74); ***ka***[1] (DBJG: 164-66))

---

mottomo もっとも   *conj.*

a conjunction used to add a comment indicating that what the speaker/writer has just expressed is not sufficient	although; though; but; yet; however 【REL. *shikashi*; *to wa iu mono no*; *tada*】

M

◆ **Key Sentence**

Sentence₁		Sentence₂	
運動は体にいいと言われている。	もっとも、	やりすぎると逆効果だ	（が）。

(They say that exercise is good for you (lit., your body), but doing too much will bring about the opposite effect.)

Formation

S₁。もっとも S₂（{が／けれども}）。

  息子はよく病気をする。もっとも大病をしたことはない（{が／けれども}）。

  (Our son often gets sick, although he has never fallen seriously ill.)

Examples

(a) あの政治家は保守的だと言われている。もっとも、時々革新的なことを言うこともあるが。

  (That politician is said to be conservative, although he sometimes makes innovative statements.)

(b) 彼は女性にとても親切だ。もっとも、それには下心がある場合が多いようだ。

(He is very kind to ladies. But, apparently, he often has an ulterior motive.)

(c) 今日は魚がよく釣れた。もっとも、いつもこのように幸運だとは限らない。

(I caught (lit., was able to catch) a lot of fish today, although I'm not always this lucky.)

(d) このドイツの車の方があの日本の車よりいいんじゃない。もっとも、僕はドイツの車を運転したことはないけどさ。

(Don't you think that this German car is better than that Japanese one? I've never driven a German car, though.)

(e) 顔写真の入った名刺というのも、強い印象を与えるからいいかもしれない。もっとも私はそこまでやりたいとは思わないけれども。

(It may be a good idea to make business cards with your picture on them because they would create a stronger impression. But I am kind of reluctant to go that far.)

(f) 若い頃は漠然としていたものが歳を重ねるごとにハッキリと見えるようになり、目標を見据えてよりポジティブに生きるようにしています。もっとも私はまだ、その途上にありますが。

(As I grow older, I begin to see more clearly things that were not clear when I was younger. I'm trying to keep the goal in focus and live more positively. But I haven't gotten there yet.)

Notes

1. *Mottomo* is a sentence-initial conjunction and is used to add a comment to supplement the information in S_1.

2. S_2 often ends with conjunctions, such as *ga* or *keredo*, which have the effect of hedging, as shown in the KS, Exs.(a) and (d)-(f).

[Related Expressions]

I. The coordinate conjunction *shikashi* "but" can replace *mottomo* in all of the KS and Exs., as shown in [1]. Note that in [1a] the sentence-final *ga* cannot be used when the conjunction is *shikashi*.

[1] a. 運動は体にいいと言われている。{もっとも/しかし}、やりすぎると逆効果だ(が)。(= KS)

　　b. 彼は女性にとても親切だ。{もっとも / しかし}、それには下心がある場合が多いようだ。(= Ex.(b))

However, *mottomo* cannot always be used in place of *shikashi*. That is, when *shikashi* expresses mere contrast, *mottomo* is not acceptable, as shown in [2].

[2]　a. 僕は憲法改正論者だ。{しかし / *もっとも}友人のKは憲法擁護論者だ。

　　　(I am for revising the current national constitution. But my friend K is for protecting it.)

　　b. 日本は島国だ。{しかし / *もっとも}韓国は大陸とつながった半島だ。

　　　(Japan is an island country. But Korea is a peninsula, connected to the continent.)

II.　Another disjunctive conjunction, *to wa iu mono no* "but," is used in the following patterns: "S₁. *To wa iu mono no* S₂" or "Quote *to wa iu mono no* ~," indicating that something unexpected from S₁ or Quote follows. In "S₁. *To wa iu mono no* S₂," *mottomo* and *to wa iu mono no* are interchangeable, as shown in [3].

[3]　a. 運動は体にいいと言われている。{もっとも / とは言うものの}、やりすぎると逆効果だ(が)。(= KS)

　　b. あの政治家は保守的だと言われている。{もっとも / とは言うものの}、時々革新的なことを言うこともあるが。(= Ex.(a))

　　c. 彼は女性にとても親切だ。{もっとも / とは言うものの}、それには下心がある場合が多いようだ。(= Ex.(b))

　　d. 今日は魚がよく釣れた。{もっとも / とは言うものの}、いつもこのように幸運だとは限らない。(= Ex.(c))

However, *mottomo* must be used in the sentence-initial position and therefore cannot be used in place of *to wa iu mono no* mid-sentence.

[4]　a. 春{とは言うものの / *もっとも}まるで初夏のようだ。

　　　(Although it is spring, it feels just like early summer.)

　　b. 日本語の先生{とは言うものの / *もっとも}日本語のことを何も知らない。

　　　(Although he is a Japanese language teacher, he doesn't know anything about the Japanese language.)

If sentences in [4] are rephrased as in [5], both *to wa iu mono no* and *mottomo* are acceptable.

[5] a. 今は暦の上では春だ。{もっとも／とは言うものの}まるでここ数日は初夏のようだが。

(It is spring on the calendar. But it has been like early summer for the past few days.)

b. 彼は日本語の先生だ。{もっとも／とは言うものの}日本語のことはまるで知らないが。

(He is a Japanese teacher. But he doesn't know anything about Japanese.)

(⇨ **to wa ie** (in this volume))

M

-muke 向け　*suf.*

a suffix that adds the meaning of "aimed at"	for; made for; for the use of; aimed at; directed towards; (directed/shipped/etc.) to 【REL. *yō*; *muki*】

◆ **Key Sentences**

(A)

	Noun		
このギター曲集は	初心者	向け	だ。
(This collection of guitar pieces is for beginners.)			

(B)

	Noun₁			Noun₂	
この秋は	アジア	向け	(の)	産業用ロボット	の販売が好調だ。
(This autumn, sales of industrial robots for Asia have been good.)					

(C)

	Noun			
D社は	携帯機器 <small>けいたいきき</small>	向け <small>む</small>	に	小型燃料電池 <small>こがたねんりょうでんち</small> を開発している。

(D Company is developing small fuel-cell batteries for portable devices.)

Formation

(i)　N 向け <small>む</small> だ

　　　デパート向けだ　(s.t. is for department stores)

(ii)　N₁ 向け <small>む</small> (の) N₂

　　　ヨーロッパ向け(の)輸出 <small>ゆしゅつ</small>　(exports to Europe)

(iii) N 向け <small>む</small> に

　　　日本人向けに　(for Japanese people)

Examples

(a) このセミナーはこれから株 <small>かぶ</small> を始める人 <small>ひと</small> 向け <small>む</small> だ。

(This seminar is for those who are going to begin (investing in) stocks.)

(b) 輸出 <small>ゆしゅつ</small> はここ数年 <small>すうねん</small> 、中国 <small>ちゅうごく</small> 向け <small>む</small> が急速 <small>きゅうそく</small> に伸びている。 <small>の</small>

(Regarding exports, for the last few years those to China have been increasing rapidly.)

(c) このサービスは、基本的 <small>きほんてき</small> にはコンシューマー向け <small>む</small> だが、法人 <small>ほうじん</small> 向けも用意する。

(This service is basically for consumers, but we will offer a version for companies, too.)

(d) 助成金 <small>じょせいきん</small> をもらって先生 <small>む</small> 向けの情報教育 <small>じょうほうきょういく</small> サイトを作ることにした。

(We've decided to get a grant and develop a website to educate teachers about information technology.)

(e) このショールームでは住宅 <small>じゅうたく</small> 向け <small>む</small> のタイル・建材 <small>けんざい</small> を展示 <small>てんじ</small> しております。

(In this showroom, we are displaying tile and construction materials for residential use.)

(f) アメリカ進出 <small>しんしゅつ</small> を考える場合は、アメリカ向け <small>む</small> の読みやすい商品説明書 <small>しょうひん</small> と価格 <small>かかく</small> 表 <small>ひょう</small> を用意することが必須 <small>ひっす</small> です。

(When you consider expanding to America, it is essential to prepare an easy-to-read product manual geared toward the U.S. and a price list.)

(g) K社は近々地図サービスと地域情報検索を国内向けに開始すると発表した。

(K Company announced that it would begin a map service and (release) a search (engine) for local information for domestic users soon.)

(h) 代表的な曲を小さなお子様向けにアレンジしました。

(We arranged well-known (music) pieces for young children.)

(i) このオペレーティングシステムは、巨大なアプリケーション向けに設計されている。

(This operating system is designed for mega-scale applications.)

Notes

1. *Muke*, the *masu*-stem of *mukeru* "to direct; to aim" is used as a suffix to add the meaning of "aiming at; directed towards/to; made for; for the use of; etc."

2. *Muke* is commonly affixed to nouns referring to people, organizations, countries or objects. N-*muke ni* modifies verbs and N-*muke no* modifies nouns. The *no* of N-*muke no* is often omitted.

3. "*no* N" in "N₁-*muke no* N₂" is sometimes omitted when it is understood from the context, as demonstrated in (1).

M

   (1) a. 輸出はここ数年、**中国向け**(**の輸出**)が急速に伸びている。(= Ex.(b))

      b. このサービスは、基本的にはコンシューマー向けだが、**法人向け**(**のサービス**)も用意する。(= Ex.(c))

[Related Expressions]

I. The suffix *yō* is similar to *muke* in terms of meaning and formation rules, as shown in [1]. (The formation rules are exactly the same as those of *muke*.)

   [1] a. このギター曲集は初心者{**向け** / **用**}だ。(= KS(A))

      b. D社は携帯機器{**向け** / **用**}に小型燃料電池を開発している。

(= KS(C))

      c. 助成金をもらって先生{**向け** / **用**}の情報教育サイトを作ることにした。(= Ex.(d))

However, there are some major differences between *yō* and *muke*. First, *yō* does not have the meaning "directed to; shipping to; to." Thus, it is not used in sentences like those in [2].

[2] a. この秋はアジア{向け／*用}(の)産業用ロボットの販売が好調だ。

(= KS(B))

  b. 輸出はここ数年、中国{向け／*用}が急速に伸びている。(= Ex.(b))

Second, *yō* is used when something is meant for both specific and general users, while *muke* is not used when something is meant for specific users, as shown in [3].

[3] a. 社長{用／*向け}の椅子
    (a chair for the president)
  b. 男性{用／*向け}トイレ
    (a restroom for men)

Third, *yō* is commonly used with nouns indicating the place where something is used, but *muke* is not.

[4] a. 教室{用／??向け}の黒板
    (blackboards for classrooms)

  b. オフィス{用／??向け}スチールキャビネット
    (steel cabinets for the office)

Fourth, *yō* is commonly used with nouns that indicate a purpose or occasion, whereas *muke* cannot be used with such nouns (e.g., [5a]-[5d]). Note that nouns before *yō* can also be the object of an action indicating purpose (e.g., [5e] and [5f]).

[5] a. 練習{用／*向け}のピアノ
    (a piano for practice)
  b. 演奏会{用／*向け}のピアノ
    (a piano for concerts)
  c. 競泳{用／*向け}水着
    (a swimming suit for competitive swimming)
  d. 正月{用／*向け}の食器
    (dishes for New Year's Day)

e. 刺身{用 / *向け}の包丁

(a knife for fixing *sashimi*)

f. 音楽{用 / *向け}CD

(CDs for recording music)

II. The suffix *muki* looks similar to *muke*, but it has a different meaning. That is, *muki* carries the meaning of "facing" or "suitable for," as shown in [6] and [7].

[6] a. 私は南向きの部屋が欲しい。

(I want a room facing south.)

b. 彼の考え方は常に前向きだ。

(He is always forward thinking.)

c. 景気がやっと上向きになってきた。

(The economy has finally turned upward.)

[7] a. この辺りは若者向きの店が多い。

(There are many shops suitable for young people around here.)

b. この話は映画よりむしろアニメ向きだ。

(This story is more suitable for *anime* than for a movie.)

c. 本日は夏向きに冷たいお料理をいくつかご紹介します。

(Today we're going to introduce some cold dishes suitable for serving in the summer.)

mushiro　むしろ　*adv.*

an adverb that indicates one of two things/people/characteristics has been chosen rather than the other to express the speaker's/writer's desire, preference or judgment	rather; instead 【REL. *kaette*; ***dochira ka to iu to***】

◆ **Key Sentences**

(A)

	Verb Phrase₁				Verb Phrase₂
		Vinf. nonpast			
夏休みは	アルバイトを	**する**	よりも	むしろ	海外旅行がしたい。

(During summer vacation I would rather travel abroad than work part-time.)

(B)

	Noun₁			Noun₂		
僕は	**すし**	より	むしろ	**さしみ**	(の方)	が好きだ。

(I prefer *sashimi* rather than *sushi*.)

(C)

	Noun₁			Noun₂	
彼は	**秀才**	というよりは	むしろ	**努力家**	だ。

(He is a man of effort rather than a man of great talent.)

(D)

	Vinf. nonpast			Vinf.past		
無為の生活を	**する**	ぐらいなら、	むしろ	**死んだ**	方が	いい。

(I would rather die than lead a good-for-nothing life.)

Formation

(i) V₁inf.nonpast より（{は／も}）むしろ V₂inf.nonpast（方が～）

　　外に行くより（は）むしろ家でテレビを見る方がいい。　(I would rather watch TV at home than go outside.)

(ii) N₁ より（{は／も}）むしろ N₂（の方）が～

　　コーヒーより（は）むしろ紅茶（の方）が好きだ。　(I like black tea rather than coffee.)

(iii) ｛V／Adj(*i*)｝inf というより（｛は／も｝）むしろ～

　　｛食べる／食べた｝というより(は)むしろ｛飲み込む／飲み込んだ｝。 (He swallows/swallowed rather than eats/ate.)

　　｛涼しい／涼しかった｝というより(は)むしろ｛寒い／寒かった｝。 (It is/was cold rather than cool.)

(iv) ｛Adj(*na*)stem／N｝｛ø／だ／である／だった／であった｝というより（｛は／も｝）むしろ～

　　丁寧｛ø／だ／である／だった／であった｝というより(は)むしろばか丁寧｛だ／だった｝。 (S.t. is/was overly polite rather than polite.)

　　先生｛ø／だ／である／だった／であった｝というより(は)むしろビジネスマン｛だ／だった｝。 (S.o. is/was a businessman rather than a teacher.)

(v) V₁inf.nonpast｛ぐらい／くらい／の／ん｝｛なら／だったら｝むしろ～

　　仕事を辞める｛ぐらい／くらい／の／ん｝｛なら／だったら｝むしろ死んでしまいたい。 (I would rather die than quit my job.)

Examples

(a) 英語は話すよりむしろ読むのが好きだ。
　　(I like reading English rather than speaking it.)

(b) 時間がある時は、観光バスに乗るよりはむしろ歩いた方がずっとよく観光できる。
　　(When you have the time, you can sightsee much better if you walk rather than ride a sightseeing bus.)

(c) 休みの日は、人の多い行楽地に行くよりは、むしろ、家でテレビでも見ている方がましだ。
　　(On a holiday it is better to watch TV or something at home rather than go to a crowded tourist spot.)

(d) 静脈を見つけ、正確に注射するという作業は、人間の手よりもむしろコンピュータを使ってロボットが行った方が、ミスが少ないと思う。
　　(I think that the action of finding a vein and injecting it accurately can be done with less failures if we use a computer and a robot rather than human hands.)

(e) 私は、健康上、肉よりむしろ魚の方を選ぶ。
　　(I choose fish instead of meat for health reasons.)

M

(f) 今年は２月よりもむしろ３月の方が寒かった。

(This year it was colder in March instead of February.)

(g) 彼らが突如大金持ちの仲間入りを果たすことができたのは、彼らの才能というよりもむしろ幸運が味方したからではないだろうか。

(The reason why they were suddenly able to join the group of very rich people may be that good fortune was on their side rather than talent (lit., their talents).)

(h) シアトルはアメリカなのですが、他の大都市とは違って、アメリカというよりはむしろカナダのような雰囲気の小ぢんまりとした街でした。

(Seattle is in the U.S. but, unlike other big cities, it is a small city with an atmosphere more like Canada than the U.S.)

(i) 今年の北海道の夏は涼しかったというよりはむしろ寒かった。

(This summer Hokkaido was cold instead of just comfortably cool.)

(j) 前の週の豪雨のため、ドナウ川の水は青いというよりはむしろ茶色に近い色だった。

(Due to the heavy rain the previous week, the (lit., water of the) Danube was brownish rather than blue.)

(k) こんなつまらない講義に出るぐらいならむしろ寮で本でも読んでいた方がました。

(Instead of attending such a boring lecture, I would rather be reading books in my dorm.)

(l) 優しくしてから突き放すくらいなら、むしろはじめから優しくするなと思う。

(If someone is going to be nice and then dump me, I would rather he just not be nice from the very start.)

Notes

1. The adverb *mushiro* is used to indicate that the speaker/writer chooses one of the two things, persons, characterizations, etc., when stating his/her desire, preference, advice, opinion, etc.

2. *Mushiro* is commonly used in the five constructions given in Formation (i)-(v). Their respective examples are: KS(A) and Exs.(a)-(c), in which two actions are compared, KS(B) and Exs.(d)-(f), in which two things are compared, KS(C) and Exs.(g)-(j), in which two characteristics of the same person/thing are compared, and KS(D), Exs.(k) and (l), in which two negative situations are compared. In all of these situations the second choice is chosen over the first one.

3. When the characteristics of a person or a thing is described, the phrase *to iu yori wa mushiro* is used, as shown in KS(C), Exs.(i) and (j). See Formation (iii) and (iv) for connections. The combination of the tense before and after *to iu yori wa mushiro* can be nonpast ~ nonpast, nonpast ~ past, past ~ past, but not past ~ nonpast.

【Related Expression】

The adverb *kaette* carries the meaning "contrary to one's expectation an opposite result occurs." The core meaning that distinguishes it from *mushiro* is "contrary to one's expectation," so it cannot replace any of the KS and Exs. except Ex.(f).

[1] a. 夏休みはアルバイトをするよりも{むしろ / *かえって}、海外旅行がしたい。(= KS(A))

b. 僕はすしより、{むしろ / *かえって}、さしみの方が好きだ。

(= KS(B))

c. 彼は秀才というよりは、{むしろ / *かえって}、努力家だ。

(= KS(C))

d. 今年は2月よりも、{むしろ / かえって}3月の方が寒かった。

(= Ex.(f))

The reason that *kaette* is acceptable in Ex.(f) is that this sentence provides a context for the meaning "contrary to one's expectation." The difference between the two versions in [1d] is that *kaette* emphasizes that something is true contrary to expectation, while *mushiro* indicates that the speaker/writer has recognized that something is true over something else. More examples follow:

[2] a. 日本人よりも、{むしろ / かえって}、外国人の方が日本文化を深く理解している場合がある。

(There are cases when foreigners rather than the Japanese understand Japanese culture more deeply.)

b. 身内よりも、{むしろ / かえって}、他人の方が親切なことも多い。

(People who are not related to you are often kinder to you than your own flesh and blood.)

(⇨ ***kaette*** (DIJG: 80-82))

M

nai de mo nai   ないでもない   *phr.*

a phrase that indicates the speaker/ writer hesitantly feels or expresses that s.t. is the case	seem to ~; somewhat; rather; may 【REL. *nai koto mo nai*; *naku mo nai*】

◆ **Key Sentence**

	Vneg		
今が私の人生で一番幸せな時期だという気が	し	ない	でもない。

(I seem to of feel that right now is the happiest time of my life.)

Formation

Vneg ないでもない

思わないでもない   (s.o. kind of thinks that ~)

食べないでもない   (s.o. may eat s.t.)

しないでもない   (s.o. may do s.t.)

Examples

(a) あの時大学を辞めたことを、今では少し早まったなと思わないでもない。

(Now I rather feel that leaving the university at that time was a bit too hasty.)

(b) そういえば、そういう話、どこかで聞いたことがあるような気がしないでもないです。

(Come to think of it, I seem to feel that I've heard something like that somewhere.)

(c) 私は「結婚しない主義」でもないし、一度結婚してみたいという気もないでもないんですが、なかなかいい相手が見つかりません。

(I am unmarried not because of principle, and I wouldn't mind getting married, but it is really hard to find a good partner.)

(d) 日本人として、アメリカ企業におけるリストラを見ると非情さを感じないでもない。

(For me, as a Japanese, the way American companies lay off workers strikes me as rather inhuman.)

(e) あなたの苦しい気持ちが分からないでもない。

(I do somewhat understand the pain you are feeling.)

(f) 白衣に眼鏡なら、一見普通の医者に見えないでもない。

(Wearing a white gown and eyeglasses, he could be taken for a doctor at first sight.)

(g) 心底謝れば許してやらないでもないけど。

(If he really apologizes to me from the bottom of his heart, then I may find it in me to forgive him(, but . . .).)

Notes

1. *Nai de mo nai* is used to express something in a hesitant manner when someone feels that something may be the case.

2. The phrase is typically used with a verb of perception, such as *kanjiru* "feel" (Ex.(d)), *ki ga suru* "feel" (KS and Ex.(b)), *ki ga aru* "feel like" (Ex.(c)), *omou* "think/feel" (Ex.(a)), *wakaru* "understand" (Ex.(e)) or *mieru* "look" (Ex.(f)). But sometimes it is used without a perception verb, as in Ex.(g). In this case, it means "may ~." More examples follow.

> (1) a. そんなに日本語を勉強したいのなら**教えないでもない**。
>
> (If you want to study Japanese that badly I may teach it to you.)
>
> b. 2年間でこれを出版することは**できないでもない**。
>
> (It may be possible (lit., may not be impossible) to publish this in two years.)

3. Adj(*i/na*) and N cannot be used with *nai de mo nai*, but can be used with *nai koto mo nai* and *naku mo nai*. Examples are shown in (2) and (3), respectively. (See Related Expressions.)

> (2) a. この小説は面白く｛*ないでもない / ないこともない / なくもない｝。
>
> (It isn't the case that this novel isn't interesting.)
>
> b. あの人は変じゃ｛*ないでもない / ないこともない / なくもない｝。
>
> (It isn't the case that he isn't strange.)

(3) a. 彼女は病気じゃ {*ないでもない / ないこともない / なくもない}。

　　　(It isn't that she isn't ill.)

　　b. 彼は学者じゃ {*ないでもない / ないこともない / なくもない}。

　　　(It isn't the case that he isn't a scholar.)

4. Because of the use of the double negative, *nai de mo nai* conveys a sense of indirectness. It is used in both spoken and written Japanese.

【Related Expression】

The phrases *nai koto mo nai* and *naku mo nai* express the idea of "seem to" or "somewhat." They can be used in place of *nai de mo nai*, as shown in [1].

　[1] a. 今が私の人生で一番幸せな時期だという気がし {ないでもない / ないこともない / なくもない}。(= KS)

　　b. あの時大学を辞めたことを、今では少し早まったなと思わ {ないでもない / ないこともない / なくもない}。(= Ex.(a))

　　c. あなたの苦しい気持ちが分かる {ないでもない / ないこともない / なくもない}。(= Ex.(e))

Nai de mo nai is used primarily with verbs of perception, but *nai koto mo nai* and *naku mo nai* can be used with any verb or Adj(*i/na*) as in [2]. In these examples, *nai de mo nai* cannot be used.

　[2] a. 彼だってアメリカのことに詳しく {ないこともない / なくもない / *ないでもない}。

　　　(It's not that he's unfamiliar with U.S. things.)

　　b. この問題は重要では {ないこともない / なくもない / *ないでもない}。

　　　(It's not that this problem isn't important.)

　　　　　　　　　　　　　　　　　(⇨ *-nai koto mo/wa nai* (DIJG: 203-05))

nai koto ni wa ないことには *phr.*

| a phrase that means "if s.t. has not taken place, s.t. else won't/can't take place" | if ~ not ~ then; unless 【REL. *nakute wa*; *nakereba*; *nakattara*】 |

◆ **Key Sentences**

(A)

	Vneg				Vneg	
この仕事が	終わら	ない	ことには、	家族と旅行に行くことも	でき	ない。

| (If I don't finish this work, I can't go on a trip with my family.) |

(B)

	Vneg				
追加予算が	下り	ない	ことには、	このプロジェクトの遂行は	無理だ。

| (Without (money from) an additional budget, it will be impossible to accomplish this project.) |

Formation

Vneg ないことには～

調べないことには分からない。 (Unless we investigate it, we can't understand.)

話してみないことには了解は不可能だ。 (Unless we talk, understanding is impossible.)

読んでみないことにはコメントできない。 (Unless we read it, comments on it are impossible.)

Examples

(a) 書き始めないことには論文ができるはずはない。

(Unless you begin writing your thesis, there's no way you'll be able to finish it.)

(b) コンピュータが作動しないことには仕事は始まらない。

　　(Unless the computer works, we can't get started on the job.)

(c) 面接を受けないことには就職はできない。

　　(You can't get a job unless you (first) have an interview.)

(d) 為替相場が安定しないことには、経済の回復もおぼつかない。

　　(Unless the exchange rate stabilizes, economic recovery will be almost impossible.)

(e) 日本語学習者は、日本に行かないことには日本語を自然に話せるようになるのは難しいだろう。

　　(If a Japanese language learner doesn't go to Japan, it will be difficult for him or her to learn to speak Japanese naturally.)

(f) 際立った才能がないことには、一流の音楽大学を出てもソリストになることは夢物語だ。

　　(Without outstanding talent, becoming a soloist, even as a graduate of a top-rated music college, is just a dream.)

Note

Nai koto ni wa introduces a condition without which it is difficult or impossible for someone to do something or for something to take place. In other words, the condition expressed in the subordinate clause indicated by Vneg *nai koto ni wa* is a necessary condition for the actualization of something expressed in the main clause. The main predicate must be explicitly negative, as in KS(A) and Exs.(a)-(c), or implicitly negative, as in KS(B) and Exs.(d)-(f).

[Related Expressions]

The phrase *nai koto ni wa* can be replaced by conditional phrases such as *nakute wa*, *nakereba* and *nakattara*, as shown below.

[1] a. この仕事が終わら{ないことには / なくては / なければ / なかったら}、家族と旅行に行くこともできない。(= KS(A))

　　b. 情報を教えていただけ{ないことには / なくては / なければ / なかったら}検討のしようがありません。

　　(Unless you give me information it is impossible to examine it.)

　　c. 為替相場が安定し{ないことには / なくては / なければ / なかったら}、経済の回復もおぼつかない。(= Ex.(d))

However, *nakereba* and *nakattara* are different from *nai koto ni wa* and *nakute wa* in that they can be used with both negative and positive predicates, as shown in [2].

[2] a. この仕事が今年中に終わら｛なければ / なかったら / *ないことには / *なくては｝、完成は来年の半ばぐらいまで延ばします。

(If I don't finish this work before the end of this year, I will just postpone its completion until the middle of next year.)

b. 情報を教えていただけ｛なければ / なかったら / *ないことには / *なくては｝自分たちで集めますから大丈夫です。(cf. [1b])

(If you can't provide us with the information, we will gather it by ourselves, so don't worry about it.)

nai made mo　ないまでも　*phr.*　<w>

| an adverbial phrase expressing the speaker's feeling that although an ideal action or state isn't possible, at least the next best action or state is or should be available | may not ~ but; even though ~ not; although ~ not |

◆ **Key Sentences**

(A)

	Vneg			
この公演は大成功とは	言え	ない	までも、	それなりの成果をもたらした。

(Although you may not be able to call this public performance a great success, it produced results of a sort.)

(B)

	Adj(*i*)stem				
彼の論文は決して	多	く	ない	までも、	その質は非常に高い。

(Although he hasn't published many papers at all, the quality (of those he has published) is extremely high.)

Formation

(i)　Vneg ないまでも

　　行かないまでも　(s.o. may not go there, but)

　　しないまでも　(s.o. may not do s.t., but)

(ii)　Adj(*i*)stem くないまでも

　　よくないまでも　(s.t. may not be good, but)

(iii)　{Adj(*na*)stem / N}{では / じゃ}ないまでも

　　元気{では / じゃ}ないまでも　(s.o. may not be peppy/healthy, but)

　　病気{では / じゃ}ないまでも　(s.o. may not be ill, but)

N

Examples

(a)　「生命とはこういうものです」とは言えないまでも、「少なくともこうではありません」とは言えるようになってくるはずだ。

　　(We may not be able to say, "This is what life is," but we should come to a point where we can say, "At least this is what it isn't.")

(b)　その彫刻は完璧とは言えないまでも、非常に可能性を感じさせる作品だった。

　　(The sculpture may not be called a perfect work, but it is (lit., was) a work that makes you feel unusual potential.)

(c)　虚偽だとは言わないまでも、かなり紛らわしい表現だ。

　　(I can't go so far as to call this wording deceptive, but it sure is misleading.)

(d)　中国語は漢字だから、読めないまでも意味はなんとなく分かるのだが、韓国語はまったく見当がつかない。

　　(If it were written in Chinese I could get a sense of what it's saying because of the characters, even though I cannot read it, but I cannot make heads or tails of Korean.)

(e) インターネットは完璧ではないまでも、生涯学習もしくは生涯教育のメディアとして、いろいろな可能性をもっています。

(The Internet is not perfect, but it does have various possibilities as a medium for life-long learning and/or teaching.)

(f) 運命には逆らえないまでも、それを味方にすることはできる。

(We may not be able to turn back Fate, but we can make it our friend.)

(g) 大方の日本人なら、「源氏物語」の原文に目を通したとまではいかないまでも、どんな話なのかは知っているだろう。

(I believe most Japanese, even though they may not have read the original *Tale of Genji*, know the basic plot of the story.)

(h) 明日は天気がよくないまでも、気温はあまり低くなりません。

(Although the weather may not be good, the temperature will not drop much.)

(i) 彼は正直者じゃないまでも、嘘つきじゃない。

(He may not be an honest person, but he isn't a liar.)

Note

The conjunctive phrase *nai made mo* expresses the idea that the speaker thinks that an ideal action or state isn't possible, but at least the next best action or state is possible or should be possible. The phrase is often used with the verb *iu* "to say," as in KS(A) and Exs.(a)-(c), but other verbs can be used, as shown in KS(B) and Exs.(d)-(g).

N

naishi (wa)　ないし（は）　　*prt. / conj.*

a particle that presents two possible choices or the minimum and maximum possible numbers/lengths/weights/etc. of something; or a conjunction that links two possible actions or events	from ~ to ~; between ~ and ~; or 【REL. *kara*; *ka*; *mata wa*; *moshikuwa*; *samo nakuba*; *aruiwa*】

◆ **Key Sentences**

(A)

	Number₁ + Counter		Number₂ + Counter		
このクラスの学生のほとんどは	３年	ないし（は）	４年	の	日本語学習歴を持っている。
(Most students in this class have three to four years of experience studying Japanese.)					

(B)

	Noun₁			Noun₂		
この論文集の論文はすべて	日本語	（か）	ないしは	英語	で	書かれている。
(The papers in this collection are written in Japanese or English.)						

(C)

S₁inf		S₂
生産量を20％減らす	（か）、ないしは	新しい市場を急遽開拓するしかない。
(We have no choice but to either reduce production by 20 percent or quickly develop a new market.)		

Formation

(i)   Number₁ (+ Counter) ないし（は）Number₂ (+ Counter)

　　　30 マイルないし（は）40 マイル　(from 30 to 40 miles)

(ii) N₁（か）ないしは N₂

　　　英語（か）ないしはドイツ語で　(in English or German)

(iii) S₁inf（か）、ないしは S₂。

　　　日本語集中講座を受ける（か）、ないしは日本へ短期留学をする。
　　　(S.o. will take an intensive Japanese course or go to Japan for
　　　short-term study.)

Examples

(a) 細菌の大きさは1ミクロンないし数ミクロンだ。

(Bacteria are between one and several microns large.)

(b) 電子メールは、忙しい人でも、1日に1回ないしは数回チェックしているはずだ。

(I expect that even busy people check their e-mail once or even several times a day.)

(c) サン・モリッツでは5つ星ないしは3つ星クラスのホテルに滞在し、4日間、スイスの冬を満喫していただきます。

(In St. Moritz, you will stay at a three to five star hotel (lit., a five to three star hotel), and fully enjoy a Swiss winter for four days.)

(d) 本冊子の購入希望者は、氏名、住所、購入希望冊数を明記の上、ファックス、ないしは電子メールで協会事務局までお申し込み下さい。

(If you would like a copy of this booklet, please send a request to the association's office via fax or e-mail with your name, address and the number of copies you want.)

(e) 本アンケートでは、2004年鉛全廃について、「必要」ないしは「やむを得ない」とするものが74％を占めた。

(In this survey, regarding the total ban on (the use of) lead in 2004, 74 percent (of respondents) indicated it would be either "necessary" or "inevitable.")

(f) 本品は1回50mg（2錠）を1日1回就寝前、ないしは1日2回、朝及び就寝前に経口服用して下さい。

(Take 50 mg (two tablets) (of this product) orally (either) once a day before going to bed, or twice daily, once in the morning and once before going to bed.)

(g) 当社は、本ウェブサイトの利用者からの問い合わせにお答えするため、ないしは、あらかじめ利用者に明示させていただいた目的の範囲で、利用者の個人情報を収集します。

(We (lit., Our company) gather our personal information from people who use our website in order to respond to their inquiries or for (lit., within the scope of) purposes made clear to the users in advance.)

N

(h) 当社は、犯罪活動の証拠となる、ないしはその一部となる顧客情報を公開することを、法律によって義務づけられることがあります。

(We (lit., Our company) may be required by law to make public such information on our clients that constitutes evidence, or partial evidence, of criminal activity.)

Notes

1. *Naishi (wa)* is used to present two possible choices or the minimum and maximum possible numbers or measurements of something.

2. When X and Y in "X *naishi (wa)* Y" are quantifiers (i.e., Number + Counter), "X *naishi (wa)* Y" means "from X to Y" or "between X and Y," as in KS(A) and Exs.(a)-(c).

3. When X and Y in "X *naishi (wa)* Y" are nouns, "X *naishi (wa)* Y" means "X or Y." In this case, the phrase does not mean "exclusively X or Y." (See Related Expression II.)

4. *Naishi wa* can also function as a conjunction linking two possible actions or events, as in KS(C) and Ex.(h). In this case, *wa* must be present.

[Related Expressions]

N

I. When X and Y in "X *naishi (wa)* Y" are quantifiers, *naishi (wa)* can be replaced with *kara* "from," as shown in [1].

    [1] a. このクラスの学生のほとんどは3年｛ないし（は）／から｝4年の日本語学習歴を持っている。(= KS(A))

       b. 細菌の大きさは1ミクロン｛ないし（は）／から｝数ミクロンだ。

                                    (= Ex.(a))

                             (⇨ ***kara***[1] (DBJG: 176))

II. *Ka*, *mata wa*, *moshikuwa*, *samo nakuba* and *aruiwa* are all synonymous with *naishi (wa)* when *naishi (wa)* means "or." However, there are some major differences between *naishi (wa)* and the other synonyms. First, when *naishi (wa)* connects two quantifiers, X and Y, it indicates that the range of something is between X and Y, as in [2a]. When the other connectors are used, they mean simply "X or Y," as in [2b] and [2c].

    [2] a. 25歳ないし（は）30歳の独身女性

       (single women between the ages of 25 and 30)

b. 25歳か30歳の独身女性

(single women 25 or 30 years old (but not the ages in between))

c. 25歳（か）｛または／もしくは／さもなくば／あるいは｝30歳の独身女性

(single women 25 or 30 years old (but not the ages in between))

Second, *naishi (wa)* cannot be used when two connected elements have an "exclusive or" relationship, i.e., when "X *naishi (wa)* Y" means "either X or Y." For example, in [3a] *naishi (wa)* is not acceptable because if "that person" is Chinese he cannot be Korean, and vice versa, i.e., *chūgoku* "China" and *kankoku* "Korea" have an "exclusive or" relationship. However, *naishi (wa)* is used when the phrase means "X or Y, or possibly X and Y." For example, in [3b] *naishi (wa)* is acceptable because it is possible that some of "those people" are Chinese and some others are Korean.

[3]　a. ?あの人の国籍は中国、ないし（は）韓国だ。

(That person's nationality is either Chinese or Korean.)

　　b. あの人たちの国籍は中国、ないし（は）韓国だ。

(Those people's nationalities are Chinese or Korean.)

Ka, *(ka) mata wa*, *(ka) moshikuwa*, *(ka) samo nakuba* and *(ka) aruiwa* are acceptable in both [3a] and [3b].

Similarly, in [4], if there is only one Tanaka in the group, *naishi (wa)* is not acceptable because this is an "exclusive or" situation.

[4]　a. 右端かその隣が田中さんだ。

(Either the person farthest to the right or the one next to him is Mr. Tanaka.)

　　b. 右端（か）、｛または／もしくは／さもなくば／あるいは／??ないし（は）｝その隣が田中さんだ。

(Either the person farthest to the right or the one next to him is Mr. Tanaka.)

(⇨ ***ka*[1]** (DBJG: 164-66); ***mata wa*** (DIJG: 171-74);
moshikuwa (in this volume); ***aruiwa*** (in this volume))

naka o 中を   *phr.*

a phrase that specifies space or time in/through which s.o./s.t. does s.t.	in the midst of; when; while; through; among 【REL. *tokoro o*; *toki ni*】

◆ **Key Sentences**

(A)

	Vinf.nonpast		
冷たい風が	｛吹く ／ 吹いている｝	中を	10キロも歩いた。

(When a cold wind was blowing I walked as much as 10 kilometers.)

(B)

	Adj(*i*)inf.nonpast		
お	忙しい	中を	いらしていただき、申し訳ございません。

(Thank you very much (lit., I'm sorry) for coming when you are (so) busy.)

(C)

	Noun Phrase			
赤十字の人たちが	ハリケーン被災者たち	の	中を	歩き回って食料を配った。

(People from the Red Cross walked among the victims of the hurricane and distributed food.)

Formation

(i)   Vinf.nonpast 中を

　　雨が｛降る／降っている｝中を　 (when it is raining)

(ii) Adj(*i*)inf.nonpast 中を

　　忙しい中を　 (when s.o. is busy)

(iii) Adj(*na*)stem な中を

　　危険な中を　 (in the midst of danger)

(iv) N の中を

嵐（あらし）の中を　(in the midst of a storm)

Examples

(a) 子供（こども）たちが遊（あそ）んでいる中を子犬がちょろちょろ走（はし）り回っていた。

(A puppy was darting around among the kids who were playing.)

(b) 公園（こうえん）では、人が集まっている中を、アイスクリーム屋が歩いていた。

(In the park, an ice cream seller was walking through the crowd of people.)

(c) 雪（ゆき）の降（ふ）る中を頑張（がんば）って走っている人を見ていたら、自分が軟弱（なんじゃく）に思えてきました。

(When I watched people out running in the snow, I began to think of myself as fragile and weak.)

(d) 私たちが呆然（ぼうぜん）として見ている中を、二人は一つの傘（かさ）の下に入って行ってしまいました。

(As we were watching with astonishment, the two walked away under the same umbrella.)

(e) 本日は、雨で足元（あしもと）が大変（たいへん）悪い中を、このようにたくさんの方（かた）にご参加（さんか）いただきまして、誠（まこと）にありがとうございました。

(Thank you very much for coming to this meeting today; it's nice to see so many of you when it is so treacherous to walk due to the rain.)

(f) 私だけ門限（もんげん）があるのでパーティーから先に帰ってきたが、楽しい中を抜（ぬ）けて帰るのはとてもつらかった。

(I'm the only one with a curfew, so I came home from the party earlier than everyone else. It was hard for me to leave and come home when I was having a good time.)

(g) 大人たちは戦後（せんご）のあの苦（くる）しい中を、気力（きりょく）をとり戻（もど）して復興（ふっこう）に精（せい）を出したのだ。

(Amidst the postwar hardship, the adults regained their spirit and worked diligently to reconstruct the country.)

(h) 我々（われわれ）は地震（じしん）で道路（どうろ）が崩壊（ほうかい）する危険（きけん）な中を車で 10 時間ぐらい走った。

(We drove our car for about 10 hours through hazardous roads which were collapsing around us during the earthquake and aftershocks.)

(i) 飛行機は嵐の中を随分と長い間飛んでいるらしく、雲に突っ込むたびに大きく揺れている。

(We seem to have been flying through this storm for a very long time, and each time the plane goes into the clouds it shakes quite a bit.)

Notes

1. *Naka o* is a phrase that marks the space or time in which someone or something does something KS(A), (C), Exs.(a)-(c), (h) and (i) refer to space, and KS(B), Exs.(d), (f) and (g) refer to time. Ex.(e) refers to a spatial/temporal situation.

2. When N is an event/action noun such as *kaigi* "conference," *kyūka* "vacation," *shigoto* "job," *benkyō* "study," *sōji* "cleaning," *ryokō* "travel" or *shutchō* "business trip," it cannot be used with *no naka o*; it has to be used with *chū* "in the midst of," the Sino-Japanese reading of *naka*.

   (1) {会議 / 休暇 / 仕事 / 勉強 / 掃除 / 旅行 / 出張} {｜*の中を /中に} 友人から電話がかかってきた。

   (I got a (telephone) call from my friend in the midst of (the/a) {conference / holidays / work / study / cleaning / travel / business trip}.

3. Space nouns that are used with *naka o* refer to something that encloses or encircles someone spatially, such as a storm, rain, snow or light, among other things, as shown in KS(A), Exs.(c) and (i).

【Related Expressions】

I. The phrase *tokoro o* can replace Adj(*i*)inf.nonpast *naka o* in time expressions, especially when the former expresses considerateness towards someone, as shown in [1].

   [1] a. お忙しい {中 / ところ} をいらしていただき、申し訳ございません。

   (= KS(B))

   b. 本日は、雨で足元が大変悪い {中 / ところ} を、このようにたくさんの方にご参加いただきまして、誠にありがとうございました。

   (= Ex.(e))

When the sentence with *naka o* does not express thankfulness, apology or politeness, *tokoro o* cannot replace *naka o*, as shown in [2].

   [2] a. みんな忙しい {中 / ?ところ} を無理して出てきたんだ。

   (All of us made the effort to come out when we were busy with other things.)

cf. みんな忙しい{中／ところ}を{ありがとう／すまないね}。

(Thank you for coming when you guys are busy.)

b. 足元が悪い{中／*ところ}を頑張って、やっとの思いで会場にたどり着いた。

(It was very treacherous to walk and I struggled to get there, but finally reached the meeting place.)

II. *Toki ni* "when" can replace *naka o* whenever the latter unambiguously expresses a time at which s.t. takes place, as shown in [3] below.

[3] a. お忙しい{中を／時に}いらしていただき、申し訳ございません。

(= KS(B))

b. 私だけ門限があるのでパーティーから先に帰ってきたが、楽しい{中を／時に}抜けて帰るのはとてもつらかった。(= Ex.(f))

c. 大人たちは戦後のあの苦しい{中を／時に}、気力をとり戻して復興に精を出したのだ。(= Ex.(g))

N

nakushite (wa)　なくして（は）　*comp. prt.*　<w>

a compound particle meaning "without s.t."

without; if it were not for ~
【REL. *nashi ni (wa)*; *nashi de (wa)*】

◆ **Key Sentences**

(A)

Noun		
努力	なくして（は）	この事業はできない。
(Without effort we won't be able to finish this undertaking.)		

(B)

Noun		Sinf.past	
山川教授 （やまかわきょうじゅ）	なくしては	今の私は存在しなかった （いま）（わたし）（そんざい）	であろう。
(Without Prof. Yamakawa, I wouldn't be what I am now.)			

Formation

N なくして(は)

協力（きょうりょく）なくして(は)　(without cooperation)

Examples

(a) コンピュータなくして現在（げんざい）の生活（せいかつ）は不可能（ふかのう）だ。

(Without computers, our current lifestyle would be impossible.)

(b) ITの活用（かつよう）なくして企業（きぎょう）の成長（せいちょう）は望（のぞ）めません。

(If we don't make good use of IT, we can't expect our business to grow.)

(c) 日本の平和（へいわ）と繁栄（はんえい）は、世界の平和と安定（あんてい）なくしてはあり得（え）ない。

(Peace and prosperity in Japan is not possible without peace and stability throughout the world.)

(d) あらゆる生物（せいぶつ）は水なくして生きていけない。

(No creature can live without water.)

(e) コミュニケーションなくしては、人間（にんげん）が関与（かんよ）する一切（いっさい）の活動（かつどう）は成立（せいりつ）し得（え）ない。

(Without communication, no human activity could occur.)

(f) 関係者（かんけいしゃ）の密接（みっせつ）な共同作業（きょうどうさぎょう）なくしてはこの計画の実現（じつげん）は不可能（ふかのう）であったろう。

(If it had not been for the close cooperation of the people involved in this project, it would have been impossible to make it a reality.)

(g) 沿道（えんどう）の人たちの声援（せいえん）なくしては、このマラソンは完走（かんそう）できなかったでしょう。

(Without encouragement from the roadside people, I couldn't have finished running this marathon.)

Notes

1. *Nakushite wa*, which means "without," can represent a counterfactual state or action, as shown in KS(B), Exs.(f) and (g).

2. The use of *wa* after *nakushite* indicates that the sentence is a conditional sentence. This means that when a sentence has a conditional meaning, *wa* is mandatory, as shown in (1).

(1) a. 山川教授{**なくしては** / ***なくして**}今の私は存在しなかったであろう。

(= KS(B))

b. 関係者の密接な共同作業{**なくしては** / ***なくして**}この計画の実現は不可能であったろう。(= Ex.(f))

When both *nakushite wa* and *nakushite* are possible as in (2), the version with *wa* emphasizes conditionality, but the version without *wa* doesn't.

(2) a. 努力{**なくしては** / **なくして**}この事業はできない。(= KS(A))

b. あらゆる生物は水{**なくしては** / **なくして**}生きていけない。(= Ex.(d))

【Related Expressions】

I. X *nashi ni (wa)* is close in meaning to X *nakushite (wa)*. The former can be used in place of the latter in all the KS and Exs.

[1] a. 努力{**なくして** / **なしに**}(は)この事業はできない。(= KS(A))

b. 山川教授{**なくして** / **なしに**}は今の私は存在しなかったであろう。

(= KS(B))

c. コンピュータ{**なくして** / **なしに**}(は)現在の生活は不可能だ。

(= Ex.(a))

d. ITの活用{**なくして** / **なしに**}(は)企業の成長は望めません。

(= Ex.(b))

However, the reverse is not true. When *nashi ni* is used to mean "without doing s.t. that should be done in advance," it cannot be replaced by *nakushite*, as shown in [2].

[2] a. 彼女(かのじょ)は別れの挨拶(あいさつ)も{**なしに** / ??**なくして**}外国に行ってしまった。

(She left for a foreign country without saying goodbye.)

b. ホームページの内容(ないよう)を事前(じぜん)の告知(こくち){**なしに** / ***なくして**}変更(へんこう)することがございます。

(The content of this website may change without prior notice.)

c. いきなり男が断りｲなしに / *なくしてｲ家に入ってきた。

(All of a sudden, a man came into our house without asking permission.)

Note that in [2] *nashi ni* does not take *wa*.

II. X *nashi de (wa)* can also replace X *nakushite (wa)* if X is not a person, as shown in [3].

[3] a. 努力ｲなくして / なしでｲ（は）この事業はできない。(= KS(A))

b. コンピュータｲなくして / なしでｲ（は）現在の生活は不可能だ。

(= Ex.(a))

c. ITの活用ｲなくして / なしでｲ（は）企業の成長は望めません。

(= Ex.(b))

d. 関係者の密接な共同作業ｲなくして / なしでｲはこの計画の実現は不可能であったろう。(= Ex.(f))

e. 山川教授ｲなくして / *なしでｲは今の私は存在しなかったであろう。

(= KS(B))

(⇨ **nashi de wa** (DIJG: 230-32))

N

---

namaji(kka)   なまじ（っか）   *adv.*

an adverb indicating that s.t. (including an action/state) has a positive value which hasn't been reached, causing s.t. negative	halfheartedly; slightly; thoughtlessly; unwisely; inadequately; imperfectly; sort of; a little; somewhat; a bit of 【REL. *chūto-hanpani/na*; *hetani*】

◆ Key Sentences

(A)

	Subordinate Clause			Main Clause
僕は	なまじ（っか）	**英語ができる**	ばかりに、	会社で重宝がられて困っています。

(Because I know a little English, the office treasures me, which is causing me problems.)

(B)

		Noun		
なまじ（っか）	{の / な}	**学問**	は、	ひけらかすと人に軽蔑される。

(People disdain those who show off (their scant knowledge) but are un-educated (lit., have inadequate scholarship).)

(C)

		Vinf.nonpast		
なまじ（っか）	政治に手を	**出す**	の	は	やめた方がよい。

(You'd better not get involved in politics halfheartedly.)

Formation

(i)　なまじ（っか）〜 Conj.

　　なまじ（っか）できるから　(because s.o. can do s.t. (a little))

　　なまじ（っか）安いために　(because s.t. is (somewhat) cheap)

　　なまじ（っか）美人なだけに　(because she is (sort of) a beauty)

　　なまじ（っか）元気なので　(because s.o. is (sort of) healthy)

　　なまじ（っか）でき{たら / ると}　(if s.o. can do s.t. (a little))

　　なまじ（っか）{安かったら / 安いと}　(if s.t. is (somewhat) cheap)

　　なまじ（っか）美人だ{ったら / と}　(if she is (sort of) a beauty)

　　なまじ（っか）元気だ{ったら / と}　(if s.o. is (basically) healthy)

(ii)　なまじ（っか）{の / な}N

　　なまじ（っか）{の / な}努力　(halfhearted efforts)

　　なまじ（っか）{の / な}勉強　(halfhearted study)

(iii) なまじ（っか）〜 Vinf.nonpast のは〜

　　　 なまじ（っか）投資をするのは危ない。　(It's dangerous to invest halfheartedly.)

Examples

(a) なまじっか手伝ってもらうより、一人でやった方が早くできそうです。

(I think it'll be quicker to do it by myself than for someone to help me in a halfhearted way.)

(b) 彼はなまじっか自信があるために、失敗した時にひどい挫折感を味わう。

(Because he has only a little self-confidence, he experiences a horrible sense of failure when something doesn't work out.)

(c) なまじっか財産など持っていたら、最低の人間になってしまうのではないかと思う。

(I think that we turn into the worst people with just a bit of wealth.)

(d) なまじ見る目が肥えてくると、アニメだったら何でもいいってわけにはいかなくなる。

(When you acquire a bit of an eye for *anime*, you discover that not every work lives up to what it's supposed to be.)

(e) なまじっか物を知ってる人よりは全然知らない人の方が、「知らないことを知る楽しみ」を感じられると思う。

(I think that a person who knows nothing can feel "the joy of discovery (lit., of knowing what he doesn't know)" more than someone who knows a little bit.)

(f) なまじ頭がいいと組織の中で協力して働くということが難しくなる。

(If a person is somewhat bright, it is more difficult for him to work cooperatively in an organization.)

(g) なまじっか元気だと、無理をしやすい。

(If you are on the healthy side, you are apt to overexert yourself.)

(h) 身体が健全に発達していなければ、なまじの美貌はかえって空しい。

(If the body hasn't developed healthily, then superficial beauty is but a hollow thing.)

(i) 電池式ブザーはなまじの武器よりも襲われた時に効果が高い上に、コストパフォーマンスに優れています。

(A battery-operated buzzer is more effective when you are attacked than an ordinary weapon and, in addition, it is more cost effective.)

(j) 体験者が語る真実は、なまじな小説よりも深く人の心を打つ。

(The truth as told by someone who experienced it moves us more deeply than a mediocre novel.)

(k) なまじ運動しているのがよくなかったんです。それを言い訳にして、以前よりもたくさん食べるようになってしまいました。

(Doing a little exercise wasn't good, because I used it as my excuse for eating more than I used to.)

Notes

1. *Namaji* has an older form *namajii*, which consists of *nama* "raw; halfway; unfinished" and *shiiru* "force s.o. to do s.t.," and means that someone is forced to do something in spite of the fact that something is halfway finished or unfinished.

2. The adverb *namaji(kka)* is used when something (including an action or a state) has a positive meaning in itself which hasn't been reached, resulting in something negative. For example, in Ex.(b), generally speaking, having self-confidence is a good thing, but because it hasn't reached a stage of full self-confidence, it breaks down when the man fails at something. In KS(B), scholarship is good in and of itself, but if it is an inadequate amount of learning, it will be a target of derision when someone shows it off.

3. *Namajikka* is more colloquial than *namaji*.

4. In some cases, English words such as "halfheartedly," "thoughtlessly," "unwisely" or "inadequately" can be used to translate *namaji(kka)*, but in others, only the context can convey the meaning, as in Exs.(f), (g) and (k). The prenominal forms, i.e., *namaji(kka) no/na*, however, can be translated as "half-hearted," "incomplete," "little," etc., as in KS(B) and Exs.(h)-(j).

【Related Expressions】

I. The adverb *namaji(kka)* can be replaced by *chūto-hanpani* without changing the meaning when a transitive verb of action or a cognitive verb (such as *shiru* "get to know," *wakaru* "can figure out") is used, as shown in [1].

[1] a. ｜なまじ(っか) / **中途半端**に｜政治に手を出すのはやめた方がよい。

(=KS(C))

b. ｜なまじ(っか) / **中途半端**に｜手伝ってもらうより、一人でやった方が早くできそうです。(= Ex.(a))

c. ｜なまじ(っか) / **中途半端**に｜物を知っている人よりは全然知らない人の方が、「知らないことを知る楽しみ」を感じられると思う。

(= Ex.(e))

If the verb is neither a transitive verb of action nor a cognitive verb, *chūto-hanpani* sounds unnatural, as shown in [2].

[2] a. 彼は｜なまじ(っか) / ??**中途半端**に｜自信があるために、失敗した時にひどい挫折感を味わう。(= Ex.(b))

b. ｜なまじ(っか) / ??**中途半端**に｜財産など持っていたら、最低の人間になってしまうのではないかと思う。(= Ex.(c))

c. ｜なまじ(っか) / ??**中途半端**に｜見る目が肥えてくると、アニメだったら何でもいいってわけにはいかなくなる。(= Ex.(d))

The prenominal forms *namaji(kka) no/na* can be replaced by *chūto-hanpana* "halfway; incomplete."

[3] a. ｜なまじ(っか)｛の / な｝ / **中途半端**な｜学問は、ひけらかすと人に軽蔑される。(= KS(B))

b. 電池式ブザーは｜なまじの / **中途半端**な｜武器よりも襲われた時に効果が高い上に、コストパフォーマンスに優れています。(= Ex.(i))

II. When *namaji(kka)* modifies a verb, *hetani* "inadequately," the adverbial form of *hetana* "unskillful," can replace the adverb, as shown in [4].

[4] a. 僕は｜なまじ(っか) / **下手**に｜英語ができるばかりに、会社で重宝られて困っています。(= KS(A))

b. ｜なまじっか / **下手**に｜手伝ってもらうより、一人でやった方が早くできそうです。(= Ex.(a))

c. 彼は｜なまじっか / **下手**に｜自信があるために、失敗した時にひどい挫折感を味わう。(= Ex.(b))

However, *hetani* cannot always replace *namaji(kka)*, because the former can also mean "unskillfully" or "carelessly," as shown in [5].

[5] a. この機械は{下手に / *なまじ（っか）}いじると壊れるよ。
(If you handle this machine carelessly, it will break down.)

b. {下手に / *なまじ（っか）}上司につっかからない方がいい。
(You shouldn't lash out at your boss.)

-nami 並み *suf.*

┌─────────────────────────────┐
│ a noun suffix that adds the meaning "to │
│ match" │
└─────────────────────────────┘

about the same level as; like; as (much ~) as; to match; to rival; on a par with; equivalent to
【REL. *to onaji kurai*】

◆ Key Sentences

(A)

	Noun		
マイクさんのゴルフは	**プロ**	並み	だ。

(Mike's golf skills are about the same level as a pro's.)

(B)

	Noun₁			Noun₂	
吉田さんは植物に ついては	**専門家**	並み	の	**知識**	を持っている。

(Regarding plants, Ms. Yoshida has as much knowledge as a specialist.)

(C)

	Noun			
日本人も	**欧米人**	並み	に	肉や乳製品を食べるようになった。

(Japanese people now eat (lit., have come to eat) as much meat and dairy products as Westerners (lit., Europeans and Americans) do.)

Formation

(i) N 並みだ

　　真冬並みだ　(s.t. is about the same as that in mid-winter)

(ii) N₁ 並みの N₂

　　大人並みの力　(power as strong as an adult's)

(iii) N 並みに

　　人並みに　(like ordinary people)

Examples

(a) 今月の降水量は平年並みだそうだ。

(It is said that this month's precipitation is about the same as (that of the same month) in an average year.)

(b) 当社に登録されている通訳の英語力はネイティブ並みです。

(The interpreters registered with our company have a native level of English proficiency.)

(c) 今日はまだ5月だというのに8月並みの暑さだ。

(Although it is still May today, it is as hot as August.)

(d) ダイエット用品、スポーツ器具、美容雑貨など、アメリカのヒット商品を現地並みの価格でお届けします。

(We deliver top-selling (lit., hit) products from America, including diet products, athletic equipment and beauty goods, at U.S. prices.)

(e) 今日はリハーサルだったが本番並みの緊張感を味わった。

(Although today's (performance) was a rehearsal, I felt the same level of tension as if it were the real performance.)

(f) やっと仕事も見つかって何とか人並みに暮らしています。

(I finally found a job, and somehow am making a go of it, living like other people do.)

(g) 私はパートなのに、正社員並みに仕事をさせられている。

(Despite the fact that I'm only a part-timer, they make me work as much as the regular employees.)

(h) 電気自動車の価格をガソリン自動車並みに下げるのは極めて難しい。

(It is extremely difficult to reduce the price of an electric car so it is on a par with a gasoline car.)

(i) ここの寿司屋は回転寿司並みに安い。

(This *sushi* bar is cheap like a conveyer belt *sushi* bar.)

Notes

1. *Nami* is a suffix that is affixed to nouns and is equivalent to *to onaji kurai* "about the same as." (See Related Expression.)

2. N-*nami* can create a noun predicate with *da*, as in KS(A), Exs.(a) and (b), modify nouns with *no*, as in KS(B) and Exs.(c)-(e), or modify verbs and adjectives with *ni*, as in KS(C) and Exs.(f)-(i).

3. When *nami no* is not a suffix, it means "ordinary; average" with a negative implication. Some examples are shown in (1).

    (1) a. 並の日本語力ではこの仕事はできない。

        (You cannot do this job with ordinary Japanese skills.)

    b. 東京では並のホテルに泊まったが、それでも高かった。

        (I stayed at an average hotel in Tokyo, but even so, it cost a lot.)

    c. 長谷川さんは並の人間ではない。

        (Mr. Hasegawa is not an ordinary human being.)

Note that the suffix -*nami* is spelled 並み but the non-suffix *nami* is spelled 並.

N

4. The common phrase *jū-nin-nami* also means "average; ordinary."

    (2) a. 私の妻は特に美人じゃありませんが、十人並み以上だと思います。

        (My wife is not an extraordinary beauty, but she is above average, I think.)

    b. 何でも十人並みにできるというのは自信にはつながらない。だから、どんな小さなことでも「これだけは誰にも負けない」と思えるものを持つことが大事だ。

        (Doing everything only as well as everyone else is no way to build confidence. Therefore, it's important to have something, no matter how small, at which you believe no one can beat you.)

【Related Expression】

Sentences with *nami* can be rephrased using *to onaji kurai* without changing the meaning, as shown in [1].

[1] a. マイクさんのゴルフはプロ{並み / と同じくらい}だ。(= KS(A))

b. 吉田さんは植物については専門家{並み / と同じくらい}の知識を
持っている。(= KS(B))

c. 日本人も欧米人{並み / と同じくらい}に肉や乳製品を食べるように
なった。(= KS(C))

nan [(Number) + Counter] **mo**　何 [(Number) + Counter] も　　*phr.*

⎰ a phrase that indicates there is a large ⎰　　many; tens/thousands/etc. of ~
⎱ number of things, people, etc.　　　　⎱

◆ **Key Sentences**

(A)

		Counter		
私は日本へは	何	**回**	も	行ったことがあるが、韓国と中国は まだだ。

(I have been to Japan many times, but I've never been to Korea or China.)

(B)

		Number	Counter		
私は日本語の辞書を	何	**十**	**冊**	も	持っている。

(I have dozens of Japanese dictionaries.)

(C)

		Number	Counter			Noun	
私は今 までに	何	**百**	**人**	も	の	**認知症患者**	を診察した。

(To date I have (medically) examined hundreds of Alzheimer's patients.)

Formation

(i)　何 (Number) + Counter も

何 (千) 人 も　(many people / thousands of people)

何 (百) 冊 も　(many volumes / hundreds of volumes)

(ii)　何 (Number) + Counter も の N

何 (百) 人 も の 学生　(many students / hundreds of students)

何 (十) 匹 も の 猫　(many cats (lit., tens of cats))

Examples

(a) マンガ図書館に何万冊も在庫があっても、人気が高いマンガだと、誰かに借り出されている可能性が高い。

(Even though *manga* libraries have tens of thousands of books in their collections, it is highly probable that the popular titles have been checked out.)

(b) 毎日のように我が家の上空をコウモリが何十匹も乱舞する。

(Dozens of bats swarm over (the roof of) our house almost every day.)

(c) ヨーロッパには「農家民宿」が何万軒もあり、都会人や観光客を受け入れている。

(In Europe, there are tens of thousands of farm houses that offer lodging to city people and tourists.)

(d) 人類は、何億年も積み重ねてきた生物としての経験を完全に捨てることなく、動物から人間へと進化した。

(Humans evolved from animals without completely discarding all the experience accumulated during hundreds of millions of years as various living organisms.)

(e) 我が社のパイロット陣はFAAの承認を得ており、何千時間もの飛行経験を持っています。

(The (group of) pilots in our company are FAA accredited and have thousands of hours of flying experience.)

(f) 阪神・淡路大震災では、住宅倒壊により何千人もの命が一瞬のうちに奪われた。

(In the Hanshin-Awaji Great Earthquake, the lives of thousands of people were taken in an instant when their houses collapsed.)

N

《 Notes 》

1. The phrase "*nan* (Number) + Counter *mo*" indicates that there is a large number of things, people, etc.

2. The number is optional, as shown in KS(A). When a number is used it has to be a number that ends in 0, such as 10, 100, 1,000, 10,000, etc.

3. When a specific counter is not available, *ikutsu mo* is used, as in (1) below.

   (1) このサイトを見ると、興味深い情報がいくつも見つかると思います。

   (If you look at this site, I think you will find many interesting pieces of information.)

4. As shown in KS(C), Exs.(e) and (f), when "*nan* (Number) + Counter *mo*" modifies a noun, the particle *no* is used between the phrase and the modified noun.

---

nani ~ nai   何〜ない   *str.*   <w>

a structure indicating that s.t. doesn't exist at all	doesn't exist at all; without [REL. *mattaku ~ nai*; *zenzen ~ nai*]

N

◆ **Key Sentences**

(A)

		Noun		Noun Phrase	
彼女は	何	不自由	ない	裕福な家庭	で育った。

(She grew up in a comfortable and rich family without inconveniences.)

(B)

		Noun			Verb
マイケルは	何	問題	なく	日本での留学生活を	続けている。

(Michael is continuing his study abroad in Japan without any problems.)

(C)

あの人は欠点が	何	一つ	ない。
(She doesn't have any weaknesses.)			

Formation

(i) 何 N₁ ない N₂

何不自由ない生活　(life without any inconvenience)

何不足ない毎日　(every day without any shortages)

(ii) 何 N なく V

何不自由なく暮らす　(live without any inconvenience)

何不足なく暮らす　(live without lacking anything)

(iii) 何一つない

長所が何一つない　(there isn't a single advantage)

失敗が何一つない　(there aren't any mistakes)

Examples

(a) 二人は結婚して、二人だけの蜜月を楽しみ、何不足ない甘い生活を送った。

(The couple got married, enjoyed their honeymoon by themselves, and led a charmed life without want.)

(b) この会社は、課長をはじめ若い社員が多く、何気兼ねなく話ができる雰囲気だ。

(In this company, there are many young employees, including the section chiefs, so it is easy to talk to one another without reserve.)

(c) あれだけの財産を手に入れたからには、一生何不都合なく暮らせると彼は思ったのであろうが、それは間違っていたのだ。

(He must have thought that once he obtained that much wealth he wouldn't want for anything the rest of his life, but he was wrong.)

(d) 日本人のホストファミリーと私は日本語で何不便なく意思疎通ができた。

(My Japanese host family and I were able to communicate in Japanese without any inconvenience.)

(e) 自然界はすばらしいエコシステムになっていて、そこには無駄な物が何一つないようだ。

(The natural world is a wonderful ecological system, and nothing in it seems to be without purpose.)

(f) 今は銀行でさえ破綻する時代だ。100％安全なものは実は何一つない。

(We are now in an age when even banks fail. In reality, nothing is 100% secure.)

Notes

1. *Nani ~ nai* is a structure that expresses the complete negation of existence of something.

2. *Naku* in Formation (ii) is the adverbial form of *nai*.

3. An emphatic expression indicating the lack of human presence is *dare hitori inai*.

   (1) そのドイツの片田舎の駅の待合室には誰一人いなかった。

   (There was not a soul in the waiting room of the station in the German countryside.)

4. The nouns used in "*nani* N *nai/naku*" are limited to *fuben/fujiyū/futsugō* "inconvenience," *fusoku* "lack" and *kigane* "reserve."

5. Except for *hito-tsu*, the combination of *ichi* with a counter cannot be paired with *nani*, as shown in (2).

   (2) a. 車は{*何一台 / 一台も}なかった。

      (There wasn't even one car.)

      b. リンゴは{*何一個 / 一個も}ない。

      (There isn't even one apple.)

[Related Expressions]

There are two expressions, *mattaku ~ nai* and *zenzen ~ nai*, similar to *nani ~ nai*. Both of them indicate complete negation. They can replace *nani ~ nai* in all cases without changing the meaning of a sentence, but the replaced versions sound more colloquial.

   [1] a. マイケルは{何 / 全く / 全然}問題なく日本での留学生活を続けている。(= KS(B))

      b. 日本人のホストファミリーと私は日本語で{何 / 全く / 全然}不便なく意思疎通ができた。(= Ex.(d))

nani mo ~ nai   何^{なに}も〜ない   *str.*   \<s\>

| a structure indicating that an action is taken for no good reason | why ~ have to ~?; it is unnecessary to ~; have no good reason to ~; not need to ~ |

◆ Key Sentences

(A)

		Vinf.nonpast				
何も	そんなに	怒^{おこ}る	こと	は	ない	よ。

(You have no good reason to get so angry.)

(B)

			Vinf.nonpast		
良性^{りょうせい}の腫瘍^{しゅよう}だから、	何も	そんなに	心配^{しんぱい}する	必要^{ひつよう}	は	ない。

(It's a benign tumor, so you don't need to worry about it too much.)

Formation

何も〜ない

何も行くことはない。   (Why do you have to go there?)

何も行く必要^{ひつよう}はない。   (It is unnecessary for s.o. to go there.)

何も行かなくても(よい)。   (You don't have to go there.)

Examples

(a) 何もいまさらみんながやっている研究をやる必要^{ひつよう}なんかないと思うだろう? それが間違^{まちが}いなんだ。

(You must be thinking there's no need to start on the research everybody is already doing. But you are wrong.)

(b) 突然携帯^{とつぜんけいたい}電話が鳴^なったのでびっくりした。友人にはすでに番号^{ばんごう}を知らせてあったから、何もそんなに驚^{おどろ}くこともないのだが、悪いことに会議^{かいぎ}中^{ちゅう}だったのだ。

(I was surprised when my cell phone rang suddenly. I had given the phone number to my friends, so it shouldn't have been a surprise, but unfortunately it happened right in the middle of a meeting.)

(c) まあ落ち着いて下さい。私たちは何もあなたが犯人だと決めてかかっている わけじゃありませんから。

(Please calm down. We certainly aren't accusing you of being the culprit.)

(d) 甘えるのは何も日本人に限ったことではない。

(It isn't just the Japanese who are psychologically dependent on others.)

(e) 彼女の性格を変えようとしているようだけど、何もそこまでしなくたってい いんじゃないか。

(You seem to be trying to change her personality, but why do you need to go that far?)

(f) 元々十分に安いのだから、何もそんなに値切らなくてもと思うんですが、そ れがゲームになってしまうんです。

(The prices are cheap enough to begin with, so there really isn't any need to haggle with the store clerk, but it gets to be sort of a game to do so.)

Notes

1. *Nani mo ~ nai* is used to indicate that an action is unwarranted. For example, in KS(A), the speaker is talking to someone who has no good reason for getting angry. In Ex.(c), the speaker and his group know that it is unwarranted to conclude that the person they are addressing is the culprit. And Ex.(d) implies that the stereotypical idea that it is only the Japanese who show psychological dependency is unwarranted.

2. Common final predicates include *koto wa/mo nai* (KS(A) and Ex.(b)), *hitsuyō (wa) nai* (KS(B) and Ex.(a)), *wake ja nai* (Ex.(c)), *ni kagitta koto de wa nai* (Ex.(d)), *-nakutatte ii* (Ex.(e)) and *-nakute mo ii* (Ex.(f)).

3. The phrase *nani mo* is often used with *sonna ni* "that much" (KS(A), (B), Exs.(b) and (f)), *soko made* "that far" (Ex.(e)) or *imasara* "at this belated time" (Ex.(a)).

nanraka no 何らかの　*phr.*　<w>

<table>
<tr><td>{ a phrase used to indicate that the exact nature of s.t. represented by the noun cannot be specified }</td><td>some; some kind of
【REL. *nan(i)ka no*】</td></tr>
</table>

◆ **Key Sentence**

	Noun		
何らかの	**原因**	で	走行中の電車が急停車した。

(Due to some (unknown) cause the train stopped suddenly.)

Formation

何らかの N

   何らかの事情　(some circumstance)

   何らかの形　(some form)

Examples

(a) 私たちが患う病気は、たいてい、何らかの意味でゲノムと関係があります。

(Most of the illnesses that we get are linked in some way with genomes.)

(b) 世界の総人口のおよそ半数の人々が、何らかの形で米を食べている。

(Approximately half the total population of the world eats rice in some form.)

(c) 何らかの理由で会議に参加できなくなった場合は、学会事務局へご連絡下さるようお願い申し上げます。

(If it turns out that you are unable to attend the conference for some reason, we would appreciate it if you would kindly contact the conference office.)

(d) 食品添加物が我々の身体に何らかの悪影響を与えると考える人は多い。

(Many people think that food additives have some bad effect on our bodies.)

(e) 火星表面の「運河」と呼ばれる溝は、何らかの液体によって作られたと考えられていた。

(The grooves on Mars' surface that are referred to as "canals" were (originally) presumed to have been caused by some liquid.)

(f) 我々はそれぞれ何らかの人生観、社会観を持って生きています。各人の生涯の生活設計に関しても、漠然とした形ではあっても、何らかのデザインをしていると思います。

(Each of us is living with a certain outlook on life and society. And no matter how vague it may be, I believe each person is designing a life plan in his/her own way.)

Note

"*Nanraka no* N" is used to indicate that the nature of something represented by N cannot be specified. The phrase is used in written Japanese or formal spoken Japanese.

【Related Expression】

In informal spoken Japanese, *nanika no* or the more colloquial *nanka no* is used in place of *nanraka no*.

[1] a. {何 / ??何ら}かの原因で走行中の電車が急停車したんだよ。(cf. KS)

  b. {何 / ??何ら}かの理由で会議に参加できなくなったら、学会事務局へ連絡してね。(cf. Ex.(c))

nanra ~ nai 何ら〜ない   *str.* <w>

a structure that is used to express a strong negative statement	not ~ at all; not any ~; nothing; no ~ whatsoever 【REL. *nani mo ~ nai*; *sukoshi mo ~ nai*; *chittomo ~ nai*; *zenzen ~ nai*; *mattaku ~ nai*】

◆ **Key Sentences**

(A)

		Vneg	
日本の大学教育の現状は	何ら	改善されてい	ない。
(The state of Japanese college education has not improved at all.)			

(B)

			Noun Phrase	Vneg	
会社側は労働組合に対して	何ら	の	誠意ある回答	も	し	なかった。
(The company (lit., company side) has failed to give any sincere reply to the labor union (whatsoever).)					

Formation

(i) 何ら N {が / も} ない

   何ら進歩がない   (there is no progress whatsoever)

   何ら応答もない   (there is no response whatsoever)

(ii) 何ら (N + Prt.) Vneg ない

   何ら返事が来ない   (no reply came)

   何ら約束をしない   (s.o. doesn't promise at all)

   何ら読んでいない   (s.o. hasn't read it at all)

(iii) 何らの N も {ない / Vneg ない}

   何らの愛情もない   (s.o. doesn't love s.o. at all)

   何らの妥協も許さない   (s.o. doesn't accept any compromise)

   何らの返事ももらっていない   (s.o. hasn't received any reply whatsoever)

Examples

(a) 私は彼女とは何ら面識もないので、彼女の能力を知る由もありません。

   (I am not acquainted with her at all, so I don't have any reason to know her ability.)

(b) ソウルの町は、人の話さえ聞かなければ東京にいるのと何ら変わりがありません。

(The city of Seoul seems no different than Tokyo, as long as you don't hear someone talk.)

(c) このドラマに登場する人物は実在する個人とは何ら関わりがありません。

(The characters appearing in this drama have no connection to any real individuals.)

(d) 1990年の入管法の改正で日系人はその在留が合法化され、日本での就労についても何ら制限を受けないことになった。

(The 1990 amendment of the immigration law legalized the residence of Japanese descendants from abroad in Japan, and they are now no longer restricted in any way from working in Japan.)

(e) 当ホテルはホテル内での紛失に関しては何らの責任も負いません。

(This hotel takes no responsibility for items lost within the hotel.)

(f) 彼女は生まれつき楽観的で、自分の将来についても何らの不安も感じていなかった。

(She was a born optimist and felt no anxiety whatsoever about her future.)

(g) この町は災害に対して何らの備えもない。

(This town has made no provision against disaster.)

(h) うちの社長は厳しくて、何らの失敗も許してくれない。

(Our company president is strict and won't accept any errors.)

Note

Nanra is used to express a strong negative statement in written or formal spoken language. As shown in the Formations, it can be used several ways as *nanra ~ ga/mo nai*, as in Exs.(a)-(c); *nanra* (N + Prt.) + Vneg *nai*, as in KS(A) and Ex.(d); *nanra no* N *mo ~ nai*, as in KS(B) and Exs.(e)-(h).

[Related Expressions]

Nani mo ~ nai, sukoshi mo ~ nai, chittomo ~ nai, zenzen ~ nai and *mattaku ~ nai* can be used in place of *nanra ~ nai* without changing the meaning of the sentence, as shown below.

[1] a. 日本の大学教育の現状は{何ら / 何も / 少しも / ちっとも / 全然 / 全く}改善されていない。(= KS(A))

b. 会社側は労働組合に対して{何らの / 何も / 少しも / ちっとも / 全然 / 全く}誠意ある回答もしなかった。(= KS(B))

The only difference among the six negative adverbs is the degree of formality. The most formal one is *nanra* and the least formal one is *chittomo*; the rest come between the two extremes.

nante[1]   なんて[1]   *phr.*   \<s\>

> a phrase used as the colloquial version of *nan to*

what; how ~ !; what a(n) ~ !; so

◆ Key Sentences

(A)

		Verb (communication)	
レポートのこと、社長は	なんて	**言っていました**	か。
(What did the president say about the report?)			

(B)

			Noun	
きのう見た映画、	なんて	いう	**映画**	だったっけ？
(What was the title of the movie we saw yesterday?)				

(C)

これぐらいの宿題、	なんて	(いう)	ことはない	よ。
(This much homework is nothing / not a big deal!)				

(D)

		Adj(*i*)inf	
日本のアニメは	なんて	面白い	んだろう。
(How interesting Japanese *anime* is!)			

Formation

(i)　なんて V　(where V = verb of communication)

　　なんて言う　(what does s.o. say?)

　　なんて書く　(what does s.o. write?)

(ii)　なんていう N

　　なんていう人ですか。　(What is his/her name?)

　　なんていう建物ですか。　(What is the name of the building?)

(iii)　なんて｛Adj(*i*)inf / Adj(*na*)stem な / N な｝んだろう

　　なんて難しいんだろう。　(How difficult s.t. is!)

　　(彼女は)なんてきれいなんだろう。　(How pretty (she) is!)

　　なんていい天気なんだろう。　(What a beautiful day!)

Examples

(a)　うちにホームステイしている留学生がテレビを観ていると「今なんて言った？」「英語だとなんて言うの？」と質問の連続だ。

(When the foreign student staying with us watches TV, he keeps asking questions like "What did he say?" or "What is that in English?")

(b)　推薦状を書くのを頼まれると、時々なんて書いたらいいのか分からないことがある。

(Sometimes I don't know what to say (lit., write) when I get asked to write a letter of recommendation.)

(c)　なんていう人か名前を忘れたけれど、なかなか魅力的な女性に出会った。

(I met a very charming lady, although I've forgotten her name.)

(d)　彼はつらい目にたくさん遭っているのに、「なんていうことはない」という感じでひょうひょうと生きている。

(He's had a rough time, but he lets it all roll off his back as if it were nothing to him.)

(e) うさぎをじーっと見てると、なんてかわいいんだろう、なんてかわいい仕草^{しぐさ}
　　をするんだろうって思った。

　　(While staring at a rabbit I admired what a cute creature he was, and
　　how he could make such cute gestures.)

(f) 自分のことを書くのって、なんて難^{むずか}しいんだろう。

　　(It is so hard to write about myself!)

Note

There are four uses of *nante*¹, as shown in Formation (i)-(iii) and KS(C).
Formation (i) (KS(A), Exs.(a) and (b)), Formation (ii) (KS(B) and Ex.(c))
and Formation (iii) (KS(D), Exs.(e) and (f)) correspond to *nan to*, *nan to iu*,
and *nanto ~ n darō* in the non-colloquial version, respectively. Formation
(iii) is used in exclamations. *(~ wa) nante (iu) koto wa nai* in KS(C) and
Ex.(d) is a fixed phrase meaning that something isn't a big deal.

N

nante²　なんて²　*prt.*　\<s\>

| a colloquial particle used to express a strong feeling such as astonishment, incredulousness, envy, disdain, dislike, happiness, etc. | that; things like 【REL. *(nado) to wa*; *nanka*; *nado*】 |

◆ **Key Sentences**

(A)

	Vinf		
小学校からのいじめが中学まで	続^{つづ}く	なんて	ひどい。
(It's terrible that bullying continues after grade school into junior high.)			

(B)

	Noun		
最近は電子メールばかり使っていて、	**手紙**	なんて	滅多に書かない。

(Lately I've been using only e-mail, and seldom write (a thing like) a letter.)

Formation

(i) {V / Adj(*i*)} inf なんて

　　私と別れるなんて、ひどい！　(It's terrible that you'd break up with me!)

　　この問題がやさしいなんて信じられない！　(I can't believe (that s.o. says) this problem is so easy!)

(ii) {Adj(*na*)stem / N} {だ / だった} なんて

　　納豆が好きだなんて、本当？　(Is it true that you like *nattō*?)

　　彼女が女優だったなんて、ちっとも知らなかった。　(I didn't know that she was an actress!)

(iii) N なんて

　　コンピュータなんて嫌いだ。　(I hate things like computers.)

Examples

(a) 生演奏で踊れるなんて、うらやましい。

　　(I'm envious that they can dance to live music (lit., a live performance).)

(b) 大勢の皆さんに家まで来ていただけるなんて、とても嬉しいです。

　　(I'm very happy that so many of you have come to my home.)

(c) 夏にエアコンをつけすぎて寒いなんて、電力浪費も甚だしい。

　　(It's horrible that they feel cold in summer while overusing their air conditioner and wasting electricity.)

(d) あの人がそんなに有名だなんてちっとも知らなかった。

　　(I had no idea he was that famous!)

(e) あなたなんて最低よ。

　　(You are contemptible!)

(f) 納豆なんて嫌いだ。

(I hate *nattō* (fermented soybeans).)

Note

*Nante*² is used to express the speaker's emotion, such as envy (Ex.(a)), happiness (Ex.(b)), anger/astonishment (KS(A) and Ex.(c)), surprise (Ex.(d)), disdain (Ex.(e)), dislike (Ex.(f)) and a sense of unimportance / feeling of cumbersomeness (KS(B)).

【Related Expressions】

I. *Nante* can be replaced by *(nado) to wa* when the former is preceded by {V / Adj(*i*)}inf or by {Adj(*na*)stem / N} {*da/datta*}. Note that the former is more colloquial than the latter.

[1] a. 小学校からのいじめが中学まで続く{なんて / (など)とは}ひどい。

(= KS(A))

b. 生演奏で踊れる{なんて / (など)とは}、うらやましい。(= Ex.(a))

c. あの人がそんなに有名だ{なんて / (など)とは}ちっとも知らなかった。(= Ex.(d))

II. *Nante* can be also replaced by *nanka* and *nado*, when the former is preceded by a noun. All three particles can express emotion, but *nado* conveys the least emotional overtone.

[2] a. 最近は電子メールばかり使っていて、手紙{なんて / なんか / など}滅多に書かない。(= KS(B))

b. 納豆{なんて / なんか / など}嫌いだ。(= Ex.(f))

---

nan to ka 何とか *adv.*

an adverb expressing that s.o. somehow does s.t., or s.t. somehow occurs

somehow; in some way; in one way or another; manage to 【REL. *dō ni ka*】

◆ **Key Sentences**

(A)

我々は今の日本の政治状況を	何とか	変えようと努力しています。

(We are making an effort to change the current Japanese political situation somehow.)

(B)

一見無理なことも、やってみれば	何とか	形になる。

(Something which appears to be impossible to do can take shape in one way or another, if you try.)

Examples

(a) この夏は友達と一緒に何とか富士山に登ってきました。

(This past summer I managed to climb Mt. Fuji with my friend.)

(b) 夜型の生活を何とかしたいと思いながら、今でもそれを続けている。

(Although I keep thinking I want to do something about my night owl lifestyle, (lit., even now) I still stay up late.)

(c) ボスにせかされているから、この書類を何とか明日までに仕上げなければならないんだ。

(My boss keeps pressing me, so somehow I have to complete this document by tomorrow.)

(d) 患者：おでこから血が出ることがあるんです。

(Patient: Sometimes my forehead bleeds.)

医者：おでこから血が？　うーん。そんな症例は聞いたことがないなあ……。

(Doctor: Your forehead bleeds? I haven't heard of a case like that before.)

患者：ほんとなんです。お願いします、先生。何とかして下さい。

(Patient: It's true. Doctor, please do something about it.)

(e) 母親：あら、有香、もう勉強は終わったの。

(Mother: Oh, Yuka, you've already finished studying?)

娘：勉強なんかやってらんないわよ。

(Daughter: I hate studying!)

母親：まったくしょうがない子ねえ。お父さん、何とか言って下さいよ。

(Mother: You're impossible! Dear, say something to her.)

(f) 何とかホームページができたのでみんなに見せたい。

(Somehow I managed to make my home page, so now I want to show it to everybody.)

(g) アメリカへ行けば何とかなるなんていう考えでアメリカに来たって、自分で何とかしなきゃ何ともならないんだ！

(If you come to the U.S. thinking that you'll get by somehow, you will amount to nothing unless you make an effort on your own.)

(h) いろんな形で支援して下さった皆様のおかげで、このプロジェクトは何とか無事に終了しました。

(Thanks to your assistance, which took all kinds of forms, this project has somehow come successfully to completion.)

Notes

1. The adverb *nan to ka* is used to convey that someone does something somehow, as in KS(A), Exs.(a)-(e) and (g) (*nan to ka suru*), or something somehow occurs, as in KS(B), Exs.(f), (g) and (h) (*nan to ka naru*).

2. *Nan to ka* is often used with verbs such as *suru*, *naru* and *iu*, as follows: *Nan to ka suru* "do something about it" in Exs.(b), (d) and (g), *nan to ka naru* "something somehow happens" in Ex.(g), and *nan to ka iu* "someone says something (so that some problem is solved)" in Ex.(e).

【Related Expression】

The adverb *nan to ka* can be replaced by another adverb, *dō ni ka*, as shown in [1].

[1] a. 我々は今の日本の政治状況を｛何とか / どうにか｝変えようと努力しています。(= KS(A))

b. この夏は友達と一緒に｛何とか / どうにか｝富士山に登ってきました。

(= Ex.(a))

c. 一見無理なことも、やってみれば｛何とか / どうにか｝形になる。

(= KS(B))

d. いろんな形で支援して下さった皆様のおかげで、このプロジェクトは
{何とか / どうにか} 無事に終了しました。(= Ex.(h))

However, if *nan to ka* doesn't include the meaning of "how," *dō ni ka* can not be used in substitution.

[2]　お父さん、{何とか / *どうにか} 言って下さいよ。(= Ex.(e))

---

nao　なお　　*adv. / conj.*　<w>

an adverb that indicates that an action or state is still going on or the degree of s.t. increases; a conjunction indicating that an additional comment follows what has just been said in the preceding sentence	still; even more; all the more for ~; additional; and; additionally; furthermore 【REL. *izen (to shite)*; *mada*; *issō*; *motto*; *sara ni*; **tada**】

◆ **Key Sentences**

(A)

			V *te*		
宮崎駿のアニメは、20 年、30 年たっても、	なお	古典アニメ として	残って	いる	だろう。
(*Anime* by Hayao Miyazaki will still remain even in 20 or 30 years as *anime* classics.)					

(B)

			Adj(*i*)	
この小説は	パリを知っている人が読めば	なお	面白い	だろう。
(This novel must be all the more interesting if you know Paris.)				

(C)

		Adj(*na*)stem		
日本へ行く前から日本が好きだったが、日本へ行ったら	なお	**好き**	に	なった。

(I liked Japan before I went there, but after going there I became even more fond of it.)

(D)

Sentence₁
来週の金曜日午後6時から拙宅で夕食会をしますので、お知らせいたします。

	Sentence₂
なお、	ご都合のつかない方はお電話下さい。

(Let me inform you that there will be a dinner at my residence starting at 6:00 p.m. next Friday. Please call us if you can't come.)

Formation

(i) なお V*te* いる

噴火はなお続いている   (the eruption is still going on)

(ii) なお Adj(*i/na*)

なおいい   (even better)

なお立派だ   (even more magnificent)

(iii) なお{Adj(*i*)stem く / Adj(*na*)stemに}(なる)

なお大きく(なる)   ((become) even larger)

なおきれいに(なる)   ((become) even prettier)

(iv) なお Number + Counter

なお10年   (another 10 years)

(v) S₁。なお S₂。

会は毎週月曜日です。なお詳しい情報は会のサイトをご覧下さい。
(The meeting is every Monday. And for detailed information, please look at the meeting's site.)

Examples

(a) 欧米やアジアでは景気は拡大し、総じて良好な状態がなお続いている。

(In Europe, the United States and Asia the economy has expanded and, generally speaking, favorable conditions continue to prevail.)

(b) テレビで「3億円強奪事件」というドラマを見たが、面白かった。実話をもとにしているから、なお面白い。

(I saw a drama called "The ¥300,000,000 Robbery" and found it interesting. It was even more so because it is based on a true story.)

(c) 考えていることを書くのは勉強になる。その文章を先生が読んで感想を書いてくれるから、なお勉強になる。

(It is instructive to write down what we think, and still more instructive when our teacher reads our essays and give comments on them.)

(d) 日本語で話すことは難しいが、書くことはなお難しい。

(It is difficult to speak in Japanese, but it is even harder to write it.)

(e) この論文を完成するまでには、なお2か月は必要だろう。

(It will take an additional two months to finish this paper.)

(f) 金沢での夏期日本語講座参加希望者は、今月末までに願書を提出して下さい。なお、奨学金応募希望者は、至急用紙を取りに学部事務所に来て下さい。

(Those of you who want to participate in the summer Japanese language program in Kanazawa, please submit your applications by the end of this month. Additionally, those who want to apply for a scholarship, please come to the department office immediately to get the form.)

(g) 私は月曜日と水曜日の午後2時から5時までは研究室にいますから、質問のある学生は自由に来て下さい。なお、それ以外の日に研究室に来たい学生は、あらかじめアポを取って下さい。

(I will be in my office from 2:00 to 5:00 p.m. on Mondays and Wednesdays, so if you have a question feel free to visit me (during those times). However, if you want to see me at another time, please make an appointment in advance.)

Notes

1. The adverb *nao* is used to indicate that something is still going on, as in KS(A) and Ex.(a), or to express an increasing degree of some state expressed by an adjective or a verb, as in KS(B), (C) and Exs.(b)-(d). It

can mean "additional" when it is used before a Number + Counter expression, as in Ex.(e).

2. The conjunction *nao* can introduce additional information related to what has been said in the preceding sentence, as in KS(D), Exs.(f) and (g).

3. The adverb/conjunction *nao* is used in formal speech or writing.

4. The adverbial use of *nao* meaning "even more" can be emphasized by adding *sara*.

(1) a. 日本へ行く前から日本が好きだったが、日本へ行ったら**なおさら**好きになった。(cf. KS(C))

b. テレビで「3億円強奪事件」というドラマを見たが、面白かった。実話をもとにしているから、**なおさら**面白い。(cf. Ex.(b))

(⇨ ***naosara*** (in this volume))

【Related Expressions】

I. The Sino-Japanese adverb *izen (to shite)* and *mada* can replace *nao* when the latter means "still," without changing the meaning.

[1] a. 宮崎駿のアニメは、20年、30年たっても、{**なお**/**依然**(として)/まだ}古典アニメとして残っているだろう。(= KS(A))

b. 欧米やアジアでは景気は拡大し、総じて良好な状態が{**なお**/**依然**(として)/まだ}続いている。(= Ex.(a))

(⇨ ***mada*** (DBJG: 224-25))

II. When *nao* is used as an adverb meaning "all the more," it can be replaced by *issō*, *motto* and *sara ni*, without changing the meaning.

[2] a. 日本へ行く前から日本が好きだったが、日本へ行ったら{**なお**/一層/もっと/さらに}好きになった。(= KS(C))

b. テレビで「3億円強奪事件」というドラマを見たが、面白かった。実話をもとにしているから、{**なお**/一層/もっと/さらに}面白い。

(= Ex.(b))

(⇨ ***sara ni*** (in this volume))

naosara   なおさら   *adv.*

| an adverb indicating that the degree of s.t. increases due to an additional circumstance | still more; much more; all the more; even more 【REL. *issō*】 |

◆ **Key Sentences**

(A)

前からタイに行きたいと思っていたが、すでに行ったことのある友人が強く勧めたので、	なおさら	行きたくなった。

(I've wanted to go to Thailand for a long time, and then a friend who has been there strongly recommended it, so I feel like going there even more now.)

(B)

悪人さえも往生するのなら、	まして	善人は	なおさら	だ。

(If even a bad person can go to heaven, then a good person has an even better chance.)

Examples

(a) 貧乏を弁解すると、なおさら貧乏くさく聞こえる。

(If you make excuses for being poor you will seem (lit., sound) still poorer.)

(b) このチーズは搾りたての新鮮な牛乳で作るから、なおさらおいしい。

(This cheese is made from milk fresh from the cow so it tastes even more delicious.)

(c) 旅で足を踏み入れるだけで、沖縄はいまだに戦争を引きずっていることを感じる。まして、現地の人ではなおさらであろう。

(When you just go there as a traveler, you get a sense that Okinawa still hasn't gotten over the war. The local people must feel that way even more so.)

(d) 英語を書くのは難しいが、正確さが要求される科学論文を書くのはなおさらだ。

(It is hard to write in English, but it is still harder to write a scientific paper that requires accuracy.)

(e) アジア諸国の学者や政府が、この教科書を詳細かつ適確に批判し、発行しないよう強く求めたにもに関わらず検定を通ったということは、なおさら重大です。

(It is all the more serious that this textbook has passed the inspection even though scholars and governments of Asian countries aptly criticized it in detail and urged the publisher not to print it.)

Note

Naosara is often used with another adverb *mashite (ya)* "still more; much more" to express a greater degree in a more emphatic way, as in Ex.(c).

(⇨ **mashite(ya)** (in this volume))

【Related Expression】

Naosara is synonymous with *issō*. *Naosara* in the KS and Exs. can be replaced by *issō*, except when the former occurs before *da* or *desu*, as in KS(B), Exs.(c) and (d).

[1] a. 前からタイに行きたいと思っていたが、すでに行ったことのある友人が強く勧めたので、{なおさら/一層}行きたくなった。(= KS(A))

b. 前からニューヨークは危ないところだと思っていたが、あのテロ事件以来、{なおさら/一層}、危険なところだと思うようになった。

(I had always thought that New York City was a dangerous place, but since that terrorist incident I've begun to think that it is even more dangerous.)

[2] a. 悪人さえも往生するのなら、まして善人は{なおさら/*一層}だ。

(= KS(B))

b. 旅で足を踏み入れるだけで、沖縄はいまだに戦争を引きずっていることを感じる。まして、現地の人では{なおさら/*一層}であろう。

(= Ex.(c))

nara de wa (no)   ならでは（の）   *phr.*   <w>

> a phrase indicating s.t. is "impossible if it's not X"

impossible if it's not ~; only possible with/by/at/etc.; not possible with/by/at/etc. other ~; very difficult with/by/at/etc. any other ~ but; you can expect only at/from/etc.; unless 【REL. *de nakereba*; *de nakute wa*; *de nai to*; *de nakattara*】

◆ **Key Sentences**

(A)

	Noun Phrase₁			Noun Phrase₂	
丸山博士の講演は、	一流の科学者	ならでは	の	示唆に富む内容	だった。

(Dr. Maruyama's lecture was rich with suggestion, the likes of which could only be heard from a first-class scientist (like himself).)

(B)

	Noun Phrase		
四季を通じて美しい景色が楽しめるのは	この地	ならでは	だ。

(Only here can we enjoy beautiful scenery through all four seasons.)

(C)

Noun Phrase		Vpot.neg		
女性	ならでは	でき	ない	仕事や役割もあるはずだ。

(There also must be jobs and roles that only women can perform (lit., that cannot be done unless you are a woman).)

Formation

(i)   NP₁ ならでの NP₂

　　　この店ならではのサービス   (service you can expect only at this shop)

(ii)   NP ならではだ

　　　学生ならではだ   (impossible unless s.o. is a student)

(iii) NP ならでは Vpot.neg ない

　　彼ならではできない　(only he can do s.t. (lit., s.t. cannot be done by anyone else but him))

Examples

(a) この大学の法律図書館には、この大学ならではの充実した資料が揃っている。

(The law library of this university houses a rich collection of documents, the likes of which do not exist at other institutions.)

(b) プロショップならではの品揃え。人気商品を特別価格でお求めいただけます。

(We have a range of products that would only be available at a shop for pros. Popular items are available at special prices.)

(c) このマンションは都心の住居ならではの便利さと快適さをお約束します。

(These condominiums promise the kind of convenience and comfort you can enjoy only in dwellings at the heart of the city.)

(d) 興味がわいたら、その分野を徹底して勉強してみる時間があるというのは学生ならではだ。

(It is only because they are students (lit., It is not possible unless they are students) that they have the time to thoroughly pursue fields they find they have an interest in.)

(e) 近郊にはゴルフコースが数多く、仕事帰りにハーフを回れるのは、緯度が高く日没の遅いカナダならではだ。

(There are many golf courses near Canadian cities, and, uniquely in Canada, where the sun sets late because of the high latitude, people play a half round on their way home from work.)

(f) 産地直送ならでは味わえない本場のおいしさをお届けいたします。

(We deliver delicious taste from the source, a taste you could not enjoy if we did not ship directly from the site of production.)

(g) 日本最高峰の富士山は、毎年夏の登山シーズンになると約20万人が山頂を目指す。登山者が長蛇の列をつくる光景は富士山ならでは見られないものである。

(In the summer climbing season every year, roughly 200,000 people aim for the summit of Mt. Fuji, the highest mountain in Japan. The long line of climbers is a scene that can't be seen anywhere but at Mt. Fuji.)

Notes

1. X *nara de wa* is equivalent to X *de nakereba* or X *de nakute wa*, which literally mean "if it is not X." Main clauses occurring with this phrase commonly involve the negative forms of potential verbs, as in KS(C), Exs.(f) and (g), or, less commonly, adjectives indicating impossibility, such as *fukanō* "impossible" or *muri* "impossible."

2. *Nara de wa* is often used as part of the structure X *nara de wa da*, as in KS(B), or X *nara de wa no* N, as in KS(A). These structures are the abbreviated forms of phrases like X *nara de wa fukanō da* "impossible if it is not X" and X *nara de wa fukanō na* N "N, which is impossible if it is not X," respectively.

3. *Nara de wa* is often used in advertisement copy, as in Exs.(b), (c) and (f).

4. X *nara de wa* is commonly used when a positive statement is made about X, although it is possible to use it to make a negative comment, as shown in (1).

   (1) a. 房子は彼女ならではの趣味の悪い服を着ていた。

      (Fusako was wearing clothes that, characteristically, showed bad taste.)

      b. そういうくだらない考えは、ジョージならでは思いつかないことだ。

      (Only George could come up with such a stupid idea.)

[Related Expressions]

Nara de wa, as it is used in KS(C), can be replaced with *de nakereba*, *de nakute wa*, *de nai to* or *de nakattara* "unless," as shown in [1].

   [1] a. 女性｛ならでは / でなければ / でなくては / でないと / でなかったら｝できない仕事や役割もあるはずだ。(= KS(C))

      b. 産地直送｛ならでは / でなければ / でなくては / でないと / でなかったら｝味わえない本場のおいしさをお届けいたします。(= Ex.(f))

Note that *de nakereba*, *de nakute wa*, *de nai to* and *de nakattara* cannot be used in place of *nara de wa* as it is used in KS(A) and (B).

   [2] a. 丸山博士の講演は、一流の科学者｛ならでは / *でなければ / *でなくては / *でないと / *でなかったら｝の示唆に富む内容だった。

(= KS(A))

b. 四季を通じて美しい景色が楽しめるのはこの地｜ならでは / *でなければ / *でなくては / *でないと / *でなかったら｜だ。(= KS(B))

narabi ni 並びに　*conj.*　<w>

| a conjunction used to combine two nouns or noun phrases | and; both ~ and ~; as well as 【REL. *to*; *oyobi*】 |

◆ **Key Sentence**

	Noun₁		Noun₂	
国連総会には	首相	並びに	外務大臣	が出席した。

(The prime minister and the foreign minister attended the U.N. General Assembly.)

N

Formation

N₁ 並びに N₂

学長並びに副学長　(the university president and the vice-president)

Examples

(a) 県並びに県内各市町村では、地域イントラネットを構築して、行政や福祉情報の円滑な提供に努めている。

(The prefecture and its municipalities have constructed local intranets, and are working to provide administrative and welfare information smoothly to their residents.)

(b) 以下は犬及びねこの引き取り並びに負傷動物の収容に関する措置要領である。

(What follows is an outline of procedures for caring for dogs and cats, and admitting injured animals.)

(c) その政党は、夫婦間における暴力の防止並びに被害者の保護に関する法律案を発表した。

(The political party announced laws for the prevention of spousal violence as well as the protection of the victims.)

(d) 今日は、大気や河川の汚染並びに酸性雨が環境に及ぼす影響についてお話しいたします。

(Today I am going to talk about the contamination of our air and rivers as well as acid rain's effect on them.)

(e) このホームページ並びにメールマガジンのスタッフをご紹介します。

(Let me introduce you to the staff of our website and mail magazine.)

(f) 本学学長の選挙資格者は、選挙公示の日における学長並びに専任の教授、准教授及び講師とする。

(Those who are qualified to be a candidate for president of this college are those who are full-time professors, associate professors and lecturers as well as the president at the time the election is announced.)

(g) 本日ここに、大統領、並びに国務長官ほか、御一行の歓迎の宴を開くことができましたことは、私の最も欣快とするところであります。

(It is my great pleasure that today we welcome the President, the Secretary of State and other honorable visitors to this reception.)

Notes

1. *Narabi ni* is a conjunction that usually combines two nouns or noun phrases, and means "and." (1a) is acceptable, but (1b) is unacceptable, because it uses *narabi ni* twice. In general, the conjunction is used only once in front of the last item. Therefore (1c) is acceptable.

(1) a. 糖尿病患者は、糖分並びに炭水化物を摂取しすぎない方がよい。

(Diabetes patients should take care not to consume excessive amounts of sugar and carbohydrates.)

b. *糖尿病患者は、糖分並びに炭水化物並びに酒類は摂取しすぎない方がよい。

(Diabetes patients should take care not to consume excessive amounts of sugar and carbohydrates and alcohol.)

c. 糖尿病患者は、糖分、炭水化物、並びに酒類は摂取しすぎない方がよい。

2. *Narabi ni* is used primarily in written Japanese, as in KS and Exs.(a)-(f), or in very formal speech, as in Ex.(g).

【Related Expressions】

Two conjunctions, *to* and *oyobi*, are related to *narabi ni*. The more commonly used is *to*, which is freely used to combine two or more nouns or noun phrases in both spoken and written Japanese.

Oyobi can also combine two nouns or noun phrases, but it is used only in written language or formal spoken language.

[1] a. 県｛並びに / と / 及び｝県内各市町村では、地域イントラネットを構築して、行政や福祉情報の円滑な提供に努めている。(= Ex.(a))

b. その政党は、夫婦間における暴力の防止｛並びに / と / 及び｝被害者の保護に関する法律案を発表した。(= Ex.(c))

However, there is a difference between *narabi ni* and *oyobi*: *Oyobi* is used to combine [A and B] and [C and D] in a schematic structure like [A *oyobi* B] *narabi ni* [C *oyobi* D], in which *oyobi* combines the basic constituents, but *narabi ni* combines the already conjoined larger items. An example follows.

[2] a. 以下は犬及びねこの引き取り並びに負傷動物の収容に関する措置要領である。(= Ex.(b))

b. 日本語には、動詞及び形容詞のように活用する品詞、並びに名詞、接続詞、及び助詞のように活用しない品詞がある。
(The Japanese language has parts of speech that are conjugated, such as verbs and adjectives, and other parts of speech which are not, such as nouns, conjunctions and particles.)

Additionally, *narabi ni* and *oyobi* can be used only once, but *to* must be used after every noun except for the final noun, as shown in [3].

[3] 糖尿病患者は、糖分｛と / *並びに / *及び｝、炭水化物｛と / 並びに / 及び｝酒類は摂取しすぎない方がよい。(= (1c))

(⇨ **to**¹ (DBJG: 473-76); **oyobi** (in this volume))

N

---

nari なり   *conj.*

~~a conjunction meaning "soon after"~~

the moment; when; as soon as; soon after; no sooner ~ than
【REL. *ya ina ya*】

◆ **Key Sentence**

	Vinf.nonpast		
妻_{つま}は私の顔を	見る	なり	泣_なき出_だした。

(My wife began to cry the moment she saw me (lit., my face).)

Formation

Vinf.nonpast なり

　知らせを聞くなり　(as soon as s.o. heard the news)

Examples

(a) 首相_{しゅしょう}は会議場_{かいぎじょう}を出るなり記者団_{きしゃだん}の質問攻_{しつもんぜ}めにあった。

(The prime minister was bombarded with questions by a group of reporters soon after he left the conference hall.)

(b) 部屋_{へや}に入るなりルームサービスの人がお茶とお菓子_{かし}を持ってきてくれた。

(No sooner had we entered our room than room service brought tea and sweets.)

(c) 編集長_{へんしゅうちょう}は私と顔を合わせるなり私をにらみつけ、「話がある」と言った。

(The chief editor glared at me when she saw me, and told me that we needed to talk.)

(d) 家に帰るまで何とかもつかと思ったが、バスを降_おりるなり激_{はげ}しい雨が降_ふり出_だした。

(I thought the weather would hold somehow until I got home, but as soon as I stepped off the bus, it started pouring.)

(e) 会議中_{かいぎちゅう}たばこが吸_すえなくて禁断症状_{きんだんしょうじょう}だった伊藤_{いとう}さんは、部屋_{へや}を出るなりたばこに火をつけた。

(Mr. Ito, who had shown withdrawal symptoms during the meeting because he was not allowed to smoke, lit a cigarette as soon as he got out of the room.)

(f) そのニュースが報道_{ほうどう}されるなり、放送局_{ほうそうきょく}に問い合わせの電話が殺到_{さっとう}した。

(Soon after the news was reported, phone queries flooded the broadcast center.)

(g) 所属レコード会社が宣伝に力を入れたため、そのアルバムは発売されるなり
ヒットチャート1位になった。

(Because the recording company made an effort to promote the album, it became No. 1 in the hit charts soon after it was released.)

Notes

1. *Nari* is always preceded by an informal nonpast verb, and the main clause is usually in the past tense. This means that the action represented by the nonpast verb is usually a past action or event and that the main clause cannot represent a future action, including a command or request, as shown in (1).

   (1) a. オフィスに{着いたらすぐ/*着くなり}電話を下さい。

   (Please give me a call as soon as you've arrived at your office.)

   b. 空港からお電話を{いただいたらすぐ/*いただくなり}課の者がお迎えに参ります。

   (Someone in our section will come to pick you up as soon as you give us a call from the airport.)

   c. 彼らは社長の許可が{出たらすぐ/*出るなり}このプロジェクトを始めるつもりだ。

   (They intend to begin this project as soon as they get the OK from the company president.)

   S₂ in "S₁ *nari* S₂" can represent a habitual or repeated action if the subject is not in the first person, as in (2). (See Note 2.)

   (2) a. アンはいつもオフィスに着くなりすぐメールをチェックする。

   (Ann always checks her e-mail as soon as she arrives at the office.)

   b. 挨拶するなり自分の部屋に入ってしまうというのはお客さまに失礼だよ。

   (It is rude to go to your room right after greeting guests, you know.)

2. In "S₁ *nari* S₂," when the subject of S₂ is the first person, the action in S₂ is usually spontaneous or uncontrollable. In (3a), for example, if the speaker stood up intentionally to greet the president, this sentence would be unnatural. Similarly, in (3b), if the speaker decided to get a can of beer from the refrigerator, this sentence would be unnatural.

(3) a. 私は社長が部屋に入ってくる**なり**｛無意識に立ち上がった／??立ち上がって挨拶した｝。

(The moment the president came into the room, ｛without thinking, I stood up／I stood up and greeted him｝.)

b. 私は家に帰る**なり**｛目眩がして玄関にしゃがみこんでしまった／??冷蔵庫からビールを取り出して一息に飲み干した｝。

(The moment I returned home, I ｛felt dizzy and squatted on my heels in the entrance hall／got a can of beer from the refrigerator and drank it in one gulp｝.)

The above restriction does not apply when the subject of S$_2$ is not in the first person, as in (4).

(4) a. 藤原さんは社長が部屋に入ってくる**なり**立ち上がって挨拶した。

(Ms. Fujiwara stood up and greeted the president the moment he came into the room.)

b. ジョンは家に帰る**なり**冷蔵庫からビールを取り出して一息に飲み干した。

(The moment John returned home, he got a can of beer from the refrigerator and drank it in one gulp.)

c. 君は先生の顔を見る**なり**何か話しに行ったけど、どうかしたの。

(You went over to talk to the teacher about something as soon as you saw him. Was something wrong?)

In first-person statements where the action in S$_2$ is controllable, other conjunctions are used, as shown in (5).

(5) a. 私は社長が部屋に入ってくる｛**とすぐ**／**と同時に**／**が早いか**／??**なり**｝立ち上がって挨拶した。

(The moment the president came into the room, I stood up and greeted him.)

b. 私は家に帰る｛**とすぐ**／**と同時に**／**が早いか**／??**なり**｝冷蔵庫からビールを取り出して一息に飲み干した。

(The moment I arrived home, I got a can of beer from the refrigerator and drank it in one gulp.)

naruhodo　なるほど　*adv.*

an adverb indicating that the speaker/writer affirms the correctness of s.t. he/she has heard/read/observed	indeed; it is true ~ (but); really; I see 【REL. *tashika ni*】

◆ **Key Sentences**

(A)

Sentence₁			Sentence₂
パリはきれいだと聞いていた	が、	なるほど	その芸術性には舌を巻いた。

(I had heard that Paris was a beautiful city, and (lit., but) indeed I was astounded by its artistry.)

(B)

	Sentence₁		Sentence₂
なるほど、	日本の官僚はいろいろと批判されている	が、	戦後の日本の復興は彼らに負うところが多い。

(It is true that Japanese bureaucrats are criticized in various ways, but we owe them for much of Japan's post-war recovery.)

(C)

A:	B:	
文化って、宗教のように倫理的な決まりが多いですね。	なるほど	ね。

(A: Culture, like religion, has a lot of ethical rules. / B: I see.)

Formation

(i)　S₁{が／けれど}、なるほど S₂。

　　若い{が／けれど}、なるほど、才能が豊かだ。　(S.o. is young, but is richly talented indeed.)

(ii)　なるほど、S₁{が／けれど}、S₂。

　　なるほど、一見くだらない{が／けれど}、研究の価値がある。　(It looks worthless at first sight, but it is worth researching.)

(iii)　なるほど(ね)。　(I see / Indeed / It makes sense.)

Examples

(a) この大学のことは大学案内で読んではいたが、実際に来てみると、なるほど、学生たちはすばらしい教育を受けているようだ。

(I had read about this college in a college guide, but by actually coming here myself I can see the students really seem to be getting a great education.)

(b) この辺りでは菜の花畑が４月中旬ごろ特にきれいだと聞いていたが、なるほど見事である。

(I had heard that the fields of rape blossoms around here are particularly beautiful around mid-April, and now that I've seen them myself, I have to say that they are indeed impressive.)

(c) 本日、川上弘美『椰子・椰子』を読了。なるほど面白い本だ。

(Today I finished reading Hiromi Kawakami's "*Yashi, Yashi* (Palm, Palm)." It's indeed an interesting book.)

(d) なるほど、これだけの規模のテロが起きると人々は恐怖に捕われるけれど、自分でコントロールできないことをくよくよ心配しても仕方がないだろう。

(It's true people are caught by fear when terrorism of this magnitude occurs, but it is no use worrying too much about what you cannot control.)

(e) なるほど日本の文化とドイツの文化は違っている点があるが、実は共通点の方が多いようだ。

(Indeed there are differences between Japanese culture and German culture, but actually it seems they have more similarities than differences.)

(f) A: 実は僕には好きな人がいるんですが、勇気がなくて告白できないんです。

(To tell you the truth, there's someone I love, but I don't have the courage to tell her.)

B: なるほど。でも、それは自分に対する自信が足りないからじゃないの？

(I see exactly what you mean. It's because you don't have enough self-confidence.)

(g) A: この使い捨てカメラって、写真を撮りたい時簡単に買えて、撮ったらそのままカメラ屋に現像に出せるのが魅力なんだ。面倒なフィルムの出し入れもないし。

(The attractive feature of this disposable camera is that you can buy one whenever you want to take a picture, and when you are done you can take it as is to a camera shop for developing. You don't need to bother putting film in and taking it out.)

B: なるほど。

(Oh, I see.)

Note

The adverb *naruhodo* is used when the speaker/writer wants to affirm what he/she has heard or read. There are three ways to use this adverb.

In the first type, the adverb is used before S₂, as shown in KS(A) and Exs.(a)-(c). In this case, the adverb is preceded by a disjunctive conjunction like *ga* or *keredo(mo)*. Here, the speaker/writer expresses what he/she has heard or read in S₁ and then confirms what is contrary to expectation in S₂. In Ex.(c), the disjunctive conjunction is missing in S₁, and what the speaker has heard or read is only implicitly expressed.

In the second type, the adverb is used at the beginning of S₁, which ends in a disjunctive conjunction like *ga* or *keredo(mo)*, as in KS(B), Exs.(d) and (e). In S₁ the speaker expresses what he/she has heard or read and gives an alternative view in S₂.

In the third type, the adverb is used almost like an interjection, *aizuchi* (i.e., a back-channel expression), as in KS(C), Exs.(f) and (g).

[Related Expression]

Every use of *naruhodo* in the KS and Exs. can be replaced by *tashika ni* without a change in meaning, except that *naruhodo* sounds more colloquial. However, there are cases in which *tashika ni* cannot be replaced by *naruhodo*, as in [1].

[1] a. 僕の自転車、{たしかに /*なるほど}ここに置いといたんだけど、ない。どうしたんだろう。

(I'm sure I placed my bike right here, but it's gone! I wonder what happened.)

b. 彼女、さっきまで{たしかに /*なるほど}ここにいたんだけど、どこに行ってしまったんだろう。

(She was here just a while ago. Where did she go?)

c. 日本の生活費は{たしかに /*なるほど}高いね。

(Living costs in Japan are no doubt high, aren't they?)

(⇨ ***tashikani ~ga*** (DIJG: 450-52))

nashi ni   なしに   *phr.*   <w>

| an adverbial phrase meaning "without (doing) s.t." | without 【REL. *nai de*; *zu ni*】 |

◆ **Key Sentences**

(A)

	VN			
料金は	予告	(すること)	なしに	変更する場合がございます。

(The fee may (lit., will sometimes) change without prior notice.)

(B)

		VN			
友達が	何の	連絡	も	なしに	いきなり訪ねてきた。

(My friend suddenly dropped by without contacting me first.)

(C)

	VN				Vpot.neg	
日本語の授業は	手続き	(すること)	なしに	は	聴講でき	ません。

(You cannot audit a Japanese class without going through the formal (registration) process.)

Formation

(i)   {N／VN (すること)／V*masu*／Vinf.nonpast こと} なしに

　　　権力なしに　(without (political) power)

　　　挨拶(すること)なしに　(without greeting)

　　　断りなしに　(without letting s.o. know s.t. in advance)

　　　(許可)を得ることなしに　(without obtaining (permission))

(ii) 何の{N / VN}もなしに

何の財産もなしに (without any estate/fortune)

何の挨拶もなしに (without any greeting)

何の断りもなしに (without s.o. knowing anything in advance)

(iii) 何の N も Vinf.nonpast ことなしに

何の許可も得ることなしに (without obtaining permission at all)

(iv) {N / VN(すること) / Vinf.nonpast こと}なしには Vpot.neg ない

コーヒーなしには生活できない (s.o. can't live without coffee)

準備運動(すること)なしには入れない (s.o. cannot enter without a warm-up)

辞書の助けなしには読めない (s.o. cannot read s.t. without the help of a dictionary)

深く考えることなしには書けない (s.o. can't write without thinking (about it) deeply)

Examples

(a) ソフトウエアの不正コピーには、許諾なしに複製されたソフトウエアや、偽造されたソフトウエアが含まれている。

(Illegal copies of software include software copied without permission and forged software.)

(b) お客様の同意なしに、第三者に個人情報を転送することはありません。

(We will never transfer private information to a third party without the customer's consent.)

(c) 男たちは何の許可もなしに事務所のコンピュータを勝手に使っていた。

(The men were using the office computers without permission.)

(d) キリスト教を理解することなしにヨーロッパの文化や社会を理解することは難しいと言われています。

(They say it is difficult to understand European culture and society without understanding Christianity.)

(e) この実験の最初の 10 年は何の成果も得ることなしに過ぎてしまった。

(The first 10 years of this experiment passed, and we had not obtained a result.)

(f) コンピュータと通信技術が飛躍的に発展するにつれ、社会生活が大きく変化し、いまやコンピュータなしには我々の生活が成立しなくなりつつある。

(With the rapid development of computers and communications technology, society has seen great changes, to the point that it is becoming harder to conduct our daily lives without computers.)

(g) 天気予報もテレビ中継も国際電話も、人工衛星の助けなしにはやっていけない時代になっている。

(We are now in an age in which weather forecasting, live TV broadcasting and international telephone calls are impossible without the help of satellites.)

(h) この掲示板では、営業目的の書き込みや著しく長い書き込みについては、断りなしに削除させていただくことがあります。

(Comments that are for sales purposes or are extremely long may be deleted from this bulletin board without prior notice.)

(i) 大事なことを何の話し合いもなしに決められて、私としては納得ができない。

(They have made an important decision on an issue without any discussion. I am dissatisfied.)

(j) 一切の政治権力なしに人々の自由を実現することは、はたして可能なのだろうか。

(I wonder if people's freedom can be realized without any political power.)

(k) 人一倍照れ屋だった父は、酒なしには人と話もできなかった。

(My father, who was twice as shy as other people, couldn't even talk with people without drinking *sake* first.)

Notes

1. ~ *nashi ni* is an adverbial phrase meaning "without (doing) s.t." The element that precedes *nashi ni* can be: (i) a *koto*-nominalized noun phrase, as shown in KS(A), (C), Exs.(d) and (e); (ii) a VN, as shown in KS(A)-(C) and Exs.(a)-(c); (iii) a V*masu* or (iv) a noun, as shown in Exs.(f)-(k).

2. Formation (ii) and (iii) are the most emphatic versions, meaning "without any."

3. *Nashi ni* is usually used in written Japanese or in formal spoken

Japanese. *Nashi* is the archaic version of *nai* "doesn't exist" and is used primarily in written Japanese.

4. When *wa* is attached to *nashi ni*, as in KS(C), Exs.(f), (g) and (k), the final predicate has to be in the negative.

【Related Expressions】

VN *nashi ni* can be replaced by Vneg *nai de* and Vneg *zu ni* if the subjects of the VN and the main verb are identical, as shown in [1].

[1] a. 料金は予告｛(すること)なしに / しないで / せずに｝変更する場合が ございます。(= KS(A))

b. 友達が何の連絡も｛なしに / しないで / せずに｝いきなり訪ねてきた。

(= KS(B))

When the subjects are different, as in Exs.(b) and (c), Vneg *nai de* and Vneg *zu ni* can be used with appropriate verbs, as shown in [2].

[2] a. お客様の同意｛なしに / を得ないで / を得ずに / *しないで / *せず に｝、第三者に個人情報を転送することはありません。(= Ex.(b))

b. 男たちは何の許可も｛なしに / 得ないで / 得ずに / *しないで / *せず に｝、事務所のコンピュータを勝手に使っていた。(= Ex.(c))

(⇨ ~**nai de** (DBJG: 271-73))

N

nasu   なす   *v.*

a verb that means "to cause s.t. to happen"

do; perform; make; change; constitute
【REL. *suru*; *okonau*; *ni/to naru*】

◆ **Key Sentences**

(A)

Noun₁			Noun₂		
災い	（を）	転じて	福	と	なす。
(One can turn misfortune into a blessing. [proverb])					

(B)

	Noun		
比喩に関しては現在多くの	研究	が	なされている。
(A large amount of research is being done on metaphors now.)			

(C)

	Noun		
人間というものは、	悪	を	なす 存在である。
(Human beings exist in order to do evil.)			

(D)

	Noun		
民主主義はアメリカ合衆国の	基盤	を	なす 思想である。
(Democracy is the founding ideology (lit., the ideology that constitutes the foundation) of the United States of America.)			

Formation

(i) N₁ を N₂ となす

   醜を美となす   (s.o. changes ugliness to beauty)

(ii) N がなされる

   外国語教育がなされる   (foreign language education is provided)

(iii) N をなす

   善をなす   (s.o. does good deeds)

   基本をなす   (s.t. constitutes the foundation)

Examples

(a) 顧客創造のためには自社製品の潜在利益を利益となす努力を払わなければならない。

(We have to make the effort to turn our products' potential profit into (real) profit in order to gain more customers.)

(b) 患者が入院時に病名や病状について理解していない場合は、必要に応じて適切な説明がなされるべきである。

(If patients do not understand the name of their disease and its symptoms at the time of hospitalization, they should be given an appropriate explanation as needed.)

(c) インターネットに関してこのような質問がなされる可能性は高い。

(Such questions are likely to be asked regarding the Internet.)

(d) 善をなすのを急げ。悪から心を退けよ。

(Hurry to do good. Turn your mind away from evil.)

(e) 権利の保護には最善の努力をなすことを目標にしている。

(For the protection of our rights we aim at doing our very best.)

(f) コンピュータサイエンスの基本をなす考え方は、様々な科学の分野で重要になってくると思われる。

(It seems that the fundamental concepts (lit., the concepts underlying the foundation) underlying computer science will become important in various fields of science.)

(g) 情報リスクマネジメントという視点で、ビジネスの根幹をなす情報システムを評価・管理することが必須だ。

(From the viewpoint of risk management, it is essential to assess and manage the informational systems that constitute the core of a business.)

Notes

1. *Nasu* is a formal, classic transitive verb that corresponds to the verb *suru*.

2. *Nasu* is used in four distinct ways. First, it means "s.o. changes s.t. into s.t. else," as in KS(A) and Ex.(a). The second meaning is "s.t. is done," as in KS(B), Exs.(b) and (c). The third meaning is "s.o. does s.t.," as in KS(C), Exs.(d) and (e), and the fourth meaning is "s.t. constitutes s.t. else," as in KS(D), Exs. (f) and (g).

3. Because the third use is limited to passive use, the active use of *nashite iru* in (1) is unacceptable. It has to be replaced by *shite iru*.

(1) 多くの学者が比喩の研究を{*なし／し}ている。
(Many scholars are doing research on metaphors.)

4. There are several frequently used idioms that include *nasu*.

(2) a. 色をなす　(s.o. turns red with anger)
b. 群れをなす　(s.o./s.t. forms a group / flocks together)
c. 恐れをなす　(s.o. shows fear)
d. 重きをなす　(s.o. is influential)

[Related Expressions]

I. *Suru* can replace *nasu* when the latter means "change s.t. into s.t. else" (Formation (i)) and "s.t. is done" (Formation (ii)), as shown in [1]. However, *nasu* is more formal than *suru*.

[1] a. ここを根拠地と{なす／する}。
(They make this place a base of operation.)

b. 比喩に関しては現在多くの研究が{なされて／されて}いる。
(= KS(B))

Note that [2] is marginally acceptable, apparently because the phrase is a set phrase.

[2] 災い(を)転じて福と{なす／??する}。(= KS(A))

Suru cannot replace *nasu* when the latter means "s.o. does s.t.," as shown in [3], or "s.t. constitutes s.t. else," as shown in [4]. Note that unlike *nasu* in [3] and [4], *nasu* in [5] can be replaced by *suru*, because *doryoku* is a VN, whereas *aku* "evil" and *zen* "good" aren't.

[3] a. 人間というものは、悪を{なす／??する}存在である。(= KS(C))

b. 善を{なす／??する}のを急げ。悪から心を退けよ。(= Ex.(d))

[4] a. 民主主義はアメリカ合衆国の基盤を{なす／*する}思想である。
(= KS(D))

b. コンピュータサイエンスの基本を{なす／*する}考え方は、様々な科学の分野で重要になってくると思われる。(= Ex.(f))

[5] 権利の保護には最善の努力を{なす/する}ことを目標にしている。

(= Ex.(e))

II. The verbs *okonau* and *suru* "do; put s.t. into practice" can replace *nasu* when the latter is used in the passive form and means "do; perform; conduct; execute," and when what is being practiced is a significant matter, as in [5]. Both *okonau* and *nasu* are formal expressions and are used in written Japanese, while *suru* is less formal and is used in spoken language.

[6] a. 比喩に関しては現在多くの研究が{なされて/行われて/されて}いる。(= KS(B))

b. 環境保護の活動が盛んに{なされて/行われて/されて}いる。

(Activities for environmental protection are being actively conducted.)

As shown in [7], *nasu*, *okonau* and *suru* are interchangeable in passive sentences with the VNs *kenkyū* "research" and *katsudō* "activity," as well as with communication-related VNs such as *giron* "discussion," *hon'yaku* "translation," *shinsei* "application," *yōkyū* "demand," and *irai* "request." However, non-communication-related VNs, such as *kensetsu* "construction," *seizō* "manufacturing," *setchi* "installment," *hakai* "destruction" (among others) cannot be used with *nasu* and *suru* in passive sentences.

[7] a. その問題に関して様々な議論が{なされて/行われて/されて}いる。

(Regarding the problem, various discussions are being conducted.)

b. この町では最近高層ビルの建設が盛んに{行われて/?なされて/*されて}いる。

(Recently, high-rises are being built robustly in this town.)

III. ~ *ni/to naru* can replace ~ *o nasu* "constitute," as shown in [8] below, without any difference in meaning except that ~ *o nasu* sounds more formal than ~ *ni/to naru*.

[8] a. 民主主義はアメリカ合衆国の基盤{をなす/になる/となる}思想である。(= KS(D))

b. コンピュータサイエンスの基本{をなす/になる/となる}考え方は、様々な科学の分野で重要になってくると思われる。(= Ex.(f))

naze ka　なぜか　　*adv.*　　<w>

an adverb indicating that the speaker/writer doesn't know the cause of / reason for s.t.	I don't know why; without knowing why; for an unknown reason 【REL. *dōshite (da) ka*; *dō iu wake (da) ka*】

◆ **Key Sentence**

このところ	なぜか	体の調子が悪い。

(I don't know why, but I haven't felt well lately.)

Examples

(a) ヨーロッパやアジアには受け入れられなかったSFが、なぜか日本には根づいた。

(Science fiction, which did not catch on in Europe and Asia, took root in Japan for some unknown reason.)

(b) なぜか僕は日本語の難しさにはまってしまった。

(For some reason, I got hooked by the difficulty of Japanese language.)

(c) 最近私が住んでいる町ではなぜか古本屋が増えている。

(I don't know why, but lately the number of used bookstores (in the town) where I live has grown.)

(d) ログインの手順を教えて下さい。なぜかできなくなってしまったんです。

(Please teach me how to log in. I don't know why, but I can't do it anymore.)

(e) 自分の文化のリズムには、なぜか体が自然と反応し、踊りたくなる。

(For some unknown reason, our bodies respond spontaneously to our own cultural rhythms, and we feel like dancing!)

Notes

1. *Naze ka* "for some unknown reason/cause" is an abbreviated form of the adverbial clause *naze ka shiranai/wakaranai keredo/ga* "I don't know why but ~."

2. *Naze ka* can be used anywhere in a sentence, as in (1).

(1) a. **なぜか**僕は日本語の難しさにはまってしまった。(= Ex.(b))

b. 僕は**なぜか**日本語の難しさにはまってしまった。

c. 僕は日本語の難しさに**なぜか**はまってしまった。

3. *Naze ka* can be replaced by *naze da ka*, although it is much less frequently used.

(2) このところ｛**なぜか / なぜだか**｝体の調子が悪い。(= KS)

【Related Expressions】

Dōshite (da) ka and *dō iu wake (da) ka*, which are more colloquial than *naze (da) ka*, can replace the latter in all the KS and Exs. without changing the meaning.

[1] a. このところ｛**なぜ（だ）/ どうして（だ）/ どういうわけ（だ）**｝か体の調子が悪い。(= KS)

b. ｛**なぜ（だ）/ どうして（だ）/ どういうわけ（だ）**｝か僕は日本語の難しさにはまってしまった。(= Ex.(b))

N

---

naze nara(ba) ~ kara da   なぜなら（ば）～からだ   *str.*   <w>

| ⎰ a structure used to introduce a reason for the statement in the preceding sentence | the reason is that ~; because 【REL. *kara*; *node*; *naze ka to iu to ~ kara da*】 |

◆ Key Sentence

Sentence₁		Sentence₂	
彼^{かれ}はみんなに好かれている。	なぜなら（ば）、	誰^{だれ}にでも親切だ	からだ。
(Everybody likes him. The reason is that he is kind to everybody.)			

Formation

S。なぜなら（ば）〜からだ。

食べない。なぜなら（ば）食欲がないからだ。　(I won't eat it. The reason is that I don't have an appetite.)

Examples

(a) 私は自分が好きです。なぜならば、今を自由に生きているからです。

(I like myself. The reason is that I am living freely in the moment.)

(b) ゲームにおいて最も重要な要素は、目的です。なぜならば、ゲームは本能ではなく理性で行われるものだからです。

(The most important element of a game is the objective. This is because games are played not by instinct but by reason.)

(c) 外国語学習者は物事を考える時、自分の母語で考える。なぜならば、目標言語では考えがまとめられないからだ。

(People who are learning a foreign language think in their mother tongue (lit., when they think). The reason is that they cannot think coherently in the target language.)

(d) 変化を遂げない経営は当然効率が悪くなります。なぜならば顧客も競合他社も常に変化しているからです。

(Management that doesn't change will become ineffective, as a matter of course. The reason is that both customers and competitors are always changing.)

(e) 近現代の日本が本当に正しい道を歩んできたのかどうかは吟味に値する。なぜならば、その過程で日本が失ったものも多いからである。

(Whether modern Japan has actually been taking the right path should be examined. The reason is that Japan has lost many things during that process.)

Notes

1. The structure *naze nara(ba) ~ kara da* is a formal way to introduce a reason for the statement presented in the preceding sentence.

2. The focus of the structure is the reason part of the sentence. (See Related Expression I.)

【Related Expressions】

I. All the KS and Exs. can be rephrased using *kara* or *node*. The major
    difference between *naze nara(ba) ~ kara da* and *kara/node* is that the
    former always focuses on the reason, whereas the latter usually focuses
    on what is stated after *kara/node*, not on the reason. The underlined part
    is under focus.

　　[1]　a. 彼はみんなに好かれている。**なぜなら**、誰にでも親切だからだ。

　　　　　　　　　　　　　　　　　　　　　　　　　　　　　　　(= KS)

　　　　→彼は誰にでも親切{**だから**/**なので**}、<u>みんなに好かれている</u>。

　　　　b. ゲームにおいて最も重要な要素は、目的です。**なぜならば**、ゲームは
　　　　　　本能ではなく理性で行われるものだからです。(= Ex.(b))

　　　　→ゲームは本能ではなく理性で行われるもの{**だから**/**なので**}、<u>ゲー</u>
　　　　　<u>ムにおいて最も重要な要素は、目的です</u>。

Because *naze nara(ba) ~ kara da* places a sharp focus on the reason,
it cannot be used in a situation where someone politely expresses the
reason why he/she cannot do something for someone, as shown in [2].
It is because the reason for closing the store is so conspicuous that it
sounds impolite in Japanese.

N

　　[2]　*来月は休業いたします。**なぜなら**店内を改装するからです。

　　　　(We will be closed next month. The reason is that we will be re-
　　　　modeling (the inside of) the store.)

　　　　→店内を改装するので来月は休業いたします。

The second difference between *naze nara(ba) ~ kara da* and *kara/node*
is that the former is used in formal written Japanese, whereas the latter
can be used in both colloquial and written Japanese, as shown in [3].

　　[3]　a. *今日はね、学校を休むよ。**なぜならば**頭がガンガン痛いからだ。

　　　　　　(I'm not going to school today. The reason is that I have a really
　　　　　　bad headache.)

　　　　→今日はね、頭がガンガン痛い{**から**/**んで**}、学校は休むよ。

　　　　b. ??あたし、彼が大好きなの。**なぜならば**、彼、とても優しいから。

　　　　　　(I like him very much. The reason is that he is so considerate.)

　　　　→あたし、彼、とても優しい{**から**/**んで**}、大好きなの。

　　　　　　　　　　　　　　(⇨ **kara**³ (DBJG: 179-81); **node** (DBJG: 328-31))

II. *Naze ka to iu to ~ kara da* can replace *naze nara(ba) ~ kara da* without the meaning of the sentence changing.

[4] a. 彼はみんなに好かれている。{なぜなら（ば）/なぜかというと}、誰にでも親切だからだ。(= KS)

b. ゲームにおいて最も重要な要素は、目的です。{なぜなら（ば）/なぜかというと}、ゲームは本能ではなく理性で行われるものだからです。

(= Ex.(b))

n bakari (ni)   んばかり（に）   *adv. phr.*   <w>

> an adverbial phrase that is used when a situation looks as if s.o. were about to do s.t. or as if s.t. were about to occur literally or figuratively

as if ~ were about to ~; almost

◆ **Key Sentences**

(A)

	Vneg				
犬は	噛みつか	ん	ばかり	に	僕に向かってほえた。
(The dog barked at me as if it were about to bite.)					

(B)

	Vneg				
どの演奏も若さと情熱が	あふれ	ん	ばかり	に	満ちていた。
(Every performance was filled with an overwhelming amount of youth and passion (lit., as if youth and passion were about to overflow).)					

(C)

	Vneg				Noun	
時折、木の枝も	折れ	ん	ばかり	の	強風	が吹いていた。

(Occasionally the wind was blowing so hard it seemed the tree branches would break.)

(D)

	Vneg			
驚いて腰を	抜かさ	ん	ばかり	だった。

(I was so frightened that it seemed I was about to lose the use of my legs (lit., to lose my lower back).)

Formation

(i) Vneg んばかりに   (Exception: する→せんばかりに)

泣かんばかりに   (as if s.o. were about to cry)

発狂せんばかりに   (as if s.o. were about to go mad)

(ii) Vneg んばかりの N

心臓が張り裂けんばかりの痛み   (heart-breaking pain (lit., pain that felt as if the heart were about to break))

(iii) Vneg んばかり{だ/だった}

家屋は倒れんばかり{だ/だった}   (it is/was as if the houses were about to collapse)

Examples

(a) その選手がシュートを決めた時、夜空に鳴り響く雷鳴をかき消さんばかりに、大歓声が競技場にとどろいた。

(When the player scored a goal, a big shout of jubilation reverberated throughout the arena, as though it would muffle the rumble of thunder in the night sky.)

(b) 樹高 10 メートルの梢から地面に届かんばかりに垂れ下がっている様子は、まさに流れ落ちる桜花の滝にふさわしい。

(The way in which the cherry blossoms are hanging from the top of the branch of the 10-meter tree, as if they were about to touch the ground, is just worthy of being called a cherry blossom waterfall.)

(c) 「風の谷のナウシカ」を娘さんに薦められて見たお父さんは、涙を流さんばかりに感激した。

(The father was so deeply moved by "Nausicaä of the Valley of the Wind," which his daughter recommended he watch, that he almost cried.)

(d) 演奏が終わるか終わらないかのうちに、この曲を知っているのは自分だと言わんばかりに拍手をする人もいます。

(Some people begin applauding just as a performance is coming to an end as if they were showing (lit., saying) how well they know the piece.)

(e) 彼に別れたいと言われた時には、私は胸が張り裂けんばかりに苦しかった。

(When he told me he wanted to break up, it was so painful I thought my chest would burst.)

(f) 彼の死を聞いた時、彼女は気も狂わぬばかりに泣き叫んだ。

(When she heard the news of his death, she screamed as if she were crazy.)

(g) 上司から叱りつけられた山崎は土下座せぬばかりに平身低頭して謝った。

(When his boss told him off, Yamazaki apologized, bowing to the ground as if he were about to get down on his hands and knees.)

(h) 彼女はいつもこぼれんばかりの笑みをたたえている。

(She is always smiling as if her smiles would overflow.)

(i) 引っ越しの時あまり重いものを持ったので、腕が肩から抜けんばかりだった。

(During the move I carried such heavy stuff that it felt as if my arms were about to fall out of their sockets (lit., come out from the shoulders).)

Notes

1. ~*n bakari ni* is an adverbial phrase that expresses a counterfactual situation in which something is about to take place. This *n* is the shortened form of the old negative marker *nu*. Thus the preceding verb has to be Vneg. As shown in Exs.(f) and (g), *nu* can replace *n*, creating a more formal written style.　　　　　(⇨ *-nu* (DIJG: 315-17))

2. The noun modification form of ~*n bakari ni* is ~ *bakari no*, as in KS(C) and Ex.(h).

3. ~*n bakari da/datta* can be used at the end of a sentence, as shown in KS(D) and Ex.(i).

---

negau / **negaimasu**   願う / 願います   *v.*

> a verb that expresses a polite request

please; ask (for)
【REL. V*te kudasai*; *o* V*masu kudasai*】

◆ Key Sentences

(A)

		V*masu*	
初めに、これだけは必ず	お	**読み**	願います。
(Please be sure to read at least this (part) first.)			

(B)

		VN	
禁煙に	ご	**協力**	願います。
(Thank you for not smoking (lit., Please cooperate with us in non-smoking).)			

Formation

(i)　お V*masu* 願います

　　　お書き願います　(please write it)

　　　お持ち願います　(please carry/take/bring it)

(ii)　ご VN 願います　(where VN = Sino-Japanese compound)

　　　ご報告願います　(please report it)

　　　ご教授願います　(please teach me)

Examples

(a) ご相談・ご意見・ご質問などがありましたら、下記へお知らせ願います。

(If you have opinions, questions, or requests for advice (lit., If there are things on which you want to consult us, your opinions and your questions), please contact us at the following (address).)

(b) 当オンラインショップで商品をご注文いただく場合は、まず最初にカタログページからご希望の商品をお選び願います。

(When you place an order for merchandise at this online shop, please first select the merchandise you want from the catalog pages.)

(c) この喫煙所は、入院しておられる患者さんの施設です。外来の方々は利用できませんのでご了承願います。

(This smoking room is for hospitalized patients' use, so please be advised (lit., understand) that outpatients are not allowed to use it.)

(d) 応募に際しては、以下の書類をEメールまたは郵便にてご送付願います。

(When you apply, please send the following documents by e-mail or regular mail.)

(e) 電車とホームの間が広く空いています。足元にご注意願います。

(There is a wide gap between the train and the platform. Please watch your step.)

(f) 学術研究を目的とする方以外の当研究所図書館の利用はご遠慮願います。

(Please refrain from using this laboratory library for any purpose other than academic research. (lit., Those whose purpose is other than academic research are asked not to use this laboratory's library.))

Notes

1. "*O* + V*masu negaimasu*" and "*go* + VN (Sino-Japanese word) + *negaimasu*" are used as polite request expressions.

2. In *go* N *negaimasu*, the N is a VN of Sino-Japanese origin. When Western borrowed words such as *adobaisu* "advice," *kopī* "copy" or *daunrōdo* "download" are used, they do not take the politeness marker *go-* or *o-*.

   (1) a. {ø /＊ご /＊お}アドバイス願います。 (Please give me advice.)

   　　 b. {ø /＊ご /＊お}コピー願います。 (Please make copies.)

   　　 c. {ø /＊ご /＊お}ダウンロード願います。 (Please download it.)

d. ｛ø /＊ご /＊お｝サイン願います。　(Please sign your name.)

3. The informal version *negau* is used in dependent clauses, as follows.

(2) a. ご協力願うこともあろうかと思いますので、その節にはどうぞよろし
く。

(I think we will ask for your cooperation (some day). In that
event, we would appreciate your consideration.)

b. お支払い願う時はあらかじめお知らせいたします。

(We will inform you in advance when we ask for payment.)

4. The past tense of *negau* can be used, as shown in (3) below.

(3) a. 学会の挨拶のため学長にご出席(を)願った。

(We asked the university president to attend the conference in
order to greet the audience.)

b. 経済界の大御所にご助力(を)願った。

(We asked for assistance from a powerful figure in the financial
world.)

[Related Expressions]

V*te kudasai* and *o*-V*masu kudasai* are also polite request forms. First,
o-V*masu negau* can be rephrased by V*te kudasai* or *o*-V*masu kudasai*, as
shown in [1a]. Second, *go*-VN *negau* can be rephrased by VN *shite kudasai*
or *go*-VN *kudasai*, as in [1b]. Third, VN *negau* can be rephrased by VN *(o)
shite kudasai*, as in [1c, d] below. The rephrased versions are less formal
than the *negau/negaimasu* version. V*te kudasai* is the least formal.

[1] a. 初めに、これだけは必ず｛お読み願います /読んで下さい /お読み下
さい｝。(= KS(A))

b. 禁煙に｛ご協力願います /協力して下さい /ご協力下さい｝。

(= KS(B))

c. アドバイス｛願います /(を)して下さい｝。(= (1a))

d. コピー｛願います /(を)して下さい｝。(= (1b))

(⇨ **~*kudasai*** (DBJG: 209-10))

Note that verbs that have special polite forms, such as *suru* (*nasaru*) "do,"
miru (*goran ni naru*) "see," *kiru* (*o-meshi ni naru*) "wear," *iu* (*ossharu*) "say,"

iku (*irassharu*) "go," *kuru* (*irassharu*) "come," *iru* (*irassharu*) "be"and *taberu* (*meshiagaru*) "eat,"cannot be used as the V*masu* in *o*-V*masu negau*.

[2] a. この書類にサインを{なさって下さい/*おし願います}。
       (Please sign this form.)

   b. この手紙を{ご覧下さい/*お見願います}。
      (Please take a look at this letter.)

   c. また{いらっしゃって下さい/お出で下さい/*お来願います}。
      (Please come back again.)

ni hikikae   にひきかえ   *phr.*

| a phrase that indicates a sharp contrast | in contrast to ~; while; whereas 【REL. *ni kuraberu to/kurabete*; *kawari ni*; *ni taishite*】 |

◆ **Key Sentences**

(A)

Noun Phrase		
几帳面な父	にひきかえ、	息子はだらしなかった。

(The son, in contrast to his meticulous father, was slovenly.)

(B)

Sentence₁			Sentence₂
この大学は教育の質がとてもいい	の	にひきかえ、	学内の設備が劣る。

(While the quality of education at this college is excellent, the quality of the campus facilities is inferior.)

Formation

(i) {N / Dem. pron.} にひきかえ

       健康な母にひきかえ   (in contrast to my healthy mother)

       {これ / それ} にひきかえ   (in contrast to this/that)

(ii) {V / Adj(*i*)} inf のにひきかえ

勉強がよくできるのにひきかえ　(s.o. is academically gifted, while ~)

部屋が広いのにひきかえ　(the room is spacious, while ~)

(iii) {Adj(*na*)stem / N} {な / だった} のにひきかえ

便利なのにひきかえ　(s.t. is convenient, while ~)

父は大学教授だったのにひきかえ　(my father was a college professor, while ~)

Examples

(a) 昨日にひきかえ今朝は快晴です。

(In contrast to yesterday, this morning is perfectly clear.)

(b) 姉は何事にも堅実なタイプなのにひきかえ、妹は奔放なタイプだ。

(My older sister is the type who's steady in any situation, while my younger sister is the free-wheeling type.)

(c) 昨年が楽しい年だったのにひきかえ、今年はいろいろな意味で試練の年だった。

(The last year was an enjoyable year, whereas this year has been a year of trials for all sorts of reasons.)

(d) 16世紀のフランスでは、貴族の食事は贅沢だったのにひきかえ、市民の食事はとても貧しいものだった。

(In France in the 16th century, the nobility ate extravagantly while the common people ate very poorly.)

(e) 我々は「Aという国は、こんなにすばらしいことをしている。それにひきかえ日本は全く駄目だ」という話をずっと聞かされ続けたものだ。

("Country A is doing this really fabulous thing. In contrast, Japan is completely useless." We have been hearing this kind of statement (continuously) for a long time.)

(f) ハーバードやMITの名前は日本で広く知られているのにひきかえ、残念ながら私が教えているプリンストンの名前はほとんど知られていない。

(Names such as Harvard and MIT are well-known in Japan while, regrettably, the name (of the school) where I am teaching, Princeton, is hardly known.)

(g) EUについては、経済問題はよく議論されてきたのにひきかえ、文化面の議論があまりなされてこなかった。

(Although the EU's economic problems have been frequently debated, its cultural issues have hardly been discussed.)

(h) このアパートは駅にとても近くて便利なのにひきかえ、部屋は狭く、家賃も高い。

(While this apartment is very close to the station and convenient, the room is small and the rent is high.)

(i) 日本の大学は、入るのが難しいのにひきかえ、出るのは簡単だと言われている。

(They say that while it is difficult to enter a Japanese university, it is easy to graduate.)

Notes

1. *Ni hikikae* is used to indicate a sharp contrast between two people/things/facts. *Hikikae* comes from the *masu*-stem of the verb *hikikaeru* "to exchange."

2. *Ni hikikae* can be used after a noun, as in KS(A) and Ex.(a); a demonstrative pronoun, as in Ex.(e); or a *no*-nominalized clause, as in KS(B), Exs.(b)-(d) and (f)-(i).

[Related Expressions]

I. In some situations, *ni hikikae* can be replaced by *ni kuraberu to* or by *ni kurabete*, as shown in [1].

[1] a. 几帳面な父に{ひきかえ／比べると／比べて}、息子はだらしなかった。(= KS(A))

b. 昨日に{ひきかえ／比べると／比べて}今朝は快晴です。(= Ex.(a))

c. 16世紀のフランスでは、貴族の食事は贅沢だったのに{ひきかえ／比べると／比べて}、市民の食事はとても貧しいものだった。(= Ex.(d))

d. 我々は「Aという国は、こんなにすばらしいことをしている。それに{ひきかえ／比べると／比べて}日本は全く駄目だ」という話をずっと聞かされ続けたものだ。(= Ex.(e))

However, when *ni hikikae* is used to mean "in exchange for ~," it cannot be replaced by either expression, as shown in [2]. Note that the structure takes the form "S₁ *no ni hikikae* S₂."

[2] a. この大学は教育の質がとてもいいのに｛ひきかえ /*比べると /*比べて｝、学内の設備が劣る。(= KS(B))

b. このアパートは駅にとても近くて便利なのに｛ひきかえ /*比べると /*比べて｝、部屋は狭く、家賃も高い。(= Ex.(h))

c. 日本の大学は、入るのが難しいのに｛ひきかえ /*比べると /*比べて｝、出るのは簡単だと言われている。(= Ex.(i))

(⇨ *ni kuraberu to/kurabete* (DIJG: 256-57))

II. In the examples in [2], another phrase *kawari ni* "in exchange for ~" can replace *ni hikikae.*

[3] a. この大学は教育の質がとてもいい｛のにひきかえ /代わりに｝、学内の設備が劣る。(= KS(B))

b. このアパートは駅にとても近くて便利な｛のにひきかえ /代わりに｝、部屋は狭く、家賃も高い。(= Ex.(h))

c. 日本の大学は、入るのが難しい｛のにひきかえ /代わりに｝、出るのは簡単だと言われている。(= Ex.(i))

(⇨ *(no) kawari ni* (DIJG: 116-21))

N

III. *Ni hikikae* can be replaced by *ni taishite*, which expresses sharp contrast without any meaning of "exchange."

[4] a. この大学は教育の質がとてもいいのに｛ひきかえ /対して｝、学内の設備が劣る。(= KS(B))

b. 我々は「Aという国は、こんなにすばらしいことをしている。それに｛ひきかえ /対して｝日本は全く駄目だ」という話をずっと聞かされ続けたものだ。(= Ex.(e))

c. ハーバードやMITの名前は日本で広く知られているのに｛ひきかえ /対して｝、残念ながら私が教えているプリンストンの名前はほとんど知られていない。(= Ex.(f))

d. EUについては、経済問題はよく議論されてきたのに｛ひきかえ /対して｝、文化面の議論があまりなされてこなかった。(= Ex.(g))

(⇨ *ni taishite/taishi* (DIJG: 275-78))

ni itatte wa   にいたっては   *comp. prt.*   <w>

a compound particle that indicates an extreme example

when it comes to ~; as for; for example
【REL. *no ba'ai (wa)*; *to kitara*】

◆ **Key Sentence**

	Noun		
人間(にんげん)の体は60％が水、魚は75％、	くらげ	にいたっては	96％が水だ。

(Human bodies are 60 percent water, while fish are 75 percent water. As for jellyfish, the figure is 96 percent.)

Formation

N にいたっては

　学生にいたっては   (when it comes to students)

Examples

(a) 私自身(じしん)は社会人になってからコンピュータを使い始めたが、新入社員は中学生の頃(ころ)から、私の子供(こども)たちにいたっては、生まれた時から家にコンピュータがある世代だ。

(I myself started to use a computer after I graduated and got a job, but the new hires got started on computers when they were still junior high school students. As for my children, they belong to the generation for whom a computer is available at home from the time of their birth.)

(b) 一年間に日本中の廃棄物(はいきぶつ)は5,160万トン、しかもこれは家庭(かてい)や飲食店(いんしょくてん)などから出る一般(いっぱん)廃棄物で、産業廃棄物にいたってはその8倍(ばい)近くの4億(おく)8百万トンも出ているのです。

(In a year, 51,600,000 tons of waste is produced across Japan. And, this is just general waste from homes and eating places. When it comes to industrial waste, as much as 408,000,000 tons of waste, or nearly eight times as much as general waste, is produced.)

(c) 少林寺拳法(しょうりんじけんぽう)では女性拳士(じょせいけんし)の数(かず)が増加傾向(ぞうかけいこう)にあり、高校や大学の部活動(ぶかつどう)にいたっては、部員(ぶいん)の半数(はんすう)近くが女性だ。

(In the case of *Shōrinji Kenpō*, the number of female practitioners is increasing; in clubs at high schools and colleges, for example, almost half of the members are girls.)

(d) 今私たちの生活には多くの椅子が使われている。ダイニングにいたっては、ダイニングテーブルと椅子は、もはや一般的である。

(Today we use many chairs in our daily life. As for the dining room, a (set of) dining table and chairs is the standard.)

(e) 日本には、一般紙やスポーツ紙、専門的な業界紙など様々な新聞があるが、雑誌にいたっては、どんな分野のものでもある。

(In Japan there are various newspapers, such as general papers, sports newspapers, or papers that specialize in certain industries, but as for magazines, they cover all fields.)

(f) アジア太平洋地域以外にも、旅行者の注目を集めている地域がある。中央アメリカは昨年、旅行者数が23％増、中東も17.5％増となった。スペインも９％増加したし、モロッコにいたっては、22％も増えた。

(Areas outside the Asia Pacific region have been drawing the attention of travelers as well. Last year Central America saw a 23 percent increase in travelers; in the Middle East, it was 17.5 percent. Spain saw 9 percent more travelers, and travel (lit., travelers) to Morocco, of all places, grew 22 percent.)

Notes

1. *Ni itatte wa* is a compound particle that indicates an extreme example. It is often the case that other examples are listed explicitly before the one introduced with this compound particle. But, as in Exs.(c) and (d), the foregoing examples are implicitly expressed. For example, in Ex.(c), the speaker/writer is implicitly comparing *Shōrinji Kenpō* groups, noting that the high school and university clubs have the largest number of female members.

2. The compound particle is used in written Japanese or in formal spoken Japanese.

3. X *ni itatte wa*, which consists of the V*te* of the verb of motion *itaru* "reach" and the topic marker *wa*, means "when (the topic) reaches X."

[Related Expressions]

I. *No ba'ai (wa)* "in the case of" can be used in place of *ni itatte wa* in all the KS and Exs., but it doesn't have the meaning of "an extreme example."

[1]　a. 人間の体は60％が水、魚は75％、くらげ{にいたって／の場合}は96％が水だ。(= KS)

　　b. 私自身は社会人になってからコンピュータを使い始めたが、新入社員は中学生の頃から、私の子供たち{にいたって／の場合}は、生まれた時から家にコンピュータがある世代だ。(= Ex.(a))

II. There is another colloquial phrase, *to kitara* "when it comes to," that can replace *ni itatte wa*, but only when the speaker/writer is criticizing a situation, as shown in [2].

[2]　a. 私の主人{にいたっては／ときたら}仕事だけで、家のことは何もしない。

　　　(When it comes to my husband, it's all about his work; he never does anything around the house.)

　　b. 衣食住の住{にいたっては／ときたら}、普通のサラリーマンには手が出ない。

　　　(Of the basics for survival (lit., housing, food and clothing), when it comes to shelter, most white-collar workers can't dream of coming up with enough money.)

N

---

ni kakawarazu　にかかわらず［関／拘／係わらず］　*comp. prt.*　<w>

⎰ a compound particle that means "re-⎱
⎱ gardless of" ⎰

regardless of; independent of; without reference to; without distinguishing; whether X or Y; whether X or not; whatever/whoever/etc.

【REL. *o towazu*】

◆ **Key Sentences**

(A)

	Noun		
当社_{とうしゃ}は	性別_{せいべつ}	に関_{かか}わらず	同様_{どうよう}に昇進_{しょうしん}できます。

(At this company, employees are (lit., you can be) promoted equally, regardless of sex.)

(B)

Noun₁		Noun₂			
出席_{しゅっせき}	か	欠席_{けっせき}	か	に関_{かか}わらず	同封_{どうふう}の葉書_{はがき}でお知らせ下さい。

(Whether or not you will attend, please inform us (of your intention) using the enclosed postcard.)

(C)

	V₁inf	V₂inf (Neg.) (V₁ = V₂)		
実際_{じっさい}に	使う	使わない	に関_{かか}わらず	レンタル料_{りょう}を払_{はら}わなければならない。

(We have to pay the rental fee whether we use it or not.)

(D)

Sinf*			
商品化_{しょうひんか}が可能_{かのう}	か{どうか / 否_{いな}か}	に関_{かか}わらず	我々_{われわれ}はこの製品_{せいひん}の研究を進める予定_{よてい}だ。

(We plan to advance the research on this product, whether it can be commercialized or not.)

*The だ after Adj(*na*)stem and N drops.

(E)

Noun			
会員_{かいいん}	であるなし	に関_{かか}わらず	商品_{しょうひん}カタログをお送りします。

(We will send you our product catalogue whether or not you are a member.)

(F)

Noun			
自覚症状	のあるなし	に関わらず	医師に相談することを勧めます。

(We recommend that you consult your doctor whether or not you have symptoms.)

(G)

	Noun		
A社は市場調査の	結果	のいかん	に関わらず

日本でのマーケティングを開始することを決めた。

(Company A has decided to begin marketing in Japan regardless of the market research results.)

(H)

	Wh-sentence.inf			
これは	どの言語を学習する	か	に関わらず	役に立つ情報だと思います。

(I think this information is useful whatever language you may study.)

Formation

(i)　N に関わらず

　　　学生数に関わらず　(regardless of the number of students)

(ii)　X か Y かに関わらず　(Y contrasts with X or is the negative form of X.)

　　　英語か日本語かに関わらず　(whether s.t. is English or Japanese)

　　　多いか少ないかに関わらず　(whether there are many or few)

　　　便利か不便かに関わらず　(whether s.t. is convenient or inconvenient)

　　　できるかできないかに関わらず　(whether s.o. can do s.t. or not)

(iii)　X Y に関わらず　(Y contrasts with X or is the negative form of X.)

　　　遅刻欠席に関わらず　(whether s.o. was late or absent)

　　　上手下手に関わらず　(whether s.o. is skillful or unskillful)

上手上手でないに関わらず　(whether or not s.o. is skillful)

うまい下手に関わらず　(whether s.o. is good or poor at s.t.)

うまいうまくないに関わらず　(whether s.o. is good at s.t. or not)

行く行かないに関わらず　(whether or not s.o. goes)

(iv) Sinf か{どうか／否か}に関わらず　(だ after Adj(*na*)stem and N is omitted.)

できるか{どうか／否か}に関わらず　(whether or not s.o. can do s.t.)

多いか{どうか／否か}に関わらず　(whether or not there are many of s.t.)

便利か{どうか／否か}に関わらず　(whether or not s.t. is convenient)

現実か{どうか／否か}に関わらず　(whether or not s.t. is a reality)

(v) {N／Adj(*na*)stem}であるなしに関わらず

国産品であるなしに関わらず　(whether or not s.t. is a domestic product)

経済的であるなしに関わらず　(whether or not s.t. is economical)

(vi) N のあるなしに関わらず

経験のあるなしに関わらず　(whether or not s.o. has experience)

(vii) N のいかんに関わらず

国籍のいかんに関わらず　(regardless of nationality)

N

(viii) Wh-sentence.inf かに関わらず

どこで使用するかに関わらず　(wherever s.t. may be used)

Examples

(a) このオンラインゲームは、性別・年齢に関わらず誰でも楽しむことができます。
(Anyone, regardless of sex or age, can enjoy this online game.)

(b) 日本で外国人が日本語を話すと、実際に上手か下手かに関わらず、「日本語が上手ですね」とほめられます。
(In Japan, when a foreigner speaks Japanese, whether they are actually good or bad, people will praise them, saying, "You speak Japanese well.")

(c) 実際にオーストラリアに行く行かないに関わらず休暇は取ろうと思っている。
(Whether or not I actually go to Australia, I'm thinking of taking some time off.)

(d) 我々は、助成金が下りるかどうかに関わらず、このプロジェクトを続ける。

(We are going to continue this project, whether we are given a grant or not.)

(e) 大学の図書館は、その大学の学生・教職員であるなしに関わらず閲覧できるのが普通だ。

((The books in) University libraries are usually available (to anyone), whether or not the user is a student, faculty member or staff member of the university.)

(f) 条例のあるなしに関わらず、公共のスペースでの喫煙は明らかなマナー違反であることを認識してほしい。

(I'd like people to recognize that whether or not there is a regulation, smoking in public spaces is clearly unacceptable behavior (lit., a violation of manners).)

(g) いかなる団体・個人についても、その意図や理由のいかんに関わらず、ここにある画像の転載・再配布等は許可しません。

(No group or individual is allowed to reproduce or redistribute the images found here, regardless of the intent or reason.)

(h) この製品の著作者及び、製造、配布に関わるいかなる者も、本ソフトウエアの使用、または使用不能によって発生する損害に対する責任は、それが直接的であるか間接的であるか、必然的であるか偶発的であるかに関わらず、負わないものとします。

(The author of this (software) product and (lit., any of) those involved in its production and distribution bear no responsibility for damage resulting from its use or the inability to use it, whether the damage is direct or indirect, or inevitable or accidental.)

Notes

1. X in "X *ni kakawarazu*" can take a variety of forms, including nouns, phrases or clauses, as demonstrated in the Formations, and it represents two or more possible conditions. This phrase is used when someone does something, something happens, or something is the case, regardless of the condition represented by X.

2. *Ni kakawarazu* should not be confused with *ni mo kakawarazu* "despite ~," which carries an entirely different meaning, as shown in (1).

   (1) ベートーベンは耳の障害にも関わらず、最後まですばらしい作品を書き続けた。

(Despite his hearing (lit., ear) problem, Beethoven kept composing wonderful works until he died.)

(⇨ ***ni mo kakawarazu*** (DIJG: 257-60))

ni kakete wa   にかけては   *comp. prt.*

a compound particle that marks s.t. in which s.o. excels or has confidence	when it comes to ~; as for; in point of; in terms of; about; regarding 【REL. *ni tsuite wa*; *ni kanshite wa*; *de wa*】

◆ Key Sentence

	Noun		
経済学のノーベル賞を受賞 したジョン・ナシュは	数学	にかけては	自分の右に出る者は いないと思っていた。
(John Nash, who received a Nobel Prize in economics, thought that when it came to math, nobody was better than he was.)			

Formation

N にかけては

音楽にかけては   (when it comes to music)

Examples

(a) ジャッキー・チェンは、アクションにかけては右に出る者がいない俳優である。
(Jackie Chan is an actor with whom none can compete when it comes to action films.)

(b) 山崎氏はこの分野の政策立案にかけては政界随一の見識と経験を持っている。
(For policy making in this field, Mr. Yamazaki has the best insight and experience in the political world.)

(c) 写真というものは絵画に比べて、その客観的再現力にかけては圧倒的にまさっている。

(Photography overwhelmingly surpasses paintings in terms of objective reproduction.)

(d) このユースホステルは年齢を問わず誰でも利用でき、快適さにかけては世界中でも最高クラスだ。

(One of the special features of this youth hostel is that people of any age can stay here (lit., use it), and when it comes to comfort, it is among the top-rated (hostels) in the world.)

(e) この工場は特殊鋼の製造にかけては世界屈指の技術を有している。

(When it comes to the production of special steels, this factory has the world's best technology.)

Notes

1. The compound particle X *ni kakete wa* is usually used with a predicate that positively evaluates X, as shown in the KS and Exs.

2. The *wa* of *ni kakete wa* cannot be omitted.

[Related Expressions]

The compound particles *ni tsuite wa* and *ni kanshite wa* mean "concerning/about ~" and can be used in place of *ni kakete wa*. The difference between these two compound particles and *ni kakete wa* is that *ni kakete wa* usually occurs with positive evaluative comments, but *ni tsuite/kanshite wa* don't always occur with such a predicate, as shown in [1] and [2]. The only difference between *ni tsuite wa* and *ni kanshite wa* is that *ni kanshite wa* is more formal than *ni tsuite wa*. *De wa* can also replace *ni kakete wa*.

[1] a. 経済学のノーベル賞を受賞したジョン・ナッシュは数学{にかけて / について / に関して / で}は自分の右に出る者はいないと思っていた。

(= KS)

b. 山崎氏はこの分野の政策立案{にかけて / について / に関して / で}は政界随一の見識と経験を持っている。(= Ex.(b))

[2] a. 彼はその問題{について / に関して / で / *にかけて}は目下検討中だ。

(He is investigating the matter right now.)

b. 地球温暖化 {について / に関して / で / *にかけて } はかなりの研究が

進んでいる。

(Regarding global warming, a fair amount of research is at an

advanced stage.)

(⇨ **ni tsuite** (DIJG: 280-83))

Since *de wa* can be used when it doesn't mark something in which someone
excels or has confidence, it can be used in cases where *ni kakete wa* cannot,
as shown in [3].

[3]　a. この問題 {で / *にかけて } は異論があった。

(There was a difference of opinion regarding this matter.)

b. コンピュータサイエンスの領域 {で / *にかけて } はさして進展はな

かった。

(In the field of computer science there was not much develop-

ment.)

(⇨ **ni kanshite/kansuru** (DIJG: 252-54))

ni katakunai　にかたくない［に難くない］　　*phr.*　<w>

| a phrase that indicates that it is not hard to imagine or guess a situation | not hard; easy ~ |

◆ **Key Sentences**

(A)

		VN	
給料が低いために教師の質が低下した	（であろう）ことは	想像	にかたくない。

(It is not hard to imagine that the quality of teachers fell because of the
low salary.)

(B)

幼い時に両親を失った彼女の生活が	{ いかに / どれほど }

			VN	
悲惨だった	か	は	推測	にかたくない。

(It is easy to guess how miserable her life was after she lost her parents.)

Formation

VN にかたくない   (where VN = Sino-Japanese compound)

{想像 / 推測 / 予測}にかたくない   (it is not hard to imagine/guess/predict)

Examples

(a) この新宅には相当お金をかけたであろうことは想像にかたくない。

(It is easy to imagine them spending a lot of money on this new house.)

(b) 日本語教育のめざましい進歩の裏には、日本語教育者・研究者の並々ならぬ努力があったことは、想像にかたくありません。

(It is not hard to imagine that behind the eye-opening progress Japanese language education has made are the extraordinary efforts of Japanese language educators and researchers.)

(c) 留学生にとって日本の伝統文化を見つけることがいかに難しくなっているかは想像にかたくないことでしょう。

(It isn't hard to imagine how difficult it has become for foreign students to find (examples of) traditional Japanese culture.)

(d) 好きな文芸の道と経営者としての責任の間で、多才な彼が苦悩していたことは想像にかたくない。

(It isn't hard to imagine that a man of his versatile talents struggled (to choose) between his beloved world of literature and his managerial responsibilities.)

(e) その青年が非常に心優しく生真面目かつ勉学熱心な人間だったことは推測にかたくない。

(It is easy to imagine that young man as a gentle, serious and diligent person.)

(f) 海外に在住して母国の軍事政権への反対活動を行っている人が帰国すれば、拘禁や拷問にさらされるであろうことは予測にかたくない。

(It isn't hard to predict that if people who live overseas and actively criticize the military regime of their country go home, most likely they will be put into prison and tortured.)

Notes

1. ~ *ni katakunai* is a phrase that means it is easy for someone to imagine or predict that a given situation will occur or has occurred. The phrase is preceded by *sōzō* "imagination," *suisoku* "guess" or *yosoku* "prediction."

2. *Ni katakunai* is commonly used as part of the sentence structure "~ *(de arō) koto wa* N *ni katakunai*," as in KS(A), Exs.(a) and (f), or "*ikani/ dorehodo* ~ *ka wa* N *ni katakunai*," as in KS(B) and Ex.(c).

3. The phrase is used only in formal spoken or written Japanese.

N

ni kimatte iru   に決まっている   *phr.*

| a phrase indicating the speaker's/ writer's strong conviction or motivation | surely; be bound to; be a given; of course; must be; we all know that 【REL. *ni chigainai*】 |

◆ **Key Sentences**

(A)

Sinf	
性格は、いい方がいい	に決まっている。
(It is a given that a good personality is preferable.)	

(B)

Sinf		
お客さまだって安く買いたい	に決まっている	じゃないか。
(Of course customers want to buy things cheaply.)		

Formation

(i) {V / Adj(*i*)} inf に決まっている

　　{来る / 来た} に決まっている　(s.o. is bound to show up / s.o. must have come)

　　{高い / 高かった} に決まっている　(s.t. must be / have been expensive)

(ii) {Adj(*na*)stem / N} {ø / だった} に決まっている

　　上手 {ø / だった} に決まっている　(s.o. is/was surely good at it)

　　日本人 {ø / だった} に決まっている　(s.o. must be / have been Japanese)

Examples

(a) ただただ漢字を書くなんて、つまらないに決まっている。

(To keep writing nothing but Chinese characters is bound to be boring.)

(b) すぐ角のたばこ屋に行く程度の用事なら、車より自転車の方が便利に決まっている。

(If you're just going on an errand to the tobacco shop around the corner, it's more convenient to go there by bike than by car—no question about it!)

(c) 立派なX染色体と小さなY染色体をつくづく見ていると、女性の方が丈夫に決まっていると思う。

(When I closely observe the magnificent X chromosome and the small Y chromosome, it seems like women are bound to be healthier.)

(d) 同じ商品なら気持ちのいい店で買うに決まっている。

(If the merchandise is the same, people will always buy at a store with a good atmosphere.)

(e) 子供は、大人が作っている社会の中で育つのだから、子供が変なのは大人のせいに決まっている。

(Children grow up in a society that adults create. So, if the children are not normal, it is a given that the adults are at fault.)

(f) 何しに来たって？ 飲みに来たに決まっているじゃないか。

((Are you asking me) what I came here for? Of course I came here to drink!)

Note

Ni kimatte iru is a stative form of *kimaru* "be decided" and is used to indicate the speaker's/writer's conjecture that something must be the case. *Kimatte iru* in the usage here is not a main verb but part of a modal verb phrase which indicates the speaker's strong conviction. It is different from *kimatte iru* in the examples in (1) below, where *kimatte iru* is the main verb.

(1) a. アルコールに強い・弱いは、遺伝的に決まっている。

(Whether you are sensitive or insensitive to alcohol is genetically determined.)

b. どの目が出るかは、サイコロを投げた瞬間に決まっているはずだ。

(The side that will appear ought to be determined the moment you throw the dice.)

【Related Expression】

Ni chigainai "must (be)" can replace *ni kimatte iru*, as shown below.

[1] a. お客さまだって安く買いたいに｛決まっている／違いない｝だろう。

(= KS(B))

b. ただただ漢字を書くなんて、つまらないに｛決まっている／違いない｝。(= Ex.(a))

But *ni kimatte iru* indicates the speaker's/writer's strong conviction, whereas *ni chigainai* indicates his/her conviction that there is no mistake on his/her part in guessing something. Therefore, when there is no room for guessing, the replacement is not possible, as shown in [2].

[2] a. 何しに来たって？ 飲みに来たに｛決まっている／*違いない｝じゃないか。(= Ex.(f))

b. 性格は、いい方がいいに｛決まっている／??違いない｝。(= KS(A))

(⇨ *ni chigainai* (DBJG: 304-06))

ni koshita koto wa nai   に越したことはない   *phr.*

| a phrase used to indicate that a state or action is more desirable | nothing is better than; if possible; be the best; be ideal; the ~ the ~ |

【REL. *~ ba ~ hodo yoi/ii*】

◆ **Key Sentences**

(A)

	Adj(*i*)inf.nonpast	
仲間<ruby>なかま</ruby>は	**多い**	に越<ruby>こ</ruby>したことはない。
(The more buddies you have the better.)		

(B)

Adj(*na*)stem		
元気	(である)	に越<ruby>こ</ruby>したことはない。
(The healthier the better.)		

(C)

	Vinf.nonpast		
虫歯<ruby>むしば</ruby>は	予防<ruby>よぼう</ruby>する	(の)	に越<ruby>こ</ruby>したことはない。
(For cavities, nothing is better than prevention.)			

(D)

	Noun		
温度<ruby>おんど</ruby>は	一定<ruby>いってい</ruby>	(である)	に越<ruby>こ</ruby>したことはない。
(A constant temperature is ideal.)			

Formation

(i)   Adj(*i*)inf.nonpast に越<ruby>こ</ruby>したことはない

　　　安いに越したことはない   (the cheaper the better)

(ii) {Adj(*na*)stem / N} (である)に越したことはない

　　静か(である)に越したことはない　　(the quieter the better)

　　英語(である)に越したことはない　　(English is the best)

(iii) Vinf.nonpast (の)に越したことはない

　　我慢する(の)に越したことはない　　(patience is the best)

Examples

(a) 環境はよいに越したことはない。

　　(A good environment is the best.)

(b) 働く時間は短いに越したことはないんじゃないの？

　　(Regarding working hours, the shorter the better, right?)

(c) 部屋は清潔に越したことはない。

　　(A clean room is best.)

(d) うちの息子はわんぱくで手に余る。まあ、元気に越したことはないけれど。

　　(My son is mischievous beyond our control, but nothing is more important than his being healthy.)

(e) 今週の土曜日から来週水曜日までの５日間、僕も夏休みに入ります。特別な予定もないけど仕事より休みに越したことはありません。

　　(I will be on summer vacation for five days from this Saturday through next Wednesday. I don't have any particular plan, but having days off is better than work.)

(f) 痛みは避けるべきものであり、ないに越したことはない。

　　(We should avoid pain, and having none is best.)

(g) クリスマスに「私にとって最高の贈り物はあなたです」なんて言葉が言えるに越したことはない。

　　(There would be nothing better than being able to say on Christmas Day, "You're the best gift I could have.")

(h) ネットワークがどれだけ発達しても、本当のコミュニケーションには、人と人とが向かい合って話すのに越したことはない。

　　(No matter how well-developed networks are, when it comes to real communication, nothing is better than talking face to face.)

Note

~ *ni koshita koto wa nai* is used when a state or an action is desirable, and often carries the implication "if possible." For example in Ex.(h), people realize that the exclusive use of face-to-face communication is difficult. But they want to experience the ideal situation, if it is possible.

【Related Expression】

~ *ni koshita koto wa nai* can be rephrased using ~ *ba* ~ *hodo yoi/ii* when the former is preceded by an *i*-adjective or a *na*-adjective, as shown below.

[1] a. 環境は｛よいに越したことはない／よければよいほどよい｝。

(= Ex.(a))

　　b. 働く時間は｛短いに越したことはない／短ければ短いほどいい｝んじゃないの？(= Ex.(b))

　　c. ｛元気であるに越したことはない／元気であればあるほどいい｝。

(= KS(B))

　　d. 部屋は｛清潔に越したことはない／清潔であればあるほどいい｝。

(= Ex.(c))

The difference between the phrases is that ~ *ni koshita koto wa nai* often implies that the speaker/writer wants an ideal situation, if possible. ~ *ba* ~ *hodo* does not imply "if possible." That is why the adverbs *dekireba*, *dekiru koto nara*, or *kanō nara* can be attached to ~ *ni koshita koto wa nai*, but not to ~ *ba* ~ *hodo yoi/ii*, as shown in [2] and [3].

[2] a. 環境は｛できれば／できることなら／可能なら｝よいに越したことはない。(cf. Ex.(a))

　　b. ??環境は｛できれば／できることなら／可能なら｝よければよいほどよい。

[3] a. 働く時間は｛できれば／できることなら／可能なら｝短いに越したことはない。(cf. Ex.(b))

　　b. ??働く時間は｛できれば／できることなら／可能なら｝短ければ短いほどいい。

Another difference is that ~ *ni koshita koto wa nai* can be used with an adverb *sukoshi de mo* "even a little more," but ~ *ba* ~ *hodo* cannot.

[4] a. 環境は少しでもよいに越したことはない。(cf. Ex.(a))

    b. *環境は少しでもよければよいほどよい。

[5] a. 働く時間は少しでも短いに越したことはないんじゃないの？

                       (cf. Ex.(b))

    b. *働く時間は少しでも短ければ短いほどいいんじゃないの？

                     (⇨ *~ **ba** ~ **hodo*** (DIJG: 6-8))

ni / to mo naru to　に / と もなると　*phr.*

a phrase that is used when s.t. or some situation is perceived to be special	when; if; as 【REL. *ni/to mo nareba*】

N

◆ Key Sentences

(A)

Noun		
桜の季節	｛に / と｝もなると	この公園は花見客でにぎわう。
(In the cherry blossom season (lit., When it becomes the cherry blossom season), this park is packed with cherry blossom viewers.)		

(B)

	Vinf.nonpast		
外国へ	行く	ともなると、	その国の言語や文化を勉強したくなるはずだ。
(When you go abroad, most likely you will want to study that country's language and culture.)			

Formation

(i)   N {に / と} もなると

   5月{に / と} もなると   (lit., when it becomes May; in May)

(ii)   Vinf.nonpast ともなると

   退職するともなると   (when s.o. retires)

Examples

(a) 正月ともなると、友人同士、お互いの家を行き来して、正月酒を楽しむ。

(On New Year's Day my friends and I go to each other's houses and enjoy New Year's Day *sake*.)

(b) ここは紅葉が始まると訪れる人が増え始め、11月半ばともなると大勢の人でごったがえす。

(When the leaves begin turning red, the number of visitors starts to increase, and in mid-November, this place is packed with people.)

(c) 社会人にもなると、先輩や友人の結婚式に招かれる機会が出てきます。

(Once you (graduate and) get out in the real world, you will start getting invited to the weddings of your elders and friends.)

(d) 高校生にもなると、自分のお小遣いくらいは、バイトして稼ぐようになる。

(When you become a high school student, you get a part-time job and start earning your own pocket money.)

(e) 大きなホテルともなると、一日に数千人もの利用者が集まってくる。

(At a big hotel, thousands of people come through daily.)

(f) 『美女と野獣』ともなると人気の作品だから、当日券なんてなかなか買えない。

("Beauty and the Beast" is a popular show, so it's hard to find same day tickets.)

(g) 大学へ進学するともなると、学問、バイト、サークルなど、人それぞれのライフスタイルができてくる。

(When you enter college, each of you will develop your own lifestyle, with studies, work and club activities.)

(h) 今年から修学旅行先が北海道になり、飛行機で行くともなると、胸を躍らせずにはいられなかった。

(Starting this year, we're going to Hokkaido for our school trip, and the thought of flying there has made us so excited we can hardly stand it.)

Notes

1. X *ni/to mo naru to* is used when a situation or thing expressed by X is perceived as special. This meaning comes from the use of the particle *mo* as in X *mo* to express the speaker's/writer's perception that X is special, as shown in (1) below.

(1) a. 夜も更けていた。

(It was late at night.)

b. 夏も終わってしまった。

(Summer is over now.)

Note that the speaker feels special about *yoru* "night" in (1a) or *natsu* "summer" in (1b).

2. *Mo* in *to mo naru to* can be omitted. The difference between "Vinf. nonpast *to mo naru to*" and "Vinf.nonpast *to naru to*" can be seen in the sentence below. In (2), the *to naru to* version is used when the speaker/writer does not think that it is a big deal to enter college.

(2) 大学へ進学すると（も）なると、学問、バイト、サークルなど、人それぞれのライフスタイルができてくる。(= Ex.(g))

3. When a noun precedes ~ *mo naru to*, the subsequent particle can be either *to* or *ni*, as shown in Formation (i). The *to* version sounds more formal than the *ni* version. When a verb precedes the phrase, only *to mo naru to* is used, as in Formation (ii).

N

[Related Expression]

The related expression *ni/to mo nareba* is freely interchangeable with *ni/to mo naru to* and, just like *ni/to mo naru to*, does not take *ni* when it is used with a verb.

[1]　a. 桜の季節｛に / と｝も｛なると / なれば｝この公園は花見客でにぎわう。(= KS(A))

b. 外国へ行く｛と / *に｝も｛なると / なれば｝、その国の言語や文化を勉強したくなるはずだ。(= KS(B))

The subtle difference between the two versions comes from the difference in the choice of conditional. For example, in [1a], the choice of *naru to* expresses the speaker's perception that the cherry blossom season and the packing of the park with cherry blossom viewers is an uncontrollable, natural situation whereas the choice of *nareba* simply expresses a condition.

(⇨ **to**[4] (DBJG: 480-82); **ba** (DBJG: 81-83))

ni mukete / **muketa**   に向けて / 向けた   *comp. prt.*

| a compound particle that indicates the destination/direction of movement, the target/direction of an action, or the goal/purpose of an action | toward; to; at; aiming at; targeting; for; for the purpose of; in order to 【REL. *ni mukatte*; *o mezashite*; *o mokuhyō ni*; *no tame ni*】 |

◆ **Key Sentences**

(A)

	Noun		
報道班は次の	目的地	に向けて	出発した。

(The team of reporters left for the next destination.)

(B)

	Noun		
このテレビコマーシャルは 20、30代の	独身女性	に向けて	発信されている。

(This TV commercial is being marketed to single women in their twenties and thirties.)

(C)

	Noun		
今、来年の	入学試験	に向けて	頑張っています。

(I'm studying hard now for the next year's entrance exam.)

(D)

	VN		
新しいエネルギーの	開発	に向けて	研究が進んでいる。

(Research is progressing toward (the goal of) developing new energy.)

(E)

Noun Phrase		Noun	
地球温暖化防止	に｛向けての／向けた｝	動き	が活発化している。

(Efforts to prevent (lit., Movement for the purpose of preventing) global warming are gaining vigor.)

Formation

(i) N に向けて

ロンドンに向けて　(toward/to/for London)

(ii) VN に向けて

体制の改革に向けて　(for the purpose of reforming the system)

(iii) N₁ に｛向けての／向けた｝N₂

21世紀に｛向けての／向けた｝社会保障　(social security for the 21st century)

Examples

(a) 救援物資を積んだヘリコプターが被災地に向けて飛び立った。

(A helicopter loaded with relief supplies left for (lit., took off toward) the site of the damage.)

(b) 機動隊はデモ隊に向けて催涙弾を発射した。

(The riot police shot tear gas bombs at the ranks of demonstrators.)

(c) K社は1月から九州で生産した高級車を中国に向けて輸出する。

(Starting in January, K Company is going to export luxury cars to China which were manufactured in Kyushu.)

(d) このプロジェクトでは、世界各国のアニメーターが世界中の子供たちに向けて作品を作り、それをそれぞれの国の言葉に翻訳します。

(In this project, animators from around the globe create works for the world's children, and then the works are translated into various countries' languages.)

(e) バレーボール協会は次のオリンピックに向けて選手の強化を急いでいる。

(The volleyball association is hurrying to strengthen its players for the next Olympic Games.)

(f) 異なる特許制度の世界的統一に向けて交渉が開始された。

(Negotiations toward the global integration of incompatible (lit., different) patent systems began.)

(g) H社は新しく開発された電池の事業化に向けて新会社を設立した。

(H Company has established a new company for the commercialization of their newly-developed battery.)

(h) 我が社は効率的な社内コミュニケーションに向けての新しいコミュニケーションシステムの導入を進めている。

(Our company is implementing a new communication system for more efficient internal communication.)

(i) M氏の提言は、新たな世紀に向けた日本外交の指針を考えていくにあたり、非常に示唆に富むものであった。

(Mr. M's proposal was full of suggestions when we began considering the guiding principles of Japan's diplomacy for the new century.)

Notes

1. *Ni mukete* is used to indicate the destination/direction of human movement, as in KS(A) and Ex.(a); the target/direction of an action, as in KS(B), Exs.(b)-(d) and (i); or the goal/purpose of an action, as in KS(C)-(E) and Exs.(e)-(h).

2. *Ni mukete* cannot be used to indicate the direction of non-human movement, as shown in (1).

   (1) a. 風が北{??に向けて / に向かって}吹いている。

   (The wind is blowing toward the east.)

   b. *川は東{??に向けて / に向かって}流れている。

   (The river is flowing toward the east.)

3. Either *ni mukete no* or *ni muketa* can be used as the noun-modification form of *ni mukete*, as in KS(E), Exs.(h) and (i).

4. *Ni mukete* is often used in titles of articles, themes of events and copy for advertisements. Some examples are shown in (2).

(2) a. 視力回復に向けて開発進む「バイオニック・アイ」

(Advances in the development of "Bionic Eyes" for the restoration of sight (lit., "Bionic Eyes," the development of which advances toward regaining sight))

b. ポリ塩化ビフェニル (PBC) 廃棄物の適正な処理に向けて

(Toward the appropriate disposal of polychlorinated biphenyl (PBC) waste)

c. 一つの世界に向けて

(Toward one world)

d. 国際シンポジウム：知的情報の流通と学術・文化の発展に向けて

(International Symposium: Toward the circulation of intellectual information and the development of art, science and culture)

e. LAN導入に向けての予備知識

(Preliminary knowledge for installing LAN (local area network))

[Related Expressions]

I. *Ni mukatte* "toward" and *ni mukete* are interchangeable when they indicate the destination/direction of human movement, as in [1].

[1] a. 報道班は次の目的地に｜向けて／向かって｜出発した。(= KS(A))

b. 救援物資を積んだヘリコプターが被災地に｜向けて／向かって｜飛び立った。(= Ex.(a))

Ni mukatte can also be used when it indicates the direction of non-human movement but *ni mukete* cannot be used in this way. (See Note 2.)

Ni mukatte cannot replace *ni mukete* when *ni mukete* indicates the target, direction, goal or purpose of an action, as shown in [2].

[2] a. このテレビコマーシャルは 20、30 代の独身女性に｜向けて／*向かって｜発信されている。(= KS(B))

b. 今、来年の入学試験に｜向けて／*向かって｜頑張っています。

(= KS(C))

c. 新しいエネルギーの開発に｜向けて／*向かって｜研究が進んでいる。

(= KS(D))

d. 地球温暖化防止に{向けての / 向けた / *向かっての / *向かった}動きが活発化している。(= KS(E))

II. *O mezashite* "aiming at," *o mokuhyō ni* "with ~ as the goal," and *no tame ni* "for the purpose of" are all synonymous with *ni mukete* and interchangeable when they indicate the goal/purpose of an action, as shown in [3].

[3] a. 今、来年の入学試験{に向けて / を目指^{めざ}して / を目標^{もくひょう}に / のために}頑張っています。(= KS(C))

b. バレーボール協会は次のオリンピック{に向けて / を目指して / を目標に / のために}選手の強化を急いでいる。(= Ex.(e))

c. 新しいエネルギーの開発{に向けて / を目指して / を目標に / のために}研究が進んでいる。(= KS(D))

d. 異なる特許制度の世界的統一{に向けて / を目指して / を目標に / のために}交渉が開始された。(= Ex.(f))

O mezashite can also be used in place of *ni mukete* when it indicates a destination / the direction of movement, as in [4].

[4] a. 報道班は次の目的地{に向けて / を目指^{めざ}して}出発した。(= KS(A))

b. 救援物資を積んだヘリコプターが被災地{に向けて / を目指して}飛び立った。(= Ex.(a))

N

~ **ni** ~ **nai**   ~に~ない   *str.*

a sentence structure meaning "s.o. cannot manage to do s.t."

cannot manage to; just cannot; cannot ~ even though ~ want to; cannot ~ despite the fact that ~ want to
【REL. *takute mo* ~ *nai*; *taku to mo* ~ *nai*; *yō ni mo* ~ *nai*】

◆ **Key Sentence**

	V₁inf. nonpast		V₂pot.neg (V₁ = V₂)	
後任者が決まらないので	辞める	に	辞められ	ない。

(Because my successor hasn't been chosen yet, I haven't been able to resign (my current position).)

Formation

V₁inf.nonpast に V₂pot.neg ない　(where V₁ = V₂)

　出るに出られない　(s.o. cannot manage to get out)

Examples

(a) 大事なお客さんからの電話がいつまで待ってもかかってこないので、帰るに帰れない。

(I've been waiting a long time for a call from an important customer, but it hasn't come, so I cannot leave the office.)

(b) みんなの前で大見えを切ってできると言ってしまったので引くに引けない。

(Because I boasted to everyone that I could do it, I cannot pull out now even though I want to.)

(c) 同窓会などで会った旧友が、何かの団体に入っていたり、何かの商品を売っていたりして、勧誘を断るに断れないケースがよくある。

(When you go to school reunions or other events, often you cannot say no to an old friend who has joined a group (and asks you to join) or is selling some product (and asks you to buy it).)

(d) 録画予約をして帰ってみたら、停電で全然録画されておらず泣くに泣けなかったという経験はありませんか。

(Have you ever had the experience of setting a programmed recording, only to come home and find that the power went out and you didn't record a thing? It makes you want to cry.)

(e) 急に今日中に終わらせなければならない仕事が入った。今日は子供の誕生日で早く帰ると約束したのに、周りの同僚も自分の仕事に必死で、頼むに頼めない。

(Unexpectedly, I got work that I have to finish today. It's my child's birthday, and I promised to come home early, but my colleagues (around me) are desperately trying to finish their own work, so I cannot (manage to) ask them to do mine for me.)

(f) 通訳の失敗談は、話として聞いている分にはおかしいものが多いが、中には深刻すぎて笑うに笑えないものもある。

(Tales of blunders by interpreters are mostly laughable incidents when heard as anecdotes, but some of them are too serious to be considered laughing matters.)

Notes

1. "V *ni* Vpot *nai*" means that someone cannot do something even though he/she wants to or is trying to. This structure is used only when someone cannot do something, not because the person is not capable of doing it, but rather because the situation does not allow him/her to do it.

2. "V *ni* Vpot *nai*" can also be used when someone is temporarily incapable of doing something for some reason, as in (1).

(1) a. 長い間、畳に正座していて痺れがきれ、立つに立てない。

(Because I've been sitting on my knees on the tatami floor for so long, my legs have fallen asleep and I can't (manage to) stand up.)

b. お尻に出来物ができているので座るに座れない。

(Because I have a boil on my bottom, I cannot (manage to) sit down.)

〔Related Expressions〕

Takute mo ~ *nai* or *taku to mo* ~ *nai* "cannot ~ even if/though ~ want to" and *yō ni mo* ~ *nai* "cannot ~ even if/though ~ try to" can express meanings similar to that of ~ *ni* ~ *nai*, as shown in [1].

[1] a. 後任者が決まらないので{辞めたくても / 辞めたくとも / 辞めようにも}辞められない。(cf. KS)

(Because it hasn't been decided who's going to be my successor, I cannot resign (the current position) even though I {want / am trying} to.)

b. 大事なお客さんからの電話がいつまで待ってもかかってこないので、{帰りたくても / 帰りたくとも / 帰ろうにも}帰れない。(cf. Ex.(a))

(I've been waiting a long time for a call from an important customer, but it hasn't come, so I cannot leave the office even though I {want / am trying} to.)

Naku ni nakenai in Ex.(d) is an idiomatic phrase and cannot be rephrased using *takute mo ~ nai*, *taku tomo ~ nai* or *yō ni mo ~ nai*.

[2] 録画予約をして帰ってみたら、停電で全然録画されておらず｛泣くに／*泣きたくても／*泣きたくとも／*泣こうにも｝泣けなかったという経験はありませんか。(= Ex.(d))

(⇨ *yō ni mo (~ nai)* (in this volume))

ni (mo) naku に（も）なく *phr.*

a phrase that means s.t. unusual happens or s.o. does s.t. unusual	unusually; more ~ than usual

◆ Key Sentence

彼女は今日は	いつ	に（も）なく	陽気だった。

(She was unusually cheerful today.)

Examples

(a) 宏は「ただいまー」といつになく明るい声で帰ってきた。

(Hiroshi came home and said "I'm home!" in an unusually cheerful voice.)

(b) 普段はたいていビールや日本酒だが、たまに柄にもなくバーにカクテルを飲みに行ったりする。

(Usually I drink beer or *sake*, but occasionally I may go out for cocktails at a bar, which is unlike me.)

(c) 今年は例年になく猛暑で、いつもは省エネを心がけている私が、いつの間にかクーラーをかけてしまっている。

(This year has been unusually hot, a real scorcher. I usually try hard to save energy, but I find myself turning on the cooler.)

(d) 気になっていた彼女が隣に座ったので、僕の心は我にもなく弾んだ。

(The woman I've got a crush on sat next to me, so my heart started pounding with excitement, which is unlike me.)

Notes

1. *Ni (mo) naku* is used with a very limited number of nouns such as *gara* "character," *reinen* "usual year" and *ware* "I," or the question word *itsu* "when," to mean that something unusual happens or someone does something unusual.

2. The use of *mo* emphasizes the unusual quality of the situation.

---

ni ōjite / ōjita   に応じて / 応じた   *comp. prt.*

a compound particle that means "in response to"

in response to; according to; depending on; appropriate for; suitable for; suited to; meet 【REL. *ni yotte*; *shidai de*; *ikan de*】

◆ Key Sentences

(A)

	Noun		
組合の	要求	に応じて	標準就業時間が短縮されることになった。

(In response to union demands, the standard work day (lit., standard work hours) will be shortened.)

(B)

Noun		
業績	に応じて	従業員全員にボーナスが支給された。

(Bonuses were distributed to all employees according to their performance (lit., achievements).)

(C)

Noun Phrase₁		Noun Phrase₂	
天候や道路状況	に応じた	適切な運転	を心がけましょう。

(Please make sure your driving is appropriate for the weather and road conditions.)

Formation

(i)　N に応じて

　　求めに応じて　(in response to s.o.'s request)

　　能力に応じて　(according to s.o.'s ability)

(ii)　N₁ に応じた N₂

　　目的に応じた教え方　(a teaching method suitable for the purpose)

Examples

(a) 当社では要請に応じて講師を学校に派遣することもできます。

(We can also dispatch a lecturer to the school in response to their request.)

(b) 病院でもらう薬は、医師が患者の体質や症状に応じて処方します。

(The drugs a patient receives at the hospital are prescribed by the doctor according to the patient's physical condition and symptoms.)

(c) 湯沸かし器の設定温度は、目的に応じてその都度調節するのが賢い使い方だ。

(A wise way of using a water heater is to adjust the (preset) temperature each time, according to the purpose.)

(d) 今年行われた「今後の大学教育のあり方に関する世論調査」によると、外国語教育の効果的だと思われる授業のあり方に関して、33.7％が「学生個人の能力に応じてクラスを分けて授業を行う」と答えた。

(According to the "Survey of How Future Higher Education Should Be," which was conducted this year, 33.7 percent (of respondents) agreed that for effective foreign language education, "classes should be taught by dividing students according to their ability.")

(e) 髪のケアには欠かせないシャンプーには症状に応じて様々なタイプがある。

(Shampoo, which is indispensable for hair care, comes in various types, depending on the condition of your hair.)

(f) 一般に供給は需要に応じて変動する。しかし、場合によって需要が供給に応じて変動するのも事実である。

(Generally, supply changes according to the demand. However, it is also true that in some cases demand changes according to the supply.)

(g) 家を購入する場合には収入に応じた物件を選ぶべきです。

(When buying a house, you should choose one that is within your means (lit., suitable for your income).)

(h) 我が社はお客さまのご予算に応じた費用対効果の高いホームページ制作を支援します。

(We support the production of highly cost-effective Web pages geared to the customer's budget (lit., suitable for the customer's budget).)

(i) 平成 15 年に公布された「個人情報の保護に関する法律」は、個人情報取扱事業者に対し、本人の求めに応じて保有個人データの開示や訂正を行うこと、また本人の求めに応じてその利用を停止することなどを義務づけている。

(The Law Regarding the Protection of Personal Information, which was promulgated in the fifteenth year of Heisei (2003), requires businesses that handle personal information to disclose or correct an individual's personal data in their possession in response to the individual's demand, or to stop using the data in response to his/her demand.)

Notes

1. The core meaning of *ni ōjite* is "in response to," as in KS(A), Exs.(a) and (i), but it is often used to mean "according to" when different actions are taken depending on differences in situations or amounts, as in KS(B), (C) and Exs.(b)-(e). Even in this use, the core meaning "in response to" is retained in that an actor (i.e., the person who takes an action mentioned explicitly or implicitly) takes different actions in response to different situations.

2. In general, when "X *ni ōjite*" is used, there is an actor, whether explicitly mentioned or not, who takes an action according to X. However, there are cases in which there is no actor involved, as in Ex.(f). This use is considered an extended use.

3. The noun modification form of *ni ōjite* is *ni ōjita*. In some contexts, *ni ōjita* may mean "appropriate for; suitable for; meet," as in KS(C), Exs.(g) and (h), which is derived from "according to." (1) provides additional examples of *ni ōjita*.

(1) a. 冷凍食品の種類に応じた解凍方法をご紹介します。

(We will show you various thawing methods suitable for different kinds of frozen foods.)

b. 地域における多様な需要に応じた公的賃貸住宅の整備が必要だ。

(It is necessary to improve public rental housing to meet the variety of needs in the area.)

c. このカメラは水中でレンズが交換できるため、被写体に応じた多彩な撮影が楽しめます。

(Because you can change the lenses of this camera in water, you can enjoy different ways of shooting according to each object.)

【Related Expressions】

I. When *ni yotte* is used in the sense of "according to; depending on," it is synonymous with *ni ōjite*, and they are interchangeable in some situations, as demonstrated in [1].

[1] a. バッター{に応じて / によって}守備位置を変える。

(We change our defensive positions {depending on / according to} the batter.)

b. 症状に{に応じて / によって}異なる治療を施す。

(We apply different treatments {depending on / based on} the symptoms.)

c. 業績{に応じて / によって}ボーナスを決める。

(We determine bonuses based on (the employee's) performance.)

However, there are situations in which *ni ōjite* cannot be used. First, X *ni ōjite* cannot be used when what is stated in the main clause is not "in response" to X, as shown in [2].

[2] a. 先生{によって / *に応じて}教え方が違う。

(The teaching style differs depending on the teacher.)

b. この本は読み方{によって / *に応じて}毒にも薬にもなる。

(This book can harm you or benefit you, depending on how you read it.)

c. 言い方{によって / *に応じて}は彼女を傷つけるかもしれない。

(Depending on how you tell (it to) her, you might hurt her.)

Second, *ni ōjite* is unnatural when the main clause involves no action as an alternative, as shown in [3a]. [3b] and [3c], however, are acceptable.

[3] a. この検査の結果{によって / ??に応じて}手術をしない可能性もある。

(Depending on the results of this examination, it is possible that we will not operate (on the patient).)

b. この検査の結果{によって / に応じて}手術をするか薬餌療法にするかを決めたい。

(Based on the results of this examination, we'd like to decide whether to operate (on the patient) or treat him/her with medication.)

c. この検査の結果{によって / に応じて}治療法を決めたい。

(We'd like to determine the treatment based on the results of this examination,)

Third, *ni ōjite* must be preceded by a noun or noun phrase, whereas *ni yotte* allows other elements to precede it, as shown in [4].

[4] a. 奨学金が<u>もらえるか</u>{<u>どうか</u> / <u>否か</u>}{によって / *に応じて}大学入学を決めます。

(I'll decide where to go to college depending on whether I get a scholarship or not.)

b. 使う言葉が<u>英語か日本語か</u>{によって / *に応じて}発表の準備の仕方が変わる。

(Depending on whether it is English or Japanese that I'm supposed to use, the way I prepare for my presentation will change.)

c. 誰が聞きに<u>来るか</u>{によって / *に応じて}話の内容を変えるつもりだ。

(I'm planning to change the content of my talk according to who's coming to listen to it.)

(⇨ ***ni yotte/yori*** (DIJG: 292-301))

II. *Shidai de* and *ikan de* also mean "depending on." However, these phrases and *ni ōjite* are not interchangeable. First, when different actions are taken in response to different situations, *shidai de* and *ikan de* cannot be used, as shown in [5].

[5] a. 業績{に応じて / *次第で / *いかんで}従業員全員にボーナスが支給された。(= KS(B))

    b. 病院でもらう薬は、医師が患者の体質や症状｛に応じて／*次第で／
    *いかんで｝処方します。(= Ex.(b))

[5a] means that the company distributed bonuses to all employees and that each employee received a different amount according to his/her performance. Similarly, [5b] means that doctors prescribe drugs for patients and that each patient receives different drugs according to his/her physical condition and symptoms. In these situations, *shidai de* and *ikan de* cannot be used.

On the other hand, *shidai de* and *ikan de* can be used in [6], where the sentence is talking about whether or not the company will distribute bonuses to its employees and not about how the amount is determined for each employee. In this case, *ni ōjite* cannot be used. (See the note on [3] above.)

[6]　業績｛次第で／いかんで／*に応じて｝従業員全員にボーナスが支給される。(cf. KS(B))

    (Bonuses will be distributed to all employees depending on the company's performance.)

Second, *shidai de* or *ikan de* can be used when no actor is involved, but *ni ōjite* cannot, as shown in [7].

[7]　a. 今年の新車の売れ行き｛次第で／いかんで／*に応じて｝この会社の将来が決まりそうだ。

    (It looks like this company's future will be determined by the sales of new cars this year (lit., according to how the sales of new cars are this year).)

    b. 実験の結果｛次第で／いかんで／*に応じて｝、大発見になる可能性もある。

    (Depending on the results, this experiment could lead to a great discovery.)

    c. 生活排水などの汚水は、その処理方法｛次第で／いかんで／*に応じて｝、周辺の水環境に悪影響を与えます。

    (Depending on the treatment method, wastewater such as residential sewage can worsen the surrounding water environment.)

        (⇨ **shidai** (DIJG: 385-90); **ikan (da)** (in this volume))

ni shiro / seyo に しろ / せよ   *phr.*

| a conjunctive phrase that carries the meaning of concession | even though (it is/was the case that); even if (it is true that); although (it is/was the case that); whatever/whoever/etc.; no matter what/who/how/etc.; whether X or Y 【REL. *ni shite mo*; *to shite mo*】 |

◆ **Key Sentences**

(A)

Sinf		
時間があまりなかった	に ｛ しろ / せよ ｝、	この仕事はひどすぎる。
(Even though he didn't have much time, this work is too sloppy.)		

(B)

Wh-sentence.inf		
誰(だれ)が書く	に ｛ しろ / せよ ｝、	絶対間違(ぜったいまちが)いがあってはいけない。
(No matter who writes it, there can be absolutely no mistakes.)		

(C)

V₁inf		V₂inf		
行く	に ｛ しろ / せよ ｝、	**行かない**	に ｛ しろ / せよ ｝、	後で電話を下さい。
(Whether you go or not, please give me a call later.)				

(D)

Wh-word		
何	に ｛ しろ / せよ ｝、	このままでは問題は解決(かいけつ)しない。
(At any rate (lit., whatever it is), leaving the situation as it is won't solve the problem.)		

(E)

	Noun		
たとえ	練習	に｛しろ／せよ｝、	真面目にやらなければならない。

(Even though it is just practice, you have to take it seriously.)

Formation

(i)   Vinf に｛しろ／せよ｝

　　　｛行く／行った｝に｛しろ／せよ｝　(even though s.o. goes/went)

(ii) Adj(*i*)inf に｛しろ／せよ｝

　　　｛高い／高かった｝に｛しろ／せよ｝　(even though s.t. is/was expensive)

(iii) Adj(*na*)stem｛ø／である／だった／であった｝に｛しろ／せよ｝

　　　不十分｛ø／である／だった／であった｝に｛しろ／せよ｝　(even though s.t. is/was insufficient)

(iv) N｛ø／である／だった／であった｝に｛しろ／せよ｝

　　　子供｛ø／である／だった／であった｝に｛しろ／せよ｝　(even though it is/was a child)

　　　誰｛ø／である／だった／であった｝に｛しろ／せよ｝　(whoever it may be／have been)

　　　いずれに｛しろ／せよ｝　(whichever it may be; at any rate)

(v) Adv. に｛しろ／せよ｝

　　　ゆっくりに｛しろ／せよ｝　(even though s.t. happens slowly)

Examples

(a) 程度の差はあるにせよ、性差別のない国はないだろう。

(Although the degree may differ from country to country (lit., there may be differences in degree), there is no country without gender discrimination.)

(b) 薬を飲むことですべての問題が解決はしないにしろ、あなたの場合は薬で症状を軽減させることが先決です。

(Even if (it's true that) taking the drug will not solve all your problems, in your case, you have to alleviate the symptoms first (by taking it).)

(c) 誰かに書いてもらうにしろ、内容は我々が考えなければならない。

(Even if we ask someone to write it for us, we will have to think of what to say (lit., the content) ourselves.)

(d) どのソフトを使うにしろ、早く使い方に慣れてもらわないといけない。

(Whichever software application you use, you must quickly get comfortable using it (lit., get used to how to use it).)

(e) 誰がそれを説明するにせよ、相手の気持ちを傷つけないように細心の注意が必要だ。

(Whoever explains it (to him) must be very careful not to hurt his feelings.)

(f) どんな事情があったにせよ、何も言わずに仕事を辞めるのは無責任すぎる。

(No matter what the circumstances were, quitting the job without saying anything is just (too) irresponsible.)

(g) ホームページの制作に関する書籍は書店の棚にあふれている状態で、自分が読むにせよ、他人に勧めるにせよ、大いに迷う。

(Books on Web page design are spilling off of bookstore shelves, and whether we want to read them ourselves or recommend them to someone else, it is hard to know what to choose.)

(h) 現政権を支持するにせよ批判するにせよ、まずはじめに問題に対する正確な理解と冷静な分析が不可欠である。

(First of all, whether you support the current administration or criticize it, an accurate understanding and a cool analysis of the problems are indispensable.)

(i) 野球にせよサッカーにせよ、プロでやっていくには並の努力では続かない。

(Whether it be baseball or soccer, you cannot stay as a professional player just with an ordinary effort.)

(j) 普通の人は、意識的にせよ無意識的にせよ、不快なことを避けようとする。

(Whether they do it consciously or unconsciously, ordinary people try to avoid unpleasant things.)

(k) 一旦ネットに発信してしまった情報は、それが真実にせよそうでないにせよ、取り消しができない。

(Whether it is true or not, once you send out information on the Internet, you can't take it back.)

(l) いずれにせよ早急に対策を考えなければならない。

(In any case, we have to think of a countermeasure immediately.)

(m)何にせよこの問題は我々だけで考えていても解決策は出てこない。

(At any rate, we cannot come up with a solution to this problem if we are thinking about it just among ourselves.)

(n) 一時的にせよ国内全空港で、航空機が約 20 分間にわたり離陸できなくなったことは深刻な問題だ。

(Although it was temporary, the fact that nationwide no airplane could take off for about 20 minutes is a serious problem.)

(o) たとえ知らずにやったことであるにしろ、彼は責任を免れないだろう。

(Even if he did it unintentionally (lit., it is something he did without knowing), he probably cannot escape the responsibility.)

Notes

1. Both *shiro* and *seyo* are imperative forms of *suru*. *Shiro* is the spoken form and *seyo*, the written form. There is no difference between *ni shiro* and *ni seyo* in terms of formality level.

2. When *ni shiro/seyo* appears in the subordinate-clause-final position, it forms a concession clause, meaning "even if S; even though S; etc." The literal meaning of *suru* in this use is "to assume."

3. In "X *ni shiro/seyo* Y *ni shiro/seyo*," X and Y are contrastive elements and they can be nouns, verbs, adjectives or adverbs, as shown in (1).

N

(1) a. ヒューマン・インターフェースにせよネットワークにせよ、この数年間でさらに大きく変わるだろう。

(Whether in human interface or networks, we will probably see further significant changes in the next few years.)

b. 会社を辞めるにせよ留まるにせよ、早く結論を出さなければならない。

(Whether you decide to stay with your company or resign, you must make your decision quickly.)

c. 高いにせよ安いにせよ、必要なら買うしかない。

(Whether it is expensive or cheap, if you need something, you have to buy it.)

d. たまにしろしょっちゅうにしろ、私用で電話をするのは勤務時間外にして下さい。

(Whether (your calls are) frequent or rare, if you use the phone for personal calls, please do it outside of your (regular) work time.)

Note that X and Y can also be phrases, as in Ex.(g).

4. A clause "X *ga* Y *de aru*" before *ni shiro/seyo* can be reduced to Y when the rest of the information is known from the context or situation. For example, the unreduced version of KS(E) is (2).

(2) たとえ<u>それが練習である</u>にしろ、真面目にやらなけらばならない。

(cf. KS(E))

(Even though it is just practice, you have to take it seriously.)

5. *Tatoe* is sometimes used for emphasis, as in KS(E) and Ex.(o).

6. The following set phrases with a Wh-word and *ni shiro/seyo* are used almost synonymously.

(3) a. 何に｛しろ / せよ｝   (at any rate; whatever it may be)

b. いずれに｛しろ / せよ｝   (at any rate; whichever it may be)

c. どちらに｛しろ / せよ｝   (at any rate; whichever it may be)

d. どっちに｛しろ / せよ｝   (at any rate; whichever it may be)

【Related Expressions】

N

I. *Ni shite mo* carries the same meaning as *ni shiro/seyo*. The connection rules are also the same. The only difference is that *ni shite mo* is less formal.   (⇨ **te mo** (DBJG: 468-70); **ni shite mo** (in this volume))

II. *To shite mo* is also synonymous with *ni shiro/seyo*. However, *to shite mo* cannot be used in the following situations:

[1] Immediately after Wh-words or noun phrases (with or without a particle) which contain a Wh-word:

a. 何｛にしろ / にせよ / *としても｝、このままでは問題は解決しない。

(= KS(D))

b. いずれ｛にせよ / *としても｝早急に対策を考えなければならない。

(= Ex.(l))

c. どんな理由（から）｛にしろ / にせよ / *としても｝何も言わずに仕事を辞めるのは無責任すぎる。

(For whatever reason, quitting the job without saying anything is just (too) irresponsible.)

[2] In the pattern "X *ni shiro/seyo* Y *ni shiro/seyo*":

    a. 行く{にしろ／にせよ／*としても}行かない{にしろ／*としても}、後で電話を下さい。(= KS(C))

    b. 野球{にせよ／*としても}サッカー{にせよ／*としても}、プロでやっていくには並の努力では続かない。(= Ex.(i))

Note that *to shite mo* can be used if it does not immediately follow Wh-words, as shown in [3].

[3] a. 誰が書く{にしろ／にせよ／としても}、絶対間違いがあってはいけない。(= KS(B))

    b. どんな事情があった{にせよ／としても}、何も言わずに仕事を辞めるのは無責任すぎる。(= Ex.(f))

ni shita tokoro de　にしたところで　*comp. prt.*

> a compound particle that means "even" or "also"

also; (even) for ~
【REL. *demo*; *mo*; ***ni shite kara ga***】

N

◆ Key Sentence

	Noun Phrase		
彼は日本語を 20 年 も勉強しているが、	その彼	にしたところで、	まだ分からない文法に 時々出くわすそうだ。

(He has studied Japanese for 20 years, but he told me that even he still encounters grammar he doesn't understand.)

Formation

N にしたところで

　その教授にしたところで　(the professor is also ~ / even the professor)

Examples

(a) 子供はいつか手の届かないところへ行ってしまうものだ。自分の子だけはそうでないと思うかもしれないが、あなたの子にしたところで同じだ。

(Children go (places) beyond their parents' reach sooner or later. You may think that your own children will be different, but they, too, will be the same.)

(b) 昔の浮気が発覚した夫は「10年たってるんだからもう時効だ」と開き直りの態度です。私にしたところで二人の子供のことを考えると離婚にはなかなか踏み切れません。

(My husband, whose past affair was discovered, turned defiant, saying, "It was 10 years ago, so it's too late (to do anything)." I, too, couldn't bear to go forward with a divorce when I thought about our two children.)

(c) 最近は万年筆で字を書く人というのを、ほとんど見なくなって残念。もっとも、そういう私にしたところで、普段使っているのはボールペンだ。

(Lately, you seldom see people writing with a fountain pen, and that makes me feel terribly disappointed. But even I usually use a ball-point pen.)

(d) 三島由紀夫は産湯に浸かった記憶があると書いているが、彼にしたところで、死ぬまでのすべての記憶があるわけではない。

(Yukio Mishima wrote that he remembered (lit., had a memory of) taking his first bath as a baby, but there's no way even he remembered everything he did from birth until death (lit., until he died).)

Notes

1. ~ *ni shita tokoro de* is used to mean "even" or "also."

2. A disjunctive conjunction such as *ga*, *shikashi* or *mottomo* tends to come right before ~ *ni shita tokoro de*, but there are cases where no disjunctive conjunction is used, as in Ex.(b) and (1) below.

(1) 僕は彼女をこれ以上傷つけたくない。研一にしたところで気持ちは同じはずだ。

(I don't want to hurt her feelings any more than this. I believe that Ken'ichi also feels the same way.)

【Related Expressions】

Demo and *mo* can always be used in place of *ni shita tokoro de*, as demonstrated in [1].

[1] a. 彼は日本語を 20 年も勉強しているが、その彼{にしたところで／でも／も}、まだ分からない文法に時々出くわすそうだ。(= KS)

b. 子供はいつか手の届かないところへ行ってしまうものだ。自分の子だけはそうでないと思うかもしれないが、あなたの子{にしたところで／でも／も}同じだ。(= Ex.(a))

But the reverse is true only in limited cases because N *ni shita tokoro de* is used only as the subject, whereas N *demo* and N *mo* can be used as the subject, as in [1], or the direct object, as in [2].

[2] a. 彼はひらがな{でも／も／*にしたところで}読めない。
(He cannot read even *hiragana*.)

b. キャロルは納豆{でも／も／*にしたところで}食べられる。
(Carol can eat even *nattō*.)

Because in N *ni shita tokoro de* the noun has to be something specific, this compound particle cannot be used when the noun is a non-specific, generic noun, as shown in [3] below. Here *kodomo* "child," *tensai* "genius" and *kokusui-shugisha* "nationalist" are presented as generic nouns. The particles *demo* and *mo* are free from this restriction.

[3] a. そんなことは子供{でも／も／*にしたところで}知っている。
(Even a child knows such a thing.)

b. そんな数学の問題、天才{でも／も／*にしたところで}解けないだろうな。
(I don't think even a genius could solve that sort of mathematical problem.)

c. 国粋主義者{でも／も／*にしたところで}その戦争に反対している人は多い。
(Even among nationalists, there are many people who are opposed to the war.)

(⇨ **demo** (DBJG: 111-13); **mo**[1] (DBJG: 247-50); **mo**[2] (DBJG: 250-53))

ni shite[1]　にして[1]　*comp. prt.*　<w>

~~~
a compound particle that indicates a
period of time/stage (in life) at which
some surprising action or state takes
place
~~~
in; at; over; while
【REL. *de*】

◆ Key Sentences

(A)

	Number + Counter		
過度の恐怖や心労は	一夜	にして	白髪をつくる。
(Excessive fear and worry will make your hair turn gray overnight.)			

(B)

	Number + Counter			
彼女は	45歳	にして	初めて	子供ができた。
(She had her first child at the age of 45.)				

(C)

	V*masu*			
外国に	居	ながら	にして	日本からの生のテレビ放送が見られるようになった。
(We can now watch live TV broadcasts from Japan while in a foreign country.)				

Formation

(i)　Number + Counter にして

　　　三歳にして　(when s.o. is three years old)

　　　大学4年にして恋を知る　(s.o. falls in love for the first time when he/she is a senior in college)

(ii)　N にして

　　　一昼夜にして　(s.t. changes in 24 hours (lit., one day and one night))

(iii) V*masu* ながらにして

　　　生まれながらにして　　(when s.o. is born)

Examples

(a) 空襲で東京の町は一夜にして焼け野原になってしまった。

(An air raid turned the city of Tokyo into a burnt field overnight.)

(b) この本は発売1週間にして売れ行きが目に見えて落ち込み始めた。

(The sales of this book began to decline visibly a week after it went on sale.)

(c) 美男美女のカップルの子にふさわしく、その女の子は生後1か月にして目鼻立ちがはっきりしていた。

(As expected of a child born of a handsome couple, the baby girl developed striking features one month after her birth.)

(d) ケプラーは若年にして地位と収入の安定を獲得し、生涯天文学の研究に打ち込む機会をも与えられたのだった。

(Kepler obtained a secure position and income at a young age, and was given the opportunity to devote his entire life to astronomy research.)

(e) 彼はなんと気の早いことに、高校1年にして大学受験日記をつけ始めた。

(He's in such a hurry! He started to keep a journal for college entrance examinations while still a freshman in high school.)

(f) 今年受験2回目にして日本語能力試験1級に合格した。

(This year, on my second try, I passed Level 1 of the Japanese Language Proficiency Test.)

(g) 今にして思えば懐かしいが、若い頃は小さなことでもくよくよ悩んでいたねえ。

(When I think about it now it makes me smile, but when I was young I worried about every little thing under the sun.)

(h) 人間は生まれながらにして健康に生きていこうとする力を持っているそうだ。

(I have heard that people are born with the ability to live in good health.)

(i) ローマは一日にして成らず。

(Rome was not built in a day.)

(j) 四十にして惑わず。五十にして天命を知る。（『論語』）

(At the age of 40 one doesn't doubt, and at 50 one knows heaven's will. (*The Analects of Confucius*))

N

Notes

1. ~ *ni shite* indicates the time during which an action takes place, as in KS(A), Exs.(a) and (i); the time at which something happens, as in Exs.(b) and (f); a stage (in life), as in KS(B), Exs.(c)-(e), (g) and (j); or the coexistence of two states or actions, as in KS(C) and Ex.(h). In all these situations, a surprising action or state is expressed in the main predicate.

2. Usually *ni shite* is used in written Japanese, but *ima ni shite omoeba* "when I think about it now" in Ex.(g) is an idiomatic phrase used in spoken and written language.

3. V*masu nagara ni shite* expresses the coexistence of two states or actions. The connected verb is limited to *iru* "exist," as in KS(C), or *umareru* "be born," as in Ex.(h).

[Related Expression]

The particle *de* can replace *ni shite* except when *ni shite* is paired with *ima* "now," as shown in [1c] below, or is used as part of V*masu nagara ni shite*, as shown in [1d].

[1] a. 過度の恐怖や心労は一夜｛にして／で｝白髪をつくる。(= KS(A))

   b. 彼女は45歳｛にして／で｝初めて子供ができた。(= KS(B))

   c. 今｛にして／*で｝思えば懐かしいが、若い頃は小さなことでもくよく
      よ悩んでいたねえ。(= Ex.(g))

   d. 外国に居ながら｛にして／*で｝日本からの生のテレビ放送が見られる
      ようになった。(= KS(C))

When the predicate doesn't indicate something surprising, *de* is acceptable but *ni shite* is not, as shown in [2].

[2] 春学期は5月10日｛で／*にして｝終わる。
     (The spring semester ends on May 10.)

(⇨ **de**[4] (DBJG: 109-10))

ni shite[2] にして[2]   *conj.*   <w>

a conjunction meaning "and" that is used to combine two noun phrases or *na*-adjectives

and; both ~ and ~
【REL. *de*】

◆ Key Sentences

(A)

	Adj(*na*)stem			
彼女は	頭脳明晰	にして	端麗な	秘書である。
(She is a bright and also beautiful secretary.)				

(B)

	Noun Phrase₁		Noun Phrase₂	
彼は	偉大な学者	にして	優れた教育者	でもあった。
(He was both a distinguished scholar and an excellent educator.)				

(C)

	Adj(*na*)stem		
あの男の性格は	粗野	にして	猛々しい。
((The character of) That man is boorish and fierce.)			

(D)

	Adj(*na*)stem		
首相の容体は	不安定	にして、	予断を許さない。
(The Prime Minister's condition is unstable and unpredictable.)			

Formation

(i) Adj(*na*)stem にして

   高価にして   (s.t. is expensive and)

(ii) NP₁ にして NP₂

   教育者にして実業家   (an educator and a businessman)

すばらしい教育者にして研究者　(a superb educator and a researcher)

聡明な指導者にして優しい人間　(a brilliant leader and a kind human being)

Examples

(a) その政治家は志操堅固にして、高潔清廉な人だった。

(The politician was a man of principle, purity and nobility.)

(b) これほど巧妙にして完璧な犯罪はないでしょう。

(No crime could be as ingenious and perfect as this one.)

(c) 彼女の絵は緻密にして軽やかな筆づかいで圧倒的な支持を集めた。

(Her paintings have become phenomenally popular (lit., gathered overwhelming support) for their elaborate and light-hearted brush strokes.)

(d) あの文法辞典は詳細にして明解な説明が施されている。

(That grammar dictionary has clear, detailed explanations.)

(e) これは堅牢にして素朴な民芸品であります。

(This is a solid and simple (example of) folk art.)

(f) この監督の映画はすべて陰鬱にして物悲しい。

(All of this director's films are gloomy and sad.)

(g) あの政治家の言動は非常識にして、絶えず批判されている。

(The way that politician speaks and acts defies common sense, and he is criticized endlessly.)

(h) 栄太は内心頑固にして決して人に使われる男ではない。

(Eita is (a man who is) stubborn of spirit, and is never taken advantage of by others.)

(i) 彼は優秀な研究者にして熱烈な教育者でもある。

(He is a superb researcher and a fervent educator.)

Notes

1. *Ni shite* meaning "and" is used to combine a *na*-adjective or a noun and another element (Adj(*na*), as in KS(A) and Exs.(a)-(e); Adj(*i*), as in KS(C) and Ex.(f); verb, as in KS(D) and Ex.(g); or N + *da*, as in KS(B), Exs.(h) and (i)).

2. *Ni shite* is used in formal speech or written Japanese.

3. This compound particle cannot be used repeatedly to combine multiple elements, as shown in (1) below.

   (1) *彼女は頭脳明晰にして端麗にして健康な秘書だ。(cf. KS(A))

4. An *i*-adjective cannot be used before *ni shite*, as shown in (2).

   (2) *あの子はかわいくにして、頭がいい。
   (The child is cute and bright.)
   →あの子はかわいくて、頭がいい。

5. It is possible to finish a sentence with "~ *ni shite* Adj(*na*)" without a modified noun, as in (3a), but more often than not the "~ *ni shite* Adj(*na*) + N" pattern is used.

   (3) a. その秘書は頭脳明晰にして<u>端麗である</u>。(cf. KS(A))
   (The secretary is bright and beautiful.)

   b. 彼女は頭脳明晰にして<u>端麗な秘書</u>である。(= KS(A))

6. There is an adverbial phrase that consists of Adj(*na*)stem *ni shite* as in *saiwai ni shite* "fortunately" or *fukō ni shite* "unfortunately."

   (4) 不幸にして彼は自分の欠点が見えていない。
   (Unfortunately he isn't aware of his weaknesses.)

N

[Related Expression]

De, the continuative form of *da*, can always be used in place of *ni shite* without changing the meaning of the sentence.

   [1] a. 彼女は頭脳明晰｛にして／で｝端麗な秘書である。(= KS(A))

   b. 彼は偉大な学者｛にして／で｝優れた教育者でもあった。(= KS(B))

   c. あの男の性格は粗野｛にして／で｝猛々しい。(= KS(C))

ni shite kara ga にしてからが　　*comp. prt.*

a compound particle indicating that s.t. unexpected occurs	even 【REL. *de sae*; *de sura*; *kara shite*; *ni shita tokoro de*】

◆ **Key Sentence**

	Noun Phrase		
ワールドカップ の時は	サッカーファンでも ない私	にしてからが	興奮状態でした。

(I am not a soccer fan, but during the World Cup, even I got excited.)

Formation

N にしてからが

首相にしてからが　(even the prime minister)

Examples

(a) 警察にしてからが、いざ事件が起きないと市民を暴力から守ってくれない。

(Even the police don't protect citizens from violence unless an incident actually occurs.)

(b) ギリシャやローマの彫刻や壁画などに、痩せた女性は皆無だ。美の女神、ヴィーナスにしてからが、かなり太めだ。

(In Greek or Roman sculptures and mural paintings there are no emaciated-looking women. Even Venus, the Goddess of Beauty, is quite full-figured.)

(c) 当代随一の知性人である彼にしてからが、恋愛にたぶらかされている。

(Even he, the greatest intellectual of the day, was deceived by love.)

(d) 息子は父から受け継いだ作風で作品を描いていたが、すでにその父にしてからが、古くさいと言われていた。

(He produced paintings in the mode he inherited from his father, but that style was already considered outdated in his father's time.)

(e) 首相の構造改革案にしてからが、官僚の強い抵抗にあっている。

(Even the prime minister's plan for structural reform met with strong resistance from bureaucrats.)

Notes

1. X *ni shite kara ga*, meaning "even X," can be used when s.t. unexpected occurs for X. In the KS, for example, the speaker didn't expect that he/ she would get excited about the World Cup soccer game because he/she isn't particularly fond of soccer, but contrary to his/her expectation, he/ she got excited when the World Cup took place.

2. X *ni shite kara ga* is always used as a subject. There is no X *ni shite kara o* or X *ni shite kara ni*.

[Related Expressions]

I. *De sae* and *de sura* can always be used in place of *ni shite kara ga*, as shown in [1], but the reverse is not true when *de sae* or *de sura* marks something other than the subject, as in [2]. *Ni shite kara ga* is used only in the subject position, but both *de sae* and *de sura* can occur in positions other than the subject position.

[1] a. ワールドカップの時はサッカーファンでもない私{にしてからが/で さえ/ですら}興奮状態でした。(= KS)

   b. 警察{にしてからが/でさえ/ですら}、いざ事件が起きないと市民 を暴力から守ってくれない。(= Ex.(a))

[2] a. 夫は簡単な家事{でさえ/ですら/*にしてからが}してくれない。
   (My husband won't do even simple household chores (for me).)

   b. 彼女は自分の町のニュース{でさえ/ですら/*にしてからが}興味を 示さない。
   (She doesn't show interest even in news from her own town.)

   (⇨ **sae** (DIJG: 363-69))

II. *Kara shite* can replace *ni shite kara ga*, as shown in [3]. But *kara shite* can also mean "viewed from," and in this sense, cannot be replaced by *ni shite kara ga*, as shown in [4].

[3] a. ギリシャやローマの彫刻や壁画などに、痩せた女性は皆無だ。美の女 神、ヴィーナス{にしてからが/からして}、かなり太めだ。

   (= Ex.(b))

   b. 当代随一の知性人である彼{にしてからが/からして}、恋愛にたぶ らかされている。(= Ex.(c))

N

[4] a. 今までの証拠{からして／*にしてからが}彼が犯人であることは確実だ。

(Based on the evidence gathered to date, it is certain he is the culprit.)

b. 外見{からして／*にしてからが}彼はビジネスマンだろう。

(Based on his outward appearance, I'd say he's a businessman.)

(⇨ *kara shite* (in this volume))

III. The phrase X *ni shita tokoro de* can replace X *ni shite kara ga* if something unexpected is expressed in the main clause, as in [5]. If not, replacement isn't possible, as shown in [6]. Since X *ni shite kara ga* expresses something unexpected, it puts more emphasis on X than X *ni shita tokoro de* does, because the subject marker *ga* of surprise is used. Therefore, X *ni shite kara ga* can carry an accusatory overtone, as shown in [5]. If the accusatory overtone isn't present, then X *ni shite kara ga* cannot be used, as shown in [6].

[5] a. 警察{にしてからが／にしたところで}、いざ事件が起きないと市民を暴力から守ってくれない。(= Ex.(a))

b. 当代随一の知性人である彼{にしてからが／にしたところで}、恋愛にたぶらかされている。(= Ex.(c))

[6] a. 大学院生{にしたところで／*にしてからが}、学者になるとは限らない。

(Graduate students do not always become scholars.)

b. 三島由紀夫は産湯に浸かった記憶があると書いているが、彼{にしたところで／*にしてからが}、死ぬまでのすべての記憶があるわけではない。

(Yukio Mishima wrote that he remembered (lit., had a memory of) taking his first bath as a baby, but there's no way even he remembered everything he did from birth until death (lit., until he died).)

(⇨ *ni shita tokoro de* (in this volume))

ni shite mo にしても *conj.*

a conjunction that represents the idea of "even if s.o. decides to do s.t.," or "even if/though s.o. decides that s.t. is true/the case"	even if (s.o. decides to / it is true that); although / even though (it is true that / it is the case that / we admit that / we agree that / etc.); whatever/whoever/etc.; no matter what/who/how/etc.; whether X or Y; as for ~, too; even (so) 【REL. *to shite mo*; ***ni shiro/ seyo***】

◆ **Key Sentences**

(A)

Sinf		
ピアノを買う	にしても、	こんな狭いアパートでは置くところがない。
(Even if we decide to buy a piano, we won't have a place to put it in such a small apartment.)		

(B)

Sinf		
美紀の言ったことは大げさだった	にしても、	すべてがウソというわけではないだろう。
(Even though (we agree that) Miki's story was exaggerated, probably not all of it was untrue.)		

(C)

Wh-sentence.inf		
誰がこの仕事をやる	にしても	失敗は許されない。
(No matter who is going to do this job, we have no room for mistakes.)		

(D)

S₁inf		S₂inf		
君^{きみ}が行く	にしても	他^{ほか}の誰^{だれ}かが行く	にしても	今回の会議^{かいぎ}はかなりの準備^{じゅんび}が必要^{ひつよう}だ。

(Whether you go or someone else does, this meeting will take a lot of preparation.)

(E)

Noun Phrase		
敬語^{けいご}の使い方	にしても	近頃^{ちかごろ}は間違^{まちが}った言い方が目につく。

(With honorific language, too, we often notice incorrect usage these days.)

Formation

(i) Sinf にしても   (だ after Adj(*na*)stem and N is omitted.)

{行く / 行った}にしても   (even if s.o. decides to go / even though (it is the case that) s.o. went)

{高い / 高かった}にしても   (even if (it is true that) s.t. is expensive / even though (it is true that) s.t. was expensive)

便利^{べんり}{ø / である / だった / であった}にしても   (even if (it is true that) s.t. is convenient / even though (it is true that) s.t. was convenient)

学生{ø / である / だった / であった}にしても   (even if (it is true that) s.o. is a student / even though (it is true that) s.o. was a student)

(ii) NP にしても

この国の文化^{ぶんか}にしても   (this country's culture, too)

Examples

(a) 今すぐ帰るにしても、飛行機^{ひこうき}の切符^{きっぷ}が取^とれるだろうか。

(Even if we (decide to) go home right now, I wonder if we will be able to get plane tickets.)

(b) 京都^{きょうと}は見るところがたくさんあるので、市内^{しない}だけ回るにしても３日くらいとっておいた方がいいでしょう。

(Kyoto has so many places to see, so even if you (decide to) stay within the city, you should plan on spending about three days.)

(c) この作品は中国大陸の影響が濃厚であるにしても、日本の画工の高い水準を示している。

(Even taking the strong influence from China into account, this work demonstrates the high quality craftsmanship of Japanese painters.)

(d) 今度の台風では最悪の事態は避けられたにしても、被害は甚大だ。

(Even though (it is true that) we could avoid a worst-case scenario, the damage from this typhoon is (still) enormous.)

(e) ニューヨークほどではないにしても、この市でもかなり質の高い音楽が聴けます。

(Even though it's not what you get in New York, you can listen to fairly high-quality music in this city, too.)

(f) 何をするにしても英語はしっかり勉強しておいた方がいい。

(Whatever you may do (in the future), you'd do well to study English hard.)

(g) 行くにしてもやめるにしても早く決めてもらえませんか。

(Whether you decide to go or not, could you make up your mind soon?)

(h) 達也にしても悪気があってあんなことを言ったわけじゃない。

(When he said that, Tatsuya didn't intend to be mean-spirited, either.)

(i) 輸入キャンピングカーの車内器具はほとんどが120Vの規格で作られているので、100V電源の日本のキャンプ場ではレンジにしてもエアコンにしても、今一つ出力が弱い。

(Because most of the appliances in imported campers are designed for the 120-volt standard, stoves and air-conditioners, for example, do not have enough output at campsites in Japan, where 100 volts is the standard.)

Notes

1. *Ni shite mo* is the concession form of *ni suru* "decide on." When *ni shite mo* is used as a conjunction, it carries the idea of concession, as in "even if someone decides to do something," "even if someone decides that something is the case," "even though we admit that something is true," etc.

(⇨ *ni suru* (DBJG: 310-11))

2. When the main clause is in the past tense, the verb preceding *ni shite mo* may be in the nonpast tense. In this case, the speaker is referring to a point in time before the action of the verb has taken place. For example, in (1a) the speaker refers to the time when the subject was about to go for his walk, and in (1b) the speaker refers to the time when the subject was about to talk to his subordinate.

(1) a. 散歩に行くにしても、一言そう言っておいてくれたら心配しなかったのに。

(When you were about to go for your walk, if you had just told me, I wouldn't have worried.)

b. 部下を叱るにしても、もう少しほかに言い方がなかったのだろうか。

(Even if he did have to tell his subordinate off, wasn't there a better way of talking to him?)

3. When the sentence that precedes *ni shite mo* contains a Wh-word, it carries the meaning of "whatever/whoever/etc." or "no matter what/who/etc. may," as in KS(C) and Ex.(f).

4. "S₁ *ni shite mo* S₂ *ni shite mo*" means "whether S₁ or S₂," as in KS(D) and Ex.(g).

5. N (or NP) *ni shite mo* is used to present another topic related to the previous discourse, as in KS(E), Exs.(h) and (i). Sometimes, two or more topics are presented by repeating *ni shite mo*, as in Ex.(i).

6. *Ni shite mo* is often used with the demonstrative *sore*, which refers to the previous statement, as in (2) and (3).

(2) 長い人生いろいろあるのは当たり前だけど、**それにしても**いやなことがあまりに多すぎる。

(Of course many things happen in a long life, but, even so, it seems like there are just too many unpleasant ones.)

(3) A: 慶子、遅いね。渋滞にあってるのかな。

(Keiko is late. I wonder if she is caught in a traffic jam.)

B: **それにしても**、遅すぎると思わない？

(Even so, don't you think she'd be here by now (lit., she's too late)?)

Sore ni shite mo is also used as a set phrase meaning "at any rate; in any case; anyway," as in (4). In these examples, the referent of *sore* is vague.

(4) a. それにしても、なぜこんなに多くのフォーマットがあるのですか。

(In any case, why are there this many (different) formats?)

b. それにしても、名古屋は本当に久しぶりだ。

(At any rate, it's really been a long time since I've been in Nagoya.)

7. With certain Wh-words *ni shite mo* is used to mean "at any rate; anyway."

(5) ｛何／いずれに／どっち｝にしても早急に結論を出さないといけない。

(At any rate, we have to make our final decision immediately.)

【Related Expression】

To shite mo, the concession form of *to suru* "assume that," is similar to *ni shite mo* in its form and meaning. However, the fundamental difference is that *to shite mo* is used to present a hypothetical situation, whereas *ni shite mo* is used to present a factual or a nearly factual situation. Thus, in hypothetical situations, as in [1], *ni shite mo* cannot be used.

[1] a. 彼が社長だった｛としても／*にしても｝この経営危機は救えないだろう。

(Even if he were the president, I don't think this management crisis could be avoided (lit., saved).)

b. 90年代のバブル経済の崩壊がなかった｛としても／*にしても｝、日本の高度経済成長はいつか止まっていたはずだ。

(Even if the collapse of the bubble economy of the '90s hadn't taken place, Japan's high-paced economic growth would have stopped sometime.)

When both *to shite mo* and *ni shite mo* can be used, the sentences have a slightly different meaning, as shown in [2].

[2] a. ピアノを買う｛にしても／としても｝、こんな狭いアパートでは置くところがない。(= KS(A))

(Even if we ｛decide to buy / consider buying｝ a piano, we don't have a place to put it in such a small apartment.)

b. 美紀の言ったことは大げさだった｛にしても／としても｝、すべてがウソというわけではないだろう。(= KS(B))

(Even ｛though (we agree that) / if we assume that｝ Miki's story was exaggerated, probably not all of it was untrue.)

It is also noted that *to shite mo* cannot be used to present a topic, as in KS(E) and Ex.(i).

[3] a. 敬語の使い方 ｛にしても /*としても｝近頃は間違った言い方が目につく。(= KS(E))

b. 輸入キャンピングカーの車内器具はほとんどが 120Vの規格で作られているので、100V電源の日本のキャンプ場ではレンジ ｛にしても /*としても｝エアコン ｛にしても /*としても｝、今一つ出力が弱い。

(= Ex.(i))

(⇨ **to suru**[1] (DIJG: 518-23))

ni todomarazu にとどまらず *phr.* <w>

{ a phrase indicating that s.t. goes beyond a spatial/temporal boundary }

doesn't stop with ~; doesn't end with ~; not limited to ~; going beyond ~; not only ~ (but also ~)
【REL. *dake de (wa) naku ~ (mo)*; *nomi narazu*】

◆ Key Sentences

(A)

	Noun			
彼の研究範囲は	哲学	(だけ)	にとどまらず、	認知心理学の領域にまで広がっている。

(His area of research is not limited merely to philosophy, but extends to cognitive psychology as well.)

(B)

	Vinf			
彼女<ruby>か</ruby>の<ruby>じょ</ruby>は小 説を広く	**読む**	（だけ）	にとどまらず、	自分でもいくつか書いて、 すでに雑誌<ruby>ざっ</ruby><ruby>し</ruby>に発表<ruby>はっ</ruby><ruby>ぴょう</ruby>している。

(Not only does she avidly read novels, she has also written a couple of
novels herself, which have been published in magazines.)

Formation

(i)　N（だけ）にとどまらず

　　　日本（だけ）にとどまらず　(s.t. is not limited to Japan, and ~)

　　　その時代（だけ）にとどまらず　(s.t. goes beyond that age ~)

(ii)　Vinf（だけ）にとどまらず

　　　｛読む／読んだ｝（だけ）にとどまらず　(not only does/did s.o. read s.t.,
　　　but ~)

(iii)　｛N／Adj(*na*)stem｝である（だけ）にとどまらず

　　　証明<ruby>しょうめい</ruby>するものである（だけ）にとどまらず　(s.t. not only serves as evidence)

　　　重要<ruby>じゅうよう</ruby>である（だけ）にとどまらず　(s.t. is not only important)

(iv)　Adj(*i*)inf だけにとどまらず

　　　面白<ruby>おもしろ</ruby>いだけにとどまらず　(s.t. is not only interesting)

N

Examples

(a) 博士<ruby>はかせ</ruby>は専門<ruby>せんもん</ruby>の数学<ruby>すうがく</ruby>にとどまらず、コンピュータサイエンスでも優<ruby>すぐ</ruby>れた研究を
している。

(The doctor is doing excellent research not only in his specialty, mathematics, but also in computer science.)

(b) 本研究室での研究は、単<ruby>たん</ruby>なる理論<ruby>りろん</ruby>にとどまらず、その応用<ruby>おうよう</ruby>も重視<ruby>じゅうし</ruby>している。

(At our lab, we don't just focus on theory, we also emphasize its
application.)

(c) 先輩方<ruby>せんぱいがた</ruby>には単<ruby>たん</ruby>に学生時代にとどまらず、卒業後<ruby>そつぎょうご</ruby>も人生<ruby>じんせい</ruby>のよき先輩として貴重<ruby>きちょう</ruby>
なアドバイスをいただいてまいりました。

(My senior schoolmates, as people more experienced in life, have given
me invaluable advice, not only when I was a student but also after I
graduated.)

(d) 本医学部は医学の専門知識だけにとどまらず、人間愛、使命感、責任感、といった人間教育にも力を注いでいます。

(This medical school not only teaches technical expertise, it also makes an effort to teach ethics (lit., human education), such as respect (lit., love) for human beings, a sense of mission and a sense of responsibility.)

(e) 室内楽では一人一人の奏者が自分のパートを理解するだけにとどまらず、他のすべてのパートも理解しなければならない。

(In chamber music, each player has to understand not only his or her own part, but everyone else's as well.)

(f) この薬は髪が薄くなるのを防ぐだけにとどまらず、白髪を黒い髪に戻します。

(Not only does this medicine prevent your hair from thinning, it brings your gray hair back to its original black color.)

(g) 本学の博士号は専門的知識における卓越性を証明するものであるにとどまらず、取得者が人間的力量の持ち主であることを宣言するものです。

(A doctorate from this university not only serves as evidence of excellence in professional knowledge, it also declares that the holder possesses great potential as a person.)

N

(h) 力学という学問は、物質世界を統制する科学技術の体系として重要であるにとどまらず、世界を認識するための体系として重要である。

(The field of mechanics is important not only as a system of science and technology that controls the material world, but also as a system for understanding the world.)

(i) 彼女の講演はただ面白いだけにとどまらず、必ず深い哲学が含まれている。

(Not only are her lectures interesting, they always have some deep philosophical meaning, too.)

Notes

1. *Ni todomarazu* indicates that something figuratively goes beyond a certain boundary. For example, in KS(A), "he" goes beyond the boundary of "philosophy" into the territory of "cognitive psychology."

2. *Todomarazu* is an archaic negative form of *todomaru* "to stay in one place for an extended period of time." The negative ending *-zu* is often used in the phrase *-zu ni* "without doing s.t."

(⇨ *~nai de* (DBJG: 271-73))

3. As shown in Exs.(g)-(i), *ni todomarazu* can be preceded by N *de aru*, Adj(*na*)stem *de aru* or Adj(*i*)inf *dake*. But the use of *i*-adjectives is rare.

[Related Expressions]

I. *Dake de (wa) naku* can replace *(dake) ni todomarazu*, as shown in [1].

[1]　a. 彼の研究範囲は哲学｛(だけ)にとどまらず／だけで(は)なく｝、認知心理学の領域にまで広がっている。(= KS(A))

　　b. 彼女は小説を広く読む｛(だけ)にとどまらず／だけで(は)なく｝、自分でもいくつか書いて、すでに雑誌に発表している。(= KS(B))

However, note the different connectors used with these two phrases.

(⇨ ***dake de (wa) naku* ~ *(mo)*** (DBJG: 97-100))

II. *Nomi narazu* can be used in place of *(dake) ni todomarazu* or *dake de (wa) naku* ~ *(mo)* without changing the meaning of the sentence.

[2]　a. 彼の研究範囲は哲学｛(だけ)にとどまらず／だけで(は)なく／のみならず｝、認知心理学の領域にまで広がっている。(= KS(A))

　　b. 彼女は小説を広く読む｛(だけ)にとどまらず／だけで(は)なく／のみならず｝、自分でもいくつか書いて、すでに雑誌に発表している。

(= KS(B))

　　c. 博士は専門の数学｛(だけ)にとどまらず／だけで(は)なく／のみならず｝、コンピュータサイエンスでも優れた研究をしている。(= Ex.(a))

　　d. 彼女の講演はただ面白い｛だけにとどまらず／だけで(は)なく／のみならず｝、必ず深い哲学が含まれている。(= Ex.(i))

Among the three, *dake de (wa) naku* ~ *(mo)* is the most colloquial and *nomi narazu* the least, with *(dake) ni todomarazu* in between.

(⇨ ***nomi narazu*** (in this volume))

ni tsuke   につけ   *conj.*

> a conjunction indicating that each time s.o. perceives s.t. he/she feels or thinks s.t. associated with it

as; every time; whenever
【REL. *tabi ni*】

◆ **Key Sentence**

	Vinf.nonpast (cognition)		
ナポリで撮った両親の写真を	見る	につけ、	あの時の楽しかった旅行を思い出す。

(When I see the photo of my parents I took in Naples, I remember what a great time we had on that trip.)

Formation

Vinf.nonpast につけ   (where V = verb of cognition)

景色を見るにつけ   (as I look at the scenery)

日記を読むにつけ   (as I read the diary)

そのことを考えるにつけ   (as I think about it)

年を感じるにつけ   (as I become conscious of my age)

その香りを嗅ぐにつけ   (as I smell the scent)

Examples

(a) 新緑の香りを嗅ぐにつけ、「ああ、春なんだなあ」と思わずのほほんとしてしまいます。

(As I smell the scent of fresh green foliage, I tell myself it's finally spring and feel really relaxed, almost without realizing it.)

(b) そのピアニストの深みのある音楽を聴き、温かい人柄に触れるにつけ、「音楽は人なり」の思いを強くしております。

(As I listen to the pianist's deeply-felt music and sense his warm personality, I feel strongly that music is man.)

(c) 深刻化する年金問題や経済問題に対する政府の無策ぶりを見るにつけ、自分

のことは自分で守るしかないと思う。

(As I watch the government's inability to deal with the increasingly serious problems related to the pension system and economy, I think that we must (do what we can to) protect ourselves.)

(d) 二十歳をはるかに過ぎても自立への見通しのつかない若者を見るにつけ、聞くにつけ、やるせない思いがあります。

(As I watch or hear about young people who are well over 20 but have no prospects for becoming independent, I feel heavy-hearted.)

(e) いじめや虐待、陰惨な事件など、子供を取り巻く不幸な状況を考えるにつけ、この国の行く末を案じずにはいられない。

(Whenever I think about the unhappy circumstances surrounding children, with the recent cases of bullying, abuse, and gruesome incidents, it makes me feel concerned about the future of this country.)

(f) 世界各地での戦いの様子を見るにつけ胸が痛む。

(As I watch the wars going on in various places around the world, my heart aches.)

(g) 最近頻発している医療ミスの記事を読むにつけ、私も被害者になる可能性があったのではと戦慄を覚えてしまう。

(Whenever I read articles about all of the medical errors that have been happening (frequently) recently, I shudder at the thought that I could have been a victim.)

(h) 年末が一気に駆け足でやってくるのを感じるにつけ、自分の年齢を思い知らされます。

(As I feel the end of the year coming at a dash, I become aware of my age.)

Notes

1. *Ni tsuke* is used when something the speaker/writer perceives causes him/her to feel or think something. The original perception is expressed by verbs of cognition such as *miru* "see," *yomu* "read," *kangaeru* "think," *kanjiru* "feel," *fureru* "touch" or *kagu* "smell." Among these cognitive verbs, *miru* and *yomu* are used most frequently.

2. *Ni tsuke* can be repeated, as shown in Ex.(d).

3. *Ni tsuke* can take the form *ni tsuke te (mo)* in all of the examples except Ex.(d), where two verbs of cognition are listed in a single sentence.

(1) 二十歳をはるかに過ぎても自立への見通しのつかない若者を見る{につけ / *につけて(も)}、聞く{につけ / *につけて(も)}、やるせない思いがあります。(= Ex.(d))

There is a slight difference in meaning between those two. *Ni tsukete mo* implies that the speaker/writer feels or thinks something, not only for the explicitly stated reason but also for some other reasons. For example, in (2), the speaker remembers the trip he enjoyed with his parents not only when he looks at the photo he took in Naples, but also by looking at or thinking about other memorable things.

(2) ナポリで撮った両親の写真を見る{につけ / につけても}、あの時の楽しかった旅行を思い出す。(= KS)

4. There are two idiomatic phrases that follow the pattern "Wh-word ~ *ni tsuke(te)*": *nani ka ni tsuke(te)* "in various ways" and *nani goto ni tsuke(te mo)* "no matter what it is." Examples follow.

(3) a. 携帯電話を持つようになって、何かにつけ(て)便利になった。

   (Now that I have a cell phone my life has become convenient in various ways.)

   b. 何事につけ(ても)熱中すると他のことが見えなくなる。

   (No matter what it is, when you get engrossed in one thing, you become blind to everything else.)

[Related Expression]

When *ni tsuke* indicates a perception that is repeated, the phrase can be replaced by Vinf.nonpast *tabi ni* "each time s.o. does s.t."

[1] a. ナポリで撮った両親の写真を見る{につけ / たびに}、あの時の楽しかった旅行を思い出す。(= KS)

   b. 世界各地での戦いの様子を見る{につけ / たびに}胸が痛む。(= Ex.(f))

Ni tsuke cannot replace *tabi ni* when the verb in the subordinate clause is not a verb of cognition, as in [2].

[2] a. 彼は飲む{たびに / *につけ}陽気になる。

   (He turns cheerful and outgoing each time he drinks.)

   b. 僕は会う{たびに / *につけ}彼女のことが好きになった。

   (I became more fond of her each time we met.)

($\Rightarrow$ ***tabi ni*** (DIJG: 442-44))

ni watatte / wataru に わたって / わたる *comp. prt.* <w>

a compound particle indicating that s.t. takes place over a particular span of time or physical space	for; over; extending; stretching; ranging; covering 【REL. *ni kakete*】

◆ Key Sentences

(A)

	Noun (time span)		
オリンピックが	16日間	にわたって	開かれた。
(The Olympic Games were held for sixteen days.)				

(B)

	Noun (space)		
干ばつのため	広範囲	にわたって	作物が被害を受けた。
(Due to the drought, crops were damaged over a wide area.)				

(C)

	Noun (time)		Noun (time)		
配管工事のため、明日	午前1時	から	午前9時ごろ	にわたって	断水する。
(Due to work on the pipes, the water supply will be cut off from 1 a.m. to about 9 a.m. tomorrow.)						

(D)

	Noun (times)		
その記事は	8回	にわたって	新聞に連載された。
(The articles appeared serially in the newspaper over eight issues (lit., extending to eight times).)				

N

(E)

Noun (time span)		Noun	
約_{やく}40年	にわたる	冷戦_{れいせん}	がついに終わった。
(The Cold War, which lasted for about 40 years, finally came to an end.)			

Formation

(i)   N にわたって

    1か月にわたって   (for one month)

    全ページにわたって   (over the entire page / all the pages)

    5回にわたって   (extending to five times)

    10キロにわたって   (extending over 10 kilometers)

    東海地方全体にわたって   (over the entire Tokai region)

(ii)   N₁ から N₂ にわたって

    1時から6時にわたって   (from 1 o'clock to 6 o'clock)

    東部から中部にわたって   (ranging from the eastern part to the central part)

(iii)   (N₁ から) N₂ にわたる N₃

    100ページにわたる報告   (a report which extends to one hundred pages)

    5月から9月にわたる乾期   (a dry season from May through September)

Examples

(a) A社の携帯電話サービスで、関東の一部で昨夜午後9時ごろから約6時間にわたって接続障害があった。

(Last night there was an interruption (lit., connection difficulties) in Company A's mobile phone service in a certain area of Kanto for about six hours starting about 9 o'clock.)

(b) コミック『ピーナッツ』は、1950年に誕生して以来半世紀以上にわたって世界中のファンを魅了してきた。

(From the time of its debut in 1950, the cartoon "Peanuts" has fascinated fans all over the world for over half a century.)

(c) その川の両側には 20 エーカーにわたって森が広がっている。

(On both sides of the river, the forest stretches for 20 acres.)

(d) 厚い雨雲が関東から九州にわたって広がっている。

(Thick clouds extend from Kanto to Kyushu.)

(e) 昨年 1 年間に両者の間で 5 回にわたって賄賂の授受があったことが明らかになった。

(It became evident that one party paid the other bribes five times during the past year.)

(f) 殺人現場は再三にわたって捜査が行われた。

(The murder site was searched many times.)

(g) 当社では、中古車の電気装置を点火装置やバッテリーを含む 5 項目にわたってチェックいたします。

(Our inspection of the electrical system in used cars covers five points, including the ignition system and the battery. (lit., Our company checks five points of used cars' electric systems, including the ignition system and the battery.))

(h) 実験の前に詳細にわたって器具の使い方の指示があった。

(Before the experiment there were detailed instructions regarding how to use the instruments.)

(i) 今回の会議では、環境保護の多岐にわたる問題について、議論が交わされた。

(At this conference many issues concerning environmental protection were discussed.)

(j) 生産段階から消費段階にわたる食品の安全性を確保することが急務だ。

(Ensuring safety from the production stage through the consumption stage is an urgent matter.)

Notes

1. As seen in the Formations, (X *kara*) Y *ni watatte* is commonly used with quantifiers (i.e., phrases with a number and a counter) of time/distance/space or nouns of time/location/space to represent a time span or a spatial expanse.

2. X *ni watatte* is also used to represent the number of occurrences or items, as shown in KS(D) and Exs.(e)-(g), or the topic area, as shown in Exs.(h) and (i).

3. *Ni watatte* commonly appears in written language, but it is also used in formal speech such as news reports.

4. When a single entity occurs with *ni watatte*, the noun must be a word which indicates the entire part of something (e.g., *zenshin* "entire body") or it must be a word meaning "entire" (e.g., *zentai* "whole"), as shown in (1).

(1) a. ｛全身／*体｝にわたって発疹が出た。

    (I had a rash all over my body.)

   b. ｛西日本全体／*西日本｝にわたって大雨が降った。

    (There was heavy rain all over western Japan.)

   c. 地震のため｛橋全体／*橋｝にわたって亀裂が生じた。

    (The earthquake caused cracks over the entire bridge.)

5. X *kara* Y *ni watatte* is commonly used when X and Y indicate specific times. Thus, the examples in (2) are rather awkward. (See Related Expression.)

(2) a. *今晩から明日の早朝にわたって大雨が降る恐れがある。

    (There is a chance (lit., fear) of heavy rain from tonight until early morning.)

   b. *昨晩から今朝にわたって地震が頻発した。

    (There were frequent earthquakes from last night through this morning.)

   c. *年末から年始にわたって来訪者が続く。

    (We will have a series of visitors from year's end through the beginning of next year.)

6. *Ni watatte* is an adverbial phrase and it modifies verbs. The adjectival form is *ni wataru*, as shown in KS(E), Exs.(i) and (j). (3) presents additional examples.

(3) a. 全560ページにわたる詳細な報告が委員会から提出された。

    (A detailed report, extending to 560 pages in all, was submitted by the committee.)

   b. メルボルンで長さ100キロにわたる巨大なアリの巣が見つかった。

    (In Melbourne, a gigantic ant's nest extending 100 kilometers was found.)

c. このプログラムは複数行にわたるひらがな文字列を一括漢字変換できる。

(This program can convert a string of *hiragana* characters extending several lines into kanji and kana all at once.)

d. 4回にわたる手術の末、彼の心臓はほぼ完全に機能を回復した。

(After four operations (lit., After a series of four operations), his heart has regained functioning almost entirely.)

【Related Expression】

X *kara* Y *ni kakete* also represents a span of time or a physical expanse.

[1] a. 配管工事のため明日午前1時から午前9時ごろ｛にわたって／にかけて｝断水する。(= KS(C))

b. 厚い雨雲が関東から九州｛にわたって／にかけて｝広がっている。

(= Ex.(d))

c. 西宮インターから芦屋インター｛にわたって／にかけて｝交通が渋滞した。

(Traffic was tied up from the Nishinomiya Interchange to the Ashiya Interchange.)

d. 左腰から左膝｛にわたって／にかけて｝まだ痺れが残っている。

(I still have numbness from my left hip to my left knee.)

However, unlike X *kara* Y *ni watatte*, X *kara* Y *ni kakete* can be used whether or not X and Y represent specific times.

[2] a. 今晩から明日の早朝｛にかけて／*にわたって｝大雨が降る恐れがある。(= (2a))

b. 昨晩から今朝｛にかけて／*にわたって｝地震が頻発した。(= (2b))

c. 年末から年始｛にかけて／*にわたって｝来訪者が続く。(= (2c))

On the other hand, X *ni kakete* cannot be used when X represents a span of time, number of occurrences or items, a topic area, or distance/area.

[3] a. 約6時間｛にわたって／*にかけて｝接続障害があった。(cf. Ex.(a))

b. オリンピックが16日間｛にわたって／*にかけて｝開かれた。

(= KS(A))

c. 私は長年{にわたって / *にかけて}その研究をしている。
(I've done research on that for many years.)

[4] a. その記事は8回{にわたって / *にかけて}新聞に連載された。
(= KS(D))

b. 当社では、中古車の電気装置を点火装置やバッテリーを含む5項目{にわたって / *にかけて}チェックいたします。(= Ex.(g))

[5] a. 干ばつのため広範囲{にわたって / *にかけて}作物が被害を受けた。
(= KS(B))

b. 5キロ{にわたって / *にかけて}交通が渋滞した。
(The traffic jam extended for five kilometers.)

c. 全身{にわたって / *にかけて}発疹が出た。(= (1a))

d. 西日本全体{にわたって / *にかけて}大雨が降った。(= (1b))

N

ni yorazu によらず   *comp. prt.*

a compound particle that means "without depending on"	without; without ~ing; regardless of; independently of; without reference to; whether X or Y; whether X or not; whatever/whoever/etc.; no matter what/who/how/etc. 【REL. *nashi de*; *ni yotte/yori*; ***o towazu***】

◆ **Key Sentences**

(A)

Noun (action)		
リストラ	によらず (に)	この会社を救う方法はない。
(There is no way to save this company without restructuring it.)		

(B)

	Noun (non-action)		
この会社では	学歴 (がくれき)	によらず、	実力(じつりょく)があればどんどん大きい 仕事をまかされる。

(At this company, if you are capable, you will be given big assignments one after another, regardless of your educational qualifications.)

(C)

Noun (Wh-word)		
何事(なにごと)	によらず	困(こま)ったことがあったらいつでも相談(そうだん)して下さい。

(Whatever it may be, if you have trouble, please consult me anytime.)

(D)

Noun₁		Noun₂			
国産(こくさん)	(である)か	輸入(ゆにゅう)	(である)か	によらず	牛肉は食べない ことにしている。

((Regardless of) Whether it is domestically produced or imported, as a rule I do not eat beef.)

(E)

	Noun			
この会社は	経験(けいけん)	のあるなし	によらず	面接(めんせつ)してくれる。

(This company will interview you regardless of your experience (lit., whether or not you have experience.)

(F)

Noun			
天候(てんこう)	のいかん	によらず	試合は予定通(よていどお)り行われます。

(No matter what the weather (lit., whatever the weather is like), the game will be held as scheduled.)

N

(G)

Wh-sentence.inf			
誰_{だれ}がそのプロジェクトを担当_{たんとう}する	か	によらず	担当者_{たんとうしゃ}には特別手当_{とくべつてあて}が支給_{しきゅう}される。

(Regardless of who it is (lit., who takes the project), the project manager will be given special compensation.)

Formation

(i) N によらず

紹介_{しょうかい}によらず　(without introduction)

学生数_{がくせいすう}によらず　(regardless of the number of students)

(ii) Wh-word (N / NP) によらず

誰_{だれ}によらず　(whoever it may be (lit., regardless of who it is))

どんな仕事によらず　(whatever work it may be (lit., regardless of what kind of work it is))

(iii) X か Y かによらず (where X, Y = contrastive words; usually nonpast forms)

・N₁ か N₂ かによらず

英語か日本語かによらず　(regardless of whether s.t. is English or Japanese)

・V₁inf か V₂inf かによらず

勝_かつか負_まけるかによらず　(regardless of whether s.o. wins or loses)

・Adj(*i*)₁inf か Adj(*i*)₂inf かによらず

高いか安いかによらず　(regardless of whether s.t. is expensive or cheap)

・Adj(*na*)₁stem か Adj(*na*)₂stem かによらず

偶然_{ぐうぜん}か意図的_{いとてき}かによらず　(regardless of whether s.t. is accidental or intentional)

(iv) X か{どう／否_{いな}}かによらず

存在_{そんざい}するか{どう／否}かによらず　(regardless of whether s.t. exists or not)

高いか{どう／否}かによらず　(regardless of whether s.t. is expensive or not)

偶然か{どう／否}かによらず (regardless of whether s.t. is coincidental or not)

学生か{どう／否}かによらず (regardless of whether s.o. is a student or not)

(v) X (Aff.) か X (Neg.) かによらず

行くか行かないかによらず (regardless of whether s.o. goes or not)

高いか高くないかによらず (regardless of whether s.t. is expensive or not)

偶然(である)か偶然でないかによらず (regardless of whether s.t. is coincidental or not)

英語(である)か英語でないかによらず (regardless of whether s.t. is English or not)

(vi) X (Aff.) + X (Neg.) によらず (where X = {V／Adj(*i*)}inf; usually nonpast forms)

行く行かないによらず (regardless of whether s.o. goes or not)

うまいうまくないによらず (regardless of whether s.o. is good or poor (at doing s.t.))

(vii) X + Y によらず (where X, Y = Adj(*i*)inf.nonpast／Adj(*na*)stem; Y = X's antonym)

上手下手によらず (regardless of whether s.o. is skillful or unskillful)

うまい下手によらず (regardless of whether s.o. is good or poor (at doing s.t.))

(viii){N／Adj(*na*)stem} であるなしによらず

会員であるなしによらず (regardless of whether s.o. is a member or not)

経済的であるなしによらず (regardless of whether s.t. is economical or not)

(ix) N のあるなしによらず

学位のあるなしによらず (regardless of whether s.o. has a degree or not)

(x) N のいかんによらず

方法のいかんによらず (regardless of the method (lit., regardless of what the method is))

(xi) Wh-sentence.inf かによらず

いかなる国における使用であるかによらず　(regardless of the country where s.t. is used (lit., regardless of in whatever country s.t. is used))

Examples

(a) 理想は武力によらず紛争を解決することだ。

(The ideal is to resolve disputes without using armed force.)

(b) 吉川さんは勤務先の斡旋によらず別の会社に再就職した。

(Mr. Yoshikawa was employed by another company without his former employer's help (lit., good offices).)

(c) 本契約は両者の合意によらずに変更されることはない。

(This contract may not be altered without the agreement of both parties.)

(d) 当ダンス教室は、いつからでも始められ、経験によらずどなたでもご参加いただけます。

(In this dance studio, students can begin at any time and anyone, regardless of experience, can join.)

(e) 当社のセールスマンの給与は勤務年数や年齢によらず、常に販売実績を基に決定される。

(The salaries of this company's sales representatives are not dependent on their length of employment or age; they are always based on sales performance.)

(f) QR の長さは P の位置によらず常に一定である。

(The distance between Q and R is always the same, regardless of where P is.)

(g) この標準テストは在籍する大学や学部によらず、また大学生であるか社会人であるかによらず、誰でも受けられます。

(Anyone can take this standardized test, regardless of what university or school you attend or whether you are a university student or a professional.)

(h) どんな仕事によらず、いつも誠実に務めなければいけない。

(No matter what job you have, you should always do the work sincerely.)

(i) 持ち物が多いか少ないかによらず、きちんと整理ができている部屋は気持ちいい。

(Whether you own a few things or many, a well-organized space makes you feel good.)

(j) 発表者がコンピュータを使うか使わないかによらず、プロジェクターとスクリーンは会場に準備しておきます。

(Regardless of whether or not the presenters use a computer, I will set up a projector and a screen at the site.)

(k) 入門コースは本会会員であるか否かによらず無料です。

(The introductory course is free whether or not you are a member of our society.)

(l) ストレスはその多少によらずいつも健康と関係する。

(Stress, regardless of how high or low it is, is always related to health.)

(m) 世の中には、潜在的な生命力のあるなしによらず、生き長らえられる人とそうでない人がいる。

(In this world some people are able to live a long time and others aren't, regardless of their potential for living.)

(n) 実験データは、どの機器を使ったかによらず1か所に集めて管理すべきだ。

(The data from the experiment should be put in one place and managed regardless of which piece of equipment it came from (lit., was used).)

Notes

1. *Ni yorazu* literally means "without depending on," but it commonly carries two meanings. That is, when the preceding element is a noun that indicates an action or the object of an action, it means "without," as in KS(A) and Exs.(a)-(c); in other cases, it means "regardless of." More specific meanings vary depending on the context, as seen in the translations of the examples above.

2. When *ni yorazu* means "without," *ni* can follow, as shown in KS(A) and Ex.(c).

3. When the X in X *ni yorazu* is a Wh-word or a noun phrase with a Wh-word, as in KS(C) and Ex.(h), *ni yorazu* indicates concession, and the whole phrase is equivalent to X *demo*, as demonstrated in (1).

(1) a. 何事｛によらず／でも｝困ったことがあったらいつでも相談して下さ
い。(= KS(C))

b. どんな仕事｛によらず／でも｝、いつも誠実に務めなければいけない。

(= Ex.(h))

(⇨ *demo* (DBJG: 111-13))

4. In general, when X *ni yorazu* means "regardless of," the X in X *ni yorazu* refers to more than one possibility. As seen in the Formations, there are a number of ways to express multiple possibilities.

【Related Expressions】

I. When *ni yorazu (ni)* means "without," it can be replaced by *nashi de*, as shown in [1].

[1] a. リストラ｛によらず(に)／なしで｝この会社を救う方法はない。

(= KS(A))

b. 理想は武力｛によらず／なしで｝紛争を解決することだ。(= Ex.(a))

c. 本契約が両者の合意｛によらずに／なしで｝変更されることはない。

(= Ex.(c))

Ni yorazu (ni) carries the nuance of "without depending on," while *nashi de* simply means "without." Note also that *nashi de* is less formal.

II. The opposite of *ni yorazu* (and other synonyms such as *ni kakawarazu* and *o towazu*) meaning "regardless of" can be expressed with *ni yotte* or *ni yori* "depending on," as in [2].

[2] a. 性別｛によって／により｝会費が異なる。
(The membership fee differs by sex.)

b. 奨学金を貰えるかどうか｛によって／により｝どの大学に行くかを決める。

(Whether or not I get a scholarship will determine where I go to college.)

(⇨ *ni yotte/yori* (DIJG: 292-301); *ni kakawarazu* (in this volume);
o towazu (in this volume))

ni yoru to によると   *comp. prt.*

| a compound particle that is used to identify the source of the information provided in the sentence | according to; based on 【REL. *ni yoreba*】 |

◆ **Key Sentences**

(A)

	Noun			
その温泉は	旅行雑誌	によると	神経痛にいい	そうだ。

(One of the travel magazines said that hot springs are good for arthritis.)

(B)

Noun Phrase		
日本の法律	によると	おおむね12歳未満の者は逮捕の対象にならない。

(According to Japanese law, generally, youths under 12 are not subject to arrest.)

(C)

Noun Phrase			
聞いたところ	によると	来年は授業料が上がる	らしい。

(Based on what I heard, (it appears that) tuition will go up next year.)

N

Formation

N によると

{新聞／法律／規則／辞書} によると   (According to the newspaper/law/rule/dictionary)

Examples

(a) 新聞の世論調査によると、内閣支持率は22％にまで急落したそうだ。

(According to a newspaper poll, the approval rating for the Cabinet dropped sharply to 22 percent.)

(b) 友達に聞いたところによると、フィンランドのメーデーは学生も集まって春を祝う祭りの日だそうだ。

(According to my friend, May Day in Finland is a day when everyone, including students, joins in a festival to celebrate spring.)

(c) H博士によると、犬は人間が歩く際に発する弱い電磁波を感じ取っている可能性があるという。

(According to Dr. H, dogs may be able to feel the faint electromagnetic waves that people generate when they walk.)

(d) 政府筋によると、政府はバイオテロリズムへの対策を研究する審議会を設置する予定であるという。

(According to government sources, the government plans to establish a panel that will study measures to cope with bioterrorism.)

(e) 法律によると、介護保険は適切な医療および福祉サービスが受けられるようにすることを目的としています。

(According to the law, the purpose of insurance for care of the elderly is to make appropriate medical and welfare services accessible.)

(f) 辞書によると、「さびしい」には「寂しい」と「淋しい」の二つの漢字が使われている。

(According to the dictionary, two characters are used for *sabishii*, 寂 and 淋.)

(g) 調査によると、高齢者に対する暴力と虐待の加害者は、家族、友人あるいは知人であることが最も多い。

(According to the survey, those who inflict violence and abuse upon the elderly are most often the victim's family, friends or acquaintances.)

(h) 懲戒処分基準によると、教職員が酒酔い運転で死亡・重傷事故を起こした場合は免職になる。

(According to the standards for disciplinary action, if a faculty or staff member driving under the influence (of alcohol) causes an accident resulting in serious injury or death, he or she will be dismissed.)

(i) 韓国人の友人によると、中国では韓国語学習者が増えているらしい。

(According to my Korean friend, the number of the learners of Korean is increasing.)

Note

Ni yoru to is used to identify the source of the information provided in the sentence. When the information is hearsay, the final predicate ends with *sōda*, as in KS(A), Exs.(a) and (b), or *to iu*, as in Exs.(c) and (d). When it is conjecture, the final predicate ends with *rashii*, as in KS(C) and Ex.(i). For objective statements based on the facts, the final predicate is not modified, as shown in KS(B) and Exs.(e)-(h).

(⇨ ***sōda***[1] (DBJG: 407-09); ***rashii*** (DBJG: 373-75))

[Related Expression]

Ni yoreba can replace *ni yoru to* without changing the meaning of the sentence.

[1] a. その温泉は旅行雑誌に｛よると／よれば｝神経痛にいいそうだ。

(= KS(A))

b. 日本の法律に｛よると／よれば｝おおむね12歳未満の者は逮捕の対象にならない。(= KS(B))

c. 聞いたところに｛よると／よれば｝来年は授業料が上がるらしい。

(= KS(C))

N

no hoka (ni) (wa) ~ nai   のほか (に) (は) ～ない

(⇨ ***yori/no hoka (ni) (wa) ~ nai*** in this volume)

nomi narazu   のみならず   *phr.*   <w>

a phrase that is used in formal writing to mean "not only"

not only ~ (but also ~); not only that
【REL. *dake de (wa) naku*; *ni kagirazu*; **ni todomarazu**; **wa oroka**】

◆ **Key Sentences**

(A)

	Noun		
我_わが社_{しゃ}は	日本国内_{にほんこくない}	のみならず、	アメリカやヨーロッパなどでもビジネス活動_{かつどう}を行っております。

(Our company does business not only in Japan but also in America, Europe, and elsewhere.)

(B)

	Vinf		
これからの企業_{きぎょう}は単_{たん}に利益_{りえき}を	追求_{ついきゅう}する	のみならず、	環境_{かんきょう}に配慮_{はいりょ}した生産活動_{せいさんかつどう}を行わなければならない。

(Today's companies should not just pursue profits; they should also consider environmental protection issues in their production activities. (lit., they must perform production activities that take the environment into consideration as well.))

(C)

Sentence₁		Sentence₂
彼_{かれ}のしたことは人間として恥_はずべきことである。	のみならず、	それは明_{あき}らかに犯罪行為_{はんざいこうい}だ。

(As a human being, he should be ashamed of what he did. Not only that, it is clearly a criminal act.)

Formation

(i)　N (Prt.) のみならず

　　　学生のみならず　(not only students)

　　　アジアからのみならず　(not only from Asia)

(ii)　{V / Adj(*i*)} inf のみならず

　　　理解_{りかい}{する / しない}のみならず　(not only does s.o. (not) understand s.t.)

　　　{難_{むずか}しい / 難しくない}のみならず　(not only is s.t. (not) difficult)

(iii) ｛Adj(*na*)stem／N｝であるのみならず

　　　不自然_{ふしぜん}であるのみならず　(s.t. is not only unnatural)

　　　学者_{がくしゃ}であるのみならず　(s.o. is not only a scholar)

(iv) S₁。のみならず、S₂。

　　　この問題_{もんだい}は難_{むずか}しい。のみならず、解決_{かいけつ}に時間もかかる。　(This problem is difficult. Not only that, it'll take time to solve.)

Examples

(a) 料金体系_{りょうきんたいけい}のみならず、サービス体制_{たいせい}も改善_{かいぜん}する必要_{ひつよう}がある。

(It is necessary to change not only the fee structure but the service system as well.)

(b) 大統領_{だいとうりょう}の決定_{けってい}には国内_{こくない}のみならず、海外_{かいがい}からも強い批判_{ひはん}の声が上がっている。

(The president's decision is being criticized heavily not only within the country but also abroad.)

(c) この会社は炭酸飲料_{たんさんいんりょう}メーカーとして世界的_{せかいてき}に有名であるのみならず、アメリカ合衆国_{がっしゅうこく}を象徴_{しょうちょう}する存在_{そんざい}の一つでさえある。

(Not only is this company famous worldwide as a carbonated beverage manufacturer, it is even an American symbol (lit., one of the entities that symbolize the United States).)

(d) この種_{しゅ}の犯罪_{はんざい}は、老後_{ろうご}の生活資金_{せいかつしきん}を根こそぎ奪_{うば}うなど、市民への経済的_{けいざいてき}な影響_{えい}_{きょう}が甚大_{じんだい}であるのみならず、精神的_{せいしんてき}打撃_{だげき}も多大_{ただい}である。

(Crimes of this kind have an enormous impact on citizens, not only economically but also psychologically, as they can completely deprive citizens of their post-retirement livelihoods (among other things).)

(e) 技術者_{ぎじゅつしゃ}は単_{たん}に技術の進歩_{しんぽ}の推進者_{すいしんしゃ}であるのみならず、人類_{じんるい}・社会に及_{およ}ぼす技術の影響_{えいきょう}についても強い責任感_{せきにんかん}を持つ自律的_{じりつてき}な行動者_{こうどうしゃ}であるべきである。

(Technology specialists should not simply play a role as promoters of technological advancement; they should also be independent actors who bear a heavy (lit., strong) sense of responsibility for the effect of technology on people and on society.)

(f) 不正軽油_{ふせいけいゆ}の製造_{せいぞう}・販売_{はんばい}・使用_{しよう}は、極_{きわ}めて悪質_{あくしつ}な脱税行為_{だつぜいこうい}である。のみならず、ディーゼル車の排気_{はいき}ガスは大気中_{たいきちゅう}の有害物質_{ゆうがいぶっしつ}を増加_{ぞうか}させるなど、環境汚染_{かんきょうおせん}の原因_{げんいん}にもなっている。

(The production, the sale, and the use of illegal diesel oil are extremely serious acts of tax evasion. Not only that, these acts result in environmental pollution because they bring about an increase in toxic substances in the atmosphere via the exhaust from diesel cars.)

(g) 私はすっかり疲れていた。肩や頸の凝るのはもちろん、不眠症もかなり甚しかった。のみならず偶々眠ったと思うと、いろいろの夢を見勝ちだった。(芥川龍之介『夢』)

(I was totally exhausted. My shoulders and neck were stiff, of course, and I was suffering from severe insomnia. Not only that, when I did finally fall asleep, I had many dreams. (from *Dreams* by Akutagawa Ryunosuke))

Notes

1. *Nomi narazu* is the combination of the particle *nomi* "only" and the negative continuative form of *nari*, the classic form, which is equivalent to *de aru* "be." Thus, the literal meaning of *nomi narazu* is "be not only ~ and."

2. *Nomi narazu* is used only in formal writing or speeches.

3. In "X *de aru nomi narazu*," X can be *na*-adjective stems and nouns, as in Formation (iii), or any other elements to which *de aru* can be affixed, as in (1).

   (1) 今すぐ謝罪すべきであるのみならず、現職を辞すべきである。

   (He should not only apologize immediately, but also resign his present post.)

4. *Nomi narazu* can appear in sentence-initial position, as in KS(C), in which case it means "not only that," where "that" refers to the statement made in the preceding sentence(s). Although *nomi narazu* in this use can be preceded by the demonstrative pronoun *sore* "that," it is usually used alone.

[Related Expressions]

I. *Dake de (wa) naku* and *nomi narazu* represent the same idea, i.e., "not only." However, besides the fact that the former is more informal than the latter, there are some syntactic differences between them.

First, the prenominal forms of *na*-adjectives cannot precede *nomi narazu*. However, *de aru* can precede both *dake de (wa) naku* and *nomi narazu*.

[1] a. 不自然な{だけで(は)なく / *のみならず}……

   (not only unnatural)

   b. 不自然である｛だけで(は)なく / のみならず｝……

Second, while *nomi narazu* can occur in sentence-initial position, *dake de (wa) naku* cannot. It needs *sore* (or *kore* depending on the situation) to refer to the statement made by the preceding sentence(s).

[2]　彼のしたことは人間として恥ずべきことである。｛のみならず / *だけで (は)なく / それだけで(は)なく｝、それは明らかに犯罪行為だ。

                                             (= KS(C))

                    (⇨ ***dake de (wa) naku* ~ *(mo)*** (DBJG: 97-100))

II. When *nomi narazu* is preceded by nouns, it can be replaced by *ni kagirazu* "not limited to," as shown in [3].

[3]　a. 我が社は日本国内｛のみならず / に限らず｝、アメリカやヨーロッパ などでもビジネス活動を行っております。(= KS(A))

     b. 料金体系｛のみならず / に限らず｝、サービス体制も改善する必要が ある。(= Ex.(a))

                           (⇨ ***ni kagirazu*** (DIJG: 249-50))

N

---

no nan no tte　のなんのって　*phr.*　\<s\>

a phrase to emphasize that s.t./s.o. is/was in an extreme state or that s.o. does/did s.t. to a great extent	so (~ that); so much/well (~ that); so ~ and 【REL. ~ *no* ~ *nai no tte*; *nante mon ja nai*; *nado to iu mono de wa nai*】

◆ Key Sentences

(A)

Adj(*i*)inf		
甘い	のなんのって	私は一口食べて全部残してしまいました。
(It was so sweet that I ate one bite and left the rest.)		

(B)

Vinf		
飲んだ	のなんのって	彼_{かれ}らは5本_{ほん}の酒_{さけ}を全部_{ぜんぶ}空けてしまった。
(They drank so much; they completely emptied five bottles of *sake*.)		

Formation

(i) {V / Adj(*i*)} inf のなんのって

　　 {効_きく / 効いた} のなんのって　 (s.t. is/was so effective that ~)

　　 {速_{はや}い / 速かった} のなんのって　 (s.t. is/was so fast that ~)

(ii) Adj(*na*)stem {な / だった} のなんのって

　　 下手_{へた} {な / だった} のなんのって　 (s.o. is/was so bad at s.t. that ~)

Examples

(a) かゆいのなんのって一晩中_{ひとばんじゅう}寝_ねられなかった。

　　 (It was so itchy that I couldn't sleep all night.)

(b) 重いのなんのって二人でも持ち上がりませんでした。

　　 (It was so heavy that even two people couldn't lift it.)

(c) 海の醍醐味_{だいごみ}を味わうなら、ホエールウォッチングだ。実際_{じっさい}に見るクジラは、大きいのなんのって、すごい迫力_{はくりょく}だよ。

　　 (If you want to experience the true charm of the ocean, try whale-watching. When seen in real life, whales are so huge they take your breath away.)

(d) もう少しで釣_つれたのに糸_{いと}が切れて魚は海の中。結構_{けっこう}大きかったので悔_{くや}しかったのなんのって！

　　 (I almost had it, but the line broke and the fish went back into the sea. It was really big, so I was *so* disappointed!)

(e) A: 試合はどうだった？

　　　 (How was the game?)

　　 B: いやもう、ひどいのなんのって、話したくもないよ。

　　　 (Oh, no, it was so terrible! I don't even want to talk about it.)

(f) 不便なのなんのって一番_{いちばん}近くのスーパーに行くのに1時間もかかるんです。

　　 (It's so inconvenient; it takes up to an hour to get to the nearest supermarket.)

(g) 朝日岳の山々はちょうど見事に色づいていてきれいなのなんのって。思わず時間を忘れて、しばらく見入ってしまいました。

(The Asahidake Mountains had just turned colors and were *so* beautiful. Without realizing it, I stared at them for a while, completely forgetting the time.)

(h) 驚いたのなんのって、しばらくは言葉も出なかった。

(I was so surprised that I couldn't even speak for a while.)

(i) この望遠鏡、よく見えるのなんのって土星の輪まではっきり見えたよ。

(I could see so well with this telescope; I could even see Saturn's rings clearly.)

Notes

1. Even when the state, event, etc., took place in the past, a nonpast form is commonly used with *no nan no tte*, as seen in KS(A), Exs.(a), (b), (e), (g) and (i).

2. Although not a commonly used, negative forms can be used in front of *no nan no tte*, as in (1).

   (1) a. 読めないのなんのって、ひらがなもまともに読めないんです。

      (His reading skill is so poor (lit., he cannot read) that he cannot read even *hiragana* correctly.)

   b. ウエイターの感じが悪い上に、出てきた料理がこれまたおいしくないのなんのって。

      (The waiter was really unpleasant, and what's more, the food that was served was so bad (lit., so not delicious).)

[Related Expressions]

I. ~ *no* ~ *nai no tte* expresses the same idea as ~ *no nan no tte*, as in [1].

   [1] a. 甘いの甘くないのって、私は一口食べて全部残してしまいました。

                                                                    (cf. KS(A))

      b. 驚いたの驚かなかったのって、しばらくは言葉も出なかった。

                                                                    (cf. Ex.(h))

Note that ~ *no* ~ *nai no tte* can also be used to mean "(say) that s.t./s.o. is ~ or that it/he/she is not ~," in which case, it is not synonymous with ~ *no nan no tte*, as shown in [2].

[2] 人は照美のことを｛冷たいの冷たくないのって /*冷たいのなんのって｝
いろいろ言うが、私は彼女が温かい人であることを知っている。

(People make various comments about Terumi, saying that she is
cold or that she is not, but I know that she is a warm person.)

II. ~ *nante mon ja nai* and its formal form ~ *nado to iu mono de wa nai*
express an idea similar to that of ~ *no nan no tte.*

[3] a. アンディのピアノは下手｛なんてもんじゃない / などというものでは
ない｝。

(Andy's piano playing is more than just bad (lit., is not something you call "bad").)

b. 彼は飲む｛なんてもんじゃない / などというものではない｝。

(He drinks so much. (lit., His (way of) drinking is not what you
usually refer to as "drinking."))

Note that ~ *nante mon ja nai* and ~ *nado to iu mono de wa nai* are
sentence-final forms while ~ *no nan no tte* is not. Thus, the sentences in
[4] are not complete by themselves.

[4] a. アンディのピアノは下手なのなんのって。(cf. [3a])

(Andy's piano is so bad, . . .)

b. 彼は飲むのなんのって。(cf. [3b])

(He drinks so much, . . .)

N

---

no nasa   のなさ［の無さ］   *phr.*

| a phrase that indicates a state where s.t. is lacking | lack of; absence of |

◆ **Key Sentence**

	Noun		
私は彼の	**常識**	のなさ	にあきれている。

| (I am appalled by his lack of common sense.) |

Formation

N のなさ

能力のなさ　(lack of ability)

元気のなさ　(lack of spirit)

Examples

(a) 跳びたいと思っても跳べない。体力、筋力のなさを痛感しました。

(I wanted to jump, but I couldn't. I became painfully aware of my lack of physical and muscular strength.)

(b) 今回の一連の貴社の対応は、私たちには全く納得できるものではなく、貴社の誠意のなさに大変な憤りを感じます。

(We cannot accept your company's response to this situation, and we are filled with anger at your company's lack of sincerity.)

(c) 辞書の使用を許可してもらったものの、時間不足で思ったように答えられない問題があり、自分の英語力のなさに落ち込みました。

(Although I was allowed to use a dictionary, because of the time constraint there were parts I couldn't answer, and I felt depressed about my lack of English proficiency.)

(d) 親しみやすさと、温かさと、飾り気のなさが、さやの絶対的な魅力である。

(Friendliness, warmth and a lack of affectation are what makes Saya so absolutely charming.)

(e) 最近の映画やドラマは、その内容のなさにがっかりさせられる。

(I am disappointed with recent movies and dramas because of their lack of content.)

(f) 調査によると日本の子供の自信のなさは世界一だそうである。

(According to a survey, Japanese children are the least self-confident in the world.)

(g) このマンガは設定は面白かったが、物語が進むにつれて話が大きくなり、リ
アリティのなさについていけなくなってしまった。

(This comic had an interesting plot, but as the story went on, it became
so exaggerated that I couldn't take the lack of reality.)

Note

~ *no nasa* is a phrase that means "a lack of s.t." *Nasa* consists of *na*, which
is the stem of the *i*-adjective *nai*, and the suffix *-sa*. In general, *-sa* is a suffix
that makes a noun out of *i/na*-adjective stem.   (⇨ *-sa* (DBJG: 381-84))

N

~ **no** ~ **no to**   ～の～のと   *str.*

a structure that states what is said by
s.o. in order to express the speaker's
disagreement or dissatisfaction

saying ~, ~, and so on; saying
~ or ~
[REL. ~ *toka* ~ *toka*; ~ *da no* ~
da no to]

◆ Key Sentences

(A)

V₁inf (Aff.)		V₂inf (Neg.) (V₁ = V₂)		
やった	の	やらなかった	のと	いつまで言っていても仕方がない。
(It is no use talking endlessly about what you did or didn't do.)				

(B)

	Adj(*na*)₁inf		Adj(*na*)₂inf (Adj(*na*)₂ = antonym of Adj(*na*)₁)	
いつまでも	好きだ	の	嫌いだ	のと

言っていないで、早く結婚相手を決めなさい。

(You should decide who you want to marry soon without saying all the time that you like (this one) or that you don't like (that one).)

(C)

	S₁inf		S₂inf		文句ばかり 言っている。
彼女は	アパートの部屋が狭い	の	場所が不便だ	のと	

(She is always complaining about how small her apartment is, how inconvenient the location is, or whatever.)

Formation

N

(i) X (Aff.) の X (Neg.) のと

　　・V₁inf (Aff.) の V₂inf (Neg.) のと　 (where V₁ = V₂)

　　　できるのできないのと　 (saying that s.t. can be done or cannot be done)

　　・Adj(*i/na*)₁inf (Aff.) の Adj(*i/na*)₂inf (Neg.) のと　 (where Adj(*i/na*)₁ = Adj(*i/na*)₂)

　　　おかしいのおかしくないのと　 (saying that s.t. is strange or not strange)

　　　好きだの好きじゃないのと　 (saying that s.o. likes s.t./s.o or does not like it/him/her)

　　・N₁ だの N₂ じゃないのと　 (where N₁ = N₂)

　　　病気だの病気じゃないのと　 (saying that s.o. is ill or not ill)

(ii) Adj(*i/na*)₁inf の Adj(*i/na*)₂inf のと　 (where Adj₂ = an antonym of Adj₁)

　　　いいの悪いのと　 (saying that s.t. is good or bad)

　　　上手だの下手だのと　 (saying that s.o. is good at s.t. or bad at it)

(iii) S₁inf の S₂inf のと

部屋が狭いの食事がまずいのと　(saying that the room is small and that meals are bad, etc.)

Examples

(a) 彼女は一緒に行くの行かぬのといつまでも煮え切らない。

(She can never decide whether she is going with me or not.)

(b) 彼らは、誰がそのことをしゃべったのしゃべらなかったのと言い争っている。

(They are arguing over who leaked or didn't leak that information.)

(c) 条件がいいの悪いのといつまで言っていても仕方がない。

(There's no point in discussing endlessly whether conditions are good or bad.)

(d) 彼女はやっと就職できたのに、やれ場所が遠いの給料が悪いのと文句ばかり言っている。

(She finally found a job, but now she can't stop complaining about how far it is, how low the salary is, and so on and so on.)

(e) コーチにフォームが悪いの力が入りすぎているのとさんざん直された。

(My coach kept correcting me, saying that my form was bad, I used too much force, and so on.)

(f) 真理は婚約者の給料が安いの背が低いのと勝手なことを言っている。

(Mari is saying selfish things such as how low her fiancé's salary is, how short he is, etc.)

Notes

1. The structure "~ *no* ~ *no to*" lists what someone says to convey the speaker's disagreement or dissatisfaction about something or someone else.

2. In "X *no* Y *no to*," Y is often the negative form of X or an antonym of X, as seen in Formation (i) and (ii). The classic verb negative ending *nu* sometimes occurs in Y, as in Ex.(a).

3. In "X *no* Y *no to*," X and Y can be imperative sentences.

(1) 母は部屋を片づけろの台所を手伝えのといつも何か言いつけてくる。

(My mother is always telling me to do something (around the house) like clean up my room or help her in the kitchen or something.)

4. When X and Y in "X *no* Y *no to*" are sentences, the information may be unspecific, as in (2).

(2) a. 隆志は給料がどうの待遇が｛どう／こう｝のと不平が多い。

(Takashi complains a lot about his work conditions: his salary, the way he's treated, etc.)

　b. 頼子は夫がどうしたの子供が｛どう／こう｝したのと文句を言わない日はない。

(There's not a day that Yoriko doesn't complain about what her husband did, what her kids did, etc.)

【Related Expressions】

I. ~ *toka* ~ *toka* can be used in place of ~ *no* ~ *no to* without changing the meaning.

[1] a. やった｛の／とか｝やらなかった｛のと／とか｝いつまで言っていても仕方がない。(= KS(A))

　b. いつまでも好きだ｛の／とか｝嫌いだ｛のと／とか｝言っていないで、早く結婚相手を決めなさい。(= KS(B))

However, the usage of ~ *toka* ~ *toka* is broader than that of ~ *no* ~ *no to*, as seen in the following examples, where ~ *no* ~ *no to* cannot be used.

[2] a. 私はバッハとかモーツアルトとかが好きだ。

(I like Bach and Mozart, among others.)

　b. 疲れた時はお風呂に入るとか早く寝るとかしなさい。

(When you are tired, you should do things like take a bath or go to bed early.)

(⇨ *toka* (DBJG: 488-90))

II. ~ *da no* ~ *da no to* can also be used in place of ~ *no* ~ *no to* without changing the meaning, although the former is not as common as the latter.

[3] a. やった｛の／だの｝やらなかった｛のと／だのと｝いつまで言っていても仕方がない。(= KS(A))

　b. 条件がいい｛の／だの｝悪い｛のと／だのと｝いつまで言っていても仕方がない。(= Ex.(c))

Note that if a *na*-adjective or a noun precedes *no*, *da* is not repeated before *no*; thus, the structure is the same structure as that of ~ *no* ~ *no to*.

[4] いつまでも好きだの嫌いだのと言っていないで、早く結婚相手を決めなさい。(= KS(B))

(⇨ ***dano*** (in this volume))

---

n to suru　んとする　*phr.*　\<w\>

> a phrase meaning for "s.o. to try to do s.t." or for "s.t. to be about to occur"
>
> try to do; be about to
> 【REL. *yō to suru*】

◆ Key Sentences

(A)

	Vneg			
教授の	言わ	ん	とする	ことが学生に伝わらないのは、たいてい教授の方が悪いのだ。

(It is usually a professor who is to blame when his students don't comprehend what he tries to convey.)

(B)

	Vneg		
太陽はまさに山の稜線に	沈ま	ん	としていた。

(The sun was about to sink behind the mountain ridge.)

Formation

Vneg んとする　(Exception: する→せんとする)

行かんとする　(s.o. tries to go there)

起きんとする　(s.o. is about to get up)

研究せんとする　(s.o. tries to do research)

Examples

(a) あの政治家は言わんとしているところがよく分からない。

(I don't comprehend what that politician is trying to say.)

(b) 善意で何事かを行わんとすると、必ずそれに水を差す人間がいる。

(Whenever someone tries to do something with good intentions, inevitably there is someone who discourages it.)

(c) 専門家でない者を排除せんとする科学者の過剰防衛には辟易させられる。

(I am fed up with overprotective scientists (lit., the overprotection of scientists) who try to eliminate nonspecialists.)

(d) 死なんとする者は本音を吐くものだ。

(A person who is about to die gives vent to his true feelings.)

(e) 暴風のために木々が倒れんとしている。

(The trees are about to be blown over by the violent wind.)

(f) まさに輝かんとする月が雲で隠れた。

(The moon, which was just about to shine, was concealed by the clouds.)

(g) 今にも崩れんとする天守閣には、城と命運をともにする城主の姿があった。

(At the castle tower, which was on the verge of collapse, stood the castle lord, ready to share its fate.)

N

Notes

1. The phrase ~ *n to suru* means "try," as in KS(A) and Exs.(a)-(c), or "be about to occur," as in KS(B) and Exs.(d)-(g).

2. The phrase is used primarily in written Japanese and has an archaic flavor.

【Related Expression】

Yō to suru carries the same meaning as *n to suru* and is more commonly used in both spoken and written Japanese, as shown below. Note that the volitional form of the verb precedes *to suru*.

[1] a. 教授の{言わん/言おう}とすることが学生に伝わらないのは、たいてい教授の方が悪いのだ。(= KS(A))

b. 善意で何事かを｛行わん / 行おう｝とすると、必ずそれに水を差す人間がいる。(= Ex.(b))

c. 太陽はまさに山の稜線に｛沈まん / 沈もう｝としていた。(= KS(B))

d. 暴風のために木々が｛倒れん / 倒れよう｝としている。(= Ex.(e))

(⇨ **miru** (DBJG: 246-47))

o chūshin ni を中心に *phr.* <w>

> a phrase that means "with s.t./s.o. at the center"

centering around; around; focusing on; mainly; primarily; with ~ as the center; with ~ as the leader; with ~ as the primary ~; take the lead 【REL. *o chūshin to/ni shite*】

◆ **Key Sentences**

(A)

Noun		
東京	を中心に	大雨が降った。
(There was heavy rain, mostly in and around Tokyo.)		

(B)

Noun		
東南アジア	を中心に	鳥インフルエンザが急速に広がっている。
(Bird flu is spreading rapidly, primarily in Southeast Asia.)		

(C)

	Noun		
この研究は	中島教授	を中心に	進められている。
(This research is progressing, with Prof. Nakajima taking the lead.)			

0

Formation

N を中心に

日本を中心に　(centering around Japan)

Examples

(a) 最近は小説よりもビジネス書を中心に読んでいる。
    (These days I mainly read business books, rather than novels.)

(b) ファーストフードのR社は近々神戸を中心に新たに25店舗を開く予定だ。

(Company R, a fast food company, plans to open 25 new stores in Kobe and neighboring cities before long.)

(c) 現在、文部科学省を中心に、義務教育改革に向けた検討が進められている。

(The Ministry of Education, Culture, Sports, Science and Technology is taking the lead in investigating compulsory education reform.)

(d) 最近の調査で、アメリカでのオンラインビデオの視聴が若い層を中心に伸びていることが分かった。

(It has become clear from a recent survey that the viewing of online videos is increasing in America—most notably among young people.)

(e) コンピュータメーカーのP社はデスクトップモデルを中心に20％以上の大幅値下げを行うと発表した。

(The computer manufacturer P announced that it would give a large price reduction of 20 percent or more for their computers, with desktop models as the primary target.)

(f) このサイトは熊本のニュースを中心に、温泉やグルメ、イベント情報などもご紹介します。

(This website highlights Kumamoto news as well as information on hot springs, gourmet foods, events, etc.)

(g) 本プロジェクトでは、言語による情報伝達と、韻律や動作、表情など、言語以外の要素との関係を中心に研究を行った。

(In this project we examined primarily the interrelationship between language-based communication and non-linguistic factors, such as meter, motions, facial expressions, etc.)

(h) この展示会はある著名な日本の建築家の作品を中心に、東京に建てられたモダンな建築について紹介している。

(This exhibition, focusing mainly on works by an eminent Japanese architect, introduces modern architecture in Tokyo.)

Notes

1. X *o chūshin ni* means that something happens or is done with X as the central or main place, object, person, etc. The specific meaning differs depending on the context.

2. X *o chūshin ni* is often in the titles of papers, articles, reports, courses, etc.

(1) a. 日英比較 —条件表現を中心に—

(A Comparison of Japanese and English: Focusing on Conditional Expressions)

b. インターネットの基礎 —ホームページ作りを中心に—

(Internet Basics: With the focus on creating Web pages)

[Related Expressions]

O chūshin to/ni shite is equivalent to *o chūshin ni* and the two can be used interchangeably, as shown in [1].

[1] a. 東京を中心{に / として / にして}大雨が降った。(= KS(A))

b. 東南アジアを中心{に / として / にして}鳥インフルエンザが急速に広がっている。(= KS(B))

c. この研究は中島教授を中心{に / として / にして}進められている。

(= KS(C))

There is no noun modification form of *o chūshin ni*. Thus, when it is necessary, the noun modification form of *o chūshin to/ni shite*, i.e., *o chūshin to/ni shita*, or *chūshin no* is used, as shown in [2] and [3].

[2] a. ここでは会話を中心{と / に}した授業が行われている。

(Here classes focusing on conversation are being taught.)

b. この辺りはトウモロコシ栽培を中心{と / に}した農業が盛んだ。

(In this area, farming, with corn cultivation as the primary business, is widespread.)

[3] a. ここでは会話中心の授業が行われている。(= [2a])

b. この辺りはトウモロコシ栽培中心の農業が盛んだ。(= [2b])

0

o kaishite / kaishita を介して / 介した　*comp. prt.* <w>

a compound particle that introduces a medium through which s.o. does s.t. or s.t. happens to s.o. or s.t.	through; via; by means of; by ~ing 【REL. *o tōshite*; *ni yotte/yori*】

◆ Key Sentences

(A)

	Noun		
今、現地の	代理人	を介して	製造元と価格の交渉をしている。

(We are negotiating the price with the manufacturer through a local agent now.)

(B)

Noun		
インターネット	を介して	音楽や映画を配信できるようになった。

(Music and movies can be distributed via the Internet now.)

(C)

	Noun		
我々は	ボランティア活動	を介して	地域の交流を図ろうとしている。

(We are trying to promote interaction among the local (units) through volunteer activities.)

(D)

Noun		Noun		
通訳	を{介しての／介した}	商談	は	効率が悪い。

(Business talks via an interpreter are inefficient.)

Formation

(i)　N を介して

　　　知り合いを介して　(through an acquaintance)

(ii)　N₁ を{介しての／介した}N₂

　　　通信網を{介しての／介した}データ送信　(data transmission via a network)

Examples

(a) 日本にいる友達を介してこの情報を手に入れた。

(I got this information with the help of (lit., through) a friend of mine in Japan.)

(b) このウイルスはそれに感染した鳥から蚊を介して人に感染する。人から人や人から蚊を介しての感染はない。

(This virus is transmitted to people from infected birds via mosquitoes. It is not transmitted between people either directly or via mosquitoes.)

(c) 自殺系サイトを介して知り合った男女が、初対面でいきなり一緒に自殺するという事件が続き、社会問題となった。

(There have been several incidents in which a man and a woman who had met through a suicide website committed suicide together right after meeting in person for the first time, and such incidents have become a social problem.)

(d) このテロ組織は海外の金融機関を介して資金の調達と仕送りをしているらしい。

(This terrorist organization seems to be collecting and distributing money via overseas financial institutions.)

(e) 記憶は再生時に脳の「海馬」という部分を介して再構成される。

(When we recall memories, they are reconstructed through the part of the brain called the hippocampus.)

(f) 新しいビジネスを生むためのアイデアは、勤務外のインフォーマルなコミュニケーションを介して、より多く得られると言われる。

(It is said that more ideas for creating new business can be obtained via informal communication outside of work.)

(g) このグループは、同じような障害で悩んでいる人々が、お互いの交流を介して問題をよりよく理解し、助け合っていけるよう、様々な支援を行っている。

(This group provides various kinds of support so that people with the same sort of disorder or disability can better understand others' problems and help each other by interacting.)

Notes

1. X *o kaishite* is used when someone does something, or something happens to someone or something, not directly, but indirectly via X. X may be a person, a living creature, an object (e.g., path, device, institution, part of a system) or an act.

2. The noun-modification forms of *o kaishite* are *o kaishite no* and *o kaishita*, as shown in KS(D) and Ex.(b). (1) provides additional examples.

(1) a. 代理人を{介しての / 介した}交渉は失敗に終わった。

(The negotiation through an agent ended in failure.)

　　b. これからはインターネットを{介しての / 介した}音楽配信が主流になるだろう。

(Music distribution via the Internet will be main stream from now on.)

[Related Expressions]

I. *O tōshite* is synonymous with *o kaishite* and can be used interchangeably in many situations, as demonstrated in [1].

　　[1] a. 今、現地の代理人を{介して / 通して}製造元と価格の交渉をしている。(= KS(A))

　　　　b. インターネットを{介して / 通して}音楽や映画を配信できるようになった。(= KS(B))

　　　　c. 我々はボランティア活動を{介して / 通して}地域の交流を図ろうとしている。(= KS(C))

However, X *o kaishite* cannot be used in the following contexts, in which X is not an active or essential medium through which something takes place.

　　[2] a. 壁を{通して / *介して}隣の部屋の話が聞こえてくる。

(I can hear the conversation next door through the wall.)

　　　　b. カーテンを{通して / *介して}家の中の様子が見えた。

(I could see what was inside the house through the curtain.)

　　　　c. この辺りは四季を{通して / *介して}気候が温暖だ。

(In this area, the weather is mild throughout the year (lit., four seasons).)

(⇨ *o tōshite* (DIJG: 330-32))

II. *Ni yotte/yori* are used to indicate means. Thus, they can be used in place of *o kaishite* in many situations, as shown in [3].

　　[3] a. インターネット{を介して / によって / により}音楽や映画を配信できるようになった。(= KS(B))

b. 我々はボランティア活動 ｛を介して / によって / により｝ 地域の交流を図ろうとしている。(= KS(C))

c. このテロ組織は海外の金融機関 ｛を介して / によって / により｝ 資金の調達と仕送りをしているらしい。(= Ex.(d))

However, when the noun preceding *ni yotte/yori* refers to a person or a living creature, *ni yotte* and its variations sound somewhat unnatural, as shown in [4]. When the preceding noun refers to a living creature (i.e., non-human), *ni yotte* and its variations are somewhat more natural than when the noun refers to a person, as indicated in [4c].

[4] a. 今、現地の代理人 ｛を介して / ??によって / ??により｝ 製造元と価格の交渉をしている。(= KS(A))

b. 日本にいる友達 ｛を介して / ??によって / ??により｝ この情報を手に入れた。(= Ex.(a))

c. このウイルスはそれに感染した鳥から蚊 ｛を介して / ?によって / ?により｝ 人に感染する。人から人や人から蚊 ｛を介しての / ?による｝ 感染はない。(= Ex.(b))

(⇨ *ni yotte/yori* (DIJG: 292-301))

0

o kinji-enai　を禁じ得ない　*phr.*　<w>

| a phrase that is used when one cannot control emotions or reactions caused by emotions | cannot hold; cannot hold back; cannot keep back; cannot help ~ing; cannot keep ~ from ~ing |

◆ **Key Sentences**

(A)

	Noun	
このような無責任な行いに対して	怒り	を禁じ得ない。
(I cannot hold back my anger at such an irresponsible deed.)		

(B)

	Vinf.nonpast		
その感動的な光景を見て、涙が	こみ上げてくる	の	を禁じ得なかった。
(Seeing the moving scene, I could not keep my tears from welling up.)			

Formation

(i)   N を禁じ得ない

　　喜びを禁じ得ない　(cannot keep back one's joy)

(ii)   Vinf.nonpast のを禁じ得ない

　　足が震えるのを禁じ得ない　(cannot keep s.o.'s legs from trembling)

Examples

(a) 24年の苦悩と空白の後、ついに実現した家族との再会に、周囲の者も涙を禁じ得なかった。

((Seeing) the family reunited, an occasion that finally became reality after twenty-four years of agony and separation, people around them couldn't help but cry, too.)

(b) その美しい早春の風景画に作者の温かい郷土愛を感じ、深い感動を禁じ得なかった。

(Looking at the beautiful early spring landscape painting, I felt the painter's love for his homeland, and couldn't help but be moved profoundly.)

(c) 出版社による無神経な個人写真の扱い方に、驚きと憤りを禁じ得ない。

(I can't hold back my surprise and anger at the publisher's thoughtless way of treating those personal photos.)

(d) 大統領の声明は、せっかく第一歩を踏み出した両国の平和統一の動きに水を差すのではないかという疑問を禁じ得ない。

(I cannot keep myself from wondering if the president's announcement will pour cold water on the two nations' hard-won first step toward peaceful unification.)

(e) 長い間憧れていた人に会う瞬間が近づいて、次第に動悸が速まるのを禁じ得なかった。

(As the moment approached when I was to meet with the person I'd admired for a long time, I could not stop my heart from beating faster and faster.)

(f) この業界の救いようのない保守性に、深いため息が出るのを禁じ得なかった。

((Looking at) this industry's hopeless conservatism, I couldn't help but let out a deep sigh.)

Notes

1. *Kinji-enai* consists of the stem of the Gr. 2 verb *kinjiru* "stop; prohibit" and the negative form of the auxiliary verb *uru/eru* "can." This is a literary expression; therefore, it cannot be used with casual words or phrases. (⇨ **uru/eru** (DIJG: 553-55))

2. The preceding element is either a noun or a verb nominalized with *no* (i.e., Vinf.nonpast + *no*). The preceding nouns represent (i) emotions such as joy, sorrow, sympathy, anger, disappointment, fear, envy, surprise, respect, doubt, and wonder, or (ii) things like tears, smiles, voices, and body movements that are caused by such emotions. The preceding verbs (or verb phrases) describe body movements that are caused by such emotions as mentioned above. Additional examples of nouns that appear before *o kinji-enai* include:

(i) Emotions:

   a. V*masu*: 戸惑い (confusion); 苛立ち (irritation, impatience); 怒り (anger); 憤り (anger, strong condemnation); 驚き (surprise); 喜び (joy)

   b. VN: 興奮 (excitement); 感嘆 (admiration); 同情 (sympathy); 失望 (disappointment); 羨望 (envy); 嫉妬 (jealousy)

   c. N: 不安 (worry, anxiety); 疑念 (doubt); 疑問 (doubt)

   d. Adj(*i*) +さ: 悔しさ (regret, vexation, chagrin); もどかしさ (irritation, impatience); 寂しさ (loneliness); むなしさ (emptiness)

   e. ～感: 不快感 (odiousness, unease); 違和感 (sense of incongruity)

   f. ～の念: 敬愛の念 (feelings of love and respect); 安堵の念 (feelings of relief or security); 畏敬の念; (feelings of reverence, awe, and respect); 嫉妬の念 (feelings of jealousy)

0

g. ～思い: 悔しい思い (feelings of regret, vexation, or chagrin); 切ない思い (heart-rending, sad and painful, or hopeless feelings)

(ii) Facial expressions, body movements, voices, etc., caused by emotions:

a. Facial expressions: 笑い (laughter, smile); 苦笑 (sour smile); 微笑 (beaming smile)

b. Body movements: 戦慄 (shivering, trembling, shuddering); 身震い (shivering, trembling, shuddering)

c. Voices, etc.: ため息 (sigh); 嘆息 (sigh); 感嘆の声 (voice of admiration); 涙 (tears)

o megutte / meguru   を めぐって / めぐる   *comp. prt.*   \<w>

a compound particle meaning "concerning; over," which is used with an issue over which different opinions, ideas, etc., are expressed or exchanged

centering around; in connection with; over; concerning; regarding; with regard to
【REL. *ni kanshite*; *ni tsuite*】

0

◆ **Key Sentences**

(A)

Noun		
モノレール建設	をめぐって	市民の意見が対立している。

(Citizens' opinions are divided over the monorail construction.)

(B)

	Noun₁		Noun₂	
無駄な	公共事業	をめぐる	批判の声	が強まっている。

((Voices of) Criticism concerning wasteful public projects is growing stronger.)

(C)

Embedded Question			
大学運営は今後どうあるべき	か	をめぐって	活発に意見が交わされた。

(Opinions were exchanged actively regarding how universities should be run from now on.)

(D)

Noun₁		Noun₂			
進攻	か	撤退	か	をめぐって	激しい議論が戦わされた。

(There was a heated discussion over whether we should advance or retreat.)

(E)

Embedded Question₁		Embedded Question₂			
新制度に即時切り替えるべき	か	来年度まで待つべき	か	をめぐって	委員の間で意見が分かれた。

(Opinions were divided among the committee members regarding whether we should shift to the new system immediately or wait until next year.)

0

Formation

(i) N をめぐって

　　　この報道をめぐって　(concerning this news report)

(ii) N₁ をめぐる N₂

　　　基礎研究をめぐる現状　(current status of (lit., around) basic research)

(iii) Embedded Question をめぐって

　　　日本がこの問題にどう対応するべきかをめぐって　(regarding how Japan should handle this problem)

(iv) N₁ か N₂ かをめぐって

　　　実行か中止かをめぐって　(concerning whether we should execute s.t., or hold off on it)

(v) Embedded Question₁ + Embedded Question₂ をめぐって

　　単独(たんどく)で行うかパートナーを探(さが)すかをめぐって　(regarding whether we want to do it by ourselves or look for a partner)

Examples

(a) 新しい歴史教科書(れきしきょうかしょ)をめぐって激(はげ)しい議論(ぎろん)が続(つづ)いている。

　　(The fierce debate over the new history textbook continues.)

(b) 審判(しんぱん)の判定(はんてい)をめぐって選手(せんしゅ)が乱闘(らんとう)し試合(しあい)が約(やく)1時間中断(ちゅうだん)した。

　　(The players had a fight over the umpire's decision, and the game was interrupted for about an hour.)

(c) 自衛隊派遣(じえいたいはけん)の是非(ぜひ)をめぐって激(はげ)しい議論(ぎろん)が交(か)わされた。

　　(There were fierce arguments over the pros and cons of dispatching the Self-Defense Forces.)

(d) 老化(ろうか)のメカニズムをめぐる研究(けんきゅう)が注目(ちゅうもく)を浴(あ)びている。

　　(Research into the mechanism of aging is drawing a lot of attention.)

(e) 我(わ)が県(けん)でもITをめぐる動(うご)きが加速(かそく)しそうです。

　　(It looks like the movement toward IT (information technology) will accelerate in our prefecture, too.)

(f) 本章(ほんしょう)では、原子力発電(げんしりょくはつでん)をめぐる最近(さいきん)の動向(どうこう)を紹介(しょうかい)すると共(とも)に、将来(しょうらい)の有力(ゆうりょく)なエネルギー源(げん)について概観(がいかん)する。

　　(This chapter introduces recent trends in nuclear power generation and gives an overview of promising energy sources for the future.)

(g) 他(た)の国(くに)でもいつ軍隊(ぐんたい)を引(ひ)き上(あ)げるべきかをめぐって議論(ぎろん)が戦(たたか)わされている。

　　(Just when the army should be withdrawn is hotly debated in other countries, too.)

(h) 深刻化(しんこくか)する少年犯罪(しょうねんはんざい)が連日(れんじつ)のように報道(ほうどう)されている中(なか)、厳罰主義(げんばつしゅぎ)か更生重視(こうせいじゅうし)かをめぐって社会(しゃかい)の対応(たいおう)が揺(ゆ)れている。

　　(While there are reports almost every day on juvenile crime, which is becoming more serious, society wavers between applying strict punishment and emphasizing rehabilitation.)

(i) 調停案(ちょうていあん)を受(う)け入(い)れるかこのまま交渉(こうしょう)を続(つづ)けるかをめぐって我々(われわれ)の間(あいだ)で意見(いけん)が分(わ)かれている。

　　(Our opinions are divided over whether we should accept the arbitration plan or continue negotiating.)

0

Notes

1. *Megutte* is a pre-verbal form (i.e., a form that modifies verbs), and *meguru* is a pre-nominal form (i.e., a form that modifies nouns). There is another pre-verbal form, *meguri. Megutte* and *meguri* can be used interchangeably, as in (1).

(1) a. モノレール建設を{めぐって / めぐり}市民の意見が対立している。

(= KS(A))

　　 b. 新しい歴史教科書を{めぐって / めぐり}激しい議論が続いている。

(= Ex.(a))

2. *O megutte* and its variations are all highly formal expressions and are used only in written language or formal presentations such as news reports.

3. X *o megutte/meguru* is used when different opinions, ideas, information, etc., about X are expressed and/or exchanged by more than one person or source. Thus, in (2) and (3), *o megutte* is not acceptable. (See Related Expressions.)

(2) a. 青木教授がヒトゲノム{*をめぐって / に関して / について}論文を書いた。

(Prof. Aoki wrote a paper on the human genome.)

　　 b. その政策{*をめぐって / に関して / について}吉村氏が意見を述べた。

(Mr. Yoshimura gave his opinion on that policy.)

(3) a. 人間の言語習得{*をめぐって / に関して / について}はまだまだ不明のことが多い。

(There are many things that are still unknown about human language acquisition.)

　　 b. その件{*をめぐりまして / に関しまして / につきまして}は、まだ報告できる段階ではありません。

(We are not yet at a stage where we can report on that matter.)

In (4), *meguru* is acceptable only when *iken* "opinion," *hōkoku* "report," and *kiji* "article" refer to more than one opinion, one report, and one article, respectively.

(4) a. モノレール建設をめぐる意見

(opinions on the monorail construction)

0

b. 環境ホルモンをめぐる報告

(reports on environmental hormones)

c. 石油資源をめぐる記事

(articles about oil resources)

Meguru is acceptable in (5) when Y in "X *o meguru* Y" refers to a single entity. This is because Y refers to a number of aspects of one thing or a number of opinions, ideas, etc., that are part of Y.

(5) a. 母子家庭をめぐる状況

(the status of single-mother families)

b. 基礎研究をめぐる現状

(the present state of basic research)

c. 憲法9条をめぐる議論

(the debate over Article 9 of the Constitution)

d. この特許をめぐる裁判

(the lawsuit over this patent)

4. *Megutte* often occurs in titles, as in (6).

(6) a. 新世紀における特許——特許政策をめぐって

(Patents in the New Century: About Patent Policies)

b. 特集「歴史の客観性をめぐって」

(Special Issue: "About the Objectivity of History")

c. パネルディスカッション：国際時代の教育をめぐって

(Panel Discussion: About Education in the International Age)

[Related Expressions]

Ni kanshite and *ni tsuite* also mean "regarding; concerning; about." However, unlike *o megutte*, these compound particles can be used even when a single opinion, view, etc. about something is referred to, as in [1], or when no specific opinion, view, etc. is referred to, as in [2].

[1] a. 青木教授がヒトゲノム｛に関して／について／*をめぐって｝論文を書いた。(= (2a))

b. その政策｛に関して／について／*をめぐって｝吉村氏が意見を述べた。(= (2b))

[2]　a. 人間の言語習得｛に関して / について / *をめぐって｝はまだまだ不明
　　　 のことが多い。(= (3a))

　　　b. その件｛に関しまして / につきまして / *をめぐりまして｝は、まだ報
　　　 告できる段階ではありません。(= (3b))

Similarly, in [3], *iken* "opinion," *hōkoku* "report," and *kiji* "article" can refer
to one or more opinions, reports, and articles, respectively. (See (4) in Note
3.)

[3]　a. モノレール建設｛に関する / についての｝意見　(cf. (4a))
　　　 (opinion(s) on the monorail construction)

　　　b. 環境ホルモン｛に関する / についての｝報告　(cf. (4b))
　　　 (report(s) on environmental hormones)

　　　c. 石油資源｛に関する / についての｝記事　(cf. (4c))
　　　 (article(s) about oil resources)

Additionally, *ni kansuru* and *ni tsuite no* can be used with events such as
conferences, gatherings, etc., whereas *o meguru* cannot, as shown in [4].

[4]　a. 先月ハイテク農業｛に関する / についての / *をめぐる｝学会に出席し
　　　 た。
　　　 (I attended an academic conference on high-tech agriculture last
　　　 month.)

　　　b. このページは陶芸｛に関する / についての / *をめぐる｝イベントの
　　　 ニュースを掲載しています。
　　　 (This page presents news about pottery events.)

　　　c. 来週、国際交流｛に関する / についての / *をめぐる｝集まりがある。
　　　 (Next week, there is a meeting about international exchange.)

　　　(⇨ **ni kanshite/kansuru** (DIJG: 252-54); **ni tsuite** (DIJG: 280-83))

omoeba 思えば　*adv.*　<w>

> an adverb that indicates feelings of nostalgia or regret when recollecting one's past experiences

come to think of it; when I think back; on reflection

◆ **Key Sentence**

思えば、	大学時代はとても楽しかった。

(When I come to think of it, I had a great time when I was in college.)

Examples

(a) 思えば、あの頃私は彼と政治問題について毎日のように議論したものだ。

(When I think back, I discussed political issues with him almost every day.)

(b) 思えば、終戦後数年は、ほとんどの日本人が野菜を庭で育てていた。

(Come to think of it, for a few years after the war, almost all Japanese people grew vegetables in their backyards.)

(c) 今思えばどうしてこんなCDを買ったのだろう。

(Now that I think about it, why did I buy such a (terrible) CD?)

(d) 思えば心筋梗塞の前兆はあった。

(Come to think of it, there were warning signs of a cardiac seizure.)

(e) 小学校３年生の時、祖母と銀座で映画を見た。今にして思えば、あれが祖母と見た最初で最後の映画だった。

(I saw a movie in Ginza with my grandmother when I was a third grader. When I think back on it now, that was the first and the last movie I ever saw with her.)

(f) 今から思えば、私が同僚の男性と結婚すると言った時、父は猛然と反対した。あの時父の忠告を聞いておけばと悔やまれる。

(As I think of it now, my father was vehemently opposed when I told him that I was going to marry my colleague. I regret that I didn't listen to his advice.)

(g) 自転車で出かけようとした途端、チェーンが外れてしまった。今から思えば、あれがケチのつき始めだった。

(The moment I went out on my bicycle, the chain came off. When I come to think of it now, that was the beginning of (a period of) bad luck.)

Notes

1. The marker of nostalgia *omoeba* is the conditional form of the verb *omou* "feel; think." The subject of the conditional always has to be the first person singular "I."

2. *Omoeba* is often used to indicate feelings of nostalgia, as in KS, Exs.(a), (b) and (e), or regret, as in Exs.(c), (d), (f) and (g).

3. *Omoeba* is often preceded by *ima*, *ima ni shite* or *ima kara*, as shown in Exs.(c) and (e)-(g).

0

o mono to mo sezu をものともせず *phr.* <w>

┌─────────────────────────────┐
│ a phrase indicating that s.o. does s.t. │
│ bravely/fearlessly in spite of unfavor- │
│ able circumstances │
└─────────────────────────────┘

in spite of ~; undaunted by ~; in defiance of ~; in the face of ~ 【REL. *ni mo kakawarazu*】

◆ **Key Sentences**

(A)

	Noun Phrase		
彼女は	重度の身体障害	をものともせず、	自分の人生をつかみとった。

(Despite severe physical handicaps, she took charge of her own life.)

(B)

	Sinf			
彼は	日本語がしゃべれ ない	の	をものともせず、	身振り手振りで日本 を旅行して歩いた。

(Undaunted by his inability to speak Japanese, he traveled around Japan communicating with gestures and signs.)

Formation

(i)　N をものともせず

　　失敗をものともせず　(in spite of the failure)

(ii)　Sinf のをものともせず　(だ after Adj(*na*)stem and N changes to な.)

　　非難されたのをものともせず　(in spite of the fact that s.o. was criticized)

　　頭が痛いのをものともせず　(in spite of the fact that s.o. has a headache)

　　場所が不便{な / である}のをものともせず　(in spite of the fact that the location is inconvenient)

　　夫が病気{な / である}のをものともせず　(in spite of the fact that s.o.'s husband is ill)

0

Examples

(a)　友人は高波をものともせず4キロを泳ぎ切った。

　　(Overcoming high waves, my friend swam (all of) four kilometers.)

(b)　子供は時差をものともせず、早速水着に着替えてワイキキビーチへ出かけた。

　　(In spite of the time difference, my child changed to her swimming suit right away and went to Waikiki Beach.)

(c)　高層ビル火災の際、消防士たちは危険をものともせずその建物の階段を駆け登っていった。

　　(At the time of the high-rise fire, firemen ran up the stairs of the building in spite of the danger.)

(d)　民衆は軍事政権の弾圧をものともせず、デモ行進を続けた。

　　(The people continued their demonstrations in defiance of the military government's oppression.)

(e) 彼女は周囲の人の批判をものともせず、自分の信じる道を進んだ。

(Ignoring criticism from the people around her, she proceeded on the path she believed in.)

(f) 高校生たちは雨が激しく降っているのをものともせず、熱心に野球の練習をしていた。

(The high school students were practicing baseball in spite of the heavy rain (lit., in spite of the fact that it was raining hard).)

(g) 美佐子は片道所要時間が２時間を越えるのをものともせず、東京の証券会社に通勤した。

(Despite the fact that it took Misako two hours each way, she commuted (every day) to a securities company in Tokyo.)

Notes

1. X *o mono to mo sezu* "lit., without making something out of X" means that one does something bravely and fearlessly in spite of existing, unfavorable circumstances.

2. *O mono to mo sezu* is preceded either by a noun or noun phrase, as in KS(A) and Exs.(a)-(e), or a *no*-nominalized noun phrase, as in KS(B), Exs.(f) and (g).

【Related Expression】

Ni mo kakawarazu "without any relation to a preceding event/situation" can replace *o mono to mo sezu* in all the KS and Exs., as shown in [1].

[1] a. 彼女は重度の身体障害 {をものともせず／にも関わらず}、自分の人生をつかみとった。(= KS(A))

　　b. 彼は日本語がしゃべれない {のをものともせず／(の)にも関わらず}、身振り手振りで日本を旅行して歩いた。(= KS(B))

However, because *ni mo kakawarazu* can be preceded by both unfavorable and favorable/neutral circumstances, *o mono to mo sezu* cannot be used to replace it, as shown in [2] below.

[2] a. 懸命の努力 {にも関わらず／*をものともせず} 健一は大学入試に失敗した。

(In spite of his extensive efforts, Ken'ichi failed the college entrance examination.)

b. あの人はよく運動する｛(の)にも関わらず／*のをものともせず｝太っている。

(He is fat, in spite of the fact that he exercises a lot.)

c. 彼は東大に入学できた｛(の)にも関わらず／*のをものともせず｝すぐやめてしまった。

(Even though he got into the University of Tokyo, he dropped out right away.)

(⇨ *ni mo kakawarazu* (DIJG: 257-60))

omou ni 思うに   *phr.*   <w>

| a phrase indicating that the subsequent statement is the speaker's/writer's personal view | in my view; it seems to me that ~; when I think (about ~); considering 【REL. *kangaeru ni*】 |

◆ **Key Sentences**

(A)

		Sentence
(私が)	思うに、	文化は宗教の一種だ。
(In my view, culture is a kind of religion.)		

(B)

Noun Phrase			Sentence
医学界の体質	を	思うに、	当然医者と製薬会社の癒着はあると思う。
(Considering the nature of the medical world, I believe there is collusion between doctors and pharmaceutical companies.)			

Formation

(i)   思うに、S。

思うに、コンピュータは良し悪しだ。   (In my view computers are good and bad.)

(ii) NP を思うに

この一年を思うに、つらいことが多かった。 (When I think about this past year, it was full of trying things.)

(a) 思うに、情報を発信するマスコミと受信する我々国民は、完全に分化され固定化されてしまっているのが現状だ。

(In my view, the present state is that the media, which distribute information, and the citizens, who receive it, are completely separate and static.)

(b) 「思うに、快楽に耽る人生ほど快楽から遠いものはない。」──ジョン・D・ロックフェラー 2 世

("I can think of nothing less pleasurable than a life devoted to pleasure." ── *John D. Rockefeller, Jr.*)

(c) 私が思うに、大学時代の部活はお薦めだ。きっと一生の宝物になるだろう。

(I would recommend joining a club activity at college. I'm sure it would be something you'd treasure for the rest of your life.)

(d) 思うに、優れた画家であっても、生命感あふれる作品を生み出せるのはほんの一時期ではないだろうか。

(It seems to me that even an outstanding painter can create dynamic artworks only during a certain period of his or her life.)

(e) 思うに、「人を使う」ことが上手な人間というのは魅力のない人間である。

(In my view, people who excel at getting things from others (lit., using people) are unattractive people.)

(f) 自分の来し方を思うに、常に幅広い好奇心を持ち続けてきたことが、研究を続ける原動力ではなかっただろうか。

(When I reflect upon my past, it appears to me that my constant sense of curiosity in everything has served as a driving power for me to keep on doing my research.)

(g) 大地震の被災者の人たちの状況を思うに、何もできずにいることが本当につらいです。

(It's painful not to be able to do anything when I think about the circumstances of people who were hit by the earthquake.)

Notes

1. *Omou ni* indicates that what follows is the speaker's/writer's personal
   view. The phrase is often preceded by *watashi ga*, as in KS(A) and
   Ex.(c). The verb *omou* may take a noun phrase + *o*, as in KS(B), Exs.(f)
   and (g).   (⇨ *o*⁴ (DBJG: 352-54))

2. *Omou ni* is sometimes used with the adverb *tsura-tsura* "carefully and
   deeply," as shown in (1).

   (1) a. つらつら思うに、カラオケは平気で歌える人と絶対歌えない人にはっ
         きり分かれるものらしい。

       (Upon careful consideration, I've come to the conclusion that *kara-
       oke* distinctly separates people according to those who can sing
       without hesitation and those who cannot.)

      b. 現代人は物質的には満ち足りているが精神的には貧しいとよく言われ
         る。つらつら思うに、想像するということがなくなったからではなか
         ろうか。

       (It is often said that people today are materially satisfied but
       spiritually impoverished. Upon careful consideration, I wonder if
       it is because we have stopped using our imagination.)

3. *Ni* in this use can also occur with similar verbs, as in *sōzō-suru ni*,
   suisoku-suru ni and *kangaeru ni*.

   (2) a. 文章から想像するに、著者は哲学に造詣が深いに違いない。

       (Guessing (lit., Imaging) from his writing, the author must have a
       profound knowledge of philosophy.)

      b. 私が考えるに、人間にとって自然が究極の教師だ。

       (In my thinking nature is the ultimate teacher for man.)

[Related Expression]

Kangaeru ni is used when the speaker/writer wants to indicate that he/she
has given careful thought to something. It is different from *omou ni* in two
ways. The first is the semantic difference. *Kangaeru* indicates that someone
exercises his/her mind in order to form an idea or arrive at a logical conclusion. *Omou* means that someone spontaneously perceives something in
his/her mind or has a view about something. Secondly, *omou ni* can be
used without any preceding elements, but *kangaeru ni* has to be used with
preceding elements that are either a phrase, as in [1b], or an adverb, as in
[1c], or a sentence, as in [1d].

So in [1a], *kangaeru ni* is unacceptable, but in [1b]-[1d] it is acceptable.

[1] a. {思うに /*考えるに}、文化は宗教の一種だ。(= KS(A))

b. 医学界の体質を{思うに /考えるに}、当然医者と製薬会社の癒着は
あると思う。(= KS(B))

c. つらつら{思うに /考えるに}、カラオケは平気で歌える人と絶対歌
えない人にはっきり分かれるものらしい。(= (1a))

d. どうして日本人はアニメが好きなのか。{思うに /考えるに}、日本
人は空想的な映像化が好きなのも一つの理由ではないだろうか。
(Why do Japanese like *anime*? In my view, one of the reasons
could be that Japanese like to make images out of their imagination.)

---

o oite hoka ni (wa) ~ nai をおいてほかに (は) 〜ない   *phr.*   \<w\>

> a phrase that means "there is nothing
> else besides X"

(there is) no ~ but X; X is the
only one; nothing else is ~ but
X; no other ~ are / do s.t. as ~
as X
【REL. *igai ni ~ nai*; *no hoka ni
~ nai*; *ichiban*; *mottomo*】

◆ Key Sentence

	Noun		
日本語を短期間で習得したいの なら	この学校	をおいてほかに (は)	ない。
(If you want to learn Japanese in a short period of time, there is no other school (that you should consider) but this one.)			

Formation

N をおいてほかに (は) 〜ない

サッカーをおいてほかに (は) 例がない   (there is no example but soccer)

リサをおいてほかに (は) いない   (there is no one else but Lisa)

Examples

(a) これほど多くの作品を手がけた監督はY氏をおいてほかにいない。

(No other director has been involved with as many works as Mr. Y.)

(b) あなたを救うのはあなた自身をおいてほかにない。

(There is no one to save you but yourself.)

(c) これほどのプロフェッショナリズムと豊かな経験を提供できる会社は、日本中で当社をおいてほかにはありません。

(There is no company in Japan but ours that can provide this level of professionalism and rich experience.)

(d) 契約に対してこれだけ無神経な国はこの国をおいてほかに思いつかない。

(I cannot think of another country that is as indifferent to contracts as this one is.)

(e) この役割をこなせるのはジェーンをおいてほかに考えられない。

(We cannot think of anyone who can handle this role but Jane.)

(f) 味のよさと形の美しさ、この二つの要件を満たす桃は、山梨県産をおいてほかにない。

(The only peaches that satisfy the two requirements of good taste and beautiful shape are the ones from Yamanashi Prefecture. (lit., No peaches satisfy the two requirements, i.e., good taste and a beautiful shape, but those from Yamanashi Prefecture.))

(g) 非母国語話者の間のコミュニケーションにおいてこれほど広範囲に用いられている言語は、英語をおいてほかには存在しない。

(There is no language but English that is used as widely for communication among non-native speakers.)

Notes

1. The predicate that follows *o oite hoka ni (wa)* is always a negative form of a verb and the verbs that commonly occur with *o oite hoka ni (wa)* are limited. They include *aru* "exist," *iru* "exist," *omoitsuku* "come to one's mind," *kangaerareru* "can think of" and *sonzai-suru* "exist."

2. *Nai* can be used instead of *inai* even when the subject of the clause with *o oite hoka ni (wa)* is human, as in Ex.(b).

3. *O oite hoka ni (wa) ~ nai* can be used as a superlative phrase. (See Related Expression II.)

[Related Expressions]

I. *Igai ni ~ nai* and *no hoka ni ~ (wa) nai* can replace *o oite hoka ni ~ (wa) nai* without a change in meaning, as shown in [1].

[1] a. 日本語を短期間で習得したいのならこの学校｛をおいてほかに／以外に／のほかに(は)｝ない。(= KS)

b. これほど多くの作品を手がけた監督はY氏｛をおいてほかに／以外に／のほかに(は)｝いない。(= Ex.(a))

c. 契約に対してこれだけ無神経な国はこの国｛をおいてほかに／以外に／のほかに(は)｝思いつかない。(= Ex.(d))

(⇨ *igai* (DIJG: 60-63))

II. *Ichiban* and *mottomo* make superlative sentences. Thus, some sentences with *o oite hoka ni (wa) ~ nai* can be rephrased using *ichiban* and *mottomo*, as in [2], although some nuances are lost in the rephrased sentences.

[2] a. 日本語を短期間で習得したいのならこの学校が｛一番だ／最もよい｝。
(cf. KS)
(If you want to learn Japanese in a short period of time, this school is the best.)

b. ｛一番／最も｝多くの作品を手がけた監督はY氏だ。(cf. Ex.(a))
(The director who has been involved with the largest number of works is Mr. Y.)

c. 非母国語話者の間のコミュニケーションにおいて｛一番／最も｝広範囲に用いられている言語は英語だ。(cf. Ex.(g))
(The language that is used most widely for communication among non-native speakers is English.)

However, when sentences with *o oite hoka ni (wa) ~ nai* represent the idea of "only X is/does s.t.," as in Exs.(b) and (e), paraphrasing using *ichiban* and *mottomo* is not possible, as in [3].

[3] a. *｛一番／最も｝あなたを救うのはあなた自身だ。(cf. Ex.(b))

b. *｛一番／最も｝この役割をこなせるのはジェーンだ。(cf. Ex.(e))

0

The sentence in [4] is acceptable, but it does not mean the same thing as Ex.(e).

[4]　{一番／最も}上手にこの役割をこなせるのはジェーンだ。(cf. Ex.(e))
　　(The person who can handle this role best is Jane.)

(⇨ **ichiban** (DBJG: 148-49))

---

ori (ni)　折(に)　　*n.*　　\<w\>

a noun indicating special or uncommon and primarily desirable occasions which s.o. takes advantage of, or where s.o. is expected to do s.t. or where s.t. desirable takes place	on the occasion; at the time; when; if; opportunity; chance 【REL. *toki*; *sai*; *setsu (ni)*】

◆ **Key Sentences**

(A)

Noun			
上京	の	折(に)	は	ぜひお立ち寄り下さい。

(When you come up to Tokyo, please be sure to stop by.)

(B)

	Vinf		
この前日本に	帰った	折(に)	高校時代の友達に会った。

(When I returned to Japan last time, I met with my high school friends.)

(C)

	Adj(*na*)stem			
援助が	必要	な	折(に)	は	早めに連絡して下さい。

(If you need any help, please contact me sooner rather than later.)

Formation

(i) N の折(に)

休暇の折(に) (on vacation)

(ii) Vinf 折(に)

京都へ{行く / 行った}折(に) (when I go/went to Kyoto)

(iii) Adj(*i*)inf.nonpast 折(に)

寒さの厳しい折(に) (at a time when it is severely cold)

(iv) Adj(*na*)stem な折(に)

暇な折(に) (when you have leisure time)

(v) Dem. adj. 折(に)

その折(に) (on that occasion; at that time)

Examples

(a) 近くにお越しの折には、ぜひ当店をご利用下さい。

(When you are in the area, please use our shop.)

(b) ロスへ出張した折に息子の様子を見るために大学の寮に寄ってみた。

(When I was on business in L.A., I stopped by my son's university dormitory to see how he was doing.)

(c) 都心に出た折に、古本屋街に足を延ばした。

(When I went into downtown Tokyo, I also went (lit., extended my trip) to the used book store district.)

(d) こういうスーツを持っていれば冠婚葬祭の折に着るものを心配しなくてもいい。

(If you have a suit like this, you don't have to worry what to wear for (lit., on the occasions of) weddings and funeral services.)

(e) 卒業の折に親に買ってもらった時計をなくしてしまった。

(I lost the watch my parents bought for me for my graduation.)

(f) 私は大きな借金をかかえて途方にくれていました。そんな折に彼から電話があったのです。

(I was saddled with debt and didn't know what to do. On that occasion, there was a call from him.)

0

Notes

1. When a verb precedes *ori (ni)*, the tense changes depending on the situation. When the action in the main clause takes place after the action in the *ori (ni)* clause, the verb tense is past; otherwise the tense is nonpast.
(⇨ ***toki*** (DBJG: 490-94))

　(1) a. 日本へ行った折に、山内さんに会うつもりだ。

　　　　(When I go to Japan (= after arriving in Japan), I intend to meet with Ms. Yamauchi.)

　　　b. 日本へ行く折に、山内さんに会うつもりだ。

　　　　(When I go to Japan (= before leaving for Japan), I intend to meet with Ms. Yamauchi.)

2. *Ori* is often used when the subject takes advantage of an occasion which is special or uncommon. For example, (2a) and (3a) are acceptable but (2b) and (3b) are not, because the occasions presented in the *ori* clauses in the (b) sentences are not considered advantageous situations.

　(2) a. ニューヨークに行った折にメトロポリタン美術館に行った。

　　　　(When I went to New York, I went to the Metropolitan Museum of Art.)

　　　b. ニューヨークに行った {*折 / 時} にハンドバッグを盗られた。

　　　　(When I went to New York, my purse was stolen.)

　(3) a. 二人きりになった折にガールフレンドに自分の気持ちを打ち明けた。

　　　　(When we were alone, I confessed my feelings to my girlfriend.)

　　　b. 二人きりになった {*折 / 時} にガールフレンドにさんざんなじられた。

　　　　(When we were alone, my girlfriend berated me endlessly.)

3. *Ori* is also used to indicate special or uncommon occasions where someone is expected to do something or something desirable takes place, as in KS(C) and Exs.(d)-(f).

4. Because *ori* is used primarily when an occasion/situation is a desirable one, it is not often used in such situations as those in (4), even though the situations are special or uncommon.

　(4) a. 火災の {??折 / 時}　(in the event of a fire)
　　　b. 台風の {??折 / 時}　(in the event of a typhoon)
　　　c. 地震の {??折 / 時}　(in the event of an earthquake)

5. Additionally, *ori* is not used when an action is routine, as in (5). (See Note 2.)

　(5) a. 毎朝顔を洗う{*折 / 時}に、ひげも剃る。

　　　(I shave when I wash my face every morning.)

　　b. 私のうちでは、夕食の{*折 / 時}にみんなでその日にあったことを話し合う。

　　　(At my home, we discuss at dinner time what each of us experienced that day.)

6. *Ori* cannot be used when the events/actions in the *ori* clause (or phrase) and the main clause are not related, as in (6).

　(6) a. 私がアメリカで勉強していた{*折 / 時}、スミスさんは日本で仕事をしていた。

　　　(When I was studying in America, Mr. Smith was working in Japan.)

　　b. 上司から電話があった{*折 / 時}、私はちょうどシャワーを浴びていた。

　　　(Just when there was a call from my boss, I was taking a shower.)

　　c. やっと仕事が終わった{*折 / 時}、もう 11 時を過ぎていた。

　　　(When I finally finished my work, it was already past 11 o'clock.)

7. *Ori* phrases/clauses represent a certain span of time. Therefore, *ori* is not used when the time span is momentary, as in (7).

　(7) a. 刑事は男が横を向いた{*折 / 瞬間 / 時}に飛びついた。

　　　(The detective jumped on the man the moment / when he turned away.)

　　b. 私はトラックが止まった{*折 / 時}に荷台から飛び下りた。

　　　(I jumped from the bed of the truck when it stopped.)

8. *Ori* is also used to present a special or uncommon occasion as the reason for the statement in the main clause. In this case, *kara* follows *ori* but *ni* cannot, as in (8).

　(8) a. 寒さの厳しい折{*に / から}、お体には十分お気をつけ下さい。

　　　(Now that the weather is severely cold, please take good care of yourself (lit., your body).)

b. 国際交流の盛んな折{*に/から}、外国からの来客を接待する機会が増えてきた。

(As international exchanges are now more frequent, there are more occasions to entertain guests from abroad.)

Ori kara in these examples is an idiomatic phrase, and in this case the *da* or *desu* before *kara* is dropped.

9. *Ori* is also used as a common noun meaning "occasion; chance" (synonymous with *kikai*). In this case *ori* occurs with either *ni* or other particles, as in (9a)-(9c), or occurs with *da* (or its variations) as a predicate, as in (9d).

(9) a. これは本題とずれるので、また別な{折/機会}に書きたい。

(This (topic) is off the main topic, so I'd like to write (about it) on another occasion.)

b. {折/機会}を見て彼に一言注意しておこう。

(I'll wait for a good time to give him a warning.)

c. 彼とはなかなか落ち着いて話をする{折/機会}がない。

(I can hardly find a good time to talk leisurely with him.)

d. これはまたとない{折/機会}だ。

(This is a golden opportunity (lit., an opportunity that will not happen again).)

【Related Expressions】

I. *Toki* "when" can be used in place of *ori* in most situations but without the nuance of "taking advantage of a good opportunity" or "doing something on a special occasion" (see Notes 2 and 3). Unlike *ori*, *toki* can be used in the following situations:

(i)   when S_1 represents an undesirable occasion (see Note 4);

(ii) when the action in S_2 is routine (see Note 5);

(iii) when the actions/events in S_1 and S_2 are not related (see Note 6);

(iv) when S_1 represents a brief moment (see Note 7).

However, *toki* cannot be used in place of *ori* in the situations described in Note 8.

[1] a. 寒さの厳しい{折 / *時}から、お体には十分お気をつけ下さい。

$$(= (8a))$$

b. 国際交流の盛んな{折 / *時}から、外国からの来客を接待する機会が
増えてきた。(= (8b))

$$(\Rightarrow \textbf{\textit{toki}} \text{ (DBJG: 490-94))}$$

II. *Sai* is also used to indicate a special occasion at which someone does something. Thus, *sai* can replace *ori* in KS(A)-(C) and in Exs.(a)-(e). (Note that demonstratives like *konna* "like this" and *sonna* "like that" do not occur with *sai* as freely as *kono* "this" and *sono* "that" do. Thus, *sai* is less natural in Ex.(f).) However, *sai* doesn't convey the nuance of "taking advantage of a good occasion." It simply indicates that the occasions mentioned are special.

Because *sai* does not convey the nuance of "taking advantage of a good occasion," it is acceptable in [2]. Note that *ori* is not acceptable in such situations. (See Note 2.)

[2] a. ニューヨークに行った{際 / *折}にハンドバッグを盗られた。(= (2b))

b. 二人きりになった{際 / *折}にガールフレンドにさんざんなじられ
た。(= (3b))

Like *ori*, *sai* is unacceptable when the actions/events in S_1 and S_2 are not related, as in [3].

[3] a. 私がアメリカで勉強していた{*折 / *際}、スミスさんは日本で仕事
をしていた。(= (6a))

b. 上司から電話があった{*折 / *際}、私はちょうどシャワーを浴びて
いた。(= (6b))

However, unlike *ori*, *sai* is acceptable with a momentary action, as in [4].

[4] a. スーツケースを持ち上げた{際 / *折}に、腰を痛めたらしい。
(I seem to have hurt my back when I lifted the suitcase.)

b. テストを提出する{際 / *折}に名前を忘れないように。
(Do not forget (to write) your name on your exam when you turn it in.)

However, *sai* cannot be used to present an occasion as a reason, as in [5].

[5] a. 寒さの厳しい{折／*際}から、お体には十分お気をつけ下さい。

(= (8a))

b. 国際交流の盛んな{折／*際}から、外国からの来客を接待する機会が増えてきた。(= (8b))

Finally, unlike *ori*, *sai* cannot be used as an independent noun.

[6] a. {折／*際}を見て彼に一言注意しておこう。(= (9b))

b. これはまたとない{折／*際}だ。(= (9d))

(⇨ *sai (ni)* (DIJG: 369-74))

III. *Setsu (ni)* also indicates a special occasion, but it is used only when the statement is directly addressed to the hearer/reader. *Setsu (ni)* is a formal expression.

[7] a. 上京の節(に)はぜひお立ち寄り下さい。(= KS(A))

b. 近くにお越しの節はお電話下さい。
(Please give me a call when you are (lit., come) nearby.)

c. その節はどうもお世話になりました。
(Thank you very much for your kindness that time.)

The sentences in [8] are unacceptable, because they are simple statements and not directly addressed to the hearer/reader like those in [7].

[8] a. この前の日本への帰国の{折／*節}に高校時代の友達に会った。
(I met with my high school friends when I returned to Japan last time.)

b. ロスへ出張の{折／*節}に息子の様子を見るために大学の寮に寄ってみた。(cf. Ex.(b))
(When I was on business in L.A., I stopped by my son's university dormitory to see how he was doing.)

Note also that *setsu (ni)* is not preceded by a clause, as in [9].

[9] a. 東京にいらっしゃる{折／時／*節}はお電話下さい。
(When you come to Tokyo, please give me a call.)

b. 援助が必要な{折／時／*節}(に)は早めに連絡して下さい。(= KS(C))

Note that *okoshi* "coming" in [7b] is not a verb.

osore ga aru　恐れがある　*phr.*

~~~
a phrase that means "it is feared
(that)"
~~~

it is feared (that); we fear
(that); we are worried/con-
cerned (that); there is a fear/
risk/chance/concern/etc.; can;
could; may; it is possible
(that); be in danger of
【REL. *kikensei ga aru*; *shinpai
ga aru*; *kanōsei ga aru*; *kamoshirenai*】

◆ **Key Sentences**

(A)

		Noun		
台風の影響で、西日本は		**大雨**	の	恐れがある。

(Due to the typhoon (lit., the typhoon's influence), there is a chance of heavy rain across Western Japan.)

(B)

	Vinf	
この戦争は第二のベトナム戦争に	**なる**	恐れがある。

(This war could become a second Vietnam War. (lit., There is a risk that this war will become a second Vietnam War.))

(C)

	Vinf	
テロリストたちが	**入国した**	恐れがある。

(There is concern that terrorists have entered the country.)

(D)

	Adj(*i*)inf	
測定誤差が	**大きい**	恐れがある。

(We are worried that the measurement errors may be large.)

(E)

	Noun		
腫瘍が	悪性	である	恐れがある。

(The tumor may be malignant.)

Formation

(i) N の恐れがある

  洪水の恐れがある (there is a fear of flood)

  爆発の恐れがある (there is a fear of explosion)

(ii) {V / Adj(*i*)} inf 恐れがある

  {傷つける / 傷つけた} 恐れがある (there is a fear that s.o./s.t. will hurt / has hurt s.o./s.t.)

  (品物が) {古い / 古かった} 恐れがある (there is a fear that s.t. is/was old)

(iii) Adj(*na*)stem {な / である / だった / であった} 恐れがある
  ("Adj(*na*)stem な" is rarely used.)

  不安定 {な / である / だった / であった} 恐れがある (there is a fear that s.t. is/was unstable)

(iv) N {である / だった / であった} 恐れがある

  不良品 {である / だった / であった} 恐れがある (there is a fear that s.t. is/was a defective product.)

Examples

(a) この地域の野生動物は絶滅の恐れがある。

  (The wild animals in this region are in danger of becoming extinct.)

(b) M社は自社の携帯電話のいくつかの機種に発熱の恐れがあると発表した。

  (Company M announced that there is a risk that some of their cellphone models may generate heat.)

(c) この薬品が目に入ると失明の恐れがあるので、保護眼鏡を着用して下さい。

  (This chemical can cause blindness (lit., when it gets in an eye), so please wear protective goggles.)

(d) 県は近く、がけ崩れなどの恐れがある場所で地形や土地利用状況などの調査を始める。

(The prefectural government will soon begin an investigation of the ground configuration, land use, etc. in places where there is some fear of landslides.)

(e) 添付書類を不用意に開けるとウイルスに感染する恐れがある。

(If you open attached files without paying close attention, you risk infecting (your computer) with a virus.)

(f) この薬は副作用がないと言われているが、8週間以上続けて服用すると肝臓に害を及ぼす恐れがある。

(This drug is said to have no side effects, but if you take it for more than eight weeks straight, there is a risk that it will damage your liver.)

(g) 選手たちが試合の中止を知らないまま、まだ練習している恐れがある。

(We're concerned that the players are still practicing, not knowing that the game has been cancelled.)

(h) 警視庁は、殺人容疑者のAが海外へ逃亡した恐れがあると発表した。

(The Metropolitan Police Office announced that there is some concern that murder suspect A has escaped overseas.)

(i) ここのカフェテリアは食材が古い恐れがある。

(The ingredients used (in the food) at this cafeteria may be old.)

(j) この薬は胎児に有害である恐れがある。

(This drug may be harmful to embryos.)

(k) 取引相手が暴力団である恐れがある。

(We're worried that we may be dealing with a (Japanese) mafia group.)

Notes

1. *Osore ga aru* is used when the speaker is concerned that something may happen or may have happened, or may be or may have been the case.

2. *Osore* is modified by either a noun (or noun phrase) or a clause. When it is modified by a clause, the clause represents a future event, a present state, or a past event, as shown in (1):

(1) a. 他人の特許権を<u>侵害する</u>恐れがある。 [Future event]

(There is a risk that we/you will infringe on others' patent rights.)

b. 他人の特許権を<u>侵害している</u>恐れがある。 [Present state]

(There is a risk that we/you are infringing on others' patent rights.)

c. 他人の特許権を<u>侵害した</u>恐れがある。 [Past event]

(There is a risk that we/you infringed on others' patent rights.)

3. Nouns that modify *osore* with the particle *no* are usually the stems of *suru*-verbs (i.e., VN), as in Exs.(a)-(c), or nouns which refer to a natural disaster, as in KS(A) and Ex.(d). When "(X *wa/ga*) N *da*" modifies *osore*, *da* changes to *de aru*, as in Ex.(k).

4. The negative form of *osore ga aru* is *osore wa nai* "there is no fear that."

(2) 他人の特許権を侵害する恐れはない。

(There is no risk that we/you will infringe on others' patent rights.)

【Related Expressions】

I. *Kikensei ga aru* "there is a danger" and *shinpai ga aru* "there is a concern" are synonymous with *osore ga aru*. However, the former is usually used when a situation is serious or critical, and the latter is usually used when the speaker expresses a personal concern.

[1] a. 震度5以上の地震では全壊の{恐れ / 危険性 / ??心配}がある。

(In an earthquake with an intensity of 5 or greater, this building is in danger of total collapse.)

b. この紛争は戦争に発展する{恐れ / 危険性 / ??心配}がある。

(This conflict is in danger of escalating into a war.)

c. 友達が道を間違う{恐れ / 心配 / ??危険性}がある。

(I {fear / am concerned} that my friend will get lost.)

d. 選手たちが試合の中止を知らないまま、まだ練習している{恐れ / 心配 / *危険性}がある。(= Ex.(g))

(We {fear / am concerned} that the players are still practicing, not knowing that the game has been cancelled.)

e. 彼が私の作ったものを食べられない{心配 / ?恐れ / *危険性}がある。

(I am concerned that he cannot eat what I made.)

f. 助手の作ったテストの問題が難しすぎる{心配 / ?恐れ / *危険性}がある。

(I am worried that my assistant's test questions will be too difficult.)

II. *Kanōsei ga aru* "there are possibilities" or *kamoshirenai* "may; might" can replace *osore ga aru*, but they do not convey the idea of fear or risk;

therefore, they are also used for events or states that are desirable, as in [2b].

[2] a. 他人の特許権を侵害する｛恐れがある／可能性<small>かのうせい</small>がある／かもしれない｝。(cf. (1a))

(There is a risk/possibility that we/you will infringe on others' patent rights. / You may infringe on others' patent rights.)

b. 奨学金<small>しょうがくきん</small>がもらえる｛可能性がある／かもしれない／*恐れがある｝。

(There is a possibility that I will be given a scholarship. / I may be given a scholarship.)

The connection rules for *kanōsei ga aru* are the same as those for *osore ga aru*. However, "N *no*" and "Adj(*na*)stem *na*" cannot precede *kamoshirenai*.

[3] a. この辺<small>あた</small>りは洪水<small>こうずい</small>の｛恐<small>おそ</small>れがある／可能性<small>かのうせい</small>がある／*かもしれない｝。

(There is a risk/possibility of flooding in this area.)

b. 彼<small>かれ</small>は精神状態<small>せいしんじょうたい</small>がまだ不安定<small>ふあんてい</small>な｛恐れがある／可能性がある／*かもしれない｝。

(There is a concern/possibility that his mental condition is still unstable.)

cf. 彼は精神状態がまだ不安定かもしれない。

(His mental condition may still be unstable.)

Note that "N *kamoshirenai*" and "N *no kanōsei/osore ga aru*" can mean totally different things, as in [4].

[4] a. この辺<small>あた</small>りは洪水<small>こうずい</small>かもしれない。[The speaker is making a guess about the state of a certain area, pointing at the location on the map.]

(There may be flooding in this area.)

b. この辺りは洪水の｛恐<small>おそ</small>れ／可能性<small>かのうせい</small>｝がある。 [Possibility of a future flood]

(There is a risk/possibility of flooding in this area.)

(⇨ **kamoshirenai** (DBJG: 173-75))

o towazu   を問(と)わず   *comp. prt.*   \<w\>

> a compound particle that means "without questioning"

regardless of; irrespective of; without reference to; whether X or Y; whether X or not; whatever/whoever/etc.; no matter what/who/how/etc.
【REL. *ni kakawarazu*; *ni kankei naku*; *ni yorazu*】

◆ **Key Sentences**

(A)

	Noun		
この会社は、経験(けいけん)があれば	学歴(がくれき)	を問(と)わず	採用(さいよう)してくれる。

(This company will employ you regardless of your educational background if you have (relevant work) experience.)

(B)

	V₁inf		V₂inf		
卒業後(そつぎょうご)	就職(しゅうしょく)する	か	進学(しんがく)する	か	を問(と)わず、

担任(たんにん)との個人面談(こじんめんだん)を受(う)けなければならない。

(You have to have an individual consultation with your homeroom teacher whether you work or go on to college after graduation.)

(C)

	Noun			
本ソフトウエアの複製(ふくせい)は	全部(ぜんぶ)	か否(いな)か	を問(と)わず	違法行為(いほうこうい)になる。

(Copying this software is (an) illegal (act) whether or not it is a complete copy.)

(D)

	X + X's antonym		
不要の電化製品、	中古新品	を問わず	買い取ります。

(We'll buy the electrical appliances which you are not using whether they are new or used.)

(E)

	Noun			
当教会は、	信者	であるなし	を問わず	挙式をお引き受けいたします。

(At this church we offer wedding ceremonies for everyone, regardless of whether or not you are Christian (lit., a believer).)

(F)

Noun			
経験	のあるなし	を問わず	誰でもこのクラブに参加できます。

(Anyone can join this club whether or not they have experience / regardless of their experience (lit., whether he/she has experience or not).)

(G)

	Noun Phrase		
A社は、	市場調査の結果	のいかん	を問わず、

日本でのマーケティングを開始する。

(Company A is beginning their marketing in Japan without considering the results of their market research.)

(H)

Wh-sentence.inf			
どのような利用である	か	を問わず	学内の施設利用は事前に大学の承認が必要だ。

(In order to use university facilities, no matter what the purpose (lit., what kind of use), you need approval from the university beforehand.)

Formation

(i)　N₁ ({、 ／と／や} N₂) を問わず

　　　　年齢を問わず　(regardless of age)

　　　　年齢、性別を問わず　(regardless of age and sex)

　　　　年齢と性別を問わず　(regardless of age and sex)

　　　　年齢や性別を問わず　(regardless of age, sex, etc.)

(ii)　X か Y かを問わず　(where X, Y = contrastive words; usually nonpast forms)

　　　・N₁ か N₂ かを問わず

　　　　　男性か女性かを問わず　(whether s.o. is a male or a female)

　　　・V₁inf か V₂inf かを問わず

　　　　　去るか留まるかを問わず　(whether s.o. leaves or stays)

　　　・Adj(*i*)₁inf か Adj(*i*)₂inf かを問わず

　　　　　暑いか寒いかを問わず　(whether it is hot or cold)

　　　・Adj(*na*)₁stem か Adj(*na*)₂stem かを問わず

　　　　　便利か不便かを問わず　(whether s.t. is convenient or inconvenient)

(iii)　X か {どう／否} かを問わず

　　　　行くか {どう／否} かを問わず　(whether s.o. goes or not)

　　　　高いか {どう／否} かを問わず　(whether s.t. is expensive or not)

　　　　便利(である)か {どう／否} かを問わず　(whether s.t. is convenient or not)

　　　　日本人か {どう／否} かを問わず　(whether s.o. is Japanese or not)

(iv)　X (Aff.) + X (Neg.) を問わず

　　　　行く行かないを問わず　(whether s.o. goes or not)

　　　　うまいうまくないを問わず　(whether s.o. is skillful or not)

　　　　上手、上手じゃないを問わず　(whether s.o. is skillful or not)

　　　　日本人、日本人じゃないを問わず　(whether s.o. is Japanese or not)

(v)　X + Y を問わず　(where X, Y = Adj(*i*)inf.nonpast / Adj(*na*)stem; Y = X's antonym)

　　　　高い安いを問わず　(whether s.t. is expensive or cheap)

　　　　上手下手を問わず　(whether s.o. is skillful or unskillful)

(vi) ｛N / Adj(*na*)stem｝であるなしを問わず

会員であるなしを問わず　(whether s.o. is a member or not)
経済的であるなしを問わず　(whether s.t. is economical or not)

(vii) N のあるなしを問わず

経験のあるなしを問わず　(whether s.o. has experience or not)

(viii) N のいかんを問わず

方法のいかんを問わず　(regardless of the method)

(ix) Wh-sentence.inf かを問わず

いかなる国における使用であるかを問わず　(in whatever country s.t.
may be used)

Examples

(a) このリゾート地は、登山、ハイキング、スキー等、四季を問わず一年中楽しめる。
(Mountain climbing, hiking, skiing, etc., can be enjoyed at this resort
area, regardless of the season.)

(b) 無線LANのおかげで、場所や時間を問わずネットへのアクセスが可能になっ
た。
(Thanks to wireless LAN, now we can access the network wherever and
whenever we need it.)

(c) 古くなったパソコン、メーカーを問わず引き取ります。
(We buy old personal computers regardless of the manufacturer.)

(d) この本は、イスラム世界に興味があるか否かを問わず、ぜひ読んでおくべき
一冊である。
(This is one book you should definitely read, whether or not you are
interested in the Muslim world.)

(e) 選挙期間中であるか否かを問わず、選挙運動またはこれに類する行為にコン
ピュータ、掲示板等学内施設を利用することを禁ずる。
(Using the campus facilities, including computers and bulletin boards,
for election campaigning or other similar activities is prohibited whether it is during an election period or not.)

(f) インストラクター募集。(男女を問わず)
(Instructors Wanted (Men or Women) [Advertisement])

(g) このDVDは映画を見た見ないを問わず、ぜひ持っておくことを勧めます。

(I recommend that you get this DVD whether you have seen the (original) movie or not.)

(h) このソフトはパソコンに精通しているいないを問わず、誰でも簡単に使える。

(Anyone can use this software easily whether he/she is familiar with personal computers or not.)

(i) クリスチャンであるないを問わず、この運動に賛同して下さる方を広く募集しております。

(We widely recruit people who agree with this movement whether they are Christians or not.)

(j) この競技にはプロアマを問わず参加が可能だ。

(It doesn't matter if you are amateur or professional; anyone can compete in this event.)

(k) 年内は平日、休日を問わず、全店朝9時から夜8時まで営業しております。

(All our stores will be open (lit., do business) from 9 a.m. to 8 p.m. on weekdays and weekends (lit., whether it is a weekday or weekend) for the rest of this year.)

(l) アメリカには、自国民であるなしを問わず、優れた才能をもつ人に機会と資金を与える懐の深さがある。

(America has a generous side (lit., deep pockets), providing opportunities and funds for people with excellent abilities, whether they are American or not.)

(m) 当行とのお取引のあるなしを問わず、国際業務に関するどのようなご質問・ご相談でもお気軽にお電話下さい。

(Please feel free to call us for any question or consultation about international business whether or not you have business with our bank.)

(n) 理由のいかんを問わず、次回の会合の欠席者は本委員会のメンバーから除外する。

(Those who miss the next meeting, regardless of the reason, will be removed from this committee.)

(o) いかなる国における利用であるかを問わず、本ソフトウエアの利用に当たっては当社と利用合意書を交わすことが必要です。

(To use this software, you must sign our user's agreement no matter where (lit., in what country) you want to use it.)

Notes

1. *Towazu* is the negative continuative form of *tou* "to question." Thus, the literal meaning of *towazu* is "without questioning."

2. As seen in Formation (i), more than one noun can precede *o towazu* without a noun-connecting particle such as *ya* or *to*.

3. The sentence-final form *o towanai* "not to question" can be used in main clauses, as in (1).

   (1) a. 買い取り品は新品中古を問いません。

      (When we buy items, we do not question whether they are new or used.)

   b. この奨学金は応募者の国籍を問わない。

      (This scholarship does not screen applicants by nationality (lit., does not question applicants' nationalities).)

4. The particle *o* before *towazu* optionally drops in advertisement, as in (2).

   (2) a. 不要の電化製品、中古新品 ｛ を / ∅ ｝問わず買い取ります。(= KS(D))

   b. インストラクター募集。(男女 ｛ を / ∅ ｝問わず) (= Ex.(f))

[Related Expressions]

Ni kakawarazu, *ni kankei naku*, and *ni yorazu* are all synonymous with *o towazu*. Thus, they can be used interchangeably, as in [1].

   [1] a. この会社は、経験があれば学歴 ｛ を問わず / に関わらず / に関係なく / によらず ｝採用してくれる。(= KS(A))

   b. 卒業後就職するか進学するか ｛ を問わず / に関わらず / に関係なく / によらず ｝、担任との個人面談を受けなければならない。(= KS(B))

   c. 本ソフトウエアの複製は全部か否か ｛ を問わず / に関わらず / に関係なく / によらず ｝違法行為になる。(= KS(C))

   d. 不要の電化製品、中古新品 ｛ を問わず / に関わらず / に関係なく / によらず ｝買い取ります。(= KS(D))

   e. 当教会は、信者であるなし ｛ を問わず / に関わらず / に関係なく / によらず ｝挙式をお引き受けいたします。(= KS(E))

f. 経験のあるなし｛を問わず／に関わらず／に関係なく／によらず｝誰でもこのクラブに参加できます。(= KS(F))

g. A社は、市場調査の結果のいかん｛を問わず／に関わらず／に関係なく／によらず｝、日本でのマーケティングを開始する。(= KS(G))

h. どのような利用であるか｛を問わず／に関わらず／に関係なく／によらず｝学内の施設利用は事前に大学の承認が必要だ。(= KS(H))

However, *ni yorazu* can be used with Wh-words or noun phrases with Wh-words, whereas *o towazu*, *ni kakawarazu* and *ni kankei naku* cannot, as in [2].

[2] a. 何事（なにごと）｛によらず／*を問（と）わず／*に関（かか）わらず／*に関係（かんけい）なく｝困（こま）ったことがあったらいつでも相談（そうだん）して下さい。

(Whatever it may be, if you ever have trouble, please consult with me.)

b. どんな仕事（しごと）｛によらず／*を問わず／*に関わらず／*に関係なく｝、それで生活（せいかつ）するとなると楽（らく）なものはない。

(No matter what the job, there's no easy work when you are making your living from it.)

Note that *ni yorazu* also means "without; without using; without relying on" in different contexts, as in [3]. In these sentences, *o towazu*, *ni kakawarazu* and *ni kankei naku* cannot be used.

[3] a. リストラ｛によらず／*を問（と）わず／*に関（かか）わらず／*に関係（かんけい）なく｝この会社（かいしゃ）を救（すく）う方法（ほうほう）はない。

(There is no way to save this company without restructuring it.)

b. 理想（りそう）は武力（ぶりょく）｛によらず／*を問わず／*に関わらず／*に関係なく｝紛争（ふんそう）を解決（かいけつ）することだ。

(The ideal is to resolve disputes without using armed force.)

Ni kakawarazu should not be confused with *ni mo kakawarazu* "although; despite."

(⇨ ***ni mo kakawarazu*** (DIJG: 257-60); ***ni kakawarazu*** (in this volume); ***ni yorazu*** (in this volume))

oyobi 及び *prt.* <w>

| a particle that connects two nouns or noun phrases | and 【REL. *to*; *soshite*; **narabi ni**】 |

◆ **Key Sentences**

(A)

	Noun₁		Noun₂	
使用した	機種	及び	ソフトウエア	を表1に示す。

| (The computer models and software we used are listed in Table 1.) |

(B)

		S₁inf		
本奨学金への応募資格は、		日本国籍を有する	こと、	及び

	S₂inf			
	国内の四年制大学に在籍する学生である		こと	である。

| (The qualifications for applying for this scholarship require (lit., are) that you be a Japanese citizen and a student at a four-year college in this country.) |

0

Formation

(i) N₁ 及び N₂

  名古屋及びその周辺 (Nagoya and the surrounding areas)

(ii) S₁inf こと、及び S₂inf こと (だ cannot be used before こと.
   Adj(*na*)stem{な / である}こと; Nであること.)

  情報を収集すること、及びそれを分析すること (collecting information and analyzing it)

  好き{な / である}こと、及び上手{な / である}こと (liking s.t. and excelling at s.t.)

  教師であること、及び父親であること (being a teacher and being a father)

Examples

(a) 室内及び廊下での喫煙は禁止されています。

(Smoking in the rooms and halls is prohibited.)

(b) 今月号では広島及び近郊他県の観光名所を紹介します。

(In this month's issue we introduce sightseeing spots in Hiroshima and neighboring prefectures.)

(c) 本店移転及び商号変更についてお知らせいたします。

(We hereby notify you of the relocation of the head office and the change of our company name.)

(d) A社は2002年及びそれ以前の製品のサポートの打ち切りを発表した。

(Company A announced that it would no longer offer technical support for products made before 2003 (lit., in and before 2002).)

(e) これは昨年度における全国の一般廃棄物の排出及び処理状況に関する報告である。

(This is a report on the status of the discharge and treatment of general waste nationwide last year.)

(f) 記者会見の前に、情報が正確であること、及びそれが公表してもいい情報であることを確認しておく必要がある。

(Before holding a press conference it is necessary to make sure that the information is accurate and that it can be (lit., it is information which can be) released to the public.)

(g) 装置には著しい破損のないこと、及びメンテナンスが規定どおり行われていることを確認した。

(We have confirmed that there is no significant damage to the device, and that it has been maintained according to the regulations.)

(h) 外国人研修生を受け入れる事業者の評価機関は、5人以上の委員からなる委員会を持つこと、及びその委員の半数以上が外国人の研修について専門知識を持つことが義務づけられた。

(It is now required that the body for evaluating companies that accept foreign interns have a committee of (lit., which consists of) five or more members, and that the majority of the committee members have (lit., be those who have) professional expertise regarding internships for foreigners.)

Notes

1. *Oyobi* is the *masu*-stem of the verb *oyobu* "to reach" and literally means "extending to." However, in modern Japanese *oyobi* also functions as a particle to connect two or more nouns (or noun equivalents); in this usage it means "and."

2. *Oyobi* is a highly formal word and is commonly used in the titles of formal documents such as laws, regulations and government reports, as in (1).

   (1) a. 動物の愛護及び管理に関する法律

   (Regulations Regarding Animal Protection and Control)

   b. スパムメールをめぐる米国及び日本における法的規制

   (Legal Restrictions in the U.S. and Japan Regarding Spam E-Mail)

   c. 対外及び対内直接投資状況

   (The Status of International and Domestic Direct Investment)

3. When there are more than two nouns, *oyobi* and the particle *to* "and" can be used together interchangeably, as in (2). (See Related Expression I.)

   (2) a. 東京と、横浜及びその周辺

   (Tokyo and Yokohama and its (i.e., Yokohama's) surroundings)

   b. 東京、及び横浜とその周辺

4. Besides nouns and noun equivalents, *oyobi* can connect nouns followed by certain particles, including compound particles such as *ni tsuite* and *to shite*.

   (3) a. 午前9時から及び午後3時からの2回、面接を行います。

   (We hold interviews at two times, 9 a.m. and 3 p.m.)

   b. 朝6時から9時まで、及び夕方5時から7時までの計5時間、検査のため装置の運転を停止する。

   (The system's operations will be stopped for inspection between 6 a.m. and 9 a.m. and from 5 p.m. to 7 p.m., for a total of five hours.)

0

c. 川辺博士にはがん治療について、及び患者の精神療法についての著述
がある。

(Dr. Kawabe has written books on cancer treatment and on the psychological therapy for cancer patients.)

d. 集団として、及び個人として、今我々が直面している問題をしっかり
考える必要がある。

(We have to think hard about the problems facing us now, both as a group and as individuals.)

5. *Oyobi* can be used to connect *na*-adjective stems when they are used without *na*, as in (4).

(4) 市民的及び政治的権利に関する国際規約

(International Agreements Regarding Civil Rights and Political Rights.)

Note here that *na* is absent after *shiminteki* "civil" and *seijiteki* "political." If *na* is required, *oyobi* cannot be used, as in (5).

(5) *便利な、及び安価な電子辞書

(a convenient and inexpensive electronic dictionary)

cf. 便利で安価な電子辞書

[Related Expressions]

0

I. *To* is similar to *oyobi* in that both connect nouns, noun equivalents, and nouns with certain particles, and mean the exhaustive "and," i.e., "X *to* Y" means "X and Y, and that's all." (cf. *ya* (DBJG: 536-38); *toka* (DBJG: 488-90))

However, *to* and *oyobi* are different in several ways. First, because *oyobi* is a highly formal and literary word, *oyobi* is unnatural in sentences describing everyday situations, as in [1].

[1] a. ビール {と / *及び} 酒を買いました。

(I bought beer and *sake*.)

b. ジョン {と / *及び} トムに電話した。

(I called John and Tom.)

Second, when more than two nouns (or noun equivalents) are listed, *to* usually occurs after each noun (*to* after the last noun is optional and is usually dropped), as in [2], while *oyobi* usually occurs only before the last noun, as in [3].

[2] a. 東京と川崎と横浜（と）

(Tokyo, Kawasaki and Yokohama)

b. ??東京、川崎と横浜

c. ??東京と川崎、横浜

[3] a. ??東京及び川崎及び横浜

(Tokyo, Kawasaki and Yokohama)

b. 東京、川崎及び横浜

Third, the position of the comma used with *to* and *oyobi* is different, as seen in [4].

[4] a. 日本国籍を有することと、国内の四年制大学に在籍する学生であること

(having Japanese citizenship and being a student at a four-year college in this country)

b. 日本国籍を有すること、及び国内の四年制大学に在籍する学生であること

(⇨ *to*[1] (DBJG: 473-76))

0

II. *Soshite* also means "and" and can be used to connect nouns and noun equivalents. Thus, *soshite* can be used in place of *oyobi*, as in [5].

[5] a. 使用した機種｛及び / そして｝ソフトウエアを表1に示す。(= KS(A))

b. 本奨学金への応募資格は、日本国籍を有すること、｛及び / そして｝国内の四年制大学に在籍する学生であることである。(= KS(B))

With regard to formality level, *soshite* can be formal or informal, and is used in both spoken and written language.

Soshite can be used when addressing a person, as in [6a]. *Oyobi* cannot be used in this way. Note that *oyobi* is acceptable in [6b] because the speaker here is not using the names (*gakusei-shokun, oyobi kyōshokuin no minasama*) as a form of address, as indicated by the particle *ni* after *minasama*.

[6] a. 浅野君、{そして / *及び}裕子さん、ご結婚おめでとうございます。
(Mr. Asano and Yuko, congratulations on your marriage.)

b. 学生諸君、{そして / 及び}教職員の皆様に一言ご挨拶申し上げます。
(I'd like to extend my greetings to you students, faculty and staff members.)

Another difference is that *soshite* can follow not only nouns or noun equivalents, but also the continuative forms of verbs, adjectives and *de aru* as well, as in [7].

[7] a. 日本へ行って、{そして / *及び}昔の友人たちに会った。
(I went to Japan and met with my old friends.)

b. この本は面白く(て)、{そして / *及び}為になる。
(This book is interesting and it's useful.)

c. この辞書は便利で(あり)、{そして / *及び}安価だ。
(This dictionary is convenient as well as inexpensive.)

d. 彼はビジネスマンであり、{そして / *及び}学者でもある。
(He is a businessman and also a scholar.)

(⇨ **soshite** (DBJG: 422-23))

---

oyoso およそ *adv.* <w>

an adverb representing the ideas "all; totally; mostly; approximately"

generally; commonly; all; quite entirely; totally; utterly; (not) at all; for the most part; mostly; almost; approximately; roughly; about; rough; general
【REL. *ippanni*; *mattaku*; *marude*; *daitai*; *ōmune*】

◆ **Key Sentences**

(A)

		Noun Phrase		
私は	およそ	名作と言われている映画	は	すべて見ているつもりだ。
(I'm convinced that I've watched all the movies that are commonly considered masterpieces.)				

(B)

		Vneg	
彼女はこういう根気のいる仕事には	およそ	向いてい	ない。
(She is not at all suited for work that requires perseverance like this work does.)			

(C)

			Verb
彼の考えていることは	およそ	想像が	つく。
(I can make a fairly good guess about what he's thinking.)			

(D)

		Number + Counter	
その学会には	およそ	1500人	の会員がいる。
(That academic association has approximately 1,500 members.)			

0

Formation

(i) およそ N は

およそ優れた研究者は　(excellent researchers in general; all excellent researchers)

(ii) およそ Adj(*i/na*)　(where Adj(*i/na*) has a negative meaning)

およそつまらない　(quite boring)

およそ不可能だ　(totally impossible)

(iii) およそ{Vneg / Adj(*i*)stem く / Adj(*na*)stem で}ない

およそ向いていない　(s.o. is not at all suited for s.t.)

およそ面白くない　(s.t. is not at all interesting)

およそ経済的でない　(s.t. is not economical at all)

(iv)　およそ {V / Adj(*i/na*) / N だ}

およそ分かる　(s.o. understands almost everything)

およそ正しい　(s.t./s.o. is about right)

およそ完成だ　(s.t. is almost complete)

(v)　およその N

およその考え　(a general idea)

およその見積もり　(a rough estimate)

(vi)　およそ Number (+ Counter)

およそ 10 万人　(approximately 100,000 people)

Examples

(a) およそ楽をして得られる技能で身につくものはない。

(Generally, none of the skills you can learn easily will become second nature.)

(b) およそ天才と言われる人は誰でも人には知れない重荷を背負っているものだ。

(Generally, anyone who is called a genius carries a heavy burden others can't see.)

(c) 我々はおよそ不合理なこの制度に長い間縛られている。

(We've been bound by this utterly irrational system for a long time.)

(d) 田宮先生は大学の政治的なことにはおよそ縁遠い人だった。

(Professor Tamiya was totally removed from university politics.)

(e) 彼には気の毒だが、彼の努力はおよそ意味のないものだった。

(I'm sorry for him, but his effort was totally meaningless.)

(f) それは彼の普段の言動からはおよそ想像できない行動であった。

(It was behavior we couldn't even have imagined based on what he usually said and did.)

(g) 仕事は午前中でおよそ片づいたので今日は早く帰れそうだ。

(I finished most of my work this morning, so it looks like I can go home early today.)

(h) その大学のおよその情報はインターネットで得られる。

(Most of the information on that university can be obtained via the Internet.)

(i) この会社の年間取引額はおよそどのくらいですか。

(Approximately what is the volume of this company's annual business?)

(j) 現在中国に生息するジャイアントパンダの数はおよそ１千頭ということだ。

(They say there are about 1,000 giant pandas living in China now.)

Notes

1. *Oyoso* is a formal expression and is usually used in formal writings or formal conversation. *Oyoso* has several different meanings depending on the context, as explained in the following notes.

2. When *oyoso* is used in a generic statement about someone or something, it means "commonly; generally; in general; all," as in KS(A), Exs.(a) and (b).

3. When *oyoso* occurs with predicates with a negative meaning, it means "quite; utterly; totally; (not) at all," as in Exs.(c) and (d). *Oyoso* cannot be used with this meaning with predicates having a positive or neutral meaning, as shown in (1).

(1) a. ｛*およそ/全く｝すばらしい話だ。

(It's quite a wonderful story.)

b. この制度は｛*およそ/全く｝合理的だ。

(This system is totally rational.)

c. 彼の言っていることは｛*およそ/全く｝正しい。

(What he says is totally correct.)

4. When *oyoso* is used with words in a negative form, it means "(not) at all," as in KS(B), Exs.(e) and (f). However, the sentences do not necessarily mean something negative, as shown in Ex.(f) and in the examples in (2).

(2) a. 彼女はおよそ間違ったことは言わない。

(What she says is always correct.)

b. 私の父はおよそ不正なことのできない性格だった。

(My father had a personality that didn't allow him to do anything unjust.)

0

5. *Oyoso* can be used as a kind of quantifier, meaning "mostly; for the most part; almost," as in KS(C), Exs.(g) and (h).

6. When *oyoso* is used with numbers, it means "approximately; about," as in KS(D), Exs.(i) and (j).

7. *Ōyoso* can be used for *oyoso* when the latter means "approximately; about," as shown in (3).

(3) a. 彼の考えていることは｛およそ / おおよそ｝想像がつく。(= KS(C))

b. その学会には｛およそ / おおよそ｝1500 人の会員がいる。(= KS(D))

【Related Expressions】

I. *Oyoso* in generic sentences can be used interchangeably with *ippanni*, as in [1].

[1] a. 私は｛およそ / 一般に｝名作と言われている映画はすべて見ているつもりだ。(= KS(A))

b. ｛およそ / 一般に｝楽をして得られる技能で身につくものはない。

(= Ex.(a))

c. ｛およそ / 一般に｝天才と言われる人は誰でも人には知れない重荷を背負っているものだ。(= Ex.(b))

II. In sentences in which *oyoso* means "quite; utterly; totally; (not) at all," *mattaku* or *marude* can be substituted, as in [2].

[2] a. 彼女はこういう根気のいる仕事には｛およそ / 全く / まるで｝向いていない。(= KS(B))

b. 我々は｛およそ / 全く / まるで｝不合理なこの制度に長い間縛られている。(= Ex.(c))

c. 田宮先生は大学の政治的なことには｛およそ / 全く / まるで｝縁遠い人だった。(= Ex.(d))

d. 彼には気の毒だが、彼の努力は｛およそ / 全く / まるで｝意味のないものだった。(= Ex.(e))

III. When *oyoso* means "mostly; for the most part; almost; approximately," it can be replaced by *daitai* or *ōmune*, as in [3].

[3]　a. 彼の考えていることは{**およそ**/**大体**/**概ね**}想像がつく。(= KS(C))

　　b. 仕事は午前中で{**およそ**/**大体**/**概ね**}片づいたので今日は早く帰れそうだ。(= Ex.(g))

　　c. その大学の{**およそ**/**大体**/**概ね**}の情報はインターネットで得られる。(= Ex.(h))

　　d. その学会には{**およそ**/**大体**/**概ね**}1500 人の会員がいる。

(= KS(D))

o yoso ni　をよそに　　*comp. prt.*　<w>

0

a compound particle that expresses s.o.'s indifference to warnings, criticism, advice, accusations, opposition, anxiety, wishes, eagerness, provocative actions, etc.

indifferent to ~; contrary to ~ ; ignoring ~; despite

◆ **Key Sentences**

(A)

	Noun Phrase		
首相は	国民の批判	をよそに	イラク戦争支持を表明した。
(Setting aside people's criticism, the prime minister declared his support for the Iraq War.)			

(B)

	Sinf		
青春時代、せいしゅん	友達がデートに明け暮れともだち　　　　　　あ　く	の	をよそに、

僕は家に一人こもって SF を読んでいた。ぼく

(During my adolescent years, I secluded myself at home and read science fiction, ignoring my friends, who were spending all their time dating.)

Formation

(i) NP をよそに

不景気をよそに　(indifferent to economic recession)ふけいき

(ii) Sinf のをよそに　(だ cannot be used before の. Adj(*na*)stem ｛な / である｝の; Nであるの.)

困っているのをよそに　(indifferent to the fact that s.o. is having trouble)こま

不便｛な / である｝のをよそに　(ignoring the inconvenience)ふべん

不況であるのをよそに　(indifferent to the state of depression)ふきょう

Examples

(a) 今回のイベントは、我々の心配をよそに多くの参加者を集め、大成功だった。こんかい　　　　　　　　われわれ　しんぱい　　　　　　　さんかしゃ　　あつ　　だいせいこう

(Despite our worries, many people participated in the event, so it turned out to be a big success.)

(b) たび重なる妻の忠告をよそに、彼は酒もたばこもやめなかった。かさ　　つま　ちゅうこく　　　　　かれ　さけ

(Ignoring his wife's repeated advice, he never quit drinking and smoking.)

(c) 彼はその恋を自身の最後の恋と感じて、周囲の警告をよそにのめり込んでかれ　　こい　じしん　さいご　こい　かん　　　しゅうい　けいこく　　　　　　　こ
いった。

(Feeling that it would be his last chance for love, he ignored the warnings of those around him, and allowed himself to get deeply involved.)

(d) 2006 年 12 月、様々な反対の声をよそに、教育基本法改正案が国会の十分なさまざま　はんたい　こえ　　　　　きょういくきほんほうかいせいあん　　　　　　　じゅうぶん
審議を経ることなく可決された。しんぎ　へ　　　　　　　かけつ

(In December 2006, the revision of the Fundamental Law of Education was passed without sufficient deliberation by the Diet, despite opposition from various sectors.)

(e) 平和を希求する市民による核兵器廃絶への切なる願いをよそに、核兵器開発、核軍拡競争は、今なおとどまるところを知りません。

(Despite the heart-felt pleas of peace-minded citizens who want to abolish all nuclear weapons, the nuclear arms race and the development of nuclear weapons still know no limits.)

(f) 多くの国々が経済発展ばかりに躍起になっているのをよそに、この国は個人の豊かな生活を基盤にした幸福を追求している。

(Contrary to the many countries in the world that enthusiastically pursue economic growth, this country is pursuing happiness based on an affluent life for individuals.)

Notes

1. *O yoso ni* expresses s.o.'s indifference to warnings, criticism, advice, rumors, accusations, opposition, anxiety, wishes, eagerness or provocative actions, among others. Note that the original meaning of *yoso* is "outside; a space where one is not involved."

2. *O yoso ni* is preceded either by a noun or noun phrase, as in KS(A) and Exs.(a)-(e), or a *no*-nominalized noun phrase, as in KS(B) and Ex.(f).

0

samo さも   *adv.*

| an adverb meaning "truly," used when describing the way s.o.'s action or behavior appears | truly; really; as if; so; that way; like that 【REL. *ikanimo*; *marude*】 |

◆ **Key Sentences**

(A)

		Adj(*i*)stem		
浩二は冷めたコーヒーを	さも	**まず**	そうに	飲んだ。

(Koji drank the cold coffee with a look that showed how bad it tasted.)

(B)

			Vinf		
古田は	さも	自分一人が	**苦労した**	ように	言っているが、

実は彼は文句を言うばかりで何もしなかったのだ。

(Furuta talks as if he suffered alone, but the truth of the matter is that he just complained and didn't do any work.)

(C)

今すぐ病院に連れて行こう。	さも	ないと	手遅れになる。

(Let's take him to the hospital right now. If we don't, it's going to be too late.)

Formation

(i)   さも {Adj(*i/na*)stem / V*masu*} そう {に / な}

     さも嬉しそうに   (looking really happy; as if s.o. were happy)

     さも嬉しそうな顔   (a face that shows s.o. is truly happy; the face of s.o. who is truly happy)

     さも不自由そうに   (as if s.o. really had trouble moving)

さも不自由そうな歩き方 (a way of walking that shows s.o. really has trouble walking; a walk that looks as if s.o. has trouble moving easily)

さも誰にでもできそうに (as if anyone could do (it))

さも誰にでもできそうな説明 (instructions that sound as if anyone could do (it))

(ii) さも～{V / Adj(*i*)}inf よう{に / な}

さも自分ができるように (as if s.o. were capable)

さも自分ができるような話し方 (a way of talking that sounds as if s.o. were capable)

さも自分が偉いように (as if s.o. were great)

さも自分が偉いような話し方 (a way of talking that sounds as if s.o. were great)

(iii) さも～ Adj(*na*)stem{な / だった}よう{に / な}

さも自分が上手なように (as if s.o. were good at s.t.)

さも自分が上手なような話し方 (a way of talking that sounds as if s.o. were good at s.t.)

(iv) さも～ N{の / だった}よう{に / な}

さも自分が専門家のように (as if s.o. were an expert)

さも自分が専門家のような話し方 (a way of talking that sounds as if s.o. were an expert)

(v) さも～{V / Adj(*i*)}inf みたい{に / な}

さも自分ができるみたいに (as if s.o. were capable)

さも自分ができるみたいな話し方 (a way of talking that sounds as if s.o. were capable)

さも自分が偉いみたいに (as if s.o. were great)

さも自分が偉いみたいな話し方 (a way of talking that sounds as if s.o. were great)

(vi) さも～{{Adj(*na*)stem / N}{ø / だった}みたい{に / な}

さも自分が上手みたいに (as if s.o. were good at s.t.)

さも自分が上手みたいな話し方 (a way of talking that sounds as if s.o. were good at s.t.)

さも自分が専門家みたいに (as if s.o. were an expert)

S

さも自分が専門家みたいな話し方　(a way of talking that sounds as if s.o. were an expert)

Examples

(a) 係員はさも面倒くさそうに私の苦情を聞いていた。

(The person in charge listened to my complaint with an expression that revealed it was truly bothersome.)

(b) 彼女はさも忙しそうにしているが、本当は大した仕事なんかないのだ。

(She acts as if she were truly busy, but really she doesn't have anything significant to work on.)

(c) 子供たちはさも退屈そうな顔をして授業を聞いている。

(The children are listening to the lecture looking really bored.)

(d) 川村はいつもその話をさも自分自身の体験みたいに話しているが、本当はそれは私が彼に話したことなのだ。

(Kawamura always tells that story as if it were his own experience, but actually I told it to him.)

(e) 部長はさも当然のごとく私に日曜出勤を命じた。

(The division chief ordered me to come to the office on Sunday as if it were a matter of course.)

(f) そのプログラムは、操作説明書を見るとさも簡単に使えそうに書いてあるが、本当にそうなのだろうか。

(When I read the operation manual, it sounds like the program is really easy to use, but I wonder if that's really true.)

(g) 男はさも親しげに私に近寄ってきた。

(The man approached me as if he knew me very well.)

(h) あの「自分はさもワインの通ですよ」って感じの戸田の話し方はまったく嫌みだ。

(Toda's way of talking (lit., That way Toda has of talking), as if he knew everything about wine, is truly offensive.)

Notes

1. *Samo* X is used when one's action or behavior appears just the way it is described by X. Because *samo* is used when describing the way one's action or behavior appears, it often occurs with such auxiliaries as *sōda*,

yōda, *mitaida*, *gotoshi* and *-geda*, as in KS(A), (B) and Exs.(a)-(g). Note that *gotoku* in Ex.(e) is the adverbial form of *gotoshi* "be like," and *-geni* in Ex.(g) is the adverbial form of *-geda* "look."

(⇨ **gotoshi** (in this volume); ~**sōda**[2] (DBJG: 410-12);
yōda (DBJG: 547-52))

2. *Samo* is usually used in adverbial or adjectival phrases or clauses rather than in main clauses, as in (1) and (2).

(1) a. 彼はさも<u>おいしそうに</u>食べる。

(He eats as though the food tastes really good.)

b. 彼はさも<u>おいしそうな</u>食べ方をする。

(He eats as though the food tastes really good.)

c. 彼の食べ方は{*さも/本当に/実に}<u>おいしそうだ</u>。

(The way he eats makes it look as though the food tastes really good.)

(2) a. 彼はさも自分一人で<u>やったように</u>話す。

(He talks as if he did it by himself.)

b. 彼はさも自分一人で<u>やったような</u>話し方をする。

(He talks as if he did it by himself.)

c. 彼の話し方は{*さも/まるで}自分一人で<u>やったようだ</u>。

(The way he talks about it makes it sound as though he did it by himself.)

3. The occurrence of the auxiliary adjective *rashii* with *samo* is limited to cases in which *rashii* means "appear; like." *Rashii* can be rephrased using *yōda* or *mitaida*, as in (3).

(3) 彼はさも革新派{らしく/のように/みたいに}<u>振る舞っている</u>が、本当は相当保守的だ。

(He behaves as if he were a progressive member, but the truth is that he is quite conservative.)

(⇨ **rashii** (DBJG: 373-75))

4. Whether or not phrases/clauses with *samo* describe a counterfactual situation depends on the context. For example, in KS(A), cold coffee usually doesn't taste good, so "*samo mazu sōni nomu*" is understood as a factual description. On the other hand, in KS(B), the main clause states that Furuta didn't do any work, so "*samo jibun hitori ga kurōshita*

yōni" is a counterfactual description. "*Samo taikutsu sōna kao*" in Ex.(c) describes the bored look of the children, but whether or not they are actually bored is unknown. Similarly, you cannot tell whether "*samo kantanni tsukae sōni*" in Ex.(f) is counterfactual or not because the program hasn't been used yet.

5. When *samo* occurs with *aru* or *nai*, it means "so; that way; like that; if not; otherwise; or else," as in KS(C). (4) provides additional examples.

(4) a. もっと真面目に勉強しなさい。さもないと卒業できませんよ。

(You should study more seriously. Otherwise (lit., if that's not the case), you won't be able to graduate.)

b. この仕事を取るか、さも{なければ / なくば}日本へ帰るしかない。

(I have to take this job or else go back to Japan.)

c. 米田は一週間で会社を辞めたそうだが、さもあろう。彼にはとても会社勤めは向かない。

(I heard Yoneda quit after a week, which is what I expected (lit., I thought so). Working for a company doesn't suit him at all.)

[Related Expressions]

I. *Ikanimo* is synonymous with *samo*, and it can be used in place of *samo* when used to describe the way someone's action or behavior appears.

[1] a. 浩二は冷めたコーヒーを{さも / いかにも}まずそうに飲んだ。

(= KS(A))

b. 古田は{さも / いかにも}自分一人が苦労したように言っているが、実は彼は文句を言うばかりで何もしなかったのだ。(= KS(B))

c. 子供たちは{さも / いかにも}退屈そうな顔をして授業を聞いている。

(= Ex.(c))

However, *ikanimo* can be used to describe the appearance of inanimate objects while *samo* cannot.

[2] a. このイチゴは{いかにも /*さも}おいしそうな色をしている。

(The color of these strawberries makes them look so delicious.)

b. {いかにも /*さも}美術館らしい建物が見えてきた。

(A building that really looked like an art museum came into sight.)

c. その部屋は {いかにも／*さも} 訪問者の気持ちを和ませるような装飾が施されていた。

(The room was decorated in such a way as to truly relax visitors' minds.)

Note that *ikanimo* can be used in main clauses while *samo* cannot. (See Note 2.)

[3] a. 彼の食べ方は {いかにも／*さも} おいしそうだ。(= (1c))

b. 彼の話し方は {いかにも／*さも} 自分一人でやったようだ。(= (2c))

[4] a. あの二人は {いかにも／*さも} よく似ている。
(Those two look so much alike.)

b. あの反論の仕方は {いかにも／*さも} 彼らしい。
(That way of arguing is just like him.)

(⇨ ***ikanimo*** (DIJG: 66-70))

II. *Marude* "as if" can be used in place of *samo* without changing the meaning when *samo* is used with *yōda* and *mitaida* in counterfactual situations, as in [5].

[5] a. 古田は {さも／まるで} 自分一人が苦労したように言っているが、実は彼は文句を言うばかりで何もしなかったのだ。(= KS(B))

b. 川村はいつもその話を {さも／まるで} 自分自身の体験みたいに話しているが、本当はそれは私が彼に話したことなのだ。(= Ex.(d))

However, *marude* cannot be used in place of *samo* when *samo* is used with *sōda* and *rashii* even in counterfactual situations, as shown in [6].

[6] a. 彼女は {さも／*まるで} 忙しそうにしているが、本当は大した仕事なんかないのだ。(= Ex.(b))

b. 彼は {さも／*まるで} 革新派らしく振る舞っているが、本当は相当保守的だ。(= (3))

S

sara ni さらに［更に］ *adv. / conj.*

an adverb/conjunction that represents the idea of "additionally" or "further"

even ~er; even more; additional; more; further; furthermore; in addition

【REL. *issō*; *nao*; *motto*; *yori*; *ato*; *mō*; *sono ue*; **hiite wa**; **katsu**; **nao**】

◆ **Key Sentences**

(A)

			Adj(*i*)
前の翻訳も難しかったが	今度のは	さらに	難しい。

(The last translation (job) was difficult, but this one is even harder.)

(B)

		Adverb	
グローバル時代に向けて 企業の国際化を	さらに	強力に	押し進める必要がある。

(In our global age, we must promote the internationalization of businesses even more forcefully.)

(C)

	Number + Counter	
さらに	500人	の人員が整理される見通しだ。

(It is expected that an additional 500 employees will be laid off.)

(D)

		Verb Phrase
我が国の経済は	さらに	悪化しそうだ。

(It looks like our nation's economy will worsen still further.)

 Formation

(i)　さらに Adj(*i/na*)

　　さらに小さい　(even smaller)

　　さらに複雑な　(even more complex)

(ii)　さらに Adv.

　　さらに慎重に　(even more prudently)

(iii)　さらに Number (+ Counter)

　　さらに 30 時間　(an additional 30 hours)

(iv)　さらに V / VP

　　さらに調査する　(s.o. investigates s.t. further)

　　さらに改良を加える　(s.o. makes further improvements)

 Examples

(a)　さらに大きいハリケーンがテキサス南部を襲った。

　　(An even larger hurricane struck South Texas.)

(b)　さらに大型のジャンボジェットが開発されることになった。

　　(It has been decided that an even larger jumbo jet will be developed.)

(c)　D社のノート型コンピュータがさらに薄くなった。

　　(Company D's laptop computers have become even thinner.)

(d)　電化製品をディスカウントショップよりさらにお安く提供しております。

　　(We provide electrical appliances even more cheaply than discount shops do.)

(e)　メモリがさらに 10 パーセント値下げされた。

　　(The price of the memory was lowered by an additional 10 percent.)

(f)　今年は主要銀行の合併がさらに進んだ。

　　(More mergers took place among major banks this year.)

(g)　鳥インフルエンザの被害がさらに広がる恐れがある。

　　(There is fear that the damage caused by bird flu will spread even further.)

(h)　センサーでデータを集め、これをさらに同一チップ上の増幅器で増幅する。

　　(Data is collected with a sensor and, furthermore, on the same chip the data is augmented with an amplifier.)

S

(i) 開店日の来場者にはもれなく記念品を差し上げます。さらに、抽選で50名
の方に当店の商品券が当たります。

(We'll give a commemorative souvenir to all customers on opening
day. In addition, we'll give a gift certificate for our store to 50 people
selected in a drawing.)

Note

Sara ni modifies adjectives, adverbs, quantifiers (i.e., numbers with or
without counters), verbs or sentences. Its meaning changes depending on
what it modifies, as seen in the examples. In general, when *sara ni* modifies
adjectives or adverbs, it means "even ~er" or "even more," as in KS(A), (B)
and Exs.(a)-(d); when it modifies numbers and units, it means "additional,"
as in KS(C) and Ex.(e); when it modifies verbs, it means "further," as in
KS(D) and Exs.(f)-(h); and when it modifies sentences, it means "further;
furthermore" or "in addition," as in Ex.(i).

【Related Expressions】

I. *Issō, nao, motto* and *yori* also modify adjectives and adverbs and convey
    a similar idea.

    [1] a. 今度の翻訳は{さらに／一層／なお／もっと／より}難しい。
         (The translation (work) this time is (even) more difficult.)

         b. グローバル時代に向けて企業の国際化を{さらに／一層／なお／もっ
            と／より}強力に押し進める必要がある。(= KS(B))

In [1a], for example, *sara ni* means "even more difficult," implying that
the previous work was difficult, too. *Issō* and *nao* also imply that the
previous work was difficult. *Motto* means "much more difficult," but it
doesn't imply that the previous work was difficult. *Yori* simply means
"more" and also does not imply that the previous work was difficult.
In addition, *yori* implies that there is not a great difference in difficulty
between the two, so it can be interpreted as "more difficult but not
much more." *Issō* is sometimes used with *nao* and *yori*, i.e., *nao issō*
"even more" and *yori issō* "even more."

When *issō, nao, motto* and *yori* modify verbs, they all mean "further"
and they can replace *sara ni*. Note that *yori* implies "further" but not
"much further."

    [2] a. 我が国の経済は{さらに／一層／なお／もっと／より}悪化しそうだ。
                                                        (= KS(D))

b. 今年は主要銀行の合併が｛さらに／一層／なお／もっと／より｝進んだ。(= Ex.(f))

($\Rightarrow$ ***nao*** (in this volume); ***yori*** (DIJG: 602-05))

II. When *ato* and *mō* modify numbers, with or without a counter, they carry the same meaning of *sara ni*, as in [3]. Of the three, *sara ni* is the most formal and *mō* is the least formal.

[3] ｛さらに／あと／もう｝500 人の人員が整理される見通しだ。(= KS(C))

III. When *sara ni* is used as a conjunction, as in Ex.(i), it can be replaced by *sono ue* "on top of that; in addition; moreover."

[4] a. 開店日の来場者にはもれなく記念品を差し上げます。｛さらに／その上｝、抽選で 50 名の方に当店の商品券が当たります。(= Ex.(i))

b. 彼は一緒にアパートを探してくれて、｛さらに／その上｝引っ越しまで手伝ってくれた。

(He looked for an apartment with me, and moreover, he even helped me move.)

($\Rightarrow$ ***sono ue*** (DIJG: 413-17))

S

sate さて　*int.*

an interjection indicating that the speaker/writer is going to talk about something different	well; now; well now; so 【REL. *tokorode*; *sā*】

◆ **Key Sentences**

(A)

	Sentence (starting a new topic)
さて、	話は変わりますが、日本では今ちょっとした韓国ブームです。

(Now, on another matter, Japan is undergoing quite a Korea boom at this time.)

(B)

	Sentence (starting a related topic)
さて、	それでは本題に入りましょう。

(Now I'm going to talk about the main topic.)

(C)

	Sentence (talking about the same topic from a different angle)
さて、	ここで今までお話ししたポイントを復習してみましょう。

(Now, let's review the points I have discussed so far.)

(D)

Sentence (presenting information)		Question
ワールドカップ開幕！	さて、	今回はどこが勝つでしょうか。

(The World Cup has begun! So, which country's going to win this time?)

(E)

	Sentence (leave-taking)
さて、	私はそろそろ失礼します。

(Well, I should be going now.)

(F)

	Question
さて、	これからどうしようか。

(Well, what shall we do now (lit., from now)?)

Examples

(a) さて、先日お願いしました契約変更の件ですが、課内部でご検討いただけましたでしょうか。

(Now, (I'd like to talk) about the contract change I requested the other day. Did you have a chance to discuss it within your department?)

(b) さて、前回の講義の続きですが、覚えていますか。

(Now, I'm going to continue where we left off in the previous lecture. Do you remember (what we covered before)?)

(c) さて、次はスポーツです。

(Now, let's turn to sports. [TV/radio news])

(d) ここに3枚のポートレートがあります。さて、吉永さんはどれでしょう。

(Here are three portraits. So, which one is Ms. Yoshinaga?)

(e) さて、もう寝ようかな。

(Well, I guess I'll go to bed now.)

(f) さて、困った。

(Well, I'm in trouble.)

(g) さて、何から始めようか。

(So, what shall we begin with?)

Notes

1. *Sate* always occurs at the beginning of a sentence and indicates that the speaker/writer is going to talk about something different from what he/she has said before. Specifically, *sate* is used in the following situations:

    (i) When the speaker/writer begins a new topic totally unrelated to what he/she has been talking about previously (often after greetings or opening remarks in letters, speeches, lectures, presentations, etc.), as in KS(A), Exs.(a) and (b).

    (ii) When the speaker/writer begins a new topic, but the previous topic and new topic are part of the same discourse, as in KS(B) and Ex.(c).

    (iii) When the speaker/writer continues on the same topic but is going to talk about it from a different angle or in a different situation, as in KS(C).

(iv) When the speaker/writer asks a question after presenting information, as in KS(D) and Ex.(d).

(v) When the speaker takes leave, as in KS(E) and Ex.(e).

2. In addition to the situations in Note 1, *sate* can be used when the speaker/writer faces a new situation and is at a loss or is thinking about what to do, as in KS(F), Exs.(f) and (g).

[Related Expressions]

I. The conjunction *tokorode* "by the way" is used to change the subject entirely and can be used as in Situation (i) in Note 1.

[1] a. ｛さて / ところで｝、話は変わりますが、日本では今ちょっとした韓国ブームです。(= KS(A))

b. ｛さて / ところで｝、先日お願いしました契約変更の件ですが、課内部でご検討いただけましたでしょうか。(= Ex.(a))

Tokorode can also be used in the situations mentioned in Note 2 if the speaker is wondering what to do and the question is not related to what was said previously.

[2] a. ｛さて / ところで｝、これからどうしようか。(= KS(F))

b. ｛さて / ところで｝、何から始めようか。(= Ex.(g))

Tokorode cannot be used in Situation (v) in Note 1.

[3] a. ｛さて / *ところで｝、私はそろそろ失礼します。(= KS(E))

b. ｛さて / *ところで｝、もう寝ようかな。(= Ex.(e))

II. The interjection *sā* "well; now," which has functions similar to *sate*, can be used in Situations (ii)-(v) in Note 1.

[4] a. ｛さて / さあ｝、それでは本題に入りましょう。(= KS(B))

b. ｛さて / さあ｝、ここで今までお話ししたポイントを復習してみましょう。(= KS(C))

c. ワールドカップ開幕！ ｛さて / さあ｝、今回はどこが勝つでしょうか。(= KS(D))

d. ｛さて / さあ｝、私はそろそろ失礼します。(= KS(E))

Sā can also be used in the situation mentioned in Note 2.

[5] a. {さて / さあ}、これからどうしようか。(= KS(F))

  b. {さて / さあ}、困った。(= Ex.(f))

sazo(kashi) さぞ（かし）   *adv.*

an adverb that is used when the speaker thinks that s.o. or s.t. is in an extreme state	I believe/I'm sure/I'm certain ~ very/really/truly ~; must be very/really/truly ~ 【REL. *kitto*】

◆ **Key Sentences**

(A)

		Adj(*na*)stem	
青森への単身赴任は	さぞ（かし）	大変	でしょう。
(Moving to Aomori (for a new assignment) without your family must be very tough.)			

(B)

		Adj(*i*)inf	
シカゴの冬は	さぞ（かし）	寒い	に違いない。
(I'm sure winter in Chicago will be very cold.)			

Formation

(i) さぞ（かし）{V / Adj(*i*)}inf {だろう / に違いない} / etc.

  さぞ（かし）喜んで{いる / いた}{だろう / に違いない} (s.o. must be / have been very pleased)

  さぞ（かし）{おいしい / おいしかった}{だろう / に違いない} (s.t. must be / have been really delicious)

(ii) さぞ（かし）Adj(*na*)stem {ø / だった}{だろう / に違いない} / etc.

  さぞ（かし）不便{ø / だった}{だろう / に違いない} (s.t. must be / have been quite inconvenient)

S

Examples

(a) 誕生日を忘れてしまったんだから、アリスはさぞ怒っているだろう。

(I forgot her birthday, so I'm sure Alice is really mad.)

(b) 彼女は大学合格の知らせを聞いてさぞ喜んだだろう。

(She must have been so happy after hearing the news that she'd been accepted (to college)!)

(c) 被災地の人々はさぞかし困っているだろうと思う。

(I imagine the people in the disaster-stricken areas are having a really hard time.)

(d) 谷本先生は長旅でさぞかしお疲れだろうと思います。

(I imagine Prof. Tanimoto is quite tired after her long trip.)

(e) もうすぐクリスマス。子供たちはさぞ楽しみなことでしょう。

(Christmas is almost here. I'm sure children are really looking forward to it.)

(f) 孝史はあの音が聞こえなかったのだから、さぞかしよく寝ていたに違いない。

(Takashi didn't hear that sound, so he must have been sleeping very heavily.)

(g) 彼はもう勝った後のことを話しているから、さぞかし自信があるんだろうね。

(He's already talking about what happens after they win, so he must be really confident.)

S

Notes

1. *Sazo* carries two meanings at the same time. One is "certainly; surely" and the other is "to a great extent; very."

2. *Sazo* usually occurs with sentence-ending phrases that express the speaker's/writer's relatively high degree of certainty, such as *darō* and *ni chigainai*, as in KS(A) and (B). *Sazo* cannot be used without such endings.

   (1) a. *青森への単身赴任はさぞ大変だ。(cf. KS(A))

   　　b. *シカゴの冬はさぞ寒い。(cf. KS(B))

   Note that phrases that express a relatively low degree of certainty cannot be used with *sazo* either, as shown in (2).

(2) a. *彼はさぞ疲れている<u>かもしれない</u>。

(He might be very tired.)

b. *彼はさぞ疲れている<u>可能性</u>が<u>ある</u>。

(It's possible he is very tired.)

3. *Sazo* is often used to express the speaker's sympathy with someone, as in KS(A), (B), Exs.(c) and (d). More examples are shown in (3).

(3) a. 私どもの手違い続きで**さぞ**お腹立ちのことでしょう。

(After a series of mistakes on our end, I'm sure you are very angry.)

b. 子供を失って純子は**さぞ**悲しんでいるだろう。

(Having lost her child, Junko must be unbearably sad.)

4. *Sazo* sometimes occurs with *koto darō/deshō*, as in Ex.(e) and (3a). This ending indicates that the speaker/writer is empathetic with the subject.

5. *Sazokashi* is more emphatic than *sazo*.

[Related Expression]

Kitto also means "surely; certainly; undoubtedly; must." However, it does not carry the meaning "to a great extent."

[1] a. 青森への単身赴任は**きっと**大変でしょう。(cf. KS(A))

(Moving to Aomori for a new assignment without your family must be tough.)

b. シカゴの冬は**きっと**寒いに違いない。(cf. KS(B))

(Chicago's winter must be cold.)

Next, *kitto* can be used with no conjecture endings, as in [2].

[2] a. 青森への単身赴任は{**きっと**/*さぞ}<u>大変だ</u>。(cf. KS(A))

(I'm sure that moving to Aomori for a new assignment without one's family would be tough.)

b. シカゴの冬は{**きっと**/*さぞ}<u>寒い</u>。 (cf. KS(B))

(Winter in Chicago is bound to be cold.)

c. 誕生日を忘れてしまったんだから、アリスは{**きっと**/*さぞ}<u>怒っている</u>。(cf. Ex.(a))

(Because I forgot her birthday, I'm sure Alice is angry.)

S

Note also that *kitto* can be used for a simple action, whereas *sazo* can only be used to describe an action taken to an extreme degree, as shown in [3].

[3] a. 彼は{きっと／*さぞ}写真を撮るだろう。

(He'll take pictures.)

b. 彼は{きっと／さぞ}たくさん写真を撮るだろう。

(I'm certain that he'll take {many / lots of} pictures.)

somosomo (no)　そもそも（の）　*adv.*

| a sentence-modifying adverb used when the speaker/writer comments on or questions a fundamental point | in the first place; to begin with; first of all; the very (beginning/ origin/etc.); original; first; fundamental 【REL. *daiichi*; *motomoto no*】 |

◆ **Key Sentences**

(A)

	Sentence (comment)
そもそも	こんなところにスーパーを造ったことが問題だ。
(The problem is that they built a supermarket in a place like this to begin with.)	

(B)

	Question
そもそも	どうしてこんなばかばかしい企画が通ったのでしょうか。
(How was such a ridiculous plan approved in the first place?)	

(C)

			Noun		
今回の 事件の	そもそも	の	**起こり**	は、	一人の社員が会社のパソコンを うちに持ち帰ったことにあった。

(This whole incident started when an employee took one of the office computers home. (lit., The very origin of this incident was in the fact that an employee took one of the office computers home.))

Formation

(i) そもそも S。

そもそもこの計画は実行不可能だ。 (In the first place, this plan can't be carried out.)

(ii) そもそもの N

そもそもの動機 (the original motivation)

Examples

(a) そもそも人間は一人で生きているのではない。

(To begin with, humans are not solitary beings.)

(b) 私はそもそも、作品のいいところをコメントしないで欠点ばかり指摘する審査のやり方に賛成できない。

(To begin with, I cannot agree with our way of judging where we point out only the flaws of a piece and never mention the good points.)

(c) そもそも電波って何なんでしょう。

(So, what are radio waves in the first place?)

(d) そもそも一体何で君がこのパーティーにいるんだ？

(To begin with, why on earth are you at this party?)

(e) 彼に期待したことがそもそもの間違いだった。

(That we were hoping for great things from him was our first mistake.)

(f) 契約書に誤訳があったのがそもそもの問題だ。

(The fundamental problem was that there was a mistranslation in the contract.)

S

(g) そもそもの目的は会員を増やすことだった。

(The original goal was to increase our membership.)

Notes

1. *Somosomo* is used when the speaker/writer makes a comment on a fundamental issue or asks a fundamental question, as in KS(A), (B) and Exs.(a)-(d).

2. *Somosomo* is also used to mean "original; fundamental," as in KS(C) and Exs.(e)-(g). In this case, the noun-modification form *somosomo no* is used.

[Related Expressions]

I. *Daiichi* "first; first of all" can be used in place of *somosomo* when it modifies sentences, as in [1].

   [1] a. {そもそも/第一}こんなところにスーパーを造ったことが問題だ。

   (= KS(A))

   b. {そもそも/第一}どうしてこんなばかばかしい企画が通ったのでしょうか。(= KS(B))

   However, *daiichi* cannot replace *somosomo* when it is used to mean "the very (beginning, origin, etc.); original; first; fundamental," as in [2].

   [2] a. 今回の事件の{そもそも/*第一}の起こりは、一人の社員が会社のパソコンをうちに持ち帰ったことにあった。(= KS(C))

   b. 彼に期待したことが{そもそも/*第一}の間違いだった。(= Ex.(e))

   c. 契約書に誤訳があったのが{そもそも/*第一}の問題だ。(= Ex.(f))

II. *Motomoto no* "original" can be used in place of *somosomo no* when the latter means "original," as shown in [3].

   [3] a. 今回の事件の{そもそも/もともと}の起こりは、一人の社員が会社のパソコンをうちに持ち帰ったことにあった。(= KS(C))

   b. {そもそも/もともと}の目的は会員を増やすことだった。(= Ex.(g))

sono mono そのもの *phr.*

| a phrase used to refer strictly to the preceding noun (phrase) or adjective | itself; themselves; very; perfect; the definition of; the picture of; absolutely; totally; utterly; perfectly 【REL. *-jitai*; *-jishin*】 |

◆ Key Sentences

(A)

Noun			
企画{きかく}	そのもの	は	悪くない。
(The plan itself is not bad.)			

(B)

	Noun		
この国は	独裁国家{どくさいこっか}	そのもの	だ。
(This country is the perfect definition of an autocracy.)			

(C)

Noun				
わいせつ画像{がぞう}	は、	それ	そのもの	が問題なのではなく、それを誰{だれ}が見るかが問題だと思う。
(I think that obscene images themselves are not the problem; who sees them is the problem.)				

(D)

	Adj(*na*)stem		
武田{たけだ}さんは今年 80 歳{さい}だが、	健康{けんこう}	そのもの	だ。
(Mr. Takeda is 80 this year and the picture of health.)			

S

Formation

(i)　N そのもの

　　　技術そのもの　　(technology itself)

　　　それそのもの　　(that itself)

(ii)　Adj(*na*)stem そのもの

　　　温厚そのものだ　　(s.o. is very gentle)

　　　温厚そのものの人柄　　(a very gentle personality)

Examples

(a)　マイナス思考ばかりしていると、人生そのものが駄目になる。

　　　(If you remain a negative thinker, your life itself will be ruined.)

(b)　私はこの団体の存在そのものを疑っている。

　　　(I doubt this group's very existence.)

(c)　我々は外務省改革にとどまらず、現在の外交そのものの転換を望む。

　　　(Not only do we want to reform the Ministry of Foreign Affairs, but we hope the current diplomacy itself will change.)

(d)　人間はその人の考えそのものである。

　　　(The epitome of a person is his or her thinking. (lit., A human being is his or her thought itself.))

(e)　私にとってバレーボールは人生そのものでした。

　　　(For me, volleyball was life itself.)

(f)　土地は、それそのものは富を生み出さないが、その上で生産、販売などの経済活動を行うことで富を生み出す。

　　　(The land itself does not produce wealth, but wealth is produced when people conduct economic activities, such as production and sales, on it (lit., by (people's) conducting economic activities such as production and sales on it).)

(g)　お年寄りを狙い、強引な方法で家屋の修理契約を結ぶ手口は卑劣そのものだ。

　　　((lit., Their way of) Aiming at the elderly and forcing them to sign a house repair contract is utterly contemptible.)

(h)　そのマニュアルは説明も図も明快そのもので、画像処理の知識がない者にもよく分かる。

　　　(The manual's explanations and figures are perfectly clear, so even people with no knowledge of image processing will be able to understand them well.)

(i) 米倉さんは誠実そのものの人柄で知られている。

(Ms. Yonekura is known for his totally sincere personality.)

Notes

1. In X *sono mono*, X is either a noun (or a noun equivalent) or a *na*-adjective stem. When X is a noun or a noun equivalent, X *sono mono* refers strictly to X and nothing else. When X is a *na*-adjective, X *sono mono* refers strictly to the essential quality of X.

2. X *sono mono* is usually used with non-human nouns, although it can be used with generic human nouns. For example, in (1) *sono mono* cannot be used, but in (2) it is acceptable. In (1), *jishin* should be used instead of *sono mono*. (See Related Expression II.)

(1) a. 私 {*そのもの / 自身} はこの合併案に特に問題を感じない。

(I don't personally feel that there is any particular problem with this merger plan.)

b. 田中さん {*そのもの / 自身}、自分の選択が間違っていたかもしれないと思い始めている。

(Mr. Tanaka himself has started to think that the choice he made might have been wrong.)

(2) a. 待遇をよくすることも必要だが、技術者そのものを増やすことが急務だ。

(We need to improve (engineers') working conditions, too, but the urgent need is to increase the number of engineers themselves.)

b. 海外では、日本人の作った製品は評価されるが、日本人そのものはあまり評価されていないような印象を受ける。

(I get the impression that people overseas think highly of products made by Japanese people, but not so highly of Japanese people themselves.)

3. *Sono mono* cannot be used with *i*-adjectives.

(3) a. このトイレは {*汚い / 不潔} そのものだ。

(This restroom is completely filthy.)

b. 彼らは {*貧しい / 貧困} そのものだった。

(They were utterly poor.)

[Related Expressions]

I. *Jitai* "itself; themselves" is synonymous with *sono mono*, as demonstrated in [1].

> [1] a. 企画｛そのもの／<ruby>自体<rt>じたい</rt></ruby>｝は悪くない。(= KS(A))
>
> b. わいせつ画像は、それ｛そのもの／自体｝が問題なのではなく、それを誰が見るかが問題だと思う。(= KS(C))
>
> c. 待遇をよくすることも必要だが、技術者｛そのもの／自体｝を増やすことが急務だ。(= (2a))

However, X-*jitai* cannot be used when X is a predicate, as shown in [2].

> [2] a. この国は独裁国家｛そのもの／*<ruby>自体<rt>じたい</rt></ruby>｝だ。(= KS(B))
>
> b. 武田さんは今年 80 歳だが、健康｛そのもの／*自体｝だ。(= KS(D))
>
> (⇨ *-jitai* (in this volume))

II. X-*jishin* "X oneself" is also synonymous with *sono mono* except that *jishin* is commonly used to refer to individuals rather than to people in general. (See Note 2.)

> [3] a. 私自身はこの合併案に特に問題を感じない。(= (1a))
>
> b. 田中さん自身、自分の選択が間違っていたかもしれないと思い始めている。(= (1b))

X-*jishin* cannot be used when X is a predicate, as shown in [4].

> [4] a. この国は独裁国家｛そのもの／*<ruby>自身<rt>じしん</rt></ruby>｝だ。(= KS(B))
>
> b. 武田さんは今年 80 歳だが、健康｛そのもの／*自身｝だ。(= KS(D))

S

sore dake それだけ *phr.*

> an adverbial phrase indicating that the degree of s.t. is proportionate to the degree of the state, action or event mentioned in the preceding sentence

that much; to the same extent; to the same degree; equally

◆ **Key Sentences**

(A)

Sentence₁			Sentence₂
この仕事は苦労（くろう）も多い	が、	それだけ	やりがいもある。
(This job is hard work, but to the same extent I also find it rewarding.)			

(B)

Sentence₁			Sentence₂
彼（かれ）らは同じ宗教内（しゅうきょうない）の派閥（はばつ）だ	から、	それだけ	憎（にく）しみも大きいのかもしれない。
(It might be that they hate each other that much more because they are in different sects of the same religion.)			

(C)

Sentence₁			Sentence₂
期待（きたい）が大きい	と	それだけ	失望（しつぼう）も大きくなってしまう。
(If your expectations are high, your disappointment will be equally high.)			

(D)

Sentence₁			Sentence₂
大きな仕事をまかされた	ということは、	それだけ	期待（きたい）されているということだろう。
(That he was assigned a big job just shows what high hopes people have for him.)			

S

Examples

(a) 株式投資は当たった時の利益は大きいが、それだけリスクも大きい。

(You can make a big profit when you invest in the right stocks, but the risk (of loss) is just as big.)

(b) たくさんのオプションがあるのはいいのだが、それだけ選択に悩むことにもなる。

(It is good to have many options, but it means that it's that much harder to choose.)

(c) 花粉症の薬は、眠くなるからそれだけ効くというわけではありません。

(It's not true of pollen allergy drugs that the sleepier they make you, the more effective they are.)

(d) できるだけ多く条件を指定すると、それだけ理想に近い人が検索されるはずです。

(If you specify as many conditions as you can, your search should turn up someone that is much closer to your ideal.)

(e) 情報の内容が二つのソースで一致するのなら、それだけ信用できるということではないだろうか。

(If information from two sources is consistent, don't you think the information is that much more reliable?)

(f) 子供にお金をかければそれだけ愛情を注いだことになる、という間違った思い込みがしばしばあるようだ。

(It seems that it's a common, and mistaken, assumption that the amount of money you spend on your children equals the amount of affection you've given them.)

(g) これに関する読者からの投書が最近増えているということは、それだけこの問題が注目されてきたということでしょう。

(The fact that we have been getting more letters from readers recently about this problem shows how much more it is drawing people's attention.)

(h) 販売経験が豊富な営業マンは、それだけ顧客の信頼も多く勝ち取るはずだ。

((Compared with those who are less experienced,) Sales representatives with a lot of experience should be all the more able to win their customers' trust.)

Notes

1. *Sore dake* represents the idea that someone or something is in a state, or something takes place, to the extent proportionate to the degree of the state, event or action mentioned in the previous sentence.

2. *Sore dake* is usually placed at the beginning of the second sentence, although it can be anywhere adverbs occur.

sore nari ni / no   それなり に / の   *phr.*

| a phrase representing the idea that s.o./ s.t. does s.t. or is in a state in his/her/ its own way, or in a way suitable to the situation or generally expected from the situation | in one's own way; accompanying; proportionate; suitable; expected; agreeable; reasonable; one's own; proper to [REL. *nari ni/no*] |

◆ **Key Sentences**

(A)

			Adj(*i*)
クラシックもジャズもロックも、聞いてみればみな	それなり	に	面白い。

(If you (really) listen to classical music, jazz and rock, each of them is interesting in its own way.)

(B)

			Noun		
外国で仕事をするのは面白いが、	それなり	の	苦労	は	覚悟しなければならない。

(Working abroad is interesting, but you must expect a certain amount of hardship, too.)

S

Formation

(i)   それなりに { V / Adj(*i/na*) / N + Cop. }

それなりに楽しめる   (s.t. can be enjoyed in its own way)

それなりにおいしい   (s.t. is tasty in its own way)

それなりに便利だ   (s.t. is convenient in its own way)

それなりに傑作だ   (s.t. is an excellent work in its own way)

(ii) それなりの N

それなりの利点   (merits proper to s.t.)

Examples

(a) 買った参考書はどれもみなそれなりに役に立っている。

(All the reference books I have bought have been helpful in their own way.)

(b) 選手たちはみんなそれなりに精一杯やっている。ただ結果が出ないだけだ。

(All the players are giving it their best in their own way. We just haven't had the (expected) result.)

(c) 天才と言われる人にはそれなりの苦しみがあると思う。

(I think people who are called geniuses suffer in their own way.)

(d) お金がなくてもそれなりに余暇を楽しむ方法はある。

(Even if you don't have money, there are ways to enjoy your leisure in your own way.)

(e) ほとんどの人は、悩みや問題があってもそれなりに暮らしているのだと思います。

(I think that even though most people have worries and problems, they are living the best they can (lit., in their own ways).)

(f) 上の地位にいればそれなりの責任がかかってくる。

(If you are in a high-ranking position, you have to assume the responsibilities that come with it.)

(g) きつい仕事にはそれなりの報酬を払うべきだ。

(For a tough assignment we should pay appropriate compensation.)

(h) 今年それなりの成績を上げることができれば、来年支店長に昇進できそうだ。

(If I can achieve the expected performance this year, it looks like I'll be promoted to branch manager next year.)

(i) それなりの収入があるのなら、結婚相手はすぐ見つかるはずです。

(If you have a reasonable income, you should be able to find someone to marry soon.)

(j) 彼が準決勝まで残ったということは、それなりの実力があるということだ。

(The fact that he made it to the semifinals means that he had the right skills to take him that far.)

(k) 彼女がみんなに好かれていないのはそれなりの理由がある。

(There's a reason no one likes her (lit., she is not liked by everyone).)

Notes

1. The literal meaning of *sore nari* is "its form," which has been extended to mean "one's way," "one's own way," "the expected way," "the way something is supposed to be," etc.

2. *Sore nari ni/no* is used in a variety of contexts and interpreted in different ways, as follows:

> (i) "in one's own way; one's own": KS(A) and Exs.(a)-(e)
>
> (ii) "accompanying": KS(B) and Ex.(f)
>
> (iii) "suitable; proper; proportionate; which should come with (it)": Ex.(g)
>
> (iv) "expected; reasonable; agreeable; which is expected from (it)": Exs.(h) and (i)
>
> (v) "which naturally leads to (it)": Exs.(j) and (k)

[Related Expression]

Nari ni/no occurs in the structure "X *(ni) wa* Y *nari ni/no*," where Y can be either the same noun as X, the corresponding personal pronoun or *sore*, as in [1]. These differences in Y make no difference in meaning.

[1] a. 彼は {それ / 彼} なりに努力しているのだ。

  (He's giving it his best effort.)

 b. 洋子には {それ / 洋子 / 彼女} なりの考えがあるようだ。

  (It seems that Yoko has her own ideas (about something).)

 c. 抽象画は {それ / 抽象画} なりに面白い。

  (Abstract pictures are interesting in their own way.)

(⇨ *nari ni* (DIJG: 227-29))

S

sue (ni) 末（に）　　*n.*

a noun that indicates the end of a period or the time after long, hard mental or physical work	after; at the end of 【REL. *ato (de)*; *nochi (ni)*; ***age-ku (ni)***】

◆ **Key Sentences**

(A)

Noun			
試行錯誤	の	末（に）、	やっと車に使える燃料電池ができた。

(After much trial and error, we finally made a fuel cell battery that can be used in cars.)

(B)

	Vinf.past		
一週間	悩んだ	末（に）、	家族をおいて単身赴任することにした。

(After considering it for a week, I decided to leave my family behind and transfer to my new job alone.)

Formation

(i)　N の末（に）

　　　今月の末（に）　(at the end of this month)
　　　交渉の末（に）　(after negotiation)

(ii)　Vinf.past 末（に）

　　　よく考えた末（に）　(after thinking hard)

Examples

(a) 両者は8時間にわたる交渉の末に、ついに合意に達した。

　　(After eight hours of negotiation, both parties finally came to an agreement.)

(b) 5時間を超える熱戦の末、タイガースが勝った。

　　(After a close game lasting more than five hours, the Tigers won.)

(c) さんざん迷った末に、友達の結婚祝いはコーヒーカップのセットを贈ることにした。

(After much hesitation, I decided to give my friends a set of coffee cups as a wedding present.)

(d) M銀行とU銀行の合併交渉は1年以上も難航した末、やっと成立した。

(After more than a year of difficult merger negotiations, M Bank and U Bank finally came to an agreement.)

(e) 下書きを20枚近く失敗した末に、やっとなんとか気に入った絵ができた。

(After almost twenty bad sketches, I finally managed to draw one I liked.)

(f) 再就職は、苦労した末、過去のコンピュータ経験を評価してくれたIT関係の会社に決まりました。

(After much trouble looking for a new job, I found one with an IT-related company that valued my previous computer experience.)

(g) 男は走って逃げ、最後には暴れ回って抵抗した末に逮捕された。

(The man tried to run away and, in the end, he was arrested after resisting violently.)

(h) この案は、各国の意見が衝突した末の「妥協の産物」だった。

(This plan was a product of compromise, reached after working through a clash of opinions between the countries.)

Notes

1. The *ni* of *sue ni* can be omitted without changing the meaning.

2. *Sue ni* is usually used when someone does something or something takes place after long, hard mental and/or physical work. Thus, *sue ni* cannot be used in the following contexts:

   (1) a. 私は宿題を{*した末に / した後で / してから}友達と食事に出かけた。

      (I went out for dinner with a friend of mine after doing my homework.)

      b. 家を{*出た末に / 出た後で / 出てから}、今日は図書館が休みであることを思い出した。

      (After leaving home, I remembered that the library is closed today.)

c. 少し{??考えた末に / ?考えた後で / 考えてから}パーティーには行か
ないことにした。

(After thinking about it for a while, I decided not to go to the
party.)

In (1c), *kangaeta ato de* is somewhat unnatural because it focuses on the
time sequence of the two actions rather than on the fact that the speaker
had to think for awhile before deciding not to go to the party.

3. When *sue ni* is used with nouns with a specific duration (a week or
longer), it means "at the end of," as in (2).

(2) a. ご注文の品は<u>5月の末</u>に入ります。

(We'll have the item you ordered at the end of May.)

b. <u>来週の末</u>に郊外に引っ越します。

(We're moving to the suburbs at the end of next week.)

c. <u>去年の末</u>に子供が生まれた。

(Our baby was born at the end of last year.)

d. ジミーとは<u>今度の連休の</u>{*末に / 終わりに}会う予定だ。

(I plan to meet with Jimmy at the end of the next string of con-
secutive holidays.)

Note that *sue ni* in (2d) is not acceptable because the duration is too
short.

[**Related Expressions**]

Ato (de) and *nochi (ni)* can be used in place of *sue ni* except when *sue ni*
means "at the end of" (see Note 3). However, *ato (de)* and *nochi (ni)* do not
carry the nuance of "after long, hard work."

[1] a. 試行錯誤の{後(で) / のち(に)}、やっと車に使える燃料電池ができ
た。(cf. KS(A))

b. 一週間悩んだ{後(で) / のち(に)}、家族をおいて単身赴任すること
にした。(cf. KS(B))

c. ご注文の品は5月の{末に / *後(で) / *のち(に)}入ります。(=(2a))

(⇨ ***ato de*** (DBJG: 78-80))

sumu 済む *v.*

| a verb that means "to be finished; to do (in the sense of being enough)" | take/cost/need/etc. only ~; do/manage (without / only with); get by / get away (without / only with); be let off (without / only with); be enough (if); be all right (if); not to have to; there is no need for 【REL. *sumaseru*】 |

◆ **Key Sentences**

(A)

	Number + Counter		
面接は めんせつ	20分	で	済んだ。 す
(The interview took only 20 minutes.)			

(B)

		Noun		
あまり難しい日本語ではなかったので、 むずか		辞書 じしょ	なしで	済んだ。 す
(Because the Japanese (in it) was not very difficult, I managed (to read it) without a dictionary.)				

(C)

	Noun		
旅行先ではどこでもクレジットカードが りょこうさき 使えたので、	現金 げんきん	がなくても	済んだ。 す
(Everywhere I traveled I was able to use my credit card, so I could travel without cash.)			

(D)

	V *te*		
これは	黙っていて だま	済む す	問題ではない。
(This is not the kind of problem where you can get away with staying silent.)			

S

(E)

	Vinf			
ちょっと顔を	**見せる**	だけで	済む	と思う。

(I think just showing up for a while will be enough.)

(F)

	Vneg			
奨学金をもらった ので、お金を	**借り**	{ ずに / なくて (も) / ないで }	済む	と思う。

(I've been given a scholarship, so I think I can get by without borrowing money.)

(G)

	Vcond		
解約したい時は、入会金だけ損を	**すれ**	ば	済む。

(When you want to cancel the agreement, all you will lose is the enrollment fee.)

Formation

(i) Number (+ Counter) で済む

    20ドルで済む (s.t. costs only 20 dollars)

(ii) N{(だけ) / なし}で済む

    電話(だけ)で済む ((just) a telephone call is enough)

    検査なしで済む (not have to have/give an examination; do without an exam)

(iii) N がなくても済む

    携帯電話がなくても済む (manage without a cell phone)

(iv) {Vte / Adj(i)stem くて} 済む

    謝って済む (get away with just apologizing)

    安くて済む (s.t. costs only a little)

(v) Vinf だけで済む

    行くだけで済む (just going is enough; get by with just going)

(vi) Vneg{ずに／なくて(も)／ないで}済む (Exception: する→せずに)

　　行か{ずに／なくて(も)／ないで}済む (do not have to go; be all right if s.o. doesn't go)

(vii){Vcond ば／Vinf.past ら}済む

　　{借りれば／借りたら}済む (be all right if s.o. borrows s.t.)

Examples

(a) この程度の翻訳なら3日で済むだろう。

(Three days should be enough for a translation like this.)

(b) この方法だと今のシステムの大部分がそのまま使えるので、新たな投資が最小で済む。

(Because this approach would allow us to use most of the current system, our new investment will be minimal (lit., we could get by with a minimal investment).)

(c) 徒歩あるいは自転車で済むところへ車で行く無駄をしていませんか。

(Aren't you being wasteful by driving places where you could walk or go by bicycle?)

(d) 15キロオーバーだったが、幸い警告だけで済んだ。

(It was 15 km/hr above (the speed limit), but fortunately I got off with just a warning.)

(e) こんな大きな失敗をして「ごめん」「知らなかった」では済まない。

(You can't excuse a major mistake like this just by saying, "Sorry," or "I didn't know.")

(f) 電動自転車はモーターの力だけで動くことはないから、法律上は「自転車」とされ、運転免許もヘルメットもなしで済む。

(Because electric bicycles are not powered solely by motor, the law classifies them as bicycles, so you can ride them without either a driver's license or a helmet.)

(g) ここからは地下鉄でどこへでも行けるから車がなくても済む。

(From here we can go anywhere by subway, so we don't need a car.)

(h) 謝って済むことと済まないことがある。

(Sometimes an apology is not enough. (lit., There are things that can be settled by apologizing and things that cannot.))

(i) ヘルメットをかぶっていたので、怪我が軽くて済んだ。

(Because I was wearing a helmet, I suffered only minor injuries.)

(j) このソフトは画面上の指示に従って操作するだけで済むので、コンピュータに弱い人でも簡単に使える。

(All you have to do to operate this software is just follow the directions on the screen, so even people who are not computer-savvy can use it with ease.)

(k) 途中で雨が降り出したが、幸い傘を持っていたのでぬれずに済んだ。

(It began to rain on the way, but fortunately I had an umbrella, so I didn't get wet.)

(l) もっと早くこのことを知っていればこんなに悩まなくて済んだのに。

(If I had only known this earlier, I wouldn't have had to worry this much.)

(m) この電子掲示板は自分のメールアドレスを公開しないで済むので安心だ。

(This electronic bulletin board is safe because you don't have to disclose your e-mail address.)

(n) 彼が一言謝ればそれで済むことだ。

(If he would just apologize, it would be enough.)

(o) これは単にソフトウエアを書き換えたら済むという問題じゃない。

(This is not a problem that can be solved by simply recoding the software.)

S

Notes

1. With quantifiers (i.e., Number + Counter), nouns, verbs, adjectives, etc., *sumu* represents the idea that s.t. will/can be done without (or only with) something or a certain action.

2. In V*te sumu*, V represents an action for which little or no effort is required, as in KS(D) and Ex.(h).

3. When the Adj(*i*)stem *kute* precede *sumu*, they represent the idea that something is insignificant or that something happened to a lesser degree than expected, as seen in Ex.(i).

[Related Expression]

Sumaseru (or *sumasu*) is the transitive form of *sumu*, meaning "to finish."

[1] a. ジョンはサンドイッチで昼食を済ませた。

(John made do with a sandwich for lunch.)

    b. 私は後任者への挨拶を電話で済ませた。

(I paid my respects (lit., finished my greetings) to my successor by phone.)

    c. 彼女は1時間でその仕事を済ませた。

(She finished the work in one hour.)

    d. 私は今回の引っ越しを20万円で済ませた。

(I managed to move for (only) 200,000 yen this time.)

S

tada ただ *conj.*

a conjunction that introduces a supplementary remark

but; however; only; the only
thing is that ~
【REL. *nao*; *mottomo*; ***tadashi***】

◆ **Key Sentences**

(A)

Sentence₁		Sentence₂
とてもいいコンピュータだと思います。	ただ	値段(ねだん)が問題ですね。

(I think this is a very good computer. But, the price is a problem.)

(B)

Sentence₁			Sentence₂
彼(かれ)はいい人だ	{が / けど}、	ただ	ちょっと考えが浅(あさ)いところが気に なる。

(He is a nice person, only I'm concerned that he is a little shallow.)

Formation

(i) S₁。ただ、S₂。

    (⇨ KS(A))

(ii) S₁{が / けど}、ただ S₂。

    (⇨ KS(B))

Examples

(a) この故障(こしょう)は直(なお)せないことはないと思います。ただ時間がかかると思います。

    (It's not impossible to repair this problem, only I think it'll take time.)

(b) とても静(しず)かでいいうちだ。ただ近くに店がないので買い物は不便だ。

    (It is a very quiet and nice house, only there are no shops nearby, so it's
    inconvenient for shopping.)

(c) この辺(あた)りは駅にもスーパーにも近くて便利(べんり)だ。ただ環境(かんきょう)があまりよくない。

    (This area is close to both the station and a supermarket, so it's con-
    venient, but the environment is not very good.)

(d) このデジカメは優れた機能をたくさん持っている。ただユーザーインターフェースが悪くて使いにくいのが難点だ。

(This digital camera has many outstanding functions. However, the problem is that it's hard to use because the user interface is bad.)

(e) たいていのことは私がいなくても他の者が代わりにやってくれるが、ただこの仕事は他の者に頼むわけにはいかない。

(For most things, if I'm not available others can do it for me; however, as far as this job is concerned, I cannot ask someone else to do it for me.)

Notes

1. *Tada* is used when the speaker/writer makes a supplementary remark. Such remarks are usually contrary to what is expected from the previous sentence. For example, if the preceding remark is positive, the supplementary remark will be negative and vice versa.

2. This conjunctional use of *tada* should not be confused with another *tada*, an adverb which emphasizes the idea of "only," as shown in (1).

   (1) a. これが彼のただ一つの欠点だ。

   (This is his only defect.)

   b. 彼女はただの一日も休んだことがない。

   (She hasn't taken even one day off.)

   c. 私はただ言われたことをやっているだけだ。

   (I'm just doing what I was told; that's all.)

   (⇨ ***tada*** (DIJG: 445-48))

3. *Tada* may appear at the beginning of a sentence when the statement that is supposed to occur before *tada* is understood from the context, as shown in (2).

   (2) A: こんなにしていただいてどうもありがとう。

   (Thank you very much for doing all this for me.)

   B: いや、ただこれは人には言わないでほしいんだ。

   (Not at all, but I'd rather you not mention it to others.)

【Related Expressions】

I. *Nao* "as another piece of information" is also used when the speaker/
writer provides additional, related information. Unlike *tada*, however,
nao does not imply that the following statement is contrary to the preceding statement.

[1] a. これを持ちまして第5回国際環境学会を閉会いたします。皆様、ご参
加ありがとうございました。{なお/*ただ}、予稿集は10月に発刊
される予定です。

(This concludes the Fifth International Conference on the Environment. Thank you very much for your participation, ladies and
gentlemen. For your information, the proceedings are scheduled
to be published in October.)

b. 会員には学会誌(年2回)と会報(年4回)が送られます。{なお/
*ただ}、来月お届けする学会誌は環境問題の特集号です。

(The Association's journals (twice a year) and the Association's
newsletters (four times a year) are sent to you. (By the way,)
the journal you'll receive next month is a special issue on
environmental problems.)

As seen in the above examples, *nao* is usually used when someone
gives formal notification to a group of people or to the general public.

(⇨ **nao** (in this volume))

II. *Mottomo* "although" is also used when one makes a supplementary
remark, and can be used in place of *tada* in most situations, as demonstrated in [2].

[2] a. とてもいいコンピュータだと思います。{ただ/もっとも}値段が問
題ですね。(= KS(A))

b. この故障は直せないことはないと思います。{ただ/もっとも}時間
がかかると思います。(= Ex.(a))

c. とても静かでいいうちだ。{ただ/もっとも}近くに店がないので買
い物は不便だ。(= Ex.(b))

Mottomo, however, cannot be used after conjunctions like *ga* and *kedo*,
as shown in [3a]. [3b] is acceptable because *mottomo* is in sentence-
initial position.

[3] a. 彼はいい人だ｛が／けど｝、｛ただ／*もっとも｝ちょっと考えが浅い
ところが気になる。(= KS(B))

b. 彼はいい人だ。｛ただ／もっとも｝ちょっと考えが浅いところが気に
なる。

(He is a nice person. But I'm concerned that he is a little
shallow.)

(⇨ ***mottomo*** (in this volume))

tadashi   ただし［但し］   *conj.*

| a conjunction indicating that there is a condition, restriction, proviso, etc., to the preceding statement. | however; but; only; here; provided that 【REL. *tada*】 |

◆ Key Sentences

(A)

Sentence₁		Sentence₂
この部屋にある雑誌や本はどれを見てもいいです。	ただし、	部屋からは持ち出さないで下さい。

(You may look at any of the magazines or books in this room. However, please do not take them out of the room.)

(B)

Sentence₁		Sentence₂
当館の開館時間は午前9時から午後6時まで。	但し、	特別行事がある場合はこの限りではない。

(This hall is open from 9 a.m. to 6 p.m. However, for special events, the hall is not limited to these hours.)

Formation

S₁。ただし、S₂。

　(⇨ KS(A) and (B))

Examples

(a) 試験の時、辞書を見てもいいです。ただし、和英辞典だけです。

　　(You may consult dictionaries during the exam. However, (you may use) only Japanese-English dictionaries.)

(b) この製品は定価の3割引きで販売しています。ただし、返品はできません。

　　(We sell this product at 30 percent off the list price. But we cannot accept returns.)

(c) 問題があったらいつでも相談して下さい。ただし、お金の問題は相談に乗れません。

　　(Please (feel free to) talk to me whenever you have a problem. However, I cannot help you with money matters.)

(d) 発表のトピックは何でもかまいません。ただし、発表時間は20分以内です。

　　(You can choose any topic for your presentation. However, the presentation should be 20 minutes or fewer.)

(e) 実習時間は午前8時30分から午後5時30分まで。但し、12時から1時までは休憩時間とする。

　　(The hours of the internship are from 8:30 a.m. to 5:30 p.m. However, there will be a break from 12:00 to 1:00.)

(f) 総会の議決は会員の過半数を以って決定される。但し、規定改定はこの限りではない。

　　(Decisions at the general meeting are passed by a majority of the members. However this does not apply to revisions of the regulations.)

(g) 第7条(出張の経路等)　出張の経路とその利用交通機関は、経済性を重視して選ぶことを原則とする。但し、特別の理由がある場合はこの限りではない。

　　(Article 7 (Routes of business trips, etc.): As a rule, for business travel, choose routes and means of transportation with economy in mind (lit., placing the most importance on economy). However, there can be exceptions when there is a special reason.)

(h) V=IR　ただし、VはAB間の電位差、Iは電流、Rは抵抗

　　(V=IR where V is the potential difference between Points A and B, I is the electric current, and R is the resistance.)

1. *Tadashi*, composed of the adverb *tada* "only" and the emphatic particle *shi*, is used when the statement made by the preceding sentence is not complete and the speaker/writer wants to complete it by adding a condition, restriction, exception or additional remark.

2. *Tadashi* often appears in highly formal documents such as rules, regulations, provisions, agreements and contracts, as in KS(B), Exs.(e)-(g).

3. *Tadashi* is also used to tell what a symbol in a formula indicates, as in Ex.(h).

4. The preceding sentence S₁ usually ends with a period, but it can be followed by *ga* or a similar conjunction, as in (1).

> (1) この部屋にある雑誌や本はどれを見てもいいですが、ただし、部屋からは持ち出さないで下さい。(cf. KS(A))

【Related Expression】

Tada is similar to *tadashi* in that they are both used when making a supplementary remark after presenting a statement. For example, *tada* and *tadashi* are both acceptable in [1].

> [1] a. ソフトウエアのアップグレードは無料です。{ただし / ただ}、CDをご希望の場合は、実費と送料（5ドル）が必要です。
>
> (To upgrade your software is free. But, if you want it on CD, you will need to pay for the cost of the CD and postage ($5).)
>
> b. この故障は直せないことはないと思います。{ただし / ただ}、時間がかかると思います。
>
> (It's not impossible to repair this problem, but I think it'll take time.)
>
> c. この辺りは駅にもスーパーにも近くて便利だ。{ただし / ただ}、環境があまりよくない。
>
> (This area is close to both the station and a supermarket, so it's convenient, but the environment is not very good.)

One of the differences is that remarks following *tadashi* usually involve something that affects the hearer directly, whereas this is not necessarily the case with *tada*. Thus, as shown in [2], if the speaker is simply telling the hearer about personal preferences or restrictions that won't affect the hearer, *tada* is natural but *tadashi* sounds rather odd.

T

[2]　a. 彼_{かれ}はいい人だ。{ただ / ??ただし}、私_{わたし}個人_{こじん}はあまり好きではない。

(He is a nice man, but I personally do not like him so much.)

　　b. ここはカニがとてもおいしいそうだ。{ただ / ??ただし}、私はアレ
ルギーのためカニは食べられない。

(I've heard that crabs here are delicious. However, I cannot eat them because of an allergy.)

Another difference is that *tadashi* is usually used to add a condition, restriction, etc., but *tada* is not (particularly in written rules, regulations, agreements and contracts). Thus, *tada* is not acceptable in the following examples:

[3]　a. 当館の開館時間は午前9時から午後6時まで。{但し / *ただ}、特別
行事がある場合はこの限りではない。(= KS(B))

　　b. 実習時間は午前8時30分から午後5時30分まで。{但し / *ただ}、
12時から1時までは休憩時間とする。(= Ex.(e))

(⇨ ***tada*** (in this volume))

---

takaga　たかが　　*noun modifier*

a noun modifier used when the speaker thinks little of the referent of the modified noun or noun phrase

only; just; mere
【REL. *tada no*; *tatta*】

◆ **Key Sentences**

(A)

	Noun Phrase		
たかが	子供_{こども}の言ったこと	だ。	そんなに深刻_{しんこく}に考えることはない。

(It's just something a child told you. You don't have to take it so seriously.)

(B)

	Noun			
たかが	漫画	（くらい）	と	馬鹿にしてはいけない。

(You shouldn't make light of it saying it's just a cartoon.)

(C)

	Noun Phrase			
たかが	車の故障	（くらい）	で	そんなに大騒ぎする必要はない。

(You don't need to make such a big fuss over a little car trouble.)

(D)

		Vinf		
たかが	無断で自転車を	借りた	くらい（のこと）	で

そんなに怒らなくてもいいでしょう。

(You don't have to get so mad at me just for borrowing your bicycle without asking.)

(E)

Noun Phrase			
人間一人の知恵	など	たかが	知れている。

(One person's wisdom doesn't amount to much.)

Formation

(i) たかが N だ

　　たかが子供だ　(s.o. is only a child)

(ii) たかが {N / Number (+ Counter)} （くらい） {と / で}

　　たかがレポート（くらい）と　(thinking/saying that it's only a report)

　　たかがレポート（くらい）で　(over just a report)

　　たかが二人（くらい）と　(thinking/saying that (there are only) two people)

　　たかが二人（くらい）で　(with just two people)

(iii) たかが〜{V / Adj(*i*)}inf くらい(のこと)で

たかが英語が{できる / できた}くらい(のこと)で (just because s.o.
can/could speak English; just for (things like) being able to speak
English)

たかが成績が{悪い / 悪かった}くらい(のこと)で (just because s.o.'s
performance is/was poor; just for (things like) s.o.'s poor
performance)

(iv) たかが〜 Adj(*na*)stem{な / だった}くらい(のこと)で

たかが料理が下手{な / だった}くらい(のこと)で (just because s.o. is/
was bad at cooking; just for (something like) being a poor cook)

Examples

(a) たかが喫煙じゃないか。どうしてそんなに犯罪者のように言われなきゃなら
ないんだ。

(It's only smoking. Why do they have to talk about us as if we were
criminals?)

(b) たかがノートくらいと言われるかもしれませんが、僕にとってはとても大事
なものなんです。

(You may say it's just a notebook, but to me it's very important.)

(c) たかが 10 万円で何ができると言うのですか。

(What do you expect us to do with only 100,000 yen?)

(d) たかがアパート探しくらいで君に面倒をかけたくない。

(I don't want to bother you with just apartment hunting.)

(e) たかが転んだくらいで救急車を呼ぶなんて大げさだ。

(It is overreacting to call an ambulance just for falling down.)

(f) 公共事業によって景気が回復する領域などたかが知れている。

(There's hardly any area in which the economy can be improved
through public projects.)

(g) たかが椅子。しかし、これによって仕事の能率が大きく左右されるし健康に
も影響する。

(It's just (a matter of) a chair. But it can affect your productivity at work
and influence your health.)

(h) たかが風邪、されど風邪。

(It's just a cold, but it is a cold.)

Notes

1. *Takaga* is used when the speaker/writer thinks something is not serious, valuable or significant, or that someone is not important.

2. *Takaga* usually modifies nouns or noun equivalents, including noun phrases ending with *kurai (no koto)* "things like ~." One exception is when *takaga* is used in the set phrase *takaga shirete iru* "not much at all," as in KS(E) and Ex.(f), in which case *takaga* modifies the predicate *shirete iru* "lit., to be known."

3. When *takaga* precedes a noun or a number with a counter, *kurai* (or *gurai*) after the noun or the counter is optional, as in KS(B), (C) and Ex.(c). However, if *takaga* precedes verbs or adjectives (not necessarily immediately), *kurai* (or *gurai*) must follow the verb or adjective, as in KS(D) and Ex.(e).

[Related Expressions]

When *takaga* modifies a number, the sentence can be rephrased using *tada no* or *tatta*, as in [1].

> [1] ｛たかが／ただの／たった｝10 万円で何ができると言うのですか。
>
> > (= Ex.(c))

The major difference between *takaga* and *tada no / tatta* is that *takaga* can be used only when the speaker thinks that something is not serious, valuable or significant, or that someone is not important. Thus in [2], *takaga* cannot be used. Note that in [1], the speaker thinks that 100,000 yen is not a significant amount of money.

> [2] この車は｛ただの／たった／＊たかが｝50 万円で買えた。
>
> (I was able to buy this car for only 500,000 yen.)

> (⇨ ***tada no*** (DIJG: 449-50))

T

ta nari (de)　たなり（で）　　*conj.*

| a conjunction indicating that a situation or condition remains unaltered | without; while ~ staying; while ~ keep ~ing 【REL. *mama (de)*】 |

◆ **Key Sentences**

(A)

	Vinf.past			
彼は椅子に	腰掛けた	なり	（で）、	ずっと黙っていた。

| (He sat in the chair and stayed there, silent the whole time.) |

(B)

	Vinf.past			Noun		
片足を	上げた	なり	の	格好	で、	数秒間目をつぶるように言われた。

| (I was told to close my eyes for a few seconds while I kept lifting one foot off the ground.) |

Formation

(i)　Vinf.past なり（で）

　　　行ったなり（で）　(s.o. went there never to return)

　　　横になったなり（で）　(s.o. lay down (without getting up))

(ii)　Vinf.past なりの N

　　　立ったなりの姿勢　(a standing posture (maintained))

Examples

(a) 純一は 17 歳の時にフランスに行ったなりで、日本には帰らず画家になって、今ではモンマルトルに住みついている。

(Junichi went to France when he was 17 and never came back to Japan; he became a painter and now has settled in Montmartre.)

(b) エリサは『源氏物語』を買ったなり、一ページも読まず、本棚に置きっぱなしだった。

(Elisa bought *The Tale of Genji*, but she left it on the bookshelf without reading a single page.)

(c) 彼は私の部屋の入り口に突っ立ったなりでニヤニヤ笑っていた。

(My sweetheart stood at the entrance to my room, grinning.)

(d) 妻がドアを開けてくれたんですけど、私はもう倒れたなりで、体が動きませんでした。

(My wife opened the door for me, but I had fallen down and couldn't move an inch.)

(e) 腰をよじったなりの姿勢で長時間座っていたので、立てないほど腰が痛くなった。

(Because I was sitting for a long time with my lower back twisted, it hurt so much I couldn't stand up.)

(f) 人形がほこりをかぶったなりで棚に乗っかっている。

(The doll sits on a shelf, covered with dust.)

Notes

1. *Ta nari (de)* conveys the idea that a condition or situation that has already happened remains unaltered.

2. *Nari (de)* sounds slightly archaic, but can be used in both spoken and written Japanese.

3. The verb of "Vinf.past *nari no* N" is limited to some movement verbs such as *ageru* "raise," *suwaru* "sit down," *koshi-kakeru* "sit down," *yojiru* "twist," etc. When the verb is used in "V$_1$inf.past *ra*, V$_2$inf.past *nari no*" (where V$_1$ and V$_2$ are identical), it means "way/style proper to s.o. or s.t.," as shown in (1). (⇨ ***nari ni*** (DIJG: 227-29))

(1) a. 50を過ぎたら、50を過ぎたなりの頑張り方がある。

   (If you are over 50 years old, there should be ways to make efforts appropriate for 50 year-olds.)

   b. 勉強しなかったらしなかったなりの結果が出る。

   (If you don't study you should get the result you deserve.)

【Related Expression】

Ta mama (de) means exactly the same as *ta nari (de)*, but, unlike *ta nari (de)*, it is commonly used in both spoken and written Japanese.

[1] a. 彼は椅子に腰かけた{なり/まま}(で)、ずっと黙っていた。

(= KS(A))

b. 妻がドアを開けてくれたんですけど、私はもう倒れた{なり/まま}
で、体が動きませんでした。(= Ex.(d))

However, there are at least two ways in which *mama (de)* and *nari (de)* differ syntactically.

First, *mama (de)* can be preceded by a negative verb, but *nari (de)* cannot.

[2] a. ドアを閉めない{まま/*なり}(で)出かけてしまった。
(I left my house without closing the door.)

b. 彼女はさよならの挨拶をしない{まま/*なり}(で)行ってしまった。
(She went away without saying goodbye.)

Secondly, *ta nari* cannot precede *da/desu* and *datta/deshita*.

[3] a. 松の木が暴風で倒れた{まま/??なり}だ。
(A pine tree remains (where it was) knocked down by a stormy wind.)

b. 彼は1964年にアメリカに行った{まま/??なり}だった。
(He went to the U.S. never to return.)

(⇨ *mama* (DBJG: 236-40))

T

tan'i de 単位で   *phr.*

a phrase that indicates the smallest amount, number or unit of s.t. (or people) involved

by the; in sets/groups/lots/etc. of; in multiples of; each; every
【REL. *zutsu*; *goto ni*】

◆ **Key Sentences**

(A)

	Number + Counter		
この ATM は	千円	単位で	お金を引き出すことができる。

(You can withdraw money from this ATM in multiples of 1,000 yen.)

(B)

	Unit		
この社内調査では	課	単位で	リサイクル実施率を調べる。

(This in-house investigation will examine the recycling rate for each section.)

Formation

(i) （Number +）Counter 単位で

　　10人単位で　(in groups of ten)

(ii) Unit 単位で

　　市単位で　(by city)

Examples

(a) 日本では湯飲みは5個単位で売られることが多い。

(In Japan, tea cups are often sold in sets of five.)

(b) B社の新しいデータ通信サービスは、最低契約量である150時間分のデータ通信を1分単位で利用できる。

(B Company's new data communication service allows the user to transmit and receive data in one-minute units for a minimum contract amount of 150 hours.)

(c) 我が社は今回のアジアからの労働者派遣が成功した場合には、次回から規模を大幅に拡大し、千人単位で派遣する予定だ。

(If our company's plan to send laborers from Asia is successful this time, next time we will greatly expand the scale and send laborers in groups of 1,000.)

T

(d) オンライン書店のZ社は、本をページまたは章単位で販売するそうだ。

(They say the online bookstore Z is going to sell books by the page or the chapter.)

(e) このプロジェクト管理ソフトの新バージョンでは、これまで日単位で行われていた計画と管理を時間・分単位で行えるようになった。

(This new version of the project management software application allows us to plan and manage (our operations) by the hour and minute, instead of the day.)

Notes

1. X *tan'i de* means that X is the smallest amount, number or unit of something (or people) involved in or required for doing something, and that greater amounts/numbers are multiples of X. For example, in KS(A), the minimum amount of money one can withdraw is 1,000 yen, and the next greater amount is 2,000 yen, etc. In KS(B), the smallest unit of the investigation is a section of the company. In this sentence, the meaning of *tan'i de* is equivalent to "every" or "each."

2. When the particle *ni* follows *tan'i*, the phrase means "every" or "each," as shown in (1).

(1) a. 研究グループ単位に特別端末が1台設置された。

(A special terminal was installed for every research group.)

b. この教科書は章単位に練習問題がつけてある。

(This textbook has a set of exercise questions in each chapter.)

Because *tan'i de* in KS(B) is equivalent to "each" (see Note 1), *tan'i ni* can replace it, as in (2).

(2) この社内調査では課単位{で／に}リサイクル実施率を調べる。

(= KS(B))

[Related Expressions]

I. *Zutsu* looks similar to *tan'i ni*, but it means "at a time; each"; therefore, the two expressions are not interchangeable. The meaning of KS(A) changes if *zutsu* replaces *tan'i de*, as shown in [1a]. *Zutsu* cannot be used in KS(B).

[1] a. このATMは千円ずつ引き出すことができる。(cf. KS(A))

(You can withdraw 1,000 yen at a time from this ATM.)

b. この社内調査では課｛単位で / *ずつ｝リサイクル実施率を調べる。

(= KS(B))

Note that *zutsu* cannot be replaced by *tan'i de* either.

[2] a. 私は毎日漢字を 5 つ｛ずつ / *単位で｝覚える。

(I memorize five kanji every day.)

b. 私たちは奨学金応募者を 2 人｛ずつ / *単位で｝面接した。

(We interviewed two scholarship applicants at a time.)

c. 子供たちにキャンディーを 5 つ｛ずつ / *単位で｝あげた。

(I gave five candies to each child.)

(⇨ ***zutsu*** (DBJG: 572-73))

II. *Goto ni* "every" can replace *tan'i ni* (or *tan'i de* when its meaning is equivalent to "every" or "each"), as shown in [3].

[3] a. 研究グループ｛単位に / ごとに｝特別端末が 1 台設置された。(= (1a))

b. この教科書は章｛単位に / ごとに｝練習問題がつけてある。(= (1b))

c. この社内調査では課｛単位で / ごとに｝リサイクル実施率を調べる。

(= KS(B))

When *tan'i de* does not mean "every" or "each," *goto ni* cannot replace it.

[4] a. このATMは千円｛単位で / *ごとに｝お金を引き出すことができる。

(= KS(A))

b. 日本では湯飲みは 5 個｛単位で / *ごとに｝売られることが多い。

(= Ex.(a))

T

Note that X *goto ni* cannot be replaced by *tan'i de* either, when X is not the smallest amount, number or unit of something (or people) involved in or required for doing something.

[5] a. そのバスは 20 分｛ごとに / *単位で｝来る。

(The bus comes every 20 minutes.)

b. お正月なので家｛ごとに / *単位で｝国旗が出ている。

(Because today is New Year's Day, the national flag is flying at each house.)

(⇨ ***goto ni*** (DBJG: 128-30))

tan ni 単^{たん}に　*adv.*

```
⌇⌇⌇⌇⌇⌇⌇⌇⌇⌇⌇⌇⌇⌇⌇⌇⌇⌇⌇⌇⌇⌇⌇⌇
an adverb that means "simply"
⌇⌇⌇⌇⌇⌇⌇⌇⌇⌇⌇⌇⌇⌇⌇⌇⌇⌇⌇⌇⌇⌇⌇⌇
```

just; only; simply; no more than; nothing but; solely; merely; alone
【REL. *tada*; *ni suginai*】

◆ **Key Sentences**

(A)

		Noun Phrase	
これは	単^{たん}に	文化^{ぶんか}の違^{ちが}いの問題	だ。

(This is simply a matter/problem of cultural differences.)

(B)

			Vinf		
この車は	単^{たん}に	ボディーのデザインを	変^かえた	だけ	だ。

(They did nothing more to this car than change the body design.)

(C)

			Adj(*na*)stem			
仕事^{しごと}が難^{むずか}しいのではなく、	単^{たん}に	私が	不器用^{ぶきよう}	な	だけ	です。

(It's not that the job is difficult; it's simply that I'm clumsy.)

(D)

		Noun Phrase		Prt.	
円高^{えんだか}の影響^{えいきょう}は	単^{たん}に	輸出^{ゆしゅつ}	だけ	に	とどまらない。

(The effects of the high yen are not limited to exports.)

(E)

		Noun Phrase	
これは	単^{たん}に	私個人^{わたしこじん}の意見	に過^すぎない。

(This is nothing more than my personal opinion.)

Formation

(i) 単に NP だ

　　単に選択の問題だ　(s.t. is simply a matter of choice)

(ii) 単に {V / Adj(*i*)} inf だけ

　　単に (英語を) {話す / 話した} だけ　(simply that s.o. speaks/spoke (English))

　　単に (手数料が) {安い / 安かった} だけ　(simply that (the handling charge) is/was low)

(iii) 単に Adj(*na*)stem {な / である / だった / であった} だけ

　　単に (周りが) 静か {な / である / だった / であった} だけ　(simply that (the neighborhood) is/was quiet)

(iv) 単に N {である / だった / であった} だけ

　　単に (先生が) 外国人 {である / だった / であった} だけ　(simply that (the teacher) is/was a foreigner)

(v) 単に NP だけ Prt.

　　単に学会の報告だけ {が / を / に / で / etc.}　(just the conference report (is/was/etc.); (read/copy/etc.) just the conference report; just (in/with/etc.) the conference report)

(vi) 単に NP に過ぎない

　　単に根拠のない噂に過ぎない　(s.t. is nothing more than a groundless rumor)

Examples

(a) それは単に解釈の問題だ。

　　(It's simply an issue of interpretation.)

(b) これは単にあなた一人の問題ではない。

　　(This is not just a problem for you alone.)

(c) この文章は単に原文を直訳しただけだ。

　　(This text is simply something that was translated literally from the original.)

(d) 当ホテルは単に安いだけでなく、行き届いたサービスで快適にお過ごしいただけます。

　　(Our hotel is not simply inexpensive; with our comprehensive array of services, you can stay (with us) in comfort.)

T

(e) 今は単に多くの利益を上げているだけでは一流企業とは言えない。

(Today, a company that simply racks up large profits cannot be called a first-class company.)

(f) このカメラは、単に被写体にカメラを向けてシャッターを押すだけで高画質の写真を撮ることができる。

(With this camera you can take high quality pictures just by holding it toward an object and clicking the shutter.)

(g) 彼は考えが一貫しているのではなく、単に頑固なだけだ。

(He is not consistent in his thinking; he's simply stubborn.)

(h) 私は単に生まれがドイツだっただけで、ドイツ語はもちろんドイツのことは何も知らない。

(Germany is no more than my birthplace (lit., It is simply that my birthplace is Germany), so I know nothing about Germany, let alone German.)

(i) 雅夫は単に数学だけができないのではない。

(It's not that Masao is poor only at math.)

(j) この場合、単にアグネスだけを非難するのは間違っている。

(In this case, it's wrong to blame only Agnes.)

(k) それは単に君の憶測に過ぎない。

(It's nothing more than your speculation.)

(l) ただ単に飲むだけの集まりなら参加しても意味がない。

(If it's just to get together and drink, there's no point in participating.)

(m) ただ単に犯行推定時間の前に現場近くにいたという事実だけで彼を犯人だと決めつけることはできない。

(You cannot decide that he is the culprit based simply on the fact that he was near the crime site before the estimated time of the crime.)

Notes

1. When *tan ni* is used with *dake* "only," *tan ni* functions simply as an emphatic element and can be omitted.

2. When *tan ni* is used in the "A *wa* B *da*" pattern, the presence of *dake* changes the meaning, as seen in (1) and (2). (Note that in (1b) and (2b) *tan ni* is emphatic and optional.)

(1) a. 彼の問題は単に技術的な問題だ。

(His problem is simply a problem of technical skills. [Talking about a soccer player.])

   b. 彼の問題は(単に)技術的な問題だけだ。

(The only problem he has is (just) technical skills.)

(2) a. 彼の問題は単に技術的な問題ではない。

(His problem isn't simply one of technical skills.)

   b. 彼の問題は(単に)技術的な問題だけではない。

((Just) Technical skills aren't his only problem.)

(1a) and (2a) are about the nature of someone's problem, while (1b) and (2b) are about the existence of a problem, more specifically, about whether or not someone has only one type of problem.

As seen in (3), *dake* cannot be used in the "A *wa* B *da*" sentence in KS(A) because this sentence is not about the existence of a problem.

(3) これは単に文化の違いの問題{ø / *だけ}だ。(= KS(A))

3. In the sentence pattern demonstrated in KS(D), either *tan ni* or *dake* or both can appear, as shown in (4). The meaning remains the same.

(4) a. 円高の影響は単に輸出だけにとどまらない。(= KS(D))

   b. 円高の影響は ø 輸出だけにとどまらない。

   c. 円高の影響は単に輸出 ø にとどまらない。

4. In KS(E), *dake* cannot be used.

(5) これは単に私個人の意見{ø / *だけ}に過ぎない。(= KS(E))

This is because (6a) is ungrammatical. The correct way to express the meaning of (6a) is (6b).

(6) a. *これは(単に)私の意見だけだ。

   (This is just my opinion.)

   b. これは{ただの / 単なる}私の意見だ。

5. The prenominal form (i.e., the form that modifies nouns) of *tan ni* is *tan naru*.

(7) それは単なる(=ただの)彼の誤解だ。

(That's simply his misunderstanding.)

(⇨ ***tada no*** (DIJG: 449-50))

6.　*Tada* may precede *tan ni* for emphasis, as in Exs.(l) and (m).

[Related Expressions]

I.　*Tada* functions in the same way as *tan ni* when it occurs with verb phrases and adjective phrases followed by *dake*.

[1]　a. この車は{単に / ただ}ボディーのデザインを変えただけだ。

(= KS(B))

　　　b. このアパートは{単に / ただ}家賃が安いだけだ。

(The rent for this apartment is cheap, and that's all.)

　　　c. このアパートは{単に / ただ}会社へ行くのに便利なだけだ。

(This apartment is convenient to the office, and that's all.)

However, in the following sentence patterns, *tada* is either unnatural or unacceptable.

[2]　a. これは{単に /*ただ}文化の違いの問題だ。(= KS(A))

　　　b. これは{単に /*ただ}あなた一人の問題ではない。(= Ex.(b))

　　　c. 円高の影響は{単に / ??ただ}輸出だけにとどまらない。(= KS(D))

　　　d. これは{単に / ??ただ}私個人の意見に過ぎない。(= KS(E))

On the other hand, in the following uses, *tan ni* is either unnatural or unacceptable.

[3]　a. 私は{ただ /*単に}弁護士だけが頼りだ。

(I have no one else to rely on but my lawyer.)

　　　b. {ただ /*単に}これだけは分かってもらいたい。

(I want you to understand (just) this, at least.)

Another difference is that *tada* can modify quantifiers but *tan ni* cannot.

[4]　a. {ただ /*単に}一人の肉親に死なれた。

(My only relative died (and I suffered).)

b. ｛ただの / *単に｝一日も休んだことがない。

(I haven't missed even a single day.)

(⇨ ***tada*** (DIJG: 445-48))

II. The sentence final phrase *ni suginai* "nothing more than" is synonymous with *tan ni*. Thus, sentences with *tan ni* meaning "nothing more than" can be rephrased using *ni suginai*, as shown in [5].

[5]　a. この車はボディーのデザインを変えた（だけ）に**過ぎない**。(cf. KS(B))

b. 仕事が難しいのではなく、私が不器用なだけに**過ぎない**。(cf. KS(C))

c. それは解釈の問題に**過ぎない**。(cf. Ex.(a))

Note that *tan ni* can be used with *ni suginai* for emphasis, as in KS(E), Ex.(k) and [6].

[6]　a. この車は**単に**ボディーのデザインを変えた（だけ）に**過ぎない**。

(cf. [5a])

b. 仕事が難しいのではなく、**単に**私が不器用なだけに**過ぎない**。(cf. [5b])

c. それは**単に**解釈の問題に**過ぎない**。(cf. [5c])

(⇨ ***ni suginai*** (DIJG: 271-74))

T

taruya　たるや　　*comp. prt.*　<w>

| a compound particle used to present a subtopic about which the writer provides surprising or impressive information | when it comes to ~; speaking of 【REL. *to kitara*; *wa*】 |

◆ **Key Sentence**

		Noun		
この湖_{みずうみ}にはここにしかいないという生物がおり、	その	数_{かず}	たるや	50種類_{しゅるい}を超_こえる。

(There are creatures in this lake that exist only here; in fact, there are more than 50 species.)

Formation

N たるや

その成績_{せいせき}たるや   (when it comes to s.o.'s performance)

Examples

(a) ノーベル文学賞_{ぶんがくしょう}はどうやって選考_{せんこう}するのだろう。1年間に世界で発表_{はっぴょう}される文学作品の数_{かず}たるや膨大_{ぼうだい}なものだと思うのだが。

(How do they ever choose (who wins) the Nobel Prize in Literature? (I think) The number of works of literature published around the world in a year must be enormous.)

(b) 1987年春_{はる}、彼_{かれ}はついにデビューを果_はたした。しかし、その初戦_{しょせん}の結果_{けっか}たるや散々_{さんざん}なものだった。

(In the spring of 1987, he finally made his debut. But, the result of that first match was so miserable.)

(c) 彼_{かれ}のバンジョーは最高だ。特にその速弾_{はやび}きテクニックたるやたぶん世界でも彼の右に出る者はいないのではないだろうか。

(His banjo playing is the best. Particularly when it comes to his fast plucking technique, I can't imagine anyone in the world who could do it better.)

(d) このダイエット教室の参加費_{さんかひ}は決_{けっ}して安くはないが、その効果_{こうか}たるや絶大_{ぜつだい}である。

(The fee for joining this diet class is certainly not cheap, but the results are tremendous!)

(e) ロボカップは、サッカーをするロボットの世界一を競う大会である。1997
年に名古屋で第1回大会が開かれて以来、国際大会が毎年開かれてきたが、
その間の「選手」の技量の向上たるや著しい。

(RoboCup is a competition where soccer-playing robots compete to be
first in the world. Since the first championship was held in Nagoya in
1997, an international competition has been held every year, and the
"players'" skills have shown remarkable improvement since the first
tournament.)

Notes

1. Etymologically, *taruya* consists of *taru*, the noun-modifying form of
   tari (the classic version of *de aru*), and the exclamatory, sentence-final
   particle *ya*. However, in contemporary Japanese, *taruya* functions as
   a topic marker, used when the speaker/writer provides surprising or
   impressive information about the topic. It is used only in writing.

2. *Taruya* is usually used to present a subtopic when the writer mentions a
   specific aspect of something or someone that has been presented earlier
   as a major topic. Note that in many of the examples above, the subtopic
   (i.e., the noun phrases marked by *taruya*) begins with *sono*, which refers
   to the major topic mentioned earlier.

[Related Expressions]

I. *To kitara* is also used to present a topic when the speaker/writer provides
    surprising information. Note that *to kitara* is used in both written and
    spoken language.

　　[1] a. この湖にはここにしかいないという生物がおり、その数｜たるや／と
　　　　　来たら｜50種類を超える。(= KS)

　　　　b. ノーベル文学賞はどうやって選考するのだろう。1年間に世界で発表
　　　　　される文学作品の数｜たるや／と来たら｜膨大なものだと思うのだが。
　　　　　　　　　　　　　　　　　　　　　　　　　　　　　　(= Ex.(a))

　　　　c. 1987年春、彼はついにデビューを果たした。しかし、その初戦の結
　　　　　果｜たるや／と来たら｜散々なものだった。(= Ex.(b))

　　　　d. 彼のバンジョーは最高だ。特にその速弾きテクニック｜たるや／と来
　　　　　たら｜たぶん世界でも彼の右に出る者はいないのではないだろうか。
　　　　　　　　　　　　　　　　　　　　　　　　　　　　　　(= Ex.(c))

II. The topic marker *wa* can be used in place of *taruya*. However, *wa* does not convey the idea that the writer is surprised or impressed by the information.

(⇨ ***wa***[1] (DBJG: 516-19))

(t)tatte[1]   （っ）たって[1]   *conj.*   \<s\>

the informal form of *te mo*

even if; if; whether; no matter what/who/how/etc.
【REL. *te mo*】

◆ **Key Sentences**

(A)

	Vinf.past		
一人で旅行に	行った	って	面白くない。

(It's not fun traveling (lit., if I travel) alone.)

(B)

	Adj(*i*)stem			
私は少しくらい	高	く	（っ）たって、	質のいいものを買うことにしている。

(I make it a rule to buy good quality things even if they are a little more expensive.)

(C)

	Adj(*na*)stem		
いくら日本語が	上手	だって	専門知識がなかったらこの翻訳はできないよ。

(No matter how good someone's Japanese is, he/she cannot do this translation without technical knowledge (in this field).)

(D)

Noun		
プロ	だって	失敗^{しっぱい}することもある。

(Even professionals make mistakes. (lit., Even if he is a professional, there are times when he makes a mistake.))

Formation

(i) Vinf.past って

　　帰ったって　(even if s.o. returns)　＝帰っても

　　見たって　(even if s.o. looks at s.t.)　＝見ても

(ii) Adj(*i*)stem く(っ)たって

　　高く(っ)たって　(even if s.t. is expensive)　＝高くても

(iii) {Adj(*na*)stem / N} だって

　　不便だって　(even if s.t. is inconvenient)　＝不便でも

　　学生だって　(even if s.o. is a student)　＝学生でも

(iv) {Vneg / Adj(*i*)stem く / Adj(*na*)stem じゃ / N じゃ} なく(っ)たって

　　行かなく(っ)たって　(even if s.o. does not go)　＝行かなくても

　　安くなく(っ)たって　(even if s.t. is not cheap)　＝安くなくても

　　便利^{べんり}じゃなく(っ)たって　(even if s.t. is not convenient)　＝便利じゃなくても

　　学生じゃなく(っ)たって　(even if s.o. is not a student)　＝学生じゃなくても

Examples

(a) 仕事を変^かえたって問題は解決^{かいけつ}しない。

　　(Even if you change your job, it won't solve the problem.)

(b) 苦^{くる}しくったって諦^{あきら}めちゃいけない。

　　(Even if it's a struggle, you shouldn't give up.)

(c) 古くたって新しくたって、よいものはよいのだ。

　　(Whether it's old or new, a good thing is good.)

T

(d) いくら通勤に便利だってこの家賃は高すぎる。

(No matter how convenient (the location) is for commuting, the rent is too high.)

(e) 誰だってそんなことを言われたら腹が立つよ。

(No matter who it is, anyone would get mad if you said that to him.)

(f) コンピュータがなくったってこの仕事はできる。

(You can do this job even if you don't have a computer,)

(g) 自分で料理しなくたって、お金さえ出せば食べたいものが簡単に手に入るようになった。

(Even if you don't cook yourself, you can easily get what you want to eat now if you just pay for it.)

Notes

1. *Tatte* is the informal form of *te mo*.

2. As seen in the Formation section, the formation rules differ significantly depending on the word's part of speech. Because the negative ending *nai* conjugates like *i*-adjectives, the informal form of *nakute mo* is *naku(t)tatte*, as shown in Formation (iv).

3. *Tatte* as the informal form of *te mo* should not be confused with *tatte* as the contracted form of *to itte mo* or *to shite mo* (see *tatte*[2] in this volume), or the colloquial form of "Vinf.past / Adj(*i*)inf.past / etc. + the quotative particle *to*," as in (1).

(1) a. 見たって言ったでしょ。＝ 見たと言ったでしょう。

(I told you I'd seen it.)

b. 聞けばよかったって思った。＝ 聞けばよかったと思った。

(I wish I had asked. (lit., I thought it would have been good if I had asked.))

c. 古田さんは英語の先生だったって聞いた。＝ 古田さんは英語の先生だったと聞いた。

(I heard that Mr. Furuta was an English teacher.)

[Related Expression]

Te mo and *tatte* are interchangeable, as shown in [1], except *te mo* is more formal and can be used in both spoken and written language.

[1] a. 一人で旅行に行っ｛たって / ても｝面白くない。(= KS(A))

b. 私は少しくらい高く｛(っ)たって / ても｝質のいいものを買うことにしている。(= KS(B))

c. いくら日本語が上手｛だって / でも｝専門知識がなかったらこの翻訳はできないよ。(= KS(C))

d. プロ｛だって / でも｝失敗することもある。(= KS(D))

(⇨ ***te mo*** (DBJG: 468-70))

(t)tatte² （っ）たって² *phr.* <s>

> the contracted form of *to itte mo* or *to shite mo*

even if (s.o. says that); even if s.o. tries to; although
【REL. *yō ni mo (~ nai)*】

◆ Key Sentences

(A)

	Vvol		
一人で	しよう	（っ）たって、	それは無理だ。

(You'll never be able to do it alone! (lit., Even if you try to do it alone, that's impossible.))

(B)

	Vinf		
今すぐ買いに	行く	（っ）たって、	もう店はみんな閉まっている。

(Even if you wanted to go buy it right now, the stores are all already closed.)

(C)

Adj(*i*)inf		
高い	(っ)たって、	100万円はしないだろう。
(Even though it's said to be expensive, my guess is it won't cost more than one million yen.)		

(D)

	Noun		
日本語教育の	経験者	(だ)ったって、	彼女はまだ日本以外で教えたことはない。
(Although she has experience teaching Japanese, she hasn't yet taught anywhere outside of Japan.)			

Formation

(i) Vvol(っ)たって

　　飲もう(っ)たって　(even if you try to drink)

(ii) Vinf(っ)たって

　　飲む(っ)たって　(even if you say you will drink)

　　飲んだったって　(even if you say you drank)

(iii) Adj(*i*)inf(っ)たって

　　高い(っ)たって　(even if you say s.t. is expensive)

　　高かったったって　(even if you say s.t. was expensive)

(iv) {Adj(*na*)stem / N}{ø / だ / だった}ったって

　　便利{ø / だ / だった}ったって　(even if you say s.t. is/was convenient)

　　学生{ø / だ / だった}ったって　(even if you say s.o. is/was a student)

Examples

(a) あの家は君が買おうったって買えるようなものじゃない。

　　(That house is not something you could buy even if you wanted to.)

(b) 僕を騙そうったってそうはいかない。

　　(It won't work if you try to cheat me.)

(c) 彼が何を言おうったってそれをとめようとは思わない。

(Whatever he may want to say, I don't think I'll stop it.)

(d) 今から帰るったってもう電車はないよ。

(There are no more trains even if (you say) you want to go home now.)

(e) 調べるったって、こんなたくさんある資料を一人で調べるのは無理だ。

(Even if you say you'll look through the materials, it's impossible for you to do it alone because there are so many.)

(f) 近いったってとても歩いて行ける距離じゃない。

(Although (I say) it's close, it's not a distance you can walk at all.)

(g) いくら簡単ったって、やっぱり最低限のパソコン知識がなくては使えない。

(No matter how simple (they say) it is, in fact you won't be able to use it without a minimum knowledge of computers.)

(h) 「断食」ったって、全く何も口に入れないんじゃない。1日に2回、野菜ジュースを飲むことはできる。

(Although I say "fasting," it's not like you can't put anything in your mouth. You can drink vegetable juice twice a day.)

Notes

1. *Ttatte* is the shortened form of *to shite mo* or *to itte mo*. When the preceding element is a volitional verb form, *ttatte* is derived from either *to shite mo* or *to itte mo*, but when other parts of speech precede *ttatte*, it is derived from *to itte mo*. (⇨ ***to suru***[1] (DIJG: 518-23))

2. *Ttatte* is commonly used in informal spoken language.

3. The initial glottal stop of *ttatte* (i.e., っ) is optional in some situations. (See Formation.)

4. When verbs precede *ttatte*, the main clause often implies that what the subject of the verb is trying to do is difficult or impossible, as in KS(A), (B), Exs.(a), (b) and (d)-(g).

T

te bakari wa irarenai てばかりはいられない *phr.*

| a phrase representing the idea that s.o. cannot just keep doing s.t. or waste time being consumed by some emotion | cannot just; cannot always; cannot just keep ~ing; cannot spend time just ~ing; cannot waste time just ~ing |

◆ **Key Sentences**

(A)

	V *te*	
過去の業績に	安住して	ばかりはいられない。

(We just cannot be content with our past performance.)

(B)

Sentence		VN		
確かにこれは深刻な事態だ	が、	議論	ばかり	してはいられない。

(Indeed, this is a serious situation, but we cannot just keep discussing it.)

(C)

Sentence			Noun	Prt.
周りの人が助けてくれる	からと言って、	いつまでも	人	に

	V *te*	
ばかり	頼って	はいられない。

(Just because the people around me have helped me out in the past, I can't depend on others endlessly.)

Formation

(i) V *te* ばかりはいられない

　　　泣いてばかりはいられない　(cannot just keep crying)

(ii) VN{してばかりはいられない / ばかりはしていられない}

　　　心配{してばかりはいられない / ばかりはしていられない}　(cannot just worry about s.t.)

(iii) N{Prt. + V*te* ばかりはいられない / (Prt.) ばかり V*te* はいられない}

> 本を読んでばかりはいられない　(cannot just read books; cannot always read books)

> 本ばかり読んではいられない　(cannot read just books; cannot always read books)

> 親から借りてばかりはいられない　(cannot just borrow s.t. from one's parents; cannot always borrow s.t. from one's parents)

> 親からばかり借りてはいられない　(cannot borrow s.t. from just one's parents; cannot always borrow s.t. from one's parents)

Examples

(a) やっと長年の夢であったマイホームを手に入れたが、喜んでばかりはいられない。これから大きなローンを返していかなければならないのだ。

(I finally own a house, which I have hoped to do for years, but I can't remain excited for long. Now I have a huge loan to repay.)

(b) リストラのショックからまだ完全に立ち直ったわけじゃないけど、いつまでも落ち込んでばかりもいられない。すぐに仕事探しを始めなければ。

(I haven't fully recovered from the shock of being laid off (lit., the restructuring shock), but I cannot waste my time just feeling depressed. I have to start looking for a job right away.)

(c) 希望の学校に入れなかったからと言って、くじけてばかりはいられない。

(I just can't let it get me down because I didn't get into the school I wanted.)

(d) 人の成功に感心ばかりしてはいられない。我々ももっと頑張らなければ。

(We can't just sit around being impressed by someone else's success. We have to work harder, too.)

(e) 障害の原因ばかり考えてもいられない。早急に失われたデータを回復する必要がある。

(We can't just keep thinking about what caused the trouble. We have to recover the lost data immediately.)

(f) 退職して悠々自適の生活ができるようになったが、家にばかりこもってもいられないのでボランティアの仕事を始めた。

(Now that I'm retired I can live as I like, but I just can't stay at home, so I've begun to do volunteer work.)

T

Notes

1. *Te bakari wa irarenai* is the negative potential form of *te bakari iru* (doing nothing but X; be doing just X). This phrase is used when someone realizes that continuing to do something or dwelling on something is counterproductive.   (⇨ ***bakari*** (DBJG: 84-87))

2. When the preceding verb is a *suru*-verb (e.g., *kenkyū-suru*), or the verb is preceded by a direct object or a noun with a particle, *bakari* may follow the *suru*-verb stem, the object or the particle, as shown in Formation (ii) and (iii). Exs.(d)-(f) and (1) present additional examples in which *bakari* precedes V*te*.

   (1) a. 後悔ばかり<u>して</u>はいられない。

      (I have to get over this feeling of regret. (lit., I cannot just keep regretting.)

   b. カップラーメンばかり<u>食べて</u>はいられない。

      (I cannot eat only cup noodles.)

   c. 日本語にばかり時間を<u>かけて</u>はいられない。

      (I can't spend all my time studying Japanese.)

   There is a subtle difference in meaning between "N + Prt. ~ *te bakari wa irarenai*" and "N (Prt.) *bakari* ~ *te wa irarenai*." For example, in (2a) the focus is on the act of depending on the speaker's parents while in (2b) the focus is on the people the speaker depends on.

   (2) a. 親に頼ってばかりはいられない。

      (I cannot just depend on my parents.)

   b. 親にばかり頼ってはいられない。

      (I cannot depend on just my parents.)

3. *Te bakari mo irarenai* is often used as a variation of *te bakari wa irarenai*, as seen in Exs.(b), (e) and (f). There is no fundamental difference between the two versions in terms of meaning or the situations in which they are used. The only difference is that *te bakari wa irarenai* conveys the nuance that the subject is only doing one thing (or experiencing just one feeling); *te bakari mo irarenai* does not imply such exclusiveness.

~ **te mo** ~ **te mo**   ～ても～ても   *str.*

| a structure meaning "even if s.o. does s.t. repeatedly" | no matter how much/often/hard/etc.; no matter how many times 【REL. *ikura ~ te mo*】 |

◆ **Key Sentence**

V₁*te*		V₂*te* (V₁ = V₂)		
考えて	も	考えて	も	思い出せない。

(No matter how much/hard I try (lit., think), I cannot remember it.)

Formation

V₁*te* も V₂*te* も   (where V₁ = V₂)

飲んでも飲んでも   (no matter how much I drink)

Examples

(a) 働いても働いてもお金が貯まらない。
(No matter how much/hard I work, I cannot save money.)

(b) 掘っても掘っても水は出てこなかった。
(No matter how much/deep I dug, I didn't hit water.)

(c) 歩いても歩いても町が見えてこない。
(No matter how far I walk, I can't see (the next) town.)

(d) 練習しても練習してもゴルフがうまくならない。
(No matter how hard I practice, my golf does not improve.)

(e) 暑い上に湿度が高いので、拭っても拭っても汗が吹き出してくる。
(Because it's hot and humid (lit., it is humid on top of being hot), I sweat no matter how many times / much I wipe (my face).)

(f) このクラスの学生は教えても教えても覚えないので、教えがいがない。
(Because the students in this class never learn no matter how many times I teach them (the same things), I feel like it's not worth teaching them.)

<hr>

Notes

1. This structure is used only with verbs. Although the main clause usually describes something undesirable, that is not always the case. For example, what is described in the main clause in (1) is not necessarily undesirable.

   (1) 彼は断られても断られても<u>あきらめない</u>。

   (No matter how many times he is refused, he never gives up.)

2. When the verb is a *suru*-verb, such as *benkyō-suru*, the stem also needs to be repeated, as shown in (2).

   (2) ｛勉強しても勉強しても／*勉強してもしても｝成績が上がらない。

   (No matter how much/hard I study, my grades do not improve.)

【Related Expression】

Sentences involving V*te mo* V*te mo* can be paraphrased using the more formal form, *ikura* V*te mo*, as in [1].

   [1] a. ｛考えても考えても／いくら考えても｝思い出せない。(= KS)

   b. ｛働いても働いても／いくら働いても｝お金が貯まらない。(= Ex.(a))

However, the reverse is not always the case, as shown in [2].

   [2] a. ｛いくら泣いても／*泣いても泣いても｝駄目だ。
      (No matter how much you cry, it won't help.)

   b. ｛いくら頼まれても／*頼まれても頼まれても｝これは引き受けられない。
      (No matter how forcefully you ask me, I cannot agree to do it.)

As seen in [2], when S$_2$ represents the speaker's reply to the hearer in response to the action represented in S$_1$, V*te mo* V*te mo* cannot be used. [3] provides more examples.

   [3] a. ｛いくら断っても／*断っても断っても｝駄目だ。
      (No matter how many times you refuse, it won't help; (therefore, you should stop refusing.))

   b. 彼女が｛いくら頼んでも／*頼んでも頼んでも｝駄目だ。
      (No matter how many times she asks, it won't work; (therefore, you should stop her from begging.))

te shikata ga nai　て仕方がない　*phr.*

a phrase that represents emotions the speaker/writer cannot control or sensations/situations he/she cannot bear

cannot help ~ing; cannot stop feeling; (so ~ and) cannot control ~; so ~ and ~ cannot bare it; so; unbearably

【REL. *te naranai*; *te tamaranai*; *(to i)ttara nai*】

◆ **Key Sentences**

(A)

	V *te*	
会社の理不尽なリストラに	腹が	立って	仕方がない。

(I'm so mad at the company's unreasonable restructuring (i.e., laying off workers) (and cannot control my anger).)

(B)

	Adj(*i*)stem		
久しぶりに妻や子供たちに会えるので	嬉し	く	て仕方がない。

(Because I get to see my wife and children for the first time in a long while, I am so happy (and can hardly control my emotion).)

(C)

	Adj(*na*)stem		
ここは何もすることがないので	退屈	で	仕方がない。

(Because I have nothing to do here, I'm unbearably bored.)

Formation

(i)　V *te* 仕方がない

　　喉が乾いて仕方がない　((I) am so thirsty (and cannot bear it))

(ii)　Adj(*i*)stem くて仕方がない

　　悲しくて仕方がない　((I) am so sad (and can hardly control (my) emotion))

(iii) Adj(*na*) で仕方がない

いやで仕方がない　((I) dislike it so much (and (I) can hardly control (my) emotion))

Examples

(a) アンディーがアメリカに帰ってまだ二日しか経っていないのに、寂しくて仕方がない。

(Although it's been only two days since Andy went back to America, I miss him so much (lit., I'm so lonely and can hardly control my emotion).)

(b) こんなすばらしい建物が取り壊されるのかと思うと残念で仕方がない。

(I feel so bad when I think that such a wonderful building is going to be demolished.)

(c) ボーイフレンドが一年の日本留学を終えて来週帰ってくる。早く会いたくて仕方がない。

(My boyfriend is coming back next week after finishing his year of study in Japan. I'm dying to see him (lit., I want to see him soon so much)!)

(d) 悪い風邪を引いたらしい。咳が出て仕方がない。

(I seem to have a bad cold. I cannot control my coughing.)

(e) ここは空港のすぐ近くなので飛行機の音がうるさくて仕方がない。

(Because this place is close to an airport, the noise from the airplanes is unbearable.)

(f) この参考書は索引が不完全なので使いにくくて仕方がない。

(Because this reference book has an incomplete index, it is so hard to use.)

(g) 私のうちは近くにスーパーもコンビニもないので不便で仕方がない。

(Because there is neither a supermarket nor a convenience store near my house, it is unbearably inconvenient.)

(h) 先週、学会で会った女性が気になって仕方がない。

(I cannot stop thinking about the woman I met at the academic conference last week.)

(i) 母親になった途端に自分の子供がよその子供より可愛く思えて仕方がない。

(As soon as I became a mother, I couldn't help thinking that my child was cuter than other children.)

Notes

1. *Te shikata ga nai* is used when the speaker cannot control his/her emotion or bodily reactions, cannot bear a sensation or external situation, or cannot help feeling something or thinking something spontaneously. Words and phrases that commonly occur with *te shikata ga nai* include the following: (Those that appear in the KS, Formations and Exs. are not included here.)

(i) Emotion:

楽しい (enjoyable), 面白い (fun), 愉快だ (fun), 悔しい (frustrating), 欲しい (want), 憎らしい (hate), 懐かしい (missed), 可哀想だ (sorry; a pity), 不愉快だ (unpleasant), 悔やまれる (regret)

(ii) Bodily reacition:

くしゃみが出る (sneeze)

(iii) Sensation:

暑い (hot), 臭い (smelly), 痛い (aching), かゆい (itchy), 苦しい (painful), だるい (languid)

(iv) External situation:

狭い (small; narrow)

(v) Spontaneous thinking:

思われる (think spontaneously), 感じられる (feel), 気がする (feel)

The feelings or sensations expressed by *te shikata ga nai* are largely negative ones, but positive ones such as *ureshii* "happy," *tanoshii* "enjoyable," *omoshiroi* "fun" and *yukaida* "fun" are also common:

2. When the subject is not in the first person, *te shikata ga nai* is followed by auxiliaries such as *yōda*, *mitaida* and *rashii*.

(1) a. 浅田さんは久しぶりに妻や子供たちに会えるので嬉しくて仕方がない {ようだ / みたいだ}。(cf. KS(B))

(Mr. Asada looks so happy (and can hardly control his emotion) because he will get to see his wife and children for the first time in a long while.)

T

b. ジョージは何もすることがないので退屈で仕方がないらしい。

(cf. KS(C))

(It seems that George is unbearably bored, having nothing to do.)

(⇨ **yōda** (DBJG: 547-52); **rashii** (DBJG: 373-75))

3. *Te shiyō ga nai* and its informal form, *te shō ga nai*, are variations of *te shikata ga nai*.

【Related Expressions】

Te naranai and *te tamaranai* are also used to express emotions the speaker/ writer cannot control or sensations he/she cannot bear. Thus, in such situations, these phrases and *te shikata ga nai* are interchangeable, as shown in [1].

[1] a. 会社の理不尽なリストラに腹が立って{仕方がない / ならない / たまらない}。(= KS(A))

b. 久しぶりに妻や子供たちに会えるので嬉しくて{仕方がない / ならない / たまらない}。(= KS(B))

c. ここは何もすることがないので退屈で{仕方がない / ならない / たまらない}。(= KS(C))

d. ここは空港のすぐ近くなので飛行機の音がうるさくて{仕方がない / ならない / たまらない}。(= Ex.(e))

e. どういうわけか、喉が渇いて{仕方がない / ならない / たまらない}。
(For some reason I'm unbearably thirsty.)

However, *te tamaranai* cannot be used with the thinking and feeling verbs, as shown in [2].

[2] a. 母親になった途端に自分の子供がよその子供より可愛く思えて{仕方がない / ならない /＊たまらない}。(= Ex.(i))

b. 最近、人命や地球環境など、とても大切なものがビジネスの道具に使われているような気がして{仕方がない / ならない /＊たまらない}。
(Recently, I cannot help but suspect that things that are very important, such as human lives and the global environment, are being used as a means for business.)

(⇨ **tamaranai** (DBJG: 445-47))

te wa irarenai てはいられない *phr.*

<table>
<tr><td>a phrase that is used when s.o. cannot be doing s.t. or be in some state due to a given situation</td><td>cannot/shouldn't be ~ing; cannot/shouldn't keep ~ing; cannot/shouldn't (stay/remain/ etc.); cannot/shouldn't waste time ~ing; cannot afford to; cannot help ~ing
【REL. *zu ni wa irarenai*; *wake ni wa ikanai*】</td></tr>
</table>

◆ **Key Sentences**

(A)

	Vte	
将来のことを考えると、いつまでもこんな仕事を	して	はいられない。

(When I think about the future, (I realize) I can't keep doing this kind of work forever.)

(B)

	Vneg		
彼女があまりにも自分勝手だったので、一言	言わ	ない	ではいられなかった。

(Because she was acting so selfishly, I couldn't resist saying something to her.)

(C)

	Noun Phrase	
彼が好きだと気づいた時から、もう	ただの友達	ではいられなくなった。

(Once I realized that I loved him, I couldn't be just a friend anymore.)

Formation

(i)　Vte はいられない

　　　　寝てはいられない　(cannot stay in bed)

(ii)　Vneg ないではいられない

　　　　話さないではいられない　(cannot keep from talking)

(iii) {Adj(*na*)stem / N} ではいられない

平静ではいられない　(cannot remain calm)

いつまでも子供ではいられない　(cannot be a child forever)

(a) もうすぐ飛行機が出るのでぐずぐずしてはいられない。

(My plane is departing soon, so I cannot afford to dawdle.)

(b) やることがたくさんあるのでパーティーなんかに行ってはいられない。

(I have so many things to do that I can't spend my time going to parties.)

(c) 自分にも同じ口癖があるので人のことを笑ってはいられない。

(I have the same speech habits, so I can't afford to laugh at other people.)

(d) あの教え方を見ていると時代錯誤を感じないではいられない。

(When I see that teaching method, I can't help thinking how outdated it is.)

(e) 忙しい時代に生まれ、時間に追われがちな今の子供たちを案じないではいられない。

(I cannot help being concerned about today's children, who were born in such a busy age and who tend to be pressed for time.)

(f) 私は一日も本なしではいられない。

(I can't go even a day without books.)

(g) よその国の事件とは言え、同じようなことはこの国でも起きる可能性がある。とても無関心ではいられない。

(Although that incident was in another country, it could happen in this country, too. I simply can't remain indifferent.)

(h) 彼女は日本中のみんなに期待されているので、もう普通の選手ではいられなくなった。

(With Japan's hopes riding on her, she can no longer be just an ordinary player.)

(i) 地球環境は急速に悪化している。いつまでもこのままではいられない。

(The earth's environment is worsening rapidly. We just can't continue to do nothing.)

Notes

1. *Te wa irarenai* (or *de wa irarenai*) is used when someone (usually the speaker/writer) cannot be doing something or be in some state due to a given situation. In some situations, "should not" is a more appropriate interpretation than "cannot."

2. *Te wa irarenai* often occurs with manner adverbs followed by *suru*, as in Ex.(a). (1) presents more examples.

(1) a. 長年勤めてきた同僚が最近リストラされた。私もうかうかしてはいられない。

   (One of my colleagues, who had worked for the company many years, was laid off recently. I can't afford to take it easy anymore.)

   b. 論文の締め切りまでまだ4か月あるとは言え、ほかにもすることがたくさんあるので、あまりのんびりしてはいられない。

   (Although I still have four months until the deadline for my paper, I cannot afford to relax too much because I have many other things to do.)

3. The literal meaning of Vneg *nai de wa irarenai* is "cannot remain not doing s.t." The phrase carries the idea of "cannot help doing s.t."

【Related Expressions】

I. Vneg *zu ni wa irarenai* "cannot help ~ing" means the same thing as Vneg *nai de wa irarenai*.

   [1] a. 彼女があまりにも自分勝手だったので、一言言わ{ないでは／ずには}いられなかった。(= KS(B))

   b. あの教え方を見ていると時代錯誤を感じ{ないでは／ずには}いられない。(= Ex.(d))

II. *Wake ni wa ikanai* "cannot; cannot help ~ing; have no choice but to ~" is used to indicate that one cannot do something due to an external circumstance. Thus, this phrase can be used in place of *te wa irarenai* in some situations, as shown in [2].

   [2] a. 将来のことを考えると、いつまでもこんな仕事をし{てはいられない／ているわけにはいかない}。(= KS(A))

　　b. 彼が好きだと気づいた時から、もうただの友達｛ではいられなくなっ
　　　た / でいるわけにはいかなくなった｝。(= KS(C))

　　c. よits国の事件とは言え、同じようなことはこの国でも起きる可能性
　　　がある。とても無関心｛ではいられない / でいるわけにはいかない｝。

　　　　　　　　　　　　　　　　　　　　　　　　　　　　　　(= Ex.(g))

Note that when the preceding verb is negative, *wake ni wa ikanai* and *te wa irarenai* express different meanings, as shown in [3]. That is, in [3a] *nai wake ni wa ikanai* indicates that the speaker/writer feels it is his/her obligation or duty to read the book, whereas in [3b] *nai de wa irarenai* indicates his/her strong desire to read the book.

[3]　a. この本を読まないわけにはいかない。

　　　　(I have no other choice but to read this book.)

　　b. この本を読まないではいられない。

　　　　(I have a burning desire to read this book.)

　　　　　　　　　　　　　　　　　(⇨ **wake ni wa ikanai** (DIJG: 581-83))

---

to atte とあって　　*phr.*　<w>

a phrase that introduces a reason when the speaker/writer considers it natural that s.o. does s.t. or is in some state, or that s.t. takes place for that reason	because ~, ~ as expected; because ~, naturally ~; because 〖REL. *node*; *kara*〗

◆ **Key Sentences**

(A)

Noun Phrase		
ボーナス後の連休	とあって、	観光地はどこも人でいっぱいだ。
(Because this is the series of holidays after the bonus season, (not surprisingly) all the tourist spots are crowded.)		

(B)

Sinf		
夏休みが始まった	とあって、	子供たちはみんな嬉しそうだ。
(Summer vacation has begun, so the children all look happy.)		

Formation

(i)　NP とあって

　　　病気とあって　(because s.o. is ill)

(ii)　Sinf とあって　(だ after Adj(*na*)stem and N is omitted.)

　　　韓国語ができるとあって　(because s.o. can speak Korean)

　　　タクシーの方が安いとあって　(because a taxi is cheaper)

　　　ノートパソコンの方が便利とあって　(because a laptop computer is
　　　　more convenient)

　　　父親が医者とあって　(because s.o.'s father is a doctor)

Examples

(a)　優勝を争うチーム同士の対決とあって、スタジアムは超満員だ。

　　　(Because this is the match between the teams competing for the cham-
　　　pionship, the stadium is packed beyond capacity.)

(b)　人気作家のサイン会とあって、本屋にはサインを求める人たちが長い列を
　　　作った。

　　　(Because it was the autograph session for a popular writer, people (who
　　　wanted his autograph) made a long line at the bookstore.)

(c)　レポートの締め切りがあさってとあって、学生たちはみんな焦っている。

　　　(Because the deadline for the paper is the day after tomorrow, the
　　　students are all panicking.)

(d)　掃除が終わったらお菓子がもらえるとあって、子供たちは一生懸命手伝って
　　　いる。

　　　(Because they know they'll get sweets after they finish cleaning, the
　　　children are doing their very best to help out.)

T

(e) 中途半端な訓練では実社会で通用しないとあって、この語学学校の指導は非常に厳しい。

(Because slapdash training does not help students function in the real world, the teaching at this language institution is very strict.)

(f) この社会人プログラムは、科目を低額で聴講できるだけでなく、自習室や図書館も自由に利用できるとあって、かなりの応募があります。

(Because this program for professionals not only allows students to audit courses cheaply but lets them use study rooms and the library freely, we receive quite a few applications.)

Notes

1. "X *to atte* Y" is used to introduce a reason when the speaker/writer considers it natural that Y is the result of X. *To atte* is not acceptable in (1), because here the information provided by X alone is not sufficient to conclude that given X, Y naturally takes place.

(1) a. 金がない{*とあって / ので / から}車を買えない。

(Because I don't have money, I cannot buy a car.)

b. 自転車が壊れた{*とあって / ので / から}バスで学校に行った。

(Because my bicycle broke down, I went to school by bus.)

2. Noun phrases or sentences precede *to atte*. When the predicate of the preceding sentence contains a noun or a *na*-adjective, *da* is omitted.

[Related Expressions]

Node and *kara* can be used in place of *to atte* to introduce a reason, as in [1]. However, *node* and *kara* do not carry the nuance that *to atte* conveys, as mentioned in Note 1.

[1] a. ボーナス後の連休{とあって / なので / だから}、観光地はどこも人でいっぱいだ。(= KS(A))

b. 夏休みが始まった{とあって / ので / から}、子供たちはみんな嬉しそうだ。(= KS(B))

(⇨ *node* (DBJG: 328-31); *kara*[3] ((DBJG: 179-81))

to atte wa   とあっては   *phr.*

a conditional phrase that indirectly presents a factual situation as a reason	if it is true that; if it is the case that; if; because; since 【REL. *(no) de areba*; *(no) nara*; *(no) da kara*; *(na) node*】

◆ **Key Sentences**

(A)

Noun Phrase		
社長の頼み	とあっては	断るわけにはいかない。

(If (it's true that) it's a favor for the president, I can't say no.)

(B)

Sinf		
全商品が３割引きで買える	とあっては、	遠方からわざわざ人が買いに来るのもうなずける。

(If (it's true that) you can buy everything at 30% off, I understand why people come from far away to shop (here).)

Formation

(i)   NP とあっては

病気とあっては   (if it's true that s.o. is ill)

(ii)   Sinf とあっては   (だ after Adj(*na*)stem and N is omitted.)

由美も行くとあっては   (if it's true that Yumi is going, too)

タクシーの方が安いとあっては   (if it's true that a taxi is cheaper)

バスの方が便利とあっては   (if it's true that the bus is more convenient)

締め切りが今週末とあっては   (if it's the case that the deadline is the end of this week)

Examples

(a) この大学が他の大学に統合されるのは残念だが、国の方針とあっては致し方ない。

(It is a pity that this university is going to be integrated into another university, but if that's the national policy, it cannot be helped.)

(b) ブラジル・ドイツ戦のすぐ後とあっては国内チーム同士の試合が物足りなく感じられたのも仕方がない。

(Because it came right after the game between Brazil and Germany, it was inevitable that people did not feel the game between the domestic teams was very exciting.)

(c) 皆が多忙な身とあっては30人以上の家族が集まれるのはクリスマスの休みしかない。

(Since everyone is so busy, Christmas vacation is the only time our family of more than 30 can get together.)

(d) スカイダイビングがここサイパンで楽しめるとあっては、挑戦してみない手はない。

(If it's true that we can enjoy skydiving here in Saipan, there's no reason not to try it.)

(e) どんなに短い作文でも、他の人に読まれ、コメントがつくとあっては、書く時の真剣味が増す。

(No matter how short your composition is, if it is read by others and they make comments, it makes you think more seriously when you write.)

(f) 役人の飲食費に税金が使われたとあっては、誰もが腹立たしく思うのは当たり前だ。しかも、そのことが明るみに出そうになると、今度は圧力をかけて「口封じ」をやったとあっては、もう救いようがない。

(If tax money was used to pay for government officials' dining and drinking, of course people would be angry. But there's no hope if the officials pressured those involved to keep their mouths shut when the practice was about to be exposed.)

Notes

1. Grammatically, *to atte wa* is a conditional phrase, but it is used when the speaker/writer presents a factual situation. This is a way to indirectly present the factual situation as a reason. The phrase can be translated as "if it's the case; if it is true" or "because; since" depending on the context.

2. As seen in Formation (ii), the *da* that follows *na*-adjective stems and nouns is omitted.

3. NP *to atte wa*, as in KS(A), is an abbreviated form of X *ga* NP *to atte wa*. X *ga* is omitted because it is understood from the context or situation. For example, the unabbreviated forms of KS(A) and Ex.(a) are (1a) and (1b), respectively.

(1) a. それが社長の頼みとあっては、断るわけにはいかない。(= KS(A))

b. この大学が他の大学に統合されるのは残念だが、それが国の方針とあっては致し方ない。(= Ex.(a))

[Related Expressions]

I. The conditional phrases *(no) de areba* and *(no) nara* can be used in the same situations in which *to atte wa* is used, as in [1].

[1] a. 社長の頼み｛とあっては／であれば／なら｝断るわけにはいかない。

(= KS(A))

b. 全商品が３割引きで買える｛とあっては／のであれば／のなら｝、遠方からわざわざ人が買いに来るのもうなずける。(= KS(B))

However, *(no) de areba* and *(no) nara* are also used when it is not certain whether a situation is factual or not. For example, [2] can be interpreted in this way.

[2] 皆が多忙な身｛であれば／なら｝30人以上の家族が集まれるのはクリスマスの休みしかない。(cf. Ex.(c))

(If we are all busy, Christmas vacation may be / is the only time our family of more than 30 can get together.)

Note that in the *to atte wa* version (i.e., Ex.(c)) the situation in the first clause is interpreted only as factual.

(⇨ *de aru* (DIJG: 30-33); *ba* (DBJG: 81-83); *nara* (DBJG: 281-84))

II. The reason phrases *(no) da kara* and *(na) node* can be used in place of *to atte wa*, as in [3]. However, the indirectness of *to atte wa* is not conveyed in these sentences. (See Note 1.)

[3] a. 社長の頼み｛だから／なので｝断るわけにはいかない。(cf. KS(A))

b. 全商品が３割引きで買える｛のだから／ので｝、遠方からわざわざ人が買いに来るのもうなずける。(cf. KS(B))

(⇨ *no da* (DBJG: 325-28); *kara*[3] (DBJG: 179-81); *node* (DBJG: 328-31))

to bakari ni　とばかりに　*phr.*　<w>

a phrase that indicates that s.o. does s.t. in order to convey s.t. or in such a way that s.o. is convinced that s.t. is the case

as if; as if to say that; as if ~ were convinced that; as if ~ believed that; as if ~ decided that

【REL. *to iwan bakari ni*; *to iu yō/fū ni*; *to*】

◆ **Key Sentences**

(A)

	Direct Quotation		
悟は	「黙ってついてこい」	とばかりに	先に立って歩き出した。

(Satoru started off (lit., began to walk ahead) as if to say: "Don't say anything and follow me.")

(B)

	Indirect Quotation		
課長は	余計な質問はするな	とばかりに	私をにらみつけた。

(My section chief glared at me as if to tell me not to ask any unnecessary questions.)

(C)

		Noun		
霧が晴れたので、私は今が		チャンス	とばかりに	写真を撮りまくった。

(The fog had cleared, so I took pictures furiously, as if it were my only chance.)

(D)

	Noun Phrase		
竹本は	この時	とばかりに	日頃の不満を吐き出した。

(Takemoto vented his long-held complaints as if he were convinced this was the time (to do so).)

Formation

(i) Direct Quotation とばかりに

「それ！」とばかりに   (as if to say, "There you go!")

(ii) Indirect Quotation とばかりに

そうはさせないとばかりに   (as if to say that s.o. wouldn't let s.o. do that)

(iii) N とばかりに

チャンスとばかりに   (as if s.o. had decided that this were s.o.'s great opportunity)

Examples

(a) 彼女は「えい！」とばかりに侵入者を投げ飛ばした。

(She threw off (lit., flung) the intruder with a yell (lit., as if yelling, "*Ei!*").)

(b) 庭園の花たちは早く撮ってとばかりに美しく咲いていました。

(The flowers in the garden were blooming beautifully, as if they wanted us to take their pictures.)

(c) 思い立ったが吉日とばかりにエアロビクスを始めました。

(I began aerobics believing that the day you think of something is an auspicious day to start it.)

(d) 新鮮な魚を食べられるのは今日が最後とばかりに、さしみを食べられるだけ食べた。

(I ate as much *sashimi* as I could, as if I were convinced it was the last day I could eat fresh fish.)

(e) 守は心の洗濯とばかりに一週間の旅行に出かけた。

(Mamoru left for a one-week trip, seemingly convinced that it would refresh his mind.)

(f) 彼らはここぞとばかりに自分たちの給料の安さを訴えた。

(Seeming to have decided that this was a great opportunity, they protested that their wages were low.)

Notes

1. *To bakari ni* is composed of the quotation particle *to*, the particle *bakari*, which means "approximately; almost" and the particle *ni*, which

indicates that the phrase is adverbial, like the final *ni* of the adverbial form of *na*-adjectives. Since the verb after *to* (e.g., *iu* "say," *shinjiru* "be convinced") is omitted, the phrase can be interpreted as "as if to say that," "as if s.o. were convinced that," "as if s.o. had decided that," etc., depending on the context.

2. The *da* before *to bakari ni* is usually omitted.

(1) a. 霧が晴れたので、私は今がチャンス<u>だ</u>とばかりに写真を撮りまくった。

(= KS(C))

b. 思い立ったが吉日<u>だ</u>とばかりにエアロビクスを始めました。(= Ex.(c))

3. The *kono toki* before *to bakari ni* in KS(D) is an abbreviated form. The unabbreviated forms is as follows:

(2) 竹本は<u>一番いいのはこの時だ</u>とばかりに日頃の不満を吐き出した。

(cf. KS(D))

(Takemoto vented his long-held complaints as if he were convinced this was the best time (lit., this is the best).)

4. The *ni* of *to bakari ni* is sometimes omitted, as in (3).

(3) a. 課長は余計な質問はするなとばかり (に) 私をにらみつけた。(= KS(B))

b. 霧が晴れたので、私は今がチャンスとばかり (に) 写真を撮りまくった。

(= KS(C))

5. The use of N *to bakari ni* is limited to situations in which the phrase expresses the idea that it is a good time to do something, as in KS(C), (D), Exs.(c) and (f).

[Related Expressions]

I. *To iwan bakari ni* "as if to say" and *to iu yō/fū ni* "in such a way that; as if to say" are synonymous with *to bakari ni* and can be used in place of *to bakari ni*. (*Iwan* is the classic form of *iwanai*.)

[1] a. 悟は「黙ってついてこい」｛とばかりに / と言わんばかりに / というように / という風に｝先に立って歩き出した。(= KS(A))

b. 課長は余計な質問はするな｛とばかりに / と言わんばかりに / というように / という風に｝私をにらみつけた。(= KS(B))

However, *to iwan bakari ni* and *to iu yō/fū ni* cannot be used when *to bakari ni* means "as if I believed; as if I were convinced," as shown in [2].

[2] a. 霧が晴れたので、私は今がチャンス｛とばかりに /*と言わんばかり
に /*というように /*という風に｝写真を撮りまくった。(= KS(C))

b. 思い立ったが吉日｛とばかりに /*と言わんばかりに /*というよう
に /*という風に｝エアロビクスを始めました。(= Ex.(c))

c. 新鮮な魚を食べられるのは今日が最後｛とばかりに /*と言わんばか
りに /*というように /*という風に｝、さしみを食べられるだけ食べ
た。(= Ex.(d))

This restriction does not apply when the subject is in the third person,
as in [3].

[3] a. 竹本はこの時｛とばかりに /と言わんばかりに /というように /とい
う風に｝日頃の不満を吐き出した。(= KS(D))

b. 守は心の洗濯｛とばかりに /と言わんばかりに /というように /とい
う風に｝一週間の旅行に出かけた。(= Ex.(e))

II. The use of *to* "(saying/thinking/believing/etc.) that" is similar to that of
to bakari ni. The difference is that *to* is used when the subject actually
says, thinks or believes something.

[4] a. 悟は「黙ってついてこい」と先に立って歩き出した。(cf. KS(A))
(Satoru said, "Just follow me," and started off.)

b. 霧が晴れたので、私は今がチャンスと写真を撮りまくった。

(cf. KS(C))

(The fog had cleared, so I took pictures furiously, believing it
was my only chance.)

To cannot be used when the preceding phrase is abbreviated, as in [5].

[5] a. 竹本はこの時｛とばかりに /*と｝日頃の不満を吐き出した。

(= KS(D))

b. 彼らはここぞ｛とばかりに /*と｝自分たちの給料の安さを訴えた。

(= Ex.(f))

(⇨ *to*³ (DBJG: 478-80))

to demo iu beki　とでも言う<ruby>言<rt>い</rt></ruby>うべき　*phr.*　<w>

| a phrase that introduces a noun (or noun phrase) to describe the nature of s.o. or s.t. | which could/may be called; which can/could be described as 【REL. *to iu*; *de aru*; *no yōna*】 |

◆ **Key Sentences**

(A)

	Noun1		Noun2	
あれは	<ruby>運命<rt>うんめい</rt></ruby>	とでも言うべき	<ruby>出来事<rt>できごと</rt></ruby>	だった。
(That was an incident that could be called fate.)				

(B)

	Noun Phrase		
これは	エッセイ<ruby>的<rt>てき</rt></ruby>なサイト	とでも言うべき	でしょう。
(This should probably be described as an essay-like website.)			

Formation

(i)　N₁ とでも言うべき N₂

　　<ruby>革命<rt>かくめい</rt></ruby>とでも言うべき<ruby>出来事<rt>できごと</rt></ruby>　(an event that could be called a revolution)

(ii)　N とでも言うべきだ

　　「<ruby>現代版<rt>げんだいばん</rt></ruby>シンデレラ」とでも言うべきだ　(we could call (her) a modern version of Cinderella)

Examples

(a) <ruby>近<rt>ちか</rt></ruby>いうちに<ruby>試用版<rt>しようばん</rt></ruby>とでも言うべきものをお<ruby>送<rt>おく</rt></ruby>りします。

(I'll send you something before long that could be called a trial version.)

(b) ミュンヘンのシンボルとでも言うべきこの<ruby>市役所<rt>しやくしょ</rt></ruby>は 1867 年から 1908 年にかけて<ruby>建<rt>た</rt></ruby>てられたものです。

(This city hall, which could be called Munich's symbol, was built between 1867 and 1908.)

(c) 我々は20世紀の技術の賜物とでも言うべき明石海峡大橋を渡った。

(We crossed the Akashi Strait Bridge, which could be described as a gift of 20th century technology.)

(d) マイホーム計画最大のポイントとでも言うべきローンの組み方には、大きく分けると公的融資と民間融資の2種類があります。

(The ways of arranging a mortgage, which could be described as the most important consideration when planning to buy a home, can be classified into two types; government mortgages and private mortgages.)

(e) 彼を一言で表現するとしたら「ネットワークの旅人」とでも言うべきだろうか。

(If I had to describe him in a word, I would call him a "network traveler.")

Notes

1. *To demo iu beki* is a type of simile and is used when the speaker/writer describes the nature of someone or something using another noun or noun phrase.

2. *Beki* is a noun-modifying form of the auxiliary *bekida* "should."

(⇨ ***bekida*** (DIJG: 11-15))

[Related Expressions]

I. *To iu* "called" appears similar to *to demo iu beki*. However, *to iu* is used when providing the generic name or the proper name of someone or something. That is, in "N$_1$ *to iu* N$_2$," N$_1$ presents the generic name of a specific set of members, as in [1a], or the proper name of a specific member in a set of entities, as in [1b]. N$_2$ presents the generic name of a class of entities which includes the member (or the set of members) identified by N$_1$.

[1] a. キリンという動物   (the animal called the giraffe)

  b. リビアという国   (the country called Libya)

(⇨ ***to iu*** (DBJG: 486-87))

II. X *de aru*, where X is a noun or noun phrase, is also used to describe someone or something. Unlike *to demo iu beki*, this phrase is used to describe an actual attribute of a person or thing. In such cases, *to demo iu beki* cannot be used.

[2] a. 日本の元首｛である /*とでも言うべき｝首相

(the prime minister, who is the head (of the government) of Japan)

b. 我々のリーダー｛である /*とでも言うべき｝田辺さん

(our leader, Mr. Tanabe)

(⇨ **de aru** (DIJG: 30-33))

III. *No yōna* is also a type of simile and can often be used in place of *to demo iu beki* when *to demo iu beki* modifies nouns or noun phrases, as in [3].

[3] a. あれは運命｛とでも言うべき /のような｝出来事だった。(= KS(A))

b. 近いうちに試用版｛とでも言うべき /のような｝ものをお送りします。

(= Ex.(a))

However, when *to demo iu beki* carries a strong sense of "should," as in Ex.(d), *no yōna* cannot be used.

[4] マイホーム計画最大のポイント｛とでも言うべき /*のような｝ローンの組み方には、大きく分けると公的融資と民間融資の２種類があります。

(= Ex.(d))

(⇨ **yōda** (DBJG: 547-52))

---

to ie domo   といえども   *conj.*   <w>

| a conjunction that expresses the idea of "even (though)" | even; any; although; though; even though
【REL. *demo*】 |

◆ Key Sentences

(A)

Noun		
医者	といえども	時に病気になることもある。

(Even doctors sometimes become ill. (lit., Even though we call them doctors, there are times when they become ill.))

(B)

	Noun		
いかなる	名人	といえども	時には失敗することもある。

(Any master sometimes makes a mistake. (lit., No matter what kind of master he/she may be called, he/she sometimes makes a mistake.))

(C)

Sinf		
東京に住んでいる	といえども	知らない都内の名所は沢山ある。

(Even though I live in Tokyo (lit., Even though I say I live in Tokyo), there are many sightseeing spots in Tokyo that I don't know.)

Formation

(i)　N といえども

　　　先生といえども　(even teachers)

(ii)　{いかなる / どんな} N といえども

　　　{いかなる / どんな}技術といえども　(any technology; no matter what kind of technology it may be)

(iii) Sinf といえども　(だ after Adj(*na*)stem and N is often omitted.)

　　　しっかり準備はしているといえども　(even though I'm well prepared)

　　　備えは万全(だ)といえども　(although the preparation is perfect)

Examples

(a) 同時通訳は一瞬といえども気が抜けない。

(In simultaneous translation, you cannot lose your concentration even for a moment.)

(b) 科学技術の分野では、たとえグループ研究といえども個人の新しい発想によるところが非常に大きい。

(In the field of science and technology, even group research is greatly dependent on individuals (coming up with) new ways of thinking.)

(c) いかなる自動翻訳機といえども、完全に機械だけで自然言語を翻訳するのは難しい。

(No matter what kind of automatic translation machine (you use), getting a natural-sounding translation solely from a machine is difficult.)

(d) 当たらずといえども遠からず。

(Close, but not quite. (lit., Although it is not exactly right, it is not far off.))

(e) 世界広しといえども、東京の神田ほど多くの古本屋が一か所に集中しているところはほかにないだろう。

(Even though the world is a big place, nowhere else are there as many used book stores concentrated in one place as there are in Kanda, Tokyo.)

(f) 筋力は少し衰えたといえども、彼はまだまだ若い選手に負けない集中力とスタミナを保っている。

(Although his strength has faded, he still maintains (levels of) concentration and stamina comparable to younger players.)

(g) いかに日本での生活が長いといえども、言葉の問題には常に遭遇する。

(Although I've lived in Japan for a long time, I constantly encounter language problems.)

(h) 天性の才能を持ち合わせているといえども、絶え間ない努力と訓練なくして今日の彼女はなかった。

(Although she has God-given talents, she couldn't be what she is now without her unceasing effort and training.)

Notes

1. *Ie domo* is the old form of *itte mo* (*te*-form of *iu* + *mo*). *To ie domo* is usually used in writing or formal speech. The colloquial version is *to itte mo*.

2. "X *to ie domo* Y" is used when Y is true although Y is not expected from/of X.

3. For emphasis, the adverb *tatoe* "even" may precede the noun or the clause before *to ie domo*, as shown in (1).

(1) a. たとえ医者といえども時に病気になることもある。(= KS(A))

b. たとえ東京に住んでいるといえども知らない都内の名所は沢山ある。

(= KS(C))

4. *Mo* is optional.

(2) a. 医者といえど(も)時に病気になることもある。(= KS(A))

b. いかなる名人といえど(も)時には失敗することもある。(= KS(B))

【Related Expression】

To ie domo can be replaced with *demo*, as shown in [1]. The latter is an informal expression.

[1] a. 医者｛といえども／でも｝時に病気になることもある。(= KS(A))

b. いかなる名人｛といえども／でも｝時には失敗することもある。

(= KS(B))

However, N *to ie domo* cannot be used in place of N *demo* unless the condition in Note 2 is met, as shown in [2].

[2] a. 私は難しい仕事｛でも／*といえども｝します。
(I will take even a difficult job.)

b. ここから｛でも／*といえども｝富士山が見える。
(Even from here you can see Mt. Fuji.)

c. この図書館は誰｛でも／*といえども｝入れる。
(Anyone can use (lit., enter) this library.)

(⇨ *demo* (DBJG: 111-13); *ikanaru* (in this volume))

T

~ **to ii** ~ **to ii** ～といい～といい   *str.*

<table>
<tr><td>a structure that introduces multiple perspectives when describing a person or a thing</td><td>in terms of both ~ and ~; in terms of ~ as well as ~; from the perspective of both ~ and ~
【REL. ~ *mo* ~ *mo*】</td></tr>
</table>

◆ Key Sentence

	Noun₁		Noun₂		
このコーヒーは	味	といい	香り	といい、	申し分ありません。
(This coffee is perfect in terms of both flavor and aroma.)					

Formation

N₁ といい N₂ といい

　色といい形といい (in terms of both color and shape)

Examples

(a) 内容といい話し方といい、見事なスピーチでした。

(It was a splendid speech in terms of content as well as delivery.)

(b) 声といい演技力といい、彼女は最高だ。

(She is the best from the perspective of both voice and acting ability.)

(c) 人柄といい才能といい、米倉さんに勝る人はいない。

(No one surpasses Ms. Yonekura in terms of both personality and ability.)

(d) 音楽の情感といい音の豊かさといい、こんな感動的な演奏を聴いたことがない。

(I've never heard such a moving performance, both in terms of the artist's emotion and the richness of the sound.)

(e) 家柄といい学歴といい、彼は非の打ちどころがない。

(He is just perfect, both in terms of his family and educational backgrounds.)

(f) スピードといいパワーといい、今の彼に勝てる選手はいない。
(No player can beat him now in terms of either speed or power.)

Notes

1. This grammatical structure is used to present multiple perspectives when describing a person or a thing. It is often used to provide the speaker's/writer's judgment of the person or the thing.

2. It is common to present just two points in this structure, although it is possible to present more than two, as in (1).

   (1) 速報性といい機能の多彩さといい情報の種類といい、インターネットニュースにかなう情報メディアはない。

   (No information media can match Internet news in terms of speed, variety of functions and kinds of information (it can integrate).)

[Related Expression]

~ *mo* ~ *mo* "both ~ and ~" can be used in place of ~ *to ii* ~ *to ii*.

   [1] a. このコーヒーは味{といい／も}香り{といい／も}、申し分ありません。(= KS)

   b. 内容{といい／も}話し方{といい／も}、見事なスピーチでした。

   (= Ex.(a))

   c. 声{といい／も}演技力{といい／も}、彼女は最高だ。 (= Ex.(b))

   (⇨ ~*mo* ~*mo* (DBJG: 255-57))

T

---

to itta   といった   *comp. prt.*

a compound particle that introduces examples	like; such as; among others 【REL. *to iu*; *to iu yōna*; *nado no*】

◆ **Key Sentences**

(A)

Noun₁, Noun₂, ...		Noun	
ドイツ、フランス、ロシア	といった	国々	が戦争に反対した。

(Countries such as Germany, France and Russia opposed the war.)

(B)

	Sentence₁, Sentence₂, ...		Noun	
このエンジンで一番困るのは	パワーが弱い、製造コストが高い	といった	問題	だ。

(The problems that are giving me the most trouble with this engine are things like weak power and high production costs.)

Formation

(i) N₁、N₂ (、……、) といった N

イヌ、ネコといったペット (pets like dogs and cats)

(ii) S₁ (、S₂、S₃、……) といった N

持ち運びしやすい、容量が大きいといった特徴 (such characteristics as portability and large capacity)

Examples

(a) 終身雇用、年功序列といった日本の伝統的な雇用形態が崩れつつある。

(Japan's traditional employment practices, such as permanent employment and seniority systems, are (in the process of) falling apart.)

(b) ここではBMWやベンツといったドイツの高級車が人気があるようだ。

(It looks like expensive German cars such as BMWs and Mercedes-Benzes are popular here.)

(c) 学校選択制、そして基礎学力の向上といったテーマが今、全国で議論されている。

(Themes like school-choice systems and the improvement of basic academic skills are being discussed all over the country now.)

(d) こんな機能があるといい、こんな情報が欲しいといったご意見・ご要望がありましたら、下記のアドレスに電子メールでお知らせ下さい。

(If you have opinions/requests such as "This kind of function would be helpful" or "I want this kind of information," please let us know via e-mail at the address below.)

(e) 一流大学から一流企業に就職すれば一生安泰の人生が送れるといった考え方はもう通用しない。

(It's no longer realistic to think that if you graduate from a first-class university and get a job at a first-class company you are set for life.)

(f) ゴミを燃やせばダイオキシンや二酸化炭素といった有害物質が排出される。またゴミの埋立地もあとわずかで満杯になる、しかも新たな埋立地がない、といった問題がある。

(If you burn trash, toxic materials such as dioxin and carbon dioxide are emitted. There is also the problem that landfills will soon be full and, to make the matter worse, no new land for landfills is available.)

Notes

1. A series of nouns, phrases or sentences can precede *to itta*.

2. *To itta* is always followed by a generic noun. The preceding nouns, phrases, etc. are examples of the entity represented by the generic noun.

3. When a series of nouns precede *to itta*, connectors like *ya*, *soshite* and *shikamo* can be used, as in Exs.(b), (c) and (f).

4. There are cases in which only one sentence precedes *to itta*, as in Ex.(e). In this case, the structure "S *to itta* N" implies that there are other things as well that are similar to what S describes.

[Related Expressions]

I. *To iu* "called" looks similar to *to itta* in form, but it is entirely different in meaning. In [1], for example, the first noun refers to something specific and the second noun refers to something generic. The whole noun phrase refers exclusively to a specific entity (the first noun) among a group of entities (the second noun).

[1] a. 田代という学生

(a student called Tashiro)

b. 数学という学問

(a subject (of study) called math)

Compare the phrases in [2] with those in [1].

[2] a. 田代、米倉といった学生

(students such as Tashiro and Yonekura)

b. 数学、物理といった科目

(courses like math and physics)

Thus, if *to iu* is used in place of *to itta*, in KS(B), for example, the sentence means that the most difficult problems are weak power and high production costs, and that's all. Note that *to iu* cannot be used in KS(A) if other countries also opposed the war.

(⇨*to iu* (DBJG: 486-87))

II. *To iu yōna* and *to itta* are completely interchangeable.

[3] a. ドイツ、フランス、ロシア｛といった／というような｝国々が戦争に反対した。(= KS(A))

b. このエンジンで一番困るのはパワーが弱い、製造コストが高い｛といった／というような｝問題だ。(= KS(B))

III. *Nado no* can also be used in place of *to itta*, but it is usually preceded by one or more nouns. The *nado no* in [4b] is not unacceptable, but it is less natural than the *nado no* in [4a].

[4] a. ドイツ、フランス、ロシア｛といった／などの｝国々が戦争に反対した。

(= KS(A))

b. このエンジンで一番困るのはパワーが弱い、製造コストが高い｛といった／などの｝問題だ。(= KS(B))

T

to ittara nai と言ったらない

(⇨ *(to i)ttara nai* in this volume)

to itta tokoro da　といったところだ　*phr.*

a phrase the speaker/writer uses to explain s.t. in a brief/rough manner	I would say ~; ~ is how I'd put it

◆ Key Sentence

9月になって猛暑も一段落	といったところです。

(I'd say the searing heat leveled off in September.)

Formation

(i)　{V / Adj(*i*)}inf といったところだ。

やっと終わったといったところだ。　(I'd say that it's finally over.)

良くもなく悪くもないといったところだ。　(I'd say that it is neither good nor bad.)

(ii)　{N / Adj(*na*)stem} といったところだ。

典型的な日本人といったところだ。　(I'd say that he/she is a typical Japanese.)

不健康といったところだ。　(I'd say that s.o. is unhealthy.)

(iii)　{Adv. / Interjection} といったところだ。

もうちょっとといったところだ。　(I'd say it will be done very soon.)

まあまあといったところだ。　(I'd say s.t. is so-so.)

Examples

(a)　ここは山というよりは、小高い丘といったところだ。

(I'd say that this is more of a (small) hill than a mountain.)

(b)　ホテルの部屋の広さはまあまあといったところでした。

(I'd say that the space in the hotel room was so-so.)

(c)　この大学の学部生と院生は合わせて 6,000 人といったところだ。

(Together, the number of undergraduates and graduates at this college is about 6,000.)

(d) ヤンキースとレッドソックスはほぼ互角といったところだ。

　　(I'd say that the Yankees and the Red Sox are even.)

(e) たった1年間の経験だけでは、図書館の「達人」と呼ばれるには、まだまだ
といったところです。

　　(With only one year of experience, I'd say I have a long way to go before people call me a library expert.)

(f) 英語の "Sorry" は日本語の「すみません」よりも「謝罪」の意味合いが強い。
いわゆる「ごめんなさい」「申し訳ありません」といったところだ。

　　("Sorry" in English is more of an apology than the Japanese "*sumimasen*." I would say that it corresponds to "*gomennasai*" or "*mōshiwake arimasen*.")

(g) この小説の主人公の男の性格を一言で表すとすれば、「自分には厳しいけれ
ど、人にはとても優しい」といったところです。

　　(If I were to describe the personality of this novel's main character in short (lit., in a word), I would say he is very hard on himself but very kind to others.)

Note

The phrase ~ *to itta tokoro da* is used when the speaker/writer wants to give a brief explanation about something, as in KS, Exs.(a), (b) and (f), or someone, as in Exs.(c)-(e) and (g).

T

to itte と言って *conj.*

| a conjunction used at the beginning of a sentence to convey the idea of "however" | however; but; having said that 【REL. *shikashi*; *shikashi nagara*; *keredomo*; *ka to itte*; *dakara to itte*; *sō ka to itte*】 |

◆ **Key Sentence**

Sentence₁		Sentence₂
あと 1000 万円あればなんとか欲しい家が買える。	と言って、	そんな大金を借りられるあてはない。

(If we had another ten million yen, we could manage to buy the house we want. Having said that, we don't know how we could borrow that much money.)

Formation

S₁。と言って、S₂。

　　時間がない。と言って、この仕事をそのままにしておくことはできない。
　　(I don't have time. But, I can't leave this job just as it is.)

Examples

(a) 外食は飽きたし自分で料理するのも億劫だ。と言って、何も食べずにいるというわけにもいかない。

(I've gotten tired of eating out, and cooking for myself is tiresome, too. But, I have to eat something (lit., I can't just not eat).)

(b) いくら考えても名案は浮かばない。と言って、何もしなければ事態は悪化する一方だ。

(No matter how hard I think, I cannot come up with a good idea. However, the situation will get only worse if I don't do anything about it.)

(c) 彼女と別れるのは絶対いやだ。と言って、妻と離婚する勇気もない。

(I definitely don't want to leave my girlfriend. Having said that, I don't have the courage to divorce my wife, either.)

T

(d) 最近は少し運動するとすぐ疲れてしまう。と言って、何もしないと体が衰えるばかりなので何かしなければならない。

(These days I get tired quickly after doing a little exercise. However, I have to do something because if I don't do anything, I'll only get weaker.)

(e) アメリカで自分の能力をためすのも面白いかもしれない。と言って、英語ができなければどうしようもないが。

(It might be interesting for you to try out your skills in America. But, it won't do any good if you cannot speak English.)

Notes

1. *To itte* literally means "saying that" (*to* is a quotation marker), and the content of what was said is the sentence immediately preceding *to*. However, this phrase functions as a conjunction at the beginning of a sentence and means "having said that; however."

2. Although it is not as common, *to itte* sometimes follows a sentence with sentence-final conjunctions like *ga* and *keredomo*. Its meaning does not change.

   (1) いくら考えても名案は浮かばない{が / けれども}、と言って、何もしなければ事態は悪化する一方だ。(= Ex.(b))

【Related Expressions】

I. Sentence-initial conjunctions that mean "however," such as *shikashi*, *shikashi nagara* and *keredomo*, can be used in place of *to itte* without a change in meaning.

   [1] a. あと 1000 万円あればなんとか欲しい家が買える。{と言って / しかし / しかしながら / けれども}、そんな大金を借りられるあてはない。

   (= KS)

   b. 外食は飽きたし自分で料理するのも億劫だ。{と言って / しかし / しかしながら / けれども}、何も食べずにいるというわけにもいかない。

   (= Ex.(a))

II. *Ka to itte* expresses the same idea as *to itte*.

   [2] a. あと 1000 万円あればなんとか欲しい家が買える。{と言って / かと言って}、そんな大金を借りられるあてはない。(= KS)

b. 外食は飽きたし自分で料理するのも億劫だ。{と言って／かと言って}、何も食べずにいるというわけにもいかない。(= Ex.(a))

III. *Dakara to itte* and *sō ka to itte* also express the same idea as *to itte*.

[3] a. あと 1000 万円あればなんとか欲しい家が買える。{と言って／だからと言って／そうかと言って}、そんな大金を借りられるあてはない。

(= KS)

b. 外食は飽きたし自分で料理するのも億劫だ。{と言って／だからと言って／そうかと言って}、何も食べずにいるというわけにもいかない。

(= Ex.(a))

However, these two conjunctive phrases can be used with another sentence-initial conjunction like *shikashi* while *to itte* and *ka to itte* cannot.

[4] あと 1000 万円あればなんとか欲しい家が買える。しかし、{だからと言って／そうかと言って／*と言って／*かと言って}、そんな大金を借りられるあてはない。(cf. KS)

(⇨ *dakara to itte* (DIJG: 21-23); *sō ka to itte* (DIJG: 397-401))

T

to iu ka　と言うか　*phr.*

<table>
<tr><td>a phrase used to restate what was just said in order to be more accurate or appropriate</td><td>or; or rather; or I'd (rather) call it; or I may call it; or I'd (rather) say; or I may say
【REL. *to iu yori*】</td></tr>
</table>

◆ **Key Sentences**

(A)

	Word₁		Word₂	
自分の	勘違い	と言うか、	**不注意**	でした。
(It was my misunderstanding . . . or carelessness, rather.)				

(B)

	Phrase₁		Phrase₂
彼のことは	諦めた	と言うか、	**もうどうでもよくなった。**
(I'm through with him . . . or rather, I don't care anymore.)			

(C)

Sentence₁		Sentence₂
我が社の話は何もできません。	と言うか、	何も話すことはありません。
(I cannot talk about our company. Or, I should say, I have nothing to say about it.)		

Examples

(a) 彼は議論好きと言うか、いつも人の意見に反対したがります。

(He is argumentative, or should I say, he always wants to disagree with others.)

(b) この事件については、私たちも驚いていると言うか、困惑しています。

(We are also surprised by this incident, or perplexed, rather.)

(c) 今日来た人は、商魂たくましいと言うか、本当に厚かましい人でした。

(The person who visited us today was an aggressive salesman, or maybe I should just say he was a really shameless person.)

(d) 何度裏切られても涙を見ると許してしまう自分に腹が立つと言うか、愛想が尽きる。

(No matter how many times I get betrayed, I end up forgiving him when I see his tears. I'm angry at myself, or I should say, I'm sick of myself. (lit., I'm angry at myself, who ends up . . .))

(e) これは何と言うか、まあ、一種の妥協でしょうね。

(What should I call it? Hmm, it's a kind of compromise, I guess.)

(f) これは日記と言うか覚え書きと言うか……。

(Should I call this a diary, or a memo . . . ?)

(g) A: あの人は奥さんですか。

　　(Is she your wife?)

　　B: うーん、と言うか、恋人みたいなもんです。

　　(Well, actually, (I'd say) she's something like a lover.)

Notes

1. *To iu ka* is used when the speaker wants to restate what he/she has just said because it is not quite accurate or appropriate.

2. A word, a phrase or a sentence can precede *to iu ka*.

3. *Nan to iu ka* is used when the speaker cannot come up with a good word, phrase, etc., as in Ex.(e).

4. *To iu ka* can be used on its own, as in Ex.(g). As this example shows, *to iu ka* is often used when the speaker wants to restate or correct what another person has just said. The more colloquial form *(t)te iu ka* is commonly used in casual speech, as shown in (1). This form is particularly common among young speakers.

　(1) A: あの人は奥さんですか。

　　　B: うーん、（っ）て言うか、恋人みたいなもんです。(= Ex.(g))

[Related Expression]

To iu yori "rather than (saying that)" is used in similar contexts. The major difference is that when "X *to iu yori* Y" is used, the speaker is certain that Y is more accurate or appropriate than X in describing the thing, person, state, etc., in question, whereas when "X *to iu ka* Y" is used, it sounds like the speaker is less certain if Y is more accurate or appropriate than X.

[1]　a. 自分の勘違いと言うより不注意でした。(cf. KS(A))

　　　(It was my carelessness more than my misunderstanding.)

　　b. 彼のことは諦めたと言うより、もうどうでもよくなった。(cf. KS(B))

　　　(I'd rather say that I don't care about him anymore than say that I am through with him.)

(⇨ **to iu yori (wa)** (DIJG: 495-97))

to iu no wa　と言うのは　*phr.*　<s>

a phrase that introduces the reason for what has just been said	(I'm saying this) because; the reason (why I'm saying this) is that; by ~ I mean that; what I mean is that 【REL. *naze ka to iu to*】

◆ Key Sentences

(A)

Sentence₁		Sentence₂	
来月の旅行は取りやめます。	と言うのは、	同じ頃に大事なお客が来ることになった	んです。

(We are cancelling next month's trip. I'm saying this because it turns out that we're going to have an important guest around the same time.)

(B)

Sentence₁			
今まで読めていた画像ファイルがほとんど読めなくなってしまいました。			

Word / Phrase		Sentence₂	
ほとんど	と言うのは、	少しですが読めるファイルもある	のです。

(Almost all the image files that I have been able to read until now have become unreadable. I say "almost" because, even though there are only a few, there are files that are still readable.)

Formation

(i) S₁。と言うのは、S₂。

行けないかもしれない。と言うのは、同じ日に試験があるんだ。 (I may not be able to go because I have an exam on the same day.)

(ii) S₁。Word / Phrase と言うのは、S₂。 (where Word/Phrase is taken from S₁)

今ならできる。今ならと言うのは、来月になると忙しくなるからだ。 (I could do it (if it's) now. I'm saying "(if it's) now" because I'm going to be busy next month.)

Examples

(a) 社長に直接話してみたらどうですか。と言うのは、実は社長も以前そういうアイディアについて話していたことがあるんです。

(Why don't you talk to the (company) president (about it)? I'm saying this because he was talking about a similar idea before.)

(b) もう少し詳しく話してもらえませんか。と言うのは、私も少し前、同じような男から同じような被害に遭ったんです。

(Could you talk about it a little more in detail? (Because) I also ran into similar trouble with the same kind of man a little while ago.)

(c) それは一度専門家に調べてもらった方がいいでしょう。と言うのは、素人が勝手に直すと、知らないうちに部品を傷めてしまう可能性があるからです。

(I think it's better to have it checked out by an expert, because if an amateur tries to fix it himself, he could damage a part without knowing it.)

(d) 最近のパソコン用OSの普及で視覚障害者が困っている。と言うのは、これらのOSは画像中心で文字情報が少なく、文字を音声で読ませる方法があまり使えないからだ。

(People with vision problems are having trouble with the spread of the latest operating systems for personal computers because these operating systems are image-oriented with little word-based information, so there's not much of a chance to use software that reads words aloud.)

(e) これらのゲームは、より正確に言えば、「一人用ゲーム」というより「一人でもできるゲーム」と言うべきでしょう。と言いますのは、これらのゲームはやり方によっては二人以上でもできるからです。

(To be more accurate, these games should be called "games that can also be played alone" rather than "games for one person." What I mean is, depending on how you play them, these games can be played by two or more people.)

(f) あの提案書はたぶん通ると思う。たぶんと言うのは、審査委員の中に一人だけ反対するかもしれないのがいるんだ。

(I think that proposal will probably be approved. I say "probably" because there is one person on the review committee who might oppose it.)

Notes

1. In very polite speech, *to iimasu no wa* is used, as in Ex.(e).

2. Sentences with *to iu no wa* often end with *n desu* or *kara desu*, because the main sentence often provides the reason for, or an explanation of, the previous statement.   (⇨ ***no da*** (DBJG: 325-28))

3. *To iu no wa* can also refer to a word or phrase in the preceding sentence, as in KS(B) and Ex.(f), in which case the speaker is providing the reason for saying the word or phrase.

4. *To iu no wa* as demonstrated here is different from "X *to iu no wa* Y *da*," which means "what is called X is Y."
   (⇨ ***to iu no wa* ~ *koto da*** (DIJG: 487-92))

【Related Expression】

To iu no wa can be replaced with *naze* (X) *ka to iu to* "the reason why (X) is that," as shown in [1].

[1] a. 来月の旅行は取りやめます。｛と言うのは / なぜかと言うと｝、同じ頃に大事なお客が来ることになったんです。(= KS(A))

b. 今まで読めていた画像ファイルがほとんど読めなくなってしまいました。｛ほとんどと言うのは / なぜほとんどかと言うと｝、少しですが読めるファイルもあるのです。(= KS(B))

~ **to iwazu** ~ **to iwazu**　〜と言わず〜と言わず　*str.*

a structure indicating that s.t. is the case not only for A and B but also for many other places, things, etc., of X, to which A and B belong	A, B and many other ~; A, B and every~ else; including; whether X or Y 【REL. ~ *darō ga/to* ~ *darō ga/to*; ~ *de arō ga/to* ~ *de arō ga/to*; ~ *de are* ~ *de are*】

◆ Key Sentence

	Noun₁		Noun₂		
友達の引っ越しを手伝ったら、翌日	肩	と言わず	腰	と言わず	体のあちこちが痛んだ。

(I helped my friend move. Then, the next day my shoulders, my back and every other part of my body ached.)

Formation

N₁ と言わず N₂ と言わず

　窓と言わずドアと言わず　(including the windows and the doors)

Examples

(a) 武史の部屋は、壁と言わず天井と言わず、いたるところにサッカーの写真が貼ってあった。

(In Takeshi's room, pictures of soccer were posted on the walls, the ceiling and everywhere else.)

(b) しばらくすると、発疹が首と言わず手足と言わず、全身に広がった。

(Some time later, a rash spread over my neck, hands, feet and all over the rest of my body.)

(c) イベント会場は廊下と言わず階段と言わず、参加者で溢れていた。

(The participants were everywhere at the event site, even in the halls and on the stairs.)

(d) 彼女が身につけているものは、靴と言わず、時計と言わず、スカーフと言わず、すべてブランドものだ。

(Everything she wears, including her shoes, her watch and her scarf, is a famous brand.)

(e) 彼は仕事中と言わず休み時間と言わず、一時もコンピュータから離れることがない。

(He doesn't leave his computer even for a moment, whether it's work time or break time.)

(f) 姉のうちは昼と言わず夜と言わず、一日中テレビをつけっぱなしにしている。

(At my (elder) sister's house, the TV set is on all the time, day or night.)

(g) 男と言わず女と言わず、誰もがこの物語のヒロインには共感するはずだ。

(Anyone—man or woman—would sympathize with the heroine of this story.)

(h) 保守と言わず革新と言わず、どんな政治家もみな選挙資金集めのために奔走する。

(Every politician, whether conservative or liberal, works hard (lit., runs around) to raise money for his/her political campaign (lit., election).)

Notes

1. A *to iwazu* B *to iwazu* is used to present examples when stating that something is the case with many other places, things, people, etc., that belong to the same category as A and B do.

2. The main clause often contains a word or phrase to indicate the idea of "every," "all" or "any," such as *itaru tokoro* "everywhere" (Ex.(a)), *zenshin* "the entire body" (Ex.(b)), and *donna seijika* "every politician" (Ex.(h)).

3. When A and B in A *to iwazu* B *to iwazu* are the only members of the group to which A and B belong, the phrase means "whether A or B," as in Exs.(e)-(h).

[Related Expressions]

When it means "whether A or B," A *to iwazu* B *to iwazu* can be rephrased using A *darō ga/to* B *darō ga/to*, A *de arō ga/to* B *de arō ga/to*, or A *de are* B *de are*.

[1] a. 彼は仕事中 {と言わず / だろうが / だろうと / であろうが / であろう

と / であれ｝休み時間｛と言わず / だろうが / だろうと / であろうが /
であろうと / であれ｝、一時もコンピュータから離れることがない。

(= Ex.(e))

　b. 男｛と言わず / だろうが / だろうと / であろうが / であろうと / であ
れ｝女｛と言わず / だろうが / だろうと / であろうが / であろうと / で
あれ｝、誰もがこの物語のヒロインには共感するはずだ。　(= Ex.(g))

(⇨ ~ de are ~ de are (in this volume))

tokoro kara　　ところから　　*phr.*

a phrase that introduces the origins of names, theories, ideas and events

because; be caused by the fact that ~; from the fact that ~
【REL. *koto kara*; *node*; *kara*】

◆ Key Sentences

(A)

	Sentence		
この宝石は	猫の目に似ている	ところから	「猫目石」と名づけられている。

(This gem is called "cat's-eye" because it resembles a cat's eye.)

(B)

Sentence		
私が両者にそのことを十分説明しなかった	ところから	誤解が生じた。

(The misunderstanding was caused by the fact that I didn't explain it to both of them fully.)

Formation

(i)　｛V / Adj(*i*)｝inf ところから

　　｛する / した｝ところから　(because s.o. does/did s.t.)

　　｛高い / 高かった｝ところから　(because s.t. is/was expensive)

(ii)　Adj(*na*)stem{な/である/だった/であった}ところから

便利{な/である/だった/であった}ところから　(because s.t. is/was convenient)

(iii)　N{である/だった/であった}ところから

日本人{である/だった/であった}ところから　(because s.o. is/was a Japanese)

Examples

(a)　田中先生はいつも蝶ネクタイをしていたところから「蝶ネクタイ先生」と呼ばれていた。

(Dr. Tanaka was called "Prof. Bow Tie" because he always wore one.)

(b)　日本は憲法が戦力の保持を禁止しているところから、「軍隊」ではなく「自衛隊」を持っている。

(Because its constitution bans the possessing of military power, Japan has "Self-Defense Forces," but not an "army.")

(c)　この説は、両者が生物的に多くの共通点を持っているところから来ている。

(This theory comes from the fact that, biologically, the two species have many things in common.)

(d)　論語に「何もしないでいるより碁を打つ方がましだ」という教えがあるところから、碁は孔子以前にかなり普及していたとみられる。

(Because the Analects teach us that "It is better to play *go* than to not do anything," it appears that *go* was already fairly popular before Confucius' time.)

(e)　そのイギリス人とは家が近くだったところから、よく遊びに行って英語や英語の歌を教えてもらったりした。

(Because my house was close to the Englishman's, I visited him often and he taught me English and English songs and other things.)

(f)　この雑誌は最初、ある有名月刊誌の別冊として刊行されたのが好評だったところから、後に単独の雑誌として独立したものだ。

(This magazine was first published as a separate volume of a famous monthly magazine and later became an independent publication because it was so well received.)

(g) 今音楽で広く使われているCDは、実はベートーベンの第九交響曲の演奏時間が 74 分間だったところからその容量が決められたということだ。

(I heard that the capacity of the CDs we use so widely now for music was settled on because a (certain) performance of Beethoven's Ninth Symphony was 74 minutes long.)

Notes

1. In addition to its literal meaning "from the place (where)," *tokoro kara* is used metaphorically to explain where names, theories, ideas, events, etc., originated. In this sense, *tokoro kara* functions as a conjunction connecting something to its reason or cause by presenting why something (or someone) was named the way it (or he/she) is, why a certain theory or idea was conceived the way it was, or what caused a certain event, etc.

2. When the reason stated in a sentence is not the origin of an event, *tokoro kara* cannot be used, as shown in (1). (See Related Expression II.)

(1) a. *学資がないところから大学進学を諦めざるを得ない。

(Because I don't have money to study, I have no choice but to give up the idea of going to college.)

b. *雨が降っているところから今日の野球の試合は中止になった。

(Because it's raining, today's baseball game was cancelled.)

[Related Expressions]

I. *Koto kara* is synonymous with *tokoro kara* and can be used to indicate the origins of names, ideas, events, etc., as reasons, as in [1].

[1] a. この宝石は猫の目に似ている{ところから／ことから}「猫目石」と名づけられている。(= KS(A))

b. 私が両者にそのことを十分説明しなかった{ところから／ことから}誤解が生じた。(= KS(B))

However, when the *koto* of *koto kara* refers to an intangible thing, *tokoro kara* cannot be used.

[2] a. 妙な{ことから／*ところから}二人の関係は悪化した。

(The relationship between the two deteriorated due to strange circumstances.)

T

　　b. そのけんかは些細な｛ことから／*ところから｝始まった。

　　(The fight started from the slightest thing.)

　　　　　　　　(⇨ ***koto***¹ (DBJG: 191-93); ***koto kara*** (in this volume))

II. *Node* and *kara* can be used in place of *tokoro kara*, as in [3], but *node* and *kara* do not imply that the clause represents the origin of a name, idea, event, etc.

　[3]　a. この宝石は猫の目に似ている｛ところから／ので／から｝「猫目石」と名づけられている。(= KS(A))

　　b. 私が両者にそのことを十分説明しなかった｛ところから／ので／から｝誤解が生じた。(= KS(B))

Node and *kara* can be used even in the situation mentioned in Note 2.

　[4]　a. 学資がない｛ので／から／*ところから｝大学進学を諦めざるを得ない。(= (1a))

　　b. 雨が降っている｛ので／から／*ところから｝今日の野球の試合は中止になった。(= (1b))

　　　　　　　　(⇨ ***node*** (DBJG: 328-31); ***kara***³ (DBJG: 179-81))

T

to mo naku　ともなく　　*phr.*　<w>

a phrase indicating that the subject does s.t. without paying much attention, or that when, where, to whom, etc., s.t. took place is unclear	without intending to; without paying much attention; unconsciously; mindlessly; don't know (exactly) who/where/etc. (but); cannot tell (exactly) who/where/etc. (but); (to/from) no particular (person, etc.) 【REL. *to mo nashi ni*; *to naku*】

◆ **Key Sentences**

(A)

	V₁inf.nonpast			V₂ (= V₁)
散歩をしているうちに、	来る	ともなく	駅まで	来てしまった。

(While I was taking a walk, I came as far as the station without intending to.)

(B)

	Wh-word	Prt.		
我が家では	いつ	から	ともなく	正月にスキーに行く習慣が始まった。

(We do not know when, but my family started a tradition of going skiing on New Year's Day.)

Formation

(i) V₁inf.nonpast ともなく V₂ (where V₁ = V₂)

見るともなく見る (look at s.t. unconsciously)

(ii) Wh-word + Prt. ともなく

どこからともなく ((cannot tell from where but) from somewhere)

誰にともなく (to no one in particular)

Examples

(a) 聴くともなく聴いていたら、だんだんその演奏に引き込まれていった。

(As I was listening to the performance without paying much attention, I was gradually pulled into it.)

(b) 大学時代のことを考えるともなく考えていると、次々にクラスメートの顔が浮かんできた。

(When I was thinking mindlessly about my university days, the faces of my classmates came to my mind one after another.)

(c) 目撃者の話を聞くともなく後ろで聞いていたが、突然その話の中に事件解決のための重要な情報が含まれていることに気がついた。

(I was listening to the witness's story from behind without paying much attention when, all of sudden, I realized that it contained an important piece of information for solving the case.)

(d) どこからともなくいい匂いが漂ってきた。

((I couldn't tell from where, but) a good smell wafted from somewhere.)

(e) 「やっと終わった」。彼は誰にともなくつぶやいた。

("Finally, it's over," he muttered (lit., muttered to no one in particular).)

(f) 二人はどちらからともなく顔を見合わせて微笑んだ。

(The two smiled at each other almost at the same time. (lit., I cannot tell which one did it first, but the two looked at each other and smiled.))

Notes

1. *To mo naku* is an abbreviated form of *to iu koto mo naku* "without (doing s.t.)." V *to mo naku* is used when one does something without paying much attention to it.

2. When a verb precedes *to mo naku*, that verb is usually repeated, as in KS(A) and Exs.(a)-(c). However, this is not always the case, as shown in (1).

   (1) いつも母がその歌をロシア語で歌うのを聞いていたので、習うともなく自然に覚えてしまった。

   (Because I always heard my mother singing that song in Russian, I learned it without even trying.)

3. "Wh-word + Prt. *to mo naku*" is used when something took place but one cannot tell exactly which person began it (*dare kara to mo naku*), the exact place it began (*doko kara to mo naku*), the exact time it began (*itsu kara to mo naku*), etc.

4. "Wh-word *to mo naku*" (i.e., with no particle) is not acceptable, as shown in (2).

   (2) a. その習慣は{*いつともなく／いつからともなく}始まった。

   (That habit began sometime (but I cannot tell when).)

   b. {*どこともなく／どこからともなく}鐘の音が聞こえてくる。

   (I hear a bell (from) somewhere (but I cannot tell where).)

[Related Expressions]

I. *To mo nashi ni* is equivalent to *to mo naku* and the two can be used interchangeably.

[1] a. 散歩をしているうちに、来る｛ともなく／ともなしに｝駅まで来てしまった。(= KS(A))

b. 我が家ではいつから｛ともなく／ともなしに｝正月にスキーに行く習慣が始まった。(= KS(B))

II. *To naku* is similar to *to mo naku* in its form and meaning, but it is used only with limited words, including those shown in [2].

[2] a. この文章はどことなく変だ。

(This passage is strange somewhere (but I cannot tell where).)

b. 哲也のことが何となく気になる。

(I'm concerned about Tetsuya somehow (lit., for some reason I don't know).)

c. 由里は誰かれとなくよく人の面倒をみる。

(Yuri gives a lot of help to anyone (without discriminating).)

d. それとなく飯田に聞いてみたらどう。

(Why don't you ask Iida about it indirectly (lit., without making the intention obvious)?)

to mo naru to　ともなると

(⇨ ***ni/to mo naru to*** in this volume)

T

to mo suru to　ともすると　*phr.*　\<w\>

| a phrase that expresses the idea that s.t. is likely to take place | tend to; apt to; be likely to; easily; be bound to 【REL. *to mo sureba*; *yaya mo suru to*; *yaya mo sureba*; *dō ka suru to*】 |

◆ **Key Sentences**

(A)

			Verb
切れ味のよい議論は	ともすると	言葉の暴力と	**なる。**

(A sharp debate is apt to lead to a violent argument.)

(B)

			Verb	
親は自分の子供には	ともすると	点数が甘く	**なり**	がちだ。

(Parents tend to be more permissive (lit., lenient in grading) when it comes to their own children.)

Formation

ともすると V

  ともすると悲観的になる   (be likely to be pessimistic)

Examples

(a) 大きな組織はともするとセクショナリズムに陥る危険性がある。

(Large organizations are likely to be in danger of falling into sectionalism.)

(b) 商品づくりにおける標準化活動はともすると社内設計部門から嫌われる。

(Activities to promote standardization in product manufacturing are bound to be disliked by the design division.)

(c) 日本ではともすると議論が感情的になってしまい、知的なディベートの場が育ちにくいと言われる。

(People say that in Japan arguments tend to be emotional, and, therefore, that it is hard to develop occasions for intellectual debate.)

(d) スポーツ選手がいい記録を出すと、世間の期待が高くなり、ともするとその重圧に押しつぶされるようなケースも出てくる。

(When athletes make good records, the public raises its expectations, and this leads to cases where athletes are more likely to be crushed by the heavy pressure.)

(e) 日本語が論理的な表現に不適だとは思わないが、日常会話的な表現を安易に使うと、ともすると論理が曖昧になりやすい。

(I don't believe that Japanese is ill-suited for expressing logic, but if you use expressions from daily conversation carelessly, your logic is apt to become ambiguous.)

(f) 国際協力と言うと、ともすると富める国が貧しい国に援助を施すというように受け取られやすい。

(When we mention international cooperation, the tendency is to interpret it as rich countries giving aid to poor countries.)

(g) 従来の音楽教育はともすると学校の中だけの活動に終始しがちであった。

(Conventional music education throughout the school year was apt to provide activities only within the school.)

(h) 長期不況のもとでは、ともすると様々な議論が極端な悲観論や危機論に傾きがちである。

(The wide-ranging debate over the long recession has tended either to be overly pessimistic or to focus on the recession as a crisis.)

(i) 現在の状況では、ともすると経済的な視点からの開発が先行し、貴重な資源を浪費したり、生活環境を損ないかねない。

(Under the current circumstances, precedence will likely be given to economically-oriented development, and (consequently) problems such as the wasting of precious resources and the destruction of our living environment may take place.)

Notes

1. *To mo suru to* literally means "if s.t. happens" or "if s.t. triggers s.t.," but in contemporary Japanese it is commonly used to mean "tend to" or "be likely to."

2. The phrase often occurs with *gachi* "tend to," as in KS(B), Exs.(g) and (h), and *yasui* "it is easy; easily," as in Exs.(e) and (f), although this use is redundant.　　　　(⇒ **-gachi** (DIJG: 47-50); **-yasui** (DBJG: 541-43))

[Related Expressions]

I. *To mo sureba*, *yaya mo suru to* and *yaya mo sureba* are all synonymous with *to mo suru to* and can be used interchangeably.

[1] a. 切れ味のよい議論は{ともすると／ともすれば／ややもすると／やや
もすれば}言葉の暴力となる。(= KS(A))

b. 親は自分の子供には{ともすると／ともすれば／ややもすると／やや
もすれば}点数が甘くなりがちだ。(= KS(B))

II. *Dō ka suru to* "it may happen that; there are a few cases" is used in
situations similar to those in which *to mo suru to*, etc., are used.

[2] a. 切れ味のよい議論は{ともすると／どうかすると}言葉の暴力となる。
(= KS(A))

b. 親は自分の子供には{ともすると／どうかすると}点数が甘くなりが
ちだ。(= KS(B))

However, while *to mo suru to*, etc., occur only with verb predicates, *dō
ka suru to* can be used with other kinds of predicates, as in [3].

[3] a. この国ではワインが安い。普段飲むものなど{どうかすると／??とも
すると／??ややもすると}ミネラルウォーターより<u>安い</u>。

(In this country, wine is cheap. It may happen that wine, which
people commonly drink, is cheaper than mineral water.)

b. 東京の都心への通勤時間は通勤距離に比例しない。{どうかすると／
??ともすると／??ややもすると}他県から通う方が都内から通うより
ずっと<u>便利なこともある</u>。

(The necessary commuting time to central Tokyo is not in proportion to the commuting distance. In some cases, it may be
much more convenient to commute from another prefecture than
to commute from within Tokyo.)

to no   との   *phr.*   <w>

| a phrase that presents the content of the referent of the following noun (e.g., a report, notice, news, view) | that 【REL. *to iu*】 |

◆ **Key Sentences**

(A)

Sinf		Noun	
経済情勢は悪化している	との	見方	が優勢だ。

(The view that the economic situation is worsening is dominant.)

(B)

Sinf			
邦画の入場者数がハリウッド映画を上回って1位になったのは初めて (だ)	との	こと	だ。

((It is said that) Apparently this is the first time that the size of the audience for a Japanese movie has exceeded that of a Hollywood movie, making it No. 1.)

Formation

Sinf との N   (だ after Adj(*na*)stem and N is often omitted.)

提案が通ったとの報告   (a report that the proposal was accepted)

危険(だ)との意見   (an opinion that s.t./s.o. is dangerous)

Examples

(a) 伊豆半島付近で地震があったとの知らせを受けた。

(I received the news that there was an earthquake near the Izu Peninsula.)

(b) 探検隊が日本時間の13時30分にベースキャンプに到着したとの報告がもたらされた。

(There was a report that the expedition party arrived at the base camp at 1:30 p.m. Japan time.)

(c) この研究テーマは社会のニーズに合っていないとの指摘がなされた。

(It was pointed out that this research topic does not meet society's needs.)

(d) 副大臣の数をあまり多くすると行政を混乱させるとの意見がある。

(There is a view that having too many vice-ministers will make governing chaotic.)

(e) 無断リンクは著作権侵害との見解が発表された。

(The view was announced that making a link (to a website) without permission infringes on the site owner's copyright.)

(f) 当地からは遠隔で不便との理由で患者さん自身が受診を希望しない場合が多い。

(Patients often don't want to come in for their examination because they are far away and it is inconvenient (to come here).)

(g) 新システムの評価はどのように行うのかとの質問に対し、ユーザーへのアンケートを行うとの回答があった。

(To the question as to how the new system would be evaluated, the response was that they would circulate a questionnaire among users.)

Notes

1. *To no* is comprised of the quotation marker *to* and the noun modifying particle *no*. *To no* is used to indicate the content of reports, news, notifications, opinions, views, suggestions, reasons, questions, etc.
   (⇨ *to*³ (DBJG: 478-80); *no*¹ (DBJG: 312-15))

2. *Da* after nouns and *na*-adjective stems is usually omitted, as in KS(B), Exs.(e) and (f).

3. *Suru* or *shita* of *suru*-verbs is sometimes omitted.

   (1) a. J銀行が中小企業の手数料を優遇(する)との報道がありました。

      (There was a report that J Bank is going to treat medium- and small-sized companies favorably in terms of handling fees.)

      b. ローマ法王ヨハネ・パウロ2世が死去(した)とのニュースが今朝流れた。

      (The news that Pope John Paul II died circulated this morning.)

4. *To no* is usually used in formal written language. Thus, sentences like (2) are not acceptable.

   (2) ジェーンが日本へ行く{*との／という}話は本当ですか。

      (Is it true that Jane is going to Japan?)

   One exception to the above is when *to no* is used in the phrase *to no koto desu*, which is used in conveying messages orally.

   (3) 森下さんが「すぐお電話下さい」とのことです。

      (Mr. Morishita said that he wanted a call (from you) immediately.)

【Related Expression】

To iu, a phrase to present information that identifies or explains the following noun, can replace *to no* in most cases.

[1] a. 経済情勢は悪化している{との / という}見方が優勢だ。(= KS(A))

b. 伊豆半島付近で地震があった{との / という}知らせを受けた。

(= Ex.(a))

To iu is less formal than *to no* and can also be used in conversation. (See (2) in Note 4.)

Note that *to iu* cannot replace *to no* when *to no* is used in the phrase *to no koto da/desu* for reporting.

[2] a. 邦画の入場者数がハリウッド映画を上回って1位になったのは初めて{との / *という}ことだ。(= KS(B))

b. 森下さんが「すぐお電話下さい」{との / *という}ことです。(= (3))

In [2], S *to iu koto da/desu* is not ungrammatical, but it means "(s.t.) means S."

Another difference between *to iu* and *to no* is that nouns can precede *to iu* but not *to no*, as shown in [3].

[3] a. 「雪国」{という / *との}小説
(the novel called "Snow Country")

b. ジャパンタイムズ{という / *との}会社
(the company called/named The Japan Times)

(⇨ **to iu** (DBJG: 486-87))

totemo ~ nai   とても～ない   *str.*

a structure that is used to deny emphatically the ability of s.o/s.t. or the possibility of an event, state or action	cannot possibly; totally impossible; there is no possibility; there is no way; not ~ at all; not ~ by any means; by no means 【REL. *tōtei ~ nai*; *mattaku ~ nai*; *kesshite ~ nai*】

◆ **Key Sentences**

(A)

			Vneg	
この仕事は	とても	私には	**でき**	ない。
(I cannot possibly do this job.)				

(B)

		Noun Phrase		
吉岡さんは	とても	私の勝てる相手	では	ない。
(Mr. Yoshioka is someone I couldn't possibly beat. (lit., Mr. Yoshioka is not someone I could possibly beat.))				

(C)

		Noun		
この病気は	とても	治る	見込み	は	ない。
(There is no possibility that he will recover from this illness.)					

Formation

(i)   とても Vneg ない

　　　とても歩けない　(cannot possibly walk)
　　　とても届かない　(do not reach at all)

(ii) とても N はない

　　　とても望みはない　(there is no (hope) at all)

(iii) とても NP ではない

とても人に見せられるものではない　(s.t. is something I cannot possibly show others (lit., s.t. is not something I can possibly show others))

Examples

(a) 私は数学ではとても彼にかなわない。

(I cannot possibly beat him in mathematics.)

(b) こんな予算ではとてもこの学校を維持していけない。

(It is totally impossible to maintain this school with a budget like this.)

(c) 今の大統領はとてもこの国を統治する能力はない。

(The current president has no ability at all to govern this country.)

(d) この病人はとても助からない。

(There is no way this patient can possibly be saved.)

(e) この地方に雪が降ることはとてもあり得ない。

(There's no way it could snow in this region.)

(f) とても我々に勝ち目はない。

(We have no chance of winning.)

(g) 経済はとてもすぐには回復しそうにない。

(It does not look like there is any chance the economy will recover soon.)

(h) 山岸さんはとても 80 歳には見えない。

(Mrs. Yamagishi does not look 80 years old at all.)

T

(i) そんな危ないところにはとても子供を行かせられない。

(I cannot possibly send my child to such a dangerous place.)

Notes

1. *Totemo ~ nai* is used to negate a statement completely. The statement is often about the ability of someone or something, as in KS(A), (B) and Exs.(a)-(c), the possibility of an event, state or action, as in KS(C) and Exs.(d)-(h), or one's desire or willingness, as in Ex.(i).

2. *Totemo ~ nai* can also be used in denying strongly that someone or something looks a certain way, as in Exs.(g) and (h).

3. *Totemo* sometimes occurs with words that contain a negative meaning rather than with the negative forms of verbs, as in (1).

(1) a. その体ではとても旅行は無理だ。

(With your condition (lit., body), there's no way you can travel.)

b. 今年中の完成なんてとても不可能だ。

(Completing it this year will be impossible.)

c. 私なんかとても駄目です。

(I am no good at all.)

4. When *totemo* is used, the speaker's/writer's statement sounds subjective. In situations like (1c), where the speaker is denying his ability at something, *totemo* also conveys a sense of modesty. (See Related Expression II.)

【Related Expressions】

I. *Tōtei ~ nai* "not at all" is synonymous with *totemo ~ nai* and the two can be used interchangeably when negating statements, although *totemo ~ nai* is not as emphatic as *tōtei ~ nai*.

[1] a. その仕事は{とても / とうてい}私にはできない。(= KS(A))

b. 吉岡さんは{とても / とうてい}私の勝てる相手ではない。(= KS(B))

c. この病気は{とても / とうてい}治る見込みはない。(= KS(C))

II. *Mattaku ~ nai* "totally not; not at all" and *kesshite ~ nai* "never" are also used for total negation. However, when these adverbs are used, the speaker's/writer's judgment of the statement sounds more objective. Thus, in [2], for example, the judgment sounds definitive.

[2] この病気は{全く / 決して}治る見込みはない。(cf. KS(C))

Similarly, in [3] the speaker/writer sounds certain about his/her judgment.

[3] その仕事は{全く / 決して}私にはできない。(cf. KS(A))

Note that *mattaku* and *kesshite* are not appropriate when the speaker/writer wants to convey modesty. (See Note 4.)

to wa   とは   *comp. prt.*

a compound particle marking an event, action or state that the speaker/ writer does not expect and that causes him/her to feel some emotion	(not think/expect/etc.) that; (be surprised / be glad / regret / etc.) that 【REL. *to iu no wa*; ***koto ni***】

◆ **Key Sentences**

(A)

Sinf		
彼が自分のベンチャー会社を立ち上げる	とは	思いもしなかった。
(I never thought that he would launch his own venture business.)		

(B)

Sinf		Predicate (emotion)
あんないい店がなくなった	とは	残念だ。
(It is too bad that such a nice shop is gone.)		

(C)

Sinf			Noun	
子供が生まれた途端にがんの宣告を受ける	とは	何という	悲劇	だ。
(What a tragedy it is for her to be told that she had cancer right after she'd had her baby.)				

(D)

Sinf	
こんな便利なサイトがあった	とは！
((a) I'm surprised that there is such a convenient website. (b) How great to have such a convenient website! (c) Who would have thought there would be such a convenient website!)	

T

Formation

(i) {V / Adj(*i*)} inf とは

   {来る / 来た} とは (驚いた) ((I'm surprised that) s.o. will come/came)

   {高い / 高かった} とは (驚いた) ((I'm surprised that) s.t. is/was expensive)

(ii) {Adj(*na*)stem / N} {ø / だ / だった} とは

   上手 {ø / だ / だった} とは (驚いた) ((I'm surprised that) s.o. is/was good at s.t.)

   医者 {ø / だ / だった} とは (驚いた) ((I'm surprised that) s.o. is/was a doctor)

Examples

(a) お父さんがそんなにお悪いとは知りませんでした。
   (I didn't know that your father was that ill.)

(b) こんなに早く自分の家が持てるとは思いもしなかった。
   (I never thought I could have my own house this soon.)

(c) ハリケーンのためにガソリンがこんなに上がるとは想像すらしなかった。
   (I would never have imagined that gas prices would go up this much because of a hurricane.)

(d) 一つのテレビドラマが日韓交流にこれほど影響を与えるとは誰が予測し得たであろう。
   (Who could have predicted that a TV drama would have this much influence on cultural exchange and travel between Japan and Korea?)

(e) 蒸したてのお芋がこんなにおいしいとは驚きました。
   (I'm surprised that fresh steamed potatoes taste this good.)

(f) まだ知り合って一週間にもならない私にお金を借りに来るとは驚きだ。
   (I was shocked that he came to borrow money from me less than a week after we first got acquainted.)

(g) こんなにおいしくて、ボリュームがあって、たったの 500 円とはありがたい。
   (It's great (lit., I'm thankful) that this (dish) tastes so good, there's a lot of it, and it costs only 500 yen.)

(h) 大勢の人が家をなくして困っているというのに、それを利用して金をもうけるとはけしからん。

(It is inexcusable that while many people have lost their houses and are suffering, some take advantage of this to make money.)

(i) バッハの最高傑作の演奏をDVDで見られるとは何という幸せでしょう！

(How happy I am to be able to watch a performance of Bach's best work on DVD!)

(j) 自分たちで嘘を広めておいて、それを既成事実にしようとは何たることだ！

(What a (shameful) thing it is to spread lies and try to convince people that they are true (lit., make them an established fact).)

Notes

1. *To wa* is commonly used with the negative forms of verbs that occur with quoted speech, as shown in (1).

   (1) a. 私は君に帰ってもいいとは<u>言わなかった</u>。
       (I didn't tell you that you could go home.)

       b. 核兵器が戦争で使われるとは<u>思わない</u>。
       (I don't think that a nuclear weapon will be used in war.)

   However, *to wa* is also used to present an event, action or state which is unexpected and causes the speaker/writer to have such feelings as surprise, happiness, sadness, anger or regret.

2. When *to wa* is used with verbs that do not express emotion, such as *omou* "think" and *yosoku-suru* "predict," the verb is sometimes paired with emphatic particles like *mo* and *sura*, as in KS(A), Exs.(b) and (c).

3. In some situations, S *to wa* is followed by *nan* { *taru* / *to iu* } N (*da*) to express the speaker's/writer's strong emotion, as in KS(C), Exs.(i) and (j).

4. The predicate after *to wa* (i.e., X in "*to wa* X") is sometimes omitted, with an optional sentence particle such as *nee*.

   (2) a. こんなことになろうとは！　[Written]
       (I'm surprised / I didn't expect / etc. that it would come to this!)

       b. こんな弱いチームに負けるとはねえ！　[Spoken]
       (I can't believe we lost to such a weak team!)

5. *Da* after nouns and *na*-adjective stems, and the conjugated part of *suru*-verbs are often omitted.

T

(3) a. あんな素敵なカップルが離婚(だ / する / した)とは！

(How sad/horrible/etc. (it is) that such a wonderful couple will get / got divorced!)

b. 申し込み手続きがこんなに面倒(だ)とは思わなかった。

(I didn't expect that the application procedure would be this cumbersome.)

c. 彼がサウジアラビアへ転勤(だ / する / させられる)とはねえ。

(Who would have thought he'd be transferred to Saudi Arabia?)

【Related Expression】

To wa in [1] is the shortened form of *to iu no wa* and is different from the *to wa* discussed above.

[1] a. ケータイ｛とは / というのは｝携帯電話のことだ。

(*Keitai* is short for *keitai-denwa* (cell phone; lit., portable telephone).)

b.「足が出る」｛とは / というのは｝出費が予定していたより多くなることだ。

("*Ashi ga deru*" means that expenses exceed the amount budgeted.)

(⇨ ***to iu no wa ~ koto da*** (DIJG: 487-92))

T

to wa ie   とは言え   *phr.*   <w>

a conjunctive phrase meaning "although it is said that"	although (it is said that / s.o. says that); even though (it is said that / s.o. says that); admitting that; that being said; however; nevertheless 【REL. *to (wa) itte mo*; *to wa iu mono no*】

◆ Key Sentences

(A)

Noun		
夏	とは言え、	ここはまだちょっと肌寒いくらいの涼しさだ。

(Although it is summer, it is still cool here—almost to the extent that it can be called a little chilly.)

(B)

Sinf		
時間がなかった	とは言え、	ジェーンにこれくらいのレポートが書けないはずはない。

((i) Even admitting that Jane didn't have much time, I don't believe that she couldn't write a (simple) report like this.
(ii) Although Jane says that she didn't have much time (or you say that Jane didn't have much time), I don't believe that she couldn't write a (simple) report like this.)

(C)

Sentence₁		Sentence₂
今度の学会が楽しみだ。	とは言え、	まだ発表準備は全然できていない。

(I'm looking forward to the next academic conference. That being said, I haven't prepared for my presentation at all yet.)

Formation

(i) Sinf とは言え (だ after Adj(*na*)stem and N is omitted.)

　　 ｛知らない / 知らなかった｝とは言え (although s.o. doesn't/didn't know)

　　 ｛寒い / 寒かった｝とは言え (although it is/was cold)

　　 不便｛ø / だった｝とは言え (although s.t. is/was inconvenient)

　　 子供｛ø / だった｝とは言え (although s.o. is/was a child)

(ii) S₁。とは言え S₂。

　　 (⇨ KS(C))

Examples

(a) 子供がやったこととは言え、これは立派な犯罪だ。

(Although this was done by a child, it practically amounts to a crime.)

(b) 予想していた返答だったとは言え、やはりそれを聞いた時はショックだった。

(Although it was the response I'd expected, it really did shock me to hear it.)

(c) ノートブック型とは言え、ディスプレイは17インチ、プロセッサーは2.4GHz、内蔵ドライブは250GBもあり、DVD/CD-RWコンボドライブ付きという優れものだ。

(Although it is a laptop, it is an excellent machine, with a 17-inch display, a 2.4GHz processor, a voluminous 250GB internal drive and a DVD/CD-RW combo drive.)

(d) 安いとは言え、都会の高級マンションだ。普通の者が簡単に買える代物ではない。

(Although I say (it is) reasonable, it is an upscale condominium in the city. It's not something ordinary people can easily afford.)

(e) いかに暫定的処置とは言え、これはずさんすぎる。

(No matter how temporary these measures are supposed to be, this is just too slipshod.)

(f) 怪我をして動けないとは言え、ものを考えることはできる。

(Even though I cannot move because of my injury, I can still think.)

(g) 毎日走っているとは言え、1キロほどジョギングするだけだから大した運動にはならない。

(Although I say I run every day, it's just one kilometer of jogging, so I don't get much exercise.)

(h) 退職したとは言え、毎日やることがたくさんあるので忙しい。

(Although I've retired, I have lots of things to do every day, which keeps me busy.)

(i) 燃料電池は将来化石燃料に代わる主要エネルギーになるだろう。とは言え、これにはまだ解決すべき技術的な問題が多く残っている。

(Fuel cells will probably become a major source of energy in the future, replacing fossil fuels. Having said that, many technical problems (with this technology) remain to be solved.)

Notes

1. *Ie* in *to wa ie* is the imperative form of *iu* "say." The imperative forms of
    some verbs convey the sense of concession (i.e., "even if; even though")
    when they are used in subordinate clauses.

    (⇨ *de are*; *ni shiro/seyo*; *wa are* (in this volume))

2. As seen in KS(B), *to wa ie* can be interpreted two ways in some situa-
    tions, i.e., "admitting that; although I admit that" and "although s.o. says
    that."

3. *To wa ie* can be used at the beginning of a sentence, as in KS(C) and
    Ex.(i). In this case, *to wa ie* means "That being said; Having said that."

4. *To wa ie* is used primarily in writing.

[Related Expressions]

I. *To (wa) itte mo* is synonymous with *to wa ie* and can be used in place of
    to wa ie without changing the meaning of the sentence, as shown in [1].

    [1] a. 夏{とは言え / と(は)言っても}、ここはまだちょっと肌寒いくらい
            の涼しさだ。(= KS(A))

         b. 時間がなかった{とは言え / と(は)言っても}、ジェーンにこれくら
            いのレポートが書けないはずはない。(= KS(B))

    Note that *to (wa) itte mo* is used in both written and spoken Japanese.

    (⇨ *to itte mo* (DIJG: 474-77))

II. *To wa iu mono no* is also synonymous with *to wa ie* and can be used in
    place of *to wa ie* in most situations without changing the meaning of the
    sentence.

    [2] a. 夏{とは言え / とは言うものの}、ここはまだちょっと肌寒いくらい
            の涼しさだ。(= KS(A))

         b. 時間がなかった{とは言え / とは言うものの}、ジェーンにこれくら
            いのレポートが書けないはずはない。(= KS(B) when it means (i))

    However, when *to wa ie* means "although s.o. (other than the first
    person) says that . . . ," *to wa iu mono no* cannot replace *to wa ie*.

    [3] 時間がなかった{とは言え /*とは言うものの}、ジェーンにこれくらい
         のレポートが書けないはずはない。(= KS(B) when it means (ii))

tsui つい *adv.*

{ an adverb used to describe s.o. doing s.t. without being able to control himself/herself or used to indicate the closeness of a time or a place } unintentionally; without being able to control oneself; without meaning to; carelessly; involuntarily; in spite of oneself; just; only

【REL. *ukkari*; *omowazu*】

◆ **Key Sentences**

(A)

		V *te*	
楽しかったので	つい	**飲みすぎて**	しまった。

(Because I had such a good time, I ended up drinking too much (without meaning to).)

(B)

	Time Adv. (close to the present time)		
つい	**さっき**	まで	山口さんが来ていたんです。

(Mr. Yamaguchi was here until just a little while ago.)

Formation

(i) つい V

    つい居眠りをする　(s.o. dozes carelessly/unintentionally)

(ii) つい Adv. (time)

    つい最近　(just recently)

Examples

(a) 人のお金を使うのは悪いとは知りながら、つい使ってしまった。

(I know it's a bad thing to use someone else's money but I just couldn't control myself (and used it).)

(b) 安かったのでつい買ってしまった。

(It was cheap, so I just bought it (even though I didn't mean to).)

(c) 恵美につい亜紀の秘密を話してしまった。

(I carelessly told Aki's secret to Emi.)

(d) 彼の仕事を見ているとじれったいのでつい手を貸してしまう。

(I feel impatient when I see him doing his work, so, without intending to, I end up extending a hand.)

(e) あの人は面白いのでついからかいたくなる。

(He's so funny it's hard to resist teasing him (lit., I come to want to tease him without meaning to)).)

(f) この店は感じがいいのでつい入ってみたくなる。

(This shop has such a good atmosphere that I can't help wanting to go in.)

(g) ついこの間、新年を祝ったと思ったら今日はもうバレンタインデーだ。

(It feels like we just celebrated New Year's the other day, and here it is Valentine's Day already.)

(h) 彼女からは、つい2、3日前にメールをもらった。

(I received an e-mail from her only two or three days ago.)

(i) ついそこに喫茶店がありますからそこで話しましょう。

(There's a tea house just over there, so let's talk there.)

Notes

1. *Tsui* is used when someone does something unintentionally. In some situations, it carries more specific meanings, such as "carelessly" or "involuntarily."

2. When *tsui* is used with time adverbs or with location nouns, it emphasizes the closeness of a moment in the past or a place, as in KS(B) and Exs.(g)-(i).

[Related Expressions]

I. *Ukkari* "carelessly" and *tsui* are used in similar situations.

[1] a. 恵美に{つい / うっかり}亜紀の秘密を話してしまった。(= Ex.(c))

b. その家の見張りをしていないといけないのに{つい / うっかり}居眠りをしてしまった。

(Although I should have been watching the house, I accidentally dozed off.)

In the above examples, *tsui* and *ukkari* can be used together, as in [2].

[2]　a. 恵美についうっかり亜紀の秘密を話してしまった。(cf. [1a])

　　　b. その家の見張りをしていないといけないのについうっかり居眠りをし
　　　　てしまった。(cf. [1b])

The difference between *ukkari* and *tsui* is that the former is used when a careless action comes from the person's absentmindedness or lack of attention while the latter is used when the person does something due to his/her lack of self-control. Thus, *tsui* cannot be used in [3a] and *ukkari* cannot be used in [3b].

[3]　a.｛うっかり／*つい｝違う物を買ってしまった。
　　　　(I carelessly bought the wrong thing.)

　　　b. 安かったので｛つい／*うっかり｝買ってしまった。(= Ex.(b))

For the same reason, *tsui* cannot be used with verbs describing uncontrollable actions, as in [4].

[4]　a.｛うっかり／*つい｝自分の駅を乗り過ごした。
　　　　(I missed my station by mistake.)

　　　b.｛うっかり／*つい｝アポイントメントを忘れてしまった。
　　　　(I carelessly forgot my appointment.)

II. *Omowazu* "unintentionally; involuntarily" is synonymous with *tsui* and can be used interchangeably in some situations.

[5]　a. 楽しかったので｛つい／思わず｝飲みすぎてしまった。(= KS(A))

　　　b. 応援している力士が負けそうになって、｛つい／思わず｝力が入った。
　　　　(When it looked like the *sumō* wrestler I supported was going to be beaten, I got tense in spite of myself.)

The difference between *omowazu* and *tsui* is that the former is used when someone does something as a natural, instinctive reaction. When a reaction is a sudden one, *tsui* cannot be used, as in [6].

[6]　a. 目の前に子供が飛び出したので｛思わず／*つい｝クラクションを鳴ら
　　　　した。
　　　　(A child ran out in front of my car, so I honked instinctively.)

　　　b. 歯医者に痛い歯を触られて｛思わず／*つい｝悲鳴を上げた。
　　　　(I yelled out in spite of myself when the dentist touched my aching tooth.)

tsuide ni ついでに *phr.*

a phrase used to express the idea that s.o. does a second thing at the same time as the first because it takes less time or effort

when; while (~ at it); as; on one's way to; since ~ (anyway); as well; at one's convenience

◆ **Key Sentences**

(A)

	Vinf		
京都へ	来た	ついでに	龍安寺の石庭を見に行こうと思っている。

(Since I'm in Kyoto, I'm thinking of going to see the rock garden at Ryoanji Temple.)

(B)

V*masu*		
頼み	ついでに	もう一つお願いしてもいいですか。

(While I'm at it, may I ask another favor of you?)

(C)

	Adj(*na*)stem		
この仕事は大変だが、	大変	ついでに	来週の分もいま片づけておけば後が楽だ。

(This job is a real chore, but while we're at it if we finish the work for next week, too, we'll have an easier time later.)

(D)

	VN		
生活費を抑えるために電気や水を節約し始めたが、	節約	ついでに	エアコンも止めることにした。

(I began to conserve electricity and water to lower my living expenses and as I'm cutting back, I decided to stop using the air conditioner as well.)

T

(E)

Noun			
話	の	ついでに	このことも言っておきます。
(While I'm telling you the story, let me add this, too.)			

(F)

Sentence₁		Sentence₂			
コピーしに行くの？	じゃ、	これも	ついでに	お願いできる？
(Are you going to make copies? Then, could I ask you to do this as well?)					

Formation

(i) Vinf ついでに

　　{行く／行った}ついでに　(when s.o. goes/went)

(ii) V*masu* ついでに

　　送りついでに　(when s.o. sends s.t. / gives a ride to s.o.)

(iii) Adj(*na*)stem ついでに

　　面倒ついでに　(since s.o. is doing a tedious thing anyway)

(iv) Adj(*i*){stem／inf.nonpast}ついでに

　　恥ずかし(い)ついでに　(since s.o. is embarrassed anyway)

(v) VN ついでに

　　発送ついでに　(while s.o. ships s.t.)

(vi) N のついでに

　　食事のついでに　(when s.o. has a meal)

　　ニューヨーク出張のついでに　(when s.o. goes to New York on
　　business)

Examples

(a) バンクーバーへ行くついでにシアトルの友達のところに寄る予定だ。

　　(I plan to stop by my friend's place in Seattle on my way to Vancouver.)

(b) 車を洗ったついでに中も掃除しておいた。

　　(When I washed my car, I cleaned the inside as well.)

(c) 叱られついでに、もう一つの失敗のことも話してしまいます。

(Since you've already told me off once, let me go ahead and tell you about another mistake I made.)

(d) 恥かきついでにもう一つお聞きしますが、アメリカも大学入試はあるんですか。

(Now that I've been embarrassed (by my ignorance) once, let me ask you another question. Are there college entrance exams in America, too?)

(e) 今回は高級ホテルに泊まっているので、贅沢ついでにホテルのレストランで食事をすることにした。

(I'm staying at a first-class hotel this time, and if that isn't luxurious enough, I've decided to have dinner at the hotel restaurant.)

(f) ご苦労ついでにこの翻訳も手伝ってもらえませんか。

(Since you're working hard anyway, could I ask you to help me with this translation, too?)

(g) 厚かましいついでにお願いがもう一つあります。

(I've already been shameless (in asking you favors), but I have another favor to ask of you.)

(h) 新しい電気自動車の取材ついでに自分も少し運転させてもらった。

(When I went to report on the new electric car, I got to drive it a little myself.)

(i) 買い物のついでに銀行に寄って少し現金を下ろしていきます。

(I'll stop by the bank and withdraw some cash when I go shopping.)

(j) 以上が今週の予定ですが、ついでに来週の予定も言っておきます。

(That is the schedule for this week, and while I'm at it, let me tell you the schedule for next week as well.)

(k) 明日用事で銀座に行くので、そのついでにデパートに寄って少し買い物をしようと思う。

(Tomorrow I'm going to the Ginza, and on my way there I'm thinking of stopping by one of the department stores and doing some shopping.)

Notes

1. "X *tsuide ni* Y" expresses the idea that someone does Y when he/she does X because that way it takes less time or effort to do Y. In this case, X is the main action. There is no convenient English equivalent

which conveys the idea of *tsuide ni*; the corresponding English differs depending on the context, as seen in the KS and Exs.

2. A limited number of adjectives can precede *tsuide ni*; mostly they describe an undesirable situation (e.g., *taihen* "difficult," *mendō* "cumbersome," *hazukashii* "embarrassing," *atsukamashii* "shameless").

3. *Tsuide ni* is often used when someone asks a favor of someone else, as in KS(B), (F), Exs.(f) and (g).

4. *Tsuide ni* can be used without modification, as in KS(F) and Ex.(j). The main action is usually mentioned in the preceding sentence.

5. *Tsuide ni* can be used with a demonstrative, as in Ex.(k), where *sono* refers to the action in the preceding sentence.

6. *Tsuide* can be used with a time noun such as *toki* and *ori*, as in (1).

(1) a. お金はついでの時に返してもらえば結構です。

(Just give me (back) the money at your convenience.)

b. 渡したいものがあるので、ついでの折でいいですから私のオフィスに寄ってもらえますか。

(I have something to give you, so could you stop by my office next time you come in this direction?)

T

tsuite wa   ついては   *conj.*   \<w\>

a sentence-initial conjunction that means "with regard to this," referring to what is stated in the preceding sentence	therefore; thus; so; because of this; for this reason; with regard to this 【REL. *ni tsuite (wa)*; *sono tame*; *sore yue*】

◆ **Key Sentence**

Sentence₁		Sentence₂
コンピュータウイルスが全国的に広がっています。	ついては、	不審なメールが届いた場合は、添付ファイルを開くことなく当該メールを削除して下さい。

(Computer viruses are spreading across the country. Because of this, if you receive a suspicious e-mail (lit., in the event a suspicious e-mail arrives), delete the e-mail without opening the attached file.)

Examples

(a) この書類は契約文の日本語抄訳です。ついては、本訳をご参照の上、ウェブの英文契約書にご同意いただく必要があります。

(This document is the abridged Japanese translation of the agreement. Therefore, it is necessary for you to refer to this translation and accept the English agreement posted online.)

(b) 11月分授業料は10月15日に指定預金口座から引き落とさせていただきます。ついては、前日までに預金残高の確認をお願いします。

(We are going to withdraw the November tuition and fees from your designated bank account on October 15. Therefore, please be sure to check the account balance by the previous day.)

(c) 夏の省エネ対策について本社から通知がありました。ついては、別紙を参照の上、夏季のエネルギー節約にご協力をお願いいたします。

(Headquarters has sent a notification with regard to summer energy conservation measures. We therefore request your cooperation with the summer energy saving in accordance with the measures listed in the attachment (lit., after referring to the attachment).)

(d) 深刻な雇用問題に対しては、再就職や雇用流動性を促進させる必要がある。ついては、以下の施策を積極的に展開されたい。

(To counter the serious unemployment (lit., employment) problem, it is necessary to promote reemployment and employment mobility. With regard to this, we'd like the following measures to be actively implemented.)

T

(e) 新しくインターネット販売の事業を始める計画です。つきましては、その資金を融資していただきたいのです。

(We plan to launch a new Internet sales business. Therefore, we would like to request financing for it.)

(f) 今月は「リサイクル強化月間」になっています。つきましては、皆様方のご理解とご協力をお願いいたします。

(This is a "recycling reinforcement month." We therefore request your understanding and cooperation.)

Notes

1. *Tsuite wa* literally means "with regard to." When it is used in sentence-initial position, as in "S₁. *Tsuite wa* S₂.", S₁ represents the reason for stating S₂.

2. *Tsuite wa* is used when making a request or giving notification, but it cannot be used in simple statements such as those in (1).

  (1) a. 長い文は耳で聞いた場合、理解するのが難しい。{*ついては / そのため} テレビやラジオのニュースでは短い文が使われる。

    (Long sentences are hard for our ears to comprehend; therefore, short sentences are used for TV and radio news reports.)

    b. 私の父は私が３つの時に交通事故で亡くなった。{*ついては / そのため}、私は父の記憶がほとんどない。

    (My father died when I was three. Thus, I have almost no memory of him.)

3. *Tsuite wa* and *tsukimashite wa* are commonly used in documents such as company memos, public notices, legal documents and formal letters.

4. The polite form *tsukimashite wa* is used in formal business conversation, as in (Ex.(e)), and in documents in which a polite tone is desirable, as in Ex.(f).

[Related Expressions]

I. The sentence-initial conjunction *tsuite wa* should not be confused with N *ni tsuite (wa)*, which means "about N; concerning N" but does not mean "therefore." (⇨ ***ni tsuite*** (DIJG: 280-83))

II. *Sono tame* and *sore yue*, which mean "therefore; for that reason; because of that," can be used in place of *tsuite wa*.

[1] a. この書類は契約文の日本語抄訳です。{ついては / そのため / それ故}、本訳をご参照の上、ウェブの英文契約書にご同意いただく必要があります。(= Ex.(a))

   b. 深刻な雇用問題に対しては、再就職や雇用流動性を促進させる必要がある。{ついては / そのため / それ故}、以下の施策を積極的に展開されたい。(= Ex.(d))

Note that *sono tame* and *sore yue* are somewhat unnatural in request sentences, as shown in [2].

[2] a. コンピュータウイルスが全国的に広がっています。{ついては / ?そのため / ?それ故}、不審なメールが届いた場合は、添付ファイルを開くことなく当該メールを削除して下さい。(= KS)

   b. 11月分授業料は10月15日に指定預金口座から引き落とさせていただきます。{ついては / ?そのため / ?それ故}、前日までに預金残高の確認をお願いします。(= Ex.(b))

As mentioned in Note 2, *tsuite wa* cannot be used with simple statements, but this is not the case with *sono tame* and *sore yue*, as shown in [3].

[3] a. 長い文は耳で聞いた場合、理解するのが難しい。{そのため / それ故 / *ついては}テレビやラジオのニュースでは短い文が使われる。

(= (1a))

   b. 私の父は私が3つの時に交通事故で亡くなった。{そのため / それ故 / *ついては}、私は父の記憶がほとんどない。(= (1b))

(⇨ **yue ni** (in this volume))

T

(to i)ttara nai　（と言）ったらない　　*phr.*

~~a phrase used to express a strong sensation or emotion~~

．

so; extremely; indescribably; indescribable; incredibly; awfully; terribly; cannot tell you / describe / etc. how; too much of
【REL. *hontō ni*; *te shikata ga nai*; *te tamaranai*】

◆ Key Sentences

(A)

	Adj(*i*)inf.nonpast	
つまらないミスで試合に負けて	悔しい	（と言）ったらない。
(I'm so mortified because I lost the game due to a stupid mistake.)		

(B)

	Adj(*na*)stem	
老眼が進んで眼鏡なしでは近くの字が読めないので、	不便	（と言）ったらない。
(My farsightedness has gotten worse so I can't read words up close without my glasses—it's so inconvenient!)		

(C)

	Adj(*i/na*)stem		
大きな書類を保存するのを忘れてコンピュータがフリーズした時の	情けな	さ	（と言）ったらない。
(The miserable feeling you get when the computer freezes and you forgot to save a large file is indescribable.)			

(D)

	Adj(*i*)inf.nonpast		
この辞書は	使いにくい	こと	（と言）ったらない。
(This dictionary is incredibly hard to use.)			

Formation

(i)　{V / Adj(*i*)} inf.nonpast（と言）ったらない

　　腹が立つ（と言）ったらない　((I'm) so mad)

　　つまらない（と言）ったらない　((it's) so boring)

(ii)　Adj(*na*)stem（と言）ったらない

　　退屈（と言）ったらない　((I'm) so bored)

(iii)　Adj(*i/na*)さ（と言）ったらない

　　その面白さ（と言）ったらない　((s.t. is) so interesting)

　　その下手さ（と言）ったらない　((s.o. is) so bad at it)

(iv)　Vinf.nonpast こと（と言）ったらない

　　疲れること（と言）ったらない　(s.t. is so tiring)

(v)　Adj(*i*)inf.nonpast こと（と言）ったらない

　　おいしいこと（と言）ったらない　(s.t. is so delicious)

(vi)　Adj(*na*)stemなこと（と言）ったらない

　　新鮮なこと（と言）ったらない　(s.t. is so fresh)

Examples

(a)　5分ごとにジェット機が離陸するのでうるさいと言ったらない。

(There's a jet taking off every five minutes—I can't even describe (to you) how noisy it is.)

(b)　いつもよくしゃべる俊子が慎一の前で赤くなって何も言えないので、おかしいったらなかった。

(It was so funny to see Toshiko, who is usually talkative, blush and turn speechless in front of Shin'ichi.)

(c)　ティムにデートをすっぽかされて頭に来るったらない。

(Tim stood me up, and that makes me so mad.)

(d)　この仕事は一日中細かい字を見ているので目が疲れると言ったらない。

(Because I look at small print all day for this job, my eyes get awfully tired.)

(e)　出張したところはインターネットも携帯も使えず、不便と言ったらなかった。

(In the area where I went on my business trip I couldn't use the Internet or my cell phone; I can't tell you how inconvenient it was.)

(f) プロジェクトに変更があるたびに関係者全員に知らせた上で承認を得なければならないので、面倒と言ったらない。

(Every time there is a change to the project, we have to notify everybody involved and get their approval, so it is incredibly tiresome.)

(g) 夏、暑い外から帰ってきた後の冷えたビールのうまさったらない。

(In summer, the taste of a cold beer is indescribably good after coming in from the heat outside.)

(h) この国ではインターネットが自由に使えないので、その不便さったらない。

(In this country we cannot use the Internet freely, so it's so inconvenient.)

(i) ハイヒールで砂利道を歩かされたので歩きにくいことと言ったらなかった。

(I had to walk on gravel in high heels, and I can't tell you how hard it was!)

(j) 雪に覆われた山々が早朝の朝日を受けて宝石のように輝く姿の美しいことと言ったらない。

(When the snow-covered mountains receive the early morning sun and sparkle like gems, they are indescribably beautiful.)

(k) 昔、痛風にかかったことがあるが、その痛みと言ったらなかった。

(I've suffered from gout before; the pain was indescribable.)

(l) 学生がいいのは、学期が終わったら次の学期の始まりまでは自由なことだ。試験やレポートが全部終わった時の開放感と言ったらない。

(One good thing about being a student is that after the term is over, you're free until the next term begins. The feeling of release after finishing all the exams and term papers is indescribable.)

Notes

1. *To ittara nai* is considered to be a shortened form of X *koto to ittara iiyō ga nai* "when you mention the fact that X, there's no way to describe it." For example, (1a) is equivalent to (1b) in meaning.

(1) a. この辞書は使いにくいことと言ったらない。(= KS(D))

b. この辞書は使いにくいことと言ったら言いようがない。

(When it comes to the fact that (lit., when you mention the fact that) this dictionary is hard to use, there is no way to describe it. = This dictionary is indescribably hard to use.)

Thus, *to ittara nai* is used when something causes the speaker a sensation or emotion that is so strong it is hard to describe.

2. *Ttara nai* is a shortened form of *to ittara nai* and is used in casual situations.

3. Words/phrases that appear before *(to i)ttara nai* can represent sensations (e.g., *oishii* "tasty," *urusai* "noisy," *atsui* "hot") or emotions (e.g., *tanoshii* "fun," *kanashii* "sad," *hara ga tatsu* "get angry"), or describe a state, event or action that causes an emotional reaction in the speaker (e.g., *jisho ga tsukainikui* "the dictionary is hard to use")

4. In some situations, *(to i)ttara nai* is preceded by noun equivalents, including Adj(*i/na*)stem + *sa*, as in KS(C), Exs.(g) and (h), Adj(*i*)stem + *mi*, as in Ex.(k), and VN + *kan*, as in Ex.(l).　　(⇨ *-sa* (DBJG: 381-84))

5. Noun phrases may occur before *(to i)ttara nai* without a specific word indicating sensation or emotion word, as in (2). The emotions implied by the noun phrases are understood from the context and/or situation.

(2) a. 良夫の歌い方ったらない。

(Yoshio's way of singing is indescribable (i.e., it's so funny, terrible, etc.).)

b. 彼がその知らせを聞いた時の顔と言ったらなかった。

(The look on his face when he heard the news was indescribable.)

【Related Expressions】

I. *Hontō ni* "really" can be used to emphasize a sensation or emotion; thus, it can be used in place of *(to i)ttara nai*, as in [1].

[1] a. つまらないミスで試合に負けて**本当**に悔しい。(cf. KS(A))

(Because I lost the game due to a stupid mistake, I'm really mortified.)

b. 老眼が進んで眼鏡なしでは近くの字が読めないので、**本当**に不便だ。

(cf. KS(B))

(Because my farsightedness has gotten worse and I cannot read words up close without my glasses, it is really inconvenient.)

c. 大きな書類を保存するのを忘れてコンピュータがフリーズした時は**本当**に情けない。(cf. KS(C))

(You feel really miserable when the computer freezes and you forgot to save a large file.)

　　　d. この辞書は**本当に**使いにくい。(cf. (KS(D))
　　　　(This dictionary is really hard to use.)

II.　*Te shikata ga nai* "cannot help feeling; extremely; so" and *te tamaranai* "unbearably; extremely; be dying to" are similar in meaning to *to ittara nai* and in some situations they are interchangable.

[2]　a. つまらないミスで試合に負けて｜**悔しい（と言）ったらない**／**悔しくて 仕方がない**／**悔しくてたまらない**｝。(= KS(A))

　　　b. 老眼が進んで眼鏡なしでは近くの字が読めないので、**不便**｜**（と言）っ たらない**／**で仕方がない**／**でたまらない**｝。(= KS(B))

　　　c. この辞書は使い｜**にくいこと（と言）ったらない**／**にくくて仕方がない**／ **にくくてたまらない**｝。(= KS(D))

However, *te shikata ga nai* and *te tamaranai* are used only to express the speaker's personal emotion or sensation (or the emotion/sensation of someone with whom the speaker is empathetic). Thus, these phrases cannot be used for generic statements, as in [3].

[3]　a. ??大きな書類を保存するのを忘れてコンピュータがフリーズした時は 情けなくて**仕方がない**。(cf. KS(C))

　　　b. ??夏、暑い外から帰ってきた後の冷えたビールはうまくて**仕方がない**。
　　　　　　　　　　　　　　　　　　　　　　　　　　　　　　　　(cf. Ex.(g))

Another difference is that *te shikata ga nai* and *te tamaranai* are used to describe a lasting state and cannot be used for a momentary reaction or a short-term state.

[4]　a. ティムにデートをすっぽかされて頭に｜**来るったらない**／***来て仕方 がない**／***来てたまらない**｝。(= Ex.(c))

　　　b. その発表は衝撃的｜**と言ったらなかった**／***で仕方がなかった**／***でた まらなかった**｝。
　　　　(The announcement was so shocking.)

　　　(⇨ ***tamaranai*** (DBJG: 445-47); ***te shikata ga nai*** (in this volume))

wa are はあれ *phr.* <w>

```
a phrase expressing the idea "even
though there is s.t."
```

even though there is; although
there is; there is ~ but
【REL. *wa atte mo*】

◆ **Key Sentence**

	Noun		
インターフェースに若干の	違い	はあれ、	この二つのプログラムは機能的には全く変わらない。

(Although their interfaces are slightly different, these two programs are just the same in terms of their functions.)

Formation

Nはあれ

いろいろ問題はあれ (even though there are various problems)

Examples

(a) 歴史の違いはあれ、米国には120万を超す非営利団体(NPO)が存在します。

(Although their histories are different (lit., there are differences in their histories), there are more than 1,200,000 non-profit organizations in America.)

(b) ほとんどの者が、程度の差はあれ、マスメディアの影響を受けていると言える。

(One can say that most people are affected by mass media, although there are differences in degree.)

(c) レベルに違いはあれ、この課にいる者は全員英語を話せる。

(Although their (skill) levels are different (lit., there are differences in thcir skill levels), everybody in this section can speak English.)

(d) 海外旅行に興味はあれ、先立つ費用がない。

(Even though I'm interested in traveling abroad, I don't have the money for it.)

(e) 若干の不満はあれ、今の職場を離れるつもりはない。

(Even though I have some complaints (lit., dissatisfaction), I don't intend to leave my current job.)

W

(f) 今まで自分を使ってくれた上司に対して感謝する気持ちはあれ、非難する気持ちは全くありません。

(I feel thankful for my boss, who has given me work to do all this time, and (lit., but) have no intention of criticizing him.)

Notes

1. *Are* in *wa are* is the imperative form of *aru* "to exist." When this form occurs in subordinate clauses, it expresses the idea of concession.

2. *Wa are* means "even though" or "although," which means that what is stated in the *wa are* clause is factual rather than hypothetical or unknown.

3. *Wa are* is basically a written expression, but can also be used in formal speech.

4. *Wa are* is sometimes followed by *do*, as in (1). The addition of *do* doesn't change the meaning but makes the phrase more "bookish."

(1) a. アンダーソン氏は海外生活の経験はあれど、アジアを経験しておらず、今回の中国赴任に若干の不安を残す。

(Although Mr. Anderson has experience living abroad, he has no Asia experience, so there is some concern about his appointment to China at this time.)

b. ゴマには白ゴマと黒ゴマのほか、黄ゴマという風味豊かなゴマもある。見た目の色の違いはあれど、栄養的な違いは微々たるものだ。

(In addition to white sesame and black sesame, there is also yellow sesame, which has a rich flavor. Although they may look different because of their colors, these types (of sesame) are almost identical in terms of nutritional value (lit., the nutritional difference is very slight).)

5. *Koso* can be used in place of *wa* in X *wa are* to emphasize the existence of X, as in (2).

(2) a. インターフェースに若干の違いこそあれ、この二つのプログラムは機能的には全く変わらない。(cf. KS)

(Although there *are* some differences in their interfaces, these two programs are just the same in terms of their functions.)

b. 今まで自分を使ってくれた上司に対して感謝する気持ちこそ**あれ**、非
　難する気持ちは全くありません。(cf. Ex.(f))
　(I do feel thankful for my boss, who has given me work to do all
　this time, and (lit., but) have no intention of criticizing him.)

【Related Expression】

Wa are can be paraphrased using *wa atte mo*, which is less formal and used
in both spoken and written language.

[1] a. インターフェースに若干の違いは{あれ／あっても}、この二つのプ
　　　ログラムは機能的には全く変わらない。(= KS)

　　b. 海外旅行に興味は{あれ／あっても}、先立つ費用がない。(= Ex.(d))

wa betsu to shite　は別^{べつ}として　*phr.*

a phrase used to present an exception or an issue the speaker/writer does not intend to cover as part of a larger statement	except for; putting/setting aside; whether X or Y 【REL. *o nozoite*; *igai wa*; *wa sate oki*】

W

◆ Key Sentences

(A)

Noun Phrase		
特殊^{とくしゅ}な場合	は別として、	手書^{てが}きのレポートを書くことは少なくなった。
(Except for special cases, there are only a few occasions now in which we write hand-written reports.)		

(B)

Sinf			
実施<ruby>じっし</ruby>できる	か（どうか）	は別として、	まず可能<ruby>かのう</ruby>な解決策<ruby>かいけつさく</ruby>をすべて リストアップしてみよう。

(Putting aside the question of whether or not each one is feasible for us to carry out, let's list all possible solutions first.)

(C)

Adj(*na*)₁ stem		Adj(*na*)₂ stem			
上手<ruby>じょうず</ruby>	か	下手<ruby>へた</ruby>	か	は別として	その人にまず翻訳<ruby>ほんやく</ruby>してもらおう。

(Putting aside the question of whether he is good or bad, let's ask that person to translate it first.)

(D)

Adj(*i*)₁inf		Adj(*i*)₂stem (Adj(*i*)₁ = Adj(*i*)₂)		
面白<ruby>おもしろ</ruby>い	（か）	面白く	ない（か）	は別として

この授業<ruby>じゅぎょう</ruby>はきっと将来役<ruby>しょうらいやく</ruby>に立つ。

(Putting aside the question of whether it is interesting or not, this class will certainly benefit you in the future.)

(E)

Sinf			
医師<ruby>いし</ruby>により薬として 使用される	場合	は別として、	麻薬<ruby>まやく</ruby>は本質的<ruby>ほんしつてき</ruby>に反社会的<ruby>はんしゃかいてき</ruby>なものとされている。

(Except for cases in which they are prescribed by doctors as medicines, drugs are considered fundamentally anti-social.)

Formation

(i)　NP は別として

　　　経験者<ruby>けいけんしゃ</ruby>は別として　(except for those with some experience)

決断の是非は別として　(putting aside the question of whether the
  decision was right or wrong)

(ii)　Sinf か（どうか）は別として　(だ after Adj(*na*)stem and N is omitted.)

うまくいくか（どうか）は別として　(putting aside the question of
  whether or not s.t. will go well)

便利か（どうか）は別として　(putting aside the question of whether s.t.
  is convenient (or not))

(iii)　X か Y かは別として　(where X, Y = contrastive words)

・N₁ か N₂ かは別として

英語か日本語かは別として　(putting aside the question of whether
  s.t. is in English or Japanese)

・Adj(*na*)₁stem か Adj(*na*)₂stem かは別として

便利か不便かは別として　(putting aside the question of whether s.t.
  is convenient or inconvenient)

・Adj(*i*)₁inf.nonpast（か）Adj(*i*)₂inf.nonpast（か）は別として

いい（か）悪い（か）は別として　(putting aside the question of whether
  s.t. is good or bad)

・V₁inf.nonpast か V₂inf.nonpast かは別として

行くか留まるかは別として　(putting aside the question of whether
  s.o. will go or stay)

(iv)　X (Aff.)（か）X (Neg.)（か）は別として　(X is usually nonpast.)

行く（か）行かない（か）は別として　(putting aside the question of
  whether s.o. will go or not)

高い（か）高くない（か）は別として　(putting aside the question of
  whether s.t. is expensive or not)

上手（か）上手じゃない（か）は別として　(putting aside the question of
  whether s.o. is good at s.t. or not)

日本人（か）日本人じゃない（か）は別として　(putting aside the question
  of whether s.o. is Japanese or not)

(v)　Sinf 場合は別として

・Vinf 場合は別として

一人で{行く／行った}場合は別として　(except for the case in which
  s.o. will go / went alone)

W

・Adj(*i*)inf 場合は別として

授業料が{高い / 高かった}場合は別として　(except for the case in which the tuition is / was expensive)

・Adj(*na*)stem{な / だった}場合は別として

場所が不便{な / だった}場合は別として　(except for the case in which the location is/was inconvenient)

・N{の / だった}場合は別として

原稿が英語{の / だった}場合は別として　(except for the case in which the manuscript is/was in English)

Examples

(a) 一部の過激派は別として、一般大衆は民主化を望んでいる。

(Except for a few extremists, the general public wants democratization.)

(b) その映画は、ストーリーは別として、音楽やアクションは楽しめた。

(Leaving the story aside, I did enjoy the music and action scenes in the movie.)

(c) 賛成していただけるかどうかは別として、私の率直な意見を述べさせていただきます。

(Setting aside the question of whether or not you will agree with me, let me present my frank opinion.)

(d) そういうところが実際にあるかどうかは別として、自分の理想とする会社はどんなところかを書いて下さい。

(Putting aside the question of whether or not such a company actually exists, please describe your ideal company.)

(e) ケーブル接続かワイヤレスかは別として、今時インターネットに接続されていないコンピュータはほとんどないと思う。

(Putting aside the question of whether a wired connection or a wireless connection is used, there are hardly any computers that are not connected to the Internet now.)

(f) いい悪いは別として、この国では患者本人に病状の事実を伝えるのが普通だ。

(Whether it is good or bad, it is a common practice in this country to tell patients (directly) the facts about their conditions.)

(g) この賞は、生活者の目に触れるか触れないかは別として、人々の生活を豊かにする技術や発明に対して与えられる。

(This award is given for technologies or inventions that make people's lives richer, whether or not they are readily recognizable (lit., to people in their ordinary daily lives).)

(h) 単身赴任など仕事上の理由がある場合は別として、夫婦が５年間も別居しているのは尋常ではない。

(Except for cases in which there is a business reason such as being sent on assignment alone, it is not ordinary for a married couple to live separately for as long as five years.)

(i) 掲示板やチャットで発言する際は、ごく親しい仲間内の場合は別として、丁寧な言葉遣いを心がけるべきだ。

(When you express your opinions on (Internet) bulletin boards or in chat rooms, except for cases in which you are talking only amongst your close friends, you should try to use polite language.)

Notes

1. *Wa betsu to shite* is used to present an exception or an issue that is not to be covered when the speaker/writer makes a statement. Thus, the phrase means either "except for" or "putting s.t. aside," depending on the context.

2. *Wa betsu to shite* cannot be used to describe a time when someone or something is available or unavailable, as shown in (1).

(1) a. 明日は午前中｛??は別として / を除いて / 以外は｝塞がっています。

(I'm occupied tomorrow except for the morning.)

b. この店は月曜日｛??は別として / を除いて / 以外は｝週六日間営業しています。

(This store is open every day (lit. six days a week) except for Monday.)

3. *Dōka* in *ka dōka wa betsu to shite* can be omitted, as in Formation (ii).

4. *Ka* is often omitted after *i*-adjectives, as shown in Formation (iii). *Ka* deletion is also common, as shown in Formation (iv).

5. In the pattern "X *no* Y *wa betsu to shite*," antonym pairs, including antonym compounds, often occur in Y, as in (2).

(2) a. その行為の是非は別として

(setting aside the question of whether the deed is/was right or wrong)

b. 結果の良し悪しは別として

(putting aside the question of whether the result is/was good or bad)

c. デザインの好き嫌いは別として

(putting aside the question of whether you like the design or not (lit., dislike it))

d. 部屋の大きい小さいは別として

(putting aside the question of whether the room is large or small)

【Related Expressions】

I.   When *wa betsu to shite* means "except for," it can be replaced by *o nozoite* or *igai wa*.

[1] a. 特殊な場合｛は別として／を除いて／以外は｝、手書きのレポートを書くことは少なくなった。(= KS(A))

b. 医師により薬として使用される場合｛は別として／を除いて／以外は｝、麻薬は本質的に反社会的なものとされている。(= KS(E))

However, as seen in Note 2, *wa betsu to shite* cannot be used to describe a time when someone or something is (un)available.

($\Rightarrow$ ***igai*** (DIJG:60-63))

II. When *wa betsu to shite* means "putting ~ aside," it can be replaced by *wa sate oki*.

[2] a. 実施できるかどうかは｛別として／さておき｝、まず可能な解決策をすべてリストアップしてみよう。(= KS(B))

b. 上手か下手かは｛別として／さておき｝、その人にまず翻訳してもらおう。(= KS(C))

wa ii to shite mo   はいいとしても   *phr.*

a phrase that conveys the meaning "even if I/we accept s.t., s.t. else is not acceptable"

be all right, but; might be all right, but; would be fine, but; would accept ~, but; even if ~ accept; even though ~ accept; although ~ accept
【REL. *wa shikata ga nai to shite mo*】

◆ **Key Sentences**

(A)

	Noun		
友達を助けようという	動機	はいいとしても	やり方が間違っている。

(Your motivation for helping your friend is all right, but your way (of doing it) is wrong.)

(B)

Noun		
私	はいいとしても	他の人がこの部屋では満足しないだろう。

(Even if I accept it, other people wouldn't be satisfied with this room.)

(C)

Sinf			
部屋が狭い	の	はいいとしても、	エアコンがないのは困る。

(I'd accept a small room, but not having an air-conditioner there is not acceptable.)

Formation

(i) N はいいとしても

　　借金はいいとしても (borrowing money may be all right, but)
　　彼はいいとしても (even if he accepts it)

(ii) {V / Adj(*i*)} inf のはいいとしても (Adj(*i*) is usually nonpast.)

　　出席できないのはいいとしても (not being able to attend may be all right, but)

W

高いのはいいとしても　(being expensive may be all right, but)

(iii) ｛Adj(*na*)stem / N｝｛な / である｝のはいいとしても

下手｛な / である｝のはいいとしても　(s.o.'s being bad at s.t. may be all right, but)

学生｛な / である｝のはいいとしても　(s.o.'s being a student may be all right, but)

Examples

(a) 著作権のあるものは、個人用のコピーはいいとしても、それを他人に配付することは違法になります。

(Regarding copyrighted materials, making copies for one's own use may be all right, but distributing them to others is illegal.)

(b) 街頭はいいとしても、電車やレストランなどの公共の場所で声高に携帯電話で話されるのは周りの者にとって極めて迷惑だ。

(Although it might be all right on the street, talking loudly on your cell phone in public places like trains and restaurants is extremely annoying to the people around you.)

(c) このような結婚式では、結婚する本人たちはいいとしても両親が承知しないだろう。

(Even if it is all right with the couple getting married, their parents probably won't approve of this kind of wedding ceremony.)

(d) この店は安いから味が少しくらい悪いのはまあいいとしても、古い材料を使うのはやめてもらいたい。

(Because this restaurant is cheap, it's all right for the food to taste a little off, but they should stop using old ingredients (for cooking).)

(e) 今の社宅は一般の賃貸に比べて格段に安いのであまり文句は言えないのだが、建物が古いのはいいとしても、傷んだところをなかなか補修してもらえないのは問題だ。

(The rent for the company house (we live in) now is much cheaper than that of ordinary houses, so we can't complain much. And even though we accept the old building, the fact that we can't get repairs done quickly when something is damaged is a problem.)

(f) ウイルスのために自分自身のコンピュータが使えなくなるのはいいとしても、何も対処しないで他の人にウイルスをまき散らすことは許されない。

(It's one thing to lose the use of your own computer (lit., It might be all right to lose the use of your own computer) because of a virus, but it's simply unforgivable to do nothing to get rid of it and thereby spread the virus to others.)

Notes

1. "X *wa ii to shite mo* S" literally means "S even if I/we assume X is all right." This sentence pattern commonly presents two things, actions or situations: X and another thing, action or situation mentioned in S, which is undesirable. The pattern is used when the speaker does not accept one thing (= S) even if he accepts the other (= X).

    (⇨ **to suru**¹ (DIJG: 518-23))

2. When a person occurs in the position of X, X *wa ii to shite mo* usually means "X may accept (it), but" or "even if X accepts it" rather than "I/we would accept X, but," as shown in KS(B) and Ex.(c).

3. The final *mo* of X *wa ii to shite mo* is sometimes dropped. The version without *mo* implies a higher degree of acceptance of X. Compare (1a) and (1b).

    (1) a. 部屋が狭いのはいいとしても、エアコンがないのは困る。(= KS(C))

    (I'd accept a small room, but not having an air-conditioner there is not acceptable.)

    b. 部屋が狭いのはいいとして、エアコンがないのは困る。

    (I accept a small room, but not having an air-conditioner there is not acceptable.)

【Related Expression】

A similar phrase X *wa shikata ga nai to shite mo* means "even if s.t. cannot be helped." This phrase implies that the speaker accepts something as unavoidable.

[1] 部屋が狭いのは仕方がないとしても、エアコンがないのは困る。

(cf. KS(C))

(Having a small room may be unavoidable, but not having an air-conditioner there is not acceptable.)

W

wa oroka はおろか   *phr.*   <w>

> a phrase that is used when s.t. is not only true with one thing or person, but also with another thing or person that is less expected or understandable
>
> let alone; not only ~ (but also ~); not to mention; to say nothing of; never mind; much less 【REL. *wa iu made mo naku*; *wa iu ni oyobazu*; *wa mochiron*; *dake de naku*; *nomi narazu*】

◆ **Key Sentence**

Noun₁		Noun₂		
インターネット	はおろか、	パソコン	も	触ったことがないのだが、講習会についていけるだろうか。

(Never having touched a computer, let alone used the Internet, I wonder if I will be able to keep up in the workshop.)

Formation

N₁ はおろか N₂ {も / でも / さえ / すら / まで}

　ひらがなはおろか漢字 {も / でも / さえ / すら / まで}   (even (in) kanji, let alone (in) *hiragana*)

Examples

(a) 最近は大学生はおろか、中高生でもかなりの者が海外旅行を経験している。

(Never mind college students, these days even junior and senior high school students often have experienced traveling abroad.)

(b) アメリカでは、隣町まで100マイル、途中ガソリンスタンドはおろか、民家さえないという場所がたくさんある。

(In America there are many places where the next town is 100 miles away and there are no houses, let alone a gas station, in between.)

(c) ハリス氏は日本の現代文学はおろか、古典にまで通じている。

(Mr. Harris is quite familiar with classics of Japanese literature, to say nothing of (his knowledge of) modern Japanese literature.)

(d) 「近くて遠い」。この表現は日本との国交がない北朝鮮はおろか、韓国との関係を指すのにもよく使われてきた。

("Near yet far." This phrase has often been used to describe Japan's relationship not only with North Korea, with which it has no diplomatic relations, but with South Korea as well.)

(e) 英語を話すのが好きなだけで、英米の文学はおろか日本の文学もろくに読んでいない学生が英米文学専攻に入ってくると悲惨だ。

(It'll be a tragedy if a student who has barely even read any Japanese literature, much less British or American literature, signs up to major in English literature just because he or she likes to speak English.)

(f) 企業は今、セキュリティのための支出を増やさなければ、セキュリティの強化はおろか、維持さえも難しくなっているという。

(It is said that it has become more difficult for businesses to maintain security, let alone enhance it, without increasing their security expenses.)

(g) このサイトは検索はおろか、本の内容紹介までしてくれるので非常に便利だ。

(Not only does this website let you search (for books), it also gives a summary of the (searched) books' contents, so it's very convenient.)

(h) 戦争はおろか食糧難すら経験したことがない者が、口先だけで戦争を議論しているのは笑止だ。

(It is laughable that those people who have never even experienced a food shortage, much less a war, make glib arguments about war.)

Notes

1. X *wa oroka* is a shortened form of X *wa iu no mo oroka da*, which literally means "it is foolish to talk about X." "N₁ *wa oroka* N₂ (*mo/sae/*etc.)" is used when something is true (or is the case) with N₁ and is expected or understandable, but is also true (or is the case) with N₂, which is less expected or understandable.

2. N₂ is often followed by particles like *mo*, *demo*, *sae*, *sura* and *made*.

[Related Expressions]

I. *Wa iu made mo naku*, *wa iu ni oyobazu* and *wa mochiron* convey the same idea as *wa oroka*, and all four expressions can be used interchangeably.

[1]　a. インターネットは｛おろか／言うまでもなく／言うに及ばず／もちろん｝、パソコンも触ったことがないのだが、講習会についていけるだろうか。(= KS)

　　　b. 最近は大学生は｛おろか／言うまでもなく／言うに及ばず／もちろん｝、中高生でもかなりの者が海外旅行を経験している。(= Ex.(a))

(⇨ ***wa iu made mo naku*** (DIJG: 568-69))

II. *Dake de naku* "not only" and the more formal phrase *nomi narazu* can be used in place of *wa oroka* in some situations, as shown in [2], although they do not carry the idea of "let alone; not to mention."

[2]　a. 最近は大学生｛はおろか／だけでなく／のみならず｝、中高生でもかなりの者が海外旅行を経験している。(= Ex.(a))

　　　b. ハリス氏は日本の現代文学｛はおろか／だけでなく／のみならず｝、古典にまで通じている。(= Ex.(c))

Thus, when the situation involves a strong sense of "let alone; not to mention," *dake de naku* and *nomi narazu* sound odd, as in [3].

[3]　a. インターネット｛はおろか／??だけでなく／??のみならず｝、パソコンも触ったことがないのだが、講習会についていけるだろうか。

(= KS)

　　　b. 英語を話すのが好きなだけで、英米の文学｛はおろか／??だけでなく／??のみならず｝日本の文学もろくに読んでいない学生が英米文学専攻に入ってくると悲惨だ。(= Ex.(e))

Note, too, that *dake de naku* and *nomi narazu* can be used with parts of speech other than nouns, as in [4].

[4]　a. 私の上司は自身よく仕事をする｛だけでなく／のみならず／*はおろか｝部下の面倒もよくみてくれる。

(Not only does my boss work hard, he also takes good care of his subordinates.)

　　　b. このレストランはおいしい｛だけでなく／のみならず／*はおろか｝値段も安い。

(Not only does this restaurant serve tasty dishes, but the prices are reasonable, too.)

c. この辺りは不便{なだけでなく / のみならず / *はおろか}環境も悪い。

(Not only is this area inconvenient, but the environment is bad, too.)

(⇨ **dake de (wa) naku ~ (mo)** (DBJG: 97-100); **nomi narazu** (in this volume))

---

wari ni (wa) 割に (は)　　*phr.*

┌─────────────────────────────────────┐
a phrase that expresses the idea that s.t. is not in proportion to what one would normally expect
└─────────────────────────────────────┘

for; despite; although; (not) as much as; (not) ~ because of that; considering
【REL. *ni shite wa*】

◆ **Key Sentences**

(A)

	Noun			
この店のサービスランチは	値段	の	割に (は)	おいしくてボリュームがある。

(The bargain lunch at this restaurant is tasty and the portions are generous for the price.)

(B)

		Vinf		
ビルは	よく	勉強している	割に (は)	成績が伸びない。

(For all his hard work, Bill's grades don't seem to improve. / Although Bill studies hard, his grades do not improve.)

(C)

	Adj(*i*)inf		
このチームは	強い	割に (は)	人気がない。

(This team is not popular despite its strength.)

(D)

	Noun			
彼は大学で	秀才	だった	割に (は)	実社会であまり成功していない。

(He's not doing very well in the business world considering that he was such a brilliant student at college. / He was a brilliant student at college, but, despite that, he is not doing very well in the business world.)

(E)

Sentence				
彼女はすばらしい研究をしている	が、	その	割に (は)	認められて いない。

(She is doing excellent research, but hasn't gained as much recognition as she deserves.)

Formation

(i) N {の / である / だった / であった} 割に (は)

値段の割に (は)   (for its price)

先生 {の / である / だった / であった} 割に (は)   (considering that s.o. is / was a teacher)

(ii) Vinf 割に (は)

よく {行く / 行った} 割に (は)   (considering that s.o. goes/went often; for as often as s.o. goes/went)

(iii) Adj(*i*)inf 割に (は)

{小さい / 小さかった} 割に (は)   (for its small size; considering that s.t. is/was small)

(iv) Adj(*na*)stem {な / である / だった / であった} 割に (は)

貧乏 {な / である / だった / であった} 割に (は)   (considering that s.o. is/was poor)

Examples

(a) 清水さんは年の割には若く見える。

(Ms. Shimizu looks young for her age.)

(b) この辺りはいつも海からの風があるので、強い日射しの割には過ごしやすい。

(Because there is always a wind coming up off the sea in this area, it is comfortable (to stay here) despite the strong sun.)

(c) このソフトは安い割には機能がよく、使いやすいです。

(For as cheap as it is, this software is easy to use and has good functionality.)

(d) この図書館は建物が立派な割には中の設備がよくない。

(Despite the impressive building, the facilities inside this library are not that good.)

(e) 多くの人が「有機野菜」表示を気にする割には、その意味を知っている人は少ない。

(Although many people pay attention to "organic vegetable" labels (on produce), few know what they mean.)

(f) シアトルなどの都市がある北部太平洋岸は比較的暖かく、緯度が北海道と変わらない割には冬の寒さも厳しくない。

(The Pacific Northwest, which is home to cities like Seattle, has a relatively mild climate, and the winter is not as bitterly cold (as one would think,) despite the fact that it is at about the same latitude as Hokkaido.)

(g) 記念すべきイベントの割には参加者が少なく物足りない気がする。

(For an event that should be commemorated, there aren't many participants; I'm not quite satisfied.)

(h) 彼は自国の大学で英語を教えていると言っているが、その割には英語が下手だ。

(He says that he teaches English at a university in his country, but despite that his English is poor.)

Notes

1. X *wari ni (wa)* is used when something is not in proportion to what one would normally expect from X.

2. *Wari* is a noun with the meaning of "proportion; ratio." Thus, it is preceded by the noun-modification forms of verbs, adjectives and N *da*, as shown in Formation (i)-(iv).

3. *Wa* after *wari ni* is optional. The presence or absence of *wa* does not change the meaning or implication.

4. When the element before *wari ni (wa)* is a predicate, it can be rephrased using "*ga, sono wari ni (wa)*," as in (1). (See KS(E).)

(1) a. ビルはよく<u>勉強している</u>が、その割に（は）成績が伸びない。

(cf. KS(B))

b. このチームは<u>強い</u>が、その割に（は）人気がない。(cf. KS(C))

c. 彼は大学で<u>秀才だった</u>が、その割には実社会であまり成功していない。

(cf. KS(D))

d. 記念すべき<u>イベントだ</u>が、その割には参加者が少なく物足りない気がする。(cf. Ex.(g))

Note that *kinen-su-beki ibento* "event that should be commemorated; memorable event" in Ex.(g) is a predicate while *nedan* "price" in KS(A) is not; therefore, KS(A) cannot be rephrased using *sono wari ni (wa)*, as in (2).

(2) *この店のサービスランチは<u>値段だ</u>が、その割にはおいしくてボリュームがある。(cf. KS(A))

【Related Expression】

Because X *ni shite wa* is used when there is some deviation from what is expected from X, *ni shite wa* and *wari ni (wa)* are used in similar situations. In [1], for example, the two phrases are almost synonymous.

[1] a. 彼は大学で秀才だった｛割に（は）／にしては｝実社会であまり成功していない。(= KS(D))

b. 記念すべきイベント｛の割には／にしては｝参加者が少なく物足りない気がする。(= Ex.(g))

However, *ni shite wa* and *wari ni (wa)* may convey different ideas in different contexts. For example, *ni shite wa* in [2a] indicates that the woman has not gained any recognition despite her good research, whereas in [2b], using *wari ni wa* indicates that she has gained recognition, but not to the degree she deserves.

[2] a. 彼女（かのじょ）はすばらしい研究をしているが、それにしては認（みと）められていない。

(cf. KS(E))

(She is doing excellent research, but even so (contrary to what we expect from that), she hasn't been recognized (for it).)

　　b. 彼女はすばらしい研究をしているが、**その割には**認められていない。

(= KS(E))

Ni shite wa cannot be used when the preceding clause has an adjective predicate, as shown in [3].

　　[3] a. このチームは強い｛**割には** / *にしては｝人気がない。(= KS(C))

　　　　b. このソフトは安い｛**割には** / *にしては｝機能がよく、使いやすいです。

(= Ex.(c))

　　　　c. この図書館は建物が立派｛**な割には** / *にしては｝中の設備がよくない。(= Ex.(d))

Note that when the preceding noun is not a predicate, *ni shite wa* cannot be used. For example, *ni shite wa* is unacceptable in [4a] but acceptable in [4b].

　　[4] a. この店のサービスランチは値段｛**の割には** / *にしては｝おいしくてボリュームがある。(= KS(A))

　　　　b. 直樹は子供｛**の割には** / にしては｝漢字をよく知っている。
　　　　　(Naoki is a child; despite that, he knows kanji well.)

(⇨ ~ni shite wa (DBJG: 309-10))

W

~ **wa** ~ **wa**　～わ～わ　*str.*　\<s\>

a structure that emphatically presents actions, events or states as examples or reasons, or indicates that s.o does s.t or s.t happens to a great extent	X and Y; for example, X and Y; because X and Y; so many; so much; one after another 【REL. ~ *yara* ~ *yara*】

◆ **Key Sentences**

(A)

S₁inf.nonpast		S₂inf.nonpast		
飛行機は 12 時間も遅れる	わ	荷物はなくなる	わ	(で)、
S₃ (main clause)				
今度の旅行は最悪だった。				
(The flight was delayed 12 hours, and my luggage was lost; this trip was the worst.)				

(B)

	V₁inf. nonpast		V₂inf.nonpast (V₁ = V₂)		
客が	来る	わ	来る	わ、	またたく間に小さい店はいっぱいになった。
(Customers came in one after another, and in the blink of an eye, the small shop had filled up.)					

Formation

(i)　S₁inf.nonpast わ S₂inf.nonpast わ

　　会議に遅れるわ名刺を忘れるわ　(s.o. was late for the meeting and forgot to bring his/her business cards)

　　交通は不便だわ家賃は高いわ　(transportation is inconvenient and the rent is expensive)

(ii)　V₁inf.nonpast わ V₂inf.nonpast わ　(where V₁ = V₂)

　　増えるわ増えるわ　(s.t. increases so much (lit., increases and increases))

Examples

(a)　仕事は増えるわ給料は下がるわ、今の状況は最悪だ。

　　(We have more work to do, and our salaries have been cut; the current situation could not be worse.)

(b) クレジットカードをなくすわ怪我をするわで、今度のスキー旅行ではひどい目に遭った。

(Having lost my credit card and gotten injured——I had an awful time on this ski trip.)

(c) 新しく雇った学生アルバイトは、仕事は遅いわ文句は多いわで、とても使いものにならない。

(The student part-timer we hired recently is (of) no help (to us) because he (lit., his work) is slow and he complains a lot.)

(d) この辺りは買い物には不便だわ環境は悪いわ、何一ついいところがない。

(There's nothing good around here——the shopping is inconvenient and the environment is bad.)

(e) 台所は何一つ手伝おうとしないわ、一緒に外食してもお金を払わないわ、もうあんな客は来てほしくない。

(She never offered to help in the kitchen or paid anything when we went out to eat; I don't want any more houseguests like that.)

(f) 面白い仕事はもらえるわ給料は上げてもらえるわ、新井君は最近いいことずくめだ。

(He gets interesting work and a raise——Arai has had a real streak of good fortune lately.)

(g) 辞書で「コウ」という発音の漢字を調べてみたら、あるわあるわ、全部で174も出ていた。

(When I looked up the kanji with the pronunciation "kou" in a dictionary, there were so many of them——174 in all.)

(h) 余程おなかが空いていたのだろう。食べるわ食べるわ、またたく間に大きな茶わんでご飯を5杯も平らげた。

(He must have been very hungry. He ate and ate, and finished five large bowls of rice in an instant.)

W

Notes

1. When sentences or phrases precede *wa*, the structure ~ *wa* ~ *wa* emphatically presents specific examples of or reasons for the statement made in the main clause, as in KS(A) and Exs.(a)-(f). Although this structure is often used to describe undesirable situations, that is not always the case, as seen in Ex.(f).

2. When the same verb occurs twice before *wa*, the structure indicates that someone does something or something happens to a great extent, as in KS(B), Exs.(g) and (h).

3. In "S₁ *wa* S₂ *wa*, S₃," the predicates in S₁ and S₂ are always nonpast regardless of the tense of the main clause (= S₃). In this respect, S₁ and S₂ are dependent on the main clause (S₃). Although in general the topic marker *wa* does not occur in dependent clauses, it can appear in S₁ and S₂ in this structure, as in KS(A) and Ex.(a).

4. *De* sometimes follows the last *wa* (i.e., just before the main clause), as in KS(A), Exs.(b) and (c).

[Related Expression]

Although it is not as emphatic as S₁ *wa* S₂ *wa*, S₁ *yara* S₂ *yara* is used in similar situations, as shown in [1]. Note that the topic marker *wa* cannot be used in S *yara*.

[1] a. 飛行機｛が／*は｝12時間も遅れるやら、荷物｛が／*は｝なくなるやら、今度の旅行は最悪だった。(cf. KS(A))

b. 仕事｛が／*は｝増えるやら給料｛が／*は｝下がるやら、今の状況は最悪だ。(cf. Ex.(a))

c. 面白い仕事｛を／*は｝もらえるやら給料｛を／*は｝上げてもらえるやら、新井君は最近いいことずくめだ。(cf. Ex.(f))

However, S₁ *yara* S₂ *yara* is unnatural when S₁ and S₂ represent states, as in [2].

[2] a. ??新しく雇った学生アルバイトは、<u>仕事が遅い</u>やら<u>文句が多い</u>やらで、とても使いものにならない。(cf. Ex.(c))

b. ??この辺りは<u>買い物に不便</u>やら<u>環境が悪い</u>やら、何一ついいところがない。(cf. Ex.(d))

If the states in [2a] are changed to actions, the sentence will sound natural.

[3] 新しく雇った学生アルバイトは、<u>仕事を怠ける</u>｛わ／やら｝よく<u>文句を言う</u>｛わ／やら｝で、とても使いものにならない。(cf. Ex.(c))
(The student part-timer we hired recently is no help because he neglects his job and complains a lot.))

The structure ~ *yara* ~ *yara* cannot be used for ~ *wa* ~ *wa* in examples like KS(B), where the same verb is repeated before *wa*.

[4] 客が<u>来る</u>｛わ / *やら｝<u>来る</u>｛わ / *やら｝、またたく間に小さい店はいっぱいになった。(= KS(B))

Wa, on the other hand, cannot be used is in the following situations:

[5] N₁, N₂, etc.:
<u>会議</u>｛やら / *わ｝<u>講習会</u>｛やら / *わ｝で最近出張が多い。
(I have been traveling a lot recently for conferences, workshops, etc.)

[6] Whether or not S:
久子は<u>来る</u>｛やら / *わ｝<u>来ない</u>｛やら / *わ｝分からない。
(We don't know whether Hisako will come or not.)

(⇨ ~ *yara* ~ *yara* (in this volume))

W

ya ina ya　やいなや ［や否や］　　*conj.*　　\<w>

a conjunction that expresses the idea that s.t. happened or s.o. did something immediately following another event or action	as soon as; no sooner ~ than; the moment; soon after; immediately after 【REL. *ya*; *totan (ni)*; *to dōji ni*; *to sugu (ni)*; *tara sugu (ni)*; *nari*; *ga hayai ka*; *shunkan ni*】

◆ **Key Sentence**

	Vinf.nonpast			Vpast
その小説は	発売される	やいなや	ミリオンセラーに	なった。

(The novel sold one million copies as soon as it went on sale.)

Formation

Vinf.nonpast やいなや

　聞くやいなや　(as soon as s.o. heard s.t.)

Examples

(a) 彼女は車から降りるやいなや報道陣やファンに取り囲まれた。

(She was surrounded by reporters and fans as soon as she got out of the car.)

(b) スタジオに着くやいなやリハーサルが始まった。

(The rehearsal began as soon as I arrived at the studio.)

(c) 秀夫はアパートに帰るやいなやベッドに倒れ込んだ。

(Hideo collapsed on his bed as soon as he returned to his apartment.)

(d) 母の顔を見るやいなや涙が込み上げてきた。

(As soon as I saw my mother (lit., mother's face), my tears welled up.)

(e) 小池氏はメディアから批判されるや否や、手のひらを返すように意見を変えた。

(No sooner was he criticized by the media than Mr. Koike abruptly (lit., as if he turned his hand over) changed his opinion.)

(f) ジョージは大学を卒業するや否やゲームソフトのビジネスを始めた。

(George started his own game software business the moment he graduated from college.)

(g) 安くておいしいと評判のそのレストランは、朝11時に開店するやいなや、常連客でいっぱいになった。

(The restaurant, which is popular for its reasonable prices and good food, was full of regular customers as soon as it opened at 11:00 a.m.)

(h) そのテレビドラマは1回目が放映されるや否や、国中に大きな韓国ブームを引き起こした。

(As soon as the first episode of the TV drama was telecast, it sparked a big Korea boom throughout the country.)

Notes

1. *Ya ina ya* is always preceded by an informal nonpast verb, and the main clause is always in the past tense. Thus, the main clause cannot be a command, a request or a volitional sentence, and it cannot represent a present habit or future action, as shown in (1) and (2). In these situations, *tara sugu (ni)* can be used.

    (1) a. ホテルに{*着くやいなや / 着いたらすぐ(に)}電話{しなさい / して下さい}。

      ({Give / Please give} me a call as soon as you've arrived at the hotel.)

      b. ホテルに{*着くやいなや / 着いたらすぐ(に)}電話しよう。

      ({Let's call / We'll call} as soon as we've arrived at the hotel.)

    (2) a. 啓次はいつも家に{*帰るやいなや / 帰ったらすぐ(に)}シャワーを浴びる。

      (Keiji always takes a shower soon after he returns home.)

      b. 友美は和男に{*会うやいなや / 会ったらすぐ(に)}そのことを話すだろう。

      (Yumi will probably tell Kazuo about it the moment she sees him.)

2. S₂ in "S₁ *ya ina ya* S₂" commonly represents an action or event that is unexpected to the speaker or writer.

3. In "S₁ *ya ina ya* S₂," when the subject of S₂ is the first person, the action in S₂ is usually spontaneous or automatic, as seen in (3).

Y

(3) a. 私は先生の顔を見る**やいなや**｛無意識に立ち上がっていた / ??立ち上がって挨拶した｝。

(As soon as I saw the teacher, I ｛stood up automatically (lit., unconsciously) / ??stood up and greeted him｝.)

　　b. 教室に入る**やいなや**｛宿題を忘れたことを思い出した / ??宿題のことを考えた｝。

(As soon as I entered the classroom, I ｛remembered that I had forgotten my homework / ??thought about my homework｝.)

【Related Expressions】

I.　*Ya* is a shortened form of *ya ina ya*, and less formal than *ya ina ya*.

[1] a. その小説は発売される｛**やいなや** / **や**｝ミリオンセラーになった。

(= KS)

　　b. 彼女は車から降りる｛**やいなや** / **や**｝報道陣やファンに取り囲まれた。

(= Ex.(a))

　　c. スタジオに着く｛**やいなや** / **や**｝リハーサルが始まった。(= Ex.(b))

II.　Vinf.past *totan (ni)* "the moment; just as" is used in situations similar to those in which *ya ina ya* can be used, as shown in [2]. Note that *totan (ni)* is preceded by verbs in the past tense.

[2] a. その小説は発売｛**されるやいなや** / **された途端(に)**｝ミリオンセラーになった。(= KS)

　　b. 彼女は車から｛**降りるやいなや** / **降りた途端(に)**｝報道陣やファンに取り囲まれた。(= Ex.(a))

　　c. スタジオに｛**着くやいなや** / **着いた途端(に)**｝リハーサルが始まった。

(= Ex.(b))

The major difference in usage between *totan (ni)* and *ya ina ya* is that *totan (ni)* is used when an action or event took place at the exact moment something else happened. *Ya ina ya* cannot be used in such situations. Thus, *ya ina ya* is unnatural in [3a] while *totan (ni)* is unnatural in [3b].

[3] a. ジェーンはその写真を｛**見た途端(に)** / ??**見るやいなや**｝気絶した。

[S₂ took place exactly the moment S₁ took place.]

(Jane fainted the moment she saw the picture.)

b. 啓次は家に｛帰るやいなや／??帰った途端(に)｝シャワーを浴びた。

[S2 did not take place exactly the moment S1 took place.]

(Keiji took a shower soon after he'd returned home.)

Totan (ni) can be used with nonpast actions, as in [4], but cannot be used with a command, a request or a volitional sentence, as shown in [5].

[4] a. 友美は和男に｛会った途端(に)／*会うやいなや｝そのことを話すだろう。(= (2b))

b. その店はバーゲンセールの日はいつも入り口のドアが｛開いた途端(に)／*開くやいなや｝客が走り込む。

(On big sale days, customers always rush into the store the moment the entrance doors open.)

[5] a. ホテルに｛*着くやいなや／*着いた途端(に)｝電話｛しなさい／して下さい｝。(cf. (1a))

(｛Give／Please give｝ me a call the moment you've arrived at the hotel.)

b. ホテルに｛*着くやいなや／*着いた途端(に)｝電話しよう。(cf. (1b))

(｛Let's call／We'll call｝ the moment we've arrived at the hotel.)

Totan (ni) has the same restrictions as those described for *ya ina ya* in Note 3, as shown in [6].

[6] a. 私は先生の顔を見た途端(に)｛無意識に立ち上がっていた／*挨拶した｝。(cf. (3a))

(The moment I saw the teacher, I ｛stood up automatically (lit., unconsciously)／*greeted him｝.)

b. 教室に入った途端(に)｛宿題を忘れたことを思い出した／*宿題のことを考えた｝。(cf. (3b))

(The moment I entered the classroom, I ｛realized I had forgotten my homework／*thought about the homework｝.)

(⇨ *totan (ni)* (DIJG: 525-28))

III. Vinf.nonpast *to dōji ni* "at the same time" can be used in situations similar to *ya ina ya*, as in [7].

[7] a. その小説は発売される｛やいなや／と同時に｝ミリオンセラーになった。(= KS)

   b. 彼女は車から降りる｛やいなや / と同時に｝報道陣やファンに取り囲まれた。(= Ex.(a))

   c. スタジオに着く｛やいなや / と同時に｝リハーサルが始まった。

(= Ex.(b))

To dōji ni is somewhat unnatural when used with a command, a request or a volitional sentence, as shown in [8], and when the sentence indicates a present habit or future action, as in [9]. (See Note 1.)

[8]　a. ホテルに着く｛?と同時に / *やいなや｝電話｛しなさい / して下さい｝。

(= (1a))

   b. ホテルに着く｛?と同時に / *やいなや｝電話しよう。(= (1b))

[9]　a. 啓次はいつも家に帰る｛?と同時に / *やいなや｝シャワーを浴びる。

(= (2a))

   b. 友美は和男に会う｛?と同時に / *やいなや｝そのことを話すだろう。

(= (2b))

To dōji ni can be used when the subject of the main clause is the first person and the action represented there is not spontaneous or automatic, as in [10]. (See Note 3.)

[10]　a. 私は先生の顔を見る｛と同時に / ??やいなや｝挨拶した。(= (3a))

   b. 教室に入る｛と同時に / ??やいなや｝宿題のことを考えた。(= (3b))

To dōji ni can also be used to present concurrent actions or states, as in [11].

[11]　a. 減量のためにダイエットをすると同時に運動もしている。

(In order to lose weight, I'm working out (lit., exercising) while I diet.)

   b. 群集が遠くに見えると同時に太鼓の音も聞こえる。

(A crowd can be seen in the distance at the same time (the sound of) drums can be heard.)

(⇨ **to dōji ni** (DIJG: 471-74))

IV. Vinf.nonpast *to sugu (ni)* means "soon after" and thus it is used in situations similar to those of *ya ina ya*. However, *to sugu (ni)* does not express as much immediacy as *ya ina ya* or *totan (ni)*.

[12] a. その小説は発売される{やいなや／とすぐ(に)}ミリオンセラーになった。(= KS)

(The novel sold one million copies {soon after / as soon as} it went on sale.)

b. 彼女は車から降りる{やいなや／とすぐ(に)}報道陣やファンに取り囲まれた。(= Ex.(a))

(She was surrounded by reporters and fans {soon after / as soon as} she got out of the car.)

c. スタジオに着く{やいなや／とすぐ(に)}リハーサルが始まった。

(= Ex.(b))

(The rehearsal began {soon after / as soon as} I arrived at the studio.)

To sugu (ni) can be used when the subject of the main clause is the first person and the action represented there is not spontaneous or automatic, as in [13]. (See Note 3.)

[13] a. 私は先生の顔を見るとすぐ(に){無意識に立ち上がっていた／挨拶した}。(cf. (3a))

b. 教室に入るとすぐ(に){宿題を忘れたことを思い出した／宿題のことを考えた}。(cf. (3b))

Unlike *ya ina ya*, the main clause after *to sugu (ni)* can be in the nonpast tense, as shown in [14], but cannot be a command, a request or a volitional sentence, as shown in [15], because *to sugu (ni)* contains the conjunction *to*. (⇨ **to⁴** (DBJG: 480-82))

Note that when the main clause is a command, a request or a volitional sentence, *tara sugu (ni)* is used. (See Related Expression V.)

[14] a. 啓次はいつも家に帰る{とすぐ(に)／*やいなや}シャワーを浴びる。

(= (2a))

b. 友美は和男に会う{とすぐ(に)／*やいなや}そのことを話すだろう。

(= (2b))

[15] a. ホテルに{着いたらすぐ(に)／*着くとすぐ(に)}電話{しなさい／して下さい}。(cf. (1a))

({Give me a call / Please call me} soon after you've arrived at the hotel.)

　　　b. ホテルに｛**着いたらすぐ(に)** /＊**着くとすぐ(に)**｝電話<u>しよう</u>。

(cf. (1b))

　　　({Let's call / We'll call} soon after we've arrived at the hotel.)

V. *Tara sugu (ni)* (i.e., Vinf.past *ra sugu (ni)*) is also synonymous with *ya ina ya* and can be used in the same way as *to sugu (ni)* (illustrated above) except that *tara sugu (ni)* can be used with a command, a request or a volitional sentence, as seen in [15]. (⇨ ***tara*** (DBJG: 452-57))

VI. Vinf.nonpast *nari* also conveys the meaning "as soon as."

[16] a. その小説は発売される｛**やいなや** / **なり**｝ミリオンセラーになった。

(= KS)

　　　b. 彼女は車から降りる｛**やいなや** / **なり**｝報道陣やファンに取り囲まれた。(= Ex.(a))

　　　c. スタジオに着く｛**やいなや** / **なり**｝リハーサルが始まった。(= Ex.(b))

The restrictions stated in Notes 1 and 2 regarding *ya ina ya* apply to *nari*, as shown in [17]-[19].

[17] a. ホテルに着く｛＊**やいなや** /＊**なり**｝電話｛<u>しなさい</u> / <u>して下さい</u>｝。

(= (1a))

　　　b. ホテルに 着く｛＊**やいなや** /＊**なり**｝電話<u>しよう</u>。(= (1b))

[18] a. 啓次はいつも家に帰る｛<u>??**なり**</u> /＊**やいなや**｝シャワーを<u>浴びる</u>。

(= (2a))

　　　b. 友美は和男に会う｛??**なり** /＊**やいなや**｝そのことを<u>話すだろう</u>。

(= (2b))

[19] a. 私は先生の顔を見る**なり**｛<u>無意識に立ち上がっていた</u> / <u>??挨拶した</u>｝。

(cf. (3a))

　　　b. 教室に入る**なり**｛<u>宿題を忘れたことを思い出した</u> / <u>??宿題のことを考えた</u>｝。(cf. (3b))

(⇨ ***nari*** (in this volume))

VII. Vinf.nonpast *ga hayai ka* also represents the idea of "as soon as," as shown in [20].

[20] a. その小説は発売される{やいなや / が早いか}ミリオンセラーになった。(= KS)

b. 彼女は車から降りる{やいなや / が早いか}報道陣やファンに取り囲まれた。(= Ex.(a))

c. スタジオに着く{やいなや / が早いか}リハーサルが始まった。
(= Ex.(b))

However, *ga hayai ka* cannot be used when the main clause represents a spontaneous action, as in [21] and [22].

[21] 母の顔を見る{やいなや / *が早いか}涙が<u>込み上げてきた</u>。(= Ex.(d))

[22] 教室に入るが早いか{宿題のことを<u>考えた</u> / *宿題を忘れたことを<u>思い出した</u>}。(cf. (3b))

Ga hayai ka cannot be used when the main clause represents a future action, including a command, a request or a volitional sentence, as in [23].

[23] a. 友美は和男に{??会うが早いか / 会ったらすぐ(に)}そのことを<u>話すだろう</u>。(= (2b))

b. ホテルに{*着くが早いか / 着いたらすぐ(に)}電話{<u>しなさい</u> / <u>して下さい</u>}。(= (1a))

c. ホテルに{*着くが早いか / 着いたらすぐ(に)}電話<u>しよう</u>。(= (1b))

(⇨ *ga hayai ka* (in this volume))

Ⅷ. Vinf.past *shunkan ni* "the moment" conveys the same meaning as Vinf.past *totan (ni)* except that *shunkan ni* means "the moment" in a more literal sense than *totan (ni)*. Thus, it sounds unnatural when there is even a slight time lag between the two actions represented by the preceding verb and the verb in the main clause, as shown in [24]. (See Related Expression II.)

[24] a. その小説は<u>発売された</u>{途端(に) / ??<ruby>瞬間<rt>しゅんかん</rt></ruby>に}ミリオンセラーに<u>なった</u>。(= [2a])

b. 友美は和男に<u>会った</u>{途端(に) / ??瞬間に}そのことを<u>話すだろう</u>。
(= [4a])

Besides the above semantic difference, *shunkan ni* has several different properties from the phrases introduced above. First, *shunkan ni* is acceptable when the main clause is nonpast, as shown in [25].

[25] a. 彼女が部屋から出てきた瞬間にカメラのシャッターを切ろう。

(I'll click the shutter button the moment she comes out of the room.)

b. カメラマンたちは、彼女が部屋から出てきた瞬間にカメラのシャッターを切るだろう。

(The cameramen will probably click the shutter buttons the moment she comes out of the room.)

c. 彼女が部屋から出てきた瞬間にカメラのシャッターを切れ。

(Click the shutter button the moment she comes out of the room.)

Second, in "S₁ *shunkan ni* S₂" the action in S₂ does not have to be spontaneous or automatic when the subject of S₂ is the first person. (See Note 3.)

[26] a. 私は彼女が部屋から出てきた瞬間にカメラのシャッターを切った。

(I clicked the shutter button the moment she came out of the room.)

b. 私は犯人が後ろを向いた瞬間に飛びかかった。

(I jumped at the culprit the moment he looked back.)

Third, *shunkan ni* can be preceded by Vinf.nonpast as well, as shown in [27]. In this case, the action in the main clause is taken just before the action represented by the verb preceding *shunkan ni*.

[27] a. ラケットがボールに当たる瞬間にシャッターを切って下さい。

(Please click the shutter button the moment the racket is about to hit the ball.)

b. ネコは鳥が飛び立つ瞬間に飛びついた。

(The cat jumped at the bird just as it was about to fly away.)

Finally, *shunkan ni* can also be preceded by "N *no*," as in [28].

[28] a. 彼は優勝の瞬間に右の拳を天に突き上げた。

(He thrust his right fist into the air at the moment of victory.)

b. 離陸の瞬間にめまいを覚えた。

(I felt dizzy at the moment of take off.)

yara やら *prt.* <s>

| a sentence-final particle that marks a self-addressed question | I wonder (if) 【REL. *darō ka*; *kashira*; *ka*】 |

◆ Key Sentences

(A)

Wh-sentence.inf		
このビルが完成するのはいつになる	の	やら。
(I wonder when this building will be finished.)		

(B)

Wh-sentence.inf		
これから先、うちの会社は一体どうなる	こと	やら。
(I wonder what will happen to our company from now on. (I'm quite worried.))		

(C)

Wh-sentence.inf			
こんな映画のどこがいい	の	やら	さっぱり分からない。
(I just don't understand what is good about this movie.)			

(D)

	Wh-word		
学生たちが	何	やら	面白そうな計画をしている。
(The students are planning something interesting.)			

▮ Formation ▮

(i) Sinf のやら　(だ after Adj(*na*)stem and N changes to な.)

　　{行く / 行った}のやら　(I wonder if s.o. will go / went)

　　{高い / 高かった}のやら　(I wonder if s.t. is/was expensive)

　　不便{な / である / だった / であった}のやら　(I wonder if s.t. is/was inconvenient)

学生｛な / である / だった / であった｝のやら　(I wonder if s.o. is/was a student)

(ii) Sinf ことやら　(だ cannot be used before こと. Adj(*na*)stem｛な / である｝こと; N であること.)

｛行く / 行った｝ことやら　(I wonder if s.o. will go / went)

｛高い / 高かった｝ことやら　(I wonder if s.t. is/was expensive)

不便｛な / である / だった / であった｝ことやら　(I wonder if s.t. is/was inconvenient)

学生｛である / だった / であった｝ことやら　(I wonder if s.o. is/was a student)

(iii) Sinf やら　(だ after Adj(*na*)stem and N is omitted.)

｛行く / 行った｝やら　(I wonder if s.o. will go / went; whether s.o. will go / went)

｛大きい / 大きかった｝やら　(I wonder if s.t. is/was large; whether s.t. is/was large)

上手｛ø / だった｝やら　(I wonder if s.o. is/was good at s.t.; whether s.o. is/was skillful)

学生｛ø / だった｝やら　(I wonder if s.o. is/was a student; whether s.o. is/was a student)

Examples

(a) 競技場ははたしてオリンピック開会までに完成するのやら。

(I really wonder if the stadium will be completed in time for the Olympic Games.)

(b) 一体いつになったら自分の家が持てることやら。

(I wonder when I'll be able to have my own house. (I feel almost hopeless.))

(c) さっきまでの元気はどこへ行ったのやら。

(I wonder where all the energy he had just a little bit ago has gone.)

(d) どこが入り口やら分からずビルの周りを何度も回った。

(Not being able to figure out where the entrance was, I walked around the building several times.)

(e) 誰も名札をつけていないので誰が誰やらさっぱり分からない。

(No one is wearing a name tag, so I simply cannot figure out who's who.)

(f) 今日はどんなご馳走を食べさせてもらえるのやら、とても楽しみだ。

(I wonder what kind of feast they'll have for me to eat today. I can't wait!)

(g) いつのまにやら外は暗くなっていた。

(It got dark outside before I realized it.)

Notes

1. The sentence-final particle *yara* is an informal expression; therefore, it does not appear in formal conversation or writing.

2. In many cases, *yara* occurs in the sentence pattern S *no yara* or S *koto yara*, where S is often a Wh-sentence. (Note that Ex.(a) is an example where S is not a Wh-sentence.) Both patterns mean "I wonder" but have different nuances: S *no yara* is used to express the speaker's uncertainty, concern, anxiety or unhappiness, while S *koto yara* is always used to express the speaker's strong concern, anxiety or unhappiness. In (1), *koto* is not acceptable because these sentences do not express any concern or anxiety.

(1) a. あんな男のどこがいい{の／*こと}やら。

(I wonder why people like (lit., what is good about) that guy.)

   b. この本はどこにしまえばいい{の／*こと}やら。

(I wonder where I should keep this book.)

   c. あの人にいつ会った{の／*こと}やら（全然覚えていない）。

(I have no idea when I met that person.)

   d. 今日はどんなご馳走を食べさせてもらえる{の／*こと}やら、とても楽しみだ。(= Ex.(f))

On the other hand, in (2), the sentences express the speaker's strong concern, anxiety or unhappiness; therefore, *no* is not acceptable.

(2) a. 彼には何度裏切られた{こと／*の}やら。

(How many times did he betray me?!)

   b. 夫ははたして無事に戦争から帰ってきてくれる{こと／??の}やら。

(I really wonder if my husband will come back safely from the war. (I'm very worried.))

Y

The sentences in (3) convey different nuances depending on whether *no* or *koto* is used. That is, the *no* version is a self-addressed question with or without the speaker's concern or anxiety, whereas the *koto* version conveys the speaker's strong concern or anxiety.

(3) a. この不況は一体いつまで続く{の / こと}やら。

(I wonder how long this recession will last.)

b. 今日はどんなものを食べさせられる{の / こと}やら。

(I wonder what they're going to make me eat today.)

c. このホールの完成はいつになる{の / こと}やら。

(I wonder when this hall will be completed.)

3. S *yara* and S *no yara* can be embedded in another clause, as in KS(C), Exs.(a) and (e), in which case *yara* is simply a marker of an internal question and does not carry the meaning "I wonder." Note that S *koto yara* cannot be embedded in another clause, as shown in (4).

(4) a. 誰が手伝ってくれる{の / *こと}やら全然知らない。

(I have no idea who's going to help me.)

b. この不況が一体いつまで続く{の / *こと}やら専門家にも全く予測がつかない。

(Even specialists cannot predict how long this recession will last.)

4. Ex.(f) presents an example of an abbreviated internal question. (5) is an unabbreviated version of Ex.(f).

(5) 今日はどんなご馳走を食べさせてもらえるのやら<u>分からないが</u>、とても楽しみだ。(cf. Ex.(f))

(I don't know what kind of feast they'll have for me to eat today, but I can't wait (to find out).)

5. Wh-word + *yara* is equivalent to Wh-word + *ka*, i.e., an indefinite pronoun or adverb; however, note that *dō yara* is not equivalent to *dō ka* "please."

(6) a. 学生たちが{何やら / 何か}面白そうな計画をしている。(= KS(D))

b. エレベーターで{誰やら / 誰か}知らない人に話しかけられた。

(Someone I don't know talked to me in the elevator.)

c. {どこやら / どこか}で大きな地震があったらしい。

(I heard that there was a strong earthquake somewhere.)

d.｛いつやら／いつか｝そういう話を友達から聞いたことがある。

(I heard a similar story from a friend of mine sometime in the past.)

e.｛どうやら／*どうか｝電車に間に合った。

(I managed to (lit., somehow or other) make it to the train.)

【Related Expressions】

I. *Darō ka* "I wonder" and *kashira* "I wonder" are also used to form self-addressed questions. Note that when the sentence ends with *yara*, as seen in the sentences in [1], the preceding clause must be followed by either *no* or *koto*, and when the preceding clause is followed by *koto*, *darō ka* and *kashira* cannot be used, as shown in [1c].

[1] a. 友美はパーティーに来られる｛*やら／だろうか／かしら｝。

(I wonder if Yumi can come to the party.)

b. 友美はパーティーに来られるの｛やら／だろうか／かしら｝。

(I wonder if Yumi can come to the party.)

c. この論文はいつ書き上げられること｛やら／*だろうか／*かしら｝。

(I wonder when I'll be able to finish this thesis. (I'm worried.))

Note also that when the preceding clause is an embedded question, *darō ka* and *kashira* cannot be used, as in [2].

[2] 明日のパーティーには誰が来る｛やら／*だろうか／*かしら｝分からない。

(I can't tell who's coming to tomorrow's party.)

(⇨ ***darō*** (DBJG: 100-02); ***kashira*** (DBJG: 181-82))

II. *Yara*, when it is used to mark embedded questions, can be replaced by *ka*, as shown in [3].

[3] a. こんな映画のどこがいいの｛やら／か｝さっぱり分からない。

(= KS(C))

b. どこが入り口｛やら／か｝分からずビルの周りを何度も回った。

(= Ex.(d))

c. 誰も名札をつけていないので誰が誰｛やら／か｝さっぱり分からない。

(= Ex.(e))

d. 今日はどんなご馳走を食べさせてもらえるの {やら / か}、とても楽しみだ。(= Ex.(f))

(⇨ ***ka²*** (DBJG: 166-68))

~ yara ~ yara   ~やら~やら   *str.*

a structure to present things, events, actions, etc., as examples, reasons or possibilities

X and Y; things like X and Y; X, Y and so on; whether X or Y; whether X or not
【REL. ~ *ya* ~ *ya*; ~ *toka* ~ *toka*; ~ *tari* ~ *tari*; ~ *ka* ~ *ka*; ~ ***wa*** ~ ***wa***】

◆ Key Sentences

(A)

	Noun₁		Noun₂			
私は	会議	やら	講習会	やら	で	このところ出張が続いている。

(I have been traveling for business a lot these days to conferences, workshops, etc.)

(B)

		Adj(*i*)₁inf.nonpast	
みんなに自分の写真をほめられて		嬉しい	やら

Adj(*i*)₂inf.nonpast			
恥ずかしい	やら	(で)	変な気持ちでした。

(When people praised the picture of me I felt strange, both happy and shy.)

(C)

	V₁inf. nonpast			V₂inf. nonpast		
今日は、上司に	叱られる	やら	財布を	落とす	やら	(で)

さんざんな一日だった。

(I got told off by my boss; I lost my wallet—it's been a horrible day today.)

(D)

	V₁inf (Aff.)		V₂inf (Neg.) (V₁ = V₂)		
久子は	来る	やら	来ない	やら	分からないから、もう行こう。

(We can't tell whether Hisako will come or not, so let's just go.)

(E)

	Adj(*i*)₁inf		
美術品のことは何も知らないので、この壺が	安い	の	やら

Adj(*i*)₂inf			
高い	の	やら	全然見当がつかない。

(Because I know nothing about art objects, I have no idea whether this pot is cheap or expensive.)

Formation

(i)　X やら Y やら

・V₁inf.nonpast やら V₂inf.nonpast やら

笑われるやら馬鹿にされるやら　(s.o. was laughed at and insulted, among other things)

今日帰るやら明日帰るやら　(whether s.o. will come home today or tomorrow)

・Adj(*i*)₁inf.nonpast やら Adj(*i*)₂inf.nonpast やら

悲しいやら悔しいやら　((I felt) sad and frustrated)

いいやら悪いやら　(whether s.t. is good or bad)

・Adj(*na*)₁stem やら Adj(*na*)₂stem やら

上手（じょうず）やら下手（へた）やら　(whether s.o. is good or poor at s.t.)

・N₁ やら N₂ やら

クッキーやらチョコレートやら　(cookies, chocolates, and so on)

本物（ほんもの）やら偽物（にせもの）やら　(real things and imitations; whether s.t. is real or an imitation)

(ii)　V₁inf (Aff.) やら V₂inf (Neg.) やら　(where V₁ = V₂)

行くやら行かないやら　(whether s.o. will go or not)

行ったやら行かなかったやら　(whether s.o. went or not)

(iii)　X のやら Y のやら

・V₁inf のやら V₂inf のやら

行くのやら留（とど）まるのやら　(whether s.o. will go or stay)

・Adj(*i*)₁inf のやら Adj(*i*)₂inf のやら

新しいのやら古いのやら　(whether s.t. is new or old)

・Adj(*na*)₁stem {な / だった} のやら Adj(*na*)₂stem {な / だった} のやら

上手なのやら下手なのやら　(whether s.o. is good or poor at s.t.)

・N₁ {な / だった} のやら N₂ {な / だった} のやら

日本人なのやらアメリカ人なのやら　(whether s.o. is a Japanese or an American)

Examples

(a) 着替（きが）えやらお土産（みやげ）やらでスーツケースはもういっぱいになってしまった。

(My suitcase is full now with a change of clothes and souvenirs and other things.)

(b) 趣味（しゅみ）のことやら家族のことやらを時々ブログに書いている。

(I write about my hobbies and my family in my blog from time to time.)

(c) 音を立ててスープを飲むやら口にものを入（い）れたまま話すやら、直樹（なおき）のテーブルマナーはひどかった。

(Naoki did things like slurping his soup and talking with food in his mouth——his table manners were horrible.)

(d) アンディと楽しそうにおしゃべりしている陽子が憎らしいやらねたましいやらで、人と話していても上の空だった。

(My mind was somewhere else when I was talking with people because I was mad at and jealous of Yoko, whom I saw talking happily with Andy.)

(e) 彼女は日本語を話すそうだが、まだ話すのを聞いたことがないので、上手やら下手やら全く見当がつかない。

(I heard that she speaks Japanese, but because I haven't heard her speak yet, I have no idea whether she's good or bad at it.)

(f) この仕事は自分にできるやらできないやら、やってみなければ分からない。

(I can't tell if I can do this job unless I try.)

(g) 彼はアメリカ生まれの生粋のアメリカ人だが、日本人なのやらアメリカ人なのやら分からないくらい、考え方が日本人的だ。

(He is a genuine born-in-the-USA American, but his ways of thinking are so much like those of Japanese people that we (almost) cannot tell whether he is a Japanese or an American. (lit., his ways of thinking are like those of Japanese people to the extent that we cannot tell whether he is a Japanese or an American.))

(h) 貸してもらえるのやらもらえないのやら分からないお金を当てにしているのはよくない。

(It's not good to count on the money before you know if they will lend it to you or not.)

Notes

1. The structure X *yara* Y *yara* is used to present things, events, states or actions as examples, reasons or possibilities.

2. When X *yara* Y *yara* presents reasons, the reason particle *de* may follow Y *yara* as in KS(B), (C) and Ex.(d).

3. The structure X *yara* Y *yara* also means "whether X or Y" when expressions like *wakaranai* "cannot figure out" and *kentō ga tsukanai* "have no idea" are in the main clause predicate, as in KS(D), (E) and Exs.(e)-(h).

4. X *yara* Y *yara* is not used in formal writing or speech.

[Related Expressions]

I. *Ya* and *toka* can also be used to present things as examples or reasons, as shown in [1]. Note that *ya* is usually not repeated after the last item.

[1] a. 私は会議｛やら / や / とか｝講習会｛やら / ∅ / とか｝でこのところ出張が続いている。(= KS(A))

b. 趣味のこと｛やら / や / とか｝家族のこと｛やら / ∅ / とか｝を時々ブログに書いている。(= Ex.(b))

However, *ya* and *toka* cannot be used when the preceding elements are not nouns.

[2] a. みんなに自分の写真をほめられて嬉しい｛やら / *や / *とか｝恥ずかしい｛やら / *や / *とか｝(で)変な気持ちでした。(= KS(B))

b. 今日は、上司に叱られる｛やら / *や / *とか｝財布を落とす｛やら / *や / *とか｝(で)さんざんな一日だった。(= KS(C))

($\Rightarrow$ ***ya*** (DBJG: 536-38); ***toka*** (DBJG: 488-90))

II. The structure X *tari* Y *tari* can also be used to present actions as reasons when X and Y are verbs.

[3] a. 今日は、上司に叱られ｛るやら / たり｝財布を落と｛すやら / したり｝(で)さんざんな一日だった。(= KS(C))

b. みんなに自分の写真をほめられて嬉し｛いやら / ??かったり｝恥ずかし｛いやら / ??かったり｝(で)変な気持ちでした。(= KS(B))

($\Rightarrow$ *~tari ~tari suru* (DBJG: 458-61))

III. The structure X *ka* Y *ka* also represents the idea of "whether X or Y," as shown in [4].

[4] a. 久子は来る｛やら / か｝来ない｛やら / か｝分からないから、もう行こう。(= KS(D))

b. 彼女は日本語を話すそうだが、まだ話すのを聞いたことがないので、上手｛やら / か｝下手｛やら / か｝全く見当がつかない。(= Ex.(e))

However, X *yara* Y *yara* can be used only when "verbs of cognition," such as *wakaru* "can tell" and *kentō ga tsuku* "guess," are in the main clause predicate. Thus, *yara* is not grammatical in [5].

[5] a. 私は電車｛か / *やら｝バス (｛か / *やら｝)で行くつもりだ。
(I'm planning on going either by train or by bus.)

Y

b. トムが行く{か/*やら}メアリーが行く{か/*やら}<u>どちらかだ</u>。
(Either Tom will go or Mary will.)

(⇨ **ka¹** (DBJG: 164-66); ~ **ka** ~ **ka** (DIJG: 87-89))

yōde wa　ようでは　　*conj.*

a conjunction that presents an undesirable situation, which is assumed to be factual	if; if it is true that; if it is the case that 【REL. *te wa*】

◆ **Key Sentences**

(A)

	Vinf.nonpast		
知らない単語が出てくるたびに辞書を	引いている	ようでは	いつまでたっても速く読めない。

(If (it is true that) you look up unfamiliar words in the dictionary every time you encounter a new one, you will never learn to read fast.)

(B)

	Adj(*i*)inf.nonpast		
アパートがそんなに	高い	ようでは	私たちは東京には住めない。

(If (it is true that) apartments in Tokyo are that expensive, we cannot live there.)

(C)

	Noun			
成績が	今まで	の	ようでは	困ります。

(If you continue to show the level of performance you have to date, we will have a problem. (lit., If your performance is like what you have exhibited up to now, it's a problem.))

Y

Formation

(i) {V / Adj(*i*)} inf.nonpast ようでは

行くようでは　(if it's true / the case that s.o. goes / is going)

弱いようでは　(if it's true / the case that s.t./s.o. is weak)

(ii) Adj(*na*)stem なようでは

下手なようでは　(if it's true / the case that s.o. is bad at s.t.)

(iii) N のようでは

2年前のようでは　(if s.t. is like two years ago)

Examples

(a) 今からそんなに文句を言っているようでは、この仕事をやり遂げるのは難しいだろう。

(If you complain like that now, it will be difficult to complete this job.)

(b) 困った時に助けてくれないようでは友達とは言えない。

(If (it is true that) he doesn't help you when you are in trouble, you cannot call him a friend.)

(c) 朝が弱いようではこの仕事は無理でしょう。

(If (it is true that) you have trouble getting up early in the morning (lit., are weak in the morning), you probably won't be able to do this job.)

(d) 千円程度の旅費払い戻しに4枚も5枚も書類が必要なようでは問題だ。

(It is a problem if (it is true that) it takes four or five forms to request a travel reimbursement for an amount as small as one thousand yen.)

(e) 今頃そんなことをしているようでは、とても締め切りに間に合わない。

(If you're doing things like that now, there's no way you'll meet the deadline.)

(f) 部下の面倒が見られないようでは上司失格だ。

(If (it is true that) you cannot take care of the people under you, you are not qualified to be their boss.)

(g) 大学の施設が現状のようでは、せっかく研究資金を増やしても有効に活用できない。

(Even if we make an effort to increase research funding, with the university facilities the way they are (lit., if the university facilities are in their present condition), we won't be able to utilize the funds effectively.)

(h) 次の試合も今日の試合のようでは、とても決勝には進めない。

(If we play the next game like (we did in) today's game, there's no way we can advance to the finals.)

Notes

1. In "S₁ *yōde wa* S₂," S₂ presents the speaker's negative comment on the undesirable situation given in S₁.

2. S *yōde wa* is used to present an undesirable situation indirectly. The indirectness is expressed with the auxiliary *yōda* "it appears that" and the conditional *te wa* "if."

(⇨ ***yōda*** (DBJG: 547-52); ***te wa*** (DIJG: 461-63))

3. Situations presented in S *yōde wa* are assumed to be factual, although there are cases in which a situation is nonfactual, as in Ex.(h).

4. As seen in KS(C), Exs.(g) and (h), *yōde* in N *no yōde wa* means resemblance (i.e., "like") rather than appearance (i.e., "it appears that"). In fact, N *no yōde wa* is somewhat unnatural when it is used to convey the way something appears, as shown in (1).

(1) a. 委員長が病気 {??のよう / ∅} では会議は開けない。

(If (it is true that) the chairman is ill (= It appears that the chairman is ill, and if that's true), we cannot have a meeting.)

b. 今回の実験が失敗 {??のよう / ∅} ではこのプロジェクトを続けるわけにはいかない。

(If (it is true that) the experiment fails this time (= It appears that the experiment will fail this time, and if that's true), we cannot continue this project.)

[Related Expression]

Te wa "if" is also used to present an undesirable situation. However, *te wa* is more direct than *yōde wa*.

[1] a. 知らない単語が出てくるたびに辞書を引いて {いるようでは / いては}、いつまでたっても速く読めない。(= KS(A))

b. アパートがそんなに {高いようでは / 高くては}、私たちは東京には住めない。(= KS(B))

(⇨ ***te wa*** (DIJG: 461-63))

yō mono nara ようものなら   *phr.*   \<w\>

| | a conjunctive phrase that presents an undesirable hypothetical situation | if ~ happen to; if ~ at all; if ~ choose to 【REL. *tari shitara*】 |

◆ **Key Sentence**

	Vvol		
山野氏は非常に時間に厳しい人で、面会時間に5分も	遅れよう	ものなら	以後二度と会ってはもらえない。

(Mr. Yamano is very strict about time; if you happen to be even five minutes late for an appointment with him, he won't meet with you again.)

Formation

Vvol ものなら

聞こうものなら   (if s.o. asks at all)

食べようものなら   (if s.o. eats s.t. at all)

Examples

(a) 私はたばこの煙に特に敏感で、近くで吸われようものならもう何事にも集中できなくなってしまう。

(I'm particularly sensitive to cigarette smoke, so when someone is smoking nearby, I cannot concentrate on anything.)

(b) ニューヨークでは信号が青に変わって一秒でも発進が遅れようものなら、すかさず後ろからクラクションを鳴らされる。

(In New York, if you happen to take even a second to move (your car) forward after the traffic light turns green, the driver behind you honks at you immediately.)

(c) この島は、晴れていれば散歩や海水浴などが楽しめるが、雨に降られようものなら何もやることがなくなる。

(On this island, you can have fun walking and swimming in the ocean on sunny days, but if it happens to rain, there's nothing to do.)

(d) この飛行機は前の座席との間隔が極端に狭いので、私のように大きい人間は、前の人に椅子を倒されようものなら、文字通り身動きできなくなってしまう。

(The seats in this airplane have an extremely small amount of space between them, so if someone in the seat ahead chooses to lean back, large people like me are stuck (lit., are in a situation in which they literally cannot move).)

(e) 最近頻繁にやってくる訪問販売は頭痛の種です。断っても簡単には帰りませんし、うっかり家の中に入れようものなら買うまで帰りません。

(The frequent visits of door-to-door salesmen these days are a real headache. The salesmen won't leave even if you say "no thanks," and if you happen to let them in the house by mistake, they won't leave until you buy (their products).)

(f) 花粉症の季節にうっかりバイクで出かけようものなら、走行中にくしゃみ連発でフルフェイスのヘルメットの中は悲惨な状態になる。

(If you happen to go out on a motorcycle in pollen season (lit., pollen allergy season) by mistake, you'll keep sneezing and be miserable inside your full-face helmet.)

(g) この魚は猛毒を持っていて、間違ってそのトゲに刺されようものなら、患部が大きく腫れ上がってしまう。

(This fish is very poisonous, and if you happen to be stung, that area will swell a lot.)

(h) 田村さんは最近漢方医学に凝っていて、うっかりそのことを聞こうものなら、たっぷり一時間はその効用を聞くはめになる。

(Ms. Tamura has taken up (studying) Chinese medicine recently and if you ask her about it by mistake, you will end up listening to (her talk about) its effects for a full hour.)

Notes

1. *Yō mono nara* is used to present a hypothetical situation that the speaker/writer or others want to avoid.

2. Only verbs can occur before *mono nara*.

3. Adverbs like *ukkari* "by accident" or *machigatte* "by mistake" are often used with *yō mono nara*, as in Exs.(e)-(h).

【Related Expression】

Yō mono nara is used in written language. A colloquial phrase equivalent to *yō mono nara* is *tari shitara*, which literally means "if s.o. does a thing like ~."

[1] a. 山野氏は非常に時間に厳しい人で、面会時間に５分も遅れ｛ようものなら／たりしたら｝、以後二度と会ってはもらえない。(= KS)

b. 私はたばこの煙に特に敏感で、近くで吸われ｛ようものなら／たりしたら｝もう何事にも集中できなくなってしまう。(= Ex.(a))

Note that *tari shitara* can be used with elements other than verbs, as in [2].

[2] a. テストの成績が｛悪かったりしたら／*悪いものなら／*悪かったものなら｝、今月の小遣いをもらえないかもしれない。

(If my grade on the test turns out to be bad, I may not get my allowance this month.)

b. 客が外国人｛だったりしたら／*ものなら／*だったものなら｝、私は緊張してしまって何も話せなくなる。

(If the customer happens to be a foreigner, I get nervous and cannot talk at all.)

---

yō ni mo (~ nai)　ようにも（〜ない）　　*phr.*

<table>
<tr>
<td>a conjunctive phrase that indicates concession: "even though s.o. tries to do s.t., he/she cannot do it for some reason"</td>
<td>even though ~ try/want to ~; even though ~ be thinking of doing ~; although ~ try/want to ~; although ~ be thinking of doing ~
【REL. *yō ttatte*; *ni mo*; *takute mo (~ nai)*; *taku to mo (~ nai)*】</td>
</tr>
</table>

◆ **Key Sentences**

(A)

	Vvol			
徹に 連絡しよう	にも	電話番号もメールアドレスも知ら	ない。	

(Even though I want to contact Toru, I don't know either her phone number or her e-mail address.)

(B)

	Vvol		Vpot.neg	
ひどく頭が痛くて	起きよう	にも	起きられ	ない。

(I have a terrible headache, and I cannot get up even though I want to.)

Formation

Vvol にも（～ない）

話そうにも（～ない）　((not) even though s.o. tries to talk)

教えようにも（～ない）　((not) even though s.o. tries to teach)

Examples

(a) 記事を書こうにも書く材料がない。

(Even though I'm thinking of writing an article, I have nothing to write about.)

(b) すしを作ろうにも材料が手に入らない。

(Even though I want to make *sushi*, I cannot get the ingredients (lit., materials).)

(c) 苦情を言おうにも誰に言っていいか分からなかった。

(Although I wanted to complain, I didn't know who to complain to.)

(d) 体を動かそうにもあちこち痛くて腕も上げられない。

(Although I'm trying to move my body, every part aches and I can't even lift my arms.)

(e) 母は僕の日本人のガールフレンドと話そうにも日本語ができなかった。

(Even though my mother wanted to talk with my Japanese girlfriend, my mother (couldn't because she) can't speak Japanese.)

(f) 気の毒に彼女は悩み事を相談しようにも相談できる人が近くにいない。

(It's sad that even though she wants to talk to someone about her troubles, she has no one to talk to near her.)

(g) カウンセリングに行こうにも、その質や学派も様々でついつい懐疑的になってしまいます。

(Although I am thinking of going for counseling, the variation in quality and schools of thought makes me skeptical.)

(h) その本は買おうにも絶版だった。

(Although I wanted to buy the book, it was out of print.)

(i) 携帯電話の電池が切れたので、電話をかけようにもかけられない。

(Because my cell phone battery is dead, I cannot make a call even though I want to.)

Notes

1. *Yō ni mo* is used when someone tries to do something or is thinking of doing something but cannot do it for some reason.

2. The main clause after *yō ni mo* presents the reason that the subject in the *yō ni mo* clause cannot do what he/she wants to do. Thus, *yō ni mo* cannot be used in (1).

   (1) a. *その仕事を一人でしようにも<u>それは無理だ</u>。

      (Even though you want to do that job by yourself, it's impossible.)

      b. *そんなことを信じさせようにも<u>誰が信じるものか</u>。

      (Even though you try to convince us, who's going to believe you?)

      c. *僕にお金を借りようにも<u>無駄だよ</u>。

      (Even though you try to borrow money from me, it's of no use.)

3. The subject of the *yō ni mo* clause is usually the first person, but third person subjects are also possible if the speaker/writer is empathetic with the subject, as in Exs.(e) and (f). Having a subject in the second person is not impossible, as shown in (2), but it is rare.

   (2) 記事を書こうにも書く材料がないだろう？

      (Even though you want to write an article, you have nothing to write about, do you?)

【Related Expressions】

I. *Yō ttatte* "even if; even though" can be used in place of *yō ni mo* in some situations.

[1] a. 徹に連絡しよう{にも / ったって}電話番号もメールアドレスも知らない。(= KS(A))

    b. 記事を書こう{にも / ったって}書く材料がない。(= Ex.(a))

    c. すしを作ろう{にも / ったって}材料が手に入らない。(= Ex.(b))

    d. 体を動かそう{にも / ったって}あちこち痛くて腕も上げられない。

(= Ex.(d))

One of the differences between *yō ttatte* and *yō ni mo* is that the main clause after *yō ttatte* does not have to be the reason, as shown in [2]. (See Note 2.)

[2] a. その仕事を一人でしよう{ったって / *にも}それは無理だ。(cf. (1a))
    (Even though you want to do that job by yourself, it's impossible.)

    b. そんなことを信じさせよう{ったって / *にも}誰が信じるものか。

(cf. (1b))
    (Even though you try to convince us, who's going to believe you?)

    c. 僕にお金を借りよう{ったって / *にも}無駄だよ。(cf. (1c))
    (Even though you try to borrow money from me, it's of no use.)

Also note that *yō ttatte* cannot be used when the main clause is in the past tense, as in [3].

[3] a. 徹に連絡しようったって電話番号もメールアドレスも{知らない / ??知らなかった}。(cf. KS(A))
    (Even though I wanted to contact Toru, I didn't know either her phone number or her e-mail address.)

    b. 苦情を言おうったって誰に言っていいか{分からない / ??分からなかった}。(cf. Ex.(c))

In terms of speech level, *yō ttatte* is more colloquial than *yō ni mo*.

(⇨ *(t)tatte*¹ (in this volume))

II. Vinf.nonpast *ni mo* can be used in place of *yō ni mo* when the sentence ends with a negative predicate, as in [4].

[4] a. 徹に連絡｛しよう／する｝にも、電話番号もメールアドレスも<u>知らない</u>。(= KS(A))

b. 記事を｛書こう／書く｝にも書く材料が<u>ない</u>。(= Ex.(a))

c. すしを｛作ろう／作る｝にも材料が手に<u>入らない</u>。(= Ex.(b))

d. 苦情を｛言おう／言う｝にも誰に言っていいか<u>分からなかった</u>。
(= Ex.(c))

When the predicate is not negative, Vinf.nonpast *ni mo* is unnatural, as shown in [5].

[5] その本は｛買おう／??買う｝にも<u>絶版だった</u>。(= Ex.(h))

III. *Takute mo (~ nai)* and *taku to mo (~ nai)* are synonymous with *yō ni mo (~ nai)* and can be used interchangeably, as shown in [6]. The difference is that the first two phrases indicate the subject's desire to do something explicitly while the third only implies that.

[6] a. 徹に連絡｛しようにも／したくても／したくとも｝電話番号もメールアドレスも知らない。(= KS(A))

b. ひどく頭が痛くて起き｛ようにも／たくても／たくとも｝起きられない。(= KS(B))

---

yori / no hoka (ni) (wa) ~ nai   より／の ほか (に)(は)～ない   *phr.*

a phrase that conveys the idea that there is no other choice than to do s.t., or that s.t. is true of only one of a select few things

there is no (other) choice but to; there is no other way than to; have to; nothing but; but; not ~ other than
【REL. *nakereba naranai*; *nakereba ikenai*; *zaru o enai*; *~ **ni** ~ **nai***】

◆ Key Sentences

(A)

	Vinf.nonpast		
公共の交通機関がないので、 自分の車で	行く	(より)	ほか (に) (は) ない。

(Since there is no public transportation, we have no other choice but to go there in your/my car.)

(B)

	Noun			Vneg	
新聞は	ニューヨークタイムズ	の	ほか (に) は	読ま	ない。

(I read nothing but the New York Times. (lit., I don't read any newspaper other than the New York Times.))

Formation

(i) Vinf.nonpast (より) ほか (に) (は) ない

買う (より) ほか (に) (は) ない　(there is no other choice but to buy s.t.)

(ii) N {より / の} ほか (に) は Vneg ない

アメリカ映画 {より / の} ほか (に) は 見ない　(I see nothing but American movies)

日本食はすし {より / の} ほか (に) は 食べない　(I don't eat any Japanese food other than *sushi*)

Examples

(a) アルバイトの仕事が駄目になったので、両親にお金を借りるよりほかになかった。

(Because I lost my part-time job, I had no choice but to borrow money from my parents.)

(b) 友人がどうして気が狂ってしまったのかは推測するよりほかにはない。

(I can only speculate as to why my friend was acting crazy.)

(c) 信号機の故障で電車が止まってしまった以上、待っているよりほかない。

(Since the train is stopped due to a signal problem we have no choice but to wait.)

Y

(d) 国際的に活躍したければ英語を学ぶよりほかはないだろう。

(A person who wants to be internationally active will have no choice but to learn English.)

(e) 秩序を回復するには権威の力を直接見せつけた容赦ない手段をとるよりほかはない。

(In order to restore order, there is no other choice than to take ruthless means, directly demonstrating the power of our authority.)

(f) モーツアルトが 35 年の生涯に 600 曲以上の作品を書いたというのには、ただただ驚くよりほかはない。

(The fact that Mozart composed more than 600 pieces during his life of thirty-five years is simply amazing (lit., leaves us no other choice than to be surprised).)

(g) 典型的な科学者のイメージに合う人はアインシュタインのほかにはいない。

(Nobody but Einstein fits the stereotypical image of a scientist.)

(h) 学会に出席している学者は数人のほかは面識がなかった。

(All but a few of the attendees of the academic conference were total strangers.)

Notes

1. Because *yori*, *ni* and *wa* are all optional in Vinf.nonpast *(yori) hoka (ni) (wa) nai*, there are several possible choices when using this phrase. Ex.(a), for example, can be rephrased in different ways, as shown in (1).

   (1) アルバイトの仕事が駄目になったので、両親にお金を借りる {よりほかに / よりほかには / よりほかは / よりほか / ほかには / ほかに / ほかは / ほか} なかった。

   The difference among the versions is very subtle: The first two versions are much more formal and are used in writing whereas the last two versions sound very colloquial and casual.

2. N_1 *wa* N_2 *no hoka ni ~ nai*, means "regarding N_1, an action or state expressed by the verb is only applicable to N_2." KS(B), Exs.(g) and (h) are examples of this.

[Related Expressions]

I. *Nakereba naranai/ikenai* can replace *(yori) hoka (ni)(wa) ~ nai* in all of the KS and Exs. when the verb is a volitional verb. If it is a non-volitional verb like *odoroku* "be surprised," *nakereba naranai/ikenai* can't be used, as shown in [1c].

[1] a. 公共の交通機関がないので、自分の車で{行くよりほかにはない／行かなければならない／行かなければいけない}。(= KS(A))

　　b. アルバイトの仕事が駄目になったので、両親にお金を{借りるよりほかになかった／借りなければならなかった／借りなければいけなかった}。(= Ex.(a))

　　c. モーツアルトが35年の生涯に600曲以上の作品を書いたというのには、ただただ{驚くよりほかはない／*驚かなければならない／*驚かなければいけない}。(= Ex.(f))

In [1a], for example, if one wants to express the idea that there is no other choice than to go by car, he/she will say *iku yori hoka ni nai*. But if one wants to express the idea that he/she has to go by car, he/she will say *ikanakereba naranai/ikenai*. (⇨ **~nakereba naranai** (DBJG: 274-76))

II. Vneg *zaru o enai* "can't help but" is very close in meaning to *(yori) hoka (ni)(wa) nai*, and it can replace all the KS and Exs. without a change in meaning.

[2] a. 公共の交通機関がないので、自分の車で{行くよりほかにはない／行かざるを得ない}。(= KS(A))

　　b. モーツアルトが35年の生涯に600曲以上の作品を書いたというのには、ただただ{驚くよりほかはない／驚かざるを得ない}。(= Ex.(f))

(⇨ **zaru o enai** (DIJG: 606-09))

Y

yoshi　よし［由］　*n.* <w>

{ a dependent noun that marks the con-
tent of what the writer has learned }
(I heard / It is said / etc.) that
【REL. *to no koto*】

◆ **Key Sentences**

(A)

	Noun			
この度は本社営業部長に	ご栄転	の	由、	誠におめでとう存じます。

(I heard of your promotion this time to manager of the headquarters'
sales department. Please accept my sincere congratulations.)

(B)

Sinf		
地球環境保護の国際会議が来年当市で開催される	由	（である）。

(It is said that an international conference on global environmental
protection will be held in this city next year.)

(C)

Sinf		
野沢先生は来年一年ドイツにいらっしゃる	由、	伺っております。

(I've been informed that next year Professor Nozawa is going to Germany for a year.)

Formation

(i)　N の由

　　　ご入院の由　(I heard of s.o.'s hospitalization)

(ii)　{V / Adj(*i*)} inf 由

　　　{行う / 行った} 由　(I heard that s.o. will do / did s.t.)

　　　{高い / 高かった} 由　(I heard that s.t. is/was expensive)

(iii)　{Adj(*na*)stem / N}{である / であった} 由

　　　不便{である / であった} 由　(I heard that s.t. is/was inconvenient)

　　　先生{である / であった} 由　(I heard that s.o. is/was a teacher)

Examples

(a) 第一子御出産の由、心からお祝い申し上げます。

(I heard that you gave birth to your first child and I send my heartfelt congratulations.)

(b) 当ホテルでのご滞在が快適でなかった由、誠に申し訳なく存じます。

(We learned that your stay at our hotel was not a pleasant one. We are very sorry for that.)

(c) 交通事故のこと伺いました。お怪我などなかった由、ほっといたしております。

(I heard about the traffic accident. I am relieved to hear that you were not hurt.)

(d) 石垣島は運よく台風の通過コースからはずれたため被害は少なかった由。

(I was informed that there was not much damage on Ishigaki Island because, luckily, the typhoon missed it (lit., swerved away from it).)

(e) 日本消費者連盟は、一部ウイスキーの不正表示に関して、公正取引委員会に申し入れる由である。

(It is said that the Japan Consumers Union is going to appeal to the Fair Trade Commission regarding the dishonest labels on some whiskies.)

(f) 懇親会にご出席の由、吉本君から連絡を受けました。

(I heard from Mr. Yoshimoto that you will be attending the reception.)

Notes

1. *Yoshi* is used to mark the content of what the writer has learned. Verbs are often omitted, as in KS(A) and (B), in which case *yoshi* also indicates the idea of "I hear; It is said; etc."

2. *Yoshi* is used only in formal written language—typically in letters to express one's congratulations, condolence, regret, relief, surprise, etc., as in KS(A) and Exs.(a)-(c). Although it is not as common, *yoshi* is also used in non-personal documents, as in KS(B), Exs.(d) and (e).

3. *Yoshi* can be followed by *da*, *de aru* or its variations, as in KS(B) and Ex.(e).

[Related Expression]

To no koto represents the same idea as *yoshi*, as shown in [1].

[1] a. この度は本社営業部長にご栄転｛の由／とのこと｝、誠におめでとう
存じます。(= KS(A))

b. 地球環境保護の国際会議が来年当市で開催される｛由／とのこと｝(で
ある)。(= KS(B))

c. 野沢先生は来年一年ドイツにいらっしゃる｛由／とのこと｝、伺って
おります。(= KS(C))

However, *to no koto* is also used in spoken language. For example, [2] can be a verbal message to the speaker's boss. *Yoshi* cannot be used in such situations.

[2] 平井さんが3時にいらっしゃる｛とのこと／*由｝です。
(I was told that Mr. Hirai is coming at three o'clock.)

yō to / ga   ようと／が   *phr.*   \<w\>

| a conjunctive phrase that expresses the idea of concession | even if; whatever/whoever/ etc.; no matter what/who/how/ etc.; whether X or Y 【REL. *te mo*; *yō tomo*】 |

◆ **Key Sentences**

(A)

	Wh-word		Vvol		
人が	何	と	言おう	｛と／が｝、	私は自分の子供を信じている。
(Whatever (other) people say, I believe my child.)					

(B)

	V₁vol			V₂vol	
頑固と	言われよう	｛と／が｝	馬鹿と	言われよう	｛と／が｝、

私は自分の信じることをやります。

(Even if people say I'm stubborn or stupid, I'll do what I believe.)

(C)

	V₁vol		V₂inf.nonpast (V₁ = V₂)		
あの教授は学生が	分かろう	｛と／が｝	分かる	まい	｛と／が｝、

かまわず授業を進めていく。

(That professor keeps lecturing (lit., advances his lecture) regardless of whether his students understand it or not.)

(D)

	Adj(*i*)₁ stem			Adj(*i*)₂ stem		
報酬が	多	かろう	｛と／が｝	少な	かろう	｛と／が｝、

私はやるべきことをやるだけだ。

(Whether the compensation is high or low, I'll just do what I have to do.)

(E)

	Adj(*na*)₁ stem			Adj(*na*)₂ stem		
英語が	上手	だろう	｛と／が｝	下手	だろう	｛と／が｝

そういうことは関係ない。

(It doesn't matter whether his English is good or bad.)

Y

(F)

Noun Phrase₁			Noun Phrase₂		
プロの作品	だろう	{と / が}	素人の作品	だろう	{と / が}

いいものは採用する。

(We'll adopt anything good, whether it's a work by a professional or an amateur.)

Formation

(i)　Vvol {と / が}

　　　話そう {と / が}　(even if s.o. talks)

　　　見よう {と / が}　(even if s.o. looks/sees)

(ii)　V₁vol {と / が} V₂inf.nonpast まい {と / が}　(where V₁ = V₂)

　　　行こう {と / が} 行くまい {と / が}　(whether or not s.o. will go)

(iii)　Adj(*i*)stem かろう {と / が}

　　　高かろう {と / が} 安かろう {と / が}　(whether s.t. is expensive or cheap)

(vi)　{Adj(*na*)stem / N} {だろう / であろう} {と / が}

　　　便利だろう {と / が} 不便だろう {と / が}　(whether s.t. is convenient or inconvenient)

　　　便利であろう {と / が} 不便であろう {と / が}　(whether s.t. is convenient or inconvenient)

　　　英語だろう {と / が} 日本語だろう {と / が}　(whether it is English or Japanese)

　　　英語であろう {と / が} 日本語であろう {と / が}　(whether it is English or Japanese)

Examples

(a)　人が何をしようと大きなお世話だ。

　　(Whatever I do, it's none of your business.)

(b) 費用がいくらかかろうとかまわない。何としてもこの訴訟に勝たなければならない。

(We don't care how much it may cost. We have to win this lawsuit by any means.)

(c) 彼はみんなが聞いていようがおかまいなしで、上司の悪口を言っている。

(He is saying bad things about his boss without regard to whether or not others are listening.)

(d) 自分の子供たちが走り回ろうが飲み物をこぼそうが、親たちは叱りもしないで自分たちの話に夢中になっている。

(Even if their children are running around or spilling drinks, the parents are too caught up in their own conversation to scold them.)

(e) 彼女が結婚しようがするまいが、そんなことは私には関係ないことだ。

(Whether she's going to marry or not, it has nothing to do with me.)

(f) 高かろうが安かろうが、必要なものなら買えばいい。

(Whether it's expensive or cheap, we should buy it if we need it.)

(g) 参加者がたとえ一人であろうとツアーは予定通り行います。

(We're going ahead with the tour as scheduled even if we have only one participant.)

(h) 日本人だろうがアメリカ人だろうが、そういうことは関係ない。好きになったら結婚する。

(It doesn't matter whether she is Japanese or American. If I fall in love (with someone), I'll marry that person.)

Notes

1. The volitional forms of verbs can indicate conjecture. Vinf.nonpast + *mai* is a negative volitional/conjecture form of verbs.

   (⇨ *-yō²* (DIJG: 599-602); *mai* (DIJG: 161-65))

2. The volitional forms of verbs, adjectives, etc., followed by *to* or *ga* indicate concession (i.e., even if; even though; whether or not; etc.). There is no difference in meaning or nuance between the *to* version and the *ga* version.

3. When a Wh-word is used in the clause, *yō to/ga* occurs once, as in KS(A), Exs.(a) and (b). When a Wh-word is not used, *yō to/ga* often occurs twice, marking two contrastive elements, as in KS(B)-(F), Exs.(d)-(f) and (h).

[Related Expressions]

I. ~*yō to/ga* can be rephrased using ~*te mo* without changing the meaning, as in [1].

[1] a. 人が何と{言おうと / 言おうが / 言っても}、私は自分の子供を信じている。(= KS(A))

b. 頑固と言われ{ようと / ようが / ても}馬鹿と言われ{ようと / ようが / ても}、私は自分の信じることをやります。(= KS(B))

c. あの教授は学生が{分かろうと / 分かろうが / 分かっても}{分かるまいと / 分かるまいが / 分からなくても}、かまわず授業を進めていく。(= KS(C))

d. 報酬が{多かろうと / 多かろうが / 多くても}{少なかろうと / 少なかろうが / 少なくても}、私はやるべきことをやるだけだ。(= KS(D))

e. 英語が上手{だろうと / だろうが / でも}下手{だろうと / だろうが / でも}そういうことは関係ない。(= KS(E))

f. プロの作品{だろうと / だろうが / でも}素人の作品{だろうと / だろうが / でも}いいものは採用する。(= KS(F))

However, ~*te mo* does not convey as strong an assertion as the other versions do. Note also that ~*te mo* is used in both written and spoken language.　　　　　　　　　　　　　　　　　(⇨ **te mo** (DBJG: 468-70))

II. ~*yō tomo* also carries the same meaning as ~*yō to/ga*, as in [2].

[2] a. 人が何と{言おうと / 言おうが / 言おうとも}、私は自分の子供を信じている。(= KS(A))

b. 頑固と言われ{ようと / ようが / ようとも}馬鹿と言われ{ようと / ようが / ようとも}、私は自分の信じることをやります。(= KS(B))

However, *tomo* cannot be used with the negative volitional form of verbs (i.e., Vinf.nonpast + *mai*) and *darō*, as in [3]. Note that *tomo* can occur with *de arō*.

[3] a. *あの教授は学生が分かろうとも分かるまいとも、かまわず授業を進めていく。(cf. KS(C))

b. 英語が上手{＊だろうとも／であろうとも}下手{＊だろうとも／であろうとも}そういうことは関係ない。(cf. KS(E))

c. 参加者がたとえ一人{＊だろうとも／であろうとも}ツアーは予定通り行います。(cf. Ex.(g))

---

yue ni　ゆえに［故に］　*conj.*　<w>

~~~
a conjunction that presents a reason or
a cause
~~~

because; because of; due to;
therefore
【REL. *tame (ni)*; *kara*; *node*;
dakara; *shitagatte*】

◆ **Key Sentences**

(A)

	Noun			
彼女はその	美貌	（の）	故（に）、	悩みも多い。

(Because of her good looks, she also has many things to worry about.)

(B)

Sinf			
結果にこだわりすぎる	（が）	故（に）、	小さなことに心を奪われることになる。

(Because you want the end result to be perfect, you end up being distracted by little things.)

(C)

Sentence₁			Sentence₂
これは極めてデリケートな問題だ。	（それ（が）／その）	故に、	慎重に取り組む必要がある。

(This is an extremely delicate problem; therefore, we must handle it very carefully.)

Y

Formation

(i) ｛N(の) / Adj(*na*)stem(な)｝故(に)

天才(の)故(に) (because s.o. is a genius)

便利(な)故(に) (because s.t. is convenient)

(ii) Sinf(が)故(に) (だ after Adj(*na*)stem and N is omitted.)

間違いを｛犯す / 犯した｝(が)故(に) (because s.o. commits/
committed an error)

｛美しい / 美しかった｝(が)故(に) (because s.o./s.t. is/was beautiful)

便利｛である / だった / であった｝(が)故(に) (because s.t. is/was
convenient)

天才｛である / だった / であった｝(が)故(に) (because s.o. is/was a
genius)

(iii) S₁。(それ(が) / その)故に、S₂。

この議論は前提がおかしい。(それ(が) / その)故に、結論も間違っている。
(This argument is based on a wrong premise. Therefore, the
conclusion is also wrong.)

Examples

(a) 彼の精神は大病の故に強靱になった。

(His mind was strengthened because of his serious illness.)

(b) 電子テキストは改変と公開が容易であるが、この特徴ゆえに公開されている
電子テキストは元データを追跡することが難しい。

(Electronic texts are easy to revise and present to the public, but because of these characteristics, it is difficult to trace publicly-displayed
electronic texts back to their original data.)

(c) 携帯電話は便利ゆえに、使い方を誤らないようにしなければならない。

(Because cell phones are convenient, we have to be careful not to use
them incorrectly.)

(d) 山は高いが故に尊からず。

(Mountains are not sacred just because they are tall.)

(e) 日本列島は南北に伸びているが故に、温度差が大きい。

(Because the Japanese archipelago extends north and south, the temperature difference (within Japan) is great.)

(f) アメリカでは今でも黒人であるが故に差別されるということがある。

(In the United States even now there are cases in which someone is discriminated against because he or she is black.)

(g) 「我思う、故に我あり。」──デカルト

("I think, therefore I am."──*Descartes*)

(h) 人はきっとミスをする。故に、それを前提とした対策を考える必要がある。

(People will certainly make mistakes; therefore, we need to think of countermeasures based on that assumption.)

(i) 俳句は言葉が最小限に抑えられている。それ故に、表現されていないことを想像しなければならない。

(*Haiku* use a bare minimum of words. Therefore, one has to imagine what is not expressed.)

Notes

1. *Yue ni* is used only in highly formal written language to express a reason for or the cause of something.

2. *Yue ni* cannot be used to represent the cause of a specific event or action, as shown in (1).

   (1) a. 地震{*(の)故に / のために}ビルが壊れた。

      (The building collapsed due to the earthquake.)

      b. その事故は飲酒運転{*(の)故に / のために}起こった。

      (The accident was caused by drunk driving.)

3. When sentences precede *yue ni*, *ga* may occur before *yue ni*, as in KS(B) and Exs.(d)-(f). This *ga* is the classic form of the noun-modification particle *no* and is optional.

4. *Ni* of *yue ni* is optional in most situations, as in (2).

   (2) a. 彼女はその美貌(の)故(に)、悩みも多い。(= KS(A))

      b. 携帯電話は便利ゆえ(に)、使い方を誤らないようにしなければならない。(= Ex.(c))

      c. 日本列島は南北に伸びているが故(に)、温度差が大きい。(= Ex.(e))

   However, *ni* must be present when S *ga yue ni* and the negative element in the main clause indicate partial negation (see Related Expression II), as in Ex.(d), or when nothing precedes *yue ni*, as in Ex.(h).

(3) a. 山は高いが**故**{に/*∅*}尊からず。(= Ex.(d))

   b. 人はきっとミスをする。**故**{に/*∅*}、それを前提とした対策を考える必要がある。(= Ex.(h))

5. *No* after nouns and *na* after *na*-adjective stems are optional, as in Exs.(b) and (c).

6. When *yue ni* is used as a sentence-initial conjunction, *sore*, *sore ga* or *sono* can precede *yue ni*, as in KS(C) and Ex.(i).

7. *Yue* can be used to form noun phrases, as in (4).

   (4) a. 福祉国家**ゆえ**の問題

      (the problem which the country has because it is a welfare state)

   b. 手作り**ゆえ**のよさ

      (the merit something exhibits because it is hand-made)

   c. コンピュータシステム**ゆえ**の限界

      (the limitation something has because it is a computer system)

8. S *yue* can be used as a predicate with the copula, as shown in (5).

   (5) a. そういう考え方しかできないのは、視野が狭い**ゆえ**である。

      (It is because of your limited viewpoint that you cannot find other ways of thinking about it.)

   b. この小説がこんなに広く読まれているのは、一つにはそのテーマの普遍性**ゆえ**だろう。

      (For one thing, it is probably because its theme is universal that this novel is read so widely.)

[Related Expressions]

I. *Tame (ni)* can be used to indicate a reason or a cause. Therefore, *yue ni* can be replaced by *tame ni*, as shown in [1].

   [1] a. 彼女はその美貌{(の)**故**(に)/のため(に)}、悩みも多い。(= KS(A))

   b. 結果にこだわりすぎる{(が)**故**(に)/ため(に)}、小さなことに心を奪われることになる。(= KS(B))

   c. これは極めてデリケートな問題だ。{(それ(が))**故**に/そのため(に)}、慎重に取り組む必要がある。(= KS(C))

Note that *tame ni* can be used to represent the cause of a specific event or action. (See Note 2.) (⇨ ***tame (ni)*** (DBJG: 447-51))

II. S *kara* and S *node* can replace S *ga yue ni* without a change in meaning.

[2] a. 結果にこだわりすぎる｛(が)故(に) / から / ので｝、小さなことに心を奪われることになる。(= KS(B))

b. 日本列島は南北に伸びている｛が故に / から / ので｝、温度差が大きい。(= Ex.(e))

However, if S *ga yue ni* and the negative element in the main clause indicate partial negation, as in Ex.(d), S *kara to itte ~ wake de wa nai* must be used instead of S *kara* or S *node*, as in [3].

[3] a. 山は高い｛が故に / *から / *ので｝尊からず。(= Ex.(d))

b. 山は高いからといって尊いわけではない。

(⇨ ***kara*³** (DBJG: 179-81); ***node*** (DBJG: 328-31);
kara to itte (DIJG: 103-05))

III. The conjunctions *dakara* and *shitagatte* can be used in place of the sentence-initial *yue ni*, as shown in [4].

[4] a. これは極めてデリケートな問題だ。｛(それ(が))故に / だから / 従って｝、慎重に取り組む必要がある。(= KS(C))

b. 人はきっとミスをする。｛故に / だから / 従って｝、それを前提とした対策を考える必要がある。(= Ex.(h))

(⇨ ***shitagatte*** (DIJG: 395-97))

Y

zu ni wa okanai　ずにはおかない　*phr.*　<w>

a phrase that expresses the idea that s.o./s.t. necessarily or naturally causes s.t. to happen	be bound to; definitely; unmistakably; unquestionably; undoubtedly; without fail; without doubt 【REL. *kanarazu*; *machigai naku*; *zettaini*; *zu ni wa orarenai/orenai/irarenai*】

◆ **Key Sentence**

	Vneg		
技術の発達は社会環境の変化を	もたらさ	ず	にはおかない。

(Technological advancements are bound to bring about changes to social environments.)

Formation

Vneg ずにはおかない　(Exception: する→せずにはおかない)

　動かさずにはおかない　(s.t. definitely moves s.t.)

Examples

(a) コンピュータの普及とインターネット利用の拡大は大きな教育の変革を促さずにはおかない。

(The spread of computers and the expansion of Internet use are bound to promote big changes in education.)

(b) この映画は観る者に感動を与えずにはおかない。

(This movie is bound to move viewers. (lit., This movie does not leave viewers without moving them.))

(c) この小説は我々に人間とは何かを考えさせずにはおかない。

(Without fail, this novel makes us think about what it is to be human.)

(d) この事故は日本とアメリカの関係に影響を及ぼさずにはおかないだろう。

(This accident will undoubtedly affect the relationship between Japan and America.)

Z

(e) 彼女は聴く者を魅了せずにはおかない音楽性とそれを表現する卓越した技術を持っている。

(She has a musicality that unfailingly captivates her audiences and the superb technique to express it.)

(f) 環境や用途に合わせて動物たちがつくりあげる構造物は、彼らの知恵と工夫がいたるところに見られ、我々の好奇心を惹起せずにはおかない。

(Structures that animals construct according to their environment and needs exhibit in every aspect their wisdom and ideas, and are bound to arouse our curiosity.)

Notes

1. X *o* Vneg *zu ni wa okanai* literally means "not to leave X without something happening to X."

2. This phrase is used when the subject necessarily or naturally causes something to happen. For example, in KS, *gijutsu no hattatsu* "technological advancements" necessarily cause *shakai-kankyō* "societal environments" to change, and in Ex.(b), *kono eiga* "this movie" naturally causes *miru mono* "the viewers" to be moved.

[Related Expressions]

I. The adverbs *kanarazu* "necessarily; certainly; surely," *machigai naku* "without fail; unmistakably" and *zettaini* "certainly; surely; absolutely" can be used in place of *zu ni wa okanai* and carry the same meaning. For example, the double-negative sentences KS and Ex.(b) can be rephrased as in the affirmative sentences [1a] and [1b], respectively.

[1] a. 技術の発達は{必ず / 間違いなく / 絶対に}社会環境の変化をもたらす。(cf. KS)

 b. この映画は{必ず / 間違いなく / 絶対に}観る者に感動を与える。

(cf. Ex.(b))

However, *zu ni wa okanai* differs from the adverbs above in that it cannot be used when no causee (i.e., a person or thing to be acted on) is involved in the event, as demonstrated in [2]-[4].

[2] a. 彼は{必ず / 間違いなく / 絶対に}来る。

(He will {certainly / unmistakably / definitely} come.)

 b. *彼は来ずにはおかない。

[3] a. このクルマは近いうちに{**必ず**／**間違いなく**／**絶対に**}壊れる。

(This car will {certainly / unmistakably / absolutely} break down before long.)

b. *このクルマは近いうちに壊れずにはおかない。

[4] a. 彼は毎晩寝る前に{**必ず**／**間違いなく**／**絶対に**}ワインを飲む。

(He drinks wine without fail before going to bed every night.)

b. *彼は毎晩寝る前にワインを飲まずにはおかない。

Another difference is that *machigai naku* and *zettaini* can also be used with adjectives and nouns, as shown in [5], whereas *zu ni wa okanai* can be used only with verbs.

[5] a. 彼は{**間違いなく**／**絶対に**}正しい。

(He is {certainly / absolutely} correct.)

b. この状況は{**間違いなく**／**絶対に**}日本チームに有利だ。

(This situation is {certainly / absolutely} advantageous to the Japanese team.)

c. 彼女は{**間違いなく**／**絶対に**}日系アメリカ人だ。

(She is {certainly / definitely} a Japanese-American.)

II. The phrase *zu ni wa orarenai/orenai/irarenai* "cannot help doing s.t." is similar to *zu ni wa okanai* in that it is used when someone or something naturally causes something to happen to someone or causes someone to do something. The major difference is that the subject in the *zu ni wa okanai* structure is the causer whereas the subject in the *zu ni wa orarenai/orenai/irarenai* structure is the causee.

[6] a. 彼女は周りにいる者を魅了せずには{おかない／*おられない／*おれない／*いられない}。 [The subject is a causer.]

(She never fails to captivate the people around her.)

b. 周りの者は彼女に魅了されずには{おられない／おれない／いられない／*おかない}。 [The subject is a causee.]

(The people around her cannot help but be captivated by her.)

In [6a], the subject is the one who causes people around her to be attracted to her (i.e., the subject is a causer). Therefore, *zu ni wa okanai* is acceptable, but *zu ni wa orarenai/orenai/irarenai* are not.

On the other hand, in [6b], the subject *mawari no mono* "the people around her" are attracted by her, i.e., the causee. In this case, *zu ni wa orarenai/orenai/irarenai* can be used but *zu ni wa okanai* cannot.

Also note that *zu ni wa orarenai/orenai/irarenai* always requires a human subject. So in [7b], where the subject is the causee but not human, *zu ni wa orarenai/orenai/irarenai* is not acceptable.

[7] a. <u>技術の発達</u>は社会環境の変化をもたらさずにはおかない。(= KS)

[subject: causer/non-human]

b. 技術の発達によって<u>社会環境の変化</u>がもたらされずには{*おられない / *おれない / *いられない}。   [subject: causee/non-human]

cf. 技術の発達によって社会環境の変化が{必ず / 間違いなく / 絶対に}もたらされる。

(Changes to social environments will {definitely / unmistakably / absolutely} be brought about by technological advancements.)

zu shite ずして *phr.* <w>

~~~
a phrase meaning "without doing s.t."
~~~

without ~ing; before (~ing); with no ~; if ~ do not; when ~ do not
【REL. *zu ni*; *nai de*】

◆ Key Sentence

	Vneg			
インカ帝国を	知ら	ず	して	南米大陸を語ることはできない。

(You cannot talk about the South American continent without some knowledge of the Inca Empire.)

Formation

Vneg ずして (Exception: する→せずして)

待たずして (without waiting)

練習せずして (without practicing)

Z

Examples

(a) 我々のチームは最終日の最終戦を待たずして優勝が決定した。

(Our team won the championship before (lit., without waiting for) the final game on the final day.)

(b) 自分の義務を果たさずして人の責任を問うべきではない。

(You should not call others to account when you have not performed your own duties.)

(c) 文雄は宝くじが当たって労せずして大金を得た。

(Fumio won the lottery, receiving a large sum of money with no effort.)

(d) 新しい議長の選出で期せずしてみんなの意見が一致した。

(In the election for a new chairman, unexpectedly (lit., without expecting), everybody agreed (on who it should be).)

(e) 今勉強せずしていつするのか？

(If we/you don't study now, when will you study?)

(f) 荒木氏は自分の設計した建物の完成を見ずして亡くなってしまった。

(Mr. Araki died before (lit., without) seeing the completion of the building he'd designed.)

(g) ウイルスに感染した電子メールを社外の個人、団体に送信してしまい、意図せずして加害者になってしまった。

(I became an offender without meaning to after sending a virus-infected e-mail to individuals and groups outside my company.)

(h) 敵を知らずしては戦えない。

(You cannot fight without knowing your enemy.)

Note

Zu shite consists of the verb negative ending *zu* and the *te*-form of *suru* and literally means "not do s.t. and ~." It is usually used in formal writing and means "without" or "without doing s.t."

[Related Expressions]

Zu ni and *nai de* are also used to mean "without doing s.t." and can replace *zu shite* without changing the meaning, as in [1].

[1] a. インカ帝国を知ら{ずして / ずに / ないで}南米大陸を語ることはできない。(= KS)

b. 我々のチームは最終日の最終戦を待た{ずして / ずに / ないで}優勝が決定した。(= Ex.(a))

c. 自分の義務を果たさ{ずして / ずに / ないで}人の責任を問うべきではない。(= Ex.(b))

However, when *zu shite* is a part of set phrases like *rōsezu shite* "with no effort" and *kisezu shite* "unexpectedly," *zu ni* and *nai de* cannot replace *zu shite*, as shown in [2].

[2] a. 文雄は宝くじが当たって{労せずして / ??労さずに / *労さないで}大金を得た。(= Ex.(c))

b. 新しい議長の選出で{期せずして / ??期さずに / *期さないで}みんなの意見が一致した。(= Ex.(d))

Because *zu shite* is used only in highly formal written language, it is awkward or unacceptable in everyday situations, as shown in [3].

[3] a. 辞書を使わ{ずに / ないで / *ずして}読んで下さい。
     (Please read it without using dictionaries.)

b. あまり勉強{せずに / しないで / ??せずして}テストを受けたのでひどい点を取ってしまった。
     (Because I took the test without studying hard, I got a terrible grade.)

(⇨ **~nai de** (DBJG: 271-73))

---

zu tomo ずとも *phr.* <w>

a conjunctive phrase that indicates negative concession, i.e., "even if ~ not"	without ~ing; even if ~ not; if ~ not 【REL. *nakute mo*; *nai de mo*】

Z

◆ **Key Sentences**

(A)

	Vneg			
今年の夏は涼(すず)しいので、エアコンを	使(つか)わ	ず	とも	過(す)ごせそうだ。
(It is cool this summer, so it looks like we can get by without using the air-conditioner.)				

(B)

	Vneg			
シカゴには親(した)しい友人が何人かいるので、ホテルに	泊(と)まら	ず	とも	よい。
(Because I have several close friends in Chicago, I don't have to stay at a hotel.)				

(C)

	Noun			
こんなに安くヨーロッパへ行けるのなら、	旅行好き	なら	ず	とも	行ってみたいと思うだろう。
(If you can go to Europe this cheaply, even if you don't especially like to travel, you'll probably want to go.)				

Formation

(i) Vneg ずとも   (Exception: する→せずとも)

使わずとも   (even if one doesn't use s.t.; without using s.t.)

(ii) N ならずとも

専門家(せんもんか)ならずとも   (even if s.o. is not a specialist)

Examples

(a) 東京(とうきょう)で会えずとも、大阪(おおさか)では必(かなら)ず会える。

((Even) if we cannot meet up in Tokyo, we will meet in Osaka for sure.)

(b) 彼(かれ)がどのくらいできるかはテストをせずとも見当(けんとう)がつく。

(I can guess how much he can do without even giving him a test.)

(c) この程度の故障ならサービスセンターに送らずともこの店で修理できます。

(We can repair this sort of trouble here at the store without sending (the product) to the service center.)

(d) この携帯電話は音声による操作が可能で、数字キーを押さずとも声だけで電話をかけられる。

(This cell phone can be voice activated, so you can make a call using just your voice, without having to punch any numbers.)

(e) これからは特別な訓練を受けずとも使えるようなユーザーインターフェースが必要となるだろう。

(From now on it will be necessary to have a user interface that doesn't require special training.)

(f) この理論は難解なので、今すぐ分からずともよい。

(This theory is hard to understand, so it is all right if you don't understand it right away.)

(g) 今回の野球ストは、これからのプロスポーツのあり方を考えさせる出来事として、野球ファンならずとも注目する人が多かった。

(Many people, even if they were not baseball fans, paid attention to the baseball strike this time because it (was an event that) made them think about what professional sports should be like in the future (lit., from now on).)

Notes

1. *Zu tomo* is a conjunctive phrase consisting of the negative ending *zu* and the conjunction *tomo* (the classic form of *te mo* "even if"). Because *zu* follows only verbs and the classic copula *nari* "be," *zu tomo* is used only with verb phrases or in the phrase N *narazu tomo*.

2. *Zu tomo* means the same thing as *nakute mo* (see Related Expressions). However, *zu tomo* is usually used in written language.

3. The phrase *zu tomo yoi* in KS(B) and Ex.(f) means "it is all right if ~ not; do not have to."

4. *Zu tomo* is sometimes used in abbreviated sentences, as in (1).

Z

(1) 将来のことは心配せずとも、私がいい仕事を見つけてあげる。

(You don't have to worry about the future. I'll find a good job for you.)

= 将来のことは心配せずともよい。私がいい仕事を見つけてあげる。

[Related Expressions]

I. Vneg *zu tomo* can be replaced by Vneg *nakute mo* without changing the meaning, as demonstrated in [1].

[1] a. 今年の夏は涼しいので、エアコンを使わ{ずとも / なくても}過ごせ そうだ。(= KS(A))

b. シカゴには親しい友人が何人かいるので、ホテルに泊まら{ずとも / なくても}よい。(= KS(B))

Narazu in N *narazu tomo* is the negative form of the classic copula *nari*. Thus, N *narazu tomo* can be replaced by N *de/ja nakute mo*, as demonstrated in [2].

[2] こんなに安くヨーロッパへ行けるのなら、旅行好き{ならずとも / でな くても / じゃなくても}行ってみたいと思うはずだ。(= KS(C))

Note, however, that *zu tomo* can be used only with verbs and N *nara*, while *nakute mo* can occur with adjectives as well, as shown in [3].

[3] a. 安く{なくても / *ずとも / *ならずとも}買うつもりだ。 (I plan to buy it even if it is not cheap.)

b. 便利{でなくても / *でならずとも / ??ならずとも}住んでみたい。 (I want to live there even if it's not convenient.)

Also note that *nakute mo* can be used in both spoken and written language.

II. Vneg *nai de mo* can also replace Vneg *zu tomo*, as shown in [4].

[4] a. 今年の夏は涼しいので、エアコンを使わ{ずとも / ないでも}過ごせ そうだ。(= KS(A))

b. シカゴには親しい友人が何人かいるので、ホテルに泊まら{ずとも / ないでも}よい。(= KS(B))

However, *nai de mo* cannot replace N *narazu tomo*, as shown in [5].

[5] こんなに安くヨーロッパへ行けるのなら、旅行好き{ならずとも / *でな いでも / *じゃないでも}行ってみたいと思うだろう。(= KS(C))

Indexes

ENGLISH INDEX

A

a bit of   *namaji(kka)*

a little   *namaji(kka)*

A, B and every~ else   *~ to iwazu ~ to iwazu*

A, B and many other ~   *~ to iwazu ~ to iwazu*

about   *ni kakete wa, oyoso*

about the same level as   *-nami*

absence of   *no nasa*

absolutely   *akumade mo, sono mono*

absolutely not   *issai ~ nai, mono ka[1]*

accompanying   *sore nari ni/no*

according to   *ni ōjite/ōjita, ni yoru to*

additional   *nao, sara ni*

additionally   *mata, nao*

admitting that   *to wa ie*

after   *ageku (ni), sue (ni)*

again   *mata*

agreeable   *sore nari ni/no*

aimed at   *-muke*

aiming at   *ni mukete/muketa*

all   *oyoso*

all the more   *naosara*

all the more for ~   *nao*

all the more reason why   *mashite(ya)*

almost   *n bakari (ni), oyoso*

almost never   *metta ni ~ nai*

alone   *tan ni*

also   *datte[2], mata, ni shita tokoro de*

although   *domo, ippō (de), mono no, mono o, mottomo, (t)tatte[2], to ie domo, wari ni (wa)*

although (it is said that/s.o. says that)   *to wa ie*

although (it is true that/it is the case that/we admit that/we agree that/ etc.)   *ni shite mo*

although (it is/was the case that)   *ni shiro/seyo*

although ~ accept   *wa ii to shite mo*

although ~ be thinking of doing ~   *yō ni mo (~ nai)*

although ~ not   *nai made mo*

although ~ try/want to ~   *yō ni mo (~ nai)*

although there is   *wa are*

always   *ippō (da)*

(not) always   *anagachi ~ nai*

among   *naka o*

among (things/people of the same kind, group, etc.)   *-dōshi*

among others   *to itta*

and   *katsu, mata, nao, narabi ni, ni shite[2], oyobi*

and (~ and)   *dano*

and ~ as well   *katsu*

and additionally   *kuwaete*

and also   *katsu*

and as one would expect   *dake atte, dake ni*

and things like that   *dano*

any   *datte[2], to ie domo*

any kind of   *ikanaru*

anything but ~   *dokoro de wa nai*

appropriate for   *ni ōjite/ōjita*

approximately   *oyoso*

apt to   *to mo suru to*

around   *o chūshin ni*

as   *ni/to mo naru to, ni tsuke, tsuide ni*

as (much ~) as   *-nami*

as ~ as possible   *dake*

as expected   *hatashite*

as for   *ni itatte wa, ni kakete wa*

as for ~, too   *ni shite mo*

as if   *ka no yōni, samo, to bakari ni*

as if ~ believed that   *to bakari ni*

D

E

give s.t. a try *hitotsu*
going beyond ~ *ni todomarazu*

H

halfheartedly *namaji(kka)*
hardly *metta ni ~ nai*
have a dash of ~ *kirai ga aru*
have a tendency to *kirai ga aru*
have a touch of ~ *kirai ga aru*
have no good reason to ~ *nani mo ~ nai*
have to *yori/no hoka (ni) (wa) ~ nai*
having said that *to itte*
here *tadashi*
how *ikan (da), ikani, ikura*
(according to) how *ikan (da)*
(depending on) how *ikan (da)*
how ~ ! *kana, koto ka, nante[1]*
how hard *ikani*
how much *ikani, ikura*
however *mottomo, tada, tadashi, to itte, to wa ie*

I

I am ~ that *koto ni*
I believe ~ very/really/truly ~ *sazo(kashi)*
I don't know why *naze ka*
I see *naruhodo*
I wonder (if) *yara*
I would say ~ *to itta tokoro da*
if *kara ni wa, mono nara, ni/to mo naru to, ori (ni), (t)tatte[1], to atte wa, yōde wa*
(even) if *kari ni*
if ~ at all *mono nara, yō mono nara*
if ~ choose to *yō mono nara*
if ~ do not *zu shite*
if ~ happen to *yō mono nara*
if ~ not *zu tomo*
if ~ not ~ then *nai koto ni wa*
if it is the case that *to atte wa, yōde wa*

if it is true that *to atte wa, yōde wa*
if it were not for ~ *nakushite (wa)*
if possible *ni koshita koto wa nai*
if s.o./s.t. were a really good/appropriate one *~ ga ~ nara*
if s.t. is right *~ ga ~ nara*
ignoring ~ *o yoso ni*
I'm certain ~ very/really/truly ~ *sazo(kashi)*
I'm sure ~ very/really/truly ~ *sazo(kashi)*
immediately after *ya ina ya*
imperfectly *namaji(kka)*
impossible *beku mo nai, mono ka[1]*
impossible if it's not ~ *nara de wa (no)*
in *ni shite[1]*
in a manner of saying *itte mireba*
in addition *kuwaete, sara ni*
in and of itself *-jitai*
in connection with *o megutte/meguru*
in contrast to ~ *ni hikikae*
in defiance of ~ *o mono to mo sezu*
in fact *hatashite*
in multiples of *tan'i de*
in my view *omou ni*
in one way or another *nan to ka*
in one's own way *sore nari ni/no*
in order to *beku, ni mukete/muketa*
in point of *ni kakete wa*
in response to *ni ōjite/ōjita*
in sets/groups/lots/etc. of *tan'i de*
in some way *nan to ka*
in spite of ~ *o mono to mo sezu*
in spite of oneself *tsui*
in terms of *kara itte, ni kakete wa*
in terms of ~ as well as ~ *~ to ii ~ to ii*
in terms of both ~ and ~ *~ to ii ~ to ii*
in the end *ageku (ni)*
in the face of ~ *o mono to mo sezu*
in the first place *somosomo (no)*
in the midst of *naka o*
in this connection *chinami ni*
inadequately *namaji(kka)*

N

naturally cannot   *mono de wa nai*
(not) necessarily   *anagachi ~ nai*
need only ~   *sumu*
needless to say   *iu made mo nai*
never   *akumade mo*
never mind   *wa oroka*
nevertheless   *to wa ie*
(there is) no ~ but X   *o oite hoka ni (wa) ~ nai*
no ~ whatsoever   *nanra ~ nai*
no matter how hard ~ try, ~ cannot ~   *dō ni mo ~ nai*
no matter how many times   *~ te mo ~ te mo*
no matter how much/often/hard/etc.   *domo, ~ te mo ~ te mo*
no matter what ~   *ikanaru*
no matter what/who/how/etc.   *datte²,   ni shiro/seyo, ni shite mo, ni yorazu,   o towazu, (t)tatte¹, yō to/ga*
no matter what/who/how/etc. ~ may be   *de are*
no more than   *tan ni*
no other ~ are/do s.t. as ~ as X   *o oite hoka ni (wa) ~ nai*
(to/from) no particular (person, etc.)   *to mo naku*
no sooner ~ than   *ga hayai ka, nari, ya ina ya*
no way   *dokoro de wa nai*
no wonder   *dake no koto wa aru*
nominally   *ichiō*
not ~ at all   *issai ~ nai, nanra ~ nai, totemo ~ nai*
not ~ by any means   *dō ni mo ~ nai, totemo ~ nai*
not ~ other than   *yori/no hoka (ni) (wa) ~ nai*
not ~ whatsoever   *issai ~ nai*
not a single ~   *hito/ichi* [Counter] *to shite ~ nai*

not any ~   *hito/ichi* [Counter] *to shite ~ nai, nanra ~ nai*
not even one   *hito/ichi* [Counter] *to shite ~ nai*
not hard   *ni katakunai*
not limited to ~   *ni todomarazu*
not need to ~   *nani mo ~ nai*
not only ~ (but also ~)   *ni todomarazu, nomi narazu, wa oroka*
not only that   *nomi narazu*
not possible with/by/at/etc. other ~   *nara de wa (no)*
not possibly   *mono de wa nai*
not to have to   *sumu*
not to mention   *wa oroka*
not to speak of   *mashite(ya)*
nothing   *nanra ~ nai*
nothing but   *tan ni, yori/no hoka (ni) (wa) ~ nai*
nothing else is ~ but X   *o oite hoka ni (wa) ~ nai*
nothing is better than   *ni koshita koto wa nai*
now   *imasara, ittan, sate*
now that ~   *kara ni wa*

O

obviously   *miru kara ni*
of course   *ni kimatte iru*
on a par with   *-nami*
on one's way to   *tsuide ni*
on reflection   *omoeba*
on the occasion   *ori (ni)*
on the other hand   *hanmen, ippō (de)*
once   *ittan, kara ni wa*
one after another   *~ wa ~ wa*
one's own   *sore nari ni/no*
oneself   *-jitai*
only   *ippō (da), (k)kiri, made (no koto) da, tada, tadashi, takaga, tan ni, tsui*
only because ~   *ba koso*
only possible with/by/at/etc.   *nara de wa (no)*

opportunity *ori (ni)*
or *aruiwa, ~ de are ~ de are, mata, moshikuwa, naishi (wa), to iu ka*
or (~ or) *dano*
or I may call it *to iu ka*
or I may say *to iu ka*
or I'd (rather) call it *to iu ka*
or I'd (rather) say *to iu ka*
or rather *to iu ka*
original *somosomo (no)*
ought not to ~ *bekarazu/bekarazaru*
over *ni shite[1], ni watatte/wataru, o megutte/meguru*

P

partly *hitotsu ni wa*
perfect *sono mono*
perfectly *sono mono*
perform *nasu*
perhaps *aruiwa*
persistently *akumade mo*
please *dō ka, negau/negaimasu*
primarily *o chūshin ni*
proper to *sore nari ni/no*
proportionate *sore nari ni/no*
provided that *tadashi*
providing that *kari ni*
putting aside *wa betsu to shite*

Q

quite entirely *oyoso*

R

ranging *ni watatte/wataru*
rarely *metta ni ~ nai*
rather *dochira ka to iu to, mushiro, nai de mo nai*
rather on the ~ side *dochira ka to iu to*
rather than otherwise *dochira ka to iu to*
really *hatashite, naruhodo, samo*
really look *miru kara ni*
reasonable *sore nari ni/no*

regarding *ni kakete wa, o megutte/ meguru*
regardless of *ni kakawarazu, ni yorazu, o towazu*
result *kai/gai*
rough *oyoso*
roughly *oyoso*

S

saying ~, ~, and so on *~ no ~ no to*
saying ~ or ~ *~ no ~ no to*
seem to ~ *nai de mo nai*
seldom *metta ni ~ nai*
setting aside *wa betsu to shite*
should *mono ka[2]*
shouldn't *bekarazu/bekarazaru, mono de wa nai*
shouldn't (stay/remain/etc.) *te wa irarenai*
shouldn't be ~ing *te wa irarenai*
shouldn't keep ~ing *te wa irarenai*
shouldn't waste time ~ing *te wa irare- nai*
simply *tan ni*
simply because *bakari ni*
simply don't/doesn't have time *dokoro de wa nai*
simply on account of ~ *bakari ni*
since *irai, (k)kiri, to atte wa*
since ~ (anyway) *tsuide ni*
slightly *namaji(kka)*
smack of ~ *kirai ga aru*
so *kono ue nai, nante[1], samo, sate, te shikata ga nai, tsuite wa, (to i)ttara nai*
so (~ that) *no nan no tte*
so (naturally) *dake atte, dake ni*
so ~ and *no nan no tte*
so ~ and ~ cannot bare it *te shikata ga nai*
so long as ~ *kara ni wa*
so many *~ wa ~ wa*
so much *~ wa ~ wa*
so much/well (~ that) *no nan no tte*

thus   *tsuite wa*
to   *beku*
to   *ni mukete/muketa*
(directed/shipped/etc.) to   *-muke*
to begin with   *somosomo (no)*
to match   *-nami*
to my/our ~   *kana, koto ni*
to rival   *-nami*
to say nothing of   *mashite(ya), wa oroka*
to the end   *akumade mo*
to the extent that ~   *ba koso*
to the same degree   *sore dake*
to the same extent   *sore dake*
together   *-dōshi*
too   *datte²*, *mata*
too late (for/to ~)   *imasara*
too much of   *(to i)ttara nai*
totally   *oyoso, sono mono*
totally impossible   *totemo ~ nai*
toward   *ni mukete/muketa*
trigger   *koto kara*
truly   *samo*
try to do   *n to suru*

U

ultimately   *akumade mo*
unbearably   *te shikata ga nai*
unconsciously   *to mo naku*
undaunted by ~   *o mono to mo sezu*
under any circumstance   *akumade mo*
undoubtedly   *zu ni wa okanai*
unintentionally   *tsui*
unless   *nai koto ni wa, nara de wa (no)*
unmistakably   *zu ni wa okanai*
unquestionably   *zu ni wa okanai*
unusually   *ni (mo) naku*
unwisely   *namaji(kka)*
utmost   *kono ue nai*
utterly   *kono ue nai, oyoso, sono mono*

V

venture to ~   *aete*
very   *kono ue nai, sono mono*
very difficult with/by/at/etc. any other ~ but   *nara de wa (no)*
via   *o kaishite/kaishita*
visibly   *miru kara ni*

W

we all know that   *ni kimatte iru*
we are ~ that   *koto ni*
we are worried/concerned (that)   *osore ga aru*
we fear (that)   *osore ga aru*
well   *sate*
well now   *sate*
what   *ikan (da), nante¹*
(according to) what   *ikan (da)*
(depending on) what   *ikan (da)*
what a(n) ~ !   *kana, koto ka, nante¹*
what I mean is that   *to iu no wa*
what kind of ~   *ikanaru*
what we call   *iwayuru*
what's more   *kuwaete*
whatever   *ikanaru*
~ whatever   *~ demo* [Wh-word] *demo*
whatever/whoever/etc.   *ni kakawarazu, ni shiro/seyo, ni shite mo, ni yorazu, o towazu, yō to/ga*
whatever/whoever/etc. ~ may be   *de are*
when   *ippō (de), naka o, nari, ni/to mo naru to, ori (ni), tsuide ni*
when ~ do not   *zu shite*
when I think (about ~)   *omou ni*
when I think back   *omoeba*
when it comes to ~   *ni itatte wa, ni kakete wa, taruya*
when one thinks/feels that ~   *ka to omou to*
whenever   *ni tsuke*
~ whenever   *~ demo* [Wh-word] *demo*
whereas   *ni hikikae*

whether   *(t)tatte*[1]

whether X or not   *ka ina ka, ni kaka-*
  warazu, ni yorazu, o towazu, ~ yara ~
  yara

whether X or Y   *~ de are ~ de are, ni*
  kakawarazu, ni shiro/seyo, ni shite
  mo, ni yorazu, o towazu, ~ to iwazu ~
  to iwazu, wa betsu to shite, ~ yara ~
  yara, yō to/ga

which can/could be described as   *to*
  demo iu beki

which could/may be called   *to demo iu*
  beki

~ whichever   *~ demo* [Wh-word] *demo*

while   *hanmen, ippō (de), naka o, ni*
  hikikae, ni shite[1]

while (~ at it)   *tsuide ni*

while ~ keep ~ing   *ta nari (de)*

while ~ staying   *ta nari (de)*

~ whoever   *~ demo* [Wh-word] *demo*

why ~ have to ~?   *nani mo ~ nai*

wish   *mono ka*[2]

with   *-dōshi*

with ~ as the center   *o chūshin ni*

with ~ as the leader   *o chūshin ni*

with ~ as the primary ~   *o chūshin ni*

with no ~   *zu shite*

with regard to   *o megutte/meguru*

with regard to this   *tsuite wa*

without   *nakushite (wa), nani ~ nai,*
  nashi ni, ni yorazu, ta nari (de)

without ~ing   *ni yorazu, zu shite, zu*
  tomo

without being able to control oneself
  tsui

without distinguishing   *ni kakawarazu*

without doubt   *zu ni wa okanai*

without fail   *zu ni wa okanai*

without intending to   *to mo naku*

without knowing why   *naze ka*

without meaning to   *tsui*

without paying much attention   *to mo*
  naku

without reference to   *ni kakawarazu, ni*
  yorazu, o towazu

wonder if   *mono ka*[2]

worth   *kai/gai*

would accept ~, but   *wa ii to shite mo*

would be fine, but   *wa ii to shite mo*

X

X and Y   *~ wa ~ wa, ~ yara ~ yara*

X is the only one   *o oite hoka ni (wa) ~*
  nai

X, Y and so on   *~ yara ~ yara*

Y

yet   *katsu, mottomo*

you are not ~, so   *de mo / ja aru mai shi*

you can expect only at/from/etc.   *nara*
  de wa (no)

JAPANESE INDEX

Note: Entries in bold-faced type appear in this book. Entries in non-bold type are included in DBJG and DIJG; "B" and "I" before the page number indicates DBJG and DIJG, respectively. X <Y> means that X is found under Y.

M

REFERENCES

Hirose, Masayoshi and Kakuko Shoji (eds.) (1994) *Effective Japanese Usage Guide—A Concise Explanation of Frequently Confused Words and Phrases,* Kodansha, Tokyo.

Kuno, Susumu, Seiichi Makino and Susan G. Strauss (2007) *Aspects of Linguistics* (『言語学の諸相』)*—In Honor of Noriko Akatsuka,* Kurosio-shuppan, Tokyo.

Kurafuji, Takeo (2004) "Plural morphemes, definiteness and the noun of semantic parameter," *Language and Linguistics* 5:1, 211-242.

Lakoff, George and Mark Johnson (1980) *Metaphors We Live By,* The University of Chicago Press, Chicago/London.

Makino, Seiichi (2002) "*Uchi* and *soto* as cultural and linguistic metaphors," *Exploring Japaneseness: On Japanese Enactments of Culture and Consciousness* (ed. by Ray T. Donahue), Ablex Publishing, London, 29-64.

―――― (2007) "The Japanese Pluralizer—*Tachi* as a Window into the Cognitive World" in Kuno, et al., 109-120

Makino, Seiichi and Mayumi Oka (in press) *A Dictionary of Japanese and English Metaphors* (『日英語共通比喩辞典』), Kurosio-shuppan, Tokyo.

Makino, Seiichi and Michio Tsutsui (1986) *A Dictionary of Basic Japanese Grammar,* The Japan Times, Tokyo.

―――― (1995) *A Dictionary of Intermediate Japanese Grammar*, The Japan Times, Tokyo.

Makino, Seiichi, Seiichi Nakada and Mieko Ohso (1999) *Kodansha's Basic English-Japanese Dictionary*, Kodansha International, Tokyo.

Martin, Samuel E. (1975) *A Reference Grammar of Japanese*, Yale University Press, New Haven, Connecticut.

Masuda, Koh (ed.) (1974) *Kenkyusha's New Japanese-English Dictionary* (fourth ed.), Kenkyusha, Tokyo.

Shirane, Haruo (2005) *Classical Japanese: A Grammar*, Columbia University Press, New York, New York.

Tsutsui, Michio (2006) "The Japanese Copula Revisited: Is *da* a Copula?" *Japanese Language and Literature* 40, 59-103.

Watt, Ito Yasuko and Richard Rubinger (1998) *Readers Guide To Intermediate Japanese*, The University of Hawai'i Press, Honolulu, Hawaii.

Wldarczyk, Andre (ed.) (2005) *Paris Lectures in Japanese Linguistics*, Kurosio-shuppan, Tokyo.

安達太郎（1999）『日本語疑問文における判断の諸相』くろしお出版

大野晋・佐竹昭広・前田金五郎編（1974）『岩波古語辞典』岩波書店

大野晋・浜西正人編（1981）『角川類語新辞典』角川書店

岡まゆみ（2004）「メタファーは OPI レベル判定のマーカーとなりうるか？」*Proceedings of the 3rd International Symposium on OPI and the 12th Princeton Japanese Pedagogy Forum* (ed. by Seiichi Makino), Princeton University, 173-191.

影山太郎（1993）『文法と語形成』ひつじ書房

加藤重広（2003）『日本語修飾構造の語用論的研究』ひつじ書房

鎌田修・筒井通雄・畑佐由紀子・ナズキアン富美子・岡まゆみ編（2005）『言語教育の新展開——牧野成一教授古稀記念論集』ひつじ書房

グループ・ジャマシイ編著、砂川有里子他著（1998）『日本語文型辞典』くろしお出版

国立国語研究所（1951）『現代語の助詞・助動詞——用法と実例』秀英出版

柴田武・山田進編（2002）『類語大辞典』講談社

白川博之監修、庵功雄・高梨信乃・中西久実子・山田敏弘著（2001）『中上級を教える人のための日本語文法ハンドブック』スリーエーネットワーク

新村出編（1998）『広辞苑』（第五版），岩波書店

瀬戸賢一（1995）『メタファー思考——意味と認識のしくみ』（講談社現代新書），講談社

―――（2001）『日本語感覚で話す英会話——日本語と英語の同じ使い方80』ノヴァ

茅野直子・秋元美晴・真田一司（1987）『副詞』（「外国人のための日本語例文・問題シリーズ」1），荒竹出版

筒井通雄（2005）「連体修飾節「N₁ の N₂」の意味解釈―各解釈の視点から―」『言語教育の新展開——牧野成一教授古稀記念論集』（鎌田修・筒井通雄・畑佐由紀子・ナズキアン富美子・岡まゆみ編），ひつじ書房

寺村秀夫（1991）『日本語のシンタクスと意味 III』くろしお出版

―――（1993）『寺村秀夫論文集 I —日本語文法編—』くろしお出版

中村明（1977）『比喩表現辞典』角川書店

名柄迪・広田紀子・中西家栄子（1987）『形式名詞』（「外国人のための日本語例文・問題シリーズ」2），荒竹出版

西原鈴子・川村よし子・杉浦由紀子（1988）『形容詞』（「外国人のための日本語例文・問題シリーズ」5），荒竹出版

西山佑司（2003）『日本語名詞句の意味論と語用論—指示的名詞句と非指示的名詞句—』ひつじ書房

仁田義雄（2002）『副詞的表現の諸相』くろしお出版

日向茂男・日比谷潤子（1989）『擬音語・擬態語』（「外国人のための日本語例文・問題シリーズ」14），荒竹出版

牧野成一（1996）『ウチとソトの言語文化学——文法を文化で切る』アルク

―――（2006）「談話における換喩の認知論的分析」日本語教育国際研究大会発表論文，コロンビア大学，8月4-5日

宮地宏・サイモン遠藤陸子・小川信夫（1991）『修飾』（「外国人のための日本語例文・問題シリーズ」17），荒竹出版

宮島達夫・仁田義雄編（1995）『日本語類義表現の文法（下）』くろしお出版

村木新次郎 （1985）「名詞と形容詞の境界」『言語』27:3, 44-49

森田良行 （1977）『基礎日本語』角川書店

―― （1980）『基礎日本語 2』角川書店

―― （1984）『基礎日本語 3』角川書店

森田良行・松木正恵 （1989）『日本語表現文型』アルク

横林宙世・下村彰子 （1988）『接続の表現』（「外国人のための日本語例文・問題シリーズ」6），
　　荒竹出版